Interaction of the "Sibling"
Byzantine and Western Cultures

Portrait of Ficino, Landino, Poliziano, and Chalcondyles (Chalcondyles at extreme right) from a fresco of Ghirlandaio in Santa Maria Novella, Florence. (See esp. pp. 222-23 for Chalcondyles' aid to Ficino in translating Plato.)

Interaction
of the
"Sibling" Byzantine and Western Cultures
in the
Middle Ages and Italian Renaissance
(330-1600)

Deno John Geanakoplos

New Haven and London, Yale University Press, 1976

Library of Congress catalog card number: 74–29722
International standard book number: 0–300–01831–2

Designed by John O. C. McCrillis
and set in Baskerville type.
Printed in the United States of America by
The Murray Printing Co., Westford, Massachusetts.

Published in Great Britain, Europe, Africa, and Asia (except Japan) by
Yale University Press, Ltd., London.
Distributed in Latin America by Kaiman & Polon,
Inc., New York City; in Australia and New Zealand by Book & Film
Services, Artamon, N.S.W., Australia; in Japan
by John Weatherhill, Inc., Tokyo.

For John and Connie, my dear children

We chant it [the *Gloria in excelsis Deo*] in Greek, according to ancient custom of the Roman church to which both Greeks and Latins once adhered. A very large part of Italy was inhabited by Greeks; hence the Greek language was not less known even to the Latins than Latin. Also, the interpreters of the *Septuagint* translated each testament from Hebrew into Greek and it was then put into Latin. . . . It is accordingly proper that Greek precede Latin as a mother her daughter, and that Latin follow Greek as a daughter her mother.

—Anonymous of Tours (Western medieval liturgist), in *Speculum Ecclesiae* 3.2.

When I look here upon the buildings . . . and the beauties of nature and of art I admire this city of Rome because of her former excellence and power. But I find the greatest joy in that, everywhere, I see the greatest similarity with our home city [Constantinople]. Even the similarity which we perceive between two different persons gives us pleasure, most of all when we see how a son resembles his father, or a daughter her mother or brothers, especially when some kinship binds us to him

The beauty of the mother [Rome] emphasizes the beauty of the daughter [Constantinople]. It is not as if we were to compare something alien to something else. Rather we compare one city with itself—the New with the Old Rome. . . . What has nature or art wrought in Rome that one cannot find in our city? Even the survivals resemble one another. If in certain respects this city [Rome] seems to surpass us, so we have other things we can show to compensate. There was and is much in our city [Constantinople] that has no counterpart in Rome, and still more has been brought to genuine perfection by us.

—The Byzantine humanist Manuel Chrysoloras, in "A Comparison of Old and New Rome" (1411).

Contents

Illustrations

Maps

Preface

This volume attempts, through a series of closely related chapters, to provide an understanding of the interaction between the cultures of two major Christian societies, the Byzantine and the Western, in the Middle Ages and the Italian Renaissance. Attention is directed to some aspects or facets of theology, political ideology, religious piety and mysticism, philosophy, and literature, as well as law, music, art, and refinements of living. In order to provide an organic unity for the chapters, the author, combining probably for the first time in this connection sociological and historical techniques, has sought in the Prologue to outline the centuries-long process of interaction, in particular of acculturation, between the two societies, and finally, in the Epilogue, to summarize the effects of this process. By means of this interdisciplinary approach, historical phases of periodization and a "typology" of acculturation are suggested as aids to interpreting the complex cultural phenomena discussed.

At the center of the discussion of relations between East and West are the Byzantine and Roman Catholic churches. With these churches today drawing ever closer together, it is hoped that this book, while identifying the forces of disunity, will help also to illuminate those more underlying factors which, from Christian antiquity onward, made for rapprochement between the churches as well as their cultures.

A word about the individual chapters and their genesis. Insofar as possible they have been chronologically arranged. The terms "Middle Ages" and "Renaissance" are used for the sake of convenience and do not imply a break in historical continuity (as they should not, I believe, in the relations of the two cultures discussed here). In part 1, "Byzantium, the Church, and the Medieval Latin World," the first chapter attempts to define what may well be, in the last analysis, the most creative, formative element in the Byzantine cultural synthesis, Orthodox Christianity, the ethos of which differs markedly from Western Christianity. The chapter, in another form, was originally read in 1970 in New York, preceding the induction ceremony of the archons into the Orthodox Patriarchal

Order of St. Andrew. Chapter 2 evaluates the significance of the close connection between religion and "nationalism" in the Byzantine state, a consideration that was frequently to complicate relations between Constantinople and the papacy, especially regarding religious union. This material was originally presented at an Eastern Orthodox-Jewish Symposium in New York City in 1972. Chapter 3, an earlier version of which appeared in my book *Byzantine East and Latin West* (Oxford, 1966), now out of print, was included at the urging of colleagues and students. It appears here in considerably revised form, including a new section on the influence of the Byzantine Church Fathers, deletion of some sections, and enrichment of many others, especially those on vocabulary borrowings, the liturgy, and art. The chapter attempts to delineate the surprisingly manifold and pervasive influences exerted by Byzantine culture on Western civilization. Though obviously it can make no claim to comprehensiveness, this chapter, so far as I am aware, is still the only attempt, at least in English, to provide a synoptic treatment of the more important aspects of this vast theme. Chapter 4 is one of the first discussions to be written on the converse question, Western influences on Byzantine civilization, despite the widespread view that virtually all medieval influence flowed from East to West. The original essay, limited to the fields of theology and literature* (where the influence is probably the most striking), was read in 1967 in Toronto at the annual meeting of the Medieval Academy of America. It has since undergone extensive changes and additions.

Chapters 5 and 6 have previously appeared in journals, the former in *Greek, Roman, and Byzantine Studies* (1966) and the latter in *Church History* (1960). They are printed here, with significant changes in text and notes, because each focuses on a substantive theme in Byzantine-Latin cultural interaction. Chapter 5 examines the influence of imperial Byzantine authority (the so-called Caesaropapism) on imperial church building, through a study of the impressive churches constructed in East and West by the two greatest builder-emperors, Constantine and Justinian. In chapter 6, a paper initially written for the Oxford Patristic Congress of 1965 and subsequently expanded, an effort is made to trace the influence of the theology of Maximos the Confessor, the Byzantine exegete of the mystical

---

*I hope soon to publish an entire monograph on the general theme of the impact of Western culture on the Byzantine. See now, however, chapter 7, on German legal influence on Byzantium.

Pseudo-Dionysian writings, on subsequent Latin and Greek theologians.

In chapter 7 an effort is made to explain the origins of the appearance in Byzantine Nicaea of curious legal phenomena—the ordeal by fire and the judicial duel, both normally connected with the Germanic West and not Byzantium, where the principles of Roman law prevailed. Finally, in chapter 8 an analysis is made of a colloquy that occurred between a Greek bishop and a Latin bishop, which supposedly took place after the attempted union of the churches at the Council of Lyons in 1274. Set forth here are many ideas and prejudices, both religious and pseudoscientific, of both the upper class and the common people—ideas that helped to make it so difficult for the two peoples to understand one another.

Part 2 of the book is concerned with cultural relations of East and West during the Italian Renaissance (ca. 1350 to 1600), more particularly before and after 1453 when Byzantium became a Turkish province and was therefore isolated from the Western world. Nevertheless, as shown in Chapter 9, learned Greek émigrés escaping to the West in a remarkable "diaspora," were able to continue the recently developed pattern of close Byzantine-Latin relations, but now entirely on Latin soil, where they established communities in Venice and Naples as well as in other Western centers. These colonies not only transmitted Greek learning to the Renaissance but, as is rarely realized, with the precipitous cultural decline of mainland Greece (a situation paralleling that of the earlier Western "Dark Ages"), consciously continued to preserve the Greek educational inheritance and thus played a major (but overlooked) role in the genesis of the modern Greek sense of national consciousness. This chapter is a much expanded version of a paper delivered at the Modern Greek Studies Association at Harvard in 1971 on the 150th anniversary of Greek Independence. Chapter 10, originally delivered as a paper at the Renaissance Symposium of the State University of New York at Binghamton in 1968, discusses the role of the Venetian-held island of Crete as a kind of halfway point in the transmission of Greco-Byzantine culture to the West during the Renaissance, a phenomenon only recently beginning to receive adequate recognition.

Chapter 11 focuses on San Bernardino of Siena, the most popular preacher of the Renaissance period, establishing not only his presence at the Council of Florence, that climactic confrontation of

Byzantine and Western churches and intellects, but showing the kind of influence he may well have exerted on the Greeks at the council. Chapter 12 (written for the Balkan Studies Conference held in Athens in 1970 but here enlarged and provided with documentation) offers new information on and clarifies the circumstances surrounding the death of the most learned of Renaissance Hellenists, Marcus Musurus. Chapter 13 discusses the career of one of the most famous of all Byzantine humanist exiles, Demetrius Chalcondyles, who taught at three major Italian humanist centers—Padua, Florence, and Milan—all of which were then at the pinnacle of their fame. The chapter concentrates especially on his tenure at Padua, providing, by means of a largely unpublished manuscript, new information concerning his inaugural address on the occasion of the establishment of the first Greek chair at that university. In order to give the reader a deeper understanding of this key event in the development of Paduan-Venetian humanism, the oration—one of the few by a Byzantine humanist to be preserved—is here presented in English translation. (See the appendix for my edition of the original Latin text.) Chapter 14, marking the final important step in East-West cultural relations, discusses, for the first time in synthesis, the return to the West during the Renaissance of the Greek Fathers of the church in translation or in the original text, concentrating particularly on the first editions to have been published. Part of this paper was read in 1974 at Cambridge University (England) at Professor Bolgar's international conference on "Classical Influences in the Renaissance, 1500–1700."

Finally, in the Epilogue, on the basis of the phases of historical periodization and the particular typology of acculturation proposed in the Prologue, an effort is made, in the light of all the material presented, to summarize and evaluate some of the principal effects of this extraordinary and ever-fluctuating interaction of over a millennium between the "sibling" but often estranged Byzantine and Latin civilizations.

For help given me in preparing for publication various aspects of the material in this book, I should like to express my apppreciation to: Professors Evan Vlachos, Demetrius Tsames, Paul Kristeller, Alexander Turyn, Father William Conlan O.P., P. Richard Metcalf, Sydney Ahlstrom, Brevard Childs, H. von Stadten; to Mary Grimes; to my assistants at one time or another at Yale

University, John Erickson, Darlene Welborn, Lawrence Le Seure, and Chris Bender; and, finally, to my secretary Ruth Kurzbauer and to my manuscript editor at Yale Press, Barbara Folsom.

New Haven, Conn.   D.J.G.
1975

Chronology of Events

Byzantine and Western, 330–1600

312	Constantine's vision and victory at the Milvian Bridge
325	First ecumenical council, at Nicaea (over Arianism)
330	Foundation of Constantinople: beginning of the "Christian" Roman (Byzantine) Empire
378	Defeat of Emperor Valens by the Goths at Adrianople
381	Second ecumenical council, at Constantinople (reaffirming anti-Arianism)
395	Official separation of eastern and western halves of the Roman Empire
431	Third ecumenical council, at Ephesus: Nestorius condemned
451	Fourth ecumenical council, at Chalcedon: Monophysites condemned
476	End of Roman Empire in the West; German states established
527–65	Reign of Justinian I: recovery of much of the West
529	Justinian Code published; soon afterward promulgation of the Pandects
532	Nika riots; St. Sophia destroyed and later rebuilt by Justinian
535–40	Byzantines recapture Sicily and Italy from Ostrogoths
553	Fifth ecumenical council, at Constantinople: concessions made to Monophysites
568	Lombards invade Italy

582–602   Creation of Exarchates of Ravenna and Carthage

610–41   Emperor Heraclius: conquest of the Persian Empire

636–46   Arabs occupy Palestine, Syria, Egypt

668–85   Reorganization of Byzantine Empire: emergence of the *theme* system

680   Sixth ecumenical council, at Constantinople: appeasement of Monophysites through Monothelitism condemned

717–41   Leo III: second defense of Constantinople against the Arabs

726 (or 730) Iconoclast decree of Leo III

750   Fall of Umayyad Caliphate. Abbassid Caliphate transferred from Damascus to Bagdad

751   Capture of Ravenna by Lombards, ending Byzantine hegemony in north and central Italy

754   Iconoclastic council at Hieria

787   Seventh ecumenical council: restoration of the icons

800   Coronation of Charlemagne: restoration of Roman Empire in the West

826   Capture of Crete by the Arabs

843   Feast of Orthodoxy and final restoration of the icons

863   Cyril and Methodius' mission to Moravia

864   Conversion of the Bulgars

867   Photius, Patriarch of Constantinople; schism with Rome (Pope Nicholas I)

902   Final fall of Sicily to the Arabs

961   Recapture of Crete from the Arabs

976–1025   Zenith of Byzantine imperial power under Basil II

989   Russia accepts Orthodox Christianity: baptism of Vladimir

1030	Normans begin conquest of Byzantine southern Italy
1054	Schism between Constantinople and Rome (Cerularius and Humbert)
1056 on	"Time of Troubles": Byzantine economic, political, and social crisis
1071	Double Byzantine defeat: at Manzikert by the Turks and at Bari by the Normans
1081	Accession of Alexius I Comnenus, "Savior" of Byzantium
1082	Byzantine alliance with Venice and grant of trading concessions to Venetians
1096	First Crusade from the West passes through Constantinople
1143–80	Reign of latinophile Manuel I Comnenus; struggle with Hohenstaufen
1147	Second Crusade from West, to recover Edessa
1182	Massacre of Latins in Constantinople
1185	Thessalonica seized and sacked by the Normans
1187	Third Crusade, after Jerusalem's fall to Saladin
1204	Fourth Crusade: Latin capture and sack of Constantinople and establishment of the Latin Empire (to 1261); acquisition of Crete by Venice
1204–61	Greek "Empire" of Nicaea in Asia Minor
1215	Fourth Lateran Council under Innocent III
1259	Byzantium defeats Latin army at Pelagonia; capture of Mistra from the Latins
1261	Michael VIII Palaeologus captures Constantinople; Byzantine Empire restored
1266	Charles of Anjou defeats Manfred and becomes king of Sicily
1281	Michael VIII excommunicated by Pope Martin IV and a crusade proclaimed against Byzantium

1282   "Sicilian Vespers": effective end of Latin attempts to recapture Constantinople

1305   "Babylonian Captivity" of the papacy at Avignon (to 1377)

1341–91   John V Palaeologus rules Byzantium

1341   Synod on Palamism, at Constantinople

1351   Synod at Constantinople approves Palamism

1361   Pilatus appointed, in Florence, to first chair of Greek in western Europe

1369   Emperor John V personally accepts Catholicism in Rome

1378   Great Schism begins in Roman church (until 1417)

1391–1425   Reign of Emperor Manuel II Palaeologus in Byzantium

1396   Chrysoloras is appointed to Greek chair in Florence, inaugurating first systematic, Western study of Greek since antiquity.

1399   Manuel II Palaeologus comes to the West (until 1402), seeking military aid against the Turks

1402   Death of Giangaleazzo Visconti of Milan, thereby ending Florentine fear of invasion; Battle of Angora: defeat of the Ottoman Turks by Timur

1409   Council of Pisa: Alexander V (Petrus Philarges) elected pope

1414   Council of Constance (to 1418)

1417   End of Great Schism: election of Pope Martin V

1422   Turks besiege Constantinople

1430   Turks conquer Thessalonica from Venice

1431   Council of Basle convened (to 1449)

1434   Cosimo de' Medici assumes power in Florence

1435   Establishment of Greek colony in Naples.

1438–39   Convocation of unionist Council of Florence between Greek and Latin churches

1444   Battle of Varna

1447–55   Pontificate of Nicholas V

1452   Union of Greek and Latin churches proclaimed at Constantinople

1453   Constantinople captured by the Ottoman Turks

1460   Mistra falls to the Turks

1462   Establishment of Platonic Academy in Florence

1463   Establishment by Venice of first Greek chair at the University of Padua (for Chalcondyles)

1467   Bessarion bequeaths his Greek library to Venice

1469   Lorenzo the Magnificent in power in Florence (to 1492)

1470   Fall of Venetian-held Negropont to the Turks

1476   Grammar of Constantine Lascaris is published in Milan, first Greek book printed in Europe

1494   Invasion of Italy by the French king, Charles VIII

1494–95   Aldus Manutius founds his Neakademia in Venice

1503   Musurus appointed professor of Greek at Padua University

1508   Cardinal Ximenes founds the University of Alcalà (Spain); Aldine press prints edition of Erasmus's *Adages*

1513–21   Pontificate of Leo X

1513   Aldine publication of Musurus' *editio princeps* of the complete works of Plato

1522   Rhodes falls to the Turks

1527   Sack of Rome

1536   Death of Erasmus

1539   Erection of Greek Church of San Giorgio in Venice

1561   Franciscus Portus settles in Geneva

1568   Pius V declares Basil, Gregory of Nazianzus, Chry-
            sostom, and Athanasius "Doctors of the Church"

1571   Turks conquer Cyprus; Battle of Lepanto

1577   Greek college of St. Athanasius founded in Rome

1596   Council of Brest

1602   Death of Margounios in Venice

1669   Turks capture Venetian-held island of Crete

Interaction of the "Sibling"
Byzantine and Western Cultures

Part 1

Byzantium, the Church, and the Medieval Latin World

Prologue: The Process of Acculturation

In recent years much has been written on Byzantium and even more on the medieval West—two cultures whose histories revert back to a common origin in the Greco-Latin world of the one Christian, Roman Empire. Despite the often absorbing, in time even dramatically hostile, nature of their relations, there is yet no comprehensive study of the interaction of the two cultures, in particular of what may be called the "acculturation" of each society toward the other during the centuries-long continuum comprising the Middle Ages and the Renaissance (330–1600). What is needed for such an investigation is, first, a delineation, at least in broad outline, of the patterns of their social interaction—patterns which may then be examined for evidence of cultural influences.

Of particular import for such a study is an analysis of the developing attitudes of the two kindred civilizations as manifested in the gradual transformation of their societies from amicable rivalry to overt hostility. Such attitudes will in turn provide the key to the degree of intercultural receptivity or repulsion which developed in the various strata of society—attitudes basic for any genuine understanding of the dynamics of cross-cultural exchange.

The acculturative process consists of three basic steps: initial encounter between cultures, interaction, and finally, the resultant rejection, "fragmentation," or assimilation of certain cultural elements on the part of one or both societies.[1] In trying to establish criteria—or as sociologists and anthropologists would say, a "typology"—for the analysis of cultural influences between the Byzantine and Latin peoples, the following modes of acculturation may be suggested: (1) the cultural dominance of one society over the other with assimilation of cultural elements by the less developed civilization from the more advanced;* (2) the amalgamation of elements of the two cultures into a new kind of synthesis; (3) the confrontation of two advanced but antagonistic societies, each challenging the dominance of the other's cultural tradition. Sometimes present

---

*Of course, the reverse process, though far less common, is also possible. See, for example, chap. 4, pp. 95–117.

3

in one or even all three modes of acculturation is the phenomenon of alienation of a particular group of society from the dominant cultural trends or processes being experienced by that society, with the consequent eruption of what sociologists term "nativistic reactions" and/or "revitalization movements." "Nativistic reaction" is characterized by an overpowering desire to hold firm and to reassert, in the face of threatening external or internal pressures, the traditional forms and beliefs of the culture. "Revitalization movement," a more comprehensive term, refers to a desire not only to revivify the traditional roots of the culture but also to strengthen them through a deeper, more creative appreciation, particularly of their historical origins.[2]

Such modes of acculturation as these are, of course, well known to the social scientist. But attention has hitherto primarily been directed to noncomplex cases of cross-cultural relations, particularly the influence of a technologically advanced society (the American or Western European, for example) on a far less developed one (say, the American Indian or central African). The history of Byzantine-Latin cultural relations, in contrast, is unique. Not only were the two cultures, originally closely related, in the main characterized by a high level of development, but between them existed a virtually unbroken continuity of connections over a vast period of time. Moreover, during the last three or four centuries of interaction, they had, on many levels, reached a condition of cultural parity.

Finally, in the pattern formed by their interrelations may be observed the full range of the various modes of acculturation mentioned above, together with instances of the phenomena of "nativistic" and "revitalization" movements. It should be observed that since little or no sociological analysis has hitherto been devoted to the encounter of two advanced cultures, there are few guidelines to follow. Hence, the modes of acculturation proposed here, and especially the categorization of mental attitudes underlying the behavior of the two peoples (a basic emphasis throughout this book),[3] may not always be consistent with established acculturation models, which have thus far been based primarily on examinations of relations between advanced and less developed societies.

What is unique, to begin with, about the interaction of the Byzantine and Latin cultures, is that they were originally "siblings," that is, they evolved from the same matrix, the Christianized Roman

Empire and its classical civilization. This fact indicates that, despite a mutual rivalry which over the centuries developed into an overwhelming hostility, there always lurked in the background the feeling that, somehow, both societies belonged together as parts of a united Christendom.[4] The configuration of cultures, however, was early on altered by two new elements: the intrusion of the barbarian Germans into the West on a scale greater than ever before, and the continual, if sporadic, influences seeping into Byzantium from the ancient, non-Roman or Asiatic East. More important in molding their cultural development was what may be considered the most creative force in the development of Byzantine and, perhaps to a lesser extent, of Western civilization—their respective forms of Christianity, each strikingly different, especially in ethos, from its counterpart.[5]

For one culture to influence another to any marked degree there must usually exist more than sporadic connections between a few individuals. That is, "contact situations" must obtain for more than brief periods and involve relatively influential groups in society.[6] Which is not to deny that charismatic individuals, themselves or through their works (if the time is "ripe"), can bring about certain alterations in the pattern of intercultural relations. Witness, in the twelfth century, the influence of the Byzantine John of Damascus on Western theology; in the fourteenth, the fascination with Thomas Aquinas on the part of some Byzantine scholars; or, still later in the Italian Renaissance, the impact of the teaching of the Byzantine Manuel Chrysoloras who, almost single-handedly, launched in the West a revival of Greek learning.[7]

A precondition to establishment of an intercultural pattern of Latin-Byzantine relations must, then, be the delineation, at least in broad contours, of the main "contact situations" of the two peoples all the way from the fourth through the sixteenth century.[8] This pattern may, for the sake of convenience, be broadly divided into four chronological phases or periods.

The first extends from the fourth to the late eleventh century, during which time Byzantine culture far surpassed that of the West and relations between the two were sporadic; the second, from the First Crusade in 1095 to the Greek recovery of Constantinople from the Latins in 1261, during which period large groups of people from the two civilizations confronted each other in the East, for the first time en masse; the third, from 1261 to the fall of Constantinople in 1453, when, again on Greek soil, the interaction between the increasingly dynamic Western and the highly developed but more static Eastern culture took on a more and more antagonistic form; and the fourth and final period, that of the Greek "diaspora," extending from approximately a half century before 1453 to the end of the Renaissance.

During this last period the previous situation was reversed, with Latin culture in certain respects surpassing the Greek (for example, in technology, social organization, and some aspects of theological speculation). Contacts now occurred primarily in the West, to which many Greek refugees fled to escape the Turkish occupation. It should be observed that the period after 1453 is, technically speaking, post-Byzantine. But, as will be shown, in the latter part of the fifteenth and in the sixteenth century Byzantine influences continued, in some cases even more strongly than before, to influence foreign areas, especially Renaissance Italy (and the world of the Orthodox Slavs).

Let us now outline the pattern of "contact situations" during our four chronological periods. In the first phase, from the fourth to the end of the eleventh century, Western society, largely as a result of the Germanic invasions (followed by those of the Arabs and Vikings) was almost completely disrupted, bringing about severe social and economic dislocation. Thus the West, culturally, sank more and more deeply into the mire of the "Dark Ages." Though the Byzantine Empire after Justinian's reign (d. 565) underwent its own lesser Dark Ages, it managed, in contrast, to remain relatively stable—in any case far more intellectually enlightened than the West. It was in this first period (and especially by the beginning of the eighth century, with the loss of Semitic Egypt, Syria, and Palestine) that Byzantium succeeded in achieving a remarkable fusion of its three basic cultural elements (Greek classical learning, Orthodox Christianity, and the Roman legal tradition) into a closely knit, viable synthesis.[9] Meanwhile, the near anarchy and disorganization of the West, with the semibarbaric customs of the Germans (witness their legal practice of the ordeal by fire, to be discussed in detail)[10] made it difficult for the West to achieve a viable integration of its own cultural components. It was not, in fact, until probably the early twelfth century that the West, after several cultural regressions, finally achieved an effective synthesis of its own main cultural elements—classical Latin learning, "Roman

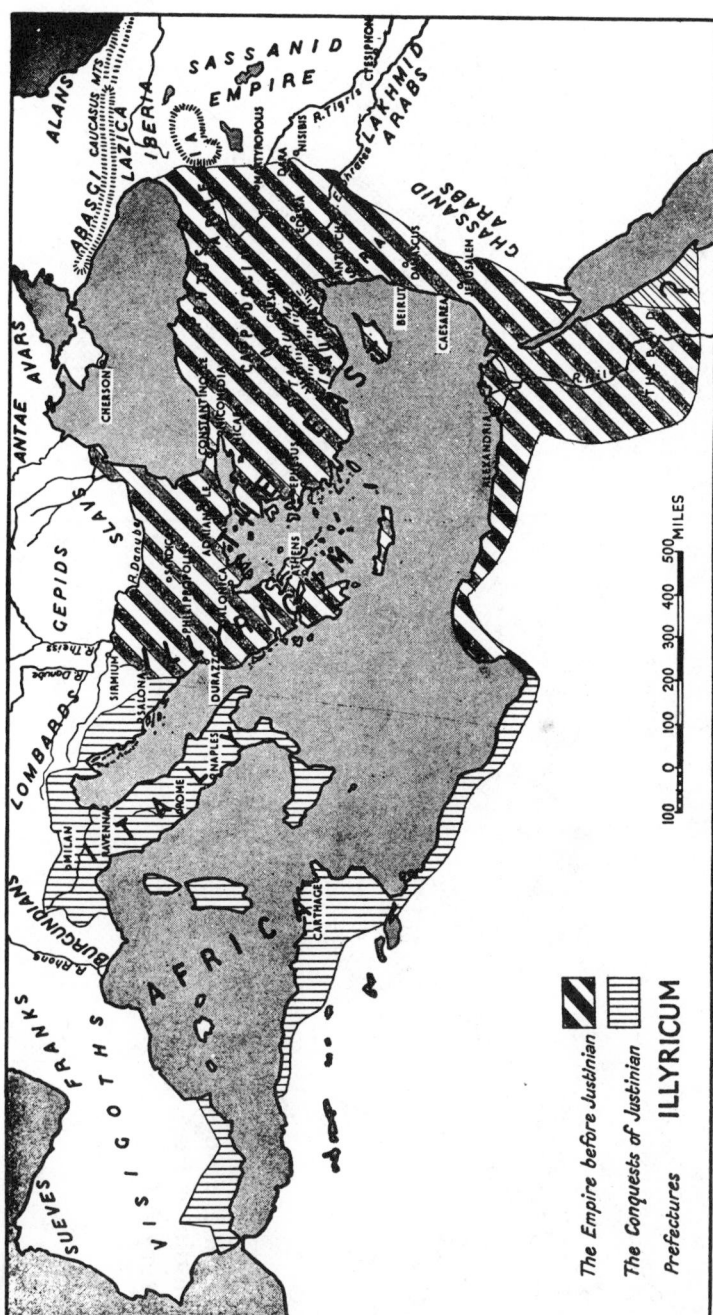

1. THE EMPIRE OF JUSTINIAN I IN 565

The Byzantine Empire in A.D. 565 under Emperor Justinian. From N. Baynes and H. Moss, eds., *Byzantium: An Introduction to East Roman Civilization* (Oxford: The Clarendon Press, 1961).

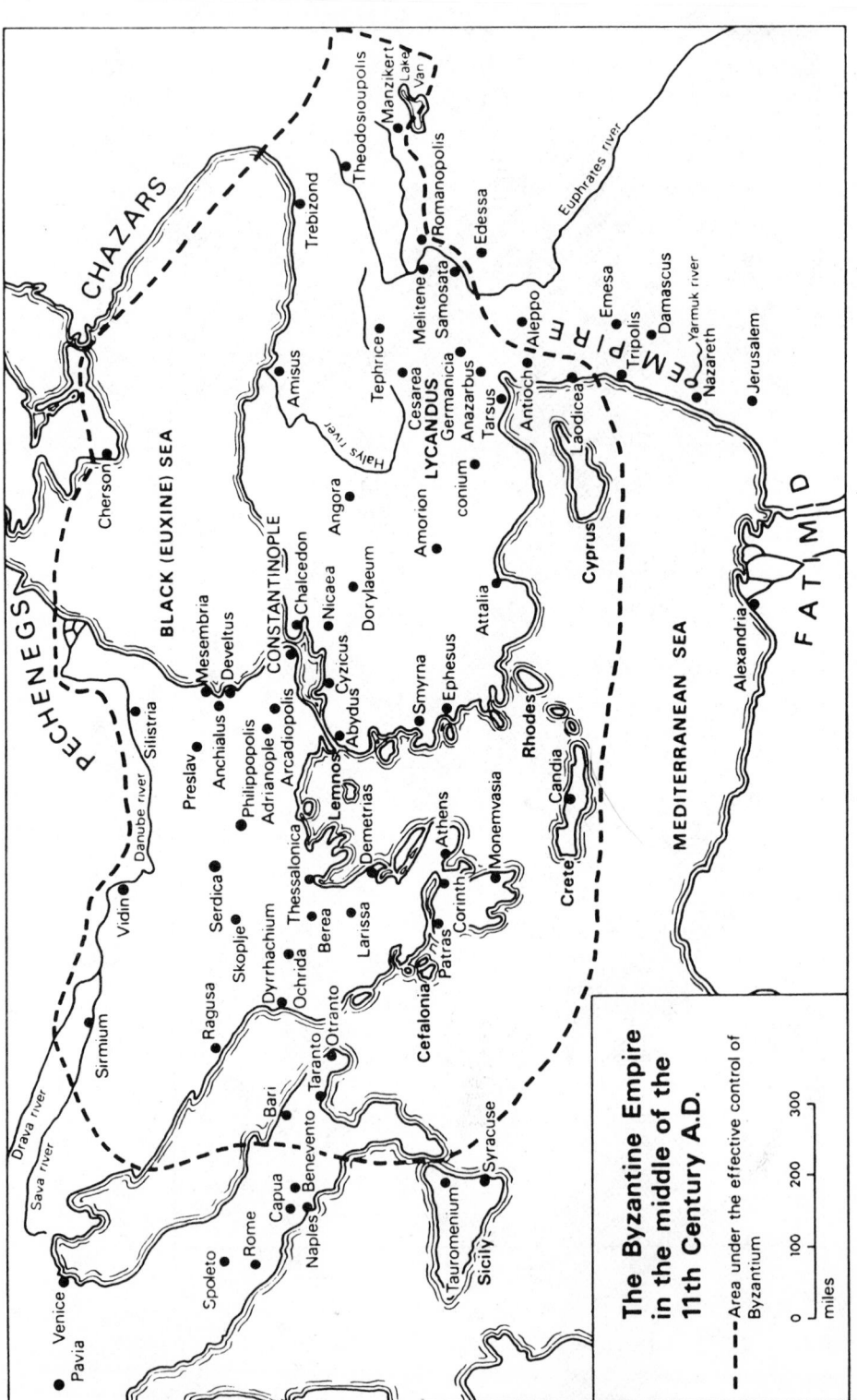

The Byzantine Empire in the mid-eleventh century A.D. From R. Jenkins, *The Imperial Centuries A.D. 610-1071* (London: Weidenfeld and Nicolson; originally published by Random House, New York, 1966).

The Byzantine Empire in the middle of the 11th Century A.D.

- - - - Area under the effective control of Byzantium

miles
0   100   200   300

CHAZARS

PECHENEGS

BLACK (EUXINE) SEA

MEDITERRANEAN SEA

FATIMID

LYCANDUS

EMPIRE

Euphrates river

Hatys river

Danube river

Drava river

Sava river

Yarmuk river

Cherson

Trebizond

Theodosioupolis

Manzikert
Lake
Van

Romanopolis

Edessa

Amisus

Melitene
Samosata

Tephrice

Cesarea
Germanicia
Anazarbus
Tarsus

Amorion
conium

Aleppo
Emesa
Damascus
Tripolis
Nazareth
Jerusalem

Antioch
Laodicea

Angora

Dorylaeum

Nicaea

Chalcedon

CONSTANTINOPLE

Cyzicus
Abydus

Smyrna
Ephesus

Attalia

Cyprus

Rhodes

Candia
Crete

Mesembria
Develtus

Anchialus
Preslav

Philippopolis
Adrianople
Arcadiopolis

Silistria

Vidin

Serdica

Skoplje

Dyrrhachium
Ochrida

Ragusa

Sirmium

Thessalonica
Berea
Larissa

Demetrias

Lemnos

Athens
Corinth
Patras

Monemvasia

Cefalonia

Otranto
Taranto
Bari

Benevento
Capua
Naples

Rome

Spoleto

Venice

Pavia

Tauromenium
Sicily
Syracuse

Alexandria

Catholic" Christianity, and, above all, the formerly disruptive but now more sophisticated Germanic influences.[11] Then for the first time the West, now reflecting the vigor of a newly mature culture, was able to break free of its confines and even to expand into the neighboring Byzantine (and Arabic) lands. It is probably no coincidence that the great Western movement of the Crusades occurred at more or less the same time as the West's growth into cultural maturity.

During this same first phase, though opportunities for contact between Greeks and Latins on a large scale were infrequent, individuals did sometimes move from one area to the other: ambassadors of popes and emperors, merchants eager for profit, adventurers seeking lands or loot, or, on rare occasions, a scholar or two curious to learn something of the past or present of the opposite half of Christendom. Nevertheless, considering the fact that Byzantine culture was, in almost all respects, far more developed and sophisticated than the Western, it may readily be conceded that whatever cultural influences existed in this period flowed from East to West, though, to be sure, there were several rather surprising exceptions (to be discussed in appropriate chapters).[12]

Two events of considerable importance for cultural interaction must be singled out in this initial period. First is the religious schism of 1054 which, according to long-standing tradition, has been taken to mark the definitive rupture, ecclesiastically speaking, between East and West. Actually, this rivalry between the two churches had seen its beginnings as early as the fourth century in the opposing claims of the patriarchs of Rome and Constantinople, in growing theological differences—note especially the diversity of Augustine's theological approach from that of the Greek Cappadocian Fathers[13] —and, no less, in cultural differences, as expressed particularly in the language and ritual of the respective liturgies. But this widening gap, exacerbated by political and social factors, reached its climax in 1054 when legates of the pope excommunicated the Greek patriarch Michael Cerularius and were themselves in turn excommunicated by a synod convoked in Constantinople by the patriarch. Nonetheless, however significant this event may seem in retrospect, the cultural and ecclesiastical relations between East and West were not, as we shall later observe, irretrievably damaged. Not only had previous religious ruptures between Rome and Constantinople been successfully healed, but to the general public of East and West, the collision of 1054 did not seem of really vital importance. It was not, in fact, until the dramatic Western "crusade" of 1204, during our second phase of East-West relations, when Constantinople was sacked and occupied by the Latins, that one may justifiably speak of a "definitive" religious schism between Rome and Constantinople.[14]

The second important event was what has been aptly termed the "political schism" of East and West. The restoration in the West of the Roman Empire in 800 by Charlemagne and the pope was accomplished in direct defiance of Byzantine claims to legitimate imperial succession to the Roman Empire. This event gave rise to the famous "two emperors" question, which was further to aggravate relations all the way to 1453.[15] Both of these events, together with the economic and social as well as political and religious barriers thus erected, seemed further to accentuate the forces of disunity in the former halves of the old Roman Empire and thus to create obstacles to effective cultural communication.

In the second chronological phase, beginning with the First Crusade of 1095, large groups of Latins, ostensibly on their way to the Holy Land, descended upon the East, thus bringing about a mass cultural encounter on Greek soil.[16] The key event in this second period was undoubtedly the conquest and sack of Constantinople in 1204 by Latin Crusader armies, resulting in the destruction of the Byzantine state and the erection of a Latin empire on its ruins. The tragedy of 1204 and the ensuing Latin occupation, with the enforced Greek conversion to the Roman faith, was a traumatic experience for the Greeks; for almost at once it transformed their political and ecclesiastical antagonism toward the West into a mass revulsion, a deep-seated hostility that began to permeate every level of society and would poison all subsequent cultural relations between the two peoples.

And no wonder, if we can believe the testimony of a French knight, Robert of Clari, regarding his participation in the events of 1204. Not only does he write about the cupidity of the Western leaders of the Fourth Crusade in rapaciously seizing the many relics of ancient Christianity preserved in Constantinople (he speaks, for example, of Latin acquisition of "two pieces of the true cross as big as a man's leg"), but he reports that it was the Latin prelates accompanying the armies who turned the expedition into a "holy war" against the

Greeks. Branding the Greeks "traitors and assassins . . . and worse than Jews," the Western clergy, he affirms, even administered absolution to all Western participants in the assault on the Greek capital.[17]

The Byzantines never really recovered from the trauma of 1204 despite the recapture by the forces of Michael Palaeologus of their capital in 1261. Henceforth, in fact, when Byzantines saw Latin expeditions labeled "Crusades" coming to "save" them from the Turks, they inevitably viewed them as robber bands seeking a repetition of the disaster of 1204.[18] And yet, paradoxically, instead of hindering the flow of one people toward the other, the establishment of Crusaders among the native Greek population brought the two peoples, willy-nilly, closer together socially and even culturally.

In this same second period, numerous examples may be cited of Byzantine-Latin social accommodation or symbiosis on both higher and lower levels of society. Westerners—soldiers, merchants, adventurers, colonists, diplomats, clerics, and friar-missionaries— now seemed to be everywhere in Constantinople and the East. Besides the foreigners (all Latins were called "Frangoi"), those who appeared to the Greeks to be ubiquitous were the Gasmules, children of mixed Greco-Latin unions who were looked down upon by all. These hybrids were believed to have inherited the "cunning of the Greeks and the boldness of the Latins"—a phrase that reveals much about the attitudes of the two peoples at the time.[19] Some Greeks disdainfully termed "Latinophrones" (Latin-minded) by their compatriots, thought it fashionable to adopt at least the trappings of Western civilization. Thus, already in the twelfth century the Byzantine emperor Manuel I Comnenus liked to surround himself with Latins in his court. He even delighted in the uniquely Western practice of the joust, often entering the arena of the Hippodrome in order to participate personally. At the same time some Greeks, primarily merchants, and even a few clerics or scholars, began to learn Latin, and on the other hand, many more Latins in the East—court administrators, merchants, mercenaries, or others—were obliged to learn Greek because of practical exigency. Gradually, certain Western expressions began to filter down to the Greek middle and lower classes, for instance, in connection with mercantile practices, in which the enterprising Latins by now had forged far ahead of the Greeks. It was also in this period of Latin penetration that certain ancient Greek works—of Aristotle, Archimedes, Galen, and others—were for the first time translated (by Latins residing in the East) into Latin, though primarily for the use of Western Scholastics.[20]

An indication, during this period, of a conscious Latin desire to penetrate Byzantine society and culture more deeply, was the plan of the Latin emperor of Constantinople, Baldwin I, seconded by pope Innocent III, "to propagate the Christian religion in the East." Thus, soon after the Latin occupation of 1204, the pope issued a decree for the establishment, in effect, of a branch of the university of Paris in Constantinople. For this purpose he invited "masters and scholars" from Paris "to go to Greece to reform the study of letters"—meaning to instruct young Greeks (and perhaps Muslims) in the Latin form of education as well as in Latin ecclesiastical rites. Whether the plan was actually implemented is doubtful. It is, nevertheless, significant as the first in a series of increasingly numerous Western attempts to infiltrate Byzantine society by striking at its most vulnerable point, the education of the young.[20a] As we shall see, this type of educational program would in time form a veritable pattern for action in future Western endeavors to dominate the East.

Despite more intensive cultural contacts, the Greek populace as a whole came more and more to regard the Latins, and especially their form of Christianity and culture, as inferior, even reprehensible. Already at the end of the twelfth century the Byzantine historian Nicetas Choniates could write with undisguised rancor:

> Between us and the Franks has opened up the widest gulf. We have not a thought in common. We are poles apart, even though we may happen to live together in the same house. They are arrogant for the most part, and proudly make pretence of an upright carriage, and affect to look down on the smoothness and modesty of our manners as base and fawning. But we regard their arrogance and boasting and over-bearing as a flux of the snivel which keeps their noses in the air, and we tread them down by the might of Christ who giveth us power to trample unhurt upon the viper and the scorpion.

And another contemporary Greek writer, John Cinnamos, resentful over the fact that, unlike the privileged Venetians, even Byzantine merchants were obliged to pay duties on goods imported to and exported from the Golden Horn, railed at the intermarriage of Latins with Byzantines, calling the Latins (absurdly) "a rotten, clownish, slavish nation.[21] It was perhaps, above all, these privileged Western merchants, even more than the Latin missionaries and mercenaries, who most irritated the Greeks.

For the Greek people in general especially after 1204, any Byzantine who even deigned to look with favor on the Latin faith came to be viewed as a traitor not only to his church but also to his "nation" and the cultural tradition that these implied. In the words of the Greek masses themselves, such a person had become "Latinized"— a term by then filled not only with religious but with ethnic and cultural overtones. Such were the effects of the collision of the two peoples and their cultures in the Byzantine East, particularly after 1204 and during the years extending up to the Greek recovery of Constantinople in 1261, the event which, as noted, put an end to the Latin Empire. Of course, all these various circumstances tended to diminish any chances for peaceful coexistence between the two peoples.

In our third period, from 1261 to 1453, a new, very disturbing factor entered the picture—the continuing threat of the Ottoman Turks to Constantinople. It was this, more than anything else, that served as the motivating factor for almost all Greek political relations, especially in the seemingly endless negotiations for ecclesiastical union between Rome and Byzantium. In fact, the problem of religious union—with the adamant papal demand for jurisdiction over the Eastern church in exchange for military aid, and the countering Greek insistence on the convocation of an ecumenical council to resolve the religious differences—may be said to have been the underlying theme which bound together almost all East-West diplomacy of the time.[21a] But the problem went far deeper than appeared on the surface. More than a dogmatic question over the *filioque*, more even than a question of Greek relief from Turkish military attacks, it was, to most Byzantines, a question of their very suvival as a people, with the individuation of their own religious and cultural tradition. In this phase, when the Byzantines fell into an increasingly defensive posture, Greek apprehensions may be said to have fluctuated not only according to the degree of anxiety the Byzantines felt over the Turkish threat, but—sometimes even more— over what they considered to be Latin aspirations to renewed domination over Constantinople.[22]

Ecclesiastical negotiations, then, became even more complex because they frequently masked deeper Greek feelings of a cultural and psychological nature. The perennial debate that raged in Byzantium over religious union with Rome, especially after the

Council of Lyons in 1274 (see chapter 8), now led some Greek intellectuals, theologians, and statesmen, for the first time in centuries, to take an interest in Latin theology. But this, in many cases, was not so much to satisfy personal curiosity as for them to be able to confront the Latins more successfully by using the Western tool of the Scholastic method.[23] In contrast to this growing group of theologians, there were others to whom the all-important fact was the salvation of the empire from the advancing Turks, an objective, they affirmed, worth a few "minor concessions" on the ecclesiastical side. For this latter group, religious considerations were therefore secondary to political expediency. These unionist *politiques,* probably somewhat greater in number than is today realized, were usually led by persons of the first rank: emperors, an occasional unionist patriarch, or at times by leading officers of the government such as the Grand Logothete (prime minister).

A somewhat different, perhaps truer, type of *Latinophilia* characterized the Byzantine idealist Demetrius Cydones, the remarkable Grand Logothete through much of the fourteenth century. Cydones, who wanted to read the Western chancery reports without interpreters, is reported to have embraced Catholicism as a result of his efforts to learn Latin by reading Thomas Aquinas! However his conversion came about, he adopted certain Latin religious beliefs and values without, in his view, compromising his loyalty to Byzantine culture. So fond, in fact, did Cydones become of the works of Aquinas that he even founded a virtual cult of Thomists in the imperial Byzantine court itself. For Cydones, however (as probably for the Byzantine prelate Bessarion a century later), the problem of religious union with Rome was basically less one of partisan loyalty to the Byzantine church or state than of fidelity to a higher ideal from which would flow, he believed, political, religious, and cultural benefits for *both* Greeks and Latins. This ideal of Cydones—the concept of the unity of Christendom as it had existed in the early centuries of Christianity—suggests that he possessed not only a broad historical vision but, more significantly, a remarkable feeling of tolerance for the divergent cultural tradition of what the average Greek had long termed the "heretical, arrogant Latins."[24]

Despite the fact that some Greek political leaders and even individual patriarchs were, in times of crisis, convinced of the need to make an accomodation to Latin ecclesiastical demands, the instinct of the vast majority of the Byzantine populace for preservation of its religious and, by extension, cultural heritage never failed. Thus, virtually all the common people, and of course the monks and the lower clergy, together with most of the middle class and part of the nobility, held fast to their religious convictions. To them Orthodoxy (literally "correct belief" in accordance with the views of the Eastern Church Fathers) was the one true faith, transmitted to them through the centuries from their forebears *(patroparadoton)*,[25] and it was their sacred duty to preserve it inviolate. Abandonment, in fact, would constitute not only betrayal of their religion and "nation" but, worse, would bring down upon their heads the full wrath of God. Indeed, a current belief held that previous Ottoman successes were owing not only to Muslim moral superiority but to the sins of the Greeks, especially the moral decadence of their clergy.[26],

Deserted by their own emperors, harassed by Greek *Latinophrones* and the violent protestations of monks against union, and courted in addition by the blandishments of papal envoys, many Greeks now suffered a kind of "identity crisis." Not comprehending, or perhaps not even wishing to comprehend, the reasoning of their *politique* leaders, these Greeks became so alienated from their government (which for the sake of political expediency was generally prounionist), that they strove all the more to preserve and even to reinforce their traditional beliefs in their religion and culture. Not that they themselves doubted their own "ethnic" identity. But what they now perceived as an internal as well as an external threat made them reassert that identity even more strongly. Thus, in order to buttress their beliefs, they reemphasized the very roots of their Orthodox religion —the seven ecumenical councils and the writings of the fourth- and fifth-century Greek Fathers of the church. What is truly remarkable, however, is that at the same time a considerable number of the intellectual elite, drawn from the upper middle class and especially the aristocracy, now began to appeal with greater fervor also to the culture of the *ancient* Greeks (Hellenes), with whom they now began, for the first time unequivocally, to indentify as their ethnic as well as their intellectual heirs.

That religious union would lead to Western political domination was not doubted by most Greeks. Not only this, many—subconsciously or otherwise—felt that within a matter of generations cultural domination by the Latins would come about, and ultimately even a considerable assimilation of the Byzantine culture into the Latin. And their fears were not without some justification, if we are to judge by the plans of two French crusader-propagandists of the fourteenth century. First was Guillaume d'Adam who, seeking to compel Greek cooperation for a joint Latin-Byzantine crusade against the Turks to recover the Holy Land, recommended forcible conversion of the Greeks, suppression of their "fanatical" monks, the burning of "heretical" Greek books, and, in order completely to "brain-wash" the East, the dispatching of the eldest son from each Orthodox family to the West to be reared in the Latin faith.[27] Second was the French publicist Pierre Dubois who, in a *mémoire* to the French king, suggested the sending of educated, noble Latin girls to the East (both to the Greeks and the Saracens) to do charity work in hospitals, the more comely to marry important Greek figures (especially clerics!) with the ultimate aim of converting the entire East to the Latin faith.[28]

More sympathetic to the Greeks, but on that account perhaps more subtly threatening, was the project of an Italian Renaissance humanist monk, the Grecophile Ambrogio Traversari (the first Renaissance humanist, as we shall see, to translate the Greek Fathers into Latin). Three years before the Council of Florence (1438–39), he suggested to Pope Eugenius IV a simple plan for proselytizing Greece through educational means. As he wrote to the pope: "I think that about a hundred very young Greek boys should be brought over [to Italy] and raised in the rites of the Latin church in our monastic house with diligence. For when they are grown, if proper care has been given them, they will serve with particular effect to restore their brethren to the faith and devotion of the Roman church, and they can then be entrusted with their own areas of the church."[29] In almost all spheres, then, political, social, and especially religious, Western plans were proposed to convert the Greeks to "Roman Catholicism" and to force them to adopt certain Western beliefs and practices.

It was no doubt in reaction to Western proposals of this kind that the Greek monk Joseph Bryennios exclaimed to his countrymen in 1400, when he heard of a new Latin expedition to "save" Constantinople from the Turks: "Do not deceive yourselves by delusive hopes that Italian allied troops will come to save us. If they pretend to rise to defend us, they will take arms only to destroy our city, our race, and our name."[30] And in the mid-fifteenth century, the fervently antiunionist George Scholarios proclaimed on the very eve of the Turkish conquest: "O miserable *Rhomaioi* [Greeks], why have you abandoned the truth . . . and why have you trusted in the Italians? In losing your faith you will lose your city."[31] In the eyes of most Byzantines he might well have added "and your sense of identity as well."

It is understandable, therefore, why the Orthodox religion with its various particularities—use of the Greek language in the ritual, the use of leavened bread in the Eucharist, and, perhaps above all, rejection of the Latin filioque—came most clearly to epitomize to the Greeks the deep cultural and psychological abyss that had opened up between the two peoples. Revealing are the epithets Latins and Byzantines were wont to hurl at each other—epithets that often conflated the religious and the ethnic. The Greeks disparagingly called the Latins "Azymites" (users of unleavened bread in the Eucharist), "Frangoi" (that is, not "Romans"), and "heretics." The Latins responded no less abusively by terming the Greeks "perfidious Greek [not "Roman"] schismatics" or "worse than the Turks."[32]

The Latins, with their supranational church under the pope and the ethnic and political individuation that it permitted, never really understood—or usually even cared to understand—the underlying cultural and ethnic fears of the Greeks. No one, that is, except for a few scholars like the thirteenth-century Latin, Humbert of Romans, or the fourteenth-century Greco-Latin, Barlaam of Calabria, both of whom had lived for years in the Greek East and could therefore comprehend the psychology of a dominated and defensive but still proud people.[33]

In this same third period (1261–1453), amid civil war, disruption of communications, and near collapse of the state structure—in short, pervasive chaos on a scale never before experienced by Byzantium—a truly remarkable but paradoxical development occurred in the East, a Greek cultural and spiritual revival which historians call the "Palaeologan Renaissance." It was the expulsion of the despised Latins from, and the Greek recovery of, their capital city, after a bitter more than half-century of Latin occupation that brought a resurgence of "national" Greek pride, confidence, and patriotism. These feelings of euphoria in turn expressed themselves concretely in a burst of spiritual, artistic, and literary creativity based in large part on a revival of the Greek religious and cultural tradition of the past, ancient as well as early Christian. One explanation for this phenomenon of revival may be that in origin the movement was, at least in its more spiritual, religious phase, inspired by the response of the many unyielding, arch-conservative Greeks to the oppressive domination (or, to make use of another term, hegemony) of the Latins, especially in the religious and cultural spheres. Byzantine cultural values could best be maintained, many in this group believed, by strictly adhering to and more strongly reasserting their religious roots in the Greek Church Fathers and the ecumenical councils. Seen in this light, the response of this group may be termed a "nativistic" Greek reaction[34] to Latin (as well as Greek Latinophile) pressures.

Another important factor in the Palaeologan Renaissance was the reaction of an intellectual group drawn almost exclusively from the higher, aristocratic class. The members of this group sought to maintain their cultural identity not only by reemphasizing the Orthodox faith, but by claiming descent from what they believed uniquely distinguished the Byzantines from all other peoples—that is, their ancient Greek forebears and their culture. This is remarkable, since for centuries to the Byzantines the term *Hellene* was distasteful and meant pagan not Christian.[35] Yet, increasingly for this group of Byzantine intellectuals of the aristocracy, including some of the civil bureaucracy, the strong reassertion of the roots of their civilization in ancient Greek literature and philosophy—a striking phenomenon bearing the characteristics of a revitalization movement—became a prime distinguishing mark of their own culture, in fact, as will be shown later, of a new kind of Greek ethnicity. After all, the West did partake of the classical inheritance even if primarily from the Latin side; and the Orthodox faith was shared with the Slavs. But the Byzantines alone could claim as their cultural patrimony *both* Orthodoxy and ancient Greek culture.

Paradoxical as the appearance of a "renaissance" may seem in light of the wretched social and political conditions of the late Byzantine period, it is compatible with the thesis of certain modern authorities, for example G. von Grünebaum. These affirm that in time of grave danger to the very fabric of a society, particularly when the peril of assimilation to another culture looms, some kind of cultural revival (or "renaissance") in the form of a virtual digging up of the past may break out among those alienated from the course of compromise or submission being followed by the leaders of that society.[36]

By the early fourteenth century this Byzantine Renaissance, now spreading in various areas of the Greek East, came to manifest itself primarily in three related yet discrete dimensions: first, a mystical, essentially nonrational movement, Hesychasm, based, so its principal proponents the monks of Mt. Athos maintained, on the writings and practices of the Fathers and earlier mystics of the Orthodox church, especially Symeon the New Theologian cf the eleventh century.[37] (Some authorities do not treat Hesychasm as part of the Palaeologan Renaissance, but it is included here because in its wider implications it reflects cultural phenomena of the period.) Second, new emphases in Byzantine art, an art less stereotyped, more humanized, displaying a richer range of colors and intensity of emotion—in short, more realistic and dramatic. This type of artistic expression is a kind of counterpart to the art of the early Italian Renaissance with its first steps toward realism and naturalism in painting[38] (as in the humanistic style of the ancients). But there appeared also in this period, it should be noted, another artistic current, one with its roots more in the traditional Byzantine religious style and which, some scholars believe, seemed in certain ways (in the use of the theme and iconography of Christ's Transfiguration, for example) to reflect in painting the mystical, contemplative spirituality of Hesychasm. Thus, attemps were made to represent the luminosity of the "uncreated" light of Mt. Tabor, which was considered to be discernible to the true Hesychast.[39]

Perhaps still more significant for our study is the renaissance's third dimension. This was a more intensive revival, from the latter part of the thirteenth or beginning of the fourteenth century, on the part of highly educated persons from among the upper and part of the middle class, of the study of ancient Greek culture—not only of the philosophy of Aristotle and the ideas (some long suspect) of Plato, but also of the great tragedies and the rhetorical and poetical works.[40] It is this broad and in some ways contradictory movement—at once spiritual, artistic, and intellectual as well, and inspired to no small extent by the need of many Byzantines for a return to the ancient Hellenic and early Christian past—that is known to modern scholars as the Palaeologan Renaissance. This is not, it should again be emphasized, to exclude other causes, social and intellectual, of this multifaceted, extraordinarily complex movement, such as other internal Byzantine and even certain Western influences,[41] which in one way or another may have challenged or in some way interacted, with the traditional Byzantine culture.

Of the three broad dimensions of the Palaeologan Renaissance—

spiritual, artistic, and intellectual[42]—it was the last, as we shall see, which came to have the most profound impact on the Latin West. With regard to painting, some recent art authorities maintain that the more humanistic, sometimes dramatic, Byzantine artistic style of the late thirteenth and fourteenth centuries somehow influenced (or at least anticipated) the style of the seminal Florentine painter of the Italian Renaissance, Giotto, in bringing similar qualities to Western Renaissance painting. Other scholars argue that this new quality, that of greater "realism" in both Byzantine and Western painting may have been the result of a certain interaction of chains of impulses between the two cultures which have not yet been fully elucidated. Still others, more plausibly perhaps, believe that, after an undisputed infusion of Byzantine influence in Western painting of the twelfth century, there occurred a parallel but independent reaching back in *both* Byzantine and Italian painting to the more humanistic and naturalistic models of the ancient past, more particularly in the West to an imitation of the early Christian frescoes and mosaics in churches of Rome. In any case, the assertion of one distinguished art historian cannot be far from the mark in stating that the solution to the problem of the almost synchronous production by Giotto of his remarkable frescoes in Padua's Arena Chapel, and of the no less remarkable Byzantine frescoes—and mosaics—in the monastery of the Chora in Constantinople, involves a psychological question of the senses, of a particular way of viewing the world, that has to be examined in the context of "the whole problem of the Byzantine and Western world in their estrangement as well as in their kinship."[43]

As for the spiritual revival, Hesychasm—an attempt at a mystical union with God through a method of contemplation and prayer—it doubtless had causes other than simply a desire on the part of the Athonite monks to reassert older East Christian religious and devotional patterns. It has even been looked upon (not so implausibly) as a means of escape from the prevailing uncertainty and despair which accompanied the social chaos of the time.[44] Concentrated on Mt. Athos, Hesychasm, with its peculiar qualities of contemplation and asceticism (for example, the technique of holding the breath while repeating the words of the "Jesus prayer"), soon made its effect felt in nearby Bulgaria, whence it was disseminated to Russia with results that extended deep into the sixteenth and later centuries. Hesychasm, on the other hand, had little if any influence on the

West, where, as we shall see, its theological beliefs in particular were considered to be "innovations" and therefore heretical.

It is sometimes affirmed that it was Hesychasm, with its strong emphasis on asceticism and evident adherence to the traditional formulaic quality of Byzantine iconography, that probably stunted the initial exuberance and experimental verve of the early Palaeologan artistic Renaissance, thereby causing a reversion of Byzantine art to its more traditionally spiritual and less humanized form. The subsequent triumph of the Hesychast monks over the state must, in any case, have been at least partly responsible for blocking the further development of the remarkable manifestations of creativity in mid-fourteenth-century Byzantine art.[45]

The intellectual phase of the Palaeologan Renaissance, with its renewed (and in some instances more profane, that is more "secular")[46] emphasis on classical Greek literature and philosophy, continued in the East as a major force until the fall of the empire in 1453. Though it was in the interest of the Turkish conquerors to keep the Greeks isolated from the Western world, the chief fruits of this extraordinary but still inadequately explored intellectual revival (which in some ways predated the better-known Italian Renaissance and in fact reveals some of the same basic characteristics) were not to be lost to the Western world, as will be discussed in several chapters below.[47]

The fourth and last period in our schema of Byzantine-Latin cultural interaction began in 1453 or, more accurately, some decades before, when, under the increasingly ominous threat of the Turks to Constantinople, more and more Greeks began to flee for sanctuary to the West, often bringing with them the revived classical learning of the Palaeologan Renaissance. This is not to say that individual Greek scholars had not exerted some influence on the West in the past Nor especially is it to affirm that these refugees had anything to do with the origins of the Italian Renaissance—a movement which, at its inception, was unquestionably the result of the interplay of internal, and especially Italian, factors.

The number of the Greek refugees waxed greater the more the Turkish menace increased, so that soon after 1453 one may justifiably speak of a veritable "diaspora" of Greeks appearing in the Western world. No longer was Constantinople or the East the focal point of contact between Byzantines and Latins. Now, rather, it was the areas of the West, especially Italy, where after 1453 a large number of Greeks had come to live and find employment. Within a few decades the various Greek colonies established in Italy consisted of virtually all social strata of the lost Byzantine homeland—aristocrats and professional men, soldiers and sailors, artisans and laborers.[48]

Most significant for East-West cultural relations in this last, post-Byzantine period (which one scholar has aptly called "Byzance après Byzance") were the scholars, especially those learned in ancient Greek literature and philosophy as revived in the Palaeologan period. As is well known, with the dawn of the Western Renaissance a vertible mania for Greek learning soon spread rapidly over the Western world, creating a particularly receptive climate for Greek studies, especially in Italy. One result was that, whereas in the medieval period when Westerners, as we shall note, tended to look upon Byzantine culture with disdain (Latin scholars had then often preferred to get at an ancient Greek work through the medium of medieval Arabic translations—second hand, as it were,)[49] now Italian humanists of the Renaissance were becoming increasingly cognizant of the greater benefits to be derived from direct access to the Byzantine texts, and even more to the Greek émigré scholars themselves.

As time passed, however, some learned Byzantine men came to receive a less cordial reception in the West—especially when Latin scholars, once having mastered Greek, began to rival (on occasion even to revile) the Byzantines not only intellectually but especially in the competition for university posts. Instructive are the cogent words of a Greek émigré, the powerfull Cardinal Bessarion who, ca. 1455, wrote lamentingly to his protégé, the Byzantine humanist Michael Apostolis: "How deeply it grieves me to see our (Greek) people suffering everywhere publicly and privately, esteemed lightly, hated, persecuted, abused. . . . Learn to bear the jealousy flourishing everywhere . . . especially against foreigners, the more so if they are learned men.[49a]

Of the various Greek colonies in the West, most outstanding was that of Venice, which by 1470 had become so large and thriving that the Greek humanist previously noted, Bessarion, could term it "a second Byzantium."[50] Many of the earlier learned Greek refugees, fleeing the Turkish seizure of their homeland, went to Venice via the Venetian-held island of Crete, which thus came to serve as a kind of "halfway point," intellectually speaking, between Byzantium and the West.[51] Greek colonies, as we shall note later, were soon established not only in Venice but in Naples, Ancona, Toledo, and still later in France, Germany, England—even Russia. Whatever the connection between the Greek colonists and Western European society, it was the individual émigré humanist who, among the many Greeks of the diaspora in the West, contributed most to the movement of the Western Renaissance. Seeking patronage and position, the Greek scholars often chose to reside in the court or residence of their patron instead of within the Greek community, with which, however, they almost invariably maintained close relations (for example, Marcus Musurus). Others obtained positions as professors of Greek at leading Western universities (at Padua, for example, as shall be described in detail),[52] but not always with the approval of their Latin competitors. Nevertheless, the nearby existence of a well-organized Greek community was vital to the Byzantine scholar-refugees in providing them with a sense of ethnic and cultural identity. It may even be said (as will later be shown) that these diaspora communities constituted, at a time when a Greek "nation" as such had ceased to exist, a fundamental but hitherto neglected factor in the emergence of the spirit of modern Greek nationalism.[53]

In establishing a permanent "contact situation" in the West, the learned diaspora Greeks thus became the main protagonists in the final chronological phase of Byzantine-Latin cultural interaction— a phase sometimes overlooked, or more often considered apart from, that of the life of Byzantium proper. The contribution of the diaspora, in fact, was in some ways more immediately productive for the West than that of the Byzantines before 1204, which, as we have already noted, may be termed rather a piecemeal "infiltration" of Byzantine culture into the Latin West. For the Greek émigrés of the fifteenth (and sixteenth) centuries, by bringing to Italy ancient Greek culture as revived by the Palaeologan Renaissance, played a central—if not the seminal—role in reorienting Florentine humanism from an essentially Latin rhetorical movement to a primarily philosophic and literary movement that emphasized ancient Greek civilization with its greater breadth and originality of thought.[54]

To write a truly systematic, detailed study of the cultural interrelations between Byzantines and Latins from the fourth through the sixteenth centuries would be, to say the least, a vast undertaking. Nor have I really attempted that here. Rather, what I have tried to do is, first to delineate in this Prologue the changing social-cultural milieux within which these cultural exchanges and interactions took place, and then, below, to provide a series of chapters illustrative of the more significant facets and dimensions of these patterns of interaction, both in the Middle Ages and in the Renaissance. Using the prologue's four phases of periodization, chronologically speaking, and the tripartite typology suggested for the various modes of cultural influence as a guide to the discussions that follow, the reader, I hope, may be helped toward a clearer understanding of the long, intricate process of acculturation between the kindred Byzantine and Latin worlds—an interaction described here in the encounter of societies, institutions, and individuals.

1

The Orthodox Church: The Primary Creative Element in Byzantine Culture

The Byzantine Empire was, technically at least, the Christian form or continuation of the old pagan Roman Empire. By the mid-seventh century, however, it had become almost entirely Greek in culture and outlook; and through the eleventh, and in certain respects up to the thirteenth or even fourteenth centuries, it remained, socially and culturally speaking, the most advanced—certainly the most sophisticated—state in the world. Its gold coin, the *nomisma*, was universally accepted as a kind of dollar of the age. And the refinements of life in Constantinople were legendary not only in the Latin and Arab worlds but even among such semibarbaric peoples as the Vikings of distant Scandinavia. Perhaps one can most readily grasp the importance of the Byzantine state by noting that at the apogee of its power in the early eleventh century, its capital city, Constantinople, contained some eight hundred thousand to one million people, while Paris, perhaps the greatest city of the West, had a mere fifty thousand inhabitants.[1]

There is no need to elaborate further on the preeminence of this state as compared to others of the age, nor to expatiate on the reasons for its decline or its remarkable longevity and tenacity of life, surrounded, as it was, almost continuously by a host of enemies. The significance of the political and economic role of Byzantium is generally recognized today; but its civilization, the accomplishments of its church in particular, are still too little appreciated. Indeed, Byzantine culture is too often regarded not only as something long since dead, but as being of little relevance to the modern Western world. Aside from long-standing Western prejudices arising from the ecclesiastical schism between Rome and Constantinople, a fundamental reason for such neglect is the simple fact that Byzantium as a state no longer exists, though to be sure the modern Greeks, because of a linguistic and religious sense of continuity, believe themselves (and probably rightly) to be the chief legatees of Byzantine civilization.[2]

Perhaps a more important reason for the neglect of Byzantium's accomplishments is the all too common view that Byzantine culture, though highly refined, was essentially uncreative and unoriginal. And that factor, rightly or wrongly, is for contemporary critics too often the primary criterion for evaluating the worth of artistic or literary expression. While realizing that without Byzantium virtually all of ancient Greek literature and philosophy would have been lost to the modern world, modern scholars at the same time tend to relegate Byzantium to the role of a mere *passive* repository of ancient culture. This is a one-sided view, for in a number of respects Byzantine civilization may be said to have been highly creative; and this creativity, as will be shown,[3] was in no small measure the result of the synthesis, the intermixture, of the thought and ideas of Hellenistic Greek culture with those of Christianity. It was the transformation effected by the amalgamation of these two forces, and especially the spiritual enrichment afforded by the peculiarly Byzantine brand of Christianity (today called Greek Orthodoxy), that gave Byzantine civilization its unique ethos and vitality.

There is no need to analyze this process of fusion between Greek philosophy and literature on the one hand and Christianity on the other or, as scholars put it more simply, between classical reason and Christian faith. It is pertinent, nevertheless, to cite the judgment of the famous German scholar Werner Jaeger, who declared that "the future of Christianity as a world religion depended on this fusion."[4] In the formative early centuries of the church, the period of the ecumenical councils, the Greek Fathers, who played the leading role, in order better to explain rationally the complexities of Christian dogma, often drew on concepts and terms from ancient Greek philosophy, from Platonism, Stoicism, and Aristotelianism.[5] And in this same early period, although many considered Christianity the enemy and even the negation of pagan Greek culture, the leading Greek Fathers advocated with certain exceptions the study of ancient Greek literature and philosophy. St. Basil himself, the "patron" of Orthodox education, in a famous discourse advised (with qualification) the Christian youth to study ancient Greek literature because its ethical values, so similar in general to those of Christianity, were presented in a style remarkable for its persuasiveness and richness.[6]

Out of the synthesis of these two elements, then—Christianity and

Greek thought—a dynamic theology was created. And it was this Greek theology that was primarily responsible for the formulation of Christian philosophy and dogma for the entire Christian church. Though certainly not overlooking the fusion of these two elements, Western scholars sometimes forget that it was the Greek East that developed the so-called apophatic approach to theology, the attempt to explain God by a process of negation—that is, by stating what God is not rather than what he is. For if one tries to define what God *is*, then by implication one tends to limit his nature; and God, of course, is uncircumscribable (*aperigraptos*).[7]

Another aspect of the Byzantine church and its activities that merits attention is the high degree of lay participation in church affairs. That was, in part, a result of the ideology of Byzantium. For church and state were closely associated, in fact intertwined. They constituted one organic structure, the whole being an imitation (*mimesis*) on earth of the kingdom of heaven above. Over this entire structure on earth presided the Basileus, or emperor, as the representative of God. As a semisacerdotal figure, though technically still a layman, the emperor possessed certain liturgical privileges reserved only for the clergy. He could cross before the Iconostasis and during the liturgy, preach to the congregation and cense the people. He could even communicate himself—that is, administer the bread and wine of the Eucharist to himself. (To be sure, only a priest could actually consecrate the bread and wine.) Yet it is of primary importance to note that, despite these extraordinary privileges, the emperor could not, on his own, pronounce on or alter church dogma:[8] for the formulation of dogma the convocation of an ecumenical council was required. Indeed, the traditional Feast of Orthodoxy, the day on which in 843 the icons were officially restored to the church, is significant precisely because certain emperors of the eighth and early ninth centuries were blocked by the church in their efforts to destroy the holy pictures and prohibit their veneration by the people.

Of special interest to modern society should be the role played in the Byzantine church by the so-called archons, the chief lay citizens in the cities of the empire. It was one of the archons' duties to protect the church in their respective areas, and in later local councils held in Constantinople, such as in the eleventh century, they even played a role in internal ecclesiastical affairs.[9] To the considerable degree of lay participation in affairs of the Byzantine church one might also add the fact of the prominence of lay theologians in Byzantium. Both of these points serve to underscore an important difference between the Greek and Roman churches in the Middle Ages. It is, in fact, only in recent years that the Roman church has been witnessing the emergence of a greater voice for laymen in ecclesiastical affairs.

In this connection, it might be pointed out that in today's so-called updating (*aggiornamento*) of the Roman church, several of the changes suggested are practices that have been common for centuries in the Orthodox church—for example, the use of leavened bread, the administering of wine in the communion cup to the laity not to the clergy alone, standing while receiving communion, and the use of the vernacular in the liturgy. There can be little doubt that the Byzantine liturgy is most moving when chanted in the original language (Greek) in which it was composed. It is noteworthy, nonetheless, that the Byzantines themselves, recognizing the significance to the masses of an understanding of the words of the liturgical ceremony, at times permitted the liturgy to be translated into other languages—the prime example being Slavonic. And that translation, fostered in the ninth century by the Greek patriarch Photius and the emperor, is the key to understanding the remarkable Byzantine success in converting the Slavic peoples to Orthodoxy in the face of the determined efforts of the Roman church, which insisted, instead, upon imposition of the Latin liturgy.[10] Not that Byzantium was always so tolerant in its approach to a "vernacular" liturgy. Witness John Chrysostom's attitude toward the Arian Goths of Constantinople in the fourth century, and evidence of other Byzantine insistence on the use of only the three "sacred" languages—Greek, Hebrew, and Latin—in preference to Slavonic.[11]

The long historical rivalry, even bitter animosity, between Rome and Constantinople is today happily diminishing, and the two churches are drawing closer to one another. Nevertheless, the most basic problem of all still remains—papal claims to jurisdiction over the entire Christian church. Several years ago in Constantinople I inquired of His Holiness, the late Patriarch Athenagoras, that most irenic of church leaders, how this seemingly insurmountable obstacle between the churches could be resolved. His answer was revealing and perhaps prophetic: "It may be that the Roman church itself will resolve this question." And recent trends in the Roman church, though diverse in scope, seem to be beginning to fulfill his prediction.

Another aspect of Byzantine ecclesiastical culture that deserves mention for its creativeness is the character of its spirituality. In Orthodox spirituality perhaps the prime concept is that of *theosis*— that is, the belief that through prayer, dedication, and contemplation (*Hesychia* in Greek) one may, already in this life, achieve a degree of mystical union with God. True, the most famous Byzantine Hesychasts, those of the fourteenth century, were monks withdrawn from the world and living on Mount Athos, and their techniques for achieving a state of contemplation were not always accepted. But their influence was felt widely in Byzantine society and soon spread to Bulgaria, whence, ultimately, they had a great influence on the Muscovite *Startsi* (holy men) who, as is well known, played a considerable role in the turbulent political and social life of sixteenth- and seventeenth-century Russia.[12]

Union with God can, of course, also be achieved through receiving the Eucharist, the partaking of the body and blood of Christ under the appearance of the bread and wine—a sacrament that possesses the same degree of efficacy for laymen, clerics, and monks alike.

The Eucharist, or Communion, is the central mystery of the sacrifice of the Mass, or the Divine Liturgy as it is called in the Orthodox church. By offering himself in preparation for communion, as an oblation in union with the sacrifice of the Mass, the communicant is able to achieve a closer union with God during the liturgy. The Orthodox liturgy, in effect the enactment of the life and passion of Christ, is in every way—visually, symbolically, and musically—a true work of art.[13] The liturgy, in particular the hymnody of the church, as is too little appreciated in the West, in fact constitutes one of the most creatively original aspects of Byzantine civilization. E. Wellesz of Oxford University maintains that the greatest Byzantine hymns, as artistic creations, are equal to, and in some cases even surpass, the best of the Roman church.[14] It must be admitted, however, that comparison is difficult to make. Take the moving Western hymn *Stabat Mater* ("The Mother was Standing"). As one listens to it one can feel the sorrow, the very human emotion of the mother as she sees her son hanging on the cross. Then consider the greatest of the Byzantine hymns, the *Akathistos Hymnos*. Here the aim is quite different, not to evoke in the listener the human emotions of this world but rather, one might say, a higher, more spiritualized emotion of the celestial world above.

This exalted quality of Byzantine hymns unfortunately cannot be adequately reproduced in translation. One can, nevertheless, note the technical devices, literary and musical, used by the Byzantine hymnographer (probably Romanus the Melodos) to produce this effect. The internal rhythm of the lines, the repetition of key phrases such as *Haire nymfe anymfefte* ("Hail bride unmarried," literally "unbrided"), the acrostic starting of each line with a new consecutive letter of the Greek alphabet, the intonation of the words chosen for their onomatopoeic effect, and finally, the remarkably pure sound of the chanting, devoid of any harmony whatever, much like Gregorian chant—all of these devices produce for the listener a lofty, ethereal quality perhaps unmatched in the entire range of liturgical literature.[15]

One can hardly speak of Byzantine hymnody without referring to the best-known cultural product of the Byzantine church, its art. Today Byzantine art is popular and widely studied, and this in part because, like most modern art, it is not literal, not merely photographic: it is symbolic, or at least semirepresentational, in character. Moreover, in its richness and variety of color, its stylization and subtlety of line, it has rarely been equaled, The extraordinary depth of expression produced by the surviving Byzantine mosaics, little pieces of colored glass placed together at different angles in order to refract light, is well known. The celebrated stained-glass windows of Gothic cathedrals produce something of the same effect, and it has recently been suggested by several Western scholars that these too may have received an initial stimulus from prototypes produced earlier by the craft of the Byzantine window glazier.[16] (Among the Byzantines, of course, the full aesthetic potential of stained glass was not realized, as it was in the West.)

As in hymnody, Byzantine painting also sought to represent the sublimity of the other world. Nevertheless, despite its remarkable qualities, some modern critics (in some cases perhaps justifiably) tend to feel surfeited with what they consider to be the overly repetitious, sometimes even stereotyped, quality of Byzantine painting But they fail to see that, in the last two centuries of the empire before its fall in 1453, one line of development in Byzantine art (and also in spirituality, as we have seen) underwent a surprising "renaissance" in which certain changes of style were manifested in Byzantine creativity. Thus we see in this new "revival" of Byzantine art—whether technically it be termed Macedonian or Constantinopolitan does not matter

—a new trend toward "realism," toward a more humanized quality which, however, in another current was combined with the older, more, traditional ethos.[17] New, more daring colors (brilliant yellows, for example) were now utilized and the figures were often elongated for special effect.[18] Such kinds of paintings may still be seen in Crete, Mistra, Constantinople, and also Mt. Athos at the Protaton in the works of the fourteenth-century Athonite arist, Manuel Panselinos.[19]

But the climax to this new artistic development was reached in two late Greek painters who worked primarily in Russia and Spain. The first, Theophanes the Greek of the fourteenth century, worked for a time in Constantinople where his works or his pupils' remain in the Church of the Chora. Little known to the Western world except to specialists, Theophanes is familiar in Russia as "Feofan Grek," who was probably (as recently stressed by V. Lazarev), the teacher of the greatest Russian painter, Rublev.[20] The best paintings of Theophanes are in the Kariye Camii and in Novgorod and in the Cathedral of the Assumption in the Kremlin itself. The second was born some fifty years after the fall of Constantinople, the great sixteenth-century painter Domenikos Theotokopoulos, better known as El Greco, who is often mistakenly referred to as Spanish. Born and raised in Crete in the early sixteenth century, he went for four years to Venice and later to Spain, where he spent the remainder of his life. But it is notable that he never failed to sign all his later paintings in Greek characters "Domenikos Theotokopoulos the Cretan." Indeed, a notarial document recently found indicates that he was probably still living in Heracleion, Crete, until the reasonably mature age of twenty-five. Hence, his technique and style as a painter were presumably to a large extent already formed before he emigrated to the West.

Both artists may perhaps be considered as the supreme exponents of the last, too little-known revival of Byzantine painting. They used the rich new colors and forms while retaining the old tradition of Byzantine symbolism. At the same time they portrayed their figures in a new way, with greater emotion and more dynamism, and sometimes in an elongated manner for greater effect. In the eyes of the viewer their works are able, as one scholar has put it, to produce the effect of man's flesh striving toward spiritual reality. (On the two "Grecos" see esp. chap. 3, Prologue, and Epilogue).[21]

In architecture, too, Byzantium was genuinely creative. In the construction of Hagia Sophia, for example, it was able to solve, for the first time on such a grand scale, the tremendously difficult technical problem of erecting a huge dome over a square space. (The Pantheon in Rome entails the easier problem of a round dome over a round area.) Incidentally, it is hard to believe, as has been confirmed, that St. Sophia's dome is actually twenty-six feet higher than vaults of the most spacious Gothic cathedral, that of Beauvais. Yet so light is St. Sophia's dome that, as several Byzantine writers put it, it seemed to hang "suspended from heaven" (see below, chapter 5).[22] No wonder that in the late tenth century, according to the primary Russian Chronicle, the Russian envoys to Constantinople reported to their master, the grand duke Vladimir of Kiev, that when assisting at the celebration of the liturgy in St. Sophia they thought they "were in heaven itself."[23]

We come finally to an aspect of Byzantine life and civilization with which the church is again closely associated but which is generally overlooked—the Byzantine administrative system. The Byzantine administrative organization, civil as well as ecclesiastic, with its many titles, ranks, insignia, and protocol, was one of the most carefully structured in history. But, like that of Washington D.C. in our day, it grew eventually so complex as to be at times almost unwieldy. Nonetheless, from two Byzantine treatises on administration that remain (the *De Cerimoniis* of Emperor Constantine VII Porphyrogenitus and the *Pseudo-Codinus,* of the tenth and fourteenth centuries, respectively),[24] one can see that the system was not static and that throughout the centuries it underwent evolution in response to the demands of a changing society.

To take one title or rank as an example, in the early centuries the Domestic was in charge of the Scholae, a branch of the guard troops of Constantinople. By the thirteenth century the title "Grand Domestic" was exalted and came to be applied to the supreme head of the state's armed forces. In the late Byzantine period, some titles, because of the constant diminution of the empire's power and the contraction of its territory, became purely honorific—that is, titles with no really functional duties attached to them. This fact and the circumstance that the Byzantines found it difficult to discard titles sometimes makes it difficult for modern scholars to ascertain exactly what each title meant at a given time.[25]

The church, though it had some services and officers in common with the state, in the main possessed its own officials and had its own carefully prepared lists of clerical and lay officials attached to or

serving it. According to an edict of the sixth-century emperor Justinian, the Cathedral of Hagia Sophia, or the "Great Church" as it was
always called, was to be provided with a huge staff of sixty priests, a
hundred deacons, forty deaconesses, ninety subdeacons, a hundred
readers, twenty-five chanters, and a hundred custodians. The lavish-
ness of the service must have been remarkably impressive.[26]

A further complication for modern historians regarding Byzantine
titles is that, after the Turkish capture of the capital in 1453, the
Greek Patriarch Gennadius continued not only to be the religious
head of the Orthodox church but was appointed by the sultan as the
"civil" head of all Orthodox people subject to the Turks, including
Bulgars, Serbs, and Albanians, as well as Greeks.[27] As heir to the
tradition of the old Empire, the patriarch during the Turkish period
("Turkokratia") introduced some new titles into the patriarchal
court that were often adapted from those of the old Byzantine imperial court. Here are a few examples of new titles or those carried on
from the patriarchal court of the earlier period, most of which are
still utilized today in the Patriarchate of Constantinople. *Megas
Chartophylax* was an old title which by the fourteenth century desig-
nated the chief patriarchal official who, along with his other duties,
administered the patriarchal chancery. *Megas Protekdikos* was a title
which seems to have been held by one who protected the rights of
ecclesiastical property. The *Megas Referendarios*, mentioned in the
ecclesiastical sources from very early times, held the delicate position
of liaison officer between the patriarch and the emperor.

Besides these, in the Byzantine and Turkish periods there were,
around the patriarch, other dignitaries of lesser importance, whose
function it was to help him carry out his many other duties. For
instance, the *Megas Rhetor* (Grand Orator) was a professor at the
patriarchal school who was especially skilled at biblical interpretation. Other dignitaries helped to keep the patriarchal records, and
were in charge of the holy vessels of the church and vestments worn
by the high prelates,[28] and, more important, of the sacred relics of
Christ and the Apostles. Of these relics Constantinople, before its sack
by the Latins in 1204, had probably possessed more than the rest
of the world combined.[29] These relics were the subject of many pages
written by several Western crusader-knights who participated in the
Fourth Crusade that seized Constantinople—notably Robert of Clari
and William Villehardouin. These eyewitnesses refer especially to the
true cross, the sponge, the crown of thorns, and the relics that served

as the special protectors of "the city," the Virgin's robe and girdle.[30] At the head of this latter group of "service" officials was the *Megas Skevophylax* (grand sacristan) and also the *Myrepsos* (overseer of the Holy Chrism). *Aktuarios* (court physician) is an interesting title utilized in the patriarchal court after 1453, which had been applied to the imperial court physician.[31] Obvious is its connection with the English word *actuary*—he who assigns insurance rates according to a calculated life span.

Constantinople was famous for its university (the first in medieval Europe), in which its civil servants were trained. But the capital city had, and still possesses, a patriarchal school for training in theological studies and ecclesiastical "letters." Certain titles, in fact, were reserved specifically for those contributing to the furtherance of education in the Orthodox church, especially laymen. Besides *Megas Rhetor* (Grand Orator) there is the title of *Didaskalos tou Evangeliou* (teacher of the Gospel), *Didaskalos tou Apostolou* (teacher of the Apostle-reading), and *Didaskalos tou Genous* (teacher of the people), the latter an old title held, among others, by the great patriot of the nineteenth-century Greek Revolution, Adamantios Koraes.[32] The *Orphanotrophos* (literally "caretaker of orphans"), a Byzantine ecclesiastic in the civil service of the imperial court, was, especially in the twelfth century, in charge of what one today would call "social work." He headed the Great Orphanage in Constantinople, which had a hospital attached to it, then the most advanced in Europe, with special doctors and wards for various diseases.[33] Naturally, in the Byzantine patriarchal court there were certain offices reserved for those in charge of liturgical ceremonies and chanting. These held such titles as *Protopsaltes* (first chanter), *Lambadarios* (in charge of candles) and so on. Another title of honor, granted to laymen as recognition of special service to the church, was that of *Ostiarios*, the person in charge of the great doors of St. Sophia.[34]

The various modern ecclesiastical *officia*, as they still exist today in the Greek ecumenical patriarchate, reach back at least five hundred and sometimes as far as a thousand years.[35] Every title has some significant historical association either with the Byzantine church or with the imperial court, both of which played, as we have seen, closely related roles in the formation of Byzantine civilization.

Indeed, the church was probably the most fundamental force in the creative vitality of Byzantine culture. The unique blend of Byzantine Christianity, Greek (more accurately "Hellenistic") learning, and certain Eastern elements in the mature Byzantine cultural synthesis, still finds its living expression in the Greek Orthodox church, particularly in the institution of the patriarchate of Constantinople. The patriarchate is, in fact, as striking an example as it is possible to find in the modern world, of the continued viability of the most creative of Byzantine institutions, the Eastern Orthodox church.

2

Religion and "Nationalism" in the Byzantine Empire and After: Conformity or Pluralism?

In examining the complex problem of the relationship between religion and nationalism, it would be hard to find a more intricate case than that of the Byzantine Empire. Many medieval historians consider the empire, especially in the sixth century under Justinian with its far-flung territories of East and West and at its height in the early eleventh, to be the classic case of a multinational state which, despite an extreme diversity of peoples, was able not only to survive but to prosper. The sense of unity that maintained this empire is believed to have come primarily from the absolute authority of its ruler, the Basileus, and—perhaps even more—from its official religion, Orthodoxy, the very name of which means "the one true religion."

Closer scrutiny, however, of this apparent unity of church and state, or more precisely of the conformity of all citizens to the religion of the state, exposes a number of difficulties and irregularities. Though by law it was necessary to adhere to Orthodoxy, there were exceptions. Jews, for instance, in the old Roman imperial tradition, were throughout the entire period more or less tolerated—if grudgingly—in the practice of their religion.[1] And at various times such groups as Arabs living *within* imperial territory were unofficially granted special permission, or at least were left unmolested, to follow the Muslim religion. An extreme example of this kind of toleration is the case of the Armenians.[2] Though essentially related to the much persecuted Monophysite groups, they, partly because of the strategic importance of Armenia as a buffer state and perhaps because of their services as soldiers or merchants, were often permitted to retain their religious beliefs even when they fled to the empire for sanctuary. Yet even the case of the Armenians is not uniform. For especially in the ninth to eleventh centuries, when entire Armenian clans emigrated to Constantinople, opportunistically or not they embraced

Orthodoxy. And when a series of Armenians ascended the imperial throne, they became more intransigently Orthodox than the Greeks themselves—to the point, it seems, of even persecuting their own former coreligionists. Another nuance making for complexity in our problem is that though hordes of barbarians or semibarbarians, especially Slavs, were converted to Orthodoxy and entered the empire, other even more numerous converted peoples remained technically *outside* the empire. Indeed, several of these Slavic nations that were at one time part of the empire were later permitted, when they became politically independent, to set up autocephalic Orthodox churches of their own. These, however, remained closely bound to, and recognized the jurisdictional authority of, the patriarch of Constantinople.[3]

With the life of the empire extending over one thousand years, the relation between religion, or its administrative aspect the church, on the one hand, and its political counterpart the state, on the other, with regard to the question of religious unity or pluralism, exhibits certain identifiable characteristics during various periods of Byzantine history. And the pattern of change or evolution permits us to advance the thesis that, in general, Orthodoxy and the sense of nationhood became more closely intertwined the more serious the crises—external and sometimes internal or both—that threatened the existence of the state. It is, of course, difficult in a chapter of this length to propose a schema that will accurately reflect all the shifting nuances of these relations. Yet for the sake of analysis we may, I think, speak of three broad chronological stages.

The first begins with Constantinople's foundation in 330 and extends until after the great crisis precipitated by the Byzantine territorial losses of Egypt, Syria, and Palestine to the Arabs in the late sixth and seventh centuries. It is at the end of this period, ca. 717, when Byzantium had been stripped of these eastern Semitic provinces —areas that had always felt somewhat alien to Asia Minor, the Balkans, and southern Italy—that for the first time we may speak of a truly Byzantine, in a sense of a more or less Greek, empire. Indeed, so deep was the trauma to the state that, to ward off the continuous threat of Arab invasion and to placate the Eastern Monophysites, whose religious views bore a distant resemblance to the Arab, several emperors even sought to "dilute" certain tenets of Orthodoxy.[4] These emperors' concept of religion was, one might say, supranational. They believed that by manipulating the religious formulas of Orthodoxy—of course they always claimed, rather, to preserve them—they could obtain beneficial political results, namely, unitary allegiance to the state, if only they could force the official organs of the church to assent. But their attempts also reveal, from the view of the dissident Monophysites, the even greater significance of the close relationship between religion and "nationalism." Historians have, in fact, long asserted that these Monophysite peoples opposed the Chalcedonian dogmatic formulation of 451, less for purely religious than for ethnic and cultural—that is, "nationalist"—reasons.[5]

It should be noted that the word *nationalism*, with its modern, strongly secular implications, is inappropriate for use in any medieval context. Henceforth I shall prefer to use the term *ethnicity*, the self-consciousness of the Byzantine people of whatever origin, that they belonged to or owed allegiance to one political organism, the empire.

The second phase for consideration would extend from about 717 to the time of the Crusades, which brought East and West into contact—indeed conflict—on a scale greater than ever before. This crusading movement culminated in the Fourth Crusade of 1204, with the seizure of Constantinople by Western armies and the dismemberment of the Byzantine Empire. In this second, middle phase, in which the empire was at first reduced in size but then once more began to grow in strength, the primary religious phenomena were the Iconoclastic struggle, the conversion of the Slavic peoples, and the schism with Rome in 1054.

With the recapture of the capital by the Greek troops of Michael Palaeologus in 1261, we may consider that a third period began, which in turn extended to 1453, the fall of Constantinople to the Turks. In this third and final stage, when the empire had become territorially a mere shadow of its former self, the identification of religion and ethnicity became even closer under the impact of the Turkish advance. But, as we shall see, the two were most truly to coincide under the more insidious danger posed simultaneously by the West which, in the eyes of most Byzantines, threatened, through ecclesiastical union with Rome, to engulf in more ways than territorially what remained of the people of the empire.

A word of caution—most of the phenomena, especially the ideologies described as belonging to the first phase, carry over into the second, and some also into the third. It is sometimes only the emphases that change; at times, in fact, there is a kind of cyclical return to earlier emphases—or to state it perhaps more precisely, the emphasis on religion remains but its conjunction with other elements is altered. The main differences, however, as we shall see, will occur in the third stage, when the political and social status of the empire has so changed, the differences between theory and reality become so glaring, that a new type of feeling emerges with which Orthodoxy can identify and strengthen itself.

Let us begin with the first phase. What distinguished the Roman Empire of Augustus from that of the Byzantines was not so much the displacement of old Rome by the new capital, Constantinople, as the creation of a *Christian* Roman Empire. Indeed, the concept of the empire, and of its ruler the emperor, was now cast into the form of Christian political theory. And an understanding of this basic Christian political ideology formulated early by Constantine's Bishop Eusebius is indispensable to any scrutiny of the relations between the Byzantine religion and its sense of nationhood.[6] According to the developed Eusebian formulation, the emperor is the vicegerent of God, the mimesis or "living icon of Christ" ("zosa eikon Christou"), and he rules the *Basileia*, the Christian commonwealth, which is in turn the terrestrial counterpart of God's kingdom in heaven. Since there was only one God, it followed inevitably that there could be only one empire and therefore only one true religion. Hence all Byzantine theoreticians and panegyrists firmly believed, without exception so far as I am aware (except perhaps at the very end), that unity of the empire entailed—nay demanded —unity of religion.[7] Otherwise the empire would become a sacrilege before God, and Constantinople would lose its claim to being God-guarded, the special preserve of the Virgin and the saints. This view, though obtaining throughout its history, was strongly reflected in the earlier periods, when the empire contained within its borders many diverse peoples: besides the Greeks of the Balkans, Asia Minor, south Italy, Sicily, and south Russia, also Copts of Egypt, in addition to Armenians, Georgians, Syrians, "Italians," Berbers, and later some of the many Slavs who were converted.

By the time of Justinian (sixth century) the culture, at least that of the upper classes in the cities, had become predominantly Greek, as had the language of the court. Yet among the lower classes of the peoples enumerated, it must be assumed that, for the bulk of those outside the towns, their primary language could not have been Greek. Hence, although Greek culture then had some importance, what basically served to preserve unity in this earlier period of a multiracial or multinational empire, would appear to have been the two *universal* Christian institutions—the emperor and the Orthodox church. As already stressed, these two were closely tied; indeed, the Byzantine church and state in many ways formed one organic unity. But of course the broad problem of the unity of church and state, which is somewhat different from that under investigation, cannot be analyzed in its entirety here.

It goes without saying that if the emperor was not considered Orthodox, allegiance to him was considered to be dissolved. This may be clearly seen in the requirement imposed by the patriarch on all emperors, beginning with Anastasius at the end of the fifth century, that each take an oath to defend the inviolability of the seven ecumenical councils and the official creeds of the church.[8] But note that this was an oath explicitly to preserve the tenets of Orthodox *religious* belief rather than of any particular *civil* aspect of government. Despite the unwritten constitution of Byzantium, no one ever really questioned the traditional absolute authority of the emperor in civil affairs.[9]

Beginning with Byzantium's foundation—and this is an ideology that persisted even until 1453—the Byzantines looked upon their empire (Basileia) as *the* political organization sanctioned by God for the world. The chief requirement for admission to this Basileia was conversion to Orthodoxy. And through this means many barbarian peoples, sometimes even of extreme cultural backwardness, were able to enter into the Byzantine *ecumene*. Once converted, another process, that of cultural adaptation or even in some cases assimilation, began. Yet though, as noted, many of those converted did enter the empire to become citizens, other peoples, such as the Moravians and especially the Russ—not to omit the Bulgars who entered but who managed forcibly to break away—remained *outside* the borders of empire. For them religious conversion, while effective, did not in itself result in a feeling of ethnic solidarity with Byzantium. True, the distant Russ, though technically not belonging to the empire, were provided with Greek metropolitans to head their church until virtually the end of the Byzantine period.[10]

Paradoxically, the Orthodox religion, rather than serving to integrate these other peoples into the empire, was able, according to certain modern historians, to provide them at critical stages of their development with a political and religious ideology that made for greater unity—an ethnicity, we might say—in their own previously disunited society. Despite these ramifications (some of which would apply to our second period as well as to the first), the rulers of such peoples as the Russ, the Bulgars, the Moravians, the Armenians (and even the Venetians) were granted and were extremely proud to accept titles in the imperial hierarchy of ranks and dignities, or, as it has been termed, in the Byzantine "family of princes." Thus, because of these specifically religious, cultural, and loose political ties—they were not ethnic—such peoples were considered part of what has been called the Byzantine "commonwealth," or as I would put it, the community of Orthodox Christendom.[11] In this unusual relationship between Byzantium and these satellites, there is often present, however, a tension which expressed itself alternately in attraction for and repulsion to the influence of Byzantium. For, as the new nations drew closer to Constantinople and the magnetism of its civilization grew overly attractive, they feared a loss of their own ethnic identity, which they sometimes expressed even in wars on Byzantium.[12]

Within the empire some exceptions were unofficially allowed to the general principle that all citizens must accept the precepts of the Orthodox faith. Mention has been made of the special cases of the Jews and the Armenians. There are also examples of Latins passing through Constantinople as pilgrims or even remaining as residents (the mercenary Western Varangian guard, for instance),[13] who were permitted to worship according to the Latin faith. There was, moreover, an Arab mosque in Constantinople and at least several Latin churches in Galata, as well as, in the eleventh and twelfth centuries, an Amalfitan monastery on Mt. Athos.[14] On the other hand, the Nestorians and, even more, the numerous Monophysite heretics of the fifth to seventh centuries and the Paulicians of the ninth and tenth, were subjected to the fullest coercion available to state power. How best to explain this paradox?

The tolerated groups were considered to be special exceptions, and the overall principle of religious unity, it must be underlined, was therefore not sacrificed. For this was considered to be absolutely indispensable for the survival of the empire as it was then constituted. In the case of small, dissident groups such as Jews and the earlier Arabs, who had no overwhelming zeal to proselytize, no real danger to the state was posed. But in the extreme intransigence of the very numerous Monophysites (comparable to that of the early

Christian martyrs) they already seemed to possess, partly because of their religious beliefs, a kind of national or ethnic unity. Since they placed allegiance to their "ethnic" traits above allegiance to the emperor, they threatened—religiously—not only to alter the purity of Orthodox dogma but—politically—to unglue the unity of the entire empire. In the case of the Paulicians, who believed that matter is evil and that therefore human institutions are invalid, the danger of destruction of the very fabric of Byzantine society and of the state organization itself was present.[15]

Accordingly, the Orthodox faith served in a very real sense as the basis not only for the emperor's authority but for the every existence of the empire, and it was therefore considered the palladium of the life of the state.[16] This must be understood not only from the theoretical side but from the practical viewpoint as well. The cumulative effect of every peasant and city-dweller every Sunday in every parish of the vast empire, hearing the purity of the faith in effect equated with the power of the empire, cannot be underestimated. And yet, paradoxically, the doctrinal views of the Nestorians and especially of the Monophysites, as related to the definition of the Council of Chalcedon, were closer to those of Orthodoxy than were those of the Jews or the Paulicians. One may recall the old adage that it is the enemy who works from within who is the more dangerous, especially if his view is very similar.

But were there other factors besides allegiance to the two universal institutions, the emperor and the church, that contributed to a sense of unity among the Byzantines? In the earliest stages of Christianity, pagan Greek culture had been the chief enemy: then, to be called a Hellene meant to be considered a pagan. But with the remarkable process of the fusion, or rather integration, of pagan literature and philosophy into Christianity—one might say the acculturation of classical learning to Christianity—it became standard for the educated classes in all areas of the empire to be instructed both in the precepts of the Orthodox religion and, to a considerable extent, in those of ancient Greek literary and philosophic learning. Nevertheless, especially in this earlier period, though we find some important scholars of the Greek classics, Orthodoxy seems, explicitly at least, to have been more emphasized than classical culture.[17] In this first period from 330 to about 717, then, we may see that in the ethnically nonhomogeneous state of Byzantium, despite the growing significance of Greek learning, the Orthodox religion in conjunction with the state was the basic factor for the preservation of political unity.

During the second period, that between the Arab conquest of the Byzantine Semitic provinces and the era of the Crusades, the empire became still more Greek in culture. And with the elimination of non-Greek elements, the consolidation of Byzantium into a more culturally homogeneous state began. It was in this period that, for reasons still unclear, several emperors tried to alter—common opinion held they were altering—the basic beliefs of Orthodoxy by decreeing the destruction of the holy icons. This brought about a dramatic struggle lasting over a century in which church and state were shaken to their very foundations. These emperors, however, were finally defeated and Iconoclasm declared heretical.

Among the theories advanced by historians for the initiation of Iconoclasm is one affirming that, aside from theological reasons, the emperor Leo III was attempting to conciliate the Arab rulers.[18] Strange as this may sound, it is not impossible, given the existence in the Arab Empire, first, of great numbers of Orthodox Christians who might be persecuted, and second, of heretical Monophysite Christians within the Byzantine Empire, whose emphasis on the singularity of Christ's nature was not far distant from Arab monotheism. What connection this point would have had with the thesis of conformity or pluralism of faith at this time can only be speculated upon. In any event, with the triumph of the icons, allegiance to the emperor after this conflict remained more or less the same as before in civil matters, though the authority of the patriarch in purely ecclesiastical affairs seems to have waxed greater. This was largely owing to the resistance of the iconophile leaders Theodore of Studius and John of Damascus, whose virtual identification of Orthodoxy with the integrity of the empire and consequent emphasis on absolute religious conformity tended to exalt the role of the faithful head of the church, the patriarch.

It was in this period that the law code, the *Epanagoge*, even if not actually promulgated, was composed, which attempted to define somewhat more clearly the spheres of authority between church and state. In this connection we find in some sources an appellation now applied to the patriarch which previously had been applied only to the emperor, "the icon of Christ." The increase in patriarchal authority, in Byzantine eyes, may be seen in the iconographic representations of emperor and patriarch standing side by side in the manner of Moses and Aaron, instead of the emperor's appearing, as formerly, in a posture very superior to that of the patriarch.[19]

It was in this second stage also that the momentous conversion of the Slavs took place. As is well known, an important if not the main reason for the ultimate success of the Byzantines in this respect was their permitting the liturgy to be translated into the vernacular language of the Slavs (thus making it immediately more meaningful to them), in contrast to the papacy, whose policy it was, in the long run, to insist on the exclusive use of Latin.[20] This is, perhaps, as striking an example as can be found to show the significance of the relation between "ethnicity" and religion. One may justifiably speculate whether such a success could have been achieved at all without recourse to use of the vernacular. In my view—though this is of course highly hypothetical—such a permissive, tolerant attitude on the part of the Byzantine authorities of church and state in the earlier period of the Persian and Arab turmoil, when the state was in a very enfeebled, condition, would have been less likely. And indeed much later, in our third period, when a much weakened Byzantium, as we shall see, was virtually to identify completely its Greek culture with its ethnic identity, such flexibility would have been even more implausible. The fact that the great Slavic conversions took place when Byzantium was entering the apogee of its political power would suggest a necessity for the precondition of political stability and imperial power during any serious activities involving changes in church practices and customs.

While the Slavs were being converted, the problem of the connection between religion and ethnicity in the form of the liturgy came again to the foreground in another respect. This time it involved a dispute between Greeks and Latins. Ill feeling between East and West had, of course, been growing from earlier times. Associated closely with the ecclesiastical rivalry of Rome and Constantinople was the Greek disdain for the West because of the "spurious" claims of the Holy Roman emperors to world hegemony and, culturally, the low level of civilization prevailing in the West up to at least the First Crusade. In this connection one point may be clarified here: that when the Greeks, as often happened, criticized Latin as a barbaric language—as even Patriarch Photius did—they often had in mind, and quite correctly, I believe, not the classical Latin of Cicero but the corrupt, vulgar Latin then prevailing in the West (see below, chap. 4, n. 49).

Ecclesiastically speaking, besides the basic question of papal claims to jurisdiction over the entire, including the Eastern, church, the significant question that now came to the fore, and with particular emphasis in the schism of 1054, was the question of the use of the azymes in the liturgy—that is, whether the Eucharistic bread should be unleavened, as was Western usage, or leavened, as was Greek custom.[21] Today this question may seem rather inconsequential; but as time went on it gradually assumed, as has not hitherto been stressed, a cultural as well as a religious meaning, and finally, because of the widening differences between East and West, strong ethnic overtones. Thus we may note that certainly by the eleventh century, and more so later, a common name applied to the Latins by the Byzantines was simply the disparaging "azymites." (see chap. 8). Once again we observe the significance of the liturgy as a bearer or expression of cultural identity. For although in the last analysis they were coreligionists, the growing antipathy between Latins and Greeks tended in the spirit of the age to find expression in the public services of the church. In the liturgy were reflected not only such basic cultural differences as language but the development of theories and practices characteristic of the mentality of each people.

It is interesting that for the Greeks the Latins, the azymites who had altered the original creed by adding the filioque, were considered heretics, whereas to the Latins the Greeks were, technically at least, schismatics. Though in a basic sense this difference reflects, rather, questions of dogma and ecclesiastical organization, one is tempted to believe that it also indicates that the Greeks, fearful of the motives of the West and increasingly on the defensive politically and culturally, already in this period felt more of an identification between ethnicity and culture than the Latins did.

We shall skip over the period of the first Crusades, with its growing estrangement of East and West, to come to the Fourth Crusade, with the sack of Constantinople by the Western armies under the banner of the cross, and the resultant division of Christendom into two opposing blocs. It was the Latin victory of 1204 more than anything else that henceforth made the religious schism final and irremediable. From this event on we can, I believe, for the first time validly speak of a "*Roman* Catholic" church in contrast to a "*Greek* Orthodox" one. In the West the Roman church, or rather the papacy, as a supranational institution (somewhat like the Byzantine Empire before its final period), remained above the "nationalism" of the developing Western nations. But in Constantinople, because of the Latin occupation of 1204 with its enforced conversion of the Greek populace to Roman Catholicism and the bitterness this engendered, the religious faith of the Greeks and their sense of ethnicity now reached the point of becoming virtually congruent. Indeed, with the Greek recovery of Constantinople in 1261 and the reestablishment of the Byzantine state, and increasingly up to 1453, the two may be said to have coincided. This may be seen in the fact that, after 1261, the Greek population as a whole refused under any circumstances to accept papal aid—and this even in the face of the attempts of such powerful princes as King Charles of Sicily to recapture Constantinople and restore the Latin Empire.[22]

The papal price for aid was always religious union with the Roman church, which of course entailed recognition of Roman claims to jurisdiction over the Eastern church. But the vast bulk of the Greeks firmly believed, or at least intuitively sensed, that this would lead, not only to political domination, but ultimately even to the gradual Latinization of the Greek people. What other interpretation can be given to the taunt cast in 1274 by the Greek rabble at the envoys of Emperor Michael Palaeologus who were returning from the West after the signing of ecclesiastical union with Rome in order to secure papal aid against Charles of Anjou? The envoys were hooted at with the abusive words:" Frangos kathestekas!" ("You have become a Frank!"—that is, "Through union you have changed your religion and become Latinized"). As George Metochites, a pro-unionist Greek envoy to Rome complained: "Instead of a conflict of words, instead of refutative proof, instead of arguments from the Scriptures, what we [envoys] constantly hear is *Frangos kathestekas.* . . . Should we prounionists, simply because we favor union, be subjected to being called supporters of a foreign nation and not Byzantine patriots?"[23] (*alloethneis hemeis all' ou philoromaioi*).

So now at the very end we see the *complete* identification of Greek culture, or *ethnic identity* as we may call it, with Orthodoxy. Earlier, when Byzantium was politically ascendant, it could afford to translate the liturgy into the native languages of projected converts. Now that it had become almost impotent politically, indeed when it was completely on the defensive, it not only did not have the strength to reach outward to convert other peoples, but it had to remain extremely wary of any foreign and especially Latin advances—and this even when it seemed that without foreign aid the empire would sure-ly fall. How else may we explain the popular intransigence in the face of Michael Palaeologus' blandishments or his brutal coercion to achieve religious union with Rome? The Byzantine people had come to believe more firmly than ever before that the purity of their Orthodox faith was their city's only protection and that the slightest deviation would bring divine punishment and the utter destruction of their empire. Such, in fact, was common Greek opinion after the Turkish capture of Constantinople in 1453—that the Greek acceptance of union, finally, at the Council of Florence in 1439, had brought down upon their heads the wrath of God for their pollution of the faith.[24]

In the protracted negotiations with Rome for religious union all the way from 1261 to 1453, the most famous example of this Greek insistence on preserving the faith intact was to be seen in the question of the filioque. In the Greek view, any addition to the creed as established by the seven ecumenical councils was sheer heresy, and they therefore branded the Latins heretics. Not even recourse to the old ecclesiastical theory of *economia* could satisfy the bulk of the populace and especially the archconservative monks who had great influence over the people. To the mass of the people, *economia* had no application where the safety of the city guarded by God—and evidently, too, where the cultural identity of the people—was concerned. As Michael himself put it, "*economia* had honorably been made use of by Greeks in the past. Only one thing now impels me to seek union [with Rome], the absolute necessity of averting the peril that threatens us."[25] But the deep-rooted suspicions of his people, the result largely of the Crusades and the years of Latin occupation, were too strong.

The most extreme statement reflecting such sentiment came from an educated Greek, the grand admiral of Byzantium, Lucas Notaras, only a few months before the capital's fall to the Turks. He is quoted as saying, "Better the turban of the Turk in Constantinople than the tiara of the Pope." A number of historians believe that he may actually have headed a party in the city who were so fearful of the loss of their national identity and culture through Latin religious union, that they preferred an Ottoman takeover to a Latin conquest. Many examples may be cited, several already utilized in the prologue, to demonstrate that this Greek fear of the West, a national trauma almost pathological in its intensity, was not groundless. On the Latin side, we may again cite the example of the cultivated humanist Petrarch, celebrated for his love of *ancient* Greek culture, who was so aroused by the Byzantine refusal to accept Latin religious rites that he wrote of "the enemy Turks and the schismatic Greeks who are worse than enemies and hate and fear us with all their souls."[26]

In the same period—again to utilize a previous example—the anti-Greek Crusader-propagandist William of Adam, recognizing clearly the role of the Orthodox religion for the preservation of Greek ethnicity, proposed to "brainwash" the Greeks by forcing every Greek family to send its oldest son to the West to be brought up in the Catholic faith. And as late as the first decades of the fifteenth century, when Alfonso of Aragon proposed to launch a crusade in aid of Constantinople, his plans included, as documents only recently have revealed, the capture of the Greek capital, not for the benefit of the Greeks but to aggrandize his own ambitions.[27]

As for the Greeks, suffice it only to demonstrate the potency of the relationship of religion and ethnicity by quoting again the typical remark of the educated Joseph Bryennios of Crete, who in 1400 wrote: "Let no one be deceived by delusive hopes that the Italian allied troops will come to save us. If they pretend to rise to defend us, they will take arms only to destroy our city, *our race, and our name.*"[28] Still later, at the Council of Florence, one Greek prelate, when urged by the Byzantine emperor to sign the union in order to bring aid to their beleagured capital, said: "I will not accept the *filioque* and become Latinized."[29] All of these examples point to the inescapable conclusion that, more than ever before, the Greeks, now in a defensive position, fearing not only Turkish attack but subversion from the Latin West as well, had come to equate their Orthodoxy with what was unique to them alone, the ancient Greek cultural heritage. And it was the conjunction of these two factors, cultural "nationalism" and religious "nationalism," that produced the ideological origins of the later, modern Greek sense of national consciousness.[30]

And yet, it has to be noted that in spite of this commonly held antagonism and distrust of the Latins, a number of Greek intellectuals, including some of the highest-ranking Greek prelates—greater in number than is usually realized—were able, in a veritable tour de force, somehow to disengage in their minds this identification of religion and ethnic identity. That Demetrios Cydones, the Grand Logothete (prime minister), Maximos Planudes, and especially the great statesman and scholar of the Renaissance, Bessarion, were able to accept the idea of religious union with Rome while at the same time believing they could retain their cultural identity, was a remarkable achievement. True, some Greeks accused Bessarion of having sold out to the pope. And all of these men were termed by the Greek rabble, which could not understand their thinking, *Latinophrones* (Latin-thinking or, as more commonly conceived of today, Latin-"lovers"), a term then particularly pejorative in its ring.

The good faith of many of these people cannot, I believe, be successfully impugned. But the answer that most of them were convinced of the superiority of the Latin faith is too simple. Actually, there is good evidence that some had, rather, begun to appreciate the advances which had been made by Latin culture, and that they saw, especially in the developing Italian Renaissance, a future role for their own Greek culture. Cydones, to take a leading example, when accused of following Thomas Aquinas to the detriment of Greek Patristic writings, is supposed in effect to have replied that Aquinas was based on Aristotle who is one of *"our own* Greeks."[31] In a few cases also, notably that of Bessarion, several of these persons may have been persuaded of the need for a return to the early Patristic unity of the church, what we would today call the "ecumenical" spirit. Moreover, for Bessarion and his teacher, the Neoplatonist Gemistos Pletho, it seemed that the advances made by the Latin West in technology and engineering might even have been utilized to revitalize the moribund Byzantine state, now in the last stage of its life.[32] That the complete merging of Orthodoxy and "national" identity was not valid—or at least less valid—for such scholars, renders them a remarkable exception, the first of a cultured group who, extending from the late fourteenth all the way to the nineteenth century, became an important part of the "diaspora," or scattered remnants of the Greek people in Western Europe. Of course, it cannot be denied that many Greeks emigrating to the West in this same period and especially after 1453 chose Catholicism simply for the sake of expediency, that is, in order to avoid persecution or for professional and political gain.

It is also worth noting that some Greek politicians of the fourteenth and fifteenth centuries, because of their aversion to the West and their equating religion and ethnic identity, looked for salvation from the Turkish danger, rather, to their fellow Orthodox Slavs of the Balkans, and especially of Russia.[33] Some little Russian help was, in fact, forthcoming in the form of alms. The emperors appealed several times to the Russian princes for assistance, but the latter were themselves at this time caught up in the storm that followed upon the Mongol conquest. Moreover, Kiev had long fallen and Moscow was too distant to be deeply concerned. Besides, in the Slavic areas, especially Moscow, the feeling had long prevailed that the Greeks, by their espousal of union with Rome at Florence, had betrayed Orthodoxy and, as the Russ believed, they themselves alone were now the true Orthodox.[34] (This belief, by the way, would seem, indirectly at least, to have contributed something to the growing ethnic feeling of the Russians.)

When the Turkish sultan Mohammed II entered Constantinople, one of his first official acts was to name George Scholarios, the rabid antiunionist, patriarch of Constantinople, and to grant him the full privileges of his predecessors not only over his Greek countrymen but over all other subject Orthodox peoples as well. Indeed, partly owing to the sultan's acts, the coincidence of religion and nationalism in its political and cultural aspects now reached its climax, becoming more complete than ever before. For George Scholarios (now called Gennadios), placed by the sultan at the head of the millet or *nation* of the Greeks, became, as such, not only the political but the religious head of *all* Balkan Christians as well, and was subject only to the high suzerainty of the sultan himself.

In the succeeding centuries, especially in the late sixteenth and early seventeenth, the occupied Greek areas in the Balkans sank to their cultural nadir. But, as is widely recognized, it was above all the Orthodox church that preserved the national identity of these Greeks. (This is not to overlook the splendid work of preservation of the spirit of a free Greek nation by the scholars of the diaspora in Western Europe—see below, chap. 9).[35] With few exceptions, the Greeks of the mainland had in general become almost illiterate, and it was in part fear of this very eventuality that moved Bessarion, as early as 1468, to bequeath his remarkable collection of some six hundred Greek manuscripts to Venice, that haven for Greek émigrés, not so much, as he prophetically implied in an earlier letter, to disseminate Greek learning to Western scholars, but so that his own countrymen could recall the actions of their ancestors and not degenerate into becoming no better than barbarians or slaves.[36] This generally overlooked statement is doubly meaningful because it comes from the pen of the very man termed derisively by many of his own Greek compatriots a *Latinophron*, a traitor to the Byzantine people—but one who actually realized, probably better than many others, the significance of the Greek cultural heritage. On the other hand, to be sure, the statement also does tend by implication to diminish the close identification between church and national identity. However, Bessarion, a churchman himself, as noted, was an ecumenical-minded Patristic scholar who looked back nostalgically to the early centuries of the church when East and West had been one.

In contrast, the Greeks of the patriarchal court in Turkish Constantinople and those who served as administrative aides and envoys of the Turks to Vienna, Moscow, and elsewhere—Greeks like the Grand Dragoman (interpreter) Panagiotes Nicousios[37]— were more conscious of their *Orthodox* inheritance as such. What they stressed was primarily their *Byzantine* heritage; and their aim, if not always explicit, was through the agency of the patriarchate to achieve a restoration of the old Byzantine Empire. Some, after 1453, placed their hopes in the Russian tsar, the sole surviving independent Orthodox ruler. Maxim the Greek, an Athonite monk who worked in Muscovy in the early sixteenth century, is often cited as having been one of such a group. But whatever may have been his political aims, his immediate religious objective was the resubmission of the Russian church to the ecclesiastical authority of the Greek patriarchate of Constantinople.[38] What finally brought on the Greek Revolution, besides the actual events of 1821, was the rise of a Greek middle class; the decline of Turkish power; the permeation of Enlightenment ideals of liberty, equality, and fraternity; and also, it should be stressed, the conjunction of ancient Greek ideals with Byzantine religious ideology.[39]

It is interesting that in the last two centuries of Byzantium's life, when the nation was threatened from without as never before, it witnessed an astonishing "renaissance" of culture, the so-called Palaeologan Renaissance. This would accord with a notable theory of modern sociology that a nation when it is most threatened is sometimes able to gather its energies and produce a revival or "revitalization" of its culture.[40] This happened to Byzantium in the late thirteenth, fourteenth, and fifteenth centuries not only in the literary and artistic spheres but also in the religious area, in the form of a new but more intensive kind of personal piety: the mystical beliefs of Hesychasm. This, some scholars claim (and in some cases rightly, though there are definite exceptions), may in some men have reflected a deepening sense of "nationality," a feeling that one was expressing traditional Byzantine beliefs and practices as opposed to Latin. Moreover, it was in this later period, when to the Greeks Orthodoxy and Greek culture became coterminous, that some of them once again began to revert to calling themselves, instead of the Byzantine name *Romans*, "Hellenes," a name which had hitherto been reserved for the pagan Greeks. This indicated that they were at last beginning to see a continuity between their ancient forebears and themselves. It did not mean, however, that any of them, except perhaps the famous Gemistos Pletho, wished to invalidate or apostatize from their Orthodox faith—that is, to separate their religion from their recently found "ethnicity."[41]

What may we conclude from this survey of the relationship between religion and ethnicity, conformity and pluralism, in the history of the Byzantine Empire and beyond? During this long period, with its shifting and later contracting political boundaries of empire, the element which seemed most steadfast in the vicissitudes of the Greek people was the Orthodox religion. True, existing even before that chronologically was the ancient Greek culture, which beyond question has always constituted the quintessence, the nucleus, of Hellenism. But in times of peace as well as in those of danger and crisis, it was the church, which early had assimilated Greek culture unto itself, that primarily served to preserve this continuity. And even in the final period of the Palaeologi, from 1261 to 1453, when a new emphasis on "nationalism" very strongly emerged, it expressed itself in a Hellenic culture for the most part still anchored in the church.

In our first and second stages, during the times when the state apparatus was powerful, it did not seem to matter that the ethnic composition of the empire was a very heterogeneous one, because the church and its ideology were successfully identified, or intertwined, with the power and ideology of the empire, itself a genuine reality. Here the state, in the person of the emperor, served as the protector of the church and the guardian of Orthodoxy, although, as we have seen, at certain points—during the Iconoclastic conflict for example—the church had to assert itself over the claims of the emperor in the matter of establishing dogma. This clearly shows, incidentally, that in strictly spiritual matters the church was stronger than the emperor.

At the same time, in our second period, when the Semitic provinces had been forcibly removed, the element of Greek culture was becoming more pervasive. And, as such, it could provide a still firmer bond of unity in the empire. It was then that the question of ethnicity began to take on some significance, not only among the Slavs—who made use of Orthodoxy and especially the Slavonic liturgy to strengthen their own emerging ethnic feelings—but among the Greeks themselves. To the latter, however, ethnicity or "national" consciousness was as yet of secondary importance, because the power of the state was still overriding and Greek culture had become dominant in the empire.

Progressively, however, by the time of our third period, and especially after the Latin occupation of Constantinople when the Byzantine state itself was destroyed—despite efforts of the successor states of Nicaea and Epirus to foster the illusion of an uninterrupted continuity of empire—relations between church and state, and in particular the question of religious conformity, began to take on a different aspect. Henceforth, even with the reestablishment of Byzantine power at Constantinople in 1261, because of the gravely growing weakness of the state, the Byzantine people had to find something besides Orthodoxy, an element that was theirs alone and that could provide them with a feeling of identity or individuality as a people. This became necessary not only because they shared Orthodoxy with another—in fact larger—ethnic group, the Slavs but, much more, in order to differentiate themselves from the hated Latins. This was all the more imperative since the very heads of their own state, the Palaeologan emperors, were continually seeking to effect ecclesiastical union with the Roman church, and some of their own leading intellectuals, the prounionists or *Latinophrones*, were, in the minds of the common people, blurring the differences between Greek and Latin to the extent that the East might even become Latinized.[42]

This new element, which emerged to undergird the people's dependence on the church, was found in the *ancient* Greek cultural tradition or heritage which, though it had begun earlier to grow in significance, was now finally made to coincide exactly with the Byzantine attachment to Orthodoxy. This is not to affirm that the state, or rather the idea of the Byzantine state, had lost all importance or potency. What in large part made for the weakening of imperial authority was, to be sure, the marked diminution of imperial territory. But at the same time the authority of the patriarch, despite, or in some ways almost because of, this territorial contraction, continued to increase, especially among the Slavs. Striking evidence for the culmination of this transposed relationship of the power of church and state, patriarch and emperor, where now the church became, rather, the protector of the state, is to be seen in the extreme statement made in 1395 by the Greek patriarch Anthony. In response to Russian disparagement of the by now almost nonexistent and decentralized authority of the Byzantine emperor, he replied pointedly to the grand prince of Moscow: "There can be no Christian church without the Emperor."[43]

In times when state power was supreme, the church could, theoretically, demand and secure conformity to the one religion on the grounds that otherwise the state would be divided and therefore weakened. But pragmatically it could and did sometimes shut its eyes in exceptional cases such as those of the Jews and Armenians. With regard to heretics such as the Nestorians, Monophysites, Paulicians, and Bogomils, however, whose numbers and proselytizing activities posed a grave danger to the very existence of the state, the thesis of conformity was, theoretically as well as in practice, insisted upon by the Byzantine authorities—often to the point of severe persecution. In the third or last period, as we have seen, the positions of church and state were reversed. As the vigor of the state dramatically declined, the church, in order to preserve political and social order, had to become the protector of the state. And the Greek people themselves, so as to bolster both church and state and, above all, to find a genuine ethnic identity of their own in the face of the collapse of empire and society, found new strength in what they believed was unique to them alone, the cultural tradition and heritage of the ancient Greeks.

In all three periods, then, it may be said that religious pluralism was, with certain non-dangerous exceptions, not tolerated in the Byzantine state. In the first period, the state authority maintained religious conformity, as it did in the second, though with certain qualifications. But in the third phase, conformity of religion increasingly coincided with the need for conformity of culture, since the state authority was weakened and the external and internal threats to the empire had become overpowering. It was the coincidence of this religious together with cultural conformity which finally produced what may be called the new, or "modern," Greek nationalism.

3

The Influences of Byzantine Culture on the Medieval West

It is frequently asserted that from a cultural point of view the chief function of Byzantium was to serve for over one thousand years as the bulwark of Christendom against invading infidel hordes, and in this capacity to preserve for the world the literary and philosophic heritage of ancient Greece.[1] There is no doubt, of course, of the signal service rendered by Byzantium as a preserver of Greek learning. After all, Greek language and literature had virtually disappeared from the German-dominated West of the so-called Dark Ages. But Byzantium was certainly more than a mere passive repository of ancient civilization. On the contrary, as her culture developed, it reflected a remarkable amalgamation not only of the philosophy and literature of Greece but of the religious ideals of Christianity—which in the East underwent a development significantly different from that of the Latin West—and thirdly, of a certain transcendent, mystical quality that may, at least partly, be attributed to the diverse influences of Syria, Egypt, the Jews, and even Persia. These three elements, then, Greco-Roman classicism (including the governmental tradition of Rome), the Byzantine brand of Christianity, and what we may call the Oriental component, were blended by the Byzantines into a unique and viable synthesis that made Constantinople, until 1204, the cultural capital of all Christendom. It was, at least in part, this many-faceted cultural amalgam that enabled Byzantium to play a far from insignificant part in the formation of Western civilization.

To analyze the Byzantine cultural influence on the West is a complex problem spanning more than a millennium of history and involving, in one way or another, most of the countries of Europe. One could perhaps make facile generalizations about the natural tendency of the less developed Western civilization to draw upon or be influenced by the more complex, sophisticated Byzantine. But we must not forget that, as the medieval period progressed, Byzantium and the West were becoming increasingly estranged—indeed, by perhaps the ninth or tenth century they had become almost two different worlds—and that many Westerners, especially those who did not come into direct contact with the East, were not receptive to Byzantine influence. To demonstrate a *definite* cultural impact of the Christian East on the West can, accordingly, sometimes be a rather difficult—even elusive—task, particularly in regard to those fields which are less tangible in nature or in which the remaining evidence is inadequate.

Now that we have pointed out some of the difficulties in tracing cultural dissemination, let us concentrate on selected areas of culture in order to show in each case what the specific Byzantine contribution seems to have been.

THE THEOLOGY AND SPIRITUALITY OF THE BYZANTINE CHURCH FATHERS

As is well known, the early theology of Christianity developed almost entirely in the Christian East. The relative ease of communication in the period before A.D. 330—the foundation of Constantinople—and especially the lack of any real language barrier (educated people in East and West generally knew both Greek and Latin) allowed the writings of the Apostolic Fathers and Apologists to be transmitted without difficulty to most areas of the Roman Empire.[2] A strong sense of the community of Christendom prevailed.[3] Gradually, however, for a number of reasons—political and ecclesiastical rivalry as well as social, economic, and cultural considerations—communications between the Greek East and Latin West became more difficult, and East and West, theologically speaking, tended to grow apart.

Basic to the differing developments in theology was, of course, the diversity of problems and situations faced by the theologians of the two regions—hence, the emphases, or shades of emphasis, in their respective theological thought. The East, though like the West insistent on *correct* belief ("Orthodoxy") and precise formulation of doctrine, tended toward a more mystical approach, that is, a type of spirituality that emphasized union with God. The West, on the other hand, though certainly sharing some of these mystical proclivities, seemed primarily to be interested in what has been called a more "legalistic" approach to theology.[4] But despite these incipient differences, certain Eastern Fathers continued for centuries to serve as the fountainhead for Western theological speculation.[5]

Of the four major Western Doctors of the Church, Ambrose, Jerome, Augustine, and Gregory (the first three belonged to the generation succeeding the principal Greek Fathers), two were students of the Greeks. Ambrose studied with the Byzantine Gregory of Nazianzus, often quoting from his works. Jerome, after learning some Greek, went to Constantinople and other Eastern areas in order to perfect his knowledge of the language, as well as of biblical exegesis. There he consulted with Gregory of Nazianzus, Gregory of Nyssa, and Amphilochius of Iconium, and read Origen.[6] Gregory the Great, who lived later (in the late sixth and early seventh centuries) never mastered Greek, though while serving as papal ambassador to Constantinople he heard Greek liturgical chanting in St. Sophia and, on that basis, may well have instituted his liturgical reform, since called the Gregorian chant.[7]

Of the works of the four leading Byzantine Fathers of the fourth and early fifth centuries—Basil, the two Gregories, and John Chrysostom—those of Chrysostom, especially his homilies and the *Catechism for Baptism*—in part because of their very practical application—were especially known in the West. John is quoted extensively not only by Ambrose, Augustine, and Jerome (one of whose favorites he was) but by virtually all Latin theologians of any consequence. Gregory of Nazianzus, the only Greek Father to be granted by the East the title of "the Theologian"[8]—an honor perhaps accorded less for his originality and profundity of theological approach than for his clear, authoritative exposition of Trinitarian doctrine—combined Greek philosophic ideas with the rhetorical style of the contemporary "Second Sophistic" movement, making effective use of its literary devices of symmetry, imagery, antithesis, comparison, and repetition of key words. He thus put into eloquently persuasive form the dogmas and beliefs that preoccupied Christendom in the period of the first two ecumenical councils. Gregory's works were popular among all classes in the East and, evidently, at least among the educated classes of the West. In any event, it may be said that his works, including his clarification of theological definitions, had a considerable impact on Western as well as Eastern theological thought.

As for Gregory of Nyssa, the greatest mystical theologian of the early Eastern church, the degree of his influence on the West (and to some extent on the East as well) is only now being clarified by research and newly published editions of his works.[9] His celebrated theological tracts, *Oration on the Divinity of the Son and Holy Spirit* and the *Life of Moses*, a prime example of the typical Eastern apophatic (that is, negative) approach to theology, were in the period of the Fathers evidently also known in the West. In the East, of course, his ideas were incorporated into the growing Byzantine mystical tradition, which in about 500 produced its greatest master in Pseudo-Dionysius. The influence of Dionysian spirituality on Western theology and mysticism (the remaining corpus of his works comprise the *Mystical Theology*, the *Divine Names*, the *Celestial Hierarchy*, and the *Ecclesiastical Hierarchy*, as well as epistles) is almost incalculable. For, because Dionysius was for long believed to be the follower of St. Paul, his work enjoyed the status of tracts written in the Apostolic period. In the East, though he was only one among other significant mystical writers—Isaac of Syria and Evagrius, for example—he became, nevertheless, subsequently a very basic fount for mystical thought. His emphasis (in his surviving works) on the negative theology (in contrast to the cataphatic, which was more typical of the West—witness Tertullian and Augustine, culminating in the thirteenth-century Thomas Aquinas) stressed the unknowability of God, the path toward union with God through the "darkness of unknowing," and the "radiance of the divine darkness."[10] For Dionysius, eternity already begins in this life through a constant striving after union with God (*theosis* in Greek), achieved by contemplation, prayer, and ascetic practices. It is possible that, after Sts. Paul and Augustine, the most profound influence on Western theological—certainly mystical—thought, was that of Pseudo-Dionysius.

Dionysius apparently had had personal experience with mystical union, an experience he termed "ineffable."[11] Hence, it is not surprising that his theological exposition was often difficult to understand, especially for those who themselves had not achieved such union. It was the contribution of the seventh-century Byzantine Father, Maximos the Confessor, to "systematize" the mystical thought of Dionysius, that is, to put into more cohesive theological form his somewhat loosely expressed and constructed mystagogy and, in particular, to apply Dionysian theology to christological themes. (On Maximos' and Dionysius' influence on the West as well as the East, see chap. 6). Maximos made other contributions to Christian theology, especially as a result of his appearance at an important local council in Rome in 649 and his fervent opposition to the heresies of Monophysitism and especially Monothelitism.

One way to assess the degree of the Eastern Fathers' theological impact on the West would be to establish the number of manuscript copies of Eastern theological works brought to and read in the West. But in view of our inability to answer precisely the important implications of this question—which manuscripts were actually read and by whom?—about all we can say with certainty is that a considerable number are still extant from this period. At any rate, the number of such manuscripts possessed by Latins seems markedly to have diminished in the fifth century with the precipitous Western cultural decline, largely as a result of the chaos attendant upon the Germanic invasions and disorganization of the empire. Several centuries later, however, the circulation of Greek theological works in some Western areas again gained a certain momentum, especially in the seventh and eighth centuries, when Greek monks fled to the West both because of the Byzantine Iconoclastic controversy and the Arabic invasions of the East.[12] The climax was reached in the twelfth century with the widespread influence exerted on the West by the theological treatise of the eighth-century Byzantine, Father John of Damascus, the *Fountain of Knowledge*, which influenced almost all Western theologians, later including Thomas and Bonaventura.[13]

Since the Greek language, from the end of the fourth through the seventh and eighth centuries, had become increasingly unknown in the West (except in a few Greek monasteries in Rome, Naples, and southern Italy),[14] the influence of the Greek Fathers had, of course, been exercised primarily through the medium of Latin translations. Indeed, Western ignorance of Greek gradually became the chief obstacle to Western knowledge of the Eastern theologians.[15]

It is commonly believed that Augustine knew only a little Greek; yet entire phrases of Greek frequently appear throughout his works. A more recent view holds that his knowledge improved during the course of his life.[16] Had he actually known Greek impeccably, one wonders what difference this might have made in the development of Western theology, and hence, perhaps, in the relations between the two churches. For Augustine (d. 430), whose theological exegesis became normative in the West virtually up to the thirteenth century, should in some ways be considered the watershed for the differing theological approaches and methods of East and West.[17] His writings on God, especially his view of the Holy Trinity, were cataphatic, concerned with grace, essence, and to a lesser degree predestination. Thus they differed from the more mystical-minded Eastern theology, which tended rather to be preoccupied with the concept of *theosis*.[18] It was Augustine's vision of the Trinity that exercised such a profound influence on subsequent Western speculation and, as a result, helped in part to bring about the later theological rift with the East, where theologians continued to hold fast to the Trinitarian views formulated by the Cappadocian church fathers.

Though Ambrose and Jerome knew Greek very well, their theological writings, in the long run, had considerably less influence on the development of medieval Western theology than those of Augustine, who is the chief pillar on which the edifice of Western theological development up to St. Thomas rests. Interestingly enough, those few Western thinkers who did not follow Augustine's path (Erigena, for example, in the ninth century, on whom see chap. 6) were those most attracted by Byzantine theological thought, especially its mysticism. The last of the four great Western Doctors of the Church, Gregory the Great, was unable, we are told, to learn Greek (perhaps he refused to do so) despite the opportunity afforded by his diplomatic residence in Constantinople.[19]

In the succeeding centuries of the Middle Ages and Renaissance, study of the chief Byzantine theologians of the Patristic era[20] began to be revived in the West, especially when the two churches found themselves in confrontation at the Council of Lyons (1274) and, above all, in Florence (1438–39).[21] Then, at a time when the question of religious union became a burning issue, theologians of both churches sought to learn more about their adversaries' views as expressed in the writings of their Church Fathers, on whom their positions were primarily based.[22] Western revival of interest in Greek patrology in the Renaissance was begun largely by the fifteenth-century Camaldolese monk, Ambrogio Traversari. He, in contact with Greek refugees, especially Demetrio Scarano (who entered the Florentine monastery of Santa Maria degli Angeli), translated from Greek into Latin such Fathers as Athanasius, Basil, Chrysostom, and several important Eastern mystics, including Dionysius, John Climacus, John Moschus, Ephraem the Syrian, and even a fourteenth-century prounionist Greek theologian,

Manuel Calecas.[23] Traversari's knowledge of the Greek Fathers was, of course, of practical aid to the supporters of the papal position at the Council of Florence.

Finally, I should indicate a point only quite recently becoming fully appreciated by Renaissance and church historians—that the revived interest in Greek patrology on the part of Western Renaissance humanists (especially Lorenzo Valla—recall his famous critical work on the New Testament, the *Annotationes*, the fruits of which Erasmus was to gather), helped them, in part through their interest in Byzantine-inspired philological criticism, to correct long unrecognized errors in Latin renderings of the Greek Fathers, and more important, of the New Testament[24] (see chap. 14). Thus they were able, generally, to come closer to the original text of the Bible and probably, by extension, to the spirit of apostolic Christianity.

PHILOSOPHY AND SCIENCE

Let us now consider the important realm of philosophic and scientific ideas. According to the famous French scholar Etienne Gilson, Western medieval and Renaissance intellectual thought underwent two fundamental crises in the course of their development, both under the impact of the reintroduction of Greek philosophy: first, in the twelfth and thirteenth centuries with the reception of Aristotle from Arabic Spain; and second, in the fifteenth century when an interest in Plato was diffused in the West following the coming to Florence of a Byzantine delegation to negotiate religious union with Rome.[25] Now it cannot, of course, be said that a knowledge of the Greek language per se was indispensable to advance in culture. After all, classical Latin was also a flexible and highly expressive language. But the point is that reception of ancient Greek philosophic works brought along with it that greatest gift of ancient Greece to the world—the emphasis on natural reason. In the period of the so-called Dark Ages such an attitude contrasted starkly with the unquestioning, superstitious Weltanschauung of the West regarding nature and the world. Hence it is clear how traumatic it must have been for the more thoughtful Western man suddenly to come upon works of Aristotle, with his convincing explanation of the cosmos based solely upon reason and entirely without reference to the supernatural elements of Christianity.

But as we have observed elsewhere, the Aristotelian philosophy and science that entered the West in the twelfth century did not come directly from Byzantium but via the Arabs of Spain. The point is that this Aristotelian thought was colored by Muslim theological interpretation which, aside from being non-Christian (as on the question of the eternity of matter), sometimes had even confused Aristotelianism with aspects of Neoplatonism.[26] It was not until after the Latin conquest of Constantinople in 1204 that most of the original Greek texts of Aristotle and other scientific writers, in more or less unadulterated form, were made available to Western scholars. It is a striking commentary on the distrust felt by the West for the Greek "schismatics," as the Byzantines were called, that for a considerable period Westerners actually preferred the second- or even thirdhand Arabic version of Aristotle to the purer version the Byzantines could provide.[27]

The introduction of the "Muslim" Aristotle from Spain provoked such a sensation in Western intellectual circles that the pope, sensing danger to the church, had to forbid the reading of portions of that author at the University of Paris, then the chief center of theological study in the West. But as usually happens with this type of censorship, the prohibition proved impossible to implement. Latin scholars, dazzled by the wealth of new material by Aristotle, and other Greek authors, simply refused to obey. And ultimately the great Dominican, Thomas Aquinas, was appointed to minimize the danger by attempting to reconcile Aristotle's cosmology with that of Catholic Christianity—with results that are well known.

It is worth noting that fully five hundred years before St. Thomas, a conciliation of Christian faith—this time of Orthodoxy—with Aristotelian reason had already been attempted in the Byzantine East by the theologian John of Damascus.[28] His treatise, the famous *Fountain of Wisdom*, is still the fundamental work for the theology of the Orthodox church and, curiously, was first translated into Latin (in the twelfth century) in Hungary, by a Byzantine-educated Venetian, Cerbanus, at the Greek monastery of Pannonhalma. Peter Lombard knew the Latin translation of John, as did others, but it was not until Aquinas that the work was very effectively used, in the composition of his celebrated *Summa Theologiae*.[29] It was also Aquinas who suggested the vast undertaking of William of Moerbeke, Latin archbishop of Corinth—a revised, literal translation made directly from the Greek of almost all of Aristotle's works, including the famous political treatise, the *Politics*.[30]

For the most part, medieval Western translations of Greek writings were limited to logical treatises, the sciences, and, to a much lesser extent, theology. Significantly, they failed to include classic Greek poetry, history, and much of philosophy[31]—that is, the more humanistic writings. And the latter works did not in general come to the West until the Renaissance. We have no time here to discuss specific works of this nature, but we should note that the original texts—say, of the Greek tragedies—had in many cases been established in Constantinople by Byzantine humanists already in the fourteenth century and then brought westward, mainly by Greek refugees or exiled scholars who settled in Venice and other Italian centers. One has only to examine a list of the personnel of the famous Academy of Aldus Manutius in Venice, which at the end of the fifteenth and early sixteenth centuries printed many first editions of these influential Greek texts, and which counted among its editors many Greeks, including the famous Cretan Marcus Musurus and the Constantinopolitan Janus Lascaris, humanist-diplomat.[32]

Of parallel significance to Aristotelianism for the development of Western thought and learning, as we have noted, was the introduction in the fifteenth century of Platonic philosophy. This, however, is to be associated exclusively with Byzantium and was not the result of mediation through the Arabs. To be sure, certain Neoplatonic works had been known to the West earlier. Already in the ninth century, during the so-called Carolingian Renaissance, the Irish scholar John Scotus Erigena had secured from the library of Charles the Bald, king of the Franks (to whose predecessor, Louis the Pious, it had been sent by the Byzantine emperor), a copy of the work of the Byzantine Neoplatonist Maximos the Confessor.[33] While writing his famous *On the Division of Nature*, Erigena also had at his disposal the work of the most highly influential mystic of the entire medieval world, the early Byzantine Dionysius the Areopagite, which Erigena translated into Latin (see chap. 6). Dante, in his *Paradiso*, drew on material from Dionysius' *Celestial Hierarchy*, and even the fourteenth-century German mystic, Meister Eckhart, owed something to the profound mysticism of Dionysius.[34]

In the Byzantine East, where pure Platonism was usually suspect to the church, the most influential revival of Platonic thought took place in the fourteenth and fifteenth centuries at Constantinople and especially at Mistra, near ancient Sparta. There the philosopher and social reformer Gemistos Pletho had founded a virtual cult of Neoplatonic studies.[35] In the West, on the other hand, Plato had been practically unknown since antiquity (despite the good intentions of Boethius in the sixth century and the pervasive Neoplatonic thought reflected in Augustine). And it was not until the coming to Italy of Pletho and other Greeks to attend the famous Council of Florence in 1438–39 that the original Platonic texts once again were brought into direct contact with the mainstream of the Western tradition. To save Constantinople, now completely surrounded by the Turks, the Greek emperor, in a last desperate measure, had assembled a large number of his prelates and officials (many of whom were also scholars) and had gone to Florence in the hope of securing military aid through religious union with the West. The papal price for Western help against the Turks, of course, was the submission of the Greek church to Rome. The proceedings of this council, the greatest medieval confrontation between East and West, lasted one and a half years. During this period Westerners had the opportunity to acquire from the Greeks a knowledge and appreciation of Platonic philosophy, along with other things, such as a new philological insight into the Greek language of the Scriptures: witness the influence on the work of Lorenzo Valla, who was present at the council.[36] Cosimo de' Medici, then ruler of Florence, was in fact so impressed by Pletho that he later founded his Platonic Academy, whence, ultimately, interest in Plato became diffused throughout the entire West.[37]

On the purely religious side, the Florentine Marsilio Ficino achieved a synthesis of Platonic and Christian thought that had an important impact on the religious outlook of many Western humanists.[38] According to some modern scholars, the reception of Plato's philosophy did more to widen the intellectual horizon of the West during the Renaissance than almost any other single factor. Certain other authorities, however, take a narrower view. They believe that the most significant contribution of Platonic philosophy consisted, rather, in an emphasis on a mathematical type of thinking derived from certain Pythagorean materials incorporated in Plato. It was this mathematical emphasis, in contrast to the medieval Western Aristotelian stress on logic that, according to this theory, paved the way for the advent of modern Western science, especially acceptance of the Copernican theory.[39]

If the Italian Ficino was responsible for producing the first complete Latin translation of the Platonic dialogues, it was, as is not always realized, a Byzantine or rather a post-Byzantine—Marcus

Musurus, the Cretan editor of the Venetian Aldine Press—who made the first printed edition of the original Greek text. To this work Musurus prefixed his famous "Hymn to Plato," a composition which, at least from the philological point of view, some scholars rank as the finest piece of Greek poetry written since antiquity.[40]

Mention must be made, if only briefly, of the most celebrated ancient Greek scientific work that passed to the West—the *Mathematike Syntaxis* of Ptolemy (better known under its Arabic title, *Almagest*), a mathematical explanation of the universe that was to dominate the astronomical thinking of the West up to the time of Copernicus. It is known that in the twelfth century the Byzantine emperor Manuel I Comnenus sent a copy of this work as a diplomatic gift to the Norman king of Sicily, Roger II. And it was from this manuscript that the first Latin version was made. But the effect of the impact made by this work was to be delayed for almost two centuries.[41]

During the Italian Renaissance the genuine revival of mathematics came about, less through the reception in the West of translations of Euclid, than through that of manuscripts of the mathematics and mechanics of Archimedes brought westward by Bessarion and other Greek exiles. Indeed, though mathematics did not occupy a formal place in the Renaissance *studia humanitatis*, it came, by the sixteenth century, to be studied by most of those worthy of the name of humanist.[42]

LITERATURE

Apart from a certain influence on Western historical writing as revealed through such works as the papal librarian Anastasius' ninth-century translation of the Byzantine chronicler Theophanes, the Byzantine influence on Western medieval literature was small. Creativity in Byzantine literature was relatively rare, except in the sometimes remarkable poetry found in the Byzantine hymnology and the unique eleventh-century epic poem, "Digenes Akritas."[43] Byzantium never produced a Dante, though probably the most learned scholar of the entire medieval world was the ninth-century patriarch Photius. This deficiency in literary creativeness is usually attributed (perhaps with certain exaggeration) to the slavish Byzantine imitation of ancient literary models. The cultured Byzantine felt that ancient Greek literature had reached such a state of perfection that in many respects it was impossible to surpass, a fact which led not only to the close Byzantine imitation of ancient rhetorical style but, more important, to the use by most writers of an artificial form of ancient Greek rather than the living vernacular spoken by the Byzantines themselves. It was this anomalous situation, somewhat analogous to that of an American attempting to write in Chaucerian English, that served in large part to stultify creativity in Byzantine literature.

Since Byzantium was the medieval repository for ancient Greek literary treasures, it was from there or from Byzantine southern Italy that they passed to the West. The medieval Greeks preserved the works of Homer, Aeschylus, Euripides, Sophocles, Aristophanes, and other poets and dramatists, when they were unknown to or had been lost to the Western world. And it is this work of preservation that some critics have termed Byzantium's most significant cultural contribution to the modern world.

While the classic dramatists were read in the East, they were never apparently performed on the stage, probably because of ecclesiastical objections to their pagan character and occasionally immoral themes. Yet it may be noted that up to the sixth century, comedies of Menander may well have been performed in Constantinople. As for Homer, he was read by all Eastern schoolboys. The eleventh-century philosopher-historian Michael Psellus, as a boy, could recite all of the *Iliad*. Nevertheless, Homer's work did not become familiar to Western scholars until the fourteenth century, when at Petrarch and Boccaccio's commission, Pilatus, a Greek of southern Italy, translated the *Odyssey* into Latin prose. The version was apparently not very successful, nor was Pilatus very effective in teaching Greek to Petrarch and Boccaccio. (Actually, it may not have been entirely Pilatus' fault, since dictionaries and other such aids were then unavailable, nor did the two Italian humanists really like Pilatus.) Nevertheless, Pilatus provided Boccaccio with material for his *Genealogy of the Gods*, the first exposition since antiquity of the Greek myths in their original pagan setting. It was at Boccaccio's initiative, moreover, that Pilatus, in 1361, was appointed at Florence to the first chair of the Greek language to be established in Western Europe.[44] A subsequent and more important holder of this post (1396) was the distinguished Byzantine nobleman Manuel Chrysoloras, during whose tenure so many leading Italian statesmen and humanists came to study with him that the formal study of classical Greek letters may be said to have begun in the Renaissance.[45]

Researchers differ sharply over the problem of the origin of the so-called Franco-Greek romances, epic poems of the fourteenth and fifteenth centuries about love and adventure that were popular in both the Greek East and the West. Some scholars believe that their genesis is to be traced to the medieval Byzantine East, others to the courtly love poems of France. Still others consider their prototype to be the novel of Greek antiquity. Certainly, in the late medieval period, Byzantine poets translated into their own language French and Italian narratives of love and combat and also, perhaps to an even greater extent, created their own works in this genre, examples being "Floire and Blanchfleur," "Lybistros and Rhodamne" and "Belthandros and Chrysantza." Moreover, it is well known that a number of twelfth-century French romances of adventure had their setting in southern Italy, Constantinople, or Rome, and that the names of some of the characters in these works are distortions from the Greek.[46] Thus, whatever the origin of the form of the so-called Franco-Greek romance, it may at least be affirmed that a mutual interaction of Byzantine and Western elements in the development of this type of literature is clearly indicated.

MEDICINE

In the early medieval period the only medical knowledge available to western Europe consisted of scattered fragments, in Latin translation, of the ancient Greek writers Hippocrates, Galen, and Dioscorides. The revival of Western medicine began in the late tenth or early eleventh century at the medical school of Salerno in southern Italy, where the traditions of Latin, Greco-Byzantine, Arabic, and Jewish medicine met and were blended. Half-legendary tradition has it that the founders of the Salerno school were: Salernus who taught in Latin, a certain Pontos who taught in Greek, Adela who instructed in Arabic, and Helinus who taught in Hebrew. Of the several elements represented here, it is generally believed that the Byzantine, aside from the ancient Greek proper, was rather negligible. But further research on the neglected field of Byzantine medicine may reveal that this view will have to be qualified. It is already known, for example, that a late twelfth-century

Latin physician at the same medical school, Roger of Salerno, was influenced by the treatises of the Byzantine doctors Aetius and Alexander of Tralles of the sixth century, and Paul of Aegina of the seventh.[47]

Arabic medicine was based largely on the ancient Greek, though in one or two areas, such as the science of vision and pharmacology, the Arabs were able to make a few original contributions. In Byzantium, naturally, the tradition of the ancients also was prevalent, and though the Byzantines seem to have made few if any important advances (our knowledge of Byzantine medicine is, however, still extremely scanty), they did achieve in certain respects a rather high state of practical application. Thus, we know that in the twelfth century the capital city, Constantinople, had two well-organized hospitals staffed by medical specialists (including women doctors), with special wards for various types of diseases and systematic methods of treatment.[48] This situation, of course, was not typical of the entire empire, nor of all classes. Yet it may be contrasted sharply with conditions in the West where, in the early period in general, apart from Salerno, gross superstition was rife.

Arabic, and to a lesser extent Byzantine, medical practice was accordingly far advanced over the contemporary Western. Eastern physicians had learned to recognize the decay of tissues and, in the case of dentistry, to treat and fill decayed teeth and do extractions.[49] With the transmission to western Europe in the twelfth and thirteenth centuries of much ancient medical learning from the Arabs of Spain, Sicily, and North Africa, and to some extent also from the medieval Greeks, the body of Western medical knowledge began to increase. It was the ancient medical and anatomical texts of Hippocrates and Galen, gradually in more complete form, both in Arabic and Greek versions, which in the fourteenth century were used in the rising medical schools of the West—at Bologna, Padua, Paris, and Montpellier. Thus the most influential anatomical textbook in the fourteenth century in the West—indeed, it was to remain the most popular until Vesalius in the sixteenth century— was the *Anatomia* of Mondino di Luzzi, a work based largely on Galen, the Byzantine Theophilus, and Arabic authorities.

Much used in the examination of the pulse and the urine, the commonest methods of diagnosis in the medieval period, was the treatise of the above-mentioned Theophilus of seventh-century Byzantium. But the principal medical work of the Byzantine era was that of the seventh-century Paul of Aegina. Emphasizing the practical aspects of medicine, its surgical section was celebrated for its excellence and had considerable influence on the medical science of the West, as well as that of the Arabs. Another Byzantine treatise, that of the thirteenth-century Nicholas Myrepsos, remained the principal pharmaceutical code of the Parisian medical faculty until 1651, while the Byzantine tract of Demetrios Pepagomenos (thirteenth-century) on gout was translated and published in Latin by the great post-Byzantine humanist, Marcus Musurus, in Venice in 1517.[50]

INDUSTRY

Before the Latin conquest of Constantinople in 1204, the Byzantines were noted for their industrial techniques—techniques carried over in some cases from the ancient Greco-Roman world, but in others involving processes perfected in Byzantium. Silk manufacture, especially the making of magnificent gold-embroidered brocades and the designing of patterns on rich materials, though partly inspired by the ancient Near East, became a specialty of the medieval Greeks. Remarkable for their longevity are some of the Byzantine textiles still remaining, such as those found in the tomb of Charlemagne dating from the ninth century. The products of Byzantine silk manufacture were so prized by the West that when, early in the twelfth century, the Norman king Roger II attacked Byzantine Greece, he took special care to transport to Palermo the most skilled Theban and Peloponnesian silk-workers. The historian of science George Sarton believes that this marked the beginning of silk production in the West.[51] But it is perhaps more likely that the production of the finer Western silk may be dated from this time.

The Byzantines had a great reputation for the casting, in Constantinople, of bronze doors—examples of which are still to be found in the cathedral of Pisa, the church of St. Paul-outside-the-Walls in Rome, at the great monastery of Montecassino, the cathedral of Amalfi,[52] and elsewhere. Byzantium until 1204 was also Europe's chief center for glass-making. After that date the industry began to revive in the West, especially in Venice. There can be little doubt that the many centuries of Venetian trade with the East, and particularly her conquest of the Greek capital in 1204, had a good deal to do with her newly found technological supremacy, for which she soon became famous. Interestingly enough, one of the best accounts we have of medieval glass-making, a treatise of the German priest Theophilus dating from the early twelfth century, prominently mentions the Byzantine methods of manufacturing certain types of glassware, such as plate glass and drinking vessels decorated with gold leaf.[53]

ADMINISTRATION, POLITICAL THEORY, LAW, AND DIPLOMACY

In contrast to the medieval West, where a relatively loose, atomized feudal system obtained, Byzantium, for most of the period, had a highly centralized state organization with a well-developed civil service—a type of government in which virtually all activities were at the command of the emperor. These two elements, the autocracy and the civil service dependent upon it, were basic factors in providing Byzantium with the strength to withstand almost continual foreign invasions and domestic crises.

The autocratic political tradition of Byzantium served as an inspiration for the development of a number of medieval Western governments. Thus, for example, part of the basis for the Norman ideas of kingship in Sicily, as well as some of the Norman court ceremonial (including the king's own costume), seem to have been borrowed directly from Byzantine usage and from the absolutist concept of the Basileus as vicegerent of God, the ruler of both state and church in the world. (The portrait of Roger II in the Martorana of Palermo is a good example.)[54] This Byzantine concept was opposed to both the earlier Western theory of pope and emperor as wielders of the two swords, and the later papal claims to universal spiritual and temporal sovereignty. We know that Roger II of Sicily, when seeking to bolster his claim to control of the Sicilian church vis-à-vis the papacy, instructed a Greek monk of his kingdom, Nilos Doxopatres, to draw up a treatise expounding the old Byzantine theory of the pentarchy, that is, of the equality of all five patriarchs, including the pope, in the governance of the Christian church. It is probable that the autocratic Byzantine type of government also inspired some of the German Hohenstaufen ideas of royal power and, according to Diehl, helped to shape the subsequent European concept of the divine right of kings.[55]

If the autocracy played a basic role in maintaining the strength of the Byzantine state, it was law which bound together Byzantine society. And it is the Roman law, codified by the Byzantine emperor Justinian and transmitted via Italy to the West,[56] which is perhaps Byzantium's chief practical legacy to the modern world. For while the West was steeped in Germanic, barbaric law with its primitive ordeals and trials by battle (see chap. 7), the Greek East was enjoying the benefits of Roman law, which had been leavened by the ideals of Stoicism and other philosophies on the basis of the long experience of the East. It is these concepts of Romano-Byzantine jurisprudence even more than the practical legal enactments themselves that have had the greatest effect on modern Western law.

Contrary to common belief, the evolution of Byzantine law did not cease with the reign of Justinian. Because of the great social changes which came about in the empire, the code had to be modified and even expanded by the Macedonian dynasty in the tenth century, at which time all laws were systematically reshaped in Greek. It was the Macedonian code, even more than that of Justinian, which occupied the central position in Byzantine jurisprudence of the tenth century and afterwards.[57] It should be noted that it was in large part because of this further development of Byzantine law that the Justinianic and Theodosian codes, which were studied later in the West by the twelfth-century Bolognese jurists, were in that century, for the Byzantines, no longer the guide to their civil law.[58]

Previously, in the eighth and ninth centuries, three other codes had been drawn up by the Isaurian dynasty: the Rural Code or farmers' law, the military code for soldiers, and an "admiralty law" based on the old Rhodian Sea Law. Of the three the latter had a considerable impact on the West. Originally developed in antiquity by the mariners and merchants of the Greek island of Rhodes, the Rhodian Sea Law had been adopted by the Hellenistic cities and then by Rome as a model of maritime law. In the Byzantine East, where it became the official or semiofficial sailor's code and "admiralty law," it offered practical, time-tested regulations for the handling of collision cases between ships and for such "proto-capitalist" problems as the relation of the owner of a ship to the cargo-owner in the event the cargo was lost.

As time went on, provisions of the code seem to have been transmitted, by custom, to the early Italian maritime cities which, as we have seen, had close relations with Constantinople. Possibly the first Italian sea code, that of Amalfi (enacted ca. A.D. 1000), seems to have been based upon it. However, as Byzantine trade declined from the twelfth century onward and Italy secured the primacy in sea power, the Rhodian Sea Law per se fell more and more into disuse. But some of its more important concepts continued to survive and inspired the development of some of the commercial and maritime practices of Genoa, Pisa, Venice, and even of the famous "Consolato del Mare," the early Spanish legal code (written down ca. A.D. 1300) of more distant Barcelona.

Regarding navigation, it appears that as the great Western commercial cities of the Mediterranean began to develop their trade, they borrowed a number of nautical and maritime terms from the Greek East. For example, the Byzantine term *skala* (landing-place or wharves for merchandise) was used in the Italian documents of Venice, Genoa, and Pisa from the eleventh century onward. The word *gripos* (a Byzantine type of net or fishing boat) and the Greek *karavi* (a large Byzantine type of vessel) also came into common usage in Italy, as did the Byzantine *palamarion* (a rope or cable), the latter found in Genoese, Venetian, as well as Catalan documents of the thirteenth century and later. Perhaps an even more interesting derivation is that of the old Viking term *dreki*, referring to the larger type of Viking ship, the prow of which was decorated with the head of a dragon or other animal, and which may well have been borrowed from the Byzantine term *drakon* (dragon). It should be observed, however, that a recent survey of nautical and maritime terms used in the Mediterranean would seem to indicate that, especially from the thirteenth century onward, more terms of this type were borrowed by the Byzantines from Western usage than vice versa. Examples are the Venetian *cassela*, chest; *marangon*, ship's carpenter; *galion*, warship (which is first mentioned in a twelfth-century Pisan document); and the Venetian term *arma*, meaning rigging of a ship.[59]

The talent for navigation demonstrated by the Byzantines up to the eleventh and twelfth centuries, though unexpressed for a long time afterward, reemerged during the Renaissance period, but now in Venice. In the early fifteenth century, when the Venetian government held a competition for a design for a speedier ship, the contest was won by a Greek émigré shipwright. Strikingly enough, his design was based on a Byzantine model of an ancient Greek vessel. As a modern specialist puts it, "The finest galley builders in the early fifteenth century were still heirs to Byzantium."[60]

An obvious but important area of cultural transmission, hitherto hardly investigated, is the possible influence of Byzantine statecraft, more precisely diplomatic practice, on the medieval West. Though Byzantine diplomatic methods were originally derived, at least in part, from Rome and the Hellenistic East, Byzantium developed these to a degree of finesse otherwise unknown in the medievel period.[61] Many Byzantine treatises dealing in whole or in part with diplomatic policy and statecraft were written (Emperor Constantine VII's *On the Administration of the Empire* and Cecaumenos' *Strategicon*, for example), which provided detailed instructions, based on both theory and experience, about the most expedient ways to handle difficult political situations. Venice, whose relations with Byzantium were always closer than those of other Western powers, seems to have profited most from the Byzantine example. Indeed, a comparison of Venetian and Byzantine diplomatic practice in the late medievel and Renaissance periods—for instance, the transmission by ambassadors of periodic reports to the home government (*relazioni*) or the organization of an intelligence service—would probably reveal no small degree of direct or indirect Byzantine influence. It may be recalled that Venice, from the eleventh and twelfth centuries onward, had a large colony in the very heart of Constantinople and that early on a substantial number of Greeks had settled in Venice.

In view of what has been discussed in this section it may be said in summary that Byzantium, with its carefully organized administrative system, offered to the feudal Western world, especially in the great capital city of Constantinople, something lost to the West since antiquity—the example of a remarkably developed and organized society under the rule of public authority. The influence of this inspiration cannot easily be measured, but it seems hard to doubt that it served as a living exemplar for the West in its transitional stage from a strictly feudal to a more centralized form of government.

Guilds

Up to perhaps the twelfth century, Constantinople was Europe's chief center of commercial activity; and, as such, its gold coin the *nomisma*, termed *bezant* by the West, was long accepted as the standard of exchange throughout Europe. Given these economic connections between East and West—interrupted, to be sure, but never wholly destroyed by the Arabic invasions—it is of no little interest that the Western guild system closely resembles, in certain respects, the system which for long obtained in Byzantium.

As we know from the tenth-century Byzantine *Book of the Prefect*, all Greek traders and merchants of the capital (and probably of the other cities as well) were organized into corporations or guilds that were under the direct control of the eparch, or prefect, of Constantinople. Cattle traders, butchers, fishmongers, bakers, spice and silk merchants of both raw and finished silk, shipwrights, even notaries, money-changers, and goldsmiths—all had to belong to the guild organization. As in the later Western system, rules were carefully prescribed: no man could belong to two guilds, the wages and hours of labor were carefully regulated, and attempts to forestall or corner the market were forbidden along with disclosure of the secrets of manufacture.[62]

An important distinction is the fact that, unlike in the West where the authority of the state had virtually disappeared, the Byzantine system was not primarily intended to serve the interests of the producers and merchants, but mainly to further governmental control of economic life in the interest of the state. What the actual degree of Byzantine influence may have been on the Western guilds has not yet been determined. And of course one cannot overlook the fact that guilds, although with a different purpose, had already existed in the late Roman world, the Byzantine being an extension of the Roman. More important, perhaps, is the fact that similar circumstances might well have evoked similar kinds of responses even in areas distant from one another. Yet until a careful and detailed comparison of the medievel guilds of East and West can prove the contrary, it is hard to believe that the long familiarity of the Italian maritime republics with Byzantine economic life—many Italian cities possessed commercial colonies in Constantinople itself—had nothing to do with the development of Western guild organization and practice.

GRACIOUS LIVING

One result of East-West contact that may not immediately come to mind is the impact of the more refined Byzantine way of life on the lower Western standard of living. In the earlier period Byzantine cloths, especially silks and silk brocades, as well as Byzantine utensils and other objects, were eagerly sought in the West, and their adoption helped to lead to what we might call a more gracious mode of living. The simpler wooden and occasional stone fortresses and residences of the Western nobles were gradually replaced during the crusading period by a type of castle with round towers, a construction which permitted better defense and deployment of forces and which may well have been inspired by Byzantine usage. The Normans in particular seemed to have learned much of what they knew about masonry construction from the Byzantines.[63] Eleanor of Aquitaine, queen of France in the twelfth century, who is often credited with introducing more refinement into the lives of the Western nobility, especially those of the women, acquired some of her tastes in the Arabic and Byzantine East while accompanying the French armies of the Second Crusade.[64] Previous to this, in the tenth century when, as we have noted, the Byzantine princess Theophano married the German emperor Otto II and brought to what she called "barbarian Germany" a large Greek entourage, she scandalized the German inhabitants by taking baths (then considered unhealthy by Westerners) and by wearing rich silken garments. One outspoken German nun said she had a dream in which Theophano appeared in hell for these transgressions! And only a few years later, after her marriage to the Venetian doge, Theophano's cousin, Maria Argyra, shocked the good Peter Damiani, an ascetic Italian monk, by introducing the use of forks to the city of Venice.[65]

The many products of exquisite Byzantine craftsmanship brought westward over the centuries—icons, ivory and jewel carvings, illuminated manuscripts, gold and silver chalices, bronze doors, intricate glassware, and other luxury goods—would seem to point to a considerable amount of Byzantine influence. But it is not always easy to determine how much of, and to what degree, western Europe was actually affected. Another way to show influence of this kind on a more or less permanent basis would be by citing examples of Western words—language is, after all, the most important bearer of ideas—the origin of which has been shown by philologists to be Byzantine. The wide range of terms adduced below will serve to suggest some of the variety of fields in which the East in one way or another influenced the West.

For example, we have from Venice the term *gondola* (a Venetian boat) which comes from the Byzantine word *kontoura*, a small boat, and which derived originally from the Greek *kontouros*, meaning short-tailed. From the area of Ravenna comes the Italian *anguria*, cucumber, which derives from the Byzantine *angurion*. In the field of administration, the English word *cadaster* (register of real estate) is from the Byzantine *katastihon*. In music, the French and English *timbre* derives from the Byzantine *tympanon* (tambourine), itself from the ancient Greek *tympanon*, a kettle-drum. The Spanish *botica* (pharmacy) comes from the Byzantine *apotheke*, meaning storehouse. And in connection with fabrics, the old French word *samit* (English *samite*, referring to a heavy silk fabric) comes from the Byzantine *examitos*, "six-threaded." With respect to furniture, the French and English word *tapis* (carpet), Catalonian *tapit*, is from the Byzantine *tapeti*. In medicine, the Spanish *quemar*, meaning to burn, comes from the Byzantine or late Greek *kaema*, meaning a cauterization (a derivative of the ancient, *kaio*, to burn).[66]

Other Western words, the provenience of which is Byzantine Greek, are: *romeo*, the widespread Western designation for pilgrim, which is from the Greek *romeos* (Roman), referring, it seems, to the famous icon of the Virgin which, during the Iconoclastic conflict, had floated all the way from Constantinople to Rome! The Greek term *Paulicians* (the heretical dualistic sect), because of mistaken Western pronunciation, was transformed in the West into *Publicani*. The Byzantine term *Tourkopouloi*, referring to men of Turkish descent who served as mercenaries in the Byzantine army, was in the West applied to bowmen in light armor, commonly in the service of the Knights Templar or the Knights of St. John (whose commander himself was called in French the *Turcopolier*). The late Byzantine term *stratiotes* (soldier) became converted, in Venetian and many other Western languages or dialects, into *stradiotto*, which is also connected with the Venetian word for street (*strada*), thus implying a wanderer as well.

In the area of medical technology the Western designation for catheter was, by the sixteenth century, *argalia* (Latin), earlier derived from the Greek *ergaleion*, meaning tool. Another Western term, the Italian *morphea* (skin disease), was borrowed directly from the Byzantine *amorphia*, meaning ugliness. The Byzantine influence in Western art left a lexical trace in the twelfth to the fifteenth centuries in the term *matizare*, to shade. This came from the Byzantine *lamma*, meaning a gradation or shading of color. Fascinatingly enough, the eighth-century archbishop Andrew of Crete used this term to compare the creative processes of the Byzantine painter with the creative acts of God. The word for the premium paid for the exchange of one currency for another (*allangion*) dates originally from tenth-century Byzantium. The West borrowed the term, which later appeared in fourteenth-century Venice as *lazius* and also in French as *agio*. In architecture, the Byzantine term *embolos*, designating a portico, turns up in Venetian, Pisan, and Genoese documents but Italianized as *embolo* referring to the warehouse and quarters of merchants. In the field of textiles, the Byzantine word for raw unfinished silk, *akatartion*, became in Italian *catarzo*, and in Spanish *cadarzo*, all with the same meaning. Again in textiles, the Greek term *triacontasimum*, an altar cloth with thirty stripes, became in Latin *triantasimum*, referring to a precious material. In fact, the very tablecloth of the knights of King Arthur's Round Table was called by the German Minnesingers, *driantasme*. The name *Malmsy* (in Venetian dialect meaning "from Malvasia") referred to a type of sweet wine originally from the town of Monemvasia in the Peloponnesus. In navigation, as already suggested, the very common Western term for a small, swift type of warship (galley) was derived from the Byzantine *galeas* (itself from the word for shark or dogfish).

Words borrowed from Latin, Arabic, and Slavic sometimes were utilized in Byzantium, and these words in turn reappeared in the West, often in very similar form. Thus, the Latin *trulla* (ladle) appeared later in Byzantine Greek as *troulos* (dome), and still later in Italian as *trullo*, an Apulian farmhouse with a conical roof. The Byzantine term *Magaritai* (from the Arabic *Muhadzirun* meaning emigrants), referring to the first followers of the Prophet to Medina, became later in the West *Margariz* (as in the *Chanson de Roland*) or *Muhadzirun*, converts to the new Islamic faith; the term ultimately, however, came also to mean renegade. And, finally, even the widespread Western term *slave*, with its many variants, was probably of Byzantine provenience. The ethnic word *Slovene* (a Slavic people) was shortened, mistakenly, to *Sklav-*, and ultimately developed, semantically, into *slave*. Both Greeks and Westerners used the term *sclavus* (or its variants) to refer to a slave.[67]

One could continue with more examples of this kind. But it may be stressed here only that in the age-old and intricate Mediterranean game of cultural give-and-take, Byzantine material was not always taken over directly by the receiving Western culture but was sometimes mediated through a third one, for instance the Arabic, just as Byzantium itself on occasion served as a mediator between other cultures.

RELIGIOUS PIETY: MUSIC AND THE LITURGY

In recent years, with the growth of interest in the Greek church, it has become increasingly evident that that element of Byzantine civilization which was able to weld together the diverse aspects of its culture and provide its greatest distinctiveness was the Orthodox religion. The peculiar ethos of Byzantine piety was expressed most clearly in the Eastern liturgy, a vivid ceremonial in which the worshiper, through personal identification with the drama transpiring in the church, was able, even more than in the Western liturgy, to experience a kind of mystical foretaste of the blessed life of the hereafter. The importance of the liturgy was so central to Byzantine culture in general that we shall devote some space to a discussion of it.

One, if not the chief example, of the artistic creations of Byzantine religious piety is the hymn—those, for example, of John of Damascus, the Patriarch Sergius, or Romanos the Melodist, who most probably wrote the celebrated Akathistos Hymnos.[68] These Byzantine hymns were a combination of metrical poetic text and music, together designed to underline and emphasize the devotional, otherworldly character of the liturgy. We are as yet not certain exactly how the musical aspect of these hymns sounded (much more work remains to be done in this area), so it would be difficult to compare their poetry to such famous Western hymn texts as the *Dies Irae* or to Jacopone da Todi's *Stabat Mater*.

For a long time musicologists have been intrigued by certain similarities found in Greek and Latin church music, and particularly by the affinity between Byzantine chant and the Western Gregorian chant as well as by the fact that certain passages of the Catholic liturgy contain isolated Greek words or phrases. One obvious explanation for such similarities is, of course, the common Syrian-Hebrew background of both Christian East and West. Significant too are the subsequent influences that flowed westward from Byzantium. We know of Byzantine colonies that had long existed in many areas of western Europe, especially those of the sixth- and seventh-century Greco-Syrian merchants in southern Gaul. More important culturally were the Byzantine monks who brought their ritual with them and who continued, in such places as the Greek monastery of Grottaferrata near Rome, to write original Greek hymns until past the eleventh century. We know that the famous fourth-century Gallic monk, St. Martin of Tours, was in contact with and deeply influenced by the great champion of Nicene orthodoxy, St. Athanasius, and the monastic tradition of the East. In Rome itself, during the first three centuries after Christ, Greek was the language of the Roman Mass and does not seem at once to have been supplanted by Latin.

Still today, in the Latin version of the Good Friday service of the Roman Church (according to E. Wellesz), one may hear sung the alternating chant, first of the Greek words "Hagios athanatos eleison hemas," then of their Latin equivalent, "Sanctus immortalis, miserere nobis." Wellesz also cites the interpolation of the Greek trisagion ("Hagios ho theos") in the Western service, which we know came to the West shortly before A.D. 529 by way of Burgundy, the rulers of which were then in close rapport with the Byzantine court.[69]

Important during the earlier Western medieval period for bilingual Greek and Latin communities in particular, were readings from the Bible in both languages. As the ninth-century Carolingian liturgist bishop, Amalrius of Metz, wrote, in defense of this custom:

> Six readings were read by the ancient Romans in Greek and Latin, and this practice is still preserved today in Constantinople for two reasons, if I do not err: first, because Greeks to whom Latin was unknown were present and because Latins were present who did not know Greek. And, second, because of the unanimity of both peoples [propter unanimitatem utriusque populi].

This theme of the "unanimity" of the two peoples, as expressed in the use of both languages in the liturgy, appears rather frequently in early Western manuscripts, for example, also in Remegius of Auxerre of the tenth century, who, in writing about the use of the Greek prayer *Kyrie eleison*, affirms that "it is recited by both Latins in Greek and by Greeks [doubtless those already in the West] in Latin, both because "certain words sound more convincing in Greek than in Latin, and also because certain words sound sweeter in Latin than Greek, and, moreover, so that we may show that we, His people, are one and that each people believes in one God."[69a]

It should be stressed, finally, that two principal reasons for the respect accorded to Greek in this early period in Western liturgical usage were, not only the fact that the New Testament was originally written in Greek, but also that the Old Testament had been trans-transmitted to the Latins in the Greek translation of the Septuagint (see Epigraph to this book, quotation from the Western liturgist, the Anonymous of Tours).

Another factor of importance for Western use of Greek was that virtually all popes of the late seventh and eighth centuries were Greeks or Syrians. Thus the Western melody "Ave [Maria] gratia plena" ("Hail Mary full of grace") has been shown to be connected directly with the Greek pope Sergius of the seventh century and was originally sung to the Greek text "chaire keharitomene." Still another, but curious, example is the Latin hymn "Ave sponsa incorrupta" of Chester (England) which includes a terribly garbled Greek line, "Karikaristo menitra toche partine," the original words of which had come from the Byzantine troparion, "chaire keharitomene theotoke parthene."[70] Of course, not all accretions of Greek phrases in Latin service books can be attributed to remnants of a common ecclesiastical heritage. In certain cases they might, rather, be ascribed to the influence of Charlemagne and his learned circle (who, according to one scholar, might even have received Byzantine influences in church music via the Muslims of southern Spain, with whom Charlemagne's court had frequent contacts). Charlemagne, we are told by his later biographer Notker, after hearing members of a Greek embassy to his court chanting their religious hymns, was so impressed that he ordered the Byzantine hymns to be translated into Latin, taking care to preserve the original Greek melody.[71]

Claims for extensive Western borrowings from Byzantine religious music are less a matter of dispute today than formerly. Nonetheless, it is not yet entirely clear what specific influence the Byzantine musical system of *octoechoi* (a grouping of tones in eight kinds of scales and constituting a melody type) may have had on the Western modal system. The most striking evidence for Byzantine influence on the Western modal system is found in Western musical treatises, particularly the *Musica Disciplina* of the ninth-century Gallic theorist Aurelian. This work, along with certain other roughly contemporary musical treatises, constitutes the first description of the theory of Western chant as it was presumably then practiced, and provided the basis for much of the subsequent theoretical work in the teaching of chant. Aurelian repeats Greek names (e.g. *nonannoeane*) for the first modes given to Western melodic formulas apparently used in the West as mnemonic devices in the teaching of chant. Aurelian records his own conversation with a Byzantine who explained that among the Byzantines the syllables of such names were utterances of rejoicing. The application of these Greek names (of modes), previous to Aurelian, suggests a direct influence of Byzantine modal theory on the codification of the Western modal system.[72]

There is a reasonable degree of agreement that, earlier, Pope Gregory the Great, in his reform of the Western ecclesiastical chant, was deeply influenced by the Eastern hymnody—and this despite the fact that as long-time papal *apocrisiarius* (ambassador) in Constantinople it is reported that he had refused to learn Greek on the grounds that the Byzantine clergy were too worldly! But it seems significant that he set about reorganizing his Schola Cantorum, a training school for instruction in the chant, immediately after his return from Byzantium, where we know that he was a frequent observer of the practice of the Byzantine chant at the cathedral of St. Sophia.[73]

The only vestiges of Byzantine secular music that remain today have to do with the acclamations, or *polychronia,* which were addressed to a newly enthroned emperor. It is worthy of note that at the coronation of Charlemagne in St. Peter's on Christmas day of the year 800, the populace assembled in the basilica burst forth, at the appropriate moment, into the imperial Byzantine *polychronion* ("May you rule many years")—a practice still preserved today in the Orthodox salutation to a newly appointed bishop (and also in the same Catholic salutation in Latin, "ad multos annos," to a newly enthroned Roman bishop). Though evidently we cannot credit the medieval Greeks with the invention of the organ, its first appearance in the medieval West seems to have been as a gift presented in 757 by the Byzantine emperor to Pepin, ruler of the Franks.[74]

Much later, in the Italian Renaissance, the Greco-Byzantine influence in music was again exercised, now for the last time—but with respect to secular music. In Italy, especially in Milan, Florence, Venice, and Rome, there were attempts on the part of humanists to restore what they thought was ancient Greek musical practice, in order, as they put it, to recapture the "maravigliosi effetti" of music. Notably, the first and greatest of these humanist theoreticians, the fifteenth-century musician Francesco Gafori, hired a translator to render into Latin from the Greek not only Ptolemy's *Harmonics* and Aristides' *De Musica,* but a commentary on Ptolemy by the fourteenth-century Byzantine scholar Manuel Bryennios.

What especially led humanists like Gafori to examine ancient musical practice was the current Renaissance interest in ancient Platonism, in which music of course had held an important place. Another sixteenth-century humanist whose aims were similar was Gioseffe Zarlino, who knew Greek as well as Hebrew and Latin, and was *maestro di cappella* at St. Mark's in Venice. Other musical theorists of the Renaissance were French poets of the circle of the

Pléiade, who in turn manifested great interest in the classical Greek meters.[75]

Much more evidence of Western indebtedness to Eastern religious music—and quite possibly a few instances of the reverse as well—will probably be found by researchers. One hindrance to such a study has been the undue emphasis placed on the schism between the two churches—a fact which has led some too readily to believe that little cultural interaction was possible, at least after 1054, the date commonly taken as marking the definitive rupture between the Greek and Latin churches. But this interpretation is probably much exaggerated, because for centuries the two great bodies of Christians had looked upon one another as part of one undivided Christian church.[76] Indeed the schism did not become truly definitive, it would seem, until as late as 1204, when the Latins captured Constantinople and forced the Greek population to accept Roman Catholicism. On the lower levels, in fact, the ordinary man of both East and West was hardly even aware of any religious rupture until long after 1054, and probably not until well into the twelfth century.[77]

Another significant subject, the study of which is only now beginning, is the influence of Byzantine piety, especially that of the Greek Basilian monks, on Western monastic life. When, during the ninth, tenth, and early eleventh centuries, many Byzantine monks fled the Arabic invasions of Sicily and southern Italy to move farther north, they brought with them the traditional ideals and practices of Byzantine monasticism, especially the ascetic type. Because of the piety of these monks they were, in this period, almost always well received, and we find examples of Byzantine-Latin symbiosis in certain Western monasteries such as the one at Montecassino, where in the late tenth century the famous Greek monk St. Nilus lived with Latin monks and wrote hymns to St. Benedict. (At this time Montecassino even had a Greek abbot.) In Rome, at Sts. Boniface and Alexius, Basilian and Benedictine monks lived together, each group under its own rule, all under a Greek abbot. The Byzantine traits that most attracted and influenced the West were the high degree of spirituality and the monks' sanctity of life (including their manner of prayer) in a period of general Western corruption and ecclesiastical degradation. The severe Basilian ideal of manual labor—at this time Western monks usually employed serfs to do their work—and the Patristic erudition of some of the

Greek monks also seem to have inspired their Western counterparts. It is interesting that the monastic houses of the West most clearly connected with the Cluniac reform movement—St. Vannes at Verdun, Cluny under Hugh, and others—had the closest relations with the Greek monks. It is therefore very possible that Byzantine influence may have played a certain indirect role in the Western reform movement of the period.[78]

Finally, in connection with the development of popular piety in particular, one might profitably investigate the influence of Byzantine ideas on Western attitudes regarding veneration of the Virgin—that is, Mariology. After all, when Mariology in the West was still in a rather undeveloped phase, the cult of the Virgin, who was looked upon as the protectress of Constantinople, was second to none in the East. In the late eleventh century a new and influential form of popular literature emerged in the West, the so-called stories of *Miracles of the Virgin*. These, more imaginative than previous legends of this type, were concerned with the miraculous intervention of the Virgin in the lives of her devotees and, as in the East, emphasized her compassion for individuals, not so much her interest in churches or religious corporations as such. Some of the stories, of course, were taken over from ancient Latin tradition, but it seems certain that a not inconsiderable number came from the Byzantine East. Thus, the famous reformer Peter Damiani, one of the earliest collectors of such stories, tells us that one of his chief sources of information was the cardinal-priest Stephen, a Burgundian who had served as papal legate to Constantinople in the famous episode that produced the schism of 1054.

No less important than the newly developing emphasis on veneration of the Virgin was the influence of the many sacred relics of the early Christian church, which had begun to flow westward already from the twelfth century and especially after the mass despoiling of the Greek churches by the Latins in 1204. This wealth of relics in certain ways helped to bring about an alteration even in the appearance of Western churches, and thus, together with the increased emphasis on Mariology, made a deep impression on the developing Western forms of public and private devotion in this period.[79]

ART

Unlike the Byzantine service to literature, which in many respects may appear to have been mainly a holding operation from antiquity, the Byzantine contribution to art was essentially original and attained a degree of expressiveness that has rarely been equaled. Byzantine art, painting in particular, has been much in vogue recently, especially because of its relatively abstract character and richness of color. We shall have to limit our remarks here to the more important aspects of Byzantine art, concentrating especially on Italy where its influence was greatest.

It is no exaggeration to say that Italy, from the sixth to the thirteenth centuries, was an artistic province of Byzantium. In its many monuments of painting and mosaics can be seen the distinctive traits of that art—its power, mysticism, color, and line—qualities which sought to represent to the viewer something more than the appearance of nature, rather to evoke emotions expressing the reality of the other world.

We may begin with the Byzantine mosaics at Ravenna, especially the portraits of the emperor Justinian, his consort Theodora, and the imperial court. The refulgent cubes (*tessera*) of colored glass and stone, set at various angles, reflect the light in such a way as to suggest the celestial richness of the court of God's vicar on earth. In these mosaics and also in the wall paintings of the Ravenna churches, in some of those of Rome throughout the various medieval centuries (the work of the artist Cavallini, for instance), and in the Norman cathedral of Monreale in Sicily with the imposing figure of the Byzantine Pantocrator in the apse, the tradition of the East is clearly apparent. Further north, in Venice, which was almost a Byzantine city, as Diehl puts it (or "another Byzantium," as Bessarion declared in the fifteenth century),[80] the mosaics of St. Mark's cathedral—the building itself is almost an exact replica of the Church of the Holy Apostles in Constantinople—also belong to the artistic sphere of Byzantium. Evidently modeled after St. Mark's is the dome structure of the church of Saint-Front in Perigeux, France; while still farther to the north, in Charlemagne's capital of Aachen, Germany, Charlemagne's palace chapel was modeled after San Vitale in Ravenna, itself an imitation of the Church of Sts. Sergius and Bacchus in Constantinople. Also to be found at Aachen are bronze doors and other specimens of Byzantine or Byzantine-inspired workmanship.[81]

While he regarded the great monuments of Byzantine art with admiration, the medieval Westerner prized even more the smaller but precious works of Byzantine craftsmen. Some ivory carvings sent as gifts to Western princes or prelates still remain, and the French monastery of St. Denis possessed textiles ornamented with Eastern-type figures. Along with their creations, the Byzantine craftsmen themselves not infrequently moved to the West; and they, probably even more than the products of their art, seem to have been responsible for suggesting new ideas and methods to local Western artists. Thus, in the seventh century, when the Greek monk and later archbishop of Canterbury, Theodore of Tarsus, came to Britain, his entourage may have included Easterners expert in the technique of sculpture. Similarly, the painted figures of the Evangelists in the Lindisfarne gospels were modeled basically on Byzantine or Italo-Byzantine originals, and we know of an intrusion of the Byzantine style in Northumbria and Mercia, and in the tenth and eleventh centuries in Wessex.[82] At Montecassino in southern Italy in the eleventh century, under the aegis of the abbot Desiderius, Byzantine art objects—bronze doors among them—were purchased in Constantinople and sent to adorn the great abbey.[83] And later, during the twelfth century, the interior of the great French monastery church of Cluny was decorated by frescoes in so Byzantine a style that they may even have been done by a native Greek.[84]

Another fascinating avenue for Byzantine influence, only recently suggested, is that of the technique of stained glass. From painted glass specimens recently discovered in the Byzantine church of the Pantokrator in Constantinople (ca. 1126), it now seems plausible that it may have been the Byzantine example which initiated or inspired the celebrated Western craft of stained glass, used to such remarkable effect in the great Gothic cathedrals.[85]

We must touch, lastly, on the difficult problem of Byzantine influence on the art of the Italian Renaissance. Scholars believe that even the beginnings of "realism" in Western painting, usually connected with the name of the Italian Giotto (as the Italian Vasari put it, Giotto freed himself from the dry "maniera greca," meaning the Byzantine style), should rather be attributed directly—or more probably indirectly—to the inspiration of twelfth- and early thirteenth-century Byzantine art.[86] Whether this be true, or whether it was the result of a parallel though independent development of Italian and Byzantine art reverting in each case to ancient Hellenistic or early Christian models (for the historical context, see my Prologue), there is no doubt that in the late thirteenth and the fourteenth centuries a good deal of Byzantine painting became more interested in showing emotion, was more dynamic and individualized—in short, more "realistic" and human. We may cite as evidence of these qualities the Byzantine masterpieces at the monastery of the Chora (Kariye Camii) in Constantinople, in the churches of Milesevo, Sopocani, and Gracanica in Byzantine Serbia (to which areas Byzantine painters and mosaicists evidently fled during the Latin occupation), to a certain extent in the churches of Mistra (near Sparta), and now also in the recently uncovered paintings at the little church of St. Nicholas Orfanos in Thessalonika. Certain similar but less developed characteristics are to be found in Italy in the works especially of the Florentine artist Cimabue, the Sienese Duccio, and certain other Italian painters.

In the view of the scholar Charles Diehl and especially a more recent authority, André Grabar, it was Italian painting, through the Byzantine influence exerted on Duccio and, more indirectly, on Giotto, that derived the greater benefit from the renewed contact of the Byzantines with paintings in the Hellenistic spirit. Despite their superb creations, the Byzantine artists who were apparently inspired by the realistic asethetic of the Hellenistic and early Christian models ultimately remained in the minority. And during the course of the fourteenth and early fifteenth centuries, when their Italian contemporaries were advancing to the freer art forms that were to become characteristic of the Italian Renaissance, much of Byzantine painting reverted to the more conventional Byzantine modes. Nevertheless, despite this reversion to the older, more traditional style, some paintings were produced during the period which equal or surpass in brilliance and decorativeness the best works of the earlier Byzantine epochs. What is also very striking is that scenes in these thirteenth- and fourteenth-century paintings display almost a new kind of experimental boldness, a heightened sense of corporeality and emotion which, in the elongated, attenuated figures and the extraordinary coloring used, in certain respects anticipated the style of El Greco.[87] (For an attempt to explain the causes and context of events for this "Palaeologan Renaissance," see the Prologue.)

It is the opinion of modern Greek art historians as well as certain Western critics that the celebrated El Greco, born Domenicos Theotokopoulos on the Venetian-held island of Crete some four or five decades after the fall of Constantinople, may be termed, from certain viewpoints, one if not the last of the "Byzantine" painters.[88] El Greco studied for four years in Venice and later adopted as his permanent

"Group of the Apostles," fragment of the fresco "Dormition of the Virgin," in the Church of Sopocani, Yugoslavia, ca. 1265. From A. Grabar, *Byzantine Painting*, Editions Albert Skira.

"The Anastasis" by Theophanes the Greek or his associates. Detail from a fresco in the Kariye Djami, Constantinople. Courtesy of Dumbarton Oaks Center for Byzantine Studies, Washington, D.C. (Note mystical light enveloping Christ; see pp. 80-81 and especially Prologue, n. 39.)

Detail, head of Adam from "The Anastasis" by Theophanes the Greek or his associates, a fresco in the Kariye Djami. Courtesy of Dumbarton Oaks Center for Byzantine Studies, Washington, D.C. (To illustrate the new dramatic realism of the Palaeologan Renaissance, second decade of the fourteenth century; see pp. 80-81.)

residence the Castilian city of Toledo. But despite the undeniable influence of these two centers on the formation of his technique and style, he never seems to have forgotten his Byzantine heritage. Indeed, a remarkable document only recently discovered seems to indicate that he lived in Crete until the age of twenty-five, not merely until eighteen, as was previously believed.[89] The point is that this greatest of all "Greek" painters may have been more deeply influenced in his early years by the Cretan-Byzantine style of his native island than some Western scholars have been willing to admit. In that period, painters were apprenticed rather early, so that by the age of twenty-five "Maestro" El Greco (as he is called in the document) should already have had some ten years' experience in the Byzantine style.

An examination of El Greco's mature work would seem clearly to indicate considerable affinity with the masterpieces of both the "Metropolitan" or "Constantinopolitan," and the "Macedonian" style of the Palaeologan and post-Byzantine periods: the importance assigned to the human figure, even to elongation for artistic effect; imaginative use of bold colors; extensive use of highlights to intensify dramatic impact (compare a similar technique of Theophanes "the Greek" in Russia, who evidently boldly used highlights to express in paint the inner light corresponding to the Hesychastic belief in the "uncreated" light of Mt. Tabor); and, most significant, El Greco's deep concern with the mystical realities of the spiritual world, so strikingly similar to the view of the painters of the Paleologan period. To be sure, El Greco seems almost entirely to have forsaken the Byzantine style during the years of his Italian sojourn. But later, in Spain, where the elements of a more abstract, traditional Byzantine style would be more appreciated by Spanish mystical Catholicism, he came to incorporate in his mature work more and more of the traits of the so-called "Constantinopolitan" and "Macedonian" schools. Of course, genius that he was, El Greco was bound by the conventions of no single style; hence one can distinguish elements or tendencies in his work that are neither Byzantine nor typical of the Renaissance ideal, as for example his near-Baroque "mannerism" and less pronounced use of line.[90]

Sometimes overlooked by modern art historians is the presence of Greek painters in Italy after the fall of Constantinople in 1453—men who continued to produce works in the more or less traditional Byzantine manner until as late as the seventeenth century. Their paintings, often referred to as belonging to the "Cretan" school, are admittedly not of primary importance. But they are frequently of quality, especially those produced by the group of painters living in the Greek community of Venice (about which I shall speak in chapter 9).

Italy, then, the prime area of Byzantine artistic influence, owed much to Byzantium: not only the models from which many Italian artists worked, not only the bronze doors, gorgeous fabrics, enamels, and richly illuminated manuscripts that were brought to the West, but, of more underlying importance, the symbolic pattern of church decoration, the iconographical schemes for important religious motifs, in some cases brought by Greek artists themselves. Thus, all through the medieval period, from the sixth century probably even to the beginnings of the Renaissance in the fourteenth, Byzantine art profoundly influenced that of Italy and, through Italy, many areas of western Europe.

Conclusion

What may we say in conclusion about the impact of Byzantine culture on the West? How is its influence to be assessed? It must be pointed out to begin with that such important facets of Western culture as parliaments and Gothic architecture, and probably the basic institutions of feudalism, manorialism, and chivalry, were essentially Germano-Latin in origin, there being little or no Byzantine influence upon them whatever. Indeed, in connection with feudalism, chivalry, and also even Scholasticism, certain influences seem, rather, to have flowed from West to East (see chap. 4). But though not a few examples may be cited of medieval Greek acculturation to individual Western practices, especially among the Byzantine upper classes, the Byzantine influence on the West seems to have been far stronger than the reverse. This was partly because, at least up to the twelfth or early thirteenth centuries, Western civilization in almost all aspects was markedly inferior to the Eastern (in classical Greek learning, of course, few Westerners could equal the Greeks until as late as the High Renaissance); and also because, owing to its developing antipathy to the West, the East in general, and the lower classes, monks, and lesser clergy in particular, strongly resisted the adoption of Latin customs.

Though it must be clear from our investigation that there was a more or less continuing Byzantine influence on Western culture from the fourth all the way to at least the end of the fifteenth century, it is no less manifest that the degree of influence varied greatly from field to field, depending not only on the pattern of contacts but on the attitudes and receptivity of the various Western areas. Italy, for example, was more deeply influenced than more distant, rather conservative France, and immeasurably more than England (the Slavic areas were, of course, the most influenced of all). Nor is it easy to ascertain how deeply the Byzantine influences we have discussed penetrated the various classes of the Western social structure, though it would seem that because of greater opportunities for "contact situations" with the East and a generally more flexible attitude, the upper classes and merchants were most affected. It should also be stressed that our judgments about the degree of influence must of necessity be tempered by the scarcity of the remaining evidence as well as by the state of scholarly research at the moment. It is easier to show, on the basis of extant artistic monuments, what the Eastern influence may have been on art than, say, on the development of the guild system, where we are reduced to hypothesis or deduction. Similarly, we should consider, I think (it is often overlooked), the evidence of such phenomena as vocabulary borrowings—borrowings which in most cases would not have taken place unless there were at least some degree of cultural transference involved. On the other hand, the mere presence in the West of a great many Byzantine luxury items should not mislead us into assigning the same importance to these as cultural agents as we would attach to the adoption of Byzantine ideas, institutions, or techniques—considerations which in the long run were to prove of more permanent value.

Bearing in mind these qualifications and the fact that Western culture was at bottom Germano-Latin, we may then affirm our findings that Byzantium, through its amalgamation of classicism and the more original "Byzantine" elements of its culture—above all, its unique brand of Christianity which permeated every facet of medieval Greek life—was able, directly or indirectly, to influence a surprisingly large number of aspects of Western cultural development. This influence can be found in certain types of art and architecture, in the sphere of industrial techniques, in law and statecraft, in some navigational terms and regulations, in the recovery of classical Greek literature and possibly the composition of the medieval romance, in forms of religious piety and liturgcal music as well as in religious thought, and, finally, in the development of a more refined, sophisticated mode of life. In all these aspects of most of the cultural areas meaningful to medieval man, there seems to have been some tangible, specific evidence of Byzantine influence in one area or another of western European society. Once more, however, it should be emphasized that these influences ranged from the very minor in some spheres to the very substantial in others.

No doubt the Byzantine contributions per se were more passive and less creative in certain fields,—for instance literature, philosophy, and science—which had in the main been taken over from the ancient Greeks and which, especially in the case of Aristotle, were first transmitted to the West via the Arabs. Yet even in their vaunted preservation of the ancient literary masterpieces, the Byzantines were able to make a few contributions of their own. For example, they developed certain philological methods of scholarship—methods which, if sometimes fautly, nonetheless had more impact than is usually realized on the development of Renaissance textual and biblical criticism[9] and thus could not help but influence the meaning and interpretation of the ancient texts transmitted (the ancient tragedies and Fathers (chap. 13–14). Even in the domain of science, despite their almost worshipful devotion to ecclesiastical tradition as well as to the authority of the ancient Greek writers, a few Byzantines seem to have broken free of these restraints and at least to have anticipated certain later Western scientific developments. Moreover, as we have observed, in several other areas there can be no doubt that the Byzantines were able to make truly *original* contributions, specifically, in art and architecture; in forms of religious piety, the liturgy, and ecclesiastical literature; in aspects of philology; and perhaps not least, in providing for the West something often overlooked by historians—a living example of a state with a highly centralized administration and tradition of statecraft under the rule of public law. Nor did Byzantine influence, as we have seen, cease in 1453. Indeed, after that date (recall the phrase "Byzance après Byzance"), Byzantine influences, through the work of learned Greek refugees, strongly affected the development of Italian, especially Florentine and Venetian, humanism. In view of these considerations it is clear that Byzantine civilization was far from being the mere "fossilization of antiquity" that Western historians were wont to term it not too many years ago.

In sum, then, it was the rich content, the diverse elements *both ancient and medieval,* of Byzantium's unique cultural synthesis, that enabled it to attract the interest of the Westerners and, little by little and despite the frequent reluctance or outright hostility of the Latins, to provide them with inspiration and guidance. And so by 1453 (when Constantinople finally succumbed to the Turks) and up to 1600, not only had Byzantium handed over its precious legacy of ancient Greek culture to the West—now prepared, in part by the East itself, to receive it—but, no less important, the West had assimilated a good deal of the products of Byzantium's *own* creativity. As a consequence of what might be called this "long-term process of acculturation," Byzantium played a much more pervasive role than is generally realized in molding the civilization of the medieval, and hence of the modern, "Western" world.

4

Western Influences on Byzantium in Theology
and Classical Latin Literature

The problem of Western cultural influence on Byzantium has not hitherto been dealt with in a synthesis that covers its many facets. Besides the fact that most medievalists focus on the formation of their own Latin culture, a primary reason for this neglect is the very inferiority, in most respects, of Western civilization to that of the Greek East, at least until the end of the twelfth century. Implicit here, of course, is the premise that an essentially less advanced culture will normally exert little or no influence on a more developed one. This argument, in the present case, seems valid enough, for the three basic elements of Western medieval civilization—the Greco-Roman (with strong accent on the Roman), the Latin Christian, and, lastly, the Germanic—were not fully integrated into a truly viable cultural synthesis until perhaps the first half of the twelfth century. It is therefore not until then, or soon thereafter, that in the higher, more intellectual spheres any real influence of West on East can be detected. In the East, in contrast to the West, the fusion of the mature, Hellenistic civilization with Patristic Christianity had been more or less fully achieved by the fifth or sixth century.

Despite this acute difference in cultural evolution, one may discern even before the twelfth century a few exceptions to the superiority of East over West in the more mundane, less intellectual areas: in military science (specifically relating to the shock tactics of the Western cavalry), in the Byzantine adoption of certain Western chivalric practices and feudal terms, in commercial and nautical terminology and usages, and, perhaps most important, in the area of Roman law and administration.[1]

Another factor leading to the neglect of our theme—one more difficult to assess—is the generally conservative attitude of the Byzantine citizen and his culture. Because of this conservatism, historians have too often concluded that Byzantine culture remained

95

static. But Byzantine culture, however tradition bound, generally succeeded in assimilating the various influences that penetrated the empire—at least the influence exerted before the Crusades by peoples of Persian, Armenian, or Arabic stock, for whose cultures the Byzantines in general had a certain amount of respect.

The case of Latin influence, however, seems to be different. The Byzantine feeling toward the West, consistently expressed throughout Byzantium's long history, was that, though both areas of East and West originally constituted segments of the one undivided Roman Empire and shared basically the same Christian religion, the Byzantines, in general culture and in theological speculation, were vastly superior. This is a significant point, for to a greater or lesser degree it served to condition Byzantine reception of Western influences, and in certain cases might even entirely inhibit receptivity. The Byzantines believed strongly that they were the true inheritors of, indeed the sole repository for, the literary and philosophic treasures of ancient Greek civilization and, from the Hellenistic and Patristic periods onward, of Greek, or what they themselves always termed "Roman," Christianity. This unqualified Byzantine feeling of superiority to the West was succinctly and accurately expressed by Gibbon in the following passage from his *Decline and Fall of the Roman Empire*:

> In every age the Greeks [Byzantines] were proud of their superiority in profane and religious knowledge; they had first received the light of Christianity; they had pronounced the decrees of the seven general councils; they alone possessed the language of Scripture and philosophy; nor should barbarians, immersed in the darkness of the West, presume to argue on the high and mysterious questions of theological science.[2]

Why, then, the Byzantines must have thought, should they bother to appreciate, much less to adopt, any of the cultural traits of the barbaric or semibarbaric West?

This disdain toward the West was, with the passing of the centuries, to become even stronger—exacerbated not only by differences of culture but by political rivalry as well. Witness the question of the "two emperors," each claiming to be the true successor to the Caesars of Rome;[3] note also the economic rivalry, which in time became expressed in a virtual strangle-hold of the Venetians and Genoese over the Constantinopolitan trade; and, most important perhaps, consider the religious schism. Here we need only mention the dispute between Patriarch Photius and Pope Nicholas and, subsequently, the acrimonious mutual excommunications of 1054. All these factors combined to produce a growing alienation of East from West which was brought to a shattering climax in 1204 with the rape and occupation of the Byzantine capital by Western armies of the Fourth Crusade. Indeed, such a massive psychological trauma was created in the Byzantine psyche as a result of the Latin conquest, the enforced Greek conversion to Roman "Catholicism," and what to many Byzantines seemed a drive toward Latinization of the Greek East by overt or covert means, that thereafter no genuine cultural interaction between the Western and Eastern worlds of Christendom would have seemed possible.

Nevertheless, this assumption, logical at it may appear, is at least in part incorrect. For, despite the eventual outbreak of overt hostility, both worlds were as a result brought into much closer contact physically. Paradoxically enough, it was precisely the effect of the Fourth Crusade and the Latin occupation of the Greek East, with the accompanying social and economic interaction of the two peoples, that made intellectual and religious exchanges between East and West more frequent and closer than ever before. Thus it is, in these last two or three centuries of Byzantine history, the thirteenth to the fifteenth, when Latin merchants and mercenaries, pilgrims and missionaries —the latter seeking tirelessly to convert the Greeks to Roman Catholicism—swarmed almost everywhere in the East, that Western influence made the greatest cultural inroads there.

In spite of the many Western influences to which, in greater or lesser degree, the Greeks were exposed, I have elected here to concentrate exclusively on two aspects of the intellectual sphere: theological influences and those based on classical Latin literature. These have been chosen for a twofold reason: first because, contrary to what one might expect, there actually was a substantial impact of Latin theology on certain Eastern thinkers, and second because, in view of the often cited Byzantine opinion of the Latins and their language as "barbarian," one is surprised to find *any* degree of influence of classical Latin literature on the East. At the end of this chapter, I shall try to draw a few conclusions as to why, given this surprising degree of Latin influence in theology and, to a lesser extent, in classical literature, Byzantine civilization remained so little affected in the long run.

THEOLOGY

Accustomed to hearing that the clearest manifestation of mutual hostility between Greeks and Latins was in connection with the church, we would naturally assume scant influence of either side on the other. Yet, oddly enough, it was in the last three centuries of the empire, the period of sharpest antagonism, that a not inconsiderable degree of Latin influence in the theological sphere seems to have made itself felt within Orthodoxy. In theology as well as general culture, the Byzantines constantly exulted in what they believed was their superiority over the Latins. And in the eyes of some Westerners, despite the growing Latin aversion for the Greeks, this was, tacitly at least, acknowledged by the fact that in the Middle Ages someone could always be found in some corner or other of the West who hungered to learn something of Hellenic antiquity and the early Eastern Fathers. Were not the latter the pristine source of the Western Christian faith as well? As E. Gilson has rightly emphasized, it was only when Westerners were able to come into contact, directly or indirectly, with representatives or works of ancient Greek or Byzantine learning, that genuine advances in medieval philosophy were made in the West:[4] witness the Aristotelian revival of the thirteenth century and the Platonic one of the fifteenth.

The notion is widespread that the Byzantines valued lightly—even disparaged—the West's literature and theology and therefore incorporated little or nothing of them into their own culture. True, the Greeks, to judge from surviving evidence, seem to have been hardly aware of the greatest Western Father, St. Augustine, or at least knew little of his works in the early period. As has been (correctly) claimed, the watershed between Byzantine and Western theology probably occurred under Augustine, whose works marked a real departure from the direction taken by the Cappadocian Fathers.[5] Yet some versions of the Latin Fathers were known early in the East. Moreover, one can enumerate even before the eleventh century a few translations of Western works into Greek, and after the twelfth and especially the thirteenth centuries, a surprisingly large number. Already in the early sixth century, for example, Emperor Justin had the historian Flavianus translated, so that he might justly assert East Rome's continuity from the empire of Augustus.[6] And in the ninth century, as Photius himself tells us, perhaps the most popular Western work of hagiography, Pope Gregory the Great's *Dialogues*, was turned into Greek from the original Latin by Pope

Zacharias (himself a Greek). Other works of Gregory, such as his *Pastoral Care*, were also translated at various times.[7] Even in the tenth century, the darkest Western hour of all, the example may be cited of Leo of Naples, who attempted to make a translation of the apocryphal story of Alexander the Great, originally written by Pseudo-Callisthenes.[8] But these works, one must grant, were not widely diffused and seem to have produced little effect on the mind of the East.

One can also mention, after the sixth century, sporadic examples of Byzantines in the East who knew Latin. To be sure, Justinian is usually cited as the last Latin-speaking Byzantine ruler. But all through the millennium of Byzantine history, one can, if one looks hard enough, find instances of imperial interpreters and envoys who had a practical knowledge of Latin for purposes of diplomacy. Thus in 1054, in the Greek counterexcommunication directed at the papal envoys of Leo IX, the name of a Spanish interpreter who obviously knew Latin is mentioned.[9] And in the sphere of law, the emperor Constantine IX of the same period prescribed that the head of the newly reestablished law school of Constantinople know Latin so as to be able to read the Justinianic legal corpus in the original.[10] This, of course, was in accord with Justinian's own injunction against translation of his famous code. Nevertheless, because of changing social conditions, Justinian's code had long since been converted into Greek.

We must move to the twelfth century, however, to the Pisan brothers Hugo Eterianus and Leo Tuscus, both in the employ of the emperor Manuel I Comnenus, to find the first significant examples since the ancient world of Westerners translating Greek Patristic works into Latin.[11] These two, one working as interpreter to the emperor, the other, as imperial adviser on questions of religious union, acquired not only a thorough command of Greek but, through perusing the numerous libraries of Constantinople, a wide familiarity with contemporary and Patristic Greek theological works.[12] During this same century may be mentioned, among others, the example of the papal envoy, the German Anselm of Havelberg, who has left us a vivid account of theological disputations held in 1136 before the emperor in Constantinople. And of course one should recall in this period the great influence the theological work of the Byzantine John of Damascus was having on a very large number of Western theologians.[13]

A parallel example in the West of the effect that Greco-Latin negotiations for religious union had on church ritual during the twelfth (and later the thirteenth) century, may be observed in the increasing number of translations made into Greek from Latin liturgies. These, however, as has earlier been shown, were primarily for the use of the Greek-speaking communities of southern Italy, which had resided there for centuries.[13a]

The beginnings, however, of a more sustained Greek interest in the West's ecclesiastical literature did not occur until one century later, after the Council of Lyons in 1274. At that conclave, though no official disputations took place, informal contacts between Greek and Latin ecclesiastics (Bonaventura, the great Latin mystic-Scholastic, represented the West) resulted for the first time in centuries in Byzantines casting about for Latin theological works to translate.[14] But the newly found enthusiasm of these Byzantines for Latin works, it should be underscored, was usually motivated less by purely intellectual fervor than by the exigencies of religion and politics. To thwart the designs of Charles of Anjou, then threatening a new Latin invasion of Byzantium, the Greek emperor Michael VIII Palaeologus looked toward effecting a reunion of the two churches in exchange for papal support for Constantinople against Charles.[15] With ecclesiastics of both sides coming into increasing contact with one another after Lyons, a more solid interest in Latin dogma and ecclesiastical literature was finally able to take root among the Greeks. And so, to best the Latins at their highly developed Scholastic argumentation, or for reasons of sheer polemic, the Greeks now found it expedient—nay indispensable—to acquire some knowledge of their opponents' methods and materials.

An example of the unexpected result such interest in Latin ecclesiastical writings might have, is that of the erstwhile, sharply anti-unionist Greek patriarch, John Bekkos. Cast into prison in 1273 by Michael VIII, he pored belligerently over the Latin Patristic texts that had been brought him, only to come to the conclusion, remarkable for his age, that the differences between East and West on the thorny problem of the procession of the Holy Ghost were relatively minor. Since G. Hofmann has recently shown that Bekkos knew no Latin, one must assume he used translations of Latin theological treatises.[16]

The Byzantine interest in Western sacred writings seems to have led, in one case at least, to an eagerness also to learn the literature of Latin antiquity, Evidently, the first recorded Byzantine after the Patristic period who evinced real interest in the profane learning of the ancient Romans seems to have been the late thirteenth-century monk Maximos Planudes. Indeed, his primary interest lay less in theology than in ancient philosophy, mathematics, Arabic (i.e. Indian) numerals, and belles lettres.[17] Planudes, it seems, even appreciated Ovid. But this eager translator, whose interest in Latin classical letters we shall concentrate on in a moment, was not occupied entirely with profane letters. He also put into Greek, Augustine's theological treatise *De Trinitate*, so basic to a Western understanding of Trinitarian doctrine—a translation that was to become popular among the growing group of Latinophile Greeks.[18] Though Planudes' interests in Latin culture were on the whole more humanistic than theological, he wrote, in his later years, two treatises directed against Latin views of the filioque.

For Greeks interested in Latin learning, a kind of nursery for the study of Latin in the East was the Dominican monastery of Pera, established across the Golden Horn from Constantinople some time after the Latin occupation in 1204 (probably before 1228). Something of a theological "college," the monastery in time became a center for the radiation of Latin theological influences throughout the entire Greek East.[19] Although Planudes himself apparently did not study there—it is clear, however, that he had close contacts with many Dominicans of the East—a considerable number of contemporary and later Greek figures took advantage of the vistas on the West opened by the monastery. Such Byzantines as Prochoros and Demetrios Cydones, Manuel Calecas, the little-known John Cyparissiotes, and the fifteenth-century patriarch Gregory Mammas, became exponents of the burgeoning cultural relations between East and West.[20]

Thus Dominicans, whether teaching in the Pera monastery or privately, turned out Byzantines such as these bilingual Greeks, who began to spread Latin ideas—their Greek opponents would say Latin religious propaganda—throughout the Byzantine Empire. Not all the activities of the monastery conduced to greater understanding, however, for some of the friars, both Latin and Greek, began to engage in polemic, writing treatises specifically against Orthodoxy. Nor were all the translations made from Latin into Greek of the same high quality as those of Planudes. Thomas Aquinas himself, in his *Contra Errores Graecorum*, it seems, used versions of polemical, anti-Greek treatises translated in the Pera monastery—versions we now know contained errors and even sometimes misrepresented Greek doctrinal views.[21]

With the increasing translation, in the later thirteenth and fourteenth centuries, of Latin theological works (resulting from more frequent political and religious contacts), Latin theological currents began to produce a very disturbing effect on traditional Greek theology. An important manifestation, at least in part, of this development is the conflict in the Byzantine world between the so-called Barlaamites and the Palamites of Mt. Athos over the quietistic doctrine of Hesychasm. The aim of the Hesychast monks was *theosis* (literally, "divinization"), or mystical union with God (see chaps. 1, 3, and 6). One aspect of this controversy was the strife between what has often (perhaps mistakenly) been taken to be the Latin-oriented theology of Barlaam, a Greek born in southern Italy, and the Byzantine theology of the archbishop of Thessalonika, Gregory Palamas. Barlaam, as John Cantacuzene and others tell us, was trained in the method of Aristotelian logic and philosophy.[22] Some modern scholars affirm that he was a Nominalist in the Western sense, though this view may partly be due to the fact that he taught (at the Chora of Constantinople) the philosophy of Pseudo-Dionysius, whose apophatic approach was in some ways perhaps similar to the views of Ockham. Gregory Palamas, on the other hand, an Athonite monk before he became archbishop, was a close follower of the Greek Patristic mystical tradition, and as such shared many of the Fathers' Neoplatonic views. Actually, it is very likely that at bottom both Barlaam and Palamas represented different strains of Byzantine theological development.[23]

The dispute between Barlaam and Palamas centered on the issue of the possibility of "knowing" God and the way such knowledge could be acquired, a question, of course, already basic for the early Fathers of the church. In his arguments Barlaam, according to certain modern scholars, reflected the Western tendency to preserve inviolate the unity of God and his attributes, thus denying that finite man could ever grasp or "know" the infinite God except through indirect, created means. Palamas, on the other hand, though also maintaining that the essence (*ousia*) of God was unknowable to mankind, believed that union with the uncreated "energies" of God could be achieved. Just as the sun has its center and rays, so too, Palamas affirmed, God has his superessential *ousia* and also his energies, the effects of which may be known or seen by man.[24]

Another figure closely involved with the Hesychast conflict was the Latin-oriented Greek, John Cyparissiotes. To escape the persecutions of the perfervid Greek Hesychast supporters, he went to the papal

Gregory Palamas, Archbishop of Thessalonica (ca. 1375), from a panel in the Museum of Fine Arts, Moscow.

court at Avignon, and in the years 1376-77 entered the service of Pope Gregory XI. There he gained the respect of the Latins who, because of his learning, called him *Sapiens*. In his writings the influence of Western Scholasticism is clearly to be seen. As is rarely realized, Cyparissiotes wrote probably the first Greek theological treatise using the dialectic method of the Western Schoolmen, *Stoicheodes eckthesis ton theologikon rheseon*;[25] and it was the first, or one of the first, of such treatises to be translated into Latin. It should be noted that the later and more famous Demetrios Cydones, unlike Cyparissiotes and despite his many Latin translations, apparently never produced an original theological treatise of his own in the Western Scholastic manner.

Up to the twelfth century, the East, except for a very few individuals,[26] knew little of the theological developments that were taking place in the West after the Patristic age. Nonetheless, after the fourth century a few Eastern theologians did possess a desire to learn something of Latin theology. This is evidenced by the fact that Planudes' Greek version of Augustine's *De Trinitate* is frequently referred to in the writings of contemporary or subsequent Greek theologians, especially of the brothers Prochoros and Demetrios Cydones of the fourteenth century.[27] Indeed, after Planudes' translation, some Byzantine scholars (such as Manuel Calecas) began to quote at length from Augustine in order to support their method of biblical exegesis and doctrinal exposition.[28]

There can be no doubt that the most significant point in the deepening acquaintance of East and West with each other's theology came in the late fourteenth century in the person of Demetrios Cydones.[29] One of the truly creative minds of Byzantium, Cydones, it has been affirmed by scholars, was initially converted to Catholicism on a purely intellectual basis.[30] Through wide-ranging reading in both Latin and Greek Patristic authors, Cydones became the first Byzantine in centuries (apart from the isolated case of Planudes, who, as noted, was mainly interested in literature) even to pose the question of whether the Latins had any philosophic or religious thought worth reading. Without exaggeration I think one may say that Cydones began to break the iron grip of prejudice against the West that had for so long bound the East.

Cydones' Latin teacher, Philip of Pera, was a friar in the Dominican house at Pera. As a textbook for his eager pupil, Friar Philip chose Thomas Aquinas's great *Summa Contra Gentiles* (which, incidentally, was written primarily against the Averroists and, to a lesser extent, the Greeks). Fascinated with Aquinas, Cydones began to turn the entire *Summa* into Greek. By 1354 he had translated four books of it, as well as part of Thomas's *Summa Theologiae* and also the *quaestio disputata* "De Potentia," which deals with the burning question of the filioque.[31] In his own *Apologia,* Cydones, after describing the impact the angelic doctor's thought had upon his thinking, relates that he presented copies of the translated Thomistic texts to the Byzantine emperor for his perusal. Remarkably, as we are told, his imperial master, John V Palaeologos, praised Cydones' undertaking as "beneficent to the Greek people."[32] (It should be noted that this emperor's mother was of the Latin house of Savoy.)

In view of the deeply rooted Greek antipathy to Latin theology, it is most interesting to note Cydones' affirmation that the Latin Fathers—Augustine, Ambrose, Jerome, Gregory the Great—had also been venerated by the Greeks before schism had separated East from West.[33] Nevertheless, though it is true that some writings of the Latin Fathers were known in the East, we cannot say that up to 1453 these early Fathers had any really formative impact on Orthodox Greek theology. As Dekkers has pointed out, even the few translations into Greek of Augustine, the greatest of the Western Fathers, were up to the eighth century made largely by non-Greeks of the East (Syrians, Copts, and Armenians) and were circulated almost exclusively in North Africa and Syria.[34]

Like Patriarch John Bekkos before him and the Cretan bishop Maximos Margounios later in the sixteenth century, Cydones found few, if any, essential contradictions between the Latin and Greek Fathers on most of the important points of doctrine.[35] Above all, and here he was unique—in a sense a precursor of the modern "ecumenical movement"—Cydones grasped the essence of the spiritual unity of the same faith that in the early church had bound East to West. He was convinced that this unity had nothing of the abstract about it; for him it was a living reality. In his *Apologia* he, in fact, advises other Greeks to study how this unity had been maintained throughout the centuries. It is this higher vision of Christendom that certain modern scholars have taken to be the mainspring of Cydones' scholarly and political life. He was, as affirmed earlier, the chief proponent of an alliance between Eastern and Western Christendom in order to push back the Turks, in contrast to other Byzantine statesmen of the period who proposed a pan-Orthodox—

that is, a Greco-Slavic—union for this same purpose.[36] Nevertheless, despite what in our time would be termed the ecumenical cast to his character, Cydones, with no small degree of "nationalistic" Greek pride, was quick to recognize in the method and material of Aquinas's *Summa Contra Gentiles*, Greek elements, and with reference to them he said, in effect (as noted before), that this was "our own Greek material." Realizing that during the medieval period far fewer translations had been made from Latin to Greek than the reverse, he noted that from antiquity Latins had continually sought to make contact with the East in order to profit from things Greek.[37]

Cydones, interestingly enough, was not only influenced by Thomas Aquinas but also by St. Augustine, whom he mentions frequently in his writings. The Augustinian element is best reflected in his work *De Processione Spiritus Sancti*. There, profusely quoting Augustine, he even accepts the Latin doctrine of the filioque, which he tried to prove to his fellow Greeks on the basis of Augustine's teachings on the procession of the Holy Spirit: "Do not doubt in any way whatever that the Holy Spirit is of the Father and the Son and proceeds from the Father and the Son."[38] Cydones tried to prove that since the three persons of the Godhead are one, and the Father begets the Son and "breathes forth" the Holy Spirit, and the Father does not differ from the Son (in essence), then the Holy Spirit must proceed from the Son as well as the Father. As is well known, the objection of the Greeks to this was on the grounds that such a definition would imply the existence of two sources, not one, for the Godhead.[39] Cydones in one place tries to explicate the Trinity by using Latin exegesis: the Son equals the *logos*, the Holy Spirit equals *agape*, and the Father, *nous*.[40] He then uses this formula again to prove that the Holy Spirit proceeds from both Father and Son.

Under the inspiration of Cydones, who was no less than Grand Logothete, a kind of prime minister of Byzantium, there soon emerged in the heart of the Byzantine court a virtual cult of Thomists. One of his chief associates in this circle was Demetrios' brother, Prochoros Cydones, who translated Aquinas's *On the Eternity of the World (Peri tes tou kosmou aidiotetos)* and also Augustine's *De Vera Religione* (written originally against the Manichaeans), as well as his *De Decem Plagis et Decem Praeceptis*. Prochoros also wrote several works based on Thomistic writings *(Peri ousias kai energeias)*.[41]

Manuel Calecas, a member of the same circle, translated into Greek Boethius's *De Trinitate* and, for the first time, a work of the proto-scholastic Anselm of Canterbury, his soteriological treatise, *Cur Deus Homo*, together with the pseudo-Augustinian *De Purgatorio*.[42] Calecas converted to the Catholic faith in 1396, and only a few years later, in 1403, entered the Dominican house on the Greek island of Mytilene. His most important original work was his apologia, *De Fide . . .* , concerning the principles of Catholicism according to Holy Scripture, the theology of which again reflects Thomistic tenets.[43] After the death of Demetrios Cydones, Calecas became the leading figure in this Greek Thomistic group, but the extent of his influence is not comparable to that of his teacher Demetrios Cydones.

We must omit here the names of others, like the fifteenth-century George Scholarius who was deeply affected by Latin Thomism. (Later, however, as the first patriarch under the Turks, he wrote a very clear exposition of Orthodoxy for the sultan Mohammed II.)[44] It should be stressed, nonetheless, that the leaders of the Thomistic movement in Byzantium were looked upon with disdain, even contempt, by most Byzantines, who considered them traitors to the Orthodox church and the nation.

But the increasing contact of the two theological systems, with the pronounced Latin theological tendencies that affected the Byzantine church in the late thirteenth and early fourteenth centuries, produced the not surprising reaction of making the naturally conservative Byzantine theologians even more conservative. Henceforth, with the exception of the Latinophile works produced, most theological treatises that were to be composed in the Byzantine East were apologetic or polemic in character, directed primarily against what they held to be the errors of the Latin church.

The connections between Latin and Greek theology in the decades before the fall of Constantinople in 1453 now became even closer. But, since they continued in essentially the same direction, we shall allude to them only briefly. Suffice it to remind the reader that the constant arguments between Eastern and Western theologians must be placed in the context of negotiations for the convocation of an ecumenical council to unite the two churches. The Greek emperor and his church sought military aid from the pope against the Turks but would make ecclesiastical concessions only after the convocation of, and discussion at, such a council. The pope, for his part, demanded submission of the Greek church to Rome before granting military aid and refused to attend an ecumenical council unless his claims to jurisdiction over the entire church were first recognized.[45]

The climax to all the East-West ecclesiastical diplomacy came, of course, at the celebrated Council of Florence in 1438–39, where, though the main purpose was ecclesiastical, the intellectual elite of Italy and the Greek East were, at dinners and elsewhere, enabled to engage in a very profitable intellectual exchange. There, for the first time since antiquity, the complete Platonic corpus in its original Greek form was reintroduced to the West, with long-range results for the history of European culture. A key point in this connection was the writing in Florence by the Byzantine Neoplatonist Gemistos Pletho, of his famous *On the Differences between Plato and Aristotle*,[46] a work to some degree anticipated by the previous intellectual ferment in Constantinople. Here, as Bessarion would do at greater length later, he suggested in effect why it was easier for Plato to be "Christianized" than Aristotle. The East, of course, had always known Aristotle and Plato in the original. But, as has hitherto not been emphasized, what helped to prepare the Greeks for the Council of Florence and especially for the argumentation occurring in Italy and the East after the appearance of Pletho's treatise was, in a way, the fourteenth-century Byzantine discussions resulting from the reception in the East of the Western Scholastic Aristotle, and especially the work of Cydones and his circle. Cydones' Thomistic circle, then, played a valuable role. In any event, despite Scholarius' own self-serving statement about the inferiority of the Greek dialectics at Florence and even the attitude of the emperor himself, some Byzantine theologians, because of their Thomistic studies, had grown better prepared to meet in disputation with the Latins at Florence.[47]

It is interesting to observe that in the theological ferment that simmered in the East before the Council of Florence and afterwards (up to 1453), two of the chief devotees of Aristotelianism and Platonism adopted different approaches to the most crucial political issue of the day—salvation of the empire. The Aristotelian Cydones, who saw in Thomism a Greek base, hoped for collaboration with the West in a great coalition to repulse the Turk and save Constantinople. The Neoplatonist Pletho, on the other hand, connected Platonism, which as late as the early twelfth century or even beyond was still looked upon in Byzantium as being tinged with paganism or "crypto-Origenism," with Greek "nationalism," and hoped, through application of ancient Platonic concepts, to bring about a regeneration of what he now termed a "Hellenic" state rather than

"Roman" (that is, Byzantine). For him, the patriotic fervor necessary for his program to revivify the Byzantine state and repulse the Turks had to come from the Byzantines' ancient Greek and not from the subsequent Roman (Byzantine) heritage.[48]

CLASSICAL LATIN LITERATURE

Ancient Latin literature, as is well known, derived much of its inspiration, its forms and style, from Greek prototypes. Byzantium, however, as heir and preserver of the Greek (more accurately Hellenistic) literary tradition, tended increasingly to disregard Latin letters after the Patristic age. More than that, in the near-anarchy of the so-called Dark Ages, when Western civilization sank to its nadir, the Greeks of the East began to look even with contempt on Western culture, terming the Latins "barbarians" and believing that the West had little of value to offer the East.[49] Fortifying this adverse Byzantine judgment toward the ancient, and even more the medieval, Latin literature, was the fact that by this time Latin, originally the language of the court in Constantinople, had in effect become a foreign language to almost all Greeks.

But even classical *Greek* literature and philosophy were not looked upon by all Byzantines, especially monks, with a favorable eye: witness, as late as the eleventh century, the case of the Neoplatonist, Grand Logothete Michael Psellos, who tells us that on a visit to a monastery in Bithynia he was looked at askance by a monk who began to cross himself when he saw Psellos reading the works of Plato.[50] Even the most erudite of all Byzantine scholars, the ninth-century patriarch Photius, in his collection summarizing numerous classical and Patristic Greek works, the *Bibliotheca*, though making some references to Latin Patristic writings, made no mention of pagan Latin authors.[51]

Latin literature, then, was not only considered alien but representative of a departed pagan culture. Moreover, in the context of the increasing political and religious alienation of East and West, it is not unduly surprising that the first example of a learned Byzantine seeking to translate Latin classical works into Greek does not occur until as late as the end of the thirteenth century. Before that, only very few isolated examples of Greek concern for ancient Latin literature can be found—of an "antiquarian" interest, so to say—though, to be sure, much investigation remains to be done on this problem as well as on that relating to Byzantine knowledge of Latin ecclesiastical literature up to the end of the Patristic period.[52] It is probably safe to say, however, that there was somewhat more Byzantine interest in Latin literature than is ordinarily believed, if one notes, for example, the existence in both West and East up to the seventh century of manuscripts containing exercises of translations from Latin to Greek and vice versa, and also of Greek papyri containing bilingual dictionaries.[53] One isolated instance, already cited in another context, is that of the sixth-century emperor Justin, who desired a Greek translation of the historical work of Flavianus in order to emphasize the continuity of East Rome from Augustus's empire. But his purpose, it should be emphasized, was purely pragmatic, not humanistic. We may also recall in the tenth century the suggestive words of the famous bishop Liutprand of Cremona, who on one of his ambassadorial visits to Constantinople said caustically to the Greek emperor Nicephoros Phocas that, though the latter might despise Latin, his very title was Roman, that he was greeted in the "Latin manner" by his subjects and courtiers, and that even the Byzantine gold coin, the *nomisma*, bore Latin inscriptions.[54]

By the tenth century at the very latest, Latin as a spoken and literary language had virtually been forgotten in the East. Apparently, the last emperor to speak Latin was the sixth-century emperor Justinian, though in the eleventh century Emperor Constantine IX ordered the head of the law school in Constantinople to learn Latin in order to understand Justinian's codes in the original.[55]

It is apparently not until after the interest generated in some circles of the East as a result of the Council of Lyons in 1274 that we find the first example of a learned Byzantine, the monk Maximos Planudes, seeking to translate into Greek, works of the ancient Latin literary tradition. Planudes translated a surprising number of works including, among others, Cato's *Dicta*, Macrobius's *Commentary on the Dream of Scipio*, Boethius's *De Consolatione philosophiae*, and possibly his *De Dialectica*, also Cato's *Distycha*, Cicero's *Somnium* and *Cato de Senectute maior*, and Ovid's *Metamorphoses* and *Epistolae Heroidum*. He even turned into Greek some works of the grammarian Donatus and, surprisingly, of the medieval physician and philosopher Petrus Hispanus (who has been identified with Pope John XXI).[56] Because of his proficiency in Latin, Planudes was in 1296 sent to the West in the capacity of imperial envoy, the Venetians even bestowing upon him, as a mark of favor, the coveted honorary citizenship of their city.[57]

Planudes, then, like Demetrios Cydones of the next century in philosophy and religion, was the first Byzantine to question the justice of the disparaging Byzantine judgment assumed in every age with regard to Latin culture. In his thirst for ancient Latin literature Planudes, who was essentially self-taught but had sporadic assistance from papal envoys occasionally appearing in Constantinople, was evidently influenced by the interest aroused in the Greek East for Latin theology as a result of the Council of Lyons in 1274. This, like the Council of Florence later, in 1438–39, with respect to Platonic philosophy, acted as a catalyst in the meeting of the two cultures. Indeed, Planudes' translation of Augustine's *De Trinitate*, evidently made soon after the assembling of the Council of Lyons, was able to provide the Greeks, especially proponents of the emperor's unionist policy, with a knowledge of Latin theological views on the much disputed filioque question.[58] Nevertheless, despite Planudes' keen interest in Latin literature as such, he seems to have been an isolated figure. Apparently he left no followers with his own deep interest in Latin letters, not even his brilliant student, the famous editor of the classical Greek tragedies, Manuel Moschopoulos.[59]

Even the influence of Cydones and his Thomistic circle, in the context of the need for learning Latin to regulate political and religious questions with the West during and after the Council of Florence, seems to have done little to stimulate Greek interest in ancient Latin literature. Certainly what little there was, did not develop with any of the same intensity as did the study of Latin theology.

To what extent did a problem exist for a Byzantine reading the Latin classical texts with regard to the reconciliation of its pagan content with Christian doctrine? Until more intensive research on individual cases is done, this question cannot really be answered adequately. It may be noted, however, that the reading of pagan Greek works in the East, especially the philosopher Plato (even Aristotle), was often looked at obliquely by the monks and perhaps some of the higher ecclesiastics. Actually, the usual medieval criterion in both East and West for the reading of pagan literature seems to have been whether or not it would be contrary to the ideals of the Christian faith. Thus, the reading of Homer and Virgil was permitted, but "immoral" sections of, say, Catullus and the Greek plays seem to have been proscribed. It may be said that in both Byzantium (at least *up to* the Palaeologan Renaissance) and the West, the classical authors were in general to be used as a means to an end rather than as an end in themselves.[60]

Most significant, however, for the rejection of ancient Latin pagan literature in Byzantium was probably the Byzantine view that it was, in effect, superfluous. The ancient Roman Cicero had already admitted that Greek philosophy far surpassed Latin and was in fact its source. Even the Byzantine scholar of the widest range of erudition, the ninth-century Patriarch Photius, in his famous *Bibliotheca*, apart from references to Augustine's *De gestis Pelagii* and to the Greek Cassian's monastic works (which, by the way, Photius read in a Greek version) makes no mention of classical or of any medieval Latin writings.[61] And as late as the Italian Renaissance, by which time contacts between East and West had become very close, few Greek humanists of the Palaeologan Renaissance as a whole appear to have learned Latin literature until they needed to come to the West for work or study. The Byzantines who learned Latin well seem limited to Bessarion, Theodore Gaza, George of Trebizond, Demetrios Chalcondyles, John Argyropoulos, and the post-Byzantines Janus Lascaris, Marcus Musurus, and Michael Marullus of the late fifteenth and early sixteenth centuries.[62] Illustrative of the typical Greek view toward Latin literature are the remarks of Chalcondyles (see chap. 13) on the occasion of his assumption of the Greek chair at Padua University.

Interesting, finally, is the attitude of the Byzantine humanist Michael Apostolis. After 1453 he lived as a refugee on Venetian-held Crete, although apparently he made several journeys to Italy. In a speech directed to the intellectuals of Italy, Michael showed that he clearly realized he was living at a turning point in history —a time in which cultural leadership was passing from the dying Byzantine world to the rising humanistic centers of Italy. Nonetheless, to his way of thinking the Italians, though heralding the dawn of a new age, were still merely the heirs of the ancient Greeks, whose superiority in literature and general culture (he affirmed) had never been surpassed.[63] The same feeling is expressed in the aforementioned discourse delivered in 1463 at the University of Padua by the Byzantine humanist Demetrios Chalcondyles on the occasion of the inauguration of Greek studies there (see chap. 13). This feeling of cultural superiority, despite the toleration for Latin literature developed for a time by Planudes and then perhaps by Cydones and his circle, was to remain entirely typical of the mentality of the Byzantines to the very end of their empire. And, as such, it goes far to explain why classical Latin literature was never able to exercise more than a slight influence on Byzantine thought.[64]

To sum up, in the early centuries of the Middle Ages when, as is well known, the superiority of Byzantine over Western civilization was unquestioned, it is not surprising that the cultural influences flowed from East to West and not in the other direction. And yet, even in these earlier centuries of the so-called Dark Ages, when a higher level of mentality, of metaphysical speculation, was almost nonexistent in the low-level, Germano-Latin society so often struggling merely to keep alive, some Western influences on the East may be observed. As the main business of the Western noble class was fighting, it developed efficient techniques of warfare. The skill in battle of the Western knights was, in fact, grudgingly admitted even by the Byzantines. And, as we have noted, certain chivalric customs, the joust for instance, were adopted by some Latinophile Greeks in the twelfth century. Moreover, certain Western terms like *kavallarius* (chevalier) were not uncommonly found as names in the East, and of course in the earlier period almost the entire legal and constitutional system of ancient Rome, along with aspects of its statecraft, was taken over by the Byzantines, though the latter developed diplomacy to a degree of finesse unknown elsewhere in the medieval world.

East and West grew out of the same matrix—the political structure of the Roman Empire and of its Greco-Roman culture—but the two fraternal civilizations had by the tenth century grown so far apart as to form almost two separate worlds of Christendom. Political, religious, and economic factors contributed to this alienation, but not least was the distinct feeling of the Byzantine throughout the entire period that he was, in virtually all aspects of higher culture, superior to the man of the West. He alone had inherited the fruits of ancient Greek culture as well as the Roman governmental tradition, and above all, the true Orthodox faith of the *Christian* Roman Empire. For him the West was no longer Roman. It had fallen to the Germanic invaders. It had become, as the Greeks put it, "Frankish," and had therefore lost the right to be called Roman. Only the Greeks were now the true "Rhomaioi." As for the proud Westerner who came in contact with Byzantines, the attitude of the latter he took as insufferable and unwarranted arrogance, especially after the Latin Crusaders, in his mind, had proved themselves vastly superior militarily to the Byzantines.

Important as these considerations may be, especially from the twelfth and thirteenth centuries onward when Western culture began to rival Byzantine, that which most truly hampered Greek receptivity to Western cultural influences was, as we have several times repeated, not only the Greek feeling of superiority but, in the latter centuries, the overt hostility of the Byzantines to the Latins. This antagonism, though in more inchoate form, had already been evident in the earlier Middle Ages. But in view of the low level of Western civilization in that period, it did not, with the few exceptions briefly alluded to above, serve to any effective degree to block any Latin influences that might flow eastward.

And yet it was precisely in the late twelfth to fourteenth centuries, when Latin oppression became greatest in Eastern political and economic life, that intellectually the deepest inroads began to be made in the East. Some Greeks, like Planudes and in the next century Cydones, the two key figures, were finally able to break the iron grip of centuries-long prejudice and even to accept the idea that Western Christianity had something of value to offer, as, for the humanist Planudes, did ancient Latin literature. But these men still took pride in the fact that the Greek heritage underlay both Latin antique literature and Latin theology. Planudes, with his apparently unique interest in Latin letters, saw in it the inspiration of Greek models. Cydones, for his part, was gratified to see that much of the Latin Thomistic achievement was based on Aristotle. It is true that in philosophy the Latins in the eleventh century made their first advance in centuries only after the reception of Aristotle, though of course by way of the Arabs of Spain. It should be noted, however, that in the latter period, when some Greeks finally become attracted by the remarkably developing dialectic of the Latin Scholastics, it was mainly for pragmatic reasons: to be able more effectively to oppose the Latins in political and ecclesiastical disputation.

On the other hand, with respect to ancient Latin literature, Planudes aside, there seems to have been very little Greek interest. As pointed out, this may well have been because Latin was far removed from Byzantine civilization. Besides being pagan, the literature was written in a language which had disappeared from the East as a spoken tongue—although originally the speech of the court at

Miscellaneous fragments of painted window glass, from the Byzantine monastery of the Pantocrator. (Nos. 2, 3, 9B, 14 and 19, colorless; nos. 4, 7, 13, and 24, green; nos. 8, 9A, 10, 15-18, 21A-C, 27, and 28, amber-yellow; nos. 20 and 25, purple-red; no. 23, pink; remainder, blue.) From A. Megaw, "Notes on Recent Work of the Byzantine Institute in Istanbul," *Dumbarton Oaks Papers* no. 17 (1963), p. 360. Courtesy of Dumbarton Oaks Center for Byzantine Studies, Washington, D.C. (See pp. 25, 79-80, showing possible Byzantine influence on Western stained-glass techniques.)

Constantinople—and was now used in a very corrupt form, the Greeks believed, by the "heretical Franks." Moreover, the Greeks already possessed Greek literature, of which the Latin literature, as even some Latins admitted, was only a pale imitation. The intense Scholastic development of the use of the Aristotelian syllogism in dialectic came as something quite new to Byzantium, and one can therefore understand its attraction for some in the East. Rhetoric, on the other hand, which was prized in Byzantium above all, was already highly developed, perhaps even overly refined. Thus, it is not strange that ancient Latin literature could provide little fresh inspiration for the Byzantine mind.

Given these various considerations, there is no doubt that the Greeks, with very few exceptions, underestimated the level which Latin culture had achieved by the fourteenth and fifteenth centuries. Dante's great *Divine Comedy*, to take but one example, reaches creative heights never approached, I believe, by any Byzantine literary work.[65] But Greek intellectuals would have nothing to do with the Western vernacular languages. Even the use of their own spoken Greek for literary purposes was by them generally deemed unworthy. And so, with one exception to be cited in chapter 13, it should not be surprising that no other evidence has, so far as I know, been found that Dante's great vernacular work was appreciated or even known to contemporary Byzantine scholars, though Dante, on his part, was unquestionably influenced—if indirectly— by the philosophy of Aristotle and the mysticism of the Byzantine Dionysius the Areopagite. It must be pointed out, on the other hand, that Dante himself—except for a bare mention of Justinian—seems to know nothing of the many remarkable theological, literary, and artistic achievements of Byzantium.

We may now ask the question: how deeply did Latin theological and literary influences actually pervade Byzantine thought of the thirteenth to the fifteenth centuries? To a startling and intensive degree, it would seem at first glance. But, one must quickly add, only within a relatively small group, in particular Demetrios Cydones' Thomistic circle at the Byzantine court—and, at that, only temporarily. Most Greeks would have nothing to do with the Latinophile Greek Thomists, though their activities must certainly have had some effect, indirectly at least, on later Greek humanists like Bessarion. That Greek cardinal was impressed by the achievement of Western theology and, as is insufficiently realized, technology, hoping the latter might somehow be used to save Byzantium from the Turks.[66] Yet, in the long run, neither Western theology nor Western philosophic ideas were able, in any organic way, to affect Byzantine thought. Its core remained entirely Greek, and what we earlier termed the "nativistic" Greek reaction to Latin influence finally triumphed. Indeed, as we have already shown, the strong attraction that Latin theology exerted on some Byzantines so repelled the majority of Greeks as to make them more conservative, more intransigent than ever, vis-à-vis the Latins.

During the last two or three centuries the Latin presence had virtually saturated the East. Nevertheless, some modern scholars fail to realize the extent of the underlying fear most Greeks had of Western domination, especially the lower classes but a large number of intellectuals and statesmen as well—fear of ultimately losing their identity as a people, in other words, of Latinization. And in view of the great mass of Latins living and working in the East and their pervasive presence in virtually all strata of Byzantine society, it cannot be denied that, though to be sure there were some Latins of good will, the Greek anxieties were far from groundless.[67] It was, then, the eternal, and admittedly in some ways unjustified, Greek feeling of cultural superiority, and even more, the almost obsessive antipathy toward religious union, itself probably a psychological defense mechanism masking a deeper fear of Latinization—that in the long run prevented Latin culture from making any really permanent inroads into medieval Greek civilization.

After 1453 the Greeks of the homeland, with the notable exception of a few areas under Venetian rule such as Crete and the Ionian isles, remained more than ever attached to their old traditional patterns of thought. Whatever Latin influence remained therefore disappeared, helped partly by the Turkish policy of keeping the Greeks out of contact with the West.[68] As has not always been realized, when in 1453 Constantinople at last fell to the Turks, the Greek East and the Latin West were cut off from each other as much by mutual distrust as by the Turkish conquest itself. Under such circumstances, any really enduring intellectual and ecclesiastical influences of the Latin West on the Byzantine mind up to 1453, however striking at the moment they occurred, could in the long run be only temporary and of relatively little consequence.

5

Church Construction and "Caesaropapism" in East and West from Constantine to Justinian

The period from the conversion of Constantine to the death of Justinian is not only that in which the crucial problem of imperial authority over the church became crystallized; it is also one of the formative eras with regard to monumental church building, perhaps the most formative in the history of the church. Each of these questions has been a separate subject of intensive study, but their correlation has been dealt with only cursorily, if at all. It is the purpose of this chapter to examine the two considerations in light of each other with the aim of deriving, in different perspective, new insights into the fundamental problem of the relationship of church and state in the early period.

Of the fifteen emperors of the Byzantine East and the somewhat greater number in the West during the time span from A.D. 312 to 565, by far the most important as regards church construction were the first, Constantine the Great, and the last, Justinian. Because of his position as the first Christian Roman emperor, Constantine's desire to commemorate the most sacred shrines of Christianity by monumental church building was only natural. Justinian, the last of this series of emperors, was as great a builder as Constantine, if not greater. And from the viewpoint of political theory, Justinian ruled in the so-called Caesaropapistic tradition established earlier by Constantine. Indeed, Justinian, historians generally agree—even those who dislike the term—was the most "Caesaropapistic" of all Byzantine emperors. In his reign, as we see clearly both from his civil and canon law, the concept of the unity of the empire was constantly emphasized—one church, one state, both under the rule of God's representative or vicegerent on earth, the Basileus. This theory of imperial rule over the Basileia, the Christian empire on earth, in imitation (mimesis) of God's rule over the divine order in heaven, was formulated largely by Constantine's adviser, Bishop Eusebius, who combined elements drawn from Christian, Hellenistic, and Roman concepts and practices.[1]

Eusebius, however, did not explicitly spell out all aspects of his theory. Indeed, what to our minds seems to be a blurring of the spheres of church and state, as well as Eusebius's impreciseness with respect to the extent of imperial control over the church, was to remain a basic problem for all later emperors and patriarchs—not to speak of modern historians.[2]

The problem of establishing a correlation between the degree of the emperor's authority over the church in theory and practice, and the amount and kind of church building accomplished in each reign, is obviously a very complex one. It involves not only the technical problem of the architecture of the churches erected but, more important, the motivations of individual emperors in such construction, and finally, of course, the possible effect of this construction in bringing the church and the faithful more closely under imperial control.

It has been suggested that literary sources are less than adequate in dealing with this problem and that archaeological remains offer perhaps the surest access to imperial church building, confirming or disproving the literary evidence.[3] Certainly, it would seem clear that for this period where the monuments are so often dilapidated or even destroyed and where the stones themselves, except through an occasional inscription, cannot speak for the emperor's motivations for building, the architectural evidence must be supplemented from other sources. A complete and balanced view of this difficult question must take into account not only the churches themselves but speeches and letters of the emperors, civil and canon law, contemporary histories, encomia—all with their doctrinal and ideological implications and all, of course, subject to rigorous scrutiny with regard to their reliability. In this chapter, which will focus primarily (but not exclusively) on the two most significant builders and examples of what, rightly or wrongly, is termed Caesaropapism, I shall try to draw from these various sources.

Constantine, in seeking to adjust to the new relationship between the Roman government and the now legally recognized Christian church, established important precedents for subsequent emperors. The reasons for Constantine's conversion to Christianity, are, of course, fundamental to any understanding not only of his policy toward church-state relations but also of his motives in building churches and shrines. Many scholars, most notably Baynes, believe that Constantine was motivated by sincerity, a sincerity, however, actuated in large part by his need to secure on his side the support of the "right God," a God who could bring him victories over his enemies.[4] If we accept this view, as I think we can, we should by extension also assume that he would have desired that his chosen God be *properly* worshiped throughout his empire.

The corollary to this theory, that of removing the "wrong" kind of worship, may also be said to have obtained for Constantine. For, in contrast to his apparent building of only two or three pagan temples (that of Tyche, for example, at the time of Constantinople's foundation, and one much later in Umbria, dedicated to his family's genius),[5] Constantine, as Eusebius points out, constructed a large number of churches with the aim of suppressing pagan worship (for instance, at Marme, in Palestine).[6] We also know from Eusebius that Constantine "forbade the immoral customs" (temple prostitution) at Heliopolis in Phoenicia, erecting a church there for which he provided a full staff of clergy.[7] Later in his reign, as attested by an edict of Constantius preserved in the Theodosian Code, Constantine forbade pagan divination under certain conditions.[8] And it is recorded that occasionally when he needed funds, he would despoil a pagan temple, melting down the gold and silver idols—something there is no record he ever did with respect to the treasures of Christian churches.

Why Constantine, despite his marked partisanship for Christianity, retained the pagan title of Pontifex Maximus, head of the state religion, is not clear. But his policy toward the pagans, which may perhaps best be termed one of grudging, even contemptuous toleration, was doubtless based on the realization that the bulk of the Roman population was still pagan. Eusebius' own attitude toward Constantine's continued toleration of paganism might be interpreted as one of anticipation, that as soon as was feasible he would entirely proscribe it.[10]

Regarding right worship *within* the Christian church, Constantine was even less tolerant of heresy than he was of paganism. As Eusebius makes plain in his *Laus Constantini*, Constantine believed that God had appointed him His representative over His earthly kingdom, a fact which, in Constantine's understanding, implied a responsibility to maintain unity in the true faith.[11] A letter of Constantine, dated 316, to his governor, Celsus, in Africa regarding the heretical Donatists of that area clearly indicates what he felt his role to be. Here Constantine announces his intention of using his own authority as emperor to settle the controversy on the spot and to teach the Donatist clergy "what worship and what kind of worship is to be given to the Divinity. . . . Is there anything more consonant with my fixed resolve and *my imperial duty* that I can do, than to scatter errors, extirpate all vain opinions and cause men to offer the Almighty a genuine religion, a sincere *concord* and a worship that is His due?"[12]

In this and similar directives[13] coming not long after the start of his reign, we can see the shape of a policy toward the church emerging, a policy which for lack of a better term has been called by modern historians, though not by those of medieval Byzantium (who would probably not have understood it) "Caesaropapism."

Constantine's building program would seem to reflect at least one aspect of his control over the church. We know that he confiscated Donatist churches in Africa[14] and, except at the end of his life, when his sympathies for or against Arianism are not always clear, that he probably did not build churches for the Arians. One exception in his policy should be noted, however, that of 330, when with the greatest reluctance he allowed the Donatists to retain a church they had seized in Cirta, Africa.[15] But it is also significant that he rebuilt another in the same area for the Orthodox.[16]

There is no doubt that Constantine wanted not only to believe, but to make certain that he had secured the stamp of divine approval for his reign. And, of course, along with his aim of providing at imperial expense larger structures to hold the growing congregations where proper worship could take place, this seeking of divine sanction was probably an underlying motivation for his building of structures to honor the holy martyrs and to enshrine the holy places connected with the life and passion of Christ.[17] The most important churches of Christendom begun or completed by him, especially in Rome, Constantinople, and the Holy Land, are well known to historians—they include St. John's Lateran and St. Peter's in Rome; St. Irene, the first St. Sophia, and at least the foundation of the Church of the Holy Apostles, all in Constantinople; the magnificent churches of Nicomedia and Antioch; and most significant of all for his contemporaries, the churches of the Holy Sepulcher and the Nativity in Palestine. We might at this point make one supplemental observation: that we seem to hear little of Constantine's church-building activities in Gaul, Spain, and aside from Constantinople, in the Balkans.[18]

In the *Vita Constantini*, which despite its detractors I think still offers certain important and acceptable material,[19] Eusebius quotes Constantine as saying that he wanted the building of the Holy Sepulcher in Jerusalem, Christianity's most sacred shrine, to be more beautiful than any other building in the empire. Constantine also wrote Macarius, bishop of Jerusalem, that "a house of prayer worthy of the worship of God should be erected near the Savior's tomb on a scale of rich and royal greatness."[20] Besides erecting new churches, Constantine, as we have heard, restored or enlarged older ones. We might make special mention of a letter he sent soon after the Council of Nicaea to his governors and bishops, explicitly directing "the heightening of the oratories and the enlargement in length and breadth of the churches of God" and urging his officials "not to spare the expenditure of money but to draw supplies from the imperial treasury itself."[21]

Whether or not Constantine was personally responsible for adopting the basilica type of church—a thorny problem that we shall avoid examining here—several important factors must have entered into the reasoning behind the decision to adopt this type of building: (1) that the basilica form could be better adapted to the growing congregations of Christians than any other existing type of building; (2) that in the Hellenistic East and pagan Rome the long, rectangular form of building with interior colonnades, called basilica, had long been a standard type of governmental structure.[22]

Regarding the first point, we might observe that in paganism, in contrast to Christianity, the worshiper did not enter the temple, the central area of which was generally small and reserved for the god's statue and officiating priests. It is instructive to note that in the sources of the period one often reads of the people's curiosity to enter into the sanctuary of pagan temples to see just what was in there, "to undress the idols," as Eusebius put it. Many pagans were, in fact, surprised that the god did nothing to avenge the sacrilege committed in his temple.[23]

With respect to the second fact, it does not have to be pointed out that the term "basilica" comes from the same root as the word *basileus*, meaning emperor, the head of the imperial government. After the period of persecution when the Christians had only just

emerged from the Catacombs, it may not have been illogical—
though some historians such as Voelkl would argue otherwise—for
Constantine to seek to exalt Christianity as the preferred religion
of the state by adapting for Christian use the semiofficial basilica
form of building. Eusebius suggests in several passages of the *Laus
Constantini* that one of Constantine's underlying aims in building
churches in Palestine was through such construction to attribute
imperial dignity to Christ. The implication is that the ruler of heaven
should not have an earthly temple less regal than the emperor, his
vicegerent on earth.[24]

Why did the bishops of Constantine's reign, Nicene and Arian
alike, seem to raise no serious objections to the imposition of Constantine's will on the church? Even Athanasius (that is, before the
reign of Constantius) made no real protest, his differences with
Constantine apparently being based, rather, on the emperor's
seemingly conciliatory attitude toward Arianism, that is, toward
false dogma.[25] Athanasius, in fact, wanted Constantine to use his
imperial authority to the full in order to suppress Arianism. The
bishops' acceptance of, or apparent concurrence in, Constantine's
authority over the church, was probably based on their need of
state support at this crucial period of the church's development, on
their gratitude for Constantine's elevation of Christianity to at least
the level of the other religions, as well as on their appreciation of the
many favors the emperor had lavished upon then, such as relief
from curial duties and the grant of extensive properties—not least
impressive of which were new churches and shrines.[26]

From the viewpoint of imperial control, however, there was
probably no sharp difference in Constantine's mind between the
spheres of church and state. Each was an important aspect of the
Basileia on earth, over which the emperor ruled as the divinely
appointed agent of God. If at times, because of temporary political
exigency, Constantine seemed unduly tolerant of the Arians or even
of the pagans—not, however, of the Donatists—he never really
deviated from his underlying conviction that he was God's vicegerent
on earth. And in his church-building program in behalf of the Nicene
Orthodox, I think we may see reflected one important side of his
concept of stewardship or, if you will, Caesaropapistic control over
the church. Constantine's aim of achieving church unity is, to be
sure, emphasized by many historians, but the corollary idea should
also be emphasized—an idea expressed or implied in Eusebius and

in Constantine's own letters: that it was his explicit *duty* as emperor to proselytize for Christianity and to promote unity within the faith.[27]

The reigns of Constantine's three sons may, in a sense, be considered an extension of their father's. Constantius, the most important of the three, was, to be sure, an Arian and attempted to force Arian beliefs on the empire.[28] But even in his partisanship of Arianism, he was in effect only following his father's policy of seeking to maintain a single faith in the church.

One modern authority has affirmed that the primary reason for Constantius' adoption of Arianism was his conviction that its beliefs would make it easier to accommodate the church to the state.[29] Support for such a view may be adduced not only by quoting Athanasius' famous statement, "The Arians have no King but Caesar," but also, by examining what seem to be the implications of the respective Nicene and Arian views toward the Trinity. According to Nicene Trinitarianism, the emperor was considered to represent God the Father. The bishops' power, however, was seen as being on the same plane as the emperor's since their authority was derived from the Logos, by them considered consubstantial with the Father. In the Arian belief, on the other hand, the emperor was viewed as superior to the bishops, since, while his power derived from God, theirs came from the Logos, for them not consubstantial with the Father, thus rendering the bishops' authority inferior to that of the emperor.[30] But the main question for us here should be—and in this context this has, so far as I know, too rarely been posed—were these differences in dogmatic implications reflected in church building? With respect to architecture there seems to have been no essential difference between Nicene and Arian churches. The differences appear, rather, in the ornamentation— such as in the mosaics at San Vitale, Justinian's Orthodox church, and Theodoric's Arian church, Sant' Apollinare Nuovo. The pictures we know of in the originally Arian church of Sant' Apollinare emphasize the humanity of Christ, while in those of the Orthodox San Vitale the emphasis is on the otherworldliness, the divinity of the court of heaven as reflected in the earthly court of Justinian.[31]

In any event, in the critical struggle between Arians and Nicenes during the reigns of Constantine's sons, it may be assumed that construction of churches with the government's financial support was one important way the emperor could effectively support the religious group he preferred—a point which, to be sure, seems obvious and which some scholars have already made. But it would be most useful to scholarship if someone—one scholar has recently attempted to do this for Constantine—would make a careful survey of all the churches erected by each of Constantine's Arian and Nicene sons to ascertain whether this thesis is borne out. From the *Ecclesiastical History* of Socrates we know, for example, that Constantius gave a Mithraeum to the Arian Christians of Alexandria to be used as a church[32]—one of the first instances of imperial assignment of a pagan temple for Arian use. Constantius also completed the construction of certain churches begun earlier by his father (one at Antioch) and himself initiated the construction of others, including that of the Holy Apostles in Constantinople, though another view has it that this was begun by Constantine.[33] How many of these churches were dedicated by Arian bishops? Did they later have to be reconsecrated by the Orthodox and, if so, were any changes made in them? Though it is difficult to answer these questions satisfactorily, they should at least be raised. Whether or not Constantius destroyed many pagan temples, we know that he was urged to exercise his imperial power to do so by such persons as the senator Julius Firmicus Maternus, who affirmed that "Christ in his graciousness had reserved for the emperor the duty of blotting out idolatry and destroying the pagan shrines."[34]

To the reign of Julian the Apostate, nephew of Constantine the Great, the Eusebian theory of imperial authority in relation to Christianity is obviously not applicable. He used his imperial authority—at least in the latter part of his reign—rather to destroy the Christian church as an institution and to restore paganism. Sometimes, in fact, it would even seem that he supported a building program favorable to non-Christians in order, obliquely, to strike at the Christian church. We know, of course, that he reopened many pagan temples and restored their revenues.[35] It should be noted that as yet Christianity had not gained a complete victory over paganism: Hellenism was still strong and not many pagan temples had been destroyed. The number of those demolished has probably been exaggerated in the dramatic stories that have come down to us concerning the role played by fanatic monks.[36] Theodoret, Sozomen, Rufinus, and Ammianus Marcellinus in their histories all speak of Julian's decree that the great Temple of the Jews in Jersualem should be rebuilt.[37] No doubt he acted to placate the Jews; but since Julian is hardly known for his philo-Jewish sentiments, it may well be suspected that, at least by implication, his decree was intended to denigrate the prestige of Christianity.

Possibly the unique example that can be cited of Julian's church building is that mentioned by Socrates, who tells us that Julian built a church in Constantinople called Anastasia.[38] It was constructed on the spot where a Novatian church (called "Alexander's church") had formerly stood. We are also told by Sozomen and Socrates that Julian required the orthodox bishop of Cyzicus to rebuild a Novatian church in his city earlier destroyed by his congregation.[39] But, it may be observed, this was a *heretical* Christian church. Julian's policy at this time seems to have been characterized by the sentiment that to prevail over one's enemies one should show favor to all dissident groups, thus serving further to divide them. At any rate, Julian's brief rule was probably too taken up with his campaigns, both military and anti-Christian, to be devoted to any kind of building on a large scale.

It is generally accepted that the definitive triumph of Christianity over paganism occurred in the reign of the emperor Theodosius the Great, a Nicene Christian. While Jovian earlier had revoked Julian's laws against Christianity,[40] Theodosius in effect dealt the death blow to pagan worship by decreeing that no more sacrifices could take place on pagan altars.[41] And it now became official government policy to begin, or at least to tolerate, the tearing down of pagan temples by Christians.[42] On the positive side of church construction, however, Theodosius did little building in the first part of his reign, though tradition has it that he did help to rebuild the church of St. Paul-outside-the-Walls of Rome.[43]

The same Theodosius was involved in two famous clashes with Bishop Ambrose of Milan over the question of imperial authority and its relationship to the church. In the case of greater interest to us here, Ambrose rebuked Theodosius because of his harshness in dealing with the Christians who had burned a Jewish synagogue in Callinicum, near the Persian frontier in Asia Minor. From the evidence of Ambrose's own letters,[44] it seems that Theodosius intended the synagogue to be rebuilt at the expense of the Christians. Ambrose was not satisfied until Theodosius had halted the imperial investigation of this incident and released the Christians from any obligation. Here, in this clash between emperor and bishop, we see an example of the church itself victoriously exerting pressure so that the ruler would not promote the building of a shrine dedicated to any religion other than Christianity. Ambrose, in fact, termed Theodosius' intent with respect to the synagogue "apostasy." The signal victory that Ambrose won over imperial power furnished a precedent for church-state relations which was later frequently to be cited by the Western church, although in the East, despite the fame of the incident at the time, the lesson was quickly lost in the face of the great growth of the emperor's power over the church.

A staunch opponent of Arianism, Theodosius nevertheless permitted his Arian Gothic *foederati* to have their own Arian church in Constantinople. This was in line with his policy of conciliation, or accommodation, toward the Goths, since they then constituted a grave threat to the imperial government itself.[45] Later, when the threat subsided, Patriarch John Chrysostom would refuse to continue this permission, though granting a church to the Goths of the Orthodox faith.[46]

Under Theodosius' sons, Honorius in the West and Arcadius in the East, there was some church building, but certainly nothing to compare with that of Constantine or later of Justinian. On the other hand, in the East under Arcadius we see a considerable amount of church construction on the part of individual patrons other than the emperor, especially his own wife Eudoxia. She contributed to the building of churches in Gaza, particularly the so-called Eudoxiana, for the construction of which (according to the contemporary writer Mark the Deacon) she assigned two hundred pounds of gold out of the revenues of the province of Palestine. This fact would seem to indicate the cooperation at least of the imperial authority in her project.[47]

Mark the Deacon makes an illuminating comment with reference to Arcadius' policy toward the pagans. When Eudoxia interceded in behalf of Porphyry, bishop of Gaza, and requested that Arcadius order the pagan temples of Gaza to be razed and replaced with Christian churches, Arcadius refused. For, though in defiance of the law the people of Gaza were idol-worshipers, they were nevertheless, Arcadius insisted, in the eyes of the imperial government, loyal citizens who paid their taxes regularly. According to Amantius the Chamberlain, who reported this conversation to Mark, the only step Arcadius would take was to agree to the closing of the temples and the removal of pagans from public office, fearing that by too harsh an action he might deprive the state of a good source of revenue. If these reports on Arcadius are accurate, it would seem that more important to Arcadius even than the exaltation of the Christian religion was the loyal observance by citizens of their duties to the state.[48]

For the reign of Arcadius' successor, Theodosius II, there is evidence of the building of churches by provincial governors and military leaders, especially in Syria.[49] Most important were the religious structures erected by Theodosius' estranged wife Eudocia. A modern authority calls her the greatest private benefactor in Palestine.[50] We are told that she placed a six thousand-pound copper cross over the Church of the Ascension in Jerusalem, gave four hundred gold pieces to a monastery nearby, and built the church of St. Stephen, also in Jerusalem, besides erecting a palace for the patriarch of Jerusalem, who was now becoming important. It has been estimated that in all she spent in Palestine 20,480 pounds of gold, that is, a million and a half gold coins, two gold coins then being enough to keep one person for a year. Whether a conclusion may be drawn here as to any connection between her efforts and those of the government to control the spread of Monophysitism in Palestine is a question that still awaits investigation.

The external difficulties of the empire, which waxed more and more serious, now prevented the emperors from undertaking much monumental church building. In Italy in 476, the Germanic invasions culminated with the deposition of the last Western Roman emperor, Romulus Augustulus. In the East the reigns of the emperors Marcian, Leo I, Leo II, and Zeno seem relatively unimportant to our problem, and we come therefore to Anastasius. To strengthen the empire, he built the famous long walls protecting the approaches to Constantinople, and he also promoted a reform of the coinage, leaving a full treasury for his successor Justin. It is of interest, moreover, that Anastasius was the first emperor to be required by the partiarch to take an oath before his enthronement that he would make no changes in the Orthodox creed—obviously to prevent partisanship on his part for the Monophysites.[51]

Under Justin, as most historians agree, the power behind the throne was his nephew Justinian. And it seems probable that Justinian did much of his less ostentatious building during his uncle's reign. As noted earlier, Justinian was at once probably the greatest of all Byzantine imperial builders and the most "Caesaropapistic" of emperors. But the question here is not why he became even more a master of the church than his predecessors—why, for example, he was able not only to secure Pope Vigilius's assent to virtually all his wishes but even to induce the fathers of the Fifth Ecumenical Council to accept his own revised Theopaschite interpretation of Chalcedonian doctrine.[52] Rather, the question is how this mastery he achieved over the church was or was not reflected in his extensive church-building program.

It was Justinian's basic political aim to restore the old Roman frontiers, to reconquer the West from the Arian Germans, and, at the same time, in the East, to preserve the loyalty of his provinces in the face of the Persian advances by placating the Monophysites.[53] In Justinian's eyes, as in Constantine's, there was no question that the concept of the unity of empire was absolutely fundamental. But to him, as to his predecessor, it meant not only imposition of one correct Orthodox faith under one emperor. Even more explicitly and emphatically than under Constantine, the law codes of Justinian—in which he is termed the Elect of God, king-priest, even archpriest (archierefs)[54]—reveal how church and state had become more closely tied together than ever before. Rather than the church's being simply a department of state, however, as some scholars have inaccurately put it, under Justinian the church and state might better be considered parallel branches of the one Christian commonwealth, Eusebius' Basileia, over which the emperor presided as God's vicegerent.

Because of Justinian's close association of church and state and the religious significance he attached to his imperial authority, not to speak of the tenacity of Byzantine ecclesiastical tradition, it seems very possible that the so-called liturgical privileges attributed to the emperors by the later Byzantine canonists may have become crystallized in Justinian's time. The canonists speak of the emperor as a kind of semipriestly figure who could perform certain liturgical functions normally reserved only to the priesthood: the emperor could, for example, preach during the religious service, enter into the sanctuary itself where the altar was, cense the people, and even take communion from the cup with his own hands without the mediation of the priest. It would be wrong, however, as Mitard and Diehl do, to call the emperor a priest. For in the last analysis he could not administer the sacraments.[55]

To what extent do we see reflected in Justinian's church-building program an emphasis on the unity of faith in the Christian empire, that is, on Orthodoxy, or right belief in the basic sense of the word?

The historian Evagrius gives us at least a hint of such an emphasis when he speaks of the Western areas reconquered from the heretic Arian Germans. In the 150 cities of Vandal Africa restored to the empire by Justinian, the emperor built "vast structures [by which] cities are adorned and the Deity propitiated,"[56] a statement that would seem to refer to Orthodox churches. One modern historian emphasizes that Justinian's construction, in former Ostrogothic territory, of the church of San Vitale at Ravenna was primarily intended to supplant Arian with Orthodox worship,[57] as seems to have been the case with his construction of the churches mentioned in Vandal Africa, for example at Septum.[58] And we have explicit evidence, often overlooked, from John of Ephesus, a Monophysite, that Justinian built 96 churches, 55 of them explicitly with imperial funds, for the use of the converted "Hellenes," that is, former pagans, in Western Asia Minor.[59] The evidence of these statements would certainly seem to indicate that Justinian, like Constantine before him, followed a policy of encouraging the construction of churches in order to combat heresy as well as paganism.

In the construction of St. Sophia in Constantinople, undoubtedly Justinian's greatest building achievement, his architects, Anthemius of Tralles and Isidore of Miletus, achieved a solution to one of the most difficult engineering problems in architectural history, the erecting of a huge, round masonry dome over a large square surface. One leading art historian, B. Smith, believes that Justinian may have been impelled to construct St. Sophia's magnificent dome less from structural or aesthetic considerations than from the influence of ideas long current in the Near East—the imagery of the dome representing heaven, that is, a kind of celestial canopy over the earth, both heaven and earth constituting halves of a great cosmic egg. These ideas are connected with the popular cult of the old pagan heroes, the Greek Dioskouroi, who were considered precursors of the Christian martyrs and whose cult, it appears, was of deep interest to Justinian.[60] Justinian's contemporary, the poet Paul the Silentiary, in his long encomium in honor of the church of St. Sophia, seems to draw precisely on the above imagery when he describes St. Sophia's dome as "the great [celestial] helmet, which, rounded in all respects like a sphere, embraces the top of the building [the church] like the radiant heavens."[61]

Justinian dedicated his cathedral of St. Sophia to the Divine Wisdom, the Logos, that is, to Christ himself. (In the *De Aedificiis*,

Procopius says explicitly that the Byzantines sometimes called God "Sophia.") [62] But it seems certain that Justinian envisioned St. Sophia as a symbol of his own imperial authority as well. We know that it was his aim to build the most magnificent church in all Christendom, and for this purpose (he was not the first Christian emperor to do so, by the way) [63] he despoiled ancient temples of their treasures. The remark that Byzantine writers report Justinian to have made at the completion of the structure, "Solomon, I have surpassed thee," [64] is particularly significant, because it emphasizes Justinian's connection with the most famous Hebrew king-priest *and* temple builder. Paul the Silentiary, in his descriptive panegyric on St. Sophia (evidently written at imperial request), speaks of the day of that church's dedication as one in which "God and the emperor are celebrated together" (*theos te kai Basileus semnynetai*). [65] And more than once in his *De Aedificiis*, Procopius, while praising Justinian's personal abilities as a kind of nonprofessional architect-engineer, attributes his success in solving difficult problems of church construction, above all, to his partnership (*syndiaprassetai*) with God. [66]

There is a very striking and effective argument, based on John Malalas, regarding the emperor's building creations, *ktiseis* [67] (the same Greek term used, incidentally, as the title of Procopius' *Buildings*), [68] in imitation of divine creativity—evidence which further emphasizes the parallel we have been drawing between God's power in heaven and his viceroy's activities on earth. In connection with this imperial ideology, it would be useful, also, if it could be determined whether or not the famous passage in Emperor Constantine VII Porphyrogenitus' *De Cerimoniis*, regarding the emperor's double throne, obtained as early as the reign of Justinian. According to this tenth-century source, the emperor's throne was a double one. The emperor usually sat on the right side, which was considered that of Christ. On Sundays and feast days, however, he sat on the left, leaving the right side vacant so as to make it visible to all that he *shared* (*synthronos*) his throne with Christ. [69]

In our analysis of the reigns of the emperors from Constantine to Justinian, we may, then, distinguish three basic interrelated purposes in their policy of constructing churches. Aside from the obvious practical desire to provide places of worship where none previously existed (as in the newly converted area of Tzanica in eastern Asia Minor, under Justinian), [70] the imperial building programs seem basically to have been motivated by: (1) a wish to promote the one true faith (as the emperors saw it) to the detriment of paganism and heresy; (2) the ideological aim (aided by what several scholars have termed "imperial propaganda")[71] of glorifying the imperial power as the representative on earth of the divine power in heaven (seen most clearly in St. Sophia); and (3) (and this is an overlapping psychological consideration that would not, of course, normally be documented in the official sources except in such a work as Procopius' vituperative anti-Justinianic *Secret History*)[72] the emperors' desire to satisfy their own personal egoism and ambition which, in the Weltanschauung of the period, they fused in their own minds with the concept of the emperor as commissioned by God to rule the earth. As Justinian put it, in a typical phrase drawn from his *Codex Justinianus* that expresses what might be called this political theology: "We rule, by the authority of God, the empire which has been entrusted to us by the majesty of Heaven."[73]

To conclude, it seems clear that in the case of virtually every emperor we have studied, there existed a definite correlation— expressed or unexpressed—between the emperor's policy of control (or lack of control) over the church, that is, his so-called "Caesaropapism," and his policy with regard to the construction of churches. In general, then, it may be said that the emperors' building of religious structures constituted an instrument, not only for the furthering of imperial control over the church, but, through imperial insistence on ecclesiastical unity as reflected in the aims of their building policy, for promoting the ultimate aim of the unity of the empire itself.

6

Maximos the Confessor and his Influence on Eastern and Western Theology and Mysticism

Maximos the Confessor, the Byzantine monk of the seventh century, is sometimes termed "the last independent-thinking theologian of the Eastern Church."[1] His works include primarily theological treatises and scriptural exegesis, especially the *Ambigua*, the *Quaestiones ad Thalassium*, the *Four Centuries on Love*, and letters. Besides his own contribution to theology, in particular to the formulation of christological doctrine (in opposition to the dangerous Monothelite heresy), he is, at least in the West, even better known as the principal exegete of the mystical writings of Pseudo-Dionysius—the latter being undoubtedly the chief influence on Western, and one of the most basic influences on Eastern, mysticism and spirituality during the entire medieval period. Maximos' main contribution in this respect was not only to systematize the many loose ideas of Dionysius but also to draw out their implications for christological theology.[2] It is the purpose of this chapter to trace, as through the links of a chain, the surprisingly widespread but not well-known influence of Maximos on subsequent theologians of both West and East and, in the process, perhaps to uncover several unknown or little-known links in this chain.

Maximos' works were apparently known throughout the entire Period of Byzantine history; yet there remains a surprising amount of research to be done in order to delineate the extent of his influence on specific Byzantine scholars and theologians, such as Anastasius in the ninth century, Euthemius Zigabenos and Symeon the "New Theologian" in the eleventh, Nicetas Choniates in the twelfth, Patriarch Gregory Palamas and Nicholas Kabasilas and their opponents Nicephorus Gregoras and the Byzantine "Scholastic" John Cyparissiotes in the fourteenth, and last of all, his impact on the sixteenth-century, post-Byzantine bishop who lived in Venice, Maximos Margounios.[3]

For the West, the chain of Maximos' influence is rather more difficult to trace, and this largely because there, much more than in the East, after the ninth century he is almost exclusively known as *the* interpreter of Pseudo-Dionysius, to whose influential mystical writings several of Maximos' writings served as commentaries.[4] But this very close Western identification of Maximos with Dionysius can nevertheless be of help in at least indicating Latin theologians who might have utilized works of the former. In the East, on the other hand, Maximos seems more often to have been used independently of Dionysius, as, for example, in connection with reaffirming and explaining points of christological doctrine to be found in earlier Byzantine Church Fathers. This distinction in the use of Maximos' work by Eastern and Western scholars of the Middle Ages is a point that should be emphasized.

The Orthodox champion against the emerging heresy of Monotheletism, Maximos came to Rome in 646, later appearing at the Lateran Council of 649 which, under his leadership, condemned Monothelitism. After this council, the first subsequent influence of Maximos' writings in the West seems to appear in the famous Carolingian philosopher John Scotus Erigena and in Anastasius, the papal librarian, both of the ninth century.[5] Erigena first translated into Latin the mystical works of Dionysius and later the *Ambigua* and *Quaestiones ad Thalassium* of Maximos, the former an exegetical commentary primarily on Gregory Nazianzenus and, to a lesser degree, on Dionysius, and the latter a commentary on difficult passages of Scripture.[6] Anastasius, the Greek librarian of Pope Nicholas I, corrected Erigena's translation of Dionysius and added to it, as an explanation, his own translation of the scholia composed by Maximos on Dionysius' mystical works.[7] It is this so-called Anastasian corpus— that is, Dionysius' writings *with* Maximos' scholia attached—that evidently became the basis, so far as I can ascertain, for all or almost all subsequent Western scholarly work on Dionysius and therefore for subsequent knowledge of Maximos as well. Influenced by this "Anastasian corpus" in the West, it would seem, were, in the twelfth century, Bernard of Clairvaux, Hugh of St. Victor,[8] and Albert the Great; in the next century Thomas Aquinas[10] and the bishop of Lincoln, Robert Grosseteste, who (as is sometimes forgotten) made a more accurate, if overly literal, translation of Maximos' prologue and scholia to the *Ecclesiastical Hierarchy*, and the *Divine Names* of Dionysius;[11] in the fourteenth century, perhaps, Meister Eckhart and the group of Rhineland mystics; and finally, in the fifteenth century, Nicholas of Cusa, and as has hitherto not been noted, his friend, the Pisan Petrus Balbus.[12]

Though Maximos' influence in one way or another thus spanned the entire period from the seventh century to the sixteenth, it is clear that much research remains to be done to establish more of the links in the chain of his influence in both East and West. The question is rendered particularly complex because of the difficulty of knowing exactly which works of Maximos, and no less important in the West, which Latin versions of him, were used by each theologian, and again more in the West than East, the problem of disentangling, in the various theologians listed above, the strands of Maximos' thought from those of Dionysius. In this chapter I shall try to fill in some of the lacunae in our knowledge of the continuity of the tradition of Maximos by showing, or where appropriate reemphasizing, his influence on certain figures—first, on the ninth-century Western Hellenophile, John Scotus Erigena, and then as a kind of contrast or parallel, on the little-known fourteenth-century Byzantine Latino-phile, John Cyparissiotes, who lived for a time at Avignon and Rome. After remarks about the use made of Maximos by several theologians in connection with the procession of the Holy Spirit, I shall conclude with a few references to the interest in Maximos' writings shown by the Renaissance scholars Nicholas of Cusa and Petrus Balbus.

After the Lateran Council of 649, Western theologians were primarily attracted to Maximos because of his scholia, that is, his interpretation of the mystical writings of Dionysius. A copy of those works, along with his own scholia and perhaps others of his works, one scholar has suggested, Maximos may have left in, the Vatican library.[13] Dionysius was believed (falsely) to have lived in, and become the first bishop of, Athens at the time of St. Paul's visit to that city, and then to have gone to Gaul, where, supposedly, he founded the monastery of St. Denys and suffered martyrdom in Paris at the hands of the pagan Germans. Western scholars have focused so intently on Maximos as the interpreter of Dionysius that they sometimes overlook other reasons for this Greek theologian's being so *persona grata* to the West, despite the growing antipathy, even that early, of some Latin theologians for the Byzantine church and state. Not only did Maximos champion the Orthodox-Catholic views against the Byzantine heresy of Monotheletism at the Lateran Council of 649, but, like Pope Martin, he suffered banishment to the Black Sea area, where he died.[14] And certainly Maximos' opposition to Byzantine imperial interference in ecclesiastical affairs made it easy for the West to identify with his anti-Caesaropapistic sentiments.

We know that in 827 the Byzantine emperor Michael II sent to the Western emperor, Louis the Pious, a copy of Dionysius' works in connection with the desire of the monks of the royal monastery of St. Denys (outside Paris) to secure the works of their supposed founder (and patron of the royal family of France), St. Dionysius. The imperfection of the translation of Dionysius made at this time by, or rather under the direction of Abbot Hilduin of St. Denys[15] prompted the new Carolingian ruler and patron of learning, Charles the Bald, to have a more accurate translation made. And it was after the completion of this translation by John Scotus Erigena that Charles the Bald, for reasons not precisely known, asked Erigena also to translate Maximos the Confessor's commentaries (*Ambigua* in Latin; *peri aporiōn* in Greek) on difficult passages found in Gregory of Nazianzus and, to a much lesser degree, in Dionysius.[16]

In his preface, which he addressed to King Charles and attached to his rendering of the *Ambigua*, Erigena himself sheds a little light on the reasons for his translation, and incidentally bespeaks his high regard for Maximos. Here is a paraphrase:

> It is a very difficult task you [Charles] have confided to me to translate this work of Maximos from Greek into Latin . . . and you requested that I do it in a hurry. . . . I have sought to achieve it as quickly as possible, and thanks to God I have finished. I would not have faced such darkness except for the fact that it is a most excellent apologia, and that I have noted that the Blessed Maximos frequently in his work affirms and clarifies the very obscure ideas of Dionysius the Areopagite, whom in the past I was also commissioned to translate.[17]

Erigena's intellectual development seems to fall into two stages—the first, in which he was under the influence of the Western Fathers, Gregory the Great and Isidore; and, more important here, the second, in which he was under the impact of Greek thought, especially that of Dionysius and Maximos. Scotus's knowledge of Greek, in spite of its many deficiencies, was rather remarkable for his time. Anastasius, Pope Nicholas' Greek librarian, though he emphasized the errors made by Erigena, thought it a miracle that a "barbarian" of such learning as Erigena could be found, as he put it, "at the ends of the

Idealized portrait of Pseudo-Dionysius the Areopagite as Apostle of the Gauls. From A. Thevet, *Pourtraits et vies des hommes illustres* (Paris, 1584). (See pp. 124-25.)

earth" ("in finibus mundi").[18] Erigena himself admits that his knowledge of Greek was insufficient to render adequately the theology and ideas of Maximos into Latin.[19] One may, in fact, note several rather obvious errors he made, for example, his rendering several times from Maximos' *Ambigua* of the word *pedais* as *pueris*.[20] We emphasize here the errors made by Erigena in translating from the Greek because it was the inadequacy of his translations of Dionysius that later induced the Western theologians John Sarrazenus and Robert Grosseteste of the thirteenth century to make new ones. The latter, so far as I can establish, was the only Western scholar after Anastasius to have translated the scholia of Maximos on Dionysius again.

Let us now examine a few theological-philosophical points or concepts which may serve to show the influence of Maximos' thought on that of Erigena. To begin with, Erigena seems to have borrowed the title of his great work, *De Divisione Naturae* (which he wrote after translating Dionysius and Maximos) from the phrase of Maximos, *peri physeōs merismou*. Besides phrases, Erigena also adopted or adapted for his work the concepts of Dionysius, in a number of cases *as interpreted by Maximos*. Erigena's doctrine of theophany, for instance, is evidently based directly on Maximos' formulation, based in turn on Dionysius. Erigena writes: "As far as the human mind ascends in love, so far the Divine Wisdom descends in mercy."[21] Here we note, in both Maximos and Erigena, that a synergism is expressed, with man, in a restricted sense raising himself to God and God at the same time extending himself to man through mercy.

On the basic question of the nature of God, we summarize Erigena's thought, in which he refers to Maximos' position on Gregory of Nazianzus: "The essence of God is incomprehensible as is the essence [*ousia*] of all that exists. But as our human intellect, which is one and invisible in itself, yet manifests itself in words and deeds, and expresses its thought in letters and figures, so the Divine Essence, which is far above the reach of our intellect, manifests itself in the created universe."[22] This striking metaphor of "letters and figures" with respect to man, and the created universe with regard to God, seems to be taken directly from Maximos' expression, *grammasi kai syllabais kai phōnais*, found in his *Ambigua*.[23] Erigena also borrowed from Maximos other terminology regarding the nature of God: for example, that the divine nature is *simplex*, or more than *simplex*—that is, not compounded, and that there is no number in

God. As Maximos himself put it: "God is . . . one, alone, primarily immovable, because he is without number, not being numerable or able to be numbered."[24]

Turning to another question connected more with doctrine than with mystical thought, it is notable that Maximos was one of the very first theologians to deal with the dogmatic question of the nature of the Trinity in a manner that foreshadowed the famous controversy over the filioque clause. In his writing Maximos developed (perhaps even coined) a formula for the relationship of the Father and the Son with respect to the procession of the Holy Spirit. It is sometimes stated that the famous compromise phrase "through the Son," in connection with the filioque, was a late achievement, especially of such theologians as Bessarion at the Council of Florence in 1438–39. And yet the same phrase, or at least something very similar, can already be found in Maximos' writing on the Holy Spirit: "For as the Holy Spirit is by nature of the substance of God the Father, thus also the Holy Spirit is by nature of the substance of the Son, so that the Holy Spirit proceeding ineffably (*aphrastōs*) from the Father in essence, and through the Son, begotten [of the Father]."[25] Latin theologians have usually interpreted this passage as supporting the Western position of the filioque, though the words *di uiou gennēthentos aphrastōs ekporeuomenon*, to me at least, seem rather to imply mediation, and not necessarily that the Holy Spirit proceeds *also* from the son.

On this question of the filioque, Erigena himself employed the expression *ex patre per filium*, a phrase probably based on the expositions of Dionysius, Gregory of Nazianzus, and especially Maximos.[26] It is interesting to observe that much later, after centuries of bitter conflict between East and West over this question, the sixteenth-century Greek humanist bishop living in Venice, Maximos Margounios, favored a similar solution, but one that also emphasized a distinction between the eternal and the temporal processions of the Holy Spirit. His views were in part, we know, based on those of Patriarch Gregory of Cyprus of the thirteenth century who, as shown by several recent scholars, had himself been affected by the teachings of Maximos.[27]

Let us turn to the influence of Maximos on the little-known four-teenth-century Byzantine theologian, John Cyparissiotes, whom we have already mentioned. Under the influence of Dominican theologians residing in the East and the Thomist circle of Cydones formed in the Byzantine court, Cyparissiotes became a Latinophile. John's main activities are closely connected with the Hesychast conflict of the later fourteenth century, in which he was, after the Italo-Greek monk Barlaam, one of the most fervid opponents of the mystical Palamite theology of the monks of Mt. Athos. For reasons probably owing to this conflict, he first left Constantinople for Cyprus, where many friends of his teacher Nicephorus Gregoras had already found refuge. Then later, apparently on the advice of his friend, the Grand Logothete Demetrios Cydones, himself a Latinophile, he went to Italy, where he entered the court of Pope Gregory XI. There, as noted earlier, his erudition earned him the Latin epithet *Sapiens*.[28]

The primary sources upon which Cyparissiotes draws for one of his two principal writings, the "scholastic" *Ekthesis stoicheiōdēs hrēseon theologikōn*,[29] which he composed in the form of ten Decades, are Dionysius and Maximos. It has been estimated by the recent editor of Cyparissiotes, B. Dentakis, that Cyparissiotes used 162 passages from Dionysius, and that the ratio of his use of Maximos to Dionysius is two to five.[30] In the Migne *Patrologia Graeca*, volume 152, we find, under the printed text of Cyparissiotes' work in the two Decades called *De Theologia Symbolica* and *De Theologia Demonstrativa*, a large number of scholia of Maximos either on Dionysius or other early Greek Fathers, which seem to be directly related to the text of Cyparissiotes. These, however, were evidently placed there to show the extensive use of Maximos, by Cyparissiotes' sixteenth-century Latin translator, Francisco Torres. The original Greek text of Cyparissiotes' work has not yet been published.[31]

Many of the main ideas of Cyparissiotes are to be found in his first Decade, entitled *De Theologia Symbolica*. Here he repeatedly quotes Maximos as an authority on explaining the nature of symbolic theology: "Maximos calls 'symbolic' also that theology which pertains to mysteries."[32]

Cyparissiotes goes on to reflect the thought of Maximos to the effect that mysteries pertaining to theology are signified in symbols—that is, symbols become the media by which we understand God, or in other words, God manifests himself in symbols.[33] Similar passages can be found in Cyparissiotes' treatment of the question of man's knowledge of God, the nature of God, and the attributes of the divine. These subjects are discussed by Cyparissiotes in the second Decade, *De Theologia Demonstrativa*, under the chapter heading, "That God is not known on the basis of natural representation, and that there is nothing [known] on the basis of intelligences or intellects, so that it is permitted to philosophize about him on the basis of his substance."[34]

This argument of the nonadmissibility of philosophizing on the nature of God is, according to Cyparissiotes himself, based directly on what Maximos had written. Thus, from century one, chapter one[35] of one of Maximos' several anti-Monothelete treatises, *Two Hundred Chapters on Theology and the Economy of the Incarnation,* he quotes Maximos: "The Holy Maximus, in his first chapter on theological matters, says, God is one, without beginning, incomprehensible, having, as it were, complete power over everything, rejecting completely the notion of when and how He is [and] known to none of those who exist, through natural representation."[36] We scarcely need note that the argument affirming man's inability logically to describe what God *is,* and stressing, rather, what we know that he is *not*—that is, the famous, so-called apophatic theology—was utilized by Greek theologians before Dionysius and Maximos. It was through their writings, especially by way of Erigena, however (see above, chap. 3), that it entered the stream of Western theology.[37]

On the subject of divine "emanations"—love, peace, goodness—a Neoplatonic concept that, with qualification, became current in the West mainly through Dionysius, Cyparissiotes, in the third Decade of this same work, *De Divinis Emanationibus,* again cites Maximos as his authority. Quoting Maximos, he writes: "Everything, Maximos says, which exists because of a cause and which is moved because of a cause, of necessity has a beginning in order to exist; that is, everything has that cause on account of which it was made so that it might be; indeed everything has, as an end to its motion, that very cause by which it is moved and toward which it is directed."[38] Cyparissiotes thus summarizes in his own words (in the title of the second chapter of his *De Divinis Emanationibus*): "That every cause and motion and beginning which is mentioned about things that are generated, is generation, which is brought about at the same time as the things themselves that have been brought about."[39]

Again under the Decade title, *De Infinitate Dei in Creaturis* (On the Infinity of God in Creatures), Cyparissiotes quotes a passage from Gregory of Nazianzus on the cause for the existence of the Son as well as the Father, citing in support Maximos' scholia on Gregory: "Therefore, unity was moved from the beginning to the number of two."[40] In the same Decade, chapter four, he cites Maximos: "Whatever things have been created in time according to time, after they have become perfected, come to an end of natural growth."[41]

On the basic problem of the Trinity, Cyparissiotes once again utilizes Maximos' theological formulation, citing his dogmatic work, referred to above: "The Centuries on Theology of God and the Son with Respect to the Incarnation." This is shown in Cyparissiotes' passage: "There is one good, absolutely without beginning and above substance, that is to say the holy unity of three persons, Father, Son, and Holy Spirit, three who are without limits, etc."[42] In the tenth Decade, on the problem of divine simplicity, Cyparissiotes, quoting from Maximos' fourth century, chapter eight, says: "Do not inquire after category and the potential of the simple and infinite substance of the Holy Trinity, lest you make it composite like creatures."[43]

It should be noted that despite his lengthy and rather impressive exegesis, Cyparissiotes in this work is not truly original, utilizing, rather, a collection of traditional Greek authorities, consisting of Cyril of Alexandria, Basil, Gregory of Nyssa, more frequently Maximos the Confessor, and above all, Dionysius.[44] The content is entirely Greek, though the method is rather like Latin Scholasticism, with its division, definition, demonstration, and resolution.

From the above exposition of passages, brief as it is, we may observe that both the Latin Erigena and especially the Greek Cyparissiotes drew heavily on the work of Maximos, whom they obviously considered an authority. Moreover, in questions important to mystical theology—the nature of God, the attributes of the divine, and even the procession of the Holy Spirit—the carefully reasoned arguments of Maximos were for Erigena and Cyparissiotes an essential, indeed sometimes the unique, authority for interpreting the often obscure passages of Dionysius.

While Cyparissiotes, as Beck and Dentakis have shown, was influenced in his method by Latin theology[45]—and he was perhaps the first and one of the very few Byzantine theologians actually to write theological tracts following the Western Scholastic method—it may in contrast be noted that his predecessor Erigena's admiration for the Greek language and Byzantine theology made him suspect to the anti-Greek pope and opponent of Photius, Nicholas I, to the degree that that pontiff, we are told, demanded to see his Greek translation.[46] Erigena's pro-Greek bias on theology and his daring praise of Constantinople over Rome, in the context of the breach taking shape between East and West under Nicholas and Photius, made him a controversial figure in the West. Regarding what he termed the jealousy of old Rome for the new Rome, that is, Constantinople, Erigena wrote as follows:

Constantinopolis florens nova Roma vocatur
Moribus et muris Roma vetusta cadis,
Transiit imperium, mansitque superbia tecum
Cultus avaritiae te nimium superat.[47]

[Flourishing Constantinople is called the new Rome.
Old Rome, your customs and walls fall.
The imperium has crossed over, but arrogance has remained
  with you,
The cult of avarice conquers you very much.]

Here, then, we have a kind of parallel: a Latin theologian, Erigena, who is pro-Byzantine, and a Byzantine theologian, Cyparissiotes, who becomes a Latinophile, both of whom draw on the Byzantine Maximos, who himself spent a great part of his career in the West and thus helped to interpret Eastern theology to the Latins. As Sherwood well puts it, the veneration for Maximos in the West was owing in part to his belonging to the "catholic"[48] —that is, ecumenical—tradition of the early period when East and West were still part of one undivided church.

In conclusion we mention two Renaissance scholars: Nicholas of Cusa, whose philosophy was a synthesis of many elements but who probably was primarily a disciple of the Dionysian-Erigenian school of thought; and Petrus Balbus, his Pisan friend, colleague, and bishop of Tropea. Nicholas, who more than once refers to Erigena under the name "Scotigena,"[49] reveals his high regard for Maximos by affirming that Erigena was on the same level "with Dionysius, Maximos, and Hugo of St. Victor," Since Nicholas' principal work, *De docta ignorantia,* shows a striking parallel to the thought and method, especially the negative theology of Erigena who borrowed heavily from Dionysius partly by way of Maximos' *Ambigua,* it is likely that Nicholas was influenced, at least indirectly, by Maximos as well.[50] But to prove this conclusively, one would have to compare the ideas and terminology of Cusanus and Maximos at length and, especially, to determine which specific works of Maximos might have been used by Nicholas. Another way of approaching this question might be to consider the influence of Nicholas' close friend, fellow student at Padua, and occasional translator from the Greek (he was a kind of secretary to Nicholas), the Pisan Petrus Balbus.[51]

An article published in *Theologia,* discussing the influence of Dionysius on Nicholas of Cusa, refers several times to Balbus's connection with Cusanus but curiously makes no mention whatever of the fact that Balbus translated certain works of Maximos: a letter of Maximos to John Cubicularius of Constantinople, *De dolore secundum deum,* and chapters from Maximos' *De Caritate.*[52] (These manuscript translations of Maximos done by Balbus are still to be found in the Laurentiana of Florence and, supposedly, in the Biblioteca Capitolare of Capua.)[53] Although Maximos' commentaries on Dionysius (via Anastasius) were certainly known to Cusanus, can we say that Cusanus knew Maximos' *Ambigua* or his *Ad Thalassium*? Cusanus knew Plato and had looked for Greek manuscripts in Constantinople itself, but I find no specific evidence for his knowledge of either of these works. Nor is Balbus's interest in Maximos referred to in Van Steenbergh's famous biography of Nicholas of Cusa. Only the more recent work of Gandillac suggests, and at that obliquely, that Nicholas' use of the words *unitas* and *entitas* corresponds to Maximos' unusual Greek term *ontotes.*[54] Nonetheless, Cusanus's at least indirect interest in Maximos via Dionysius, together with his friend Balbus's actual translation of several of Maximos' lesser works, suggest the probable influence of Maximos' thought on that of the great Cusanus—a possibility which I believe warrants closer investigation.

From our exposition we may tentatively conclude that the influence of Maximos on the theological development of both East and West was perhaps more extensive than, or at least somewhat different from, what is generally believed. As in tracing a textual tradition, we have been able to add the names of a few more individuals to the chain of those who seem to have been affected by his writings. I should stress once again that Maximos' influence in the East differed from what it was in the West. In the East other works of Maximos such as the *De Caritate, Quaestiones ad Thalassium,* his *Mystagogia,* and minor works on dogmatic points, were in some ways no less influential than his commentaries on the mystical works of Dionysius, probably owing to the fact that before Dionysius a strong tradition of Christian mysticism already existed in the East. After the eighth century, the primary emphasis in the Byzantine East was on the preservation of the theological pronouncements of the ecumenical councils and the teachings of the Greek Fathers. Thus Maximos' ideas,

independent as they may in some ways have been—recall the charac-
terization of him cited above[55]—were in later centuries used to
strengthen what was already accepted rather than to bring about
innovations in theological thought. Even in reading the Byzantine
Cyparissiotes, who actually adopted the Western Scholastic method
of exegesis, we see that his use of Maximos did not serve as a basis for
any new departures in theological thought.

In the West, on the other hand, it would appear that Maximos'
Ambigua and the *Quaestiones ad Thalassium* were translated only by
Erigena and that the West's knowledge of these works derives exclusively from Erigena's faulty translation. Of the many other works
of Maximos, possibly aside from a few small anti-Monothelete tracts
in connection with his appearance at the Lateran Council of 649, it
seems that before Cyparissiotes (who, it is believed, wrote his chief
work at the papal court)[56] and Balbus, no other works of Maximos
were known to the Western Middle Ages, except for the not very influential twelfth-century translation of his *De Caritate* by the monk
Cerbanus,[57] and of course his celebrated scholia on Dionysius' four
mystical works, translated by Anastasius (and later by Grosseteste).
Nonetheless, it may be said that through these scholia Maximos was
primarily responsible for fixing definitely in the West the Catholic
interpretation of Dionysius. And the use of these scholia as *the*
indispensable interpretation of Dionysius' mystical theology probably helped in no small measure to inspire not only Erigena but such
synthetic thinkers as Hugo of St. Victor, presumably Cusanus, and
possibly Ficino,[58] to shape their ideas into new patterns of thought.
Generalizations have too easily been made about the extent of Maximos' influence in the East, and even more in the West, often with
too little qualification. I hope that the results of the research presented here may help to bring about a further clarification of this
question, especially with regard to the continuity of the process of
transmission.

7

Ordeal by Fire and Judicial Duel at Byzantine Nicaea (1253): Western or Eastern Legal Influence?

Trials by ordeal of fire and judicial duel were common methods of "proving" innocence or guilt in the Latin West during the Middle Ages. In the Byzantine East, however, where the principles of Roman law still prevailed, such practices should presumably have been unknown, or at least not resorted to. It is therefore extraordinary to find the ordeal by fire and judicial combat elaborately mentioned at the trial for treason of the Byzantine noble, Michael Palaeologus, at Nicaea in the year 1253.

Michael Palaeologus, subsequently Byzantine emperor and restorer of Constantinople to the Greeks (1261–82), as a young man of twenty-one, was accused on hearsay evidence of plotting against the throne. Taken before his sovereign. John Vatatzes, emperor of Nicaea (one of the Greek "successor" states after the Latin conquest of Constantinople in 1204),[1] he was ordered, rather than undergoing a regular trial, to prove his innocence by submission to the ordeals of fire and combat. It is with the origins of these two barbaric practices and the reason for their remarkable appearance on this occasion that this investigation is concerned.

That the ordeal by fire was not a native Byzantine institution seems clear from the remarks of even the contemporary Greek historians who discuss this trial. According to George Acropolites, when Palaeologus cleverly insisted that he would undergo the ordeal only if the Metropolitan Phocas would first grasp the hot iron in his own hands and then pass it on to him, that worthy prelate, judiciously declining the honor, said: "This is not a part of our Roman institutions or even of our ecclesiastical tradition, or of our laws, or received earlier from our divine and holy [ecclesiastical] canons. The practice is barbarous and unknown to us and invoked only by imperial command."[2] George Sphrantzes, writing later in the fifteenth century about this recourse to the ordeal, puts practically the same words into the mouth of the bishop (patriarch?) Arsenius (whom he mistakenly cites as being present): "There is no law or custom among the Romans and wise Greeks to torture those on trial and especially the nobles in this way, but the practice is barbaric and inappropriate and the law is heathen."[3] Similar is the testimony of Demetrius Chomatianos, the noted Greek bishop and canonist living in Ochrida (in Byzantine Bulgaria) in the early thirteenth century: "It is entirely unknown not only to ecclesiastical but also to civil practice. Why? First because it has come from a barbarian people, and second because it is not looked upon with a good eye. . . . [It is] barbaric and foreign to our observances and holy canons."[4] From the testimony of all these writers it is obvious that the practice was not indigenous to the Byzantines but seems to have been imported from elsewhere—but where?

The origin of the Byzantine use of this ordeal has been attributed to three peoples. The first theory holds that it came from the ancient Greeks, a view championed by the modern Greek Byzantinist, P. Koukoules.[5] He cites verses from the *Antigone* of the ancient tragic poet Sophocles, which mention such an ordeal by fire: "And we were ready to take bars of hot iron in our hands / and to walk through fire and to call the Gods to witness."[6] But this evidence seems far from conclusive when one recalls that much more than a millennium had intervened between the composition of the *Antigone* and the date of this trial. Moreover, in this long interval it is difficult to discover other instances of the ordeal by fire in Byzantine sources.[7] As additional proof of his theory, Koukoules cites the *modern* Greek expression, "I will walk on hot coals if it is not so."[8] Furthermore, Koukoules makes no attempt to explain away the statements, cited above, of Chomatianos and the Greek historians. More to the point, as Koukoules himself suggests, even if the practice had actually been carried down from the ancient Greeks, it is very questionable that the Byzantines would have referred to the ancient Greeks as *barbaroi*, as they did in the texts in question. *Hellenes*, the term normally used by the Byzantines to refer to the ancient Greeks, connoted "pagans" (who were learned), but never "barbarians."[9]

A second theory has been advanced by another Greek scholar, Constantine Sathas.[10] He affirms that the practice was derived from Albanians living in Macedonia and Cyprus, and was brought to

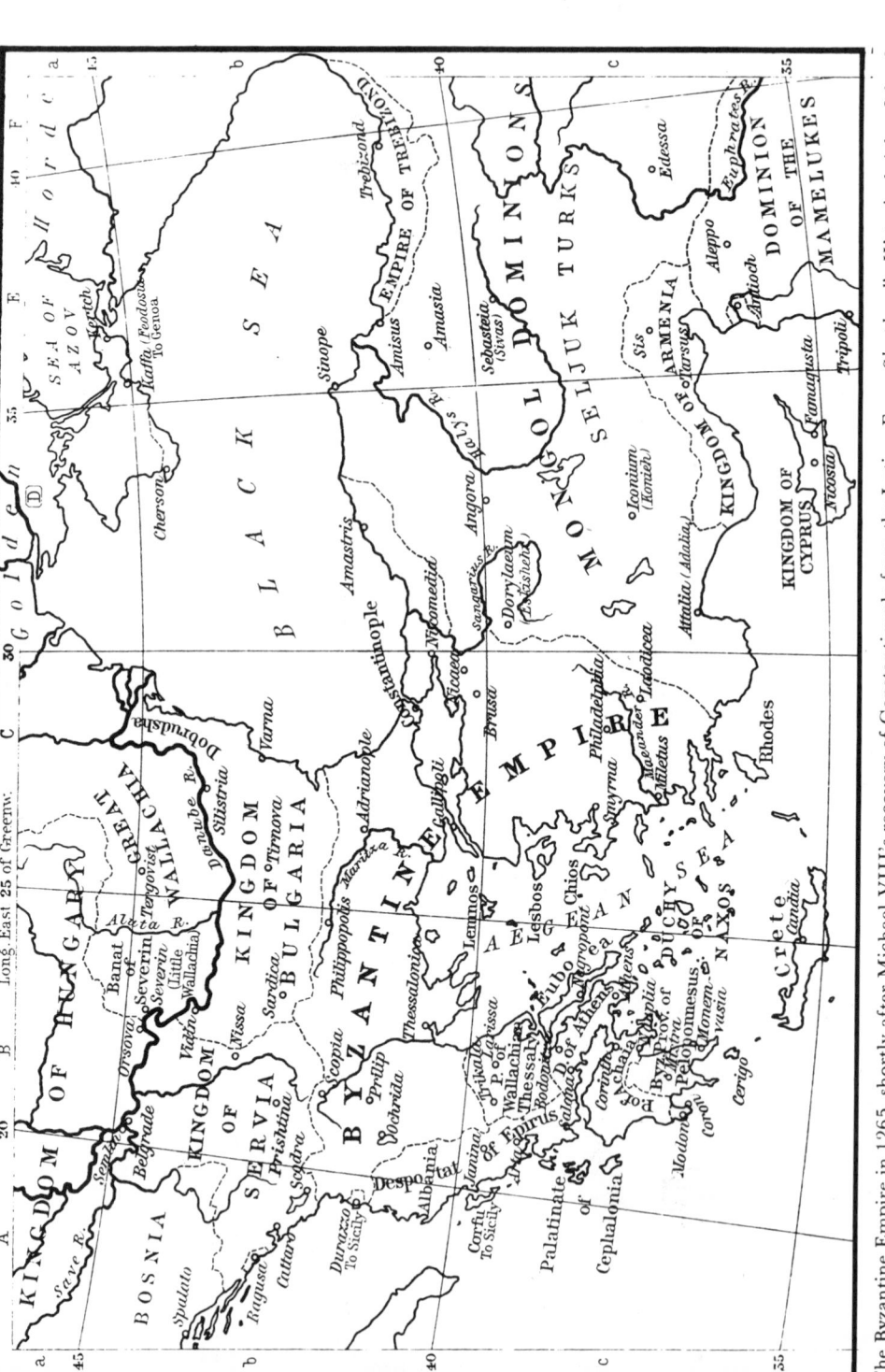

The Byzantine Empire in 1265, shortly after Michael VIII's recovery of Constantinople from the Latins. From *Shepherd's Historical Atlas*, 9th ed., map no. 89 (New York: Harper & Row, 1964).

Nicaea by the emperor John Vatatzes, himself an Albanian.[11] Unfortunately, this entire thesis is suspect because Sathas has failed even to demonstrate the Albanian ancestry of Vatatzes. That emperor, it appears, was actually born in Didymotichon, Thrace, in 1201, a date much too early for the migrations of the Albanians to those areas.[12] But then, Sathas, a patriotic nineteenth-century Greek with more than a trace of anti-Latin animus, and a much better philologist than historian, was notorious for making wild statements, especially regarding Albanian-Greek relations.[13]

Nonetheless, Sathas is the only scholar who attempts to explain several strange phrases uttered by Michael Palaeologus at the time of his trial, when he said to the judges: "I really am not the type to perform miracles. . . . If a red-hot iron should touch the hand of a living man, I do not see how he could escape being burned, unless he be carved from stone by Phidias or Praxiteles, or fashioned from bronze."[14] A classical scholar reading this passage might believe mention of the two ancient sculptors to be merely one more example of Byzantine fondness for display of classical knowledge, either on the part of Michael or the historian of the event, Acropolites. According to Sathas, however, Michael was simply recalling a popular Byzantine tradition that viewed Phidias and Praxiteles as supernatural beings made of marble and bronze, who could undergo without danger the most awful trials and ordeals.[15] The roots of this story, according to Sathas, lie in Phidias' acquittal from Athenian charges of calumny made on the grounds that he had engraved his name and that of Pericles on the base of his chryselephantine statue of Athena. Popular Byzantine belief transformed the acquitted Phidias, along with Praxiteles, into a philosopher (!), and finally into a magician capable of holding in his hands masses of red-hot iron without suffering injury. A somewhat similar story, according to Sathas, was current in medieval Rome, where, however, the two sculptors were portrayed as nude philosophers. This is attested by the famous *Mirabilia Romae*, written anonymously in Rome about 1200.[16] It is tempting to accept this remarkable explanation of Michael's allusion to the celebrated sculptors. However, since Sathas offers no confirmation whatsoever for the story, and since there seems to be no other evidence in the Byzantine sources to corroborate it, the existence of the legend in Byzantium must be considered as something less than established fact.[17]

The third theory is that the ordeal by fire was derived from the

Latins, among whom it was known as *ferri candentis judicium*.[18] Among
those who have supported this view are H. C. Lea, who states that
the practice became "partially domesticated" among the Greeks,
probably as a result of the Latin domination of Constantinople.[19]
A. Gardner, a modern historian of Nicaea, writes, "There is no doubt
that in its developed form this ordeal was introduced from the West
and was despised on the same ground as other Western institutions."[20] L. Bréhier, the scholar of Byzantine institutions, remarks
more inclusively that it was "empruntée à l'occident et aux peuples
barbares voisins de Byzance."[21] Z. von Lingenthal, in his old but
celebrated work on Byzantine law, notes that Western influence was
very strong during this period in Nicaea.[22] Even the leading Greek
specialist on the history of Nicaea, A. Miliarakis, upholds the view of
Latin provenience.[23] The French legal historian G. Mortreuil, however, who rejects Western influence on Byzantine law, is silent on
this particular matter.[24] Although these scholars in the main agree,
then, on a Latin origin, few have attempted to define its mode of
transmission to Nicaea, and those who have, have not done so conclusively. All, it seems, have assumed such a transference almost
exclusively on the grounds of the mere similarity existing between
this Byzantine practice and that of the Latin West.

One modern scholar, the Hungarian G. Czebe, while supporting
the theory of Latin provenience, offers an interesting new theory for
a definite mode of transmission.[25] His thesis is that the practice was
borrowed by the Byzantines—Nicaea specifically—from the Frankish law code, the Assizes of Jerusalem, via Cyprus, where an anonymous writer of the twelfth century had translated the Assizes into
vulgar Greek,[26] and whence the code was disseminated to parts of
the Greek East. According to him, the term *jouisse* or *joi* (ordeal of
fire) of the Assizes of Jerusalem, is to be found in the vulgar Greek
version, transliterated as *zouis*.[27] This, of course, at once poses the
question as to why Acropolites, Pachymeres, and Sphrantzes did not
utilize this Greek expression in their accounts. Czebe's reply is that
they, like almost all Byzantine writers of the period, were purists and
thus preferred the more classical Greek terms: for example, Pachymeres, *mydron*;[28] Acropolites, *he dia mydrou apodeixis*;[29] Sphrantzes,
sideron en te flogi.[30] Czebe, moreover, points out that centuries before,
Sophocles in his *Antigone*, verse 264, had employed exactly the same
expression as Pachymeres, *mydrous*.[31]

Although Czebe's thesis of Cyprus as the ordeal's channel of transmission seems credible at first glance, it is based on several false premises. Unduly stressing the importance of the written word, he implies that it was the translation of the Jerusalem Assizes into Cypriot Greek which made possible the transmission of the Latin practice to Byzantine Nicaea. Evidently, he had overlooked the fact that different peoples, even if ignorant of or imperfectly acquainted with one another's languages, can sometimes borrow practices from each other, provided that there is some sort of prolonged contact between them. The mere sight of such striking practices as the Latin ordeals by fire or combat may very well have been sufficient to fix either one in the mind of an inquisitive, intelligent Byzantine. As proof, one may cite the case of Anna Commena, who, in her famous *Alexiad*, described her impressions of the Latin judicial duel, which she saw for the first time during the passage of the Western knights of the First Crusade through Constantinople (1096).[32] So far as is known, she had little, if any, knowledge of French or Latin.

Furthermore, the fact that the contemporary Greek historians did not employ the Frankish-Cypriot terms (*jouisse, joi*) need not necessarily demonstrate, as Czebe states, that it was merely their purism which made them disregard these words. On the contrary, their silence may just as easily indicate ignorance of the terms. Finally, Czebe has neglected to demonstrate what should be an essential part of his proof, namely, the existence of close cultural connections between Cyprus and Nicaea. Indeed, it is difficult to find more than very few evidences of contact between the two states at this time.[32a] Besides the fact that they were not on particularly friendly terms, another reason may be the considerable distance between them, and especially the difficulty of communications, which involved a relatively long sea route or the traversing of enemy Turkish or Mongol territory.

It seems, therefore, that if we are to attribute to the Latins the origin in Nicaea of the use of the ordeal by fire, we must seek another channel of transmission. The strong possibility, of course, should not be overlooked that the Nicene Byzantines had already learned of this kind of ordeal from those Latins who passed through Constantinople during the period of the Comneni and Angeli (circa 1095–1204).[33] At that time, that is during the first four Crusades, relations between the two peoples had grown more and more frequent, especially during the Latin occupation of Constantinople. Since, apparently, no specific documentary evidence has been found of Byzantine adoption of such an institution at that time, we will confine our analysis to the Nicene period (1204–61), in which the event under discussion occurred.

A hypothesis which obviates the objections to Czebe's thesis and which has the added merit of simplicity, is that the Nicenes learned of this ordeal from the Latins residing in Nicaea itself. We know that the ordeal by fire was practiced in Latin Constantinople (1204–61), since it is described in the Assizes of Romania, a law code based on the Assizes of Jerusalem, and which was adopted by the Latin rulers of Constantinople in 1204 at the time of the capital's conquest.[34] The fact that the Assizes of Romania were written in Old French, a language alien to Nicaea, may have at first been a hindrance to any possible transmission; but to reiterate, when institutions continue to be practiced and cultural contacts are frequent, it is possible for practices to be transmitted regardless of linguistic considerations.

The relations between Nicaea and Latin Constantinople, situated only about eighty miles apart with the Bosporus between, afforded excellent opportunity for contact, despite their usual enmity. John Vatatzes, the Nicene emperor, for example, had seized important territories such as Adrianople and Gallipoli, which had belonged to the Latins for some twenty-five years and in which Latin institutions had doubtless been practiced. Moreover, his wife's sister, Eudocia, was married to Ansel de Cayeux, a Latin noble of Constantinople,[35] and he himself had married Anne, the daughter of the Western emperor Frederick II,[36] from whose entourage he could easily have learned of the practice. Most important, a number of Latins were living in Nicaea itself, employed either as mercenaries or as part of the imperial guard. Acropolites, in fact, mentions the presence at this very trial of certain Latins "who were eager to see Palaeologus acquitted.[37] Doubtless they belonged to the mercenary Latin contingent of the Nicene army, over which Michael himself held the rank of Grand Constable, a title derived from the Normans of Sicily. Such Latin troops had often fought for Greek rulers against their fellow Latins of Constantinople and had even been excommunicated by the papacy for aiding the "schismatic" Greeks.[38] According to Pachymeres, Palaeologus himself was commander of these Latin troops,[39] and in that capacity must have often observed them carrying on Western practices. More examples could be cited, but these seem sufficient to indicate that relations between the two capitals, despite the wars often raging between them, were close, and furthermore, that the Nicenes had to look no farther than their own city to observe Latin practices.[40]

It remains now to discuss not only the first appearance of these two institutions of the ordeal among the Byzantines but, more especially, the reasons for their use at this particular trial of Michael Palaeologus. On the basis of another passage in Pachymeres, we learn specifically that the ordeal by fire first appeared in Nicaea during the reign of Vatatzes (1222–54) and that under him it became fairly common. According to Pachymeres' description, the Greek practice was similar to the Latin.[41] As for the judicial duel, the first mention of it in Byzantine sources seems to be in Anna Comnena, who called it *polemos* and wrote that it was "a Latin institution hitherto unknown to the Greeks."[42] (The Latin-style tournaments introduced to Constantinople by the Byzantine emperor Manuel I [1143–80] are not, of course, to be confused with the judicial duel).[43] It is only with the trial of Palaeologus, however, that we apparently have the first reference to its actual use by Byzantines. Indeed, from the beginning of the twelfth century and the work of Anna Comnena up to 1253, the date of this trial, the Byzantine sources seem to be silent regarding the duel. It must be noted, nevertheless, that such an argument *ex silentio* does not necessarily mean that it had never hitherto been employed, or even that its first appearance was subsequent to that of the ordeal by fire. Despite the growing Greco-Latin ill-feeling, it is not at all impossible that one or even both practices had been utilized during the Comnenan-Angelid period, when Greco-Latin relations had become increasingly close, but that no record has remained of their use.

If it be admitted that both institutions were already known to the Nicenes at the time of this trial, how can we explain the preference of the emperor John Vatatzes (who prided himself on his "Roman" legal heritage) for Palaeologus' submission to ordeal by fire instead of a duel? Why, furthermore, did Palaeologus refuse the ordeal by fire and, rather, suggest judicial combat? Above all, why did Vatatzes invoke practices so fundamentally alien to Byzantine judicial procedure in the first place?

To begin with, Vatatzes must have realized that, since Palaeologus faced no formal charge but only a vague accusation of treason based on hearsay evidence, it would be difficult to bring him to trial under the procedures of Roman law.[44] The unilateral form of the ordeal by fire would be more appropriate in this case, where an accuser was (apparently) lacking to oppose Michael in a judicial duel. Furthermore, according to Acropolites, Vatatzes, already personally suspicious of Palaeologus, hoped for his conviction, or at least humiliation.[45] Moreover, it may be assumed that, among the Greeks, as was certainly the case among the Latins, it was considered something of a stigma for a noble to undergo the ordeal by fire. As is well-known, the Latins of the West regarded the judicial duel as more proper for members of the nobility, and this attitude may well have been reflected among those Nicenes who were familiar with the practice.[46]

Palaeologus, therefore, well-educated and doubtless acquainted with at least the principles of Roman law, refused to submit to the ordeal by fire despite Vatatzes' insistence. As he declared proudly, "Since I am a Roman, born of Romans, I should be tried according to Roman law and written traditions."[47] Finally, it was Palaeologus himself who suggested that he submit to trial by duel.[48] In this way (since an opponent would presumably be provided), he would at least have a "fighting chance" and could avoid public humiliation.

Omitting other more irrelevant details of the trial, it need only be said that Vatatzes, "influenced by the prevailing sentiment in favor of Palaeologus" (to quote Acropolites), finally canceled the inquest and released his prisoner.[49]

To demonstrate conclusively the connection between the Byzantine judicial duel and its Latin prototype, we may further point out certain similarities existing between the practice as recounted in Acropolites and that described in the work of the contemporary Latin writer of Jerusalem, John d'Ibelin. The latter provides a very good description of the Latin trial by judicial combat as practiced in contemporary Frankish Syria.[50] In both Nicaea and Syria the protagonists dueled on horseback;[51] in both places, death was the penalty for the defeated;[52] and both prescribed that the duel should be fought only at the command of the sovereign.[53]

Finally, from a curious but overlooked passage in Pachymeres,[54] who notes that in Vatatzes' reign in Nicaea it was not unusual for an accused person to prove his innocence by undergoing the ordeal of red-hot iron, we might point out resemblances between the Latin ordeal by fire and the Nicene practice. In both cases the victim was expected to fast before the ordeal; his hand had to be purified; and on the day of the trial he would grasp the hot iron (called "the holy one" in Pachymeres) in his hands, and walk three times around a table. Obviously, the Greek and Latin rituals in this ordeal were strikingly similar.

In view of the above analysis, it may be stated in summary that the origins of both the ordeal by fire and the judicial duel, as they appear at this trial of Michael Palaeologus, can safely be traced to Latin influence—if not to that transmitted previous to 1204, certainly to that exerted during the reign of Vatatzes in Nicaea. More significant even than the knowledge of the particular institutions transmitted, is the light this knowledge casts on Greco-Latin relations in the later Middle Ages. For this study reveals that, despite increasing religio-political differences and popular antipathies—even sharp hostility—separating the two peoples, a certain cultural interchange was at work between them. More particularly, this instance provides us with a specific example of cultural transmission from Latins to Greeks (even though it had no lasting significance), a fact of special interest because most scholars casually assume that such influences always flowed in the other direction.

8

A Greek Libellus against Religious Union with Rome after the Council of Lyons (1274)

In the four centuries after 1054, the generally accepted date of the schism between the Byzantine and Latin churches, two attempts were made, in general council, to unite them. The first occurred at the Council of Lyons in 1274 and the second at that of Florence in 1438–39. At both councils religious union was officially proclaimed, but in each case it turned out to be ephemeral; for the motives of the protagonists, emperors as well as popes, were inspired far less by purely religious considerations than by the political or ecclesiastical advantages to be gained. Thus, on the Byzantine side, Emperor Michael Palaeologus at Lyons was motivated toward union primarily by fear of a new Latin invasion on the part of the king of Sicily, Charles of Anjou, whose vaulting ambition extended to Constantinople. And later, the underlying aim of John VIII Palaeologus at Florence was, through union, to secure political and military aid from the popes to ward off the now extremely grave threat of the Turks to his empire. On the Western side, at Lyons as well as Florence, both Pope Gregory X and his later successor Eugenius IV were, more than anything else, inspired by a desire, through union, to secure the jurisdictional and theological subordination of the Greek church to Rome.

Much has been written about both councils, about their proceedings, and in particular about the dogmatic and ecclesiastical points at issue: the double procession of the Holy Ghost (that is, the celebrated filioque question), the doctrine of purgatory, the crucial problem of papal claims to supremacy over the Greek church, and various liturgical disputes regarding the *azymes* (use of leavened or unleavened bread in the Eucharist) and the *epiklesis* (involving the question of invocation of the Holy Spirit as the precise moment at which the miracle of "transubstantiation" takes place in the liturgy). Nonetheless, despite the publication of numerous studies of a theological or historical nature that primarily reflect the views of the high clergy and the upper classes, little information has hitherto been available on attitudes prevalent on the less enlightened level of the common people, that is, on popular beliefs and popular piety. This is particularly true regarding the Council of Lyons and its aftermath.[1]

It is the purpose of this chapter, at least in part, to elucidate some such attitudes of the masses, as well as of the more learned class, by discussing a document containing the text of a colloquy that probably took place shortly after the convocation of the Council of Lyons, namely, during the turmoil in Constantinople attendant upon attempts of Emperor Michael Palaeologus to force ecclesiastical union upon the bitterly recalcitrant Byzantine populace. For, after the signing of union at Lyons by Michael's chief ambassador, the layman George Acropolites (who was accompanied by a former patriarch, the incumbent one being opposed to union!), sentiment against union became so vocal—indeed so violent—in Constantinople that Michael was constrained to issue orders that anyone overtly or even covertly opposing union—for example, by secretly circulating or even reading propagandistic tracts against it—would be subject to the death penalty.[2]

The following document is a striking example of one such *libellus*[3] directed not only against the Latins but, even more, against the emperor and his followers (including, probably, the new unionist patriarch, John Bekkos). Not everything recorded should be taken literally, of course, for some of the Greek accusations against the Latins expressed here are clearly erroneous or exaggerated. Moreover, in order to emphasize his points the more strongly, the anonymous Greek writer utilizes against the Latins not only invective but in places satire as well. Finally, the point should be made that the Greek text of the document contains numerous grammatical errors and strange forms, a fact which sometimes makes it very difficult to understand.

The document falls into two parts, the first having as its subject the mysteries of the visible and invisible world, and the second, various errors imputed to the Latins by the Greeks. It is to be noted that in both parts of the colloquy the role of the Latin protagonist is simply to pose questions to the Greek protagonist and thus to provide a pretext for the latter to inveigh against the "falsity" of Latin religious beliefs and practices.

The document begins with a statement regarding the appearance in Constantinople during the reign of Michael, the patriarchate of Arsenios and the consulate of Euphrosinus,[4] of a certain John who, as the text reads, "came from the Pope with a mule bridled." This John is no doubt meant to be identified with the famous prounionist Byzantine Franciscan, John Parastron, well known at the time for his conciliatory attitudes and actions, and in particular for acting as go-between for the pope and emperor in the long unionist negotiations.[5] That the author of the tract was indeed a Greek antiunionist, is clear from the rather snide remark made to the effect that John appeared "with a bridled mule on which there was a basket enclosing an image of the pope" and that also present was Bekkos, the prounionist patriarch. Notably, Bekkos is described here as wearing, in Latin style, "the mitre and with a ring on his finger" which, as the text reads, "is the sign of the pope."[6]

In the next sentence the emperor Michael is depicted as emerging from the imperial palace while holding the bridle of the papal mule and with six cardinals standing on either side of him. The simultaneous appearance in Constantinople of no less than a dozen cardinals is, of course, highly unlikely. But what is really important is the intended meaning of this scene. The emperor is portrayed here as performing before the pope (or rather before his image, which is set in the back of the basket on the mule!) the subservient Western act of *stratordienst*, in apparent imitation of the Western emperor's holding of the bridle of the papal mule as the pope rode down the street in the manner of Christ and the Apostles entering Jerusalem on Palm Sunday. Here, Michael's performance is deftly described in ironic terms in order to make the emperor appear ridiculous before his Greek subjects. One may recall the famous scene in St. Mark's Square involving the German emperor Frederick Barbarossa and Pope Hadrian, and an episode in the earlier career of Michael Palaeologus himself, when, before he became emperor, he purposely held the bridle of the mule of the newly elected patriarch Arsenios in order to flatter that prelate and thus to render easier his subsequent usurpation of the throne.[7]

The document continues that "the Emperor, making obeisance before the image of the pope, affirmed, 'Long live my lord the Pope,' after which the Cardinal blessed Michael and his son." Thereupon, Michael, followed by the cardinals, entered the palace, where he had the pope's name inserted into the diptychs, that is, the tablets from which the names of those commemorated at Eucharist were read publicly (an act signifying communion between the churches). Any possible doubt as to bias on the part of the anonymous author is completely dissipated by the statement he attributes here to the cardinals, that "the Pope has sent us to your Majesty so that all Christians may partake of the communion of the unleavened bread," after which the *libellus* adds, "which is of course a heresy"—a phrase referring to the much disputed liturgical question of the *azyma*.[8] The author then lists the Byzantines who partook of this Latin form of the eucharistic sacrament, including such historically authentic, prounionist figures as the logothete Theodore Muzalon, his father-in-law John Papylas (the "beardless one"), Meletios, Gennadios, and Maleas the Protopapas. All or most of these are mentioned in Pachymeres' famous history of Michael's reign and are here referred to as "[men] of bad conscience."[9]

To dramatize the anti-Orthodox feeling of the Greek people, a basic aim of the document, the author now introduces the "champion of the Christian [Orthodox] people, [Manuel] Holobolos," the famous monk and the head and *rhetor* of the Patriarchal School in Constantinople, whose pupils are here said to number 336 [10] (the digits three and six are very likely of biblical significance). More intriguing, however, is the treatise's statement, probably symbolic, that Holobolos and his students had "preserved unblemished their foreskin."[11] This curious phrase may perhaps be explained as representing their manhood in the sense of their preservation of the "purity" of the Orthodox faith, as opposed to the supposed impurity of those Greeks who had accepted the *azyma*, the *filioque*, and religious union with Rome in general. The phrase, on the other hand, may also imply that the ardent Orthodox Holobolos and his followers had rejected the "Judaizing" practice of circumcision. As is well known, the Latin use of unleavened (*azyma*) instead of leavened bread in the Eucharist was condemned by the Greeks (among other reasons) as being a Jewish practice.[12] (Incidentally, when in 1054 the Latin *azyma* had first officially been condemned by Patriarch Michael Cerularius, the practice of unleavened bread on the part of the Armenians was at the same time also attacked by the mystical theologian, Nicetas Stethatus on the grounds of "Judaizing."

Now introduced is the chief protagonist of the colloquy, Constantine, here called Panagiotes, probably a fictitious name, who represents and articulates the Orthodox point of view toward Latin beliefs, especially of the common people. The name Panagiotes derives from *Panagia* (the all-holy Virgin), and in this context may be a suggestive allusion to *Panagiotatos*. The term "Panagiotatos," of course, is that normally applied to the Ecumenical Patriarch of Constantinople. Here "Panagiotes" is probably to be taken as symbolic of the defenders of Orthodoxy against the *kainotomias*, that is, the innovations (as the Orthodox would say) of the Latin church. Thus, Panagiotes is here presented as the pious Greek champion who, in the ensuing debate, expresses the views cherished for centuries by the Orthodox populace. It is interesting to note that before the colloquy begins, Michael (the treatise reads) had warned Constantine not to engage in discussion with any of the Latin representatives until the emperor could be present. The heart of the discussion, in any event, consists of the debate which now transpires publicly between the Greek bishop, Constantine Panagiotes, and the unnamed leader of the Roman group of cardinals, here contemptuously termed, besides "Cardinal" and "the Frank" [Latin], "Azymita" (azymite), that is, "partaker of unleavened bread." Clearly, by 1274 the term "azymite" had become highly significant in the Byzantine mind as connoting one with Latin or "Latinizing" views.[13]

After some initial skirmishing, doubtless embodying certain popular beliefs which perhaps derive from apocryphal versions of stories in the Old and New Testaments, the cardinal inquires of Panagiotes, "How many natures [in Christ] do you accept?" The Greek counters soundly with: "Do you mean before or after the Incarnation?" After the Greek has expressed the traditional Orthodox view of the divine and human natures in Christ and the three hypostases of Father, Son, and Holy Spirit in the Trinity ("three in one, and one in three, one substance"), he stresses the incorruptibility of the Divinity. To illustrate this teaching he quotes from David (whom he calls "the Prophet"),[14] "And he poured out of the one into the other even to the dregs, but still the sediment was not poured out."[15] Reflected here, probably, is the Eastern emphasis on the ineffable divine essence of Christ, in that, even in his act of sacrifice in emptying himself to redeem humanity, Christ still maintained his divine essence intact.

After several remarks concerning the relationship of the persons of the Trinity, including brief mention of the problem of the procession of the Holy Spirit, the cardinal says: "I ask you. Does dry weather cause the river to become lower and the river to have no passage?"[16] Panagiotes, on his part, seems to have taken this curious remark to be an allegorical reference to the miraculous conception and incarnation of Christ, which, according to Eastern and Western belief, did not affect Mary's ever-virginal state, even while Christ was issuing from her womb.[17] Thus the Panagiotes answers: "Weather without rain is like my Super-holy Theotokos [who did not need impregnation] and the river lacking a channel [a passage] is Christ, whose Divinity man cannot comprehend."[18]

After a further exchange of this rather mystifying kind of repartee, the cardinal touches on the difficult question of the fate of the soul after death, asking, "Where are the souls of the just men?" Panagiotes replies, "In Paradise, those of the sinners in Hell," quite possibly an allusion, in the dichotomy expressed, to the Greek belief in heaven and hell, though not in the Latin doctrine of purgatory.

After an exchange on the repose of the souls in paradise, "like doves," and the souls of sinners in hell, "like tortoises,"[19] the cardinal begins a fascinating discussion on the structure of heaven, that is, on the cosmography of the universe. This is once again of special astronomical, even of astrological, interest because it probably reflects popular Byzantine conceptions of the cosmos at the time. The Latin first asks the Greek how many heavens there are, to which the (unchristian) answer is: "One uniform heaven in the shape of a sphere like a copper hammer and like ice."[20] When the cardinal asks what is above heaven, the Greek's answer is, "Water, and above it darkness and fire, and above them an ark, and still higher a throne, and above the throne, the Divinity, and above that, the Everlasting Light"—(shades of the Apocalypse or, in view of the seven levels mentioned, of the common ancient and medieval Christian tradition about "seven heavens").

At this juncture the Latin, again contemptuously referred to by the author as the "Azymite," inquires, "What is below heaven?" to which the reply is, "Air, ether, and clouds." To the query "What is below the earth?" Panagiotes affirms, "Water, and underneath the water, darkness, and underneath it fire, and below, Hades, and beneath that Erebos [a mythical pagan Greek land of everlasting darkness between Earth and Hades] and then Tartarus which the sinners deserve."[21] These curious references, some of which, to be sure, are found in the Fathers and Revelation, may also be carry-overs from pre-Christian pagan times or conceivably taken from such later Byzantine, semipopular lore as Cosmas Indicopleustes.[22]

After a further exchange, the Latin inquires: "Are the stars in the sky odd or even?" Replies the Greek, shrewdly, "If they were twice as many their number would be even because now it is odd." The cardinal asks, "How many are the battalions of the angels?" Panagiotes: "There are ten angels' battalions, each with twelve legions, each legion with twelve thousand. Of these, 144 thousand were lost, became demons, and there remained nine divisions: the Angels, Archangels, Thrones, Dominations, the many-eyed beings, the Seraphim, and of six-winged, the Cherubim. And there remained 1,106 good angels. The heaven is 946 feet from the earth but the span of Christ is equal to 1,000 human spans."[23]

The source or inspiration for many of these strange numbers and figures would seem ultimately to be the Apocalypse of St. John, although mystical views of Pseudo-Dionysius and Nicetas Stethatus (of the mid-eleventh century) may also be reflected here. Nevertheless, one cannot escape the feeling that the Byzantine ecclesiastical protagonist, in as serious a manner as he can summon, is at the same time not so subtly trying to ridicule the Latins and their Greek supporters, by playing with numbers in imitation of the Scholastic manner, which was then, of course, the prevailing philosophic method in the West.[24]

At this point parts of the dialogue become particularly obscure in meaning—a circumstance perhaps owing to the fact that the bases for some of the opinions expressed are probably to be found in apocryphal sources known only to Byzantine popular tradition and which may now even be lost. In one place Panagiotes says: "Mankind will be judged and divided into nine battalions: i.e. kings, patriarchs, archbishops, bishops, priests, sub-deacons, deacons, readers, and [note this especially] all the Christian people [probably laymen]." This remarkable division of Christian society after the Last Judgment is somewhat reminiscent of the division of the heavenly host and the earthly ecclesiastical hierarchy of Dionysius the Areopagite—recall his *Celestial Hierarchy* and *Ecclesiastical Hierarchy*—but especially of the work of the Byzantine Nicetas Stethatus who, in his mystical *Contemplation of Paradise*, emphasizes the number nine (three triads).[25]

Other examples of popular views of church teachings may be noted in the text, as when Panagiotes, in response to a question of the Latin, remarks that God created heaven *before* he created earth. (One recalls here, of course, the Old Testament statement: "In the beginning God created the heaven *and* the earth.") To strengthen the reference implied here to the concept of time, the Greek prelate cites Chrysostom, that "every builder must first construct the foundation, then cover it, but God first covered [the world with the roof of heaven] and then created the foundation [earth]. . . . Heaven [the roof, that is] must be larger than the earth so that the earth may not be damaged."[26]

Many more ideas are now expressed by the Greek—and since it is a Greek document Greek ideas are obviously far more prominent than Western—one being that paradise is fourfold,[27] and that "near paradise there exists a place *between* mortality and immortality." Is this possibly an oblique reference to a kind of limbo (like the Latin purgatory) after death and before the Last Judgment (the Greek church does not accept a purgatory) or, possibly, of the kind of paradise first experienced by Adam in the Garden of Eden? The passage that follows sounds like a mingling of phrases from expressions of St. Paul, especially of the first several chapters of Genesis, and of Nicetas Stethatus' *Contemplation of Paradise*. In further describing paradise, Panagiotes speaks of red water in the sea and an even line of mountains. Mentioned also *in extenso* is the Tree of Life, so prominently described in Genesis and the Apocalypse.[28] But here the speaker may have confused or conflated material taken from other treatises as well (e.g. that of Nicetas Stethatus), which discuss, besides the paradise tree of Genesis, two fountains at the roots of a tree covering paradise and containing all manner of plants, but with trees excluded. One of these fountains flows with milk and honey (a phrase obviously taken from the Promised Land passage in the Old Testament); the other is the spring from which four rivers emerge— Pishon, Gihon, the Tigris, and the Euphrates (the latter phrase is directly taken from Genesis).[29]

In a subsequent passage, the Byzantine, responding to a query of the cardinal, replies that thunder and lightning are "the sound of your [God's] thunder in the whirlwind."[30] Discussing the four images of man (a phrase taken from the Apocalypse of St. John)[31]—an eagle, a bull, a lion, and a man—as the four Evangelists, Panagiotes cites Jeremiah (a mistake, apparently, for Ezekiel, 10: 14): "The eagle sings, the bull snorts, the lion roars, and man speaks." Then, fascinatingly, the dialogue takes a more intellectual (or pseudo-scientific) turn when the Greek asserts that, according to philosophy (is this perhaps from the pre-Socratics, Aristotle, or possibly Archimedes?), "when two clouds collide and attack each other, two winds come out of them, one cold, the other warm, with a noise produced from their collision."[32] Unexpectedly, Panagiotes then quotes the ancient Greek Hermogenes ("the rhetor of rhetors," as he calls him here), saying, "When the water of Heaven falls down from a place and the water collides, a noise is produced."[33] Interestingly enough, this may be the first, or one of the very first, references to the name of Hermogenes to appear in connection with Westerners in the medieval period.

Then, perhaps surprisingly for a fervent ecclesiastic, Panagiotes in the text cites the names of the Greeks Demosthenes and Achilles (Achilles Tatios, the Alexandrian?), affirming that "three hundred angels hold up the sky with twelve columns and twelve arches, and three hundred angels hold up the earth with twelve columns and twelve arches."[34] He adds (nonbiblically, and rather surprisingly, it would seem) that "it is for this reason that heaven is called twelve-hilled and seven-hilled."[35] He continues in this vein for several more statements, relating how, with the collision of the angels with each other, "a great sound is produced, from which collision comes fire, in turn producing lightning."

There follows a rather lengthy passage regarding the sun, which, it is stated, "is divided into three, into flesh in imitation of the incarnation of Christ, into light in imitation of both the flesh [of Christ] and of the Father, and into both rays of the Son and the fire of the Holy Spirit." This description of the sun, and especially the mention of its rays and the Son, is suggestive of the doctrine, later fully developed by the Hesychast Gregory Palamas, concerning the distinction between the essence and the uncreated energies of God, for which the sun and its rays were frequently used as an analogy.[36]

After a description of how the setting sun delivers its light to Christ, the giver of life, a bit of astronomical or astrological lore is displayed. The Greek declares that the sky revolves three times during the day and three times at night, "round and round like a mill." (One may think here of Ptolemy's *Cosmographia*, Plato's *Timaeus*, or, more probably, of popular lay astronomical beliefs of the period.) When the Latin inquires why the sun and moon do not turn with the sky, the Greek replies: "Whatever are suspended from the sky below the clouds are like the candles in the Church and are distant from the sky three hundred of God's feet" (recall that earlier he had said that a divine "foot" equaled a thousand human feet).

Then, again in a curious admixture of pagan, biblical, and Christian lore, Panagiotes, in response to a question of how the sun rises, relates that "Christ the Son of God gives the crown to the angels, they put it on the sun and it rises, and, at once, two birds called griffins [a pagan mythical creature], of which one is called phoenix, with each other dampen the sun so that the sun may not scorch the earth. And because of the heat of the fire, the feathers of the birds are burnt and only their flesh remains. And again they fly toward the ocean and wash themselves and once more grow feathers. And the cocks imitate these birds and derive their names from these birds. . . . They have blood under their armpits; the blood agitates them and they scratch with their beaks. And as they are irritated by the blood, they awake and, having foreknowledge of the noise made by the birds, by the grace of Christ they make manifest the resurrection of Christ."

This passage, very obscure and not easily interpreted, seems, among other things, to suggest an analogy between the pelican, which, it was believed, feeds its young with its own blood, and Christ, who fed mankind with his own blood and body by being pierced in the side and dying on the cross, and continues to nourish mankind through his blood and body in the Eucharist. (This analogy between the blood of Christ and the pelican is, incidentally, prominently mentioned in the famous "He Zoe en Tafo" of the Holy Friday service of the Orthodox church.)[37]

In a humorous passage suggesting that the Byzantine is once again ironically imitating Scholastic terminology, the Panagiotes, in response to the Azymite's question, "How many tips does my beard have?" asserts, "Tell me how many roots there are and I will tell you how many they are at the tip." (One may recall by analogy the supposed Scholastic query, "How many angels can stand on the head of a pin?") In the course of another ironic exchange, revealing a strangely humanistic touch, Panagiotes says the Latin knows six of the arts of letters—philosophy, oratory, grammar, Greek (text reads "roman") and Latin, plus (he emphasizes) the teaching of the devil— while he, as a mere student, knows only three: the implication is clear—the Father, Son, and Holy Spirit.

The disputation now turns to matters of popular devotional and liturgical beliefs. Thus the Greek asks, "Why do the Franks [i.e. the Latins] not call the super-holy Theotokos the Mother of God but Santa Maria, that is, make her *simply a Saint*?" (Is not this, by the way, remarkable evidence that in this period of the later Middle Ages the Byzantines were, still perhaps, greater devotees of Mariology than the Latins?)[38] The Byzantine continues, "We call her the *super-holy* Theotokos because she bore the King of heaven and earth." Then, turning specifically to liturgical practices, the Orthodox inquires of the Latin, "Why do you not use three fingers to cross yourself from your face down to your breast and your navel, while bearing on yourself the symbol of my Jesus Christ, the sign of the cross,[39] but rather you cross yourselves from the opposite side?" This no doubt refers to the Greek practice (still followed) of making the sign of the cross with three fingers of the right hand (the two others being kept closed) and touching the forehead, breast, and shoulders, first the right then the left. In the thirteenth century (evidently *before* composition of this *libellus*), a change had come about in Latin practice, with all fingers instead being joined and extended, and the left shoulder being touched before the right.[40] In the two practices described here, we may well have concrete evidence of the change that occurred in the Latin practice of making the sign of the cross—a change which has not been well documented.

Then, regarding still another liturgical practice, the Greek inquires why the Latins "do not worship and kiss the holy icons with love and faith but you fall on your knees and, while whispering, make the sign of the cross on the ground with two fingers, kiss the cross, and then [arising] you trample upon it." This may be a popular Greek misconception about certain Latin practices, such as genuflection and possibly even prostration. (Prostration is still practiced in the Roman church during the rite of ordination and also when the cardinals in consistory prostrate themselves before the pope.)

Panagiotes, who by now is doing almost all the talking, further asks why the Latins eat strangled meat[41]—a practice already complained of at the time of Patriarch Photius—and why the Latins bleed themselves in a glass (open their veins, that is) "and then you wash it and drink from it." This probably refers to the Latin practice of bleeding themselves as a supposed health measure, and perhaps to an erroneous Greek belief in what they referred to as the Latin "impurity" of placing the blood in a glass after bleeding and then later drinking from the same glass.[42] As if to prove this accusation of "impurity" of practice, the Greek then accuses the Latins of feeding dogs from their own plates, then washing the dishes and eating from them. This may well refer to the common practice of Western feudal nobility of feeding their dogs under the table by handing down their plate to them. It is interesting that in a Russian text of the later medieval period, the very same complaint is made—that the Latins eat from the same dishes as their dogs.[43]

The Greek continues, "Why do you eat hedgehogs, bears, and crows, things abominable and polluted?" To which the cardinal replies, "When Peter got hungry, did not the angel say, 'Get up Peter, slaughter [animals], then eat?' " But the Greek argues back that Peter did not eat defiled things, but rather that these are beliefs. (What all this probably refers to is the passage in Acts in which Peter, in a trance, sees many animals appear and is ordered by God to eat. But when Peter refuses on the grounds that he cannot eat unclean animals, God replies that what He has created and purified is not unclean.)[44] Then, in line with old Orthodox traditional belief, the Greek accuses the Latin of eating meat and cheese the first day of Lent, "when demons shudder and angels exult and we Christians abstain even from water, whereas you do not fast during the whole of Lent." These remarks again provide evidence of the existence of specific differences in liturgical practices between the two churches, dating from as early as, or earlier than, the thirteenth century—the kind of information one is much less likely to derive from more formal historical sources.

In the course of the discussion, the Byzantine prelate accuses the Latin of not chanting the Hallelujah until Holy Friday,[45] of walking barefoot in church, and of taking the cross from one corner to another on the grounds that Christ went to Jerusalem and returned[46] (referred to here, if inaccurately, may be the Latin devotional practice of the stations of the cross). Again the Greek alludes to the practice of Latin women eating cheese, eggs, milk, and butter on the Saturday and Sunday of Lent and abstaining only from meat. (In actual fact, on the plea of grave sickness, a Catholic could eat meat on Ash Wednesday and Good Friday.) Panagiotes further touches on the much disputed problem of the celibacy of the clergy, which he questions, though first citing St. Basil on aspects of celibacy. Then he alludes to Christ's (Paul's?) directions that a virgin boy marry a virgin girl because of the weakness of the flesh. He notes that to the (Greek) church, marriage was considered a "treasure." He then paraphrases the famous biblical words, " 'Let no man put asunder those whom God has joined together,' for the church is heaven on earth." It is for this reason (because the priest is a man, that is), the

Byzantine claims, that the church permits a priest to marry, though the Latins do not.

Then, in perhaps the most strikingly scathing, scurrilous, anti-Latin passage,[47] which deserves to be quoted at length, Panagiotes affirms that, instead of marriage, Latin priests have recourse to concubinage. In his words, "Instead you have concubines, and your priest sends his servant to bring him his concubine and he puts out the candle and then he 'mounts' (*anerchetai*) her for the whole night. Then he goes out of his cell and asks forgiveness before his fellow priests who do the same, [hypocritically] offering as an excuse, 'Forgive me, my brothers, but I have had an erotic dream (*efantasteka*)'[48] and he receives pardon. Then he enters into the church to celebrate the liturgy."

In a final passage on the celebration of the liturgy, the Greek remarks that the Latin priest holds the body of Christ—that is, the host—in his belt and breeches (today Catholic priests have a special container for carrying the Eucharist, called, from the Greek word *pyx*, box) and—note the curious juxtaposition of ideas here—he may go to urinate and meet a woman. He thus (according to the Greek) sins in his soul; but the Latin priest then says, "There is no water" (that is, to cleanse himself?). The Greek then remarks that (despite all these transgressions) the Latin priest is not at all hindered from celebrating the liturgy, indeed, from celebrating it many times a day ("five or ten times even") on the same altar. According to Orthodox practice, it should be observed, the liturgy can be performed only once a day by the same priest on the same altar—a fact that does not obtain for the Roman church. Moreover, the occasional Latin practice of a priest celebrating Mass absolutely alone, and the frequent Western medieval abuse of the practice of saying many Masses for the dead, may have served as the basis for some Greek objections.

Panagiotes, in conclusion, notes that the Latin priest, during the liturgy, may go, if he wishes, to satisfy his need: so "removing his robes, he goes to satisfy the needs of the body [though still 'unclean,' the Byzantine implies], whereupon he again enters the church."[49] This entire curious passage, however grossly exaggerated, very probably reflects certain popular Greek views on the mores of the Latin secular clergy—whom many lower- (and some upper-) class Greeks envisioned as not only very materialistic-minded but, frequently, sexually immoral as well.

The Greek text of the dialogue, in the Vienna manuscript from which we have been quoting, breaks off at this point. But on the basis of another passage found in a Paris manuscript (this passage is lacking in all the numerous Slavic versions) we are able to complete the Greek text of the colloquy.[50] Thus, in a kind of epilogue to the piece, the text continues to reveal that Constantine Panagiotes, whose anger and rage at the Latins and—even more—at the emperor and the prounionist Greeks, has been steadily increasing, at the end hurls anathema at the Latin heretics in general, and the Greek "azymites" in particular. (Clearly, it was the use of the *azyma*—after all, it concerned the Eucharist itself—which seemed to him most to symbolize the pro-Latinism of the unionist Greeks.) Whereupon Panagiotes, the staunch defender of Orthodoxy who, with imprecations and curses castigates emperor, patriarch, and cardinals in succession, is now (according to the manuscript) condemned to death. Finally and in conclusion, the anonymous writer of the *libellus* reveals, almost triumphantly, his own pro-Orthodox sentiments by awarding Panagiotes, posthumously, the crown of a martyr.

In order to provide a kind of parallel Latin view of Greek "errors" in religious beliefs and practices, we may briefly cite here a contemporary report of the official papal envoy, the Franciscan Jerome of Ascoli, which he sent to the pope on his way back to the West from Constantinople to attend the Council of Lyons. (Jerome, incidentally, may have been the model for the cardinal in this colloquy.) In this, Jerome affirms, among other things, that the Greeks considered fornication a less serious sin than a third marriage—indeed, for Greeks fornication is not a "mortal" sin—that the Greeks rebaptize Latin converts, and that the Greeks had long opposed the Roman church, since they had already excommunicated the pope and all the Latins at the Council of Nicaea in 325 (!).[51]

In summation of the analysis of the Greek *libellus* provided here, it may be said that we have before us a remarkable document—highly biased though it is—a text which, like few others in medieval annals, reveals not only differences in doctrine but especially in beliefs and practices as conceived of in the popular Orthodox mind. Sections of the colloquy concern matters, dogmatic and especially liturgical, that were not formally discussed either at ecumenical or other councils (certainly not at Lyons, where no discussions, officially at least, took place), or about which formal pronouncements were never made by the church. Hence the text is able to give us valuable insight into the religious mentality, mixed with aspects of pseudoscientific lore and superstition, of the common people as well as the more learned class, although almost exclusively from the Byzantine point of view. The document thus provides us with a deeper awareness of some of the more intangible factors which, in the later Middle Ages, made understanding so difficult between the mass of the Greek and Latin peoples.

Part 2

Byzantium, Greco-Byzantine Learning, and the Italian Renaissance

9

The Greeks of the Diaspora: The Italian Renaissance and the Origins of Modern Greek National Consciousness

When, in 1455, Bessarion, the most influential of the Greek scholars who emigrated to Italy as a result of the Turkish threat to and capture of Constantinople, wrote to his protégé Michael Apostolis directing him to collect Greek manuscripts from whatever sources he could, he explained the reasons for his commission as follows:

> As long as the common and simple hearth of the Greeks [Constantinople] remained standing I had no concern with gathering [Greek] manuscripts. But when it fell, I conceived a great desire to acquire all these works not so much for myself . . . but for the sake of the Greeks who are left now, as well as for those who may have a better fortune in the future. . . . Otherwise, they [the Greeks] would lose even these few vestiges of those excellent and divine authors which have been saved from what we have lost in the past, and they [the Greeks] would differ in no way from barbarians and slaves.[1]

Almost four centuries later, in 1838, a few years after the outbreak of the Greek Revolution, Kolokotrones, one of the heroes of that war (and himself no intellectual), declared in a speech delivered on the Greek mainland:

> Many among the Greek scholars who have fled to the West have translated books and sent them to Greece. We owe a great debt of gratitude to these scholars, for as soon as a young man of the people [in Greece] had mastered the elements of reading and could read these books, he realized what kind of ancestors we had and how great were the exploits of Themistocles and Aristides and of the other Greeks, and at the same time he became conscious of the terrible situation under which we were living.

> Thus we decided to follow the example of our forefathers in order
> to be happier [the implication is, to seek to live in freedom].[2]

The first quotation, penned at the beginning of the Turkish occupation of Byzantine Constantinople, is significant no more for its indication of the contribution made by Greek learning to the Italian
Renaissance, important as that is, than for Bessarion's clear implication of the role of ancient Greek culture in enabling future generations of Greeks to maintain, during the period of subjugation, a
knowledge of the past heritage and thus a sense of cultural and ethnic
identity.

The second quotation, from a speech given almost four hundred
years later, soon after the violent birth of modern Greece, seems to
bear out the intent of Bessarion's emphasis on education and the role
in its preservation played by the diaspora, that is, Greeks living
abroad. It is the main theme of this chapter, then, within the four
centuries intervening between the two passages quoted (the so-called
Turkokratia, when a Greek nation as such had completely disappeared), to analyze the activities of the more important Greek
communities of the diaspora in the West, concentrating especially on
the educated classes, and thus to show how these Greeks in exile
helped lead to the emergence of what is often termed the "new national consciousness" of the early nineteenth century. The role of the
diaspora Greeks of Russia and the Slavic East is outside the scope of
this discussion.

Many modern historians explain the apparently sudden emergence
of a strong Greek desire for liberation in the years shortly before
1821 primarily in terms of Enlightenment and French revolutionary
influences on Greeks living in such centers as Vienna, Paris, Budapest,
and Odessa, and exemplified in the creation of the secret society,
the Philike Hetaireia.[3] At the same time, they may mention a few
sporadic Greek revolts that took place in the Morea or Epirus, incited for selfish motives by one or another of the great powers. However valid this approach—and there is certainly something to be said
for it—it fails to take into account the contribution of the many Greek
communities established outside the Balkans earlier. For especially
in the western European communities was preserved a continuous
sense of a distinct and proud people with a long tradition, and almost
an obsession—not always explicit to be sure—for the re-creation of an
independent Greek nation.

Now, to pose the problem of the development of a feeling of nationalism exclusively in terms of a continued interest in the ancient
Hellenic culture is an oversimplification. Yet there can be little doubt
that what, in the last analysis, made the Greek people feel different
from all others was the knowledge of the accomplishments of the
ancient Greeks and necessarily, a priori, a sense of identification with
them as ancestors.

The role of the Orthodox church in preserving the feeling of ethnic
identity, or national consciousness, during the Turkish occupation is
not to be slighted. In the sixteenth and seventeenth centuries, the
worst period of domination (the true "Dark Ages" for the Greek
homeland), the lower clergy, though in large part barely educated
themselves, performed a most valuable service in preserving Orthodoxy against a not inconsiderable number of conversions to Islam and
resultant Turkicization.[4] For among the Greeks of the mainland from
the sixteenth to the early seventeenth century, even a simple ability
to read and write was, with few exceptions, largely nonexistent. And
there it was primarily the church, especially through the local clergy
with their sermons and implied or explicit identification of the
genos with Orthodoxy, that did most to preserve the idea of a national
identity.[5] Yet without disparaging this contribution, we should recognize that the Orthodox church performed much the same service
for other Orthodox, the Slavic peoples of the Balkans. These shared
the same faith, formulas, and practices, but their liturgy was in
Slavonic; and this significant linguistic factor, along with a different
medieval historical development, contributed to the Slavic feeling of
differentiation from the Greeks.

That the religious factor was, however, not always indispensable to
the development of a Greek national consciousness is indicated by the
fact that some of the most important diaspora Greek intellectuals
during the Renaissance or later became Uniates or, on rare occasions,
even Roman-rite Catholics. Yet from their pens came some of the
most moving and patriotic appeals for aid in the regeneration of
Greece as a nation.[6]

In examining the question of ideologies contributing to the nationalism of modern Greece, it may be argued that, throughout the
Turkish occupation, some Greeks, especially in Constantinople,
seemed to envision a kind of revival of the old Byzantine, that is,
Roman, state. But apparently what they had in mind was not the
earlier multinational Byzantine state—in the sixteenth and seven-

teenth centuries this would have been highly unrealistic—but something more akin to an ethnically Greek state united under the Orthodox religion.

The difference between the ideology of restoration of a Greek nation on the ancient model as opposed to one on the Byzantine, though not lacking importance, can perhaps be overemphasized. After all, the basic characteristic of both seems to be the ancient Hellenic cultural tradition, which is reflected also, *mutatis mutandis*, in the Greek Orthodox church. The Phanariots of the later seventeenth and eighteenth centuries, ensconced in a position of authority in Constantinople, were, to be sure, often loath to risk damage to their exposed position through overt revolt. Yet it would seem that even they, though envisioning a Greek restoration centering in Constantinople rather than Athens, in the last analysis based their ideology primarily on the Greek cultural legacy reflected in a common language and literature as well as in the Orthodox religion.

It was among the diaspora Greeks, however, where learning was much more common, intensive, and diffused, that the sense of identification with the ancients was most clearly and explicitly realized. And this because, disencumbered of the Turkish oppression, they were able to establish and maintain an educational system which had as its foundation ancient Greek history and learning. In the Renaissance, the exiles' sense of individuation was often heightened by the attitude of Italian humanists, who not only admired their skill in ancient learning but sometimes flattered them as being the progeny of the ancients. As the humanist pope Pius II affirmed upon hearing of Constantinople's fall to the Turks in 1453: "This is the second death of Homer and Plato."[7]

With these briefly drawn considerations in mind, let us now set forth the more meaningful aspects of the history of the main disapora centers in western Europe.[8] Thousands of Greeks fled the Turkish occupation of their homelands, coming to the West not only from Constantinople and the Greek mainland, but from the Greek islands and even from threatened, but as yet unconquered, Venetian-held areas of the old Byzantine East. This emigration did not pour into the West at a constant rate but seems to have occurred in spurts. It began almost imperceptibly in the last quarter of the fourteenth century after the initial Ottoman threats to Constantinople, then speeded up considerably in the decades before 1453. We should note the attraction of Italy for Greek intellectuals in particular. The favorable reception accorded them at the Council of Florence in 1438–39 afforded an awareness of the professional academic opportunities awaiting them in the wake of the Western revival of interest in Greek studies.[9] New waves of Greek émigrés flowed westward after the fall of Venetian Negropont in 1470, again with the conquest of Cyprus in 1571, and even as late as 1689, the Turkish conquest of Venetian Crete.

The colonies of this Greek diaspora included virtually all strata of society: scholars and diplomats, printers, merchants and craftsmen, artists, parish priests, laborers, and soldiers or sailors who served in Western armed forces. The further away the émigrés moved, the more, it seems, they tended to become merchants or shopkeepers. Almost none turned to agriculture, although some émigrés had originally been peasant farmers in their homeland. Of course, the fact that many came without funds meant they lacked the capital to buy land. Nevertheless, once arrived in the West, they immediately adapted to an urban life style.

The communities most important for the preservation of the Greek tradition and for the ultimate establishment of a politically independent nation were those of Venice—together with its satellite city Padua—Naples, and Ancona—all in Italy; Toledo and lesser towns in Spain; Lyons and perhaps Paris in France. These colonies were most important during the fifteenth to approximately the early seventeenth centuries, after which there emerged to prominence the newer Greek communities of Trieste, London, Livorno, and especially Budapest, Vienna, and Odessa. The Greek community of Venice, however, still maintained a certain significance even up to the outbreak of the Greek revolution in 1821. Indeed, it may be said that of all the communities active during this long preparatory period, Venice held the primacy. It was the largest, longest-lived, and in general made the greatest contribution to the development of modern Greece.

THE GREEK COMMUNITY OF VENICE

From the earliest medieval centuries individual Byzantines had lived in Venice, a satellite if not a possession of Byzantium, which was thus early influenced by Byzantine culture and, increasingly from the late fifteenth century onward, by ancient Greek civic and intellectual ideals. When Constantinople fell in 1453, many Greeks, especially the educated ones, found it not difficult to flee to nearby Venetian-held Crete, the most important former Byzantine territory still free of the Turk. There, under an increasingly enlightened Venetian government, they could speak their own language, practice their religion with only sporadic interference, and thus escape the blight of Turkish oppression. From Crete it was an easy step to proceed to Venice, and it was therefore not long before the solid nucleus of a Greek-speaking community had been established in that city.

In 1494 the Greek community of Venice (which called itself the Brotherhood of St. Nicholas), after the filing of a petition, was recognized as a formally organized legal entity by the Venetian Council of Ten. It thus assumed a place, later the chief place, as one of the corporately constituted foreign communities of Venice, others being those of the Slavs, Albanians, and Armenians. Its legal foundation, it seems, was mainly owing to Venetian recognition of the contribution rendered to the Venetian state by the Greek *estradioti*, light horsemen serving in the Venetian military forces who had come primarily from Epirus or Albania.[10] Waxing richer because of the expanding activities of its many merchants (in the Greek quarter, called Campo dei Greci, the merchants possessed their own docks on the Rio dei Greci), the Greek community soon began to make plans for the construction of a church, the typical nerve center for every diaspora community. This construction, it should be noted, was due essentially to the patriotic initiative of Greek shipowners, captains, and seamen who, on each voyage to Venice, made a more or less voluntary contribution to the treasury of the colony.[11] The result, finally, was the erection in 1539 of the impressive church of San Giorgio dei Greci. For the building of this edifice in the Byzantine style (aside from the campanile), the colony procured the services of several famous Italian architects. The considerable work of ornamentation, however, was executed in the still viable Byzantine style of painting by Greeks of the community who had come from Crete or the Venetian-held Ionian islands.[12]

Even before this, however, in 1468, the distinguished Byzantine prelate Bessarion, who had supported religious union with Rome and had become a Roman convert, was so impressed with the increasing interest of the Venetians in classical Greek studies and with the refuge Venice offered to his compatriots, that he had termed Venice "almost a second Byzantium" ("quasi alterum Byzantium")[13] and, as we have already noted, bequeathed his famed collection of Greek manuscripts to her. Venice rapidly became a magnet for the emigration of many highly educated Greeks who sought to find employment in or near Venice or Padua.

In about 1500, the colony numbered close to 5,000, increasing in later years to possibly 10,000 out of a total Venetian populace of about 110,000.[14] One of the principal services rendered by this growing community in the Renaissance was to provide a second or substitute homeland for Greeks in exile. The refuge that was afforded by Venice—where one could live as a Greek while residing in the most dynamic and richest of Western cities—was common knowledge in the entire Greek world from the late fifteenth century almost to the time of the Greek Revolution. This fact is especially notable for the period of the Renaissance, the fifteenth to seventeenth centuries. One should therefore abandon the traditional stock picture of the poor Greek scholar escaping alone to the West, clutching his precious manuscripts in his hands, and with no specific destination in mind.[15] From the correspondence of Greek humanists like Marcus Musurus, John Gregoropoulos, Michael Apostolis, Demetrius Ducas, and others, it is clear that they looked upon the community of Venice as a second homeland.[16] By a curious irony, Venice, the arch-villain of the Fourth Crusade, which had been primarily responsible for abolishing the Byzantine state, was now in the position of acting as host, the chief receptacle as it were, for a large-scale Greek emigration to the West.

Among the most important Greek scholars whose careers centered wholly or partly in Venice, one of the earliest is Michael Apostolis of Constantinople. Living for the most part in Venetian Crete, he corresponded with Greek and Latin humanists in Venice or elsewhere, collected books for Bessarion's library, and seems to have founded a kind of school for scribes. Nevertheless, despite his desires, he was never able to acquire a post teaching Greek in an Italian academic institution. In this sense, therefore, his career may be considered more typical of the numerous émigré or refugee scholars from the East who never succeeded in making a successful career in the West. Michael also wrote one of the earliest appeals to a Western ruler (other than the pope), with the aim of relieving the Greeks from Turkish oppression. Addressing the Holy Roman Emperor, Frederick III, he appealed to him to "destroy this accursed race of Turks and restore the Greeks to their rightful heritage." The tenor of this letter would seem to indicate that Apostolis' views are in the Byzantine tradition. For he seeks restoration of the old Roman or Byzantine political unity, with Frederick's son, in fact, to be enthroned as ruler of the East. Unfortunately, this highly rhetorical appeal provides no concrete details as to any proposed administrative organization or the possible role of the Greek church vis-à-vis Rome.[17]

More closely associated with the life and government of Venice was a man who was very probably the greatest Hellenist of the entire Western Renaissance, Marcus Musurus. Born on the Venetian-held island of Crete, Musurus studied in Venice with several eminent scholar-émigrés, notably Janus Lascaris, who with Bessarion acted as the patron of his fellow Greek intellectuals. Musurus' contributions to scholarship and to Greek patriotism are manifold and intertwined. As principal editor of the famous Aldine Press, he edited no less than eleven or twelve of the most important ancient Greek authors, among them the three tragedians and the complete corpus of Plato. His work necessitated the making of crucial decisions on textual readings, some of which, despite the advances of modern philology, are still accepted today. Moreover, as professor at the University of Padua and later in Venice, he taught no less than twenty-five of the West's subsequently noted humanists, who on their return to their homelands spread the seeds of interest in ancient Greek learning.

Musurus converted to Catholicism—a not uncommon occurrence for post-Byzantine humanists employed in Italy. But though such conversion entailed acceptance of papal primacy, it allowed for preservation of the Greek ritual, which for the sophisticated scholar-Greek of the diaspora (unlike for the more fanatic and simpler Greeks of the mainland) did not necessarily mean repudiation of one's ethnic distinctiveness. Musurus always remained a fervent Greek patriot. Thus, his celebrated "Hymn to Plato," which he prefixed to his Aldine *editio princeps* of the complete works of Plato and dedicated to the Hellenophile Pope Leo X, was in reality a plea to the spirit of Plato to so move the pope that he would launch a crusade to save "fainting Greece from the Turkish wolflike tyranny." This poem, the theme of which is the resurrection of the Greek nation, is considered by some scholars to be the finest piece of poetry written in the Greek language since antiquity.[18]

The capital contribution to Hellenic learning of the Italian Aldus Manutius is well known. In Venice, he published first editions of virtually all the principal ancient Greek literary works except Polybius. His printshop provided employment for a large number of

Greek inhabitants of the Greek community, especially Cretans, who worked as editors, transcribers, typesetters, or laborers. Researches suggest that not he, but his friend the Cretan émigré Zacharias Calliergis, may deserve credit for conceiving the idea of printing the first complete corpus of Greek literary works. It would be very strange indeed had no learned Greek émigré seen, in the revolutionary new invention of printing now rooted so strongly in Venice, an opportunity to make use of his special learning for commercial profit, while doing something perhaps to ameliorate the plight of his oppressed compatriots. Such, indeed, may have been the case with the publication in 1499 of Calliergis' *Etymologicum Magnum*.[19] Probably edited by Musurus, who worked for Calliergis before going to Aldus, the work's title page and opening pages reproduce the old Byzantine ornamentation and utilize as Calliergis' printer's mark, the imperial Byzantine double-headed eagle.

In any event, Calliergis was the first, or one of the very first, to devote a considerable part of his printing production, in Venice and later in Rome, to the publication of Orthodox liturgical books.[20] This particular contribution of his, and of many later Greek presses in the Venetian Greek community, had the pragmatic purpose of providing much needed materials for worship, especially in the occupied East. And in the preservation of the Greek tradition, it ranks second only to the printing of the ancient literature. Indeed, the printing of Orthodox books in Venice was so enduring that even today on Mt. Athos, the citadel of Orthodoxy, most liturgical books in use have issued from Venetian Greek presses. (A qualification must be adduced in connection with Orthodox Russia, where sometimes another reaction was produced. There, for example, in the mid-seventeenth century, when Asenios Sukhanov returned to Moscow from Mt. Athos with Greek liturgical books printed in Venice, some Russians looked upon them suspiciously as being "contaminated" by Roman Catholicism.)[21]

In these various endeavors of the Venetian community, the number of Cretan names we find is striking. No less so are the large number of stemmata of Cretan families to be found in the sixteenth to seventeenth centuries in the Grand Aula of the University of Padua, an indication of the surprising number of Cretans who studied there.[22] Among the principal Cretan scholars is Demetrius Ducas, who edited for Aldus the *Rhetores Graeci* and Plutarch's *Moralia* (Ducas later worked in Spain); also, the Cretan Arsenios Apostolis, whose character was so shady that even his patriotism seems equivocal. Finally, we might single out the Cretan Franciscus Portus, who taught at Ferrara and later at Geneva, Switzerland, and who is almost the only Greek émigré intellectual who converted to Calvinism. Yet he is best known for his edition of the scholia on Homer and for his erudite teaching of ancient Greek philology in Geneva.[23]

Among other Greek literati in the Venetian colony was Demetrius Chalcondyles, who later taught also in Florence. The text of the (essentially still unpublished) discourse he delivered (in Latin) in 1463 before the Venetian Signoria on his assumption of the newly established chair of Greek at the University of Padua, is full of references to the culture of his ancient forebears (see chap. 13 and Appendix for translation and Latin text). It concludes with a moving exhortation to the doge to launch an expedition to save from the Turk "oppressed Hellas, prostrate like the damned in Dante's *Inferno*."[24]

Modern historians almost invariably overlook these patriotic appeals to heads of Western governments by the Greek diaspora scholars as boring, rhetorical effusions of patriotism, or, more often, simply as irrelevant to the development of humanism. But the patriotism of these Greek humanists, especially their interest in securing aid for the resurrection of a Greek nation, cannot easily be separated from their scholarly work. Indeed, virtually all of them took advantage of their position and whatever rhetorical virtuosity they could summon to appeal on behalf of their lamented country.

Some of these apostrophes are, to be sure, excessively rhetorical and do at first glance seem of little interest to Western scholarship. But among the most eloquent, besides those of Musurus and Chalcondyles, are those of Bessarion. As virtual prime minister to several successive popes, he made it his lifework to travel throughout Europe seeking to persuade various powers, especially Venice and the papacy, to launch a joint expedition to expel the Turk from Constantinople. Another such appeal, unknown to Westerners, was written by Antonios Eparchos of Corfu.[25]

Not all these scholars lived, technically, within the confines of the Greek colony. Janus Lascaris, though associating freely with his Greek compatriots, went as papal envoy to Madrid, where he too made an appeal to Charles V on behalf of his countrymen.[26] The humanist Constantine Lascaris wrote exhortations for aid from Messina,[27] and in Paris the second-generation Greek and member of the Pléiade, Nicholas Vergikios, wrote nostalgic poetry in French about his homeland, Crete.[28] But as late as the seventeenth century, Venice remained the primary center for such appeals for the regeneration of a Greek nation.

In not a few cases the diaspora scholars dangled before Western sovereigns the hope that, through military intervention, the latter could become rulers of a revived Byzantine, or perhaps even a new "Hellenic," nation. The sometimes pathetic appeals of these humanist émigrés deserve a special place in the history of the emergence of the modern Greek spirit of nationalism. For through their appeals, however rhetorical, they managed to keep before the crowned heads and intellectuals of Europe the image of the Greeks as an individual, still existent people, who though in bondage, would one day rise as a new nation from their prostrate position.

A few words on the activities of the nonscholarly inhabitants of the Venetian community. Most notable are the famous *estradioti*, the Greek light cavalry who served in the Venetian land forces. Their almost legendary exploits are mentioned in the Venetian sources, especially in Marino Sanuto's famous *Diarii* and in the decisions of the Council of Ten. These Greek troops, of course, needed little encouragement to combat an enemy anathema to themselves as well as Venice. It is not well known that at this time *estradioti* also served in the German armies, fought against the Spaniards, or—more often, as we shall see—in the late sixteenth and seventeenth centuries, were used by Spanish rulers in their wars against the Turks.[29] To mention only one *estradiot*, Michael Marullus, his family was originally from Constantinople but he himself was born in Ancona. A close friend of Lorenzo the Magnificent of Florence, Marullus later became celebrated as a poet of sensitive, lyric Latin verses, some evoking nostalgia for his lost Greek homeland.[30]

Nor were artisans or artists lacking in the Venetian community. The most renowned artist is, of course, El Greco, who, born in Crete, spent some years in the Greek colony before proceeding to Spain.[31] But merchants and their enterprises became, in time, probably the leading element in the colony. Indeed, the most flourishing era for the colony was the immediate post-Renaissance period, that is, after 1600 or 1650, when many of the merchants became wealthy. It was then that as a group or, more often in the Greek fashion, individually, they began to take an increasing interest in the spread of Greek learning to the Greek homeland and to other areas inhabited by Greeks. A Cypriot, Thomas Flanginis, in 1626 took the step of establishing in

Greek church of San Giorgio as it was in the late eighteenth or early nineteenth century. Courtesy of the Biblioteca Marciana, Venice. (See pp. 168-69.)

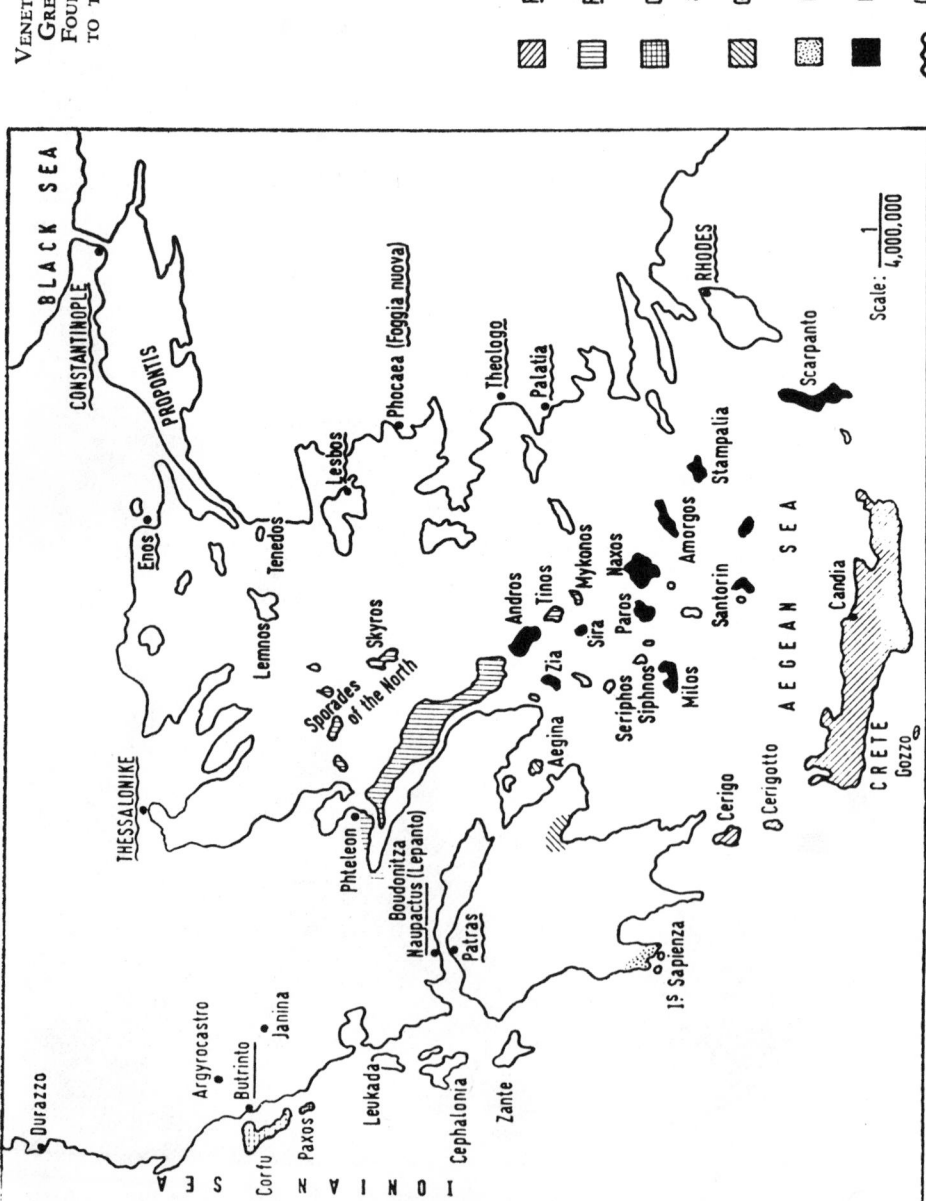

Venetian colonies in the Greek East from the Fourth Crusade (1204) to the Renaissance period. From D. Geanakoplos, *Byzantine East and Latin West* (Oxford: Basil Blackwell, 1966).

VENETIAN COLONIES IN THE GREEK EAST FROM THE FOURTH CRUSADE (1204) TO THE RENAISSANCE

Regno of Candia.

Regno of Negropont.

Government of Corfu and dependencies.

Government of Nauplia.

Coron and Modon.

Protectorates of the Aegean.

(Venetian) trading posts.

The Italian city-states in the Renaissance. From P. MacKendrick, D. Geanakoplos, and J. Hexter, *Western Civilization*, vol. 1, ed. W. Langer (New York: Harper & Row–American Heritage, 1968).

Venice what remained for about two centuries the most famous higher school established by a Greek for Greeks in Europe.[32] This so-called Flangeneion school became, in fact, a kind of nursery for the subsequent establishment of Greek schools in many areas of the Greek East. In the rolls of the Venetian community (often referred to as the "Brotherhood of the Greek Nation") we find records revealing that on many occasions rich Greek merchants would send or bequeath funds for the establishment of schools not only in the Ionian isles, but even more important, during the late seventeenth and eighteenth centuries, on the Greek mainland. These merchants, especially after the fall of Cyprus in 1571, were largely Cypriots and, still later, Greeks from Epirus.[33] To be sure, during this period the policy of the declining Turkish state had for political reasons become less repressive in Greece. But this fact does not diminish the significance of the schools, elementary as most had to be, that were established in Greece as the result of the initiative and generosity of the Greek merchants of Venice.

With Napoleon's conquest of Venice in 1797, the Greek community, along with Venice's own decline and loss of independence, lost a good deal of its former importance and wealth. Its rich library, for example, was destroyed or lost. But by then its work had been accomplished.[34]

THE GREEK COMMUNITY OF NAPLES

Second to Venice in importance was the Greek diaspora community of Naples, whose period of efflorescence was also the sixteenth and seventeenth centuries. In the early Middle Ages, Naples had been a Byzantine possession, but what was to be technically a Greek settlement in a Latinized Naples was not established until 1435. In contrast to the Greek colony of Venice, which was dedicated to peaceful commercial and scholarly pursuits, the history of the Naples colony was, almost from its foundation, largely military and political in character. The Neapolitan Greeks were the first of the Western diaspora colonies to participate in attempts at rebellion in the Greek peninsula and, in fact, in almost every kind of anti-Turkish action organized outside as well as within occupied Greece. As a Spanish possession, the kingdom of Naples shared the Spanish rulers' ambitions in the Balkan peninsula. Moreover, the historical Spanish hostility to the Muslims coincided with Greek hatred for the Turk. Since Naples and Sicily were situated directly across from Greece, the Spanish viceroy from Madrid stationed in Naples had constantly to maintain powerful military forces in order to repulse a possible Turkish naval attack. The numerous Turkish pirates in the Mediterranean were a constant threat as well. In view of these conditions, the Greek inhabitants of Naples sought in large numbers to enroll in the Sicilian navy and cavalry forces. Not only could they vent their hatred against the Turks, but they could thus earn the means to maintain their families and sustain their burgeoning community. Indeed, who knew if some day they might not turn their military experience to the liberation of the Greek mainland?

The interests of the very few historians who have worked on the history of the Neapolitan Greek colony (there as yet exists no fully detailed, systematic study) have primarily focused on the religious conflicts of its church, that of Sts. Peter and Paul, against the claims of local Catholic ecclesiastical authorities. But indications exist in Spanish and Venetian documents that the activities of these Greeks of south Italy and Sicily, from the end of the fifteenth to the late seventeenth century, were much more than religious.[35]

Though commercial activity is often mentioned, the most frequent references relate to a surprising number of attempts at revolt on the Greek mainland. These were usually directed from the Greek community of Naples and involved Greeks working for the Spanish government. In such attempts to foment revolt, members of the Greek colony were used in order to maintain contact with relatives or friends in Greece, something they could do because of their knowledge of Turkish and Greek. In time, a veritable network of agents, spies, and saboteurs was organized, whose activities covered the areas from Constantinople, Negropont, and the Morea, to Cairo and Alexandria.[36]

Greek agents were also valuable to the Spanish government in transmitting information on the position of the Turkish fleet, rebellions of pashas, actions of the Janissaries, and especially Turkish plans for future military action. Though the network of Greek agents involved the eastern Sicilian and Calabrian coastal cities, the meeting place and center of organization was the Greek church of Sts. Peter and Paul in the Greek quarter of Naples. In a Venetian source, this church is revealingly referred to as being located "alla strada delli

greci, populatissima di quella natione e di donne infami napole-
tane"[37] ("on the street of the Greeks, vastly populated by that people
[or "nation"] and by infamous Neapolitan women").

The one who presided over such meetings was ordinarily the priest
of the Greek community,[38] himself usually a graduate of the Greek
College of St. Athanasius in Rome. This college had been founded in
1577 by the papacy, with the specific aim of training young Greeks to
spread the gospel of Rome in the East. Although in some cases this
worked out well for Rome (young Greeks were even imported from the
Balkans or the Venetian-held Greek islands to attend St. Athanasius),
in numerous others the Greeks made use of the education provided to
help their own people.[39] Indeed, whether returning to Greece or
remaining abroad, not a few reverted to the Orthodox faith. All, it
would seem, took pride in the Orthodox ritual, acceptance of which
to many Greeks was now the real "cultural" test of whether one was
a Greek or not. In any event, though more Greeks than is generally
realized accepted papal supremacy, virtually all seemed to maintain
a sense of Greek patriotism and an unceasing desire to see their homeland freed of the Turk.

In the early sixteenth century, the Neapolitan noble Giovanni
Lomellino sent many Greek spies to the Greek mainland to promote
rebellion. In a report he wrote in 1530 to Emperor Charles V
(whose support he sought) he stated that the people of Greece
"stand with open arms ready to aid and that Spain should take
'Romanya.' "[40] Several implications may be drawn from this
phrase: namely, that the Greeks of the Balkans in the early sixteenth
century were not so docile as is usually believed, and that Spain's
sphere of interest in this period extended to the former Byzantine
territories—which are here termed "Romania" in the old Byzantine
style, though it may be noted that the term "Greeks" is also used in
the sense of a separate people or nation.

Especially stirred up by the sending of men, arms, and provisions
directly from or through the instrumentality of the Greek colony of
Naples, were the ever-warlike Epirots, in particular those of Chimara.
The latter we find in revolt at least six times from 1566 to 1596 and,
later, during almost the entire first half of the seventeenth century.
Two Greek agents of the Spanish viceroy, both residents of the Naples
community, were the Corfiot Pietro Longos and the Cypriot-Epirot,
Geronimo Combia. Combia, especially, had connections not only
with Epirus but with Negropont, Constantinople, and, after Cyprus's

fall in 1571, with several Cypriot attempts at revolt.[41] After 1575, we find three hundred Greco-Albanians of Epirus registered in the light cavalry (*estradioti*) of the Neapolitan kingdom. Later, at the end of the sixteenth century, the well-born Cypriot copyist of the Neapolitan community, Giovanni Agiomavros, sought to aid Cyprus in its struggle against Turkey. This fact shows that participation in the colony's revolutionary activities was not limited to those of the political and military professions.[42]

A key date in the opposition of Spain and Western Christendom as a whole to the Turks was the defeat of the Turkish fleet in 1571 at the famous naval battle of Lepanto, fought in Greek waters. Numerous Greeks and Albanians of Naples and Sicily participated on the Christian side.[43] This engagement should occupy a prominent place in the development of the idea of modern Greek independence; for one insufficiently stressed reason for the Turkish defeat was the rebellion, at the crucial moment, of the sultan's numerous Greek rowers, who, seizing the Turkish galleys, joined and fought against their masters alongside the Christian allies. Many of these Greeks, unable to return home after the battle, settled in Naples, where they were compensated by King Philip II with pensions or posts in the Sicilian fleet. Other Greeks, such as Marcos Raftopoulos and Theofilos Venturas, assumed dangerous missions to the Greek East or sought ever more vocally to persuade the Spanish government to support movements on behalf of the Greek liberation. After 1600 the revolutionary activities of the Neapolitan Greeks were intensified since they accorded well with the general policies of the Spanish king, Philip III.[44]

During this period far fewer records exist of Greek intellectuals—professors, printers, editors, and artists—living in the Naples community than in Venice. And yet Greek had been spoken continuously in southern Italy from antiquity. Besides the eleventh-century Byzantine John Italus and the fourteenth-century Byzantine, proto-Renaissance humanists Barlaam and Pilatus,[45] the no less important post-Byzantine humanist, Constantine Lascaris, deserves mention. Lascaris spent the last phase of his life (that is, the late sixteenth century) teaching in Sicilian Messina. He left behind, among other works, a remarkable lament for the fall of Constantinople and a moving description of his own penury in exile.[46] More pertinent, his writings betray the same intense patriotism, even anguished concern, over the loss of his homeland that seems to be found in the works of virtually all Greek scholars of the Renaissance. An oblique expression of his desire to preserve the Greek cultural heritage can be seen in his famous Greek grammar, the *Erotemata*, which is written in typical Byzantine style and, printed in 1476 in Milan, is considered by many to be the first Greek book printed in the West.[47]

The military efforts of the Neapolitan Greek colony and its close relations with the Spanish viceroys evoked a sharp reaction from the sultan, who finally forced the patriarch of Constantinople to excommunicate all those Orthodox who engaged in any conspiratorial contact with the Spaniards of Naples.[48] This might at first glance be taken as another example of the so-called perfidy of the Phanariots. One must not forget, however, that the patriarch was directly under the thumb of the sultan and that not infrequently he issued directives which he expected, or perhaps even hoped, would be ignored by the more distant members of his flock.

The Greek colonization of Spanish Naples and Sicily intensified still more after 1650. Spanish authorities began to organize, in the Kingdom of the Two Sicilies, a military unit called the "Royal Macedonian Regiment," which consisted largely of newly arrived émigrés in Naples from Epirus and later from the Ionian isles, Macedonia, the Cyclades islands, and the Morea. Spanish interests in Greece, especially commercial ones, continued as late as the early nineteenth century. Such activities led to the development of a modern Spanish Philhellenism that is reflected in the literary production of certain Iberian romantic writers, especially Catalan, some of whom, such as de los Casas and the Sevillian Joseph García, even participated in the Greek War of Independence.[49]

As time went on, individual Greeks were offered refuge by the Spanish rulers in Spain itself. That such Greeks engaged in many kinds of activities is shown by the career of the well-known soldier of fortune Pedro de Candia. Cretan-born, he was knighted by the Spanish king for leading the gunners of Pizarro in the conquest of Peru.[50] When the Cretan painter El Greco came to the Spanish capital of Toledo, he lived in or had close contacts with what has been termed a Greek colony, though it was then probably quite small. It now seems clear that he was preceded in Spain by at least two other talented Greek painters, both—like himself—called El Greco (the Greek).[51] And in a recent work it has been shown that he had contacts with the royal scribe and librarian of the Escurial, another Cretan, Nicholas de la Torre.[52] El Greco, too, as is proved by the Greek signature on all his paintings, was proud of his lineage and appeared on several occasions in court to testify on behalf of fellow Greeks seeking to ransom a friend or relative from Turkish captivity in Greece.[53]

The leading post-Byzantine Greek scholar to appear in Spain was the Cretan Demetrius Ducas, who went there at the request of the Spanish cardinal Ximenes, probably in 1513, to edit the Septuagint version of the Old Testament. He was also, as has recently been shown, probably the chief editor of an even more important work, the first published edition of the Greek text of the New Testament. An indication of Ducas' patriotism is his publication at his own expense, just before this, of the very first Greek books in Spain (Greek grammatical tracts and Musaeus' poem, "Hero and Leander"). Later, in Rome, he edited and printed the Orthodox liturgies of Sts. Basil and Chrysostom.[54]

OTHER GREEK COMMUNITIES IN ITALY

Several other Greek communities of western Europe and their activities may be mentioned here. Of the Greek colony at Ancona the most notable representative was the aforementioned Michael Marullus;[55] another was John Gemistos, probably the grandson of the celebrated Gemistos Pletho, and secretary to the government of Ancona.[56] The sizable Greek community of Livorno, situated near Pisa, was founded in the latter part of the eighteenth century, in 1768, thus reversing roles, as it were, with the Pisans who had a colony in medieval Constantinople.[57] The last important colony of the numerous Greek communities founded in Italy was that of Trieste. It flourished in the preceding years, and its history is closely connected with the Greek Revolution.

Other cities of Italy, notably Renaissance Florence, Siena, and Rome, certainly included among their citizenry a number of Greeks; but reliable evidence about them is difficult to find. Moreover, it is doubtful whether they were ever formally organized or sufficiently numerous to be termed "communities."[58]

Given the difficulty of fomenting successful revolt in Greece itself, one may well ask whether any of the diaspora colonies ever conceived the idea of establishing a Greek nation or state in exile. Such a remarkable though logical phenomenon did in fact occur in the late fifteenth century in connection with Siena and Venice. At this time the wealthy émigré to Venice, Anna Notaras, daughter of the last Byzantine grand duke (in effect prime minister), made appeal to the Sienese government for the establishment of what she termed "a new Greek nation," to be located in the Tuscan Maremma area of Siena.[59] The project was apparently unsuccessful and we have no evidence of further developments. (The Maremma was an infertile and rather marshy area.) Nonetheless, the significance of this plan, however small, should not be minimized; for it suggests that hidden away in the archives may perhaps be found other evidence to reinforce the theory that, long before 1821, educated Greeks of the far-flung diaspora had already envisioned the founding of a new Greek state, even if outside the Balkan peninsula.

In this regard, a perusal of the many and sometimes eloquent appeals of Greek scholars to Western rulers may indicate (as a few do) that their authors were actuated, not only by a desire to see their Balkan compatriots emerge to freedom, but, by implication, to establish if necessary a new Greek nation, at least temporarily.[60] In any event, to arrive at solid historical conclusions such writings must be studied more systematically and in comparative fashion. In the case of Anna, the fact that she was the daughter of a Byzantine official must not induce one to assume automatically that her proposed state was intended as a successor to Byzantium. Even if such were the case, she no doubt had in mind, rather, the example of the extremely diminished Byzantine Empire in its last century or so of existence when it had become a purely Greek state, though the fiction of "Rome" was maintained virtually until the end in Byzantine court circles. Moreover, Anna herself, having lived for some time in Venice, was by now (ca. 1470) influenced by Western political conceptions. We know that she was a devotee of Bessarion who, as is clear from one of his letters, had himself been deeply influenced by Western politics, technology, and socio-economic ideas.[61]

Besides the well-known proposals of Bessarion shortly before 1453 for reform of the Byzantine state on the basis of Western models, we may cite a more radical plan, put forth in the same years and derived essentially from Platonic ideas. This plan came from the pen of the Byzantine philosopher Gemistos Pletho.[62] Pletho had been in Florence at the time of the great church council (1438–39), had lectured to the Florentine humanists on Plato, and was well acquainted with ancient political writers such as Isocrates and Aelius Aristides. His interest in Western as well as Greek political ideas is proved by a copy (now in Milan) of Leonardo Bruni's autograph of his famous Constitution of Florence, on which are inserted comments written in Pletho's own hand.[63] One scholar believes that Pletho had in mind not a utopian regeneration of Byzantium but the creation of a new form of state, to be located in the Morea and to be imbued with much of the political and cultural ideology of Plato. A prime ideal in its fromation was to be the use of the term "Hellene" (Greek) to refer to its people rather than "Byzantine" (Roman), and, though some scholars do not accept this, it seems also to have entailed disestablishment of the Christian religion.[64]

Pletho's plan, with its emphasis on the political example of the ancient Greeks, has been termed a key manifestation of Neo-Hellenism by some modern scholars. They also believe, however, that this development of a "national consciousness" in the last century of the Palaeologan period was, on the Greek mainland, cut off abruptly by Constantinople's fall in 1453 and the conquest of the Morea in 1460. Though the impetus for this sense of Greek "national consciousness" was, in fact, lost on the Greek mainland, it is the thesis of this chapter that it was able to continue uninterruptedly and to undergo even further development among the Greek communities of the diaspora.[65]

NORTHERN EUROPE

In northern Europe, Greek communities were also established, especially in the later Renaissance and afterward. But one may say in general that the farther away from Constantinople and the East the émigrés traveled, the less numerous and more isolated their groups or settlements tended to become. Thus France, more distant and with fewer political and commercial connections with Greece, received fewer émigrés. In the sixteenth century, the nucleus of a Greek colony seems to have existed in Lyons, at which time silk-workers were settled, apparently to establish a silk industry in competition with the Italians.[66] As might be expected, Greeks also appear relatively early in the French capital, Paris. With the beginnings of interest in Greek studies in France in the later fifteenth and sixteenth centuries, one finds a number of Greek savants in the French capital.

Best known of these scholars are: Janus Lascaris, who became envoy of the French king to Venice; also George Hermonymus, who was a capable copyist of texts despite Erasmus's and Budé's denigration of his abilities; further, the expert calligrapher Angelos Vergikios, official scribe to the French king, whose first name is supposed to have inspired the coinage of the phrase "to write like an angel"; and Antonios Eparchos, who presented a number of Greek manuscripts to King Francis I, which were to constitute the nucleus for the royal library at Fontainebleau and later for the famous Greek collection in the Bibliothèque Nationale.[67] At least one Greek achieved a high post in the French military service, Bissypat, who has been mentioned in connection with Columbus, thus helping to give rise to the very curious myth of Columbus's supposed Byzantine ancestry. Bissypat was apparently descended from the aristocratic Byzantine family of Disypatos, of which the name Bissypat is supposedly a Western corruption.[68]

From the time of Theodore of Tarsus, first archbishop of Canterbury in the seventh century, a number of Byzantine visitors came off and on to distant England. In the twelfth century an account was written about England by a Greek, or half-Greek, with the curious name of Fitzstephen.[69] In the mid-fourteenth century, the Cretan Franciscan Petrus Philarges studied at Oxford, and at the very end of the same century the Byzantine emperor Manuel II and his entourage came to England, seeking aid against the Turks.[70] Then in the fifteenth and sixteenth centuries, during the English Renaissance, several Byzantine humanists, such as Andronicos Callistos and Hermonymos, appeared in London to teach Greek.[71] In the seventeenth century an annual bursary scholarship was established at Oxford for a student to be brought from Greece.[72] Despite these evidences of the presence of learned Greeks in England, the existence of a colony of Greeks in London before the late seventeenth or, more probably, the eighteenth century may be questioned. Still, documents found in the Cretan section of the Venetian archives, relating to transactions for the export of wines and cloth between Crete and England, attest to the possibility of more such emigration than is realized.[73] Certainly by the time of the Greek Revolution the Greek colony in London was well established.

Small groups of Greeks also appeared in Germany in the late fifteenth and sixteenth centuries. The names of Greek scribes, for example one Michael Markokephalites, appear on documents associated with the Council of Trent—scribes in the service of the learned Spanish Hellenist Mendoza. At the end of these documents, the copyists have frequently written "done by the hand of such and such."[74] The close and protracted connections between the Reformation figure Melanchthon and, more important, the Hellenist Martinus Crusius of Tübingen University on the one hand, and the partiarchal court of Constantinople in the mid-sixteenth and seventeenth centuries on the other, are well known. Crusius, who was interested not only in ancient but in Byzantine ecclesiastical texts, even visited Greece and as a result composed his famous *Turcograecia*.[75] These texts for a short time apparently produced a few ripples of unrest in Germany over the plight of the enslaved Greeks. Nor must we overlook as being outside our theme the relations of the celebrated seventeenth-century Greek patriarch of Constantinople, Cyril Lukaris, with the Calvinists. For through his many contacts with the West, his study at the Venetian University of Padua, his appearance at the Council of Brest in 1596, and his many exchanges with Protestant intellectuals, Cyril came to the realization that education was the best means of uplifting the spirits of his people and ultimately leading them to freedom.[76] In this he shared the sentiments of the Western diaspora Greeks who, however, had the advantage of working apart from the stultifying atmosphere of Turkish Constantinople. Whether or not Cyril was a real Calvinist, there is no doubt that he was, in his own way, a true patriot, and that through advancement of Greek learning—it was he who established the first Greek press in the East—he envisioned the improvement of the lot of his people.

Other examples, such as the wide connections with many European intellectuals of the sixteenth-century bishop living in the Venetian community, Maximos Margounios,[78] could be cited. But these are enough to show that the Greeks of the western European diaspora, after the fifteenth century, were becoming more numerous, richer, and better organized. They still lamented the plight of their compatriots in the homeland, but now, gradually, they began more actively to do what they could to promote education not only abroad but, more particularly, in Greece itself.

THE GREEK REVOLUTION AND THE DIASPORA

With the outbreak of the French Revolution, itself preceded by the intellectual movement of the eighteenth-century *philosophes*, scholars seem to agree that a new phase began to emerge in the history of modern Greece. It was, according to this view, these secular French ideas of liberty, equality, and fraternity which, together with the expansion of a nascent middle class, primarily inspired the Greeks and ultimately brought the homeland to revolution. Especially instrumental in this respect were, it is affirmed, the newer Greek colonies in Odessa, Vienna, and Paris, which became the centers of the secret *Philike Hetaireia*.[79] The importance of these considerations should not be underestimated. Yet one should point out that without the vital link provided for so long by the Greek diaspora colonies established earlier in the West, these later factors might not have exerted the influence they did. Because of the increasing ignorance and almost total lack of schools in Greece proper until the mid-seventeenth century, the Hellenic classical tradition in Greece (with very few exceptions) was growing weaker and weaker.[80] The Phanariots of Constantinople, especially in the Patriarchal School that continued to exist after the fall of Constantinople, stressed the Christian Byzantine tradition far more than the classical political ideology.[81] Thus it was that the diaspora centers, especially Venice and Naples, served to perpetuate the ancient tradition and were its chief—indeed almost sole—effective bearers.

But why, then, did no successful revolt against the Turks take place from the diaspora areas? The fact is that these colonies, however wealthy and educated, were few in number and separated by too great distances to undertake joint effective action against the powerful Turk. The territorial contiguity that would have provided a greater sense of cohesion and strength was lacking. Nor were they always, one suspects, free of rivalry, as was the case with Naples and Venice. True, they were imbued with the same ideas, especially the feeling of being legatees of the ancient culture, and they almost invariably paid at least lip service to the patriarch in Constantinople.[82] The political cohesion of each colony was, moreover, enhanced by the erection and maintenance of a church building. But one should not forget, finally, that the communities were under the surveillance of their host city. And that host, however tolerant, after the reactionary triumph of the Holy League in 1815, could not permit any seditious or revolutionary conduct on the part of its subjects, especially foreigners.

In the last analysis, the revolution had to come from the homeland itself, from the Greek peninsula, less likely from Constantinople, and least likely from the weaker Greeks of Asia Minor. As noted, the Phanariots of Constantinople and Asia Minor, though usually well educated, were engrossed in their own schemes and loath to risk danger to their exposed position. Arnold Toynbee somewhere suggests that, had the Greek Revolution not occurred when it did, in a matter of decades the Phanariots might have taken over the entire Ottoman administration from within.[83] And who knows, then, what kind of Greek nation or possibly even hybrid Greco-Turkish union (as some Greeks envisioned) might have resulted? Accordingly, it was among the long-suffering, simpler, and more numerous Greeks of the mainland that the revolution began. And yet this movement was not nearly so abrupt as has been portrayed; the way had been paved by the earlier diaspora colonies. Not only did they preserve the vital sense of national identity through emphasis on a historical continuity from the time of the ancient Greeks, but they managed effectively to disseminate education about the ancient past to the populace of the mainland.

That the Greeks of the homeland, from sometime in the fifteenth century to almost the last part of the seventeenth, had fallen into almost total cultural darkness, has already been emphasized.[84] Kakrides and other modern Greek scholars maintain that as late even as the eighteenth century the vast majority of those living in Greece still did not appreciate the ancient cultural inheritance, though they always clung to the Orthodox faith. They had a vague feeling, to be sure, that they were somehow connected with the ancient inhabitants of Greece, but they tended to view them as supermen, giants of physique as well as intellect.[85] Actually, these Greeks of the seventeenth and eighteenth centuries were groping for some means of identification with the ancients. The folklore of the period reveals that many in fact were unclear as to how to refer to themselves, a few combining the terms "Greek" and "Roman" ("Byzantine") in the hybrid term "Romeoellenes."[86] At least in some areas of the mainland, then, the Greeks lacked a consistent ideology—a quality important for the emergence of a true sense of nationhood.

The catalytic agent most responsible for producing, finally, a clear sense of the past on the mainland was, I believe, the educational work of the more historically aware Greeks of the diaspora. What the diaspora Greeks, and especially those of Venice, were able to do for the Greeks of the homeland was to juxtapose, or perhaps better to superimpose, the classical tradition of antiquity onto the Christian tradition of Byzantium and thus to recover for the Greeks of the continent a sense of the *entire* history of their past. When this happened, the ground was truly prepared for the late eighteenth-century French revolutionary ideologies which, in turn, were able to bring about the birth of modern Greek nationalism.

The clearest manifestation of the dissemination of this Greek cultural tradition is the work of the diaspora colonies in education. For the disastrous period of the sixteenth century, when Greek civilization almost entirely collapsed on the mainland, Paparego-poulos, the national historian of Greece, has been able to find the names of only some 230 Greeks who might be called "scholars," or who at least possessed more than a rudimentary learning. But of this number, it should be noted, more than 170 were from the Greek community of Venice and its possessions in the Greek East, from Italy, or from elsewhere in the West. Of the remaining sixty who came from the Turkish-occupied area which today constitutes Greece, about forty-five are referred to in the documents simply as "educated clerics and monks," no other evidence about them having survived. The remaining fifteen with two exceptions, Theodosios Zygomalas and Nicholas Malaxos, are known only for their interest in liturgical and religious matters.[87] Through the munificence of the Venetian Greeks, Paparegopoulos affirms, there were subsequently established, in the seventeenth and eighteenth centuries, schools in Italy and, most significant, in Greece itself, such as those at Athens, Patras, Patmos, still later in Thessaly and Macedonia, but above all at Ioannina in Epirus.[88]

Regarding the role of the diaspora communities in education, the highest praise belongs to Venice, from which radiated the inspiration that saw the foundation of schools for the first time in centuries in many areas of Greece. As noted, the center of the Venetian community's educational activities was the Flangeneion school[89] and, specifically for higher studies, the University of Padua, which, in the sixteenth and seventeenth centuries, became in effect *the* university of the diaspora. (Patriarchs Cyril Lukaris and Meletios Pigas, among others, studied there.)[90]

Had the diaspora colonies remained insulated from contact with the Balkan peninsula, their influence might well have produced no important results for the emergence of an independent Greece. But because of its educational contribution, the diaspora helped to revive or, as some would say, to create a *new* national consciousness. In a basic sense, however, it was not new at all. For, as we have tried to show, the neo-Hellenism characteristic of the Greek state of 1821 had already appeared in the last century or so of Byzantium's life; but instead of disappearing, this sense of nationality or ethnic individuation was preserved and in some ways developed further by the diaspora Greeks. Thus Veludes'and Paparegopoulos' remarks that the Greek community of Venice, through its work of education, constituted the seedbed of modern Greece,[91] are to a considerable extent justified. Although it would be too strong to say that without the work of the diaspora the Greek Revolution would not have occurred, one may state with conviction that it would very probably have taken place later than it did.

It is my view, and I believe this point has escaped the notice of scholars of modern nationalism, that one of the factors that rendered the Greek Revolution unique, that made it the earliest to take place effectively in the nineteenth century, was precisely the educational preparation for nationhood provided by the diaspora communities. This was characteristic, it would seem, of no other European people then aspiring to national liberation (one might recall in this respect the only recently founded state of Israel). Thus the words of Kolokotrones, quoted at the start of this chapter, with their emphasis on the educational significance of the diaspora Greek scholars, seem, in the light of the material presented, to bear out the prophetic words of Bessarion linking together Hellenic education and a sense of nationhood. The apparently sudden emergence of a new Greek nation in 1821 can thus be explained not only by the persistence of the Christian Orthodox tradition, by the ideological influences of the Enlightenment and the French Revolution, and by internal conditions in the Balkans resulting from the Turkish Empire's decline, but, no less important, by the contribution of the Greeks of the diaspora, who for almost four centuries *were* the Greek nation in exile.[92]

10

Crete: Halfway Point between East and West
in the Renaissance

Not too long ago scholars naïvely believed that one, perhaps even the basic, cause of the Italian Renaissance was the revival of Greek learning resulting from the influx to the West of Byzantine refugee scholars fleeing the Turkish conquest of Constantinople in 1453. However, the great advances made in Renaissance studies have shown conclusively that, not only must the date for the appearance of the Renaissance's principal intellectual factor—humanism—be pushed back long before 1453, but that at its inception the humanist movement was essentially of Latin rather than Greek inspiration. Nonetheless, despite these qualifications, it may plausibly be affirmed that, insofar as the cultural development of the Renaissance is concerned, the factor which more than any other served to widen its intellectual horizon was the reception and increasing use by the humanists of original texts of new or unknown works of Greek antiquity, especially those of literary and philosophic content. Now this learning, hitherto largely lacking in the West, could have come from only one place, its repository for one thousand years, the Byzantine East, particularly from its capital city of Constantinople and from Thessalonika, and to a certain extent from southern Italy, where up to at least the sixteenth century some Greek texts and a knowledge of Greek were preserved.

But what was the avenue or avenues for the transmission of this Greek heritage? It is still generally accepted as true, though we must certainly deemphasize the importance of the Greek refugees for the *origins* of Italian humanism, that most of the Greek literary works, the Platonic corpus, and even certain writings of Aristotle did come to the West in this manner, though during the period extending before, as well as after, 1453.

As we examine this broad flow of Greeks moving westward, a veritable diaspora, we see that it tends to follow certain lines, to form a kind of pattern. And it is this pattern of transmission from East to West, or rather one neglected aspect of it, that will be my focus of attention here. Aside from a few preliminary Greek figures (almost always overlooked by Renaissance historians) like the Cretan Peter Philarges, who came in 1357 to Padua to study and then later was actually elected pope as Alexander V,[1] and Simon Autumano, who briefly taught Greek in Florence (1380–81),[2] the emigration of Greek scholars to the West tended to concentrate at three important centers. The first and best known of these was the Florence of the Medici. There the formal beginning of this period of Florentine primacy in Greek studies is accredited to one Greek, the nobleman Manuel Chrysoloras.

Originally dispatched to the West by the Byzantine emperor in order to seek military and political aid against the Turks for beleaguered Constantinople, in 1396–97 Chrysoloras was invited by the Florentine government to teach Greek at its *studium*. As the Italian humanist Leonardo Bruni put it, a little exaggeratedly though more or less correctly, this was the first time in seven hundred years that the Greek language had been taught in the West—that is, since the time of the Germanic invasions! And in actual fact the systematic study of Greek language and literature during the Renaissance may be said to begin at this time. Indeed, because of the large number of students he taught, who in turn became devotees of Greek learning, Chrysoloras succeeded in making Florence, from 1396 to about 1490 or so, the first great center for Greek studies in western Europe.[3]

A second important area for Greek study developed a little later, in the mid-fifteenth century in Rome, in part concurrent with the establishment there of the Greek cardinal Bessarion after the abortive Council of Florence and his appointment as chief minister to the pope. Under the patronage of the learned Bessarion, there soon gathered in the papal curia an entire circle of Greek and also some Latin scholars, including George of Trebizond, all of whom were interested in the furtherance of Greek studies.[4] They made some rather important translations from Greek into Latin. These two phases of the development and transmission of Greek learning in the West, in Florence and Rome, are of course well known. But there is a third phase which follows and which, in certain ways, is more important than either of the other two for the dissemination of Greek learning throughout the West in general. This period, extending from the last decade of the fifteenth century through the first half or so of the sixteenth, is connected with the city of Venice. During that time Venice took over the primacy from Florence to become the leading center in all Europe not only for Greek studies but for intellectual activity in general.[5]

As I have shown elsewhere, one important factor in this development, hitherto neglected by Western historians, was the existence in Venice of a large, thriving Greek colony. And from its population, such scholars as the great Italian printer of Greek, Aldus Manutius, a prime mover in this Venetian period, could draw to secure the skilled labor so necessary for the collation of Greek texts and their editing for the press.[6] Not that all the inhabitants of the Greek community were learned or that all Greek émigré scholars actually lived within the confines of this colony. The community was nevertheless a magnet that attracted most Greeks, especially cultured ones, to Venice. They termed it, in fact, their second homeland, and frequently they visited friends or relatives there. Some of them taught in the school established by the now formally organized Greek community, in the nearby chancery of Venice, or perhaps even at the famous University of Padua, which in 1405 had become the possession of Venice.

Despite this rather lengthy introduction, it is not my purpose here to delineate the history of the Greek colony of Venice, which I have tried to do in some detail in the previous chapter. Rather, I want to discuss the significance, in the process of the dissemination of Greek letters from East to West and especially from Venice to the rest of the West, of an area insufficiently studied in this connection: the island of Crete. Today the study of the archaeology of ancient Crete is attracting much attention; and historians of modern Greece are increasingly aware of the part played by Crete in the emergence of the modern Greek nation. But how many scholars are cognizant of the astonishing number of intellectuals and painters produced by that Aegean island in the period from about 1400 to 1600? From that small barren island literally scores of boys or young men went forth who were later to play a significant role in the diffusion of Greek letters. Along with its choice oils and wines, which were justly famous, Crete exported scholars and even painters (El Greco, to name only one) who held positions of influence in the world of letters and art, in areas extending all the way from Spain eastward to Russia.

Contrary to what is usually believed, Crete was not altogether barren intellectually in the early fifteenth century, some degree of culture having remained from the Byzantine and Venetian periods. But its emergence to genuine importance begins with the emigration to the island of many Byzantine intellectuals fleeing the Ottoman occupation of Constantinople. At that time, indeed since 1204, Crete had been under Venetian domination, and it was to remain so until 1669. Hence it was, and this is a very important point, the only substantial Greek-speaking area not as yet to fall under the yoke of the Turks. But the narrow environment of Crete, which lacked institutions of higher learning and possessed little wealth, offered little opportunity to ambitious men of letters who might seek professional recognition, say, by occupying a university chair. Thus, after a residence of some length on the island (where some of them might study at the *scriptorium* newly established at Candia by Constantinople-born Michael Apostolis), many intellectuals, either born in Constantinople or in Crete itself, began to look elsewhere for employment. And quite naturally their gaze fell upon Venice, the master of the island and at this time, perhaps, Europe's richest city. Soon after 1453, therefore, we see numerous Cretans moving to and establishing themselves in the city of the lagoons, often settling in the Greek quarter located only a few hundred yards from St. Mark's Basilica itself.[7]

At this point I shall discuss this movement by concentrating on the careers and activities in Venice of some of the more important of these Cretans—men of letters whose work made Crete, in the transmission of Greek learning, a kind of halfway point between the old, perishing Byzantine world and the rising Italian centers of humanistic endeavor.

What offered many opportunities to the skilled Hellenist was the developing Venetian interest in Greek literature, itself fostered by the humanistic ideals of Florence and nearby Padua, and now especially furthered by the demands of the newly established Greek press. In Venice a Hellenist could work either as a scribe for a wealthy patron, as a teacher in a Venetian school, at the nearby University of Padua, or, finally and most commonly, as a typesetter or editor in one of Venice's numerous Greek presses. The most famous of all was the workshop of Aldus Manutius. But there also existed a number of Cretan presses, which have hitherto attracted little attention.

In the history of printing it was a Cretan of Latin parentage, Demetrius Damilas, who in 1476 at Milan printed what scholars have usually considered to be the first entirely Greek book published in Europe, the *Erotemata* of the Byzantine Constantine Lascaris. Not long afterwards, in 1486 in Venice, the Greek Cretans Laonikos and Alexander produced what I take to be Venice's first Greek books, the *Psalter* and Homer's *Batrachomyomachia*.[8] It should be observed that these appeared almost a decade before the first production of the great Italian printer, Aldus Manutius, to whom Western scholars have usually awarded the credit for initiating the work of the Venetian Greek press. It is very possible, indeed, and this is my own view, that Aldus's aim of printing for the first time all the major Greek classical works was anticipated by the Cretan printer, Zacharias Calliergis.

Calliergis was, like his fellow-countrymen, a patriotic Greek, as is shown by the fact that his first book, the *Etymologicum magnum* (the greatest of all Byzantine dictionaries), was produced in imitation of Byzantine manuscripts, utilizing as his printer's marks the Byzantine double-headed eagle and manuscript ornamentation. Calliergis employed on his staff only Cretan compatriots. But though his works were of the finest execution, often surpassing in quality even those of Aldus, Calliergis went out of business, evidently for financial reasons;[9] whereupon, it should be noted, his workmen were hired en masse by his friend and rival Aldus. This did not end Calliergis' career, incidentally, for he is later to be found working in Rome, where he was attracted by the promotion of humanistic learning on the part of the Medici pope, Leo X. There in the papal capital he established the first Greek press, printing among other things a valuable edition of Pindar, Theocritus, Greek liturgical works, and others. The Calliergian edition of Pindar, because of its important scholia, was more significant than the earlier Aldine *editio princeps*.[10]

The career of the great Aldus is, of course, too well known to require discussion here in any detail. Suffice it to point out that in his so-called Aldine Academy of thirty-six members, more than a dozen were Greek-born, most of whom were Cretans employed by him. Of his many collaborators, Aldus, in his own words, prized above all the aid of Marcus Musurus. This Cretan, as earlier noted, edited for Aldus no less than eleven or twelve first editions of the ancient Greek masterpieces—including the works of Plato, Aristophanes, Hesychius, and others. Musurus had gone to Florence from his native island as a young man. There he had studied Greek literature, primarily with the famous Byzantine teacher Janus Lascaris.[11]

Musurus' knowledge of Greek was phenomenal, as is clearly attested in the text of his many editions, some emendations of which, either intuitive or based on older Palaeologan, Byzantine tradition, especially of his predecessors Demetrios Triklinios and Manuel Moschopoulos of the fourteenth century, are still accepted by scholars.[12] Especially unique was his knowledge of the difficult meter of ancient Greek lyric poetry and tragedy, which was quantitative rather than qualitative, as in modern western European languages.[13] His famous edition of Plato's *Dialogues* (which, by the way, was at least as important as Marsilio Ficino's translation of the Platonic corpus into Latin) contains as a preamble a poem addressed to his patron, Pope Leo X. In this, Musurus apostrophizes Plato and pleads to the pope for the liberation of his forebear's ancient homeland of Constantinople from the Turks. (Compare this plea with that in the Byzantine Chalcondyles' address, chap. 13 below.) Although the content of the poem is not too interesting to us, the remarkable polish and elegance, the sheer technical skill of composition, which utilizes the almost forgotten quantitative meter of the ancient Greeks, is such that it may be ranked as the finest Greek poem to have been composed since the time of the ancient world.[14]

However important his editing work for Aldus, no less significant in disseminating Greek learning was Musurus' career as professor of Greek at the University of Padua and subsequently in Venice itself. Around him gathered a very large number of students, potential humanists we might say, who assembled from all areas of western Europe to hear his lectures. When these men returned to their homelands, they carried back with them the inspiration and knowledge received from Musurus. His period of instruction of Greek in Venice —where he taught, among other things, the Greek tragedies and lyric poetry as well as Aristotle's *Poetics* (a fact that has been little noted)[15] —constitutes an important landmark in the development of Western Greek studies, a landmark comparable perhaps only to the success achieved by Chrysoloras the century before in Florence.

Let me enumerate a few of Musurus' students, all names well known in the development of Renaissance learning: Lazzaro Bonamico, Raffael Reggio, Girolamo Aleandro, who later helped to inaugurate Greek teaching in Paris, John Conon, possibly the true founder of Greek studies in Germany, Germain de Brie and Jean de Pins of France, Janus Vertessy from Hungary, Gelenius from Prague who later went to Basle, and many others.[16] Best known of all is the great Erasmus, who tells us himself that he heard Musurus' lectures. (He called Musurus "very skilled in both Greek and Latin.") On

intimate terms with Musurus, Erasmus borrowed rare or still unknown Greek manuscripts from his library,[17] including works of
Plato, Plutarch, Hermogenes,[18] Aristotle's *Rhetoric*, and the valuable
scholia on Homer of Eustathius of Thessalonika (so vital for the manuscript tradition of Homer), as well as the large collection of ancient
Greek and Byzantine sayings compiled by the Cretan Michael
Apostolis. The latter collection was secured by Erasmus from Michael's son, the Cretan humanist Arsenios Apostolis, who also lived in
Venice at this time and was associated with the Aldine circle.[19]

As shown elsewhere, much of this new material Erasmus incorporated into the famous Aldine edition of his celebrated *Adages*. It
was this work, critics agree, that was primarily responsible for bringing him his reputation as Europe's leading scholar. Erasmus is generally regarded by historians as the chief link between the Italian and
Northern phases of the movement of the Renaissance. But scholars
often fail to realize to what extent his work in Greek scholarship
(which to him was much more important than Latin), was indebted
to personal contacts with his Cretan friends in Venice, especially with
Musurus, for whom he had a great regard and affection.

Musurus is certainly the most important Cretan scholar to appear
in the West. Indeed, it is my impression that he was probably the
Hellenist with the widest and most perfect knowledge of Greek
language and literature to appear during the entire period of the
Western Renaissance.[20] Musurus died in 1515 but other, though less
talented, Cretans took up his work in Venice. The emigration of
Cretans to Venice, in fact, continued throughout the entire sixteenth
and even early seventeenth centuries. One might mention here, at
the end of the sixteenth, still another scholar, able but again little
known to Western historians, Maximos Margounios. Margounios
was a Cretan bishop-humanist residing in the Greek colony in
Venice, who not only sponsored a new approach with regard to
union of the Greek and Latin churches, but wrote poetry and published first editions of Greek or Byzantine texts, such as that of John
Chrysostom. He also had many contacts by way of correspondence
with a large number of Western humanists in England, France,
Italy, and especially those in Tübingen, Germany, including Martin
Crusius.[21]

As more and more specialists in Greek appeared in Venice from
the East and as Latin Hellenists, too, became better trained by these
same Greeks, what may be termed a surplus of Hellenists developed

in Venice. Hence, many now decided to emigrate to the culturally undeveloped areas of the North. There, especially in France and Spain, Greek printing had not yet made its appearance, or was just on the point of doing so. So, Cretans, one by one or in small groups, gradually made their way northward to find employment and new outlets for their talents. Usually, however, they would first pass through Venice, that funnel, one might say, for the passage of Greeks coming from the East.

One of the first Cretan intellectuals to appear in Spain was Demetrius Ducas. Summoned to Spain around 1513 by Cardinal Ximenes from the Aldine Academy to teach Greek for the first time at that prelate's new University of Alcalá, Ducas was also called upon to participate in Ximenes' great project, the editing for the press of the famous Complutensian Polyglot Bible. Meanwhile, Ducas on his own published the first two Greek books to appear in Spain.[22] Moreover, he not only edited (as is well known) the Septuagint Greek text of the Old Testament for Ximenes but was probably (as is still little known) the chief editor for the Greek text of the much more important New Testament. This latter point I have tried to show primarily on the basis of a comparison of the Greek and Latin introductions to the Greek text.[23] Believing the Greek an exact equivalent of the Latin, scholars have hitherto read only the Latin introduction and neglected the Greek. But the Greek contains some significant phrases omitted from or altered in the Latin text. Where the Latin (both introductions are written by the editor or editors) records "it seems to us," the Greek reads "it seems to me." The Greek text also contains a reference to certain "ancient inscriptions on stones in Constantinople," which most probably only a Greek like Ducas, and not his Spanish collaborators, could have seen or even known about. Moreover, it is most interesting that of the five epigrams placed at the end of the introduction by the editors, that of Ducas precedes those of the others. Finally, the nuances of style reflected in the introduction would induce one to believe that only a person highly skilled in Greek, like Ducas, could have composed it. All of which considerations lead to the conclusion that Ducas was probably primarily responsible for the edition of the basic Greek text of the Complutensian New Testament.[24]

The name of Ducas has been long confused by scholars with those of at least two other Demetrioi; indeed, one important Spanish scholar, who makes only a brief reference to his teaching at Alcalá, calls him Lucas! Hence no biography was written about him until the main facts of his career were established. The last mention I could find of him was as "publicus professor" of Greek in 1526–27, in the papal University of Rome, and as editor of several Greek liturgical works, including those of Sts. Chrysostom and Basil.[25] It is interesting to observe that, like others of his Cretan compatriots, Ducas, too, was interested in publishing Byzantine liturgical works. This phenomenon, the publication by Greek scholars in the West of Greek liturgical works, is a phase of the Renaissance that needs investigation. Ducas' contributions in particular have been almost entirely ignored by modern scholars, except for brief mentions of him in Legrand's *Bibliographie Hellénique*.[26]

Other Cretans followed the pioneer efforts of Ducas in Spain, including several Greek painters, all of whom were simply known as "Greco," the Greek. The climax came in the person of the great El Greco of Toledo, who was born Domenicos Theotocopoulos at or near the Cretan town of Candia, today called Herakleion. El Greco's career is well known and there is no space here to delineate it again in detail. Suffice it to emphasize a few little-known or completely unknown points: that he was preceded in Spain by several other Greek painters (for example, in Barcelona); that there already existed a Greek colony in Toledo before his arrival; and that (as recent scholarship has shown) El Greco's technique of painting was probably largely formed before he went to Spain and even before he went to Venice.[27] A recently discovered notarial document signed by "Menegos Theotokopoulos" (*Menegos* is the Greek diminutive for *Domenikos*), "Maestro" of painting, shows that he was evidently still living in Candia, the capital city of Crete, in his twenty-fifth year and had achieved the title of "Maestro."[28] Hence the common belief that he went to Venice to learn painting at the early, still very immature age of eighteen must be discarded, and we should probably instead believe that he had already acquired a good deal of his remarkable technique of painting on Crete, which was still under Byzantine and Venetian cultural influences. Thus the view must be abandoned that all or most of El Greco's technique and style was acquired after he emigrated to Venice and Spain. This new view is reinforced when we observe certain striking similarities in paintings of the so-called Macedonian and Metropolitan schools on the one hand, and in certain works of El Greco himself[29] (see above, pp. 20, 31, and esp. 90). But let us return now to the sphere of letters.

In France the first appearance of Cretan émigrés can probably be connected with the rising French interest in humanistic studies at the end of the fifteenth century. We have already mentioned the isolated, anticipatory case of the Cretan, Petros Philarges, who in 1357, at the age of seventeen, became a Franciscan. (St. Francis, by the way, is the only Latin saint to be venerated by Greeks, specifically on the island of Crete.) He then went to study in Padua, and later became an important professor of Scholasticism at the University of Paris.[30] Finally, he was elected pope at the Council of Pisa (1409), the only Greek since the early medieval period to attain this supreme ecclesiastical post, though in the fifteenth century the great Greek cardinal Bessarion missed election to the papal throne twice only by the narrowest of margins.

Also in the fifteenth century, a Cretan printer named John Kres appeared in Brittany and set up a press. But Greeks, and especially Cretans, did not go in greater numbers to Paris until the noble Byzantine, Janus Lascaris, had firmly established Greek studies there. He had gone to Paris after the French invasion of Italy in 1494.[31] In 1535 the post of librarian of the French Royal Library at Fontainebleau was awarded to the Cretan Angelos Vergikios. Vergikios, the most important Cretan to appear in France, had first settled in Venice, and came to Paris possibly at the invitation of the French ambassador to Venice, Jean de Pins. Rising steadily in his profession of scribe, Vergikios was finally appointed *écrivain ordinaire* (official scribe) to the king himself. Besides this, he taught to supplement his income. As noted earlier, he copied many important manuscripts in a hand so beautiful that the words "to write like an angel" are supposed (though probably wrongly) to apply to him. Some modern scholars believe that the original letters cut for the royal Greek press in France by Garamont and then by Henry Stephanus were modeled on the handwriting of Vergikios.[32] (Similarly, it was formerly believed that the Aldine "Italic" script was modeled on the calligraphy of Musurus.) Other Cretans worked with Angelos in Paris, including his son Nicholas, who had been born in Crete. Nicholas knew French so well that he could write competent French poetry and mingled with the famous literary group called the Pléiade.

England, too, had its share of Greek refugees, George Hermonymos, Andronicos Callistos, John Servopoulos—though it is difficult in every case to establish who was born a Cretan.[33] There is evidence,

in any event, of considerable trading activity between England and
Crete in this period, not only in wines and oils but in other products,
such as cloth.[34] And there is little doubt that a scholar or two must
have followed in the wake of this commercial activity.

In Germany there are also traces of Cretans, especially of copyists
like John Episkopopoulos and certain printers of Greek who appeared at the Council of Trent.[35] There are records, too, of Cretans
who went to the Slavic areas farther eastward, including Russia,
the Ukraine, Poland, and the Balkans and Turkey. And the Cretan
patriarch of Alexandria, Meletios Pegas, shortly after 1593 wrote to
and urged the Russian tsar Theodore to establish a Greek school and
printing press in Moscow.[36]

One Cretan whose career is so extraordinary that it deserves
treatment at greater length is Franciscus Portus. Though he was
born in Rethymno, Crete, his forebears had originally come from
Vicenza, Italy. He was a nonconformist with a caustic train of
mind. Like other Cretans he gravitated early to Venice, studying
philosophy at the University of Padua and teaching Greek in the
city's Greek colony. But he soon found employment at the famous
Renaissance court of Modena, where he taught Greek. Leaving
Modena, where he was suspected of Protestant sympathies, he
enjoyed a reputable career as professor of Greek at Ferrara. After
wandering for a time in Europe, he finally settled down, in 1561,
in Geneva, Switzerland. There for two decades, in that center of
Calvinism, he taught Greek with great éclat at the municipal
academy. Geneva, in fact, became a notable center of Greek studies,
in large part through his efforts. One of his pupils was the celebrated
philologist Isaac Casaubon, who succeeded him in his Greek chair.
In Geneva many important Greek editions and Latin commentaries
of such authors as Pindar, Apollonius, Sophocles, Xenophon,
Thucydides, Aristotle, Euripides, and Hermogenes, were published
by Portus. (His commentaries on and edition of Homer, by the way,
are especially important and are still of some use today.)[37] There he
enjoyed the close friendship of Theodore Beza and even of Calvin
himself. Portus, in fact, wrote polemical pamphlets supporting the
Calvinist cause against the French king and the Catholics. He was, so
far as I can tell, the only Greek intellectual who converted to Calvinism, if we except the celebrated but questionable case of the
seventeenth-century patriarch of Constantinople Cyril Lukaris.[38]
Portus, extraordinary family included his Cretan-born son, Emilius,

later professor of Greek at Lausanne and Heidelberg in Germany, and a nephew, John Casimatis of Crete, who achieved fame as a poet at Ferrara.[39]

In the careers of the many Cretan Hellenists mentioned—unfortunately we have had time to allude only briefly to the names of one or two Cretan painters—we may see the significance of the role played by Cretans in the diffusion of Greek scholarship to the West. Like the émigrés of the early period, their movements, too, seemed to follow a certain pattern. First, as emphasized earlier, they moved from Crete to Venice, and from there, as greater opportunity beckoned, they went to the North. It is striking, as Greek studies developed and inevitably Greek presses appeared, that the names of Cretans are to be associated with almost all of these early presses— in Spain with Ducas, in Paris with Vergikios, in Geneva with Portus, and earlier with Damilas in Florence, with Laonikos and Alexander in Venice, and with Calliergis in Rome. In the corollary field of teaching, so important for diffusing Greek at a time when the West still had an imperfect knowledge of the literary works of ancient Greece, some of the greatest Greek teachers were Cretans. The most influential of all was Musurus, and, as noted, the scores of embryonic humanists who heard him lecture, on their later return to their homelands went back in the capacity of bearers, or in some cases even of pioneers, of Greek studies.

More research remains to be done on the careers of many lesser-known Cretans in this diaspora.[40] And when this task has been accomplished a more complete picture of the activities and contributions of the Cretans in the West will be provided. One may make a few generalizations now, however, by analyzing the lives of the Cretans already mentioned. All of these men carried with them not only ancient Hellenic learning but the methodology, the pedagogy, used in the Byzantine schools of Constantinople and Crete. This is a fact that to date has been rarely noted. And it is deserving of special study to find out in what ways the passing of ancient learning through the filter of Byzantium affected it—in other words, to ascertain the influence of Byzantine methods of teaching and interpretation on Western ones.

Another factor that should not be overlooked is the pervasive patriotism of these Cretans for their race and island, and the degree to which it served as an inspiration to them to preserve their own heritage for future generations of Greeks—all in the light of the fact, as they themselves often mention, that Greek learning was in danger of being lost in the East under the Turkish occupation.[41]

And, finally, one cannot overlook the influence on these Cretans of the Venetian environment, a significant factor, of course, in Crete itself from the time of the Venetian occupation of the island in 1204. As Western scholars are almost entirely unaware, later in the seventeenth century there was to be a remarkable literary renaissance on Crete itself; and this appears to have been the product of Venetian-Byzantine cultural amalgamation, which produced a true hybrid Cretan-Venetian culture.[42]

To conclude, then, in the light of our presentation, I think it may be said that the basic contribution of the Cretan intellectuals of the fifteenth and sixteenth centuries was the forging of connecting links between the Hellenism of the old Byzantine East and the rising, youthful Hellenism of the Renaissance West. In this way, the island of Crete, through the work of its distinguished sons, served as an important halfway point between East and West. And as such, Crete during the Renaissance played a significant, if still inadequately appreciated, role in the process of the diffusion of Greek letters, not only to Italy, but—especially from Venice—throughout other areas of the Western world.

11

San Bernardino of Siena and the Greeks at the Council of Florence (1438–39)

Many celebrated figures of the Italian Renaissance appeared at the Council of Florence, doubtless the greatest confrontation, ecclesiastically and intellectually speaking, between the medieval Byzantine and Latin worlds. Leonardo Bruni, Pier Paolo Vergerio, Ambrogio Traversari, and Nicholas of Cusa, among others, represented the Latins; and Gemistos Pletho, Bessarion, George Scholarios, Mark of Ephesus, and others, the Greeks. To this significant group of humanists and clerics who participated in the religious and intellectual exchanges (which one modern scholar has termed a veritable "seminar" for the Western humanists),[1] we might also add the name of the foremost Western "popular" preacher of the day, Bernardino.

San Bernardino of Siena, though an evangelical preacher noted more for religious fervor than for intellectual capacity, nevertheless had more than a slight interest in classical learning. This, in fact, he made skillful use of, often incorporating allusions and quotations from ancient classical authors into his popular sermons, delivered in the open air before huge crowds of Sienese and Florentines, in order not only to reach a wider audience of educated as well as less literate people but to increase the rhetorical impact of his preaching. It is not our purpose here to determine whether, or to what degree, Bernardino was a humanist (a thorny problem depending in considerable part on questions of definition).[2] Rather, I shall discuss the fact of his presence at the council—a circumstance hitherto observed by only a few scholars.[3] In addition, I shall adduce another little-known allusion to him from the work of a leading fifteenth-century Byzantine historian; and, finally, an attempt will be made to reconstruct the possible influence of Bernardino on the Greeks at the council.

Bernardino's rhetorical skill in preaching, that is, his ability to move his audience, was almost legendary throughout Italy. As founder of the Observance, a more rigorous group of Franciscans than the larger, traditional group of Conventuals, he was hardly less known for his emphasis on right living and for his sharp criticism of the sinfulness and corruption of the life of the worldly Florentines and Sienese.[4] Many of his characteristics remind one of his earlier Franciscan predecessor, St. Bonaventura, who in 1274 had participated in a similar unionist council between Latins and Greeks, that of Lyons.

Bonaventura, who there had replaced St. Thomas Aquinas as principal spokesman for the Western side in whatever discussions were to take place (Thomas actually died on his way to Lyons), evidently, like his later counterpart Bernardino, through private conversations and the sincerity and force of his personality, had impressed the Greek delegation. The Greeks, it is reported, affectionately referred to Bonaventura as "Eutychios," a near-literal Greek rendering of Bonaventura. We are told that Greeks, conversing in private sessions with Bonaventura, were attracted by the magnetism of his personality.[5] Bonaventura apparently knew something of contemporary Greek theology, having written two small pieces on the basic theological and liturgical questions of the filioque and the azymes.[6] At Lyons, however (unlike later at Florence), no public, official disputations had taken place between the two sides, a primary reason for the Greek people's subsequent rejection of the validity of the Council of Lyons. The Council of Lyons had, in fact, been almost predestined to failure, the then Byzantine emperor Michael VIII Palaeologus seeking religious union primarily from motives of political expediency, and the pope basically in order to exalt papal authority through submission of the Greek church to Rome.

By the time of Florence, the political and military situation had become even more threatening, indeed almost hopeless, for the Greeks; for Constantinople was now faced by an almost perpetual siege by the Ottoman Turks. Only gradually did the Greeks—or more exactly, a small minority of them—come to realize that military aid, and therefore hope for salvation from the Turks, could come only at the price of ecclesiastical submission to Rome. It is, accordingly, in the context of this set of circumstances that, at the request of Pope Eugenius IV, many Latins, including Bernardino, appeared in 1439 in Florence to meet with the Greeks in council. A host of Westerners, along with a huge seven-hundred-man Greek delegation, therefore assembled, first at Ferrara and later at Florence, to which city the council was moved for various reasons.[8]

Bernardino's name is not mentioned in the official or semiofficial acts of the council, neither in the so-called *Acta Graeca* nor in the private Latin account of Andrea of Santa Croce. Moreover, the primary Greek historian of the Florentine council, the Grand Ecclesiarch of St. Sophia, Sylvester Syropoulos, also fails to mention him.[9] Since Bernardino was famed much more for his preaching than for his theological acumen, it would not be surprising if he did not participate (at least not publicly) in the abstruse arguments over questions of the filioque, azymes, purgatory, and the problem of papal supremacy over the Greek church. Nonetheless, as vicar-general of the Franciscan Observantists, we can accept the fact that he was invited by the pope to attend the council, along with heads of other Western religious orders.

This is corroborated by an anonymous Franciscan account included in a collection edited by the sixteenth-century Carthusian chronicler, Laurentius Surius (in his *Vita Sancti Bernardini Senensis*), as quoted in the seventeenth-century, more or less official history of the Franciscan order, the *Annales Minorum* of Lucas Waddingus.[10] As the anonymous Franciscan records: "now by the example of his life, now by private talks and public sermons" Bernardino was able "to help bring the Greeks to union." Carried away by admiration for Bernardino, the chronicler goes on to say that, though Bernardino knew no Greek, he "reflected on the precious boon granted to the Apostles by our Lord, the ability to speak in languages." Then, the account continues, Bernardino, murmuring a prayer, ascended the pulpit of the Florence cathedral, and after suddenly and miraculously receiving this gift of tongues, began to preach in Greek, instructing the Greeks in the Catholic faith with so much learning that all marveled and said "he knew Greek no less well than if he were born in Greece." In explanation the Franciscan chronicler offers only this simple line: "Then God was moving his tongue and speaking through him."[11]

We can perhaps appreciate what appears to be the chronicler's obvious exaggeration when we recall the great esteem in which he must have held his famous coreligionist Bernardino. But there appears to be only one other reference, and that oblique, in the sources on Bernardino's interest in Greek. This is mentioned as

occurring in 1423, at which time, we are told, he was present at
lectures of the great Italian Hellenist, Guarino of Verona.[12] But in
all probability Bernardino heard only a few of Guarino's lectures
and, if he had acquired any knowledge of Greek, it was only a few
words or halting phrases.[13] Nevertheless, it is noteworthy that this
faculty of the "gift of tongues" (rather than "glossolalia," a kind of
gibberish) was, in this period, sometimes attributed to other saints,
including a number of famous Franciscans. For example, in a collection of medieval English Franciscan accounts, we read of the fourteenth-century "John of England, a Franciscan monk [who] went to
Sclavonia where he preached the word of God in the Illyrick language by the inspiration of the Holy Ghost, having no knowledge
of that tongue [but] by the gift of tongues."[14]

From the similarity of circumstances and expressions used in these
two accounts, that of the anonymous Franciscan on Bernardino, and
that of the anonymous medieval English Franciscan on John of
England, one may hazard the suggestion that reference to acquisition
of the gift of tongues may have been a kind of *topos* in medieval
Franciscan accounts. The imputation of the divine gift of tongues,
attached to the names of charismatic Franciscans by sometimes
overzealous Franciscan admirers, reminds one of the early Western
medieval practice of hagiographers who often indiscriminately
transferred "stock" miracles from the life of one saint to another.[15]
In any event, it would appear to be outside the realm of possibility
that Bernardino could have addressed the Greeks in a discourse in
their own language. Certainly he could not have engaged in effective
argument with them in Greek on the technically abstruse points of
theology or ecclesiology at issue at the time.

On the other hand, there is nothing to prevent us from believing
that Bernardino could easily have made use of others, Latins or
Greeks, to act as interpreters for him. We know that in Florence men
were present who were learned in both languages ("in utriusque
linguis"), such as the Latin Camaldolese, Ambrogio Traversari, and
Leonardo Bruni of Arezzo; and a number of Greek prounionists:
the Archbishop Bessarion of Nicaea, Archbishop Andreas of Latin-
held Rhodes, and Nicholas Secundinus—the two latter officially
employed as interpreters by the papal Curia.[16] Though the precise
method of their function is not entirely clear, Bernardino would
certainly have had recourse to them had he wished to converse with
any of the Greeks, which seems very likely.

It is of interest that the great humanist Lorenzo Valla, who was also present in Florence (incidentally, he composed a treatise on the much debated question of the procession of the Holy Spirit—filioque —in which he seemed to support the Greek view),[17] calls Bessarion "in Rome the most Latin of the Greeks and in Constantinople the most Greek of the Latins [*Latinorum graecissimus, Graecorum latinissimus*]." This undoubtedly referred primarily to Bessarion's linguistic proficiency in the two tongues. Bessarion, one of the leading Greek personalities in Florence, after being named a cardinal of the church by the pope, was still later appointed to head a papal commission which finally approved the canonization of Bernardino. This fact could well suggest previous contacts in Florence between Bessarion and Bernardino.[18]

That Bernardino's reputation remained in the memory of at least some Greeks after Florence may perhaps be evidenced by the near-contemporary Byzantine historian, Laonicus Chalcondyles, who, in his well-known *History of the Turks*(in Greek), mentions him in a passage. In this account, which reveals Chalcondyles as a humanist-imitator of the language and style of Thucydides, Chalcondyles' primary concern was to exalt the deeds of the Turkish conqueror of Constantinople, his master and employer, Mehmet II.[19] But Laonikos thereby sought, it seems, not only to curry favor with the sultan but to explain to his very troubled Greek compatriots (as the ancient Greek historian Polybius did centuries before with regard to the rise of Rome and decline of Greece) the equally remarkable rise to eminence of Renaissance Italy and the total destruction of the Byzantine state, in particular the loss of their "God-guarded" capital, Constantinople. For in the terrible catastrophe of 1453 most Byzantines were firmly convinced that they were being punished by God for their sins.[20]

Chalcondyles, in his short but fascinating excursus on Bernardino, affirms that after Bernardino's death many churches in Italy were dedicated to him, statues even being erected in his honor.[21] As a pupil at Mistra in the Peloponnese, of the celebrated Byzantine philosopher Gemistos Pletho (at Florence Pletho had dazzled the Italian humanists with his exposition of the Platonic dialogues, including his famous explication, "On the Differences between Plato and Aristotle"), Chalcondyles may have heard about the sessions at Florence from Pletho, Bessarion, or, no less likely, from his own cousin, the Athenian humanist Demetrius Chalcondyles, who was later to become far better known in Italy than Laonikos. At this time Demetrius had not yet gone to Italy, but in 1448 he would go to teach Greek at Perugia University; later, in 1463 as we shall see, he became the first occupant of the chair of Greek studies at Padua University; and, subsequently, he taught Greek in Florence and Milan.[22] To return to Laonikos Chalcondyles—in his account he drew an analogy between Bernardino, the Italian saint, and a hero (*heroi*) of old, affirming that in erudition Bernardino ranked among "the first" (*ta prota*) in the West. As the Greek passage reads, "[Bernardino] reached the heights both in wisdom and contemplation."[23]

The fact that the anonymous Franciscan probably exaggerated in his account of Bernardino should not induce us to dismiss the mention of Bernardino's presence at the council peremptorily. We may, in fact, draw a useful inference from this—that Bernardino's example of piety and his vivid sermons (public or private and whether completely understood or not) probably exerted some beneficial influence on the Greeks. The Greeks were always impressed by skillful rhetoric, and, as is known especially through the intimate, detailed record of the Greek historian at the council, Sylvester Syropoulos, vacillated between acceptance of union and rejection of it, not only on dogmatic, ethnic, and psychological grounds, but (this is a lesser point, to be sure) because of what many believed was the too often reprehensible morality and arrogance of the Latin clergy.[24] One is again reminded in this regard of Bernardino's Franciscan confrère Bonaventura, of two centuries earlier. For it was precisely the example of Bonaventura's purity of life, his sense of moral righteousness, integrity, and amiability that apparently made such a favorable impression on the Greeks at Lyons. On Bernardino, besides the evidence already cited, we might adduce the perhaps overly effusive opinion of the famous contemporary Florentine bookseller and humanist Vespasiano, who writes that "in no other man was there to be found such a wonderful concourse of talents."[25]

If we can accept the evidence of the anonymous Franciscan account of Bernardino's life as well as Chalcondyles' words in praise of him, it would seem that Bernardino's career had made a vivid impression in certain circles of the East as well as the West. Indeed, it is not at all unlikely that when Pope Eugenius summoned Bernardino to Florence, he had partly in mind the impression his personality and reputation for purity of life might make on the Greek clergy, in particular on the intransigently antiunionist Greek monks.

For it is to them that the rather austere reform program of the Observantist Franciscan friars would have been most appealing. The broader implication here is not only that the clergy and the monks of each side could mix and learn more about each other but, more important, that there was also at Florence, besides the high-level intellectual and theological exchanges, a certain interchange between the two sides on a more informal, private level. Except for the private, rather formal, banquets presided over by Cosimo de' Medici, at which Pletho, Bessarion, and other Byzantines expounded on the texts of the Platonic and Aristotelian philosophies, the possi-bility of contact on other levels than this has been largely ignored by historians of the council.

We know from many testimonies that, with respect to the famous question of poverty, Bernardino held to a middle course between the views of the very strict Spiritual Franciscans (by now heretical) and those of the far more relaxed Conventuals. Throughout his entire life Bernardino never, in fact, ceased to preach his views (called the "Observance"—that is, a *stricter observance* of St. Francis's rule): to live a simpler, more severe life with respect to food, clothing, and housing, and to have absolutely no individual possessions. To adhere best to these prescriptions, a friar, it would appear, should lead an ascetic life. It does not seem too much to believe, then, that through the living example of Bernardino's sincere kind of piety and ex-emplary conduct, at least some of the Greeks, might have gained a more favorable impression of the Roman church, especially regard-ing the personal morality and social ethics of the Latin monastic clergy, than was all too often projected in the East by their brethren of the secular clergy, the proud prelates of the Roman Curia.[27] The example set by Bernardino's piety and forthrightness is, it would seem, precisely referred to in the words of the anonymous Franciscan, as noted above: "Now through the example of his life, now by private talks and public sermons, [he helped] to bring the Greeks to union."[28]

Among those in whom Bernardino's example might, in particular, have struck a responsive chord were the Hesychast Greek monks—to whose long tradition of contemplation and asceticism a number of Greek monks and clerics at Florence, including Mark of Ephesus, still adhered.[29] (Whether they were technically "Hesychasts" or "Palamites" need not concern us here.)[30] Nevertheless, at Florence, if we examine the sources, we see that the Greek Hesychasts did not

Emperor John VIII Palaeologus and Patriarch Joseph at the Council of
Florence, detail from the "Miracle of San Bernardino," attributed to an anony-
mous painter from Urbino. Courtesy of the Galleria Nazionale dell'Umbria.
(See pp. 202-03.)

so much as open their mouths on the beliefs of Hesychasm. It was, in fact, the emperor himself who forbade his clergy even to bring up the subject.[31] The Hesychast theology of the divine energies as contrasted with that of the divine essence, and their explanation of the light of Mt. Tabor as seen by human eyes, were views apparently considered too hazardous to defend effectively before the Latins. Indeed, it is highly probable that the emperor (and his unionist-minded prelates) wished to avoid providing any opportunity of being accused of propounding dogma which, according to the Latin view, was not part of that formulated by the early church fathers. And this especially since the question of the "addition," or innovation, of doctrine (witness the filioque problem) was precisely the chief accusation always leveled by the Greeks against the Latins. Moreover, it goes without saying that in Florence the emperor wanted to present a united Greek front against the Latins.

Nevertheless, despite the *official* silence of the Greek delegation in Florence on Hesychastic theology, one may venture the opinion that exchanges of a friendly nature on Hesychastic ascetical practices and beliefs did take place *in private* between Bernardino and the Greek representatives. This is particularly likely since, as certain modern scholars believe, the form of the Jesus prayer as recited by Bernardino was similar to (if not indirectly derived from) the famous centuries-old Jesus prayer of the Greek Hesychasts: "Lord Jesus Christ have mercy upon me." (Some authorities hold that both Eastern and Western forms of the prayer derived from early Greek tradition, especially stemming from the "Kyrie eleēson" of the Greek liturgy of John Chrysostom, which, in time, passed in the West to such persons as St. Bernard of Clairvaux, St. Bonaventura, and from him later to his devotee San Bernardino.)[32]

Bernardino's constant emphasis on the very name of Jesus, as evidenced in his famous anagram of Greek letters (IHC, the acronym for Jesus), which, inscribed on a placard, he carried everywhere, and which he insisted that Italian towns adopt in place of their factional party slogans, would have pleased the Greek Hesychasts in particular. For they, too, emphasized the Holy Name in their Jesus prayer, the repetition of which, together with certain exercises, was to them a means of attaining a state of contemplation and inner peace.[33]

One could speculate on what might have happened had Bernardino, the fervent Western preacher and moralist, come into collision, directly or through interpreters, with the foremost Greek preacher

Portrait of San Bernardino of Siena by Pietro di Giovanni di Ambrogio. Courtesy of the Pinacoteca Nazionale di Siena. (Note the Greek acronym for the name of Jesus, IHS; see pp. 202-03.)

Portrait of Mark of Ephesus from an illuminated manuscript, no. 19, fol. 350v. Courtesy of the Benaki Museum, Athens. (See pp. 202-03.)

and spokesman, the equally fiery Mark of Ephesus. Mark, as noted in the Prologue, was the intransigent champion of the independence of the Greek church vis-à-vis Rome, and Bernardino was no less unyielding on matters of faith.[34] That there was nevertheless a friendly rapport between Mark and at least one Latin unionist, is indicated by a Latin source for the council, which affirms that Ambrogio Traversari, the affable Camaldolese monk who knew Greek very well and was, in fact, the chief Latin interpreter there, was permitted by Mark Eugenikos to go through his library in search of manuscripts.[35]

Bernardino's contacts with the Greeks, as we have tried to delineate here, would seem significant for informal, unofficial relationships between members of the two ecclesiastical delegations. Indeed, a similarity of interests between Bernardino and the Greek clerics, especially many of the monks—emphasis on Jesus prayer, on personal piety and morality, and on eloquence in preaching, not to speak of possible humanistic proclivities—may well have made a considerable impression on the Greeks and thus, at least indirectly, contributed to the successful outcome of the council, however ephemeral.

12

Marcus Musurus: New Information on the Death of a Byzantine Humanist in Italy

The question of the circumstances surrounding the death in 1517 of the Renaissance's greatest Hellenist, the Cretan scholar Marcus Musurus, particularly the curious story of his reputed death from "envy" at not being named a cardinal by the pope, has not yet been satisfactorily resolved.[1] We know that about a decade before his death he had enjoyed a remarkable tenure of teaching Greek at the University of Padua and then in Venice, during which time at least two dozen of Europe's leading humanists (including Erasmus) had studied Greek language and literature with him. Subsequently, apparently in response to a summons from Pope Leo X, he had come to Rome to aid in the direction of a new Greek college founded by Leo.[2] Very probably, in moving from Venice to the papal capital, now increasingly characterized by a lavish patronage of artists and scholars, he saw an opportunity for the material advancement of his career. In any case, he must have become increasingly aware of the political decline of Venice and its replacement by Rome as the leading center of humanist scholarship in Europe.

In two documents found in the Venetian archives, certain interesting references are made to Musurus' death.[3] It is the purpose of this chapter to see if, through an examination of these sources, more light can be shed on the circumstances surrounding his demise and particularly his state of mind at that time.

The problem arises because of a report of the famous Italian historian, Paolo Giovio, to the effect that Musurus' death was actually due to envy and disappointment at not being named to the cardinalate. As Giovio puts it (certainly with at least a little exaggeration since one does not die exclusively of envy!), Musurus, "driven by insane ambition which led him to an archbishopric [that of Monemvasia in Greece], aspired overhastily to the cardinalate." Giovio adds that Musurus often complained that none of the Greeks, to their great

225

shame, had achieved this high office of cardinal.[4] This last statement is, of course, manifestly wrong, since Giovio—or Musurus—had apparently forgotten that, some seventy years before, Bessarion and Isidore of Kiev had both been made cardinals by Pope Eugenius IV after the Council of Florence, and that one century before Musurus' time, a fellow Cretan, Petros Philarges, had actually achieved the supreme rank of pope under the name of Alexander V (1409–10). Indeed, at the Council of Constance in 1414, the Byzantine humanist-diplomat Manuel Chrysoloras, too, had been one of the prime candidates for the office of pope.[5] Nevertheless, it is true that in Musurus' own day no Greek had risen to the office of cardinal (though Janus Lascaris, Musurus' own teacher in Greek earlier at Florence, is reported to have been offered a cardinal's hat but rejected it).[6]

Giovio's charge of envy on the part of Musurus, it should be noted, is contradicted by another contemporary, the only other writer of the period to allude to the story, Lilio Gyraldi. Gyraldi affirms that it was, in fact, those who concocted the report who were envious— those who saw this as the sole means of defaming "this most learned and modest person." Gyraldi goes on to say that Musurus, while alive, was "well spoken of by all."[7]

The first of our documents is actually a report or dispatch of the *orator* (ambassador) of Venice to the papacy, Marco Minio, addressed to the doge of Venice on 26 October 1517,[8] that is, some nine days after the presumed death of Musurus, which, according to the contemporary Venetian historian-diarist Marino Sanuto, occurred on 17 October 1517.[9] However, the new document in question differs in chronology from Sanuto because, also on 26 October 1517, Minio writes that "in his [Musurus'] letter he signified to you that he greatly desired to return to lecture [in Venice], nor did the things here [in Rome] much satisfy him, but it pleased our Lord God to call him to Himself, and on Sunday at the hour of ten he died."[10] Since 26 October 1517 fell on a Monday, the previous Sunday was not, then, the 17th but the 25th of October.[11]

A more significant point is the question of the exact meaning, and especially the implications, of Minio's phrase "nor did things much satisfy him here [in Rome] [ne delle cose de qui molto si sodisfaceva]." According to Marino Sanuto's *Diarii*, "Musurus wanted to come to Venice to lecture but he had need first of sending some short letters in regard to benefices and he would be in Venice at the start of the Studio [the university year]." Our newly found document

corroborates Sanuto's statement regarding Musurus' desire to return
to Venice to teach. What is more to the point, however, is Sanuto's
statement that Musurus would not go to Venice until he had made
arrangements for his benefices[12] (probably meaning, more specifically, the stipends derived from them). We know that Musurus
had earlier been appointed archbishop of Monemvasia in Greece
and also bishop of Hierapetra in Crete, though he never actually
appeared in either place to perform his duties.[13] Probably Marcus
received a stipend for his teaching at the Greek college in Rome
in addition to money from his sees in (Venetian-held) Monemvasia
and Crete.

It is possible to construe Sanuto's statement as meaning that
Musurus (who, as we know, was already in holy orders) also held
various benefices in Rome not involving the care of souls, in which
case, of course, before moving, he would have had to find a vicar to
take his place in the papal capital so that he could continue in Venice
to collect the income from his benefices. As is well known of the
medieval period, if one held a benefice (as in the case of Petrarch
much earlier) that did not involve the care of souls, one could appoint
a vicar or clerk to perform the necessary duties of the office, which
generally amounted only to the saying of a requisite number of
Masses. It is probable that Musurus' income from Monemvasia was
not great, and of course upon leaving for Venice he would have had
to give up his stipend for teaching at the college in Rome (though
at the same time this would be replaced by a Venetian salary). However valid all these speculations may be, we should take note here of
a second (unpublished) document in trying to clear up the reason
for his discontent in Rome and to determine whether, as Giovio
puts it, it was connected with his "insatiable" ambition and envy at
not being named to the cardinalate.

According to this new document, written also by Marco Minio
to the doge of Venice but dated earlier than the first, that is, on 1
October 1517, "the making of cardinals was considered and the
great *partito* [affair] was proposed (*vien posto*) to his holiness the
pope, besides the necessity of money, [a condition] in which he [then]
found himself—I believe, because of holding this new election, he
thought of creating ten [posts costing] forty to sixty thousand ducats
for each [candidate] that wishes to spend, and among the others was
named a son of Dom Francesco da Ramada. . . . But certainly it is
a thing of little dignity for this order [cardinalate], for aside from

the great number, because of the obligation imposed on them [to offer this great sum], they lose every sense of honor. But the device is fine for the pope."[14] The above passage is difficult to read in the original document, some words or phrases being unclear, but the general meaning of the passage as a whole certainly seems to emerge.

Here we have material for new speculation on Musurus' attitude. He might have been angered by this flagrant flouting of decorum and the demand for what constituted a bribe of forty to sixty thousand ducats. Instead, then, of "sickening and dying of envy," as Giovio would have it, Musurus may have been incensed at the necessity of paying a bribe for the cardinalate. Or it is possible that, as a normally ambitious person, he may have been somewhat upset that he himself lacked the money to pay it.[15] However, in this case, if we take October 1 as the date for the proposal of the payment for the cardinalate, there remains only an interval of twenty-five days in which the psychological condition Giovio supposes responsible for Musurus' death could have developed.

The modern German historian of the seventeenth century, O. Freher, erroneously says that Musurus did in fact become a cardinal.[16] We know, in any case, from our first document of Marco Minio that Musurus did move in high curial circles. He was vice-secretary as well as a favorite of Cardinal Giulio de' Medici, the future Clement VII and cousin of Pope Leo, and thus presumably was on good terms with the group immediately surrounding the pope. Also, we learn from our second document, again a report of Minio to the doge, that Musurus' friend and former mentor Janus Lascaris (here called "Zuan Lascari") was named by him, in his will, as one of his executors, along with his old patron, Prince Alberto Pio of Carpi.[17]

It is plausible, then, that Marcus would have had some reason to aspire to being named to the cardinalate. Nevertheless, without other supporting evidence our document cannot effectively support the theory of Giovio that Musurus was "so chagrined and jealous at not being named cardinal that his body rapidly wasted away and he died." Yet at the same time it is not impossible, as noted earlier, that the demand for a bribe did upset him at least to some degree, when he saw others with money far less worthy than he being appointed (for example, the son of Dom Francesco da Ramada).[18] Chagrin, therefore, may have been a contributing factor leading to his death, though it was almost certainly not the principal cause, in view of

Sanuto's positive statement (which there is no reason to challenge) in his *Diarii*, that "Musurus had been sick for two months and had become consumptive [lo episcopo Mussuro . . . e stato amalato do mexi, era venuto eticho]."[19]

In a letter of the Bolognese professor-humanist Paolo Bombasio, he wrote, on 6 December 1517, to his friend (and Musurus') Erasmus, that the reason Musurus did not teach long at Pope Leo's Greek college in Rome was that Musurus "died in the autumn of 1517 of dropsy," and therefore not, as Giovio affirmed, of shame at not being named a cardinal. Though Bombasio's statement disagrees slightly regarding the precise disease that carried off Musurus, it nevertheless offers additional new testimony to render worthless Giovio's extraordinary aspersion cast on Musurus' character.[19a]

There are a number of attestations to the high quality of Marcus' character and moral conduct throughout his career, for example, on the part of Sanuto, Gyraldi, Alberto Pio, prince of Carpi, and also in the second letter of Minio dated (as noted) 1 October 1517, which describes "Marcus Musurus Cretensis" as "virtutibus ac prestanti doctrina verumque scientia ornatus."[20] Thus, in view of the information provided in the documents presented here, though we still cannot make a categorical judgment, it would seem very likely that Giovio's charge against Musurus of insane jealousy that drove him, or at least contributed, to his death, is without any real substance. It may, indeed, be merely another of the defamatory stories so typical of the Italian Renaissance, which in this case may have been given more than usual credence because of Musurus' foreign Greek background.

Our new documents, then, besides casting grave doubts on the credibility of Giovio's story regarding Musurus' mental attitude before his demise, also provide us with a few new facts: first, that he died between October 24 and 25 and not on October 17, as Sanuto says.[21] (Let us not·forget that Sanuto was then living in distant Venice, while Minio was residing in Rome where Musurus died.) Another new point is that a logical explanation for Musurus' failure to achieve the cardinalate is the fact that Pope Leo required from each potential candidate payment of forty to sixty thousand ducats, a large sum which Musurus could undoubtedly ill afford. Nevertheless, this demand may seem less reprehensible if we recall that Leo was engaged in war at this time and that the expense of maintaining a rich, humanist court was considerable, the Medici family fortune itself not being what it used to be.[22] Interesting also is the information that the pope was not at Musurus' funeral but hunting somewhere on the outskirts of Rome,[23] a fact which may or may not indicate that Musurus, at that particular moment, was not in his good graces. In addition, Minio explicitly states what Sanuto had already suggested—that Musurus was not satisfied with living in Rome.

Finally, we learn that at Musurus' funeral a great number of distinguished personages were present: Musurus' friend Giulio de' Medici, cousin of Pope Leo and himself later Pope Clement VII,[24] bishops, the envoy of the Holy Roman emperor, that of Portugal,[25] and Marco Minio himself as envoy of the government of Venice.[26] The document does not state categorically whether Janus Lascaris or the prince of Carpi were present at Musurus' obsequies, but since they are explicitly named as executors of Musurus' will, we may safely assume that such was the case.[27]

To summarize, then, although we may not have uncovered anything of great significance to contradict what modern scholars have written about Musurus' career in general, we have been able to add several interesting details that serve to round out our knowledge of the circumstances surrounding the death of this most erudite of all the Hellenists in the Western Renaissance. Musurus was a man of high character and repute, considerably superior to any other Greek émigré, except possibly Bessarion or Janus Lascaris. Hence, in view of all the above reasons and implications, it would seem that the defamatory story of Paolo Giovio about this learned scholar of the Renaissance may finally be laid to rest once and for all.

13

The Career of the Byzantine Humanist Demetrius Chalcondyles at Padua, Florence, and Milan

The humanist movement in the Italian Renaissance began as a Latin revival, but it was probably the restoration of Greek letters which did more than anything else to expand the intellectual horizon of Renaissance humanism.[1] In the history of this Greek revival the most significant role was played by the Greek scholar-exiles from the Byzantine East. Knowledge of the activities of these Greek scholars and their contribution to the Renaissance has increased in recent years. But the careers of many, including even some of the more important, refugees are still not sufficiently known. More precisely, their contribution has not yet adequately been integrated into the mainstream of Italian humanistic development.

One such career is that of Demetrius Chalcondyles, a Byzantine humanist (born in Athens before Constantinople's fall) about whom very little has been written in English. His career is of importance not only because of his many editions of ancient Greek works but equally because of his teaching in Florence, Padua, and Milan, three of the chief centers of humanistic development. This chapter will examine his tenure of teaching in Florence and Milan, and more especially at Padua—the latter a period about which very little has been known. Information about this Paduan phase of his career will be gleaned from the essentially unpublished text of a document containing the famous address he delivered in 1463 on the occasion of the inauguration of Greek studies at the great University of Padua.

The career of Chalcondyles may conveniently be divided into three broad phases, each concerned with his instruction of Greek: the Paduan phase (he was at Padua from 1463 to 1472), then the Florentine (1475 to 1491) and, finally, the Milanese (he instructed at Milan until his death in 15'1).[2] About his earliest years, that is, those he spent in Greece before his arrival in Italy, almost nothing is known. He was born in August, it seems, of 1423 in Athens rather than Constantinople, as some authorities have believed. His family, one of the most powerful and noble of Athens, could trace its lineage as far back as the twelfth century. Demetrius' family had lived in Athens under the domination of the various Western conquerors following the Fourth Crusade in 1204: the French, the Catalans, and finally the Florentine family of the Acciaiuoli. It was probably because of differences with the latter that the entire Chalcondyles family, sometime in the late fourteenth century, moved to the Peloponnesus. There they settled in or near the Byzantine city of Mistra, where in this period the famous Byzantine Platonist Gemistos Pletho was teaching. What made the family move back to Athens, it may be conjectured, was the gradual stabilization of conditions in Greece after the Turkish conquest of Athens in 1456. Aside from these few references to his family life, we have no information on Chalcondyles up to the time of his arrival in Italy in 1449, when he was little more than twenty-five years of age.[3] As we learn from the report of an Italian pupil of his, Giovanni Campani, he came directly to Rome from Athens. This would indicate that he did not travel via Venice, the usual funnel for Greek émigrés coming to Italy. Rather than making a long sea voyage, he crossed, it seems, by sea from Ragusa to Ancona, after which he journeyed on land to Rome.

We may assume that, like other contemporary Greek intellectuals, Demetrius' aim was to find support in Rome in the circle of the most eminent Byzantine exile of the age, the powerful Roman cardinal and scholar John Bessarion. As patron of the Greeks, Bessarion had surrounded himself in Rome with a remarkable circle of Greek (and some Latin) humanists, whose primary activity was copying Greek manuscripts and translating them into Latin.[4] Despite Demetrius' purpose, however, his principal patron and guide throughout most of his life was not to be Bessarion but, rather, another Byzantine humanist of a somewhat earlier generation. This was Theodore Gaza of Thessalonika, whose pupil Demetrius became, and to whom Demetrius bound himself in an intimate and enduring friendship.[5]

In 1452, for reasons not entirely clear but which doubtless had to do with his inability to support himself properly in Rome, Demetrius went to Perugia. Exactly how long he stayed there is not certain. At any rate, he was in Rome again in 1455, living for a time in the orbit of Bessarion and his court. It was some years later, in about 1462, that Demetrius became involved in the famous quarrel among the

Greeks over the relative merits of the philosophy of Plato and Aristotle. His role, a secondary one, consisted of replying to a tract written by another Greek then residing in Crete, Michael Apostolis, who, in order to curry favor with his patron Bessarion, had launched a violent verbal attack on the Aristotelian Theodore Gaza.

But Apostolis' plan backfired. For Bessarion, though himself a Platonist, was angered. And when Chalcondyles—we may recall that he was Gaza's friend and pupil—took it upon himself to reply to Apostolis (his response has unfortunately not survived), Bessarion was gratified. The incident, relatively unimportant in itself, is of some significance, not only because it marked the beginning of the celebrated Renaissance conflict over the philosophies of Aristotle and Plato, but also because of the attention it inevitably directed to the *original* texts of the two philosophers, which in turn led to a more intensive study and clarification of their respective views. Thus, in the long run, it helped enormously to widen the philosophic horizon of the entire Renaissance. As for Chalcondyles, it reveals something of his loyalty and friendship, that, despite his personal inclination toward Plato, he could take up the cudgels on behalf of an Aristotelian.[6]

Except for a few rather vague hypotheses, little else may be adduced regarding this phase of Demetrius' career. The important question certainly is how he managed to secure appointment to the first chair of Greek to be created at the celebrated University of Padua. As we shall note shortly, our new document will enable us to answer not only this question but others—such as what courses he taught, the quality of his Latinity at this time (for the document is written in Latin), and finally, how he sought to justify, in his own eyes as well as those of his audience, the creation of a chair of Greek studies at Padua.

Let us pause briefly to indicate some of the more illustrious of the many pupils Chalcondyles taught during his tenure at Padua. His most learned student was undoubtedly the young Byzantine Janus Lascaris, to whom Chalcondyles, whose attitude was so different from that of a good number of the jealous Greek humanists of the time, never ceased to be devoted. Also, Giovanni Lorenzo, the Venetian (who later, in 1466, as Demetrius tells us in an epigram, helped Demetrius correct—that is, edit for the press—the famous Byzantine *Planudean Anthology*). Other pupils of Demetrius at Padua were the Italian humanists Varino Favorino Camerti, Niccolò

Leonico Tomeo, Agostino Baldo, Andrea Brenta, and, finally, the copyist of Chalcondyles' inaugural discourse at Padua, the German student and later well-known physician from Nürnberg, Hartmann Schedel.[7]

Why did Chalcondyles, apparently well liked and prosperous at Padua, leave his post to go to Florence in 1472? We should not forget that by the mid-fifteenth century Florence had become unquestionably the world's leading humanist center, and that it must therefore have been the ambition of many learned Greek émigré-scholars, to go to that city and to succeed to the chair held over half a century before by their celebrated Byzantine country-man, the great Manuel Chrysoloras. As will be recalled, it was with Chrysoloras' teaching, begun at the Florentine *studium* in 1397, that Greek studies may be said effectively to have been initiated in the Renaissance.

There are two other relevant facts to explain Chalcondyles' departure for Florence. First, that the previous holder of the chair, the Greek John Argyropoulos, for reasons still obscure, had in July of 1471 left the chair vacant. And second, that Demetrius Chalcondyles (so several historians believe, perhaps exaggeratedly) may have become unhappy at Padua because his appointment had to be renewed each year—a circumstance which may have made him feel insecure at what he felt was the need continually to demonstrate his worthiness.[8] Of course, one cannot rule out the possibility of discord over some other matter—say, over his stipend. Another plausible reason for Demetrius' departure for Florence may have been simply the fact that, since the Council of Florence in 1438–39 and especially after the tenure of John Argyropoulos, the chair of Greek at Florence had become the most coveted in all of Italy.

Meantime, that is, during the four-year period the Florentine post was vacant, an incident worthy of special notice occurred in the life of Demetrius. On a trip he made from Padua to Bologna in order to pay his respects to Bessarion, he was (as we learn from a letter written by Demetrius himself to a friend),[9] treated by Bessarion with un-warranted contempt and haughtiness. Bessarion, it seems, hardly condescended to give him an audience and said almost nothing to him, indeed barely deigned to mention his name. As Chalcondyles himself rather jaundicedly puts it: "In the past I considered him [Bessarion] arrogant and scurvy-ridden, but not at all deprived of judgment. But now I adjudged him even worse. When others realize he is only 'an ass clothed in the skin of a lion,' all will disparage him."[10] This statement may well strike us as rather astonishing in view of Bessarion's reputation for magnanimity to his fellow Greek exiles, in particular when we see later how effusively Demetrius himself was to praise Bessarion for, as he says, securing for him his post at Padua. In any event, the remark militates against almost all other testimony we have about Bessarion, presenting him in a new light and disclosing a side to his nature quite contrary to that usually attributed to him.

The main impediment to Demetrius' nomination to the Florentine post seems to have been the presence in Florence of still another Greek savant, Andronikos Callistos, who may well already have been teaching privately in the city on the Arno. In fact, it was only after Callistos' departure from Florence for Milan in March of 1475 that Demetrius appeared in Florence. His coming was evidently in part the result of intervention in his favor by the Italian Hellenist Francisco Filelfo, who addressed two letters to the young but influential Florentine humanists, Alemanno Rinuccini and Donato Acciaiuoli.[11] Whatever the extent of the influence exercised by these three humanists in Demetrius' favor, it is clear that, in September of 1475, Chalcondyles was officially appointed to the famous *cathedra* of Greek in Florence.

Thus, finally, as Cammelli rather floridly puts it,[12] Demetrius, in the joy of realizing his dream, could forget the disappointments of his first arrival in Italy, his long peregrinations from city to city in vain search of a post, the difficulties that had embittered his last years at Padua, and the new anxieties he had suffered to find a new position. And indeed, after twenty-six years in a foreign land, Demetrius could now, in fact, look forward to a serene and tranquil period of his life in Florence. For he was to spend an uninterrupted sojourn of sixteen years there, marred only by the death of his close friend Theodore Gaza, which occurred in the very year he assumed his new position. Though no Vespasiano da Bisticci (the famous Florentine biographer) has left us intimate glimpses of Chalcondyles' life in Florence (as he did for Chalcondyles' predecessor, Argyropoulos), we know enough about Demetrius' career there to derive a fairly clear picture of the deep impression his teaching and personality made on the Florentine intellectual community.

It was during the long tenure of his predecessor, the brilliant John Argyropoulos, that the atmosphere had been prepared for Demetrius' talents in literature as well as philosophy to show to their best advantage. The famous Platonic Academy of Florence was created by Cosimo de' Medici in 1462—an event which, as Della Torre puts it, "transported the ancient learning of Athens to the banks of the Arno."[13] Nevertheless, it is often overlooked that, previous to this academy and for a time, in fact, contemporary with it, there existed in Florence another academy, one devoted to the cult of Aristotle. This latter was in its later years under the leadership of Argyropoulos, as the Platonic Academy was to be under that of Marsilio Ficino. Though both academies thus seemed originally to be rivalrous in scope, largely as the result of Argyropoulos' influence a period of relative peace between them gradually came about. (Indeed, Argyropoulos himself in his *private* instruction in his home may be said to have initiated the teaching of Platonism in Florence.)

In the conflict generated by the Greeks at the Council of Florence over the relative primacy of Aristotle or Plato, the last word was spoken, in 1469, by Bessarion in his *In Calumniatorem Platonis*. One year before, in 1468, Cristoforo Landino had composed his *Disputationes Camaldolenses*, in which *both* academies were depicted as playing an important role. Evidence that conciliation rather than rivalry, or at least not hostility, had now become the order of the day, is attested to by the fact that Demetrius, a professed Platonist, seemed to owe his appointment to the Florentine *studium* mainly to two Aristotelians, the young Rinuccini and Acciaiuoli.

Despite the increasing pacification of the two groups, it cannot be denied that the coming of Demetrius signified a triumph for the Platonic faction in Florence. Indeed, the most luminous period of the Platonic Academy, from 1470 to 1492, when it was under the aegis of Lorenzo the Magnificent, may be said to have coincided almost exactly with the period of Demetrius' tenure in the Greek chair at Florence. (Chalcondyles arrived in 1475 and left Florence at the end of 1491.) Interestingly enough, Lorenzo the Magnificent, an early disciple of Argyropoulos and one who had himself initially begun to specialize in the teaching of Aristotle, now became the great partisan of the Platonic Academy under Ficino.[14]

The precise courses that Chalcondyles taught at Florence are not reported to us, though several surviving documents (two, for example, dating from 1484 and 1489) state that Chalcondyles was engaged in the teaching of moral philosophy and the Greek authors, presumably literary.[15] These and other bits of information permit us to assume that Chalcondyles taught *both* Greek literature and Greek philosophy.

In this flourishing period of his career and of the humanistic primacy of Florence, Chalcondyles had as colleagues in the *studium* a group of humanists of unique brilliance and learning, not only Angelo Poliziano, the Florentine Hellenist and most influential figure at Lorenzo's court, but the Platonist Cristoforo Landino, and others. The list of Demetrius' students, some of whom subsequently became noted humanists in their own right, is impressive. Among the Florentines were Piero de' Medici (son of Lorenzo) and Pietro Dalian. Among the many non-Italian students who came to hear him were, notably, the Englishmen William Grocyn and Thomas Linacre, both of whom later returned to their homeland much the richer for their study with Chalcondyles. Also John Reuchlin, later to become the most celebrated of German humanists who, after some years, even followed Chalcondyles to Milan in order to continue studying with him there.[16] The great success and popularity achieved by Chalcondyles in Florence is attested to by the unanimous praise accorded him from all quarters and by the breadth of his reputation, which soon spread to all the learned circles of western Europe.

The only rivalry or rancor (or even suggestion of it) that seems, then, to have clouded his life—and this is disputed by certain historians—was in connection with the Florentine humanist Angelo Poliziano. Some scholars affirm that Poliziano, after learning all he could from the Greek émigrés, began to denigrate them and their contribution to humanism, and to consider his mastery of Greek language and literature superior to theirs. One critic, indeed, believes that Chalcondyles, a man without a homeland, objected to the following words of Poliziano, delivered publicly from his chair in the *studium* to the humanists of Florence: "In your city, O Florentines, Greek learning again lives. Your youth now speaks the Greek language with such Attic purity that it would seem that Athens, which is now in the hands of the barbarians, has itself been transplanted to your Florence and become one with it."[17]

It may be noted that the hypothesis of rivalry and ill-feeling between Poliziano and Chalcondyles is strongly supported by the contemporary writer Paolo Giovio. But, as scholars have noted (see chap. 12), Giovio's "evil tongue" was always prone to find evidence of malice in the characters of those he discussed. Giovio, for example, by implication even attacks the honor of Demetrius' wife—Demetrius had married extremely late in Florence—who, remarkably, bore ten children when Demetrius was between the ages of seventy-one and seventy-seven.[18]

Chalcondyles' influence on Florentine culture was not limited to the teaching of Greek but also extended to publication. Most important was his two-volume edition, printed in 1488, of the Greek poet Homer, the first great work to be printed in Greek.[19] This was published at the expense of two young Florentine pupils of Chalcondyles, Bernardo Nerli and Piero de' Medici, who, as Chalcondyles himself gracefully put it, "could easily have spent their money on some other trifle [*epinoia tini*]."[20] In the Greek preface to this edition of Homer, Chalcondyles relates how difficult it was to reconstruct the text of "this supreme guide to all men in the life of wisdom," since the manuscripts he had used were so mutilated. The first volume of Homer contains, besides the *Iliad,* the life of Homer by Herodotus and Plutarch and the oration on Homer by Dio Chrysostom. Volume 2 contains the *Odyssey,* the *Batrachomyomachia (The Battle of the Mice and Men),* and the *Hymns,* the latter supposedly written by Homer.[21] Chalcondyles affirms that he utilized in his edition the famous scholia of the twelfth-century Byzantine scholar, Eustathius of Thessalonica. But several modern critics (Camelli and Ferrai among them) remark that actually this edition differed little from the "vulgate" Byzantine version of the period.[22] It should be noted that more truly critical editions of Homer were not to be produced until later in the sixteenth century, especially in 1577 by Henry Stephanus, whose edition was based on all the codices and scholia then known.

Let us now consider the third and last phase of Chalcondyles' career—his tenure in Milan after the felicitous years in Florence. Once again a certain mystery exists regarding his departure from his chair in Florence. This circumstance reminds us that Chalcondyles seems only too typical of most of the Greek refugee-exiles who, far from their homeland and possessed of a nostalgia for their country, often suffered from a kind of wanderlust. In the case of Demetrius, there is evidence of several invitations made to him to teach elsewhere than in Florence (in Ragusa and possibly Rome). But he did not accept, though he himself may well have solicited the offers. Finally, however, again at the recommendation of Filelfo, he did accept the offer of the wealthy and powerful duke Ludovico il Moro to assume the position of professor of Greek at his court in Milan.[23]

Before the arrival of Demetrius, Greek letters had not been systematically cultivated in Milan despite the teaching there intermittently (privately or publicly) of several Greek scholars: the great Manuel Chrysoloras (called by Giangaleazzo in 1400; Manuel's one student in Milan had been Umberto Decembrio); briefly, Demetrius Castrenos, Andronicus Callistos, and the extremely erudite Byzantine, Constantine Lascaris.[24] With respect to Constantine, in 1462 forty-seven leading Milanese citizens (including Pier Candido Decembrio, son of the Milanese humanist, Umberto) appealed to their government to have the chair of Greek letters bestowed upon "Constantine the Constantinopolitan [Lascaris]," whereupon Lascaris assumed the post, publicly teaching in Milan for two years. But in 1474 Lascaris suddenly abandoned Milan and moved to Messina to occupy its *cathedra* of Greek.[25]

It was probably only natural that at this juncture the Milanese ruler, the learned Mycenas Ludovico il Moro, bethought himself of Demetrius Chalcondyles, whose reputation had by now spread throughout all of Italy. And so with the arrival in Milan of Demetrius in 1477, one may say that the Greek chair had finally been permanently filled. As Camelli affirms with no more than slight exaggeration, the center of Greek studies in Renaissance Italy now moved from Florence to Milan.[26] An indication of the enthusiasm engendered by Chalcondyles' teaching is provided by a secretary of il Moro who, upon hearing Demetrius' inaugural lecture, wrote that Demetrius showed "vast erudition and knowledge not only of Greek literature but also of Latin"—evidence of how much Demetrius' Latin must have improved since his Paduan days.[27]

The period of Demetrius' Milanese sojourn deserves further scholarly investigation. But it may be said briefly that the personality and erudition of Demetrius complemented well the brilliant coterie of intellectuals and artists assembled by il Moro, the ruler of Milan. There, celebrated artists such as Leonardo da Vinci and Bramante mingled with almost equally famous humanists. The list of Demetrius' pupils in Milan, if not quite so brilliant as that in Florence, is almost as large. It includes, among others, Baldassare Castiglione (later the celebrated author of *The Courtier*), Lilio Gyraldi, Benedetto Giovio, brother of Paolo Giovio, the celebrated German, John Reuchlin (mentioned above), and even, it seems, the great printer of Venice, Aldus Manutius. Besides teaching, Demetrius found time to maintain an extensive correspondence with such scholars as the most able

Hellenist of the French humanists, Guillaume Budé (who later studied Greek in Paris under Demetrius' best pupil, Janus Lascaris). It was Budé who now termed Chalcondyles "the master of our times."[28] Even more significantly, Chalcondyles also devoted his considerable energies to the editing and translating of Greek authors for the press. Notably he translated Galen's *On Anatomy* (first printed in Bologna in 1529). His edition of the orator Isocrates was printed in Milan in 1493, and the voluminous edition of the Byzantine *Suda Lexicon,* appeared in 1499. As Chalcondyles himself accurately pointed out in his preface, the Suda *Lexicon* was "a mine of information for the scholar."[29]

But as happened with respect to more than one humanist center in Italy, political and military events following upon the French invasion of Italy in 1494 now overwhelmed Milan. In 1499, in fact, the French king Louis XII captured il Moro himself and took him as prisoner to France. The glory of Milanese humanist culture seemed to have ended. Chalcondyles' fortunes in particular are unknown during these years. Nevertheless, a statement of Marino Sanuto that in 1500 Demetrius competed with others for a chair in Venice would seem to indicate his financial need. Moreover, we have evidence that in 1500 he was in Ferrara for a time.[30] His tribulations, however, seem to have come to a happy end in 1501 when the new French rulers of Milan recalled him and restored him to his old post. Henceforth, for ten more years, until his death in 1511 at the advanced age of eighty-eight, Chalcondyles was able to reap a second and renewed success in Milan. The happiness of his last years was disturbed, however, by the unexpected, tragic deaths of several of his sons (as noted, he had ten children in all) who, while still in their mid-twenties, had as budding Hellenists already exhibited some of the talent of their father.[31]

During Chalcondyles' nine-year tenure at Padua, his sixteen at Florence, and his almost twenty years at Milan, he achieved a record which in length of teaching and brilliance—except, of course, for the eventful short years of Chrysoloras in Florence, and possibly those of Musurus later in Padua—cannot be matched by any other Byzantine or Latin teacher of Greek in the Italian Renaissance. It would seem more than coincidental that his teaching in Lorenzo's Florence and il Moro's Milan coincided almost exactly with two of the most brilliant periods of humanistic development in the entire Renaissance.

After this delineation of Demetrius' career, let us return to the document we alluded to earlier—Chalcondyles' inaugural speech (or speeches) delivered in 1463 on the establishment of the new chair of Greek studies at Padua University.[32] The precise circumstances of Chalcondyles' appointment at Padua, particularly the person or persons to whom he owed his nomination, have not hitherto been clarified, though scholars have suspected as preparing the way, the Byzantine Theodore Gaza (his old teacher and patron), Francesco Filelfo, and Palla Strozzi.[33] Whatever their efforts behind the scenes, we may now learn from the unpublished text of Chalcondyles' oration precise details on who was most directly responsible for establishment of the chair. As Chalcondyles puts it: "Through the most illustrious and outstanding authority of the Venetians at the request of the most reverend my Lord Cardinal personal legate of the Holy See . . . and patron of Constantinople, and by the favor and help of the Magnificent Rector and of the excellent scholars [does this refer to Gaza, Filelfo, and Strozzi, or, more probably, to the faculty of Padua University?] I was accordingly appointed publicly to lecture on Greek letters."[34] The words *my Lord Cardinal*, of course, denote the great patron of the Greeks in Italy, the Byzantine-born John Cardinal Bessarion, to whose select intellectual circle in Rome Chalcondyles seems to have belonged earlier. A convert to the Roman church after the Council of Florence, Bessarion was now, it seems, papal governor of Bologna and envoy to Venice, to which city, with its large Greek community, he was later to leave his famous collection of Greek codices.[35]

Let us move now to our manuscript itself—that is, to Chalcondyles' inaugural speech. After a brief introduction, four separate sections may be distinguished. The first two, very brief in scope, are evidently preambles to the two long discourses which constitute parts three and four of the manuscript. Section three undoubtedly constitutes *the* famous inaugural oration delivered by Chalcondyles, as was the custom in Renaissance Italy when one assumed a new university chair. The fourth section, again a lengthy oration, was most probably written (and evidently delivered by Chalcondyles) in the next year, 1464, that is, at the beginning of the succeeding year's course. The practice of giving a kind of second inaugural address at the commencement of the second year of a new course was not remarkable, indeed even rather common, in Renaissance Italy.[36]

In view of the composition of Chalcondyles' audience, both speeches and their preambles, as would be expected, are composed in Latin. In his brief introduction to the manuscript containing Chalcondyles' speeches, the scribe of the manuscript, Hartmann Schedel, later to become famous as a physician-humanist from Nürnberg, Germany,[37] introduces and emphasizes the significance of Chalcondyles as a scholar: "Demetrius the Athenian was that Greek who publicly expounded (*exposuit*) to us first at Padua the *Erotemata*, then Hesiod." Then Schedel, quoting from a preface of Marsilio Ficino which had been appended to Ficino's own famous translation of Plato's *Dialogues*,[38] first printed in 1484 (but of which the translation was finished earlier, in 1468 or 1470), interpolated the fascinating information, quoted from Ficino himself, that before publishing his celebrated translation of Plato, Ficino had "consulted with several critics for this work: Demetrius the Athenian, no less [expert] in philosophy and eloquence than others of the race of Attica."[39] In the published edition, Ficino adds the names of the Florentines Georgius Antonius and Joannes Battista, and also, though Schedel omits them here, the names of Angelo Poliziano, Cristoforo Landino, and Bartolomeo Scala.[40] But note that of all these famous names Chalcondyles is listed first. That Chalcondyles and Ficino had discussions in Florence, and in particular at the home of Bernardo Bembo, is attested elsewhere by Ficino himself, in his *Theologia Platonica*, book 6, chapter 1.[41]

From these opening remarks of Schedel, we are able to garner several interesting nuggets of completely new information. First that at Padua Chalcondyles lectured on the ancient Greek poet Hesiod and the *Erotemata* (grammar), probably that of Chrysoloras. It is thus clear that Chalcondyles taught not only the rudiments of Greek grammar but poetry—that is, literature, in particular the work of Hesiod, evidently his chief composition, the famous *Works and Days*. This is especially significant since this is probably the first time that works of Hesiod, as yet very little known in western Europe, had been taught at a Western university. (The *Works and Days* was, in fact, first published later in 1493 by Bonus Accursius in Milan, edited incidentally, by Chaldondyles himself.[42] Let us not overlook, too, the reference to Ficino's consultation with Demetrius before publication of his translation of Plato's *Dialogues*, an achievement recognized as seminal in the development of Renaissance Platonism.[43] Moreover, one wonders, unless too much is read into the words, whether it is possible to see in Ficino's reference, quoted by Schedel, to Chalcondyles as expert in *both* philosophy and eloquence, an allusion to the transformation taking place in Italian—particularly Florentine—humanism as the result of the Council of Florence and more recently of John Argyropoulos' philosophic teaching in Florence—that is, a shift from an emphasis on rhetoric to one on metaphysical philosophy.[44]

Chalcondyles' inaugural speech, as revealed by its preamble, is addressed to the "Magnificent Rector and distinguished doctors and you other most erudite men"—presumably the assembled faculty of Padua, and, no doubt, the Venetian officials present as well. With typical exaggerated Renaissance (not to speak of Byzantine) modesty, Demetrius then enters the body of his discourse. "Assuredly, most cultivated and wise men, you have accustomed yourselves to exercise in all things the greatest courtesy (*humanitatem*) and gentleness. But this same kindness, may you be willing to show to me, a new man (*homini novo*), who is of mediocre erudition in Latin letters, and may you with a cheerful frame of mind hear my speech."[45]

Of little interest is the second preamble inserted in the manuscript which, as noted, was probably delivered by Demetrius the following year at Padua as introductory to the second oration. This preamble is very similar to the first but is even more florid. There is one important passage, however, that may be quoted: "When . . . I was appointed publicly to teach Greek letters, it seemed good to say something not off the subject—how much utility, how much embellishment and perfection (*ornamenti perfectionisque*) they [Greek letters] bring and how the study of Greek literature has explained and does explain Latin letters."[46]

Here Demetrius informs the assembled faculty of what he considers to be a special dividend they may expect from his instruction of Greek. Not only would a knowledge of Greek help the Paduan student more easily to explain Latin literature; it would, Demetrius indicates, aid the student in the formation of a better style. This remark was apparently calculated to appeal to the contemporary rhetorical interests of leading Italian humanists, as well, of course, as to reflect the more pragmatic propaganda of the Greek refugee scholars, to whose obvious professional interest it was to foster the desire of Western humanists to learn their language.

It should not surprise us that the Byzantine Chalcondyles begins his oration with a long justification for study of the Greek language. Such an apologia was common enough in humanist speeches of the period, or might conceivably even suggest that Greek studies were still considered by some to be not really indispensable to a university curriculum. We might recall the early case of the humanist Giovanni Conversino da Ravenna, who was ignorant of Greek (he called anyone who addressed him in the language "barbarian")[47]; and also that, probably in 1405, Cardinal Dominici in Florence violently attacked Coluccio Salutati for his interest in the classics (including ancient Greek literature)[48]; and that in Venice itself, in around 1416, the secretary to the Venetian senate and chancellor of Crete, Lorenzo de' Monaci, a friend of both the great Florentine humanist Leonardo Bruni and the Venetian Francesco Barbaro, expressed profound hostility to everything Greek and declared that both the study of Greek and translations from that language were useless.[49] Of course, even at this relatively mature date (1463) in the development of the Renaissance, Demetrius' apologia at the beginning of his second discourse might also simply reflect the age-old Byzantine feeling of intellectual superiority to the Latins.

Chalcondyles continues in the same vein: "I believe that no one of you is ignorant that the Latins received every kind of liberal arts from the Greeks. And it is also well known that the originators of all these arts were Greek and that the very name of the arts was inspired by the Greek. So let me begin with the small things themselves and with the very rudiments of grammar, poetry, the oratorical art, history, logic, mathematics, natural philosophy, medicine, and then of divine science [theology] itself.[50] For who, even moderately learned, is unaware that they [the Greeks] were the inventors? Or that everything or some of the things which were received from others, they [the Greeks] themselves made more perfect and then transmitted to the Latins? . . . The Latins, following the Greeks even to the very elements of literature, are rightly thought, therefore, to have excelled other nations in every kind of learning, as in warfare. Since therefore they [Latins] had received literary studies (*studia litterarum*) and every craft (*omnes artes*) and they follow the inventors (*ductores*) themselves, no one could deny that the study of Greek letters offers much fruit to the Latins in every kind of learning. And about the things, first of all, which pertain to grammar, I shall say something. Since Latin grammar is joined to Greek and seems to depend upon it, how can anyone have a complete grasp (*cognitionem*) of it unless he knows Greek letters; nor can he know the derivation of very many words and their specific meanings, nor the declension of many nouns, nor the quantity of syllables, nor want to speak correctly and elegantly (*recte ac eleganter*) if he is ignorant of Greek letters."

Chalcondyles proceeds to elaborate on the necessity of knowing Greek for a more perfect knowledge of Latin.[51] He observes that "no one can say rightly, I believe, that some Latin authors wrote some works concerning these things and therefore it is not necessary to know Greek literature.[52] For they [the Latin authors] speak thus about these things [Greek letters] so that the learners may have knowledge of them, so that they may not be completely ignorant of them . . . . [Indeed, how could anyone] desirous to quench his thirst seek the swamp (as I should say) rather than the fountain and, being hungry, prefer to have dessert instead of solid food?[53] In the same way, I think this should be said about those things that seem to pertain to poets, oratory, and every branch of speaking (*genus dicendi*), since no one considers that a poem or an oration may be written without nouns (*nominibus*), correct diction (*recta locutione*), figures [of speech], brilliant shadings (*coloribus*) and subject matter (*argumentis*).[54] And since both skills [he refers here to poetry and oratory] have been handed down abundantly and copiously by them and have been put to use in their Latin poems, orations, and histories most fully and perfectly, the old Latin authors (*auctores*), the poets, the orators, and also the historians, confirm my opinion: none of them [the Roman authors] was ignorant of Greek letters. Indeed, several (*complures*) of them venerated Greek literature so thoroughly, that one wonders whether they knew Greek or Latin literature better."[55] Here he quotes Cicero, that "hero" of the early Italian Quattrocento, who, Chalcondyles declares, always coupled Greek and Latin. He also cites Brutus and Favorinus and other Latin authors. Demetrius here affirms: "nor would those most learned men [the ancient Romans] have devoted so much effort to this literature unless they had believed that they could have secured a great benefit from them, and they realized that Greek literature was an aid and an embellishment (*ornamento*) [i.e. in style] to the Latin literature and to their own works." Chalcondyles then cites Horace's famous words, from his *Art of Poetry*: "Turn over the Grecian models both night and day."[56]

It may be said that this reference, meager as it is, reveals something of Chalcondyles' somewhat limited knowledge of Latin poetry.[57] For though expert in Greek literature, the usual Byzantine

or post-Byzantine humanist in the West disdained or even consciously neglected Latin literature, especially poetry, as being
inferior to Greek.[58] Of all the Greek refugees, very few besides
Theodore Gaza, Janus Lascaris, Michael Marullus, and probably
Bessarion, ever learned Latin thoroughly enough to write it elegantly.[59] Turning to philosophy—and Padua, let us recall, was famous
for its Averroism—Chalcondyles remarks with no little justification
that "the texts themselves of Aristotle . . . have been rather badly
and improperly translated into the Latin language" and "in order
that those who apply themselves chiefly in their own fountain of
philosophy [is he here referring to the Averroists and Thomists of
Padua?] might understand them [the works of Aristotle] fully and
correctly, they should learn this literature."

This important passage, it seems to me, may indicate how much
Chalcondyles and other Byzantine scholars were distressed by the
many inadequate Latin translations of Greek philosophic (and
literary) works being circulated in the West. True, the Florentines,
especially Bruni, had tried to get away (but not without criticism)
from the crabbed, overly literal style of the medieval translators from
the Greek, and under the tutelage of such Byzantines as Chrysoloras,
Argyropoulos, and later this same Chalcondyles, were gradually
producing Latin versions that adhered more to the spirit than the
letter of the original text. One feels, nonetheless, that in his complaint Chalcondyles seems unaware of, or underestimates the significance of, the translations of Leonardo Bruni in particular, in helping
to establish a new and broader horizon for the study of the original
Aristotelian texts.[60]

Chalcondyles moves on to a reference to medicine, astrology
(which here probably means the "science of the stars," namely,
astronomy),[61] and the other arts, "since, as I believe, most things are
[included] in those disciplines (scientiis) which, unless one has Greek
literature, cannot very easily be understood." One particularly notes
here Chalcondyles' mention of medicine—which was not included in
the curriculum of studies generally considered to be humanistic—
that is, was not part of the studia humanitatis. At Padua University,
however, medicine was very closely connected with the faculty of
arts, so much so that, unlike at many other universities, both were
listed under the same rubric, as the "faculty of arts and medicine."
Thus, in relating medical terms, especially their etymological roots,
to the study of Greek grammar, Demetrius must have been catering

to the pride of the celebrated Paduan medical school, and showing how, from a humanistic point of view, Greek could be helpful in this respect too.

Then, more directly addressing the Paduan youth, or those who "have expended much strength and effort on virtues and the liberal arts," Chalcondyles exhorts them to the study of Greek so that they can reap a "delightful fruit, a fruit nourishing the mind." In seeking to induce them to such an endeavor, which, as he affirms, may at first glance seem to them onerous at this stage, he argues that, even if one starts the study of Greek rather late, "you will not find great difficulty . . . because Greek letters seem to have no small similarity and relationship to Latin letters. . . . And even if someone in some manner should believe that those letters are difficult to learn, yet you should not avoid any kind of toil or difficulty because of the hope of fruit and usefulness (*utilitas*) to be derived from them."[62] Note here especially his reference to *utilitas*, a term often used by the humanists —the Schoolmen, incidentally, also used this term—in seeking to justify the profit to be gained from the study of ancient literature in order to make it useful to their contemporary world. To bolster this angument, Demetrius quotes, in good humanist fashion, from a classical Greek poet whose works, perhaps more than those of any other, emphasized the work ethic—Hesiod: "To virtue the gods joined much sweat." This is undoubtedly a paraphrase of a famous passage from Hesiod's chief composition, the *Works and Days*. Since this work had not yet been published and was little known in the West, the particular passage was probably not familiar to the scribe, who, in our manuscript, has tried—badly—to reproduce the original Greek letters in Latin characters.[63]

To cap his argument to the Paduan students on the value of Greek, Chalcondyles promises, on his part, to spare no effort to instruct them effectively. And here he states—and this is a salient point— what *exactly* his teaching will consist of. He will teach, he affirms, a "beginning course in grammar, poetry [meaning literature], and oratory (*in his principiis grammatice et in poetis ac oratoribus*)"[64] In other words, this instruction of his was to include, not only the basic grammar, but the more advanced material of the Greek orators and poets. Note that philosophy is not mentioned here, though Platonism, as already noted, had begun to be important in not distant Florence somewhat earlier, because of Pletho at the Council of Florence and, after 1456, with John Argyropoulos' instruction at the Florentine *studium*; and Chalcondyles himself, still later of course, was to become famous as a professor of Platonism in Florence. Nevertheless, it would appear that at this time Padua University and its patron, the Venetian government, were probably more interested in the more practical benefits to be derived from the study of Greek, among other things, in connection with medicine and, perhaps, with the training of government secretaries and statesmen through Greek rhetorical studies.[65]

Then, inevitably, as with every ethnically conscious Greek émigré, Chalcondyles loses no opportunity to impress upon the government and intellectuals of Venice the melancholy fate of his enslaved fellow countrymen. Lamenting their plight, he remarks especially on Bessarion's aim "for the recovery of wretched Greece (*Graecie misere*) which, most cruelly overrun and oppressed by them [the Turks], suppliantly implores the aid of all Christians and most of all the Latins, and from these Latins entreats this reward (*remuneracionem*). So that, just as she [Greece] had expended for them [the Latins] all of her most precious and outstanding possessions liberally and without any parsimony, and had restored into her state with her hand and force of arms Italy, long ago oppressed by the Goths, they [the Italians] should in the same way now be willing to raise up prostrate and afflicted Greece and liberate her by arms, from the hands of the barbarians." (He refers here, of course, to the analogy of Justinian's sixth-century reconquest of Italy from the Ostrogoths.) Note here also the rare reference, one of the few on the part of Byzantine refugee scholars, to Byzantium. The Greek exiles obviously preferred to remind Westerners of their intellectual debt to ancient Greece rather than to Byzantium which, in Western eyes, because of the lingering heritage of the Middle Ages, was still looked upon by many as being schismatic and even somewhat opprobrious.

Chalcondyles continues, mentioning the *utilitas* that will accrue to all Christendom if Greece is liberated. Then he singles out Venice, the state which had lost most through the Turkish capture of Constantinople: "Which [liberty] Greece will obtain, especially from the most illustrious lordship of the Venetians, through its [Venice's] authority and most holy and pious wish to be liberated from the infidels with God's favor and to be restored to her pristine state, [then] Greece will give undying thanks to Venice (*dominio*) for such lasting benefit." He closes his inaugural address with a curious and striking analogy between the fate of the damned in Dante's *Inferno*

and the prostrate condition of Greece, and finally with this protesta-
tion of modesty: "I wanted to say these things before you despite the
meagerness of my learning (*doctrina*) and my talent (*ingenii*)."[66]

Chalcondyles' analogy between the supine condition of the
suffering Greeks and the damned in Dante's *Inferno*, besides revealing
the unique phenomenon of a Byzantine scholar's all too rare knowledge of Italian literature, may also reflect a standard Byzantine belief
that Constantinople had fallen to the infidel Turks as a result of
Byzantine sins, the Turks having been sent by God as a scourge to
chastise them until such time as the Greeks might be deemed worthy
of resurrection as a nation. More relevant politically—and Chalcondyles no doubt was aware of the situation—is the fact that in the
very same year this discourse was delivered (1463), Venice, after ten
unsuccessful years of attempted appeasement of the Turks, had
finally changed its policy. She was now engaged in the opening
stages of a desperate struggle over the preservation of her territories
in the former Byzantine East, now threatened by the Turks.[67]

At this point the manuscript continues with the second discourse
of the following year, 1464. The fact that Chalcondyles covers very
much the same material as in the first speech, though at times more
emphatically, may perhaps suggest that it is a later version by
Chalcondyles of the earlier speech transcribed by the copyist. More
likely, however, in view of the title, "Oratio secunda Greci Studii
habita Padue," of the date inserted in the margin of the manuscript
(1464), and, thirdly, of the statement of Schedel at the end, that the
orations were copied "from the hand of the famous Greek [Chal-
condyles]," it seems, rather, to be a speech delivered, in the not
extraordinary custom of the age, at the beginning of the second year
of Chalcondyles' course in Greek.[68]

We know that many humanists, especially the earlier Florentines,
were interested in what they considered the more practical—that is,
the rhetorical, ethical, and historical—aspects of liberal studies
(*studia humanitatis*) and less in the metaphysical or philosophic side.
They wanted to study ancient letters, the *studia humanitatis*, not only
for the benefit of the student's intellectual and moral development,
but even more for the benefit (*utilitas*) of their city-state and society
as a whole. With this practical scope in view—and Chalcondyles
certainly must have had some knowledge of the ideals of the Florentines—it may be understood how Chalcondyles' mention of the
Greek historians at this point in his second oration might well have

appealed to his audience. Indeed, if we may draw such an implication from his use of the words *hystoriis* in the first oration and *hystoriarum* in the second, Chalcondyles, in his second-year Greek course, may also have taught some Greek history.[69] History, to quote the famous Italian humanist dictum, was "philosophy teaching by example," and one should recall that Padua was at this time a famous center of Aristotelian philosophic teaching, though not yet in the original Greek text. Whether Chalcondyles intended parts of his speech to cater to current humanist taste in Florence as well as Padua cannot, of course, be determined.

Chalcondyles concludes his second "inaugural" oration with another appeal to the Paduan students to join their efforts to his own in this venture and thus "to imitate your ancestors." Once more he thanks Bessarion and the signoria (*dominium*) of Venice, as well as the "magnificent rector" and all others who have shown interest in obtaining the chair for him.

To sum up, the document we have sought to analyze, and from which we have quoted the more important passages, is significant for a number of reasons. Though its existence has been noted by one or two modern scholars, it has never hitherto been edited, nor has anyone quoted from it except for some isolated phrases. True, a cursory reading of the text would seem to indicate merely another highly rhetorical, and less elegant than usual, humanist oration. But our analysis, we believe, has provided us with some interesting new data for the study of Italian humanism. To begin with, it provides evidence hitherto lacking about one of the more notable but lesser-known episodes in the transmission of Greek learning,[70] so basic for the evolution of Renaissance humanism. More concretely, the speech supplies us with, if not one of the first mentions of Hesiod in Renaissance intellectual circles, certainly with the first specific instance of the *teaching* of Hesiod in a Western scholarly institution.

Besides confirming that the (German) scribe Hartmann Schedel was in truth a pupil of Chalcondyles, the document seems to provide evidence, through Schedel's Greek inserted into the text, of the state of his knowledge of Greek at the time he copied down the discourse in 1464, more probably in 1466, or possibly even later.[71] Moreover, by emphasizing Bessarion's primary role in the establishment of this Paduan chair, the oration reemphasizes his devotion to humanist learning and to the welfare of his fellow Greek émigrés. In particular, it provides a cogent and heretofore unknown example of his, as well as Chalcondyles', unceasing efforts to ameliorate the condition of their unfortunate fellow Greeks under Turkish subjugation, by appealing publicly for aid to the powerful signoria of Venice.[72]

More directly connected with the sphere of Italian humanism, the discourse, although couched in what to our taste may seem extravagant and at times even empty language, discloses the importance Chalcondyles and other late Byzantines attached to the study of Greek oratory and poetry, as well as history and philosophy.[73] From as far back as the time of Cicero, whom Chalcondyles several times cites as being immersed in Greek studies, the Western world identified *humanitas* with *paideia*, the Greek term for education of the young, but in the broad sense of humane culture as a whole.

Chalcondyles' emphasis here on poetry (and at this time one thought primarily of epic more than lyric poetry) and its conjunction with oratory, is particularly interesting because, through the didactic quality of the epic the youth could be provided with ideal, moral models to follow, and in oratory he could put to practical use the virtues thus learned from epic poetry. As for history, Lorenzo Valla had well expressed, for the Italian humanists, its close connection with oratory, in his famous statement that "oratory is the mother of history." Finally, oratory, history, and philosophy were in some sense related by the Italian humanists in their famous dictum, already quoted, that "history is philosophy teaching by example."[74]

That Chalcondyles, a Platonist by inclination, may in subsequent years have taught some aspects of Platonic philosophy at Padua, as he did later in Florence (witness the corroboration in the manuscript's introduction of his advice to Ficino on his translation of Plato), is not entirely to be excluded.[75] Yet it seems likely that Padua, which originally hired him to teach the Greek language, was more interested in his knowledge of Aristotle than Plato.

Whether Chalcondyles had in mind the various nuances mentioned above in the development of Italian humanism when he delivered his speeches at Padua, cannot, of course, be ascertained. But it is of no little interest, I believe, that in the period of the Palaeologan Renaissance, the various subjects here mentioned by Demetrius were all considered important and were studied in sequence, from the so-called *enkyklios paideia* (a difficult term that may be translated here as "encompassing knowledge"), that is, largely grammar, then extending to rhetoric and history, and finally to philosophy, the capstone of all Byzantine secular learning, just as theology was considered the end of all Byzantine ecclesiastical learning.[76]

Even more important, Chalcondyles' views, though full of tiresome, effusive pride in Greek culture, give *specific* reasons why a knowledge of Greek literature can benefit Latin—for example, in providing a better understanding of the fine points of grammar, in making it possible to acquire a more powerful and elegant style and also more meaningful content and ideas or arguments (*argumentis*). (An excellent field for investigation in this respect would be the influence of the greatest of ancient rhetoricians, Hermogenes,[77] on the West via the Greek refugee-humanists, and also the influence on the Renaissance of the textual emendations made in the ancient Greek works, especially the plays, by the Palaeologan scholars, Triklinios, Magister, and Moschopoulos.[78]

Finally, though the discourse is written in not very elegant Latin and in a language not native to Chalcondyles, we must mention here an important point almost entirely overlooked by modern Renaissance historians—that in order to understand the full implications of the Western revival of Greek, we must try to learn more about the style of late Byzantine—that is, Palaeologan—rhetoric, the modern study of which is still in its infancy but some elements of which are, I strongly suspect, manifested in this speech of Chalcondyles. For as one important nineteenth-century Italian scholar, Ferrai, put it—and I would put it even more strongly—Chalcondyles' teaching at Padua and Florence is an echo of "the last Byzantine Hellenism."[79]

Although I am not aware of any extant Byzantine orations given in Constantinople upon the assumption of a university chair, a careful study of the many encomia delivered before the Byzantine imperial court on an emperor's enthronement, on an emperor's death, or on the city of Constantinople itself, would, I believe, show certain parallels between them and this discourse of Chalcondyles.[80] Of course, it should again be stressed that Chalcondyles had taught in Italy before coming to Padua and that there are very probably Latin influences to be found here as well as Byzantine. Nevertheless, to really comprehend the manner in which the Italian humanists received the Greek classics, and the interpretation they attached to them, it would seem necessary to know more of the way in which the Byzantine preservers and transmitters of this heritage organized and, in particular, taught these classics; for Greek literature came to the

West only through the long filter of Byzantium, whose teaching and appreciation of classical Greek learning itself underwent several phases, culminating in the so-called Palaeologan Renaissance. Byzantium was not merely a repository of ancient Greek learning: it was in some ways also a modifier of it.

At any rate, there can be no doubt that for Chalcondyles, a son of Byzantium transplanted to the West, a thorough knowledge of all the main aspects of Greek culture, of "eloquence" in the broadest Western humanist sense and not merely in the narrow technical one, was central to the more perfect development of Latin literature in the Renaissance. As Chalcondyles repeatedly affirms, if to the eminently practical Romans the study of Greek literature and history—he even points out that the Romans sent their sons to be educated in Greece[81] —was found to be so helpful, why could these same studies, as exemplified in his course of grammar, oratory, and poetry, not be equally profitable to the later Quattrocento Italian humanists, who prized that civilization above all? With this argument Demetrius Chalcondyles of Athens made to his always pragmatic Veneto-Paduan audience his most telling point for the benefits to be derived from the study of Greek.

The career of Demetrius Chalcondyles deserves more attention than has hitherto been accorded it, for his contribution to the development of Italian humanism matches that of the greatest of Byzantine humanists in the West—Chrysoloras, Argyropoulos, and Musurus. While to Chrysoloras goes the honor of instituting the systematic teaching of Greek in the West during the Renaissance, to Argyropoulos a good deal of the credit for transmuting Florentine humanism from an emphasis on rhetoric to one on metaphysical philosophy, and to Musurus the palm for the broadest erudition and publication of the greatest number of Greek first editions, it was Chalcondyles whose teaching career outlasted that of any other Greek émigré in the West and, more important, took place in three major centers of the Italian Renaissance—Padua, Florence, and Milan—when they were all at or near the pinnacle of their humanistic achievement.

TRANSLATION OF CHALCONDYLES' DISCOURSES ON THE INAUGURATION OF GREEK STUDIES AT PADUA UNIVERSITY (1463)*

[Preface of the scribe: Demetrius the Athenian was that Greek who publicly expounded to us at Padua first the *Erotemata*, then Hesiod. Marsilio Ficino, in his preface to the works of Plato, makes mention of Demetrius in this manner: "Lest perhaps you think, friend reader, that such a great work is edited without design, know that when I had composed it [and] before I published it, I consulted several critics about this work: Demetrius the Athenian no less [expert] in philosophy and eloquence than others of the race of Attica, Georgius Antonius [and] Joannes-Battista, Florentines who are most skilled in the Latin and Greek languages."]

Magnificent rector, distinguished doctors, and you other most erudite men: Although I do not see that I am able to make a speech on the study of Greek letters worthy either of the subject or of your ears, I—very little experienced as I am in such things and, moreover, with little talent and slight learning, [although] I can give little satisfaction to you very learned and wise men—nevertheless, because the newness in particular of the subject and especially the custom of inaugural addresses seem to require it, have undertaken this task (as they say) with a dull Minerva [i.e. without skill].

Assuredly, most cultivated and wise men, you have accustomed yourselves to exercise in all things the greatest courtesy (*humanitatem*) and gentleness. But may you be willing to show this same kindness to me, a new man (*homini novo*), who is of mediocre erudition in Latin letters, and may you hear my speech with a cheerful frame of mind.

When, then, through the most illustrious and outstanding authority of the Venetians, at the request of the most reverend my lord cardinal, personal legate (*de latere*) of the Apostolic See, and by the favor and help of the Magificent Rector and of the excellent scholars, I was accordingly appointed publicly to lecture on (*legere*) Greek letters, for that reason it seems appropriate to mention how much

*As recorded (in Latin) by his pupil, the subsequently famous German physician, Hartmann Schedel. The above is my translation.

254

usefulness, style (*ornamento*), and perfection these studies [of Greek] offer to Latin letters, and how much they have explained and do clarify Latin. It does not seem necessary to say anything more.

[Schedel's heading: Another preamble of the same Greek in the following year—that is, 1464—in the *studium* of Padua.]

Today is for me a most joyful and, at the same time, a very sad day: most happy indeed that such a gathering of very famous and learned men has deigned to be present for my discourse. If in any way this speech can be worthy and pleasing to your ears I shall truly have accomplished nothing happier for me; nothing sweeter is more desirable; sad, indeed, because with so little talent and mediocre knowledge, and with such meager and poor eloquence (*eloquencia*), I am about to deliver an oration before men who are the most famous and distinguished of any place on earth and are endowed with every kind of wisdom, knowledge, and eloquence. Who could be either so eloquent or able in knowledge and ability? Who would not be numbed before your gaze—you who are so important and wise, who would not tremble or hesitate? But since I recall your knowledge, your humanity and gentleness toward all, I have not in the least doubted that you will show yourselves to be sympathetic and well disposed even to a man who is new (*homini novo*) and completely unaccustomed, and who has very little experience (*exercitato*) in matters of this kind, and is learned in small degree in Latin letters, even if my speech is thin and worthy neither of the dignity of the occasion, about which it is important to say something, nor worthy of wisdom (*sapientia*). When, therefore, through the very illustrious and renowned authority of the Venetians (*inclito dominio Venetorum*), at the request of the most reverend my lord cardinal, personal legate (*legati de latere*), and by the favor and help, desire, and agreement of the distinguished rector and excellent scholars I was appointed publicly to teach Greek letters, it seemed good to say something not off the subject—how much utility, style, and perfection (*ornamenti perfectionisque*) they bring, and how the study of Greek literature has explained and does explain Latin letters. Therefore, magnificent and most kind men, I should like you to consider this matter for a little while here, and that you should want to listen to my discourse, according to your custom, benignly and with cheerful disposition.

[Schedel: Here begins the speech of the famous Greek presented in his inaugural lecture (*in principio lecture*) in the famous Paduan gymnasium (i.e. university).]

I believe that none of you is ignorant that the Latins received every kind of liberal arts (*liberalium artium*) from the Greeks. And it is also well known that the originators of all these arts were Greek and that the very names of the arts were derived from the Greek. So let me begin with the small things themselves and with the very rudiments (*ipsorum elementorum*) of grammar, poetry, the oratorical art, history, logic, mathematics, natural philosophy, medicine, and then of divine science itself—(for who, even moderately learned, is unaware that they [the Greeks] were the inventors (*inventores*)? Or that everything or some of the things that were received from others they [the Greeks] themselves made more perfect and then transmitted to the Latins?) They [the Greeks] flourished so much in every kind of virtue and learning (*in omni genere virtutis doctrinaque*), that it is well authenticated: to no one did they yield in anything during the time in which they flourished. The Latins, having followed the Greeks even to the very elements of literature, are rightly thought to have excelled other nations in every kind of learning, as in warfare. Since, therefore, they had received literary studies (*studia litterarum*) and every craft (*omnes artes*) and they follow the inventors (*ductores*) themselves [the Greeks], no one could deny that the study of Greek letters offers much fruit to the Latin in every kind of learning.

And about these things, first of all those pertaining to grammar, I shall say something. Since Latin grammar is joined to Greek and seems to depend upon it, how can anyone have a complete grasp (*cognitionem*) of it unless he knows Greek letters? Nor can he know the derivation of many words and their specific meanings, nor the declension of many nouns, nor the quantity of syllables, nor want to speak correctly and elegantly (*recte ac eleganter*) if he is ignorant of Greek letters. No one can say rightly, I believe, that some Latin authors wrote some works concerning these things and that therefore it is not necessary to know Greek literature. For they [the Latin authors] speak thus about these things [Greek letters] so that the learners may have knowledge of them, so that they may not be completely ignorant of them, so that they might speak about this not imperfectly regarding those who have touched a bit there as at the fountain itself (so to speak)—as if anyone desirous of quenching his thirst would seek the swamp rather than the fountain and, being hungry, would prefer to have dessert instead of solid food! In the same way I think this should be said about those things that seem to pertain to poets, oratory, and every branch of speaking (*genus dicendi*), since no one would maintain that a poem or an oration can be written without nouns (*nominibus*), correct diction (*recta locutione*), figures [of speech], brilliant style (*coloribus*), and subject matter (*argumentis*). And since both skills have been handed down abundantly and copiously by them and have been put to use in their [Latin] poems, orations, and histories most fully and perfectly, the old Latin authors (*auctores*), the poets as well as the orators and historians, confirm my opinion: none of them [Latin authors] was ignorant of Greek letters. Indeed, several (*complures*) of them venerated Greek literature so thoroughly that one wonders whether they knew Greek or Latin literature better.

It is reported that M. Cicero himself confessed that he always joined Greek to Latin in order to serve his purpose and that he made no distinction between a knowledge of the Latin and Greek languages. But you know these things far better than I. And it is maintained that Brutus left to posterity letters written most elegantly in Greek, most weighty and full of meaning (*gravissimas sententiosissimasque*). Moreover, Favorinus the Latin was an outstanding orator, as testifies Philostratus in his book which he composed on the lives of the Sophists, and many others seem to have turned out to be very expert in Greek literature, then, whose names would take too long to enumerate. Nor would these most learned men [Latins] have devoted so much effort to this literature if they had not believed they could secure a great benefit from it, and they realized that Greek literature was an aid and a [rhetorical] embellishment (*ornamento*) to Latin literature and to their own works, as can be clearly recognized from the opinion of Horace, a most serious and very good poet, who speaks thus about the Greeks: "The Muse bestowed on the Greeks talent (*ingenium*), gave the Greeks talent to speak with a round mouth (*ore rotundo*) [i.e. to speak elegantly]." And elsewhere, urging the Latins to these studies, he exhorts them, "Turn over the Grecian models both night and day." What should I say about philosophy itself, regarding which those who apply themselves chiefly in their own fountain of philosophy [i.e. Thomism?] should learn this literature [Greek] in order that they might understand them [their own works] more fully and more correctly? Indeed, even if one may gather no other fruit from these studies, one can gain a better understanding of the texts themselves of Aristotle, which are otherwise accessible only in rather bad and inept Latin translations. I omit to note how much sweetness (*succi*) and fruit in this philosophy they can in abundance derive from other Greek books, and how much better and more fully they can understand the thoughts and opinions of other philosophers through these same Greek authors. They [the Latins] seem to see them [Greek thoughts and opinions] now, as it were, without the shadow of darkness [when they know Greek].

In the same way, I might speak about medicine, astrology [astronomy], and other arts, since the Greeks assert that they were the founders of all of them and since most things, I think, in those disciplines (*scientiis*) cannot very easily be understood unless one has Greek literature. Wherefore, distinguished and learned youths, you who have expended much strength and effort on virtues and the liberal arts (*virtutibus liberalibusque artibus*), having followed the examples of your old authors and many reasons (*rationibus*), may you be willing to devote yourself with all your strength to Greek letters and to gather from these letters a delightful fruit—a fruit that nourishes the mind. But if you possess a ready and eager enough mind, you will perceive indeed that I have advised you correctly. And then you will be neither more dissatisfied (if I am not mistaken) because you began them, nor displeased because you began to study those letters rather late. Nor, moreover, will you have great difficulty, as perhaps you thought, in learning this literature, since these [Greek] letters seem to bear no small similarity and relationship to Latin letters.

And if someone in some manner should believe that those letters are difficult to learn, nevertheless you should not avoid any kind of toil or difficulty because of the hope of fruit and usefulness (*utilitatis*) to be derived from them. This chiefly you should keep in mind: that nothing good can be acquired without labor and difficulty, as Hesiod the poet also says: [a garbled line of the Greek text of Hesiod is inserted here]. Which verses one may interpret thus: "To virtue the gods (*superi*) joined much sweat."* Who is able at the sàme time to attribute vice to himself? And I, indeed, who intend to teach you these letters, God willing, although I do not know that I possess the knowledge to teach you the higher and more difficult things, yet I shall bend every effort to satisfy you in this beginning course in grammar (*in hiis principiis grammatice*) and in the poets and orators, and insofar as I can, to disclose a shorter and better way to attain

*Here in the MS a Latin transliteration of the garbled Greek text is also given: "Aretes drosa te apro peden ethasca tin men ti kako tis ike ikinis sneletha" (see original text, below).

Portrait of Cardinal Bessarion from an illuminated manuscript in the
Grottaferrata Monastery. (See pp. 238-39.)

these letters. Finally, I promise I shall put at your service all my efforts in these letters. It remains for all of you to turn your attention to these letters and through your skill and vigilance to reflect that I am ready and eager to teach you. On the other hand, once again this lectureship (*lectura*) is instituted at this famous university for its honor, expansion, and utility. You and I together should first give great and undying thanks to the most illustrious and celebrated lordship of the Venetians which because of its generosity, readily granted the request for this lectureship.

Then we should give thanks to the most reverend lord cardinal and patriarch of Constantinople, *legatus de latere* of the Apostolic See and my matchless lord, who, since he is most skilled in both languages (*in utraque lingua*) and very wise, and since he understands how much fruit these letters can offer, demonstrate, and produce, at once accepted the wish (*voluntatem*) of the university. Without any delay whatever, he did not at all neglect to ask [the assent of] the most illustrious lordship and to secure it at once. May omnipotent God always keep the dominion [of Venice] with Him, safe and prosperous—both because of their [the Venetians'] piety and worship of Him, and because of the very good will and mind they direct against the abominable, monstrous, and impious barbarian Turks on behalf of the faith and for the benefit (*utilitate*) of all Christians and the recovery of pitiable Greece (*Gracie misere*) which, most cruelly overrun and oppressed by them, suppliantly implores the aid of all Christians, and most of all of the Latins, and from these Latins entreats this reward (*remuneracionem*). So that, just as she [Greece] had expended in their behalf [the Latins] all of her most precious and outstanding possessions liberally and without any parsimony, and had restored with her hand and force of arms the state of Italy [*Italia*], long ago oppressed by the Goths, they [the Latins] should in the same way now be willing to raise up prostrate and afflicted Greece and liberate it by arms from the hands of the barbarians. Which Greece will obtain, especially from the most illustrious lordship of the Venetians through its [Venice's] authority and most holy and pious wish, to be liberated from the infidels with God's favor and aid and restored to her pristine state, [then] Greece will give undying thanks to Venice (*dominio*) for such lasting benefit. And she [Greece] will think that it [Venice] has appeared for her salvation, just like those who saw Christ descend into hell for their liberation from evil, as in Dante's Inferno.

I wanted to say these things before you in accordance with the meagerness of my learning (*doctrine*) and talent (*ingenii*). Nor do I seek to instruct you because I think you are ignorant of these things, but in order to keep the custom in an inaugural address of this kind (*in huiuscemodi principiis*) and so as not at all to seem to have neglected my duty of exhorting youth toward these studies. But even though I should accomplish nothing worthy either of your expectation or your dignity, still may you extend, in accordance with your humanity and custom (*humanitate ac consuetudine*), forbearance toward me who, though troubled by various ill-fortunes and misfortunes (*variis casibus ac infortuniis*), have not, indeed, attained mediocre learning; nor, if I, being able, were to have much greater learning and talent, should I think that I could ever satisfy such men [as you]. May I thank you, men of such wisdom and dignity, because you have so kindly and courteously been willing to hear me.

[End of the first speech of a very distinguished Greek.]

[Schedel: Second oration of a Greek, at the beginning of studies, delivered in Padua in the year of our Lord 1464, the 10th day of November.]

Magnificent Rector, distinguished doctors, and other illustrious men, I would wish to have the strength of talent and learning, along with eloquence (*eloquencia*), to be able to say something about the study of Greek letters, something suitable to Greek letters which might indeed be worthy of your expectation. For in this way I would think that the worthiness and usefulness of those studies might be adequately explained and, I should think, satisfy your wisdom in some way. But since I see in me small learning and very slight eloquence, I fear that I may seem inept in speaking to you serious men— men most skilled in this branch of knowledge [i.e., oratory]. [I fear] that I may say something worse than the subject of the occasion requires. But when I consider how you have always been benign and humane to all accustomed to speak here, and that you grant to everyone as much kindness as the talent and ability of each seems to warrant, I, profiting therefore from your kindness and not from my erudition, have decided to say here what should be said about these studies, especially since it behooves me to follow the custom, now long observed and approved, in these inaugural addresses (*principiis*).

Therefore, to make a beginning here, I think that the study of Greek literature has been of great use and rhetorical embellishment (*ornamento*) in the first place (*in primis*) for the human race, and that no one imbued with some study of letters is ignorant. For who could be so inexpert and so uncultivated in liberal arts (*liberalium artium*) as not to know that every branch (*genus*) of knowledge was cultivated and flourished especially among the Greeks, who were the originators and cultivators of almost all the sciences? Anyone may easily recognize how much all the nations of the earth follow them, with how much veneration they have pursued them [the Greek authors]. The Greeks, had they not been skilled in these things [Greek literature], never would have been able (unless I am mistaken) to attain perfection in knowledge, when in this literature the bases and principles of all the sciences are established and discussed and thoroughly interpreted. The more they became learned and expert in these sciences, the more they burned with zeal for the study of these [Greek] letters. Just as, in fact, the Romans, who shone no less, perhaps, in the liberal arts than in arms in past times, clearly demonstrate.

Because almost all of these [Romans] understood their own language no less than Greek, and they preferred to express the feelings of their minds and the meaning (*rerum vim*) and nature of things more often in Greek than in Latin. For no one who observes is undecided about this: the books of almost all the most worthy authors are filled with Greek words and opinions, so that, not only did they realize that this fruit could be obtained from Greek literature, but they also saw that they drew from it a fuller knowledge of their own language, since none of them [the Latins] was ignorant that Latin eloquence took its origin from Greek [eloquence], and that it [Latin eloquence] had, as it were, a parent [in Greek]. What should I say to men skilled in every kind of ability, who, each one in his own art [skill] would like to write and bring something to light? How much fruit and how much fertility can they draw from the Greek sources, as divine Cicero declared! Since each man may reflect on the [Greek] sources (*fontibus*) in his mind, and since we do have very worthy examples of those first famous men before our eyes, I cannot, indeed, be astonished enough. Why have so many of these people been filled with idleness and laziness so that they completely neglect these literary studies [Greek]?

But if unlearned men unskilled in good letters do so [i.e. do not study Greek], and they do not take delight in the liberal arts or do not want to praise talent (*ingenium*), that seems not in the least remarkable, for such men do not at all like to devote themselves to literary studies—indeed, all studies seem to be the greatest burden for them [the unskilled]. But they are not averse to them, like frenzied (*frenesi*) captives wanting to consult skilled doctors or any others for their health. But when I see erudite and learned men do this [not take up this study], I am indeed overcome by the greatest astonishment. For, by the immortal gods, these letters can offer both knowledge and a fuller and certainly stronger end (*sermonem pleniorem ac certe firmiorem finem*) and no little fruit in all branches of knowledge; add to this embellishment and fullness [of expression] (*ornamentum et copiam*) in many other things and also in historical matters.

What is it that causes one to avoid these studies? Work, of course, and the difficulty of the undertaking or the extremely great distances involved (*locorum maxima intervalla*). But it is a shame for men endowed with virtue and skill to want to avoid anything good and to shun virtue on account of some one (*aliquid*) of these [i.e. work, difficulty, or distance], even should we be incited to this [pursuit of virtue and the good] by nothing else than the examples of those old and famous men whom I have enumerated, both Latin and Greek, who, for the sake of learning, traveled through almost the whole world, terrified by no danger or task.

The Romans, moreover, who were masters on land and sea [and] learned, in addition, at home and in school in almost every branch of knowledge (*scientia*) that exists, were accustomed to send their children to Athens. But you who do not need to undergo great labor or a long journey for the sake of these studies, up to now have you not neglected and hesitated to seize (*arripere*) them? To barbarians (*barbaris*) unskilled in every good art, this laziness may be permitted, this inertia allowed, I say. But I should not like this to be said arrogantly by me, or for you to think [that] of me. For I do not arrogate to myself so much authority (*provinciam*), nor am I so lofty that I should not be able to understand that I am of little importance. I have said these things, accordingly, to show that those early and almost divine men avoided no labor, no greatest distance of places, for the sake of virtue (*virtutis*). We, however, stand so far from them that at times we seem to condemn and reject the things that [for us] are very close at hand and which they found situated far from their fatherlands yet bent every effort to acquire. Moreover, the matter [of learning Greek] is not so arduous so that whoever wants to devote himself to this literature can profit much in a short time, inasmuch as it [Greek literature] has such an accord (*convenientiam*) and so great a relationship (*necessitudinem*) (as I should say) with Latin, that whoever knows the one may very easily acquire the other—which we also learn from many experiences. For some foreigners (*externi*) have wanted to learn this literature who seem rather distant (*alieni*) from them [i.e. Greek letters], and have very rapidly acquired not a little proficiency in these letters.

Wherefore you young people, who are in the most flourishing period of your life in which you are able to learn much, and who burn with a desire for all manner of knowledge, exert yourselves and add these studies to your others, and may you in this imitate your ancestors. Gather eagerly the fruit offered to you from this literature. You will always find me, in teaching of these letters, to be most eager to help you, and my small ability, whatever it may be, and my teaching (*doctrina*) of these letters and finally all the strength within [me], I certainly intend to expend (*impendere*) most freely. Know for certain (*pro certo habetote*) that I shall make you learned in the study of these letters, and in a short time I shall perhaps provide [you with] no mediocre knowledge of them.

And for the privilege which this distinguished university has conferred upon me by its consent and request (*consensu et rogatu*) and which I obtained by the intercession (*intercessione*) of the most serene, my lord the most remarkable and wise Nicene cardinal, from the most illustrious and munificent lordship of the Venetians, I shall return this reward and favor with all my ability.

I give the thanks I can, not those I should, to you, most magnificent and humane rector, to whom I shall always confess that I am bound on account of your singular virtues and your outstanding learning, and to you, most wise doctors, and to the rest of the men because of your kindness and enthusiasm in obtaining this lectureship of mine—to you men endowed with virtue and learning—because you have deigned to listen to me so kindly and with benevolent mind.

End

[Schedel: Thus end happily the speeches of the very distinguished Greek, my teacher in the *studium* of Padua, at the beginning of his lectureship, which were very elegantly read aloud. I, Hartmann Schedel of Nuremberg, Paduan doctor of arts and medicine, have written them down at the beginning of the course of study, from the hand of the aforesaid Greek when he taught the beginning course in Greek letters. Praise be to God.]

14

The Last Step:
Western Recovery and Translation of the Greek
Church Fathers and Their First Printed
Editions in the Renaissance

An important aspect of Byzantine-Latin relations long neglected by modern scholars is the recovery by the West during the Renaissance of the entire corpus of the Greek Church Fathers. In contrast to widespread concern with the revival of ancient Greek learning, the development of the Western Renaissance interest in Patristic Greek writings has hitherto received comparatively little attention. Nevertheless, there seems to be no question that the more prominent of the early Quattrocento Florentine humanists—Niccoli, Traversari, and to a lesser extent Bruni and Poggio—in the period between the teaching of Chrysoloras in Florence (1397–1400) and the advent of the Greeks at the Council of Florence (1438), were attracted almost as much by writings of the ancient Greek Fathers as by the classical Greek learning of antiquity. This chapter will concentrate on the initial phase of the process of the Greek Fathers' recovery during the early Renaissance and then, more particularly, on the printing of the first editions of these Fathers, starting with 1470, the probable date of the first edition, and extending to the later sixteenth century, by which time the entire corpus had been disseminated throughout the West.[1]

As we have seen, Greek was largely lost to the medieval Western world; but some works of the Greek Fathers were known in Latin translation.[2] Indeed, we might suspect that the medieval West knew somewhat more about these Greek writings than has yet been realized. At any rate, among the best known of such works were the sermons and commentaries of Chrysostom, Basil, and a few of Origen. Familiar also, again in translation, were Greek ascetic and moral discourses of Basil, Ephraem, and especially Chrysostom's *De Patientia Job*, as were the church histories of the fourth-century Byzantine, Eusebius. In pure theology only two Greek Patristic works seem to appear repeatedly in Western medieval literature: John of Damascus in the twelfth century (with his Aristotelian approach), and the mystical writings of Pseudo-Dionysius, whose corpus had been widely circulated (as we have seen in chap. 6) from John Scotus Erigena's time onward. But Dionysius was, technically at least, not viewed in the same light as the other Greek Fathers, since he was believed to have been a disciple of St. Paul.[3]

Renaissance humanists naturally drew heavily on this earlier medieval Greek tradition. Yet though humanist interests, in particular those of the editors of the Greek first editions, were often similar to those of the Scholastics, they were in some ways quite different. A few theories may be adduced for the changes wrought by and in Renaissance attitudes toward these works. Early Italian humanist translators of the Greek Fathers—with the possible exception of Ambrogio Traversari—were in general more interested than medieval scholars had been in the style of the works. Whereas the medieval translator (William of Moerbeke, for instance) had produced word-for-word versions, the Renaissance humanists, in an effort to reproduce the eloquence of the style, made freer translations which, in many cases (though not always), were more faithful to the content of the text. One may recall in this respect the dispute involving the bishop of Burgos in Spain who, lacking any knowledge of Greek, in 1430 criticized humanist Leonardo Bruni's translation of a classical Greek text, preferring instead the Scholastic, more literal rendering of William of Moerbeke.[4]

The humanists in some instances also effected a change in attitudes toward certain works of the Greek Fathers which had for centuries been considered heretical. Notable is the case of Origen—his biblical *Commentaries* had, of course, always been widely read—many more of whose works now became popular in the Renaissance largely because of the Neoplatonic ideas embodied therein and because of his felicitous manner of expression.[5]

To take another example, the humanists also reoriented medieval views toward the Byzantine Eusebius' *Preparatio Evangelica*, in which that author had sought to point out the precursors of the Christian Gospel.[6] However, humanistic attitudes toward certain other Greek Fathers, Chrysostom and Basil in particular, differed little from the

Scholastic, since their "orthodoxy" had never been questioned—a circumstance reflected in the many translations of their works.

The leading advocate of the revival of Christian antiquity in the early Italian Renaissance was certainly the Florentine Ambrogio Traversari. It is to him that we owe the translation into Latin, many for the first time, of more than twenty Greek Patristic works. As a monk (later minister-general of the Order) of the Camaldolese convent of Santa Maria degli Angeli in Florence, Traversari early became fascinated by ancient learning, both Greek and Latin, but with particular interest in the Greek Patristic writings. According to his own testimony, he began to learn Greek on his own, not through formal study with the humanists but simply by comparing individual words from the Greek Psalter and the New Testament with their corresponding Latin versions.[7]

A Byzantine refugee from Constantinople, Demetrius Scaranus (he has been almost completely slighted by historians), was of considerable help to Traversari in his work on the Patristic Greek texts.[8] Scaranus, who spent the last decade or more of his life at Ambrogio's monastery, performed for Traversari the difficult but fundamental task of transcribing the sometimes almost undecipherable manuscripts of centuries past. These Traversari had managed to secure either directly from the Greek East or from the libraries of Italian or Byzantine humanists in Italy, such as Chrysoloras, Guarino, Corbinelli, or Filelfo.[9] But Scaranus was probably more than a scribe, if we can believe a letter of Traversari to his supporter in his Patristic venture, Niccolò Niccoli.[10]

Contrary to what is sometimes believed, Traversari did not study Greek with the Byzantine Manuel Chrysoloras.[11] Nonetheless, the two did later meet and the famous Byzantine professed much esteem for Traversari's learning. Indeed, in view of Chrysoloras' similar interests in Greek Patristic writing as well as the classics (see Epigraph, the quotation from him stressing similarites between old Rome and Constantinople), Chrysoloras encouraged Traversari in his project of translating the Fathers. Traversari, it would seem, unlike many other Italian humanists, was interested in the Greek Fathers not for antiquarian reasons but, more importantly as he saw it, for the light they could cast on beliefs and practices of the early period of Christianity, when the Eastern and Western churches, ecclesiastically and culturally, were still one. Indeed, in 1424 he even translated a late Byzantine treatise (which he dedicated to the pope), the

Portrait of Ambrogio Traversari, from "De Vita et Moribus Philosophorum" (manuscript, Plut. 65.22). Courtesy of the Biblioteca
Medicea Laurenziana, Florence. (See pp. 246-47.)

Manuel Chrysoloras, engraving in I. Bullart, *Académie des sciences et des arts* (Amsterdam, 1682). (See pp. 246-47.)

Adversus Graecos of the fourteenth-century Latinophile Byzantine, Manuel Calecas. Evidently, it was the practical purpose of Traversari to promote the union of the churches through expounding a near-contemporary Byzantine theologian's support for the Latin view of the double procession of the Holy Spirit.[12]

Among some notable Latin translations of the Greek Fathers made by Traversari—treatises, letters, and sermons—were those of his favorite John Chrysostom (whose eloquence especially attracted him), of Basil, Athanasius, Gregory of Nazianzus, Ephraem the Syrian, and the Pseudo-Dionysius. He also translated (apparently at the suggestion of Chrysoloras) a very important work of early Byzantine monasticism, sixth-century John Climacus' *Ladder of Paradise*.[13] As a participant in the theological disputations at the Council of Florence, Traversari acted as an official interpreter and sometimes, because of his known sympathy for and understanding of the Byzantines, was called upon to serve as a kind of mediator or conciliator between the two parties.[14] His knowledge of Byzantine theology, derived from his study of the Greek Fathers, thus had its pragmatic side, though at this council his allegiance was certainly to the papacy.

Having discussed the work of the initiator of Renaissance interest in the Greek Fathers, let us turn to the printing of the first editions of these works—an undertaking that would enable them to be more easily and widely disseminated. What was the chief criterion of selection for the first Greek Patristic works to be printed, at least for the first that seems to have appeared, Basil's famous *Discourse to Christian Youth on Studying the Greek Classics*? This work, discovered—or rather rediscovered—in the West about 1400, was first translated into Latin (after 1410) by Leonardo Bruni of Florence, pupil of the Byzantine professor Manuel Chrysoloras.[15]

Where could the humanists, whose zeal for classical learning was not infrequently under attack, find more powerful vindication for study of the classical, and especially the pagan Greek, literary heritage than in this work of Basil? Indeed, the prime purpose of Basil's *Discourse* had been precisely to justify (with distinct qualification) study of the Greek classics by showing their utility for the Christian believer of Basil's own time.[16] The work thus gave cogent support to the Renaissance humanist emphasis on the *studia humanitatis*—a curriculum of study that stressed, among other things, classical literature as a preparation for the study of Sacred Scripture. It could hardly have been coincidental, then, that Basil's work, which had

Head of Leonardo Bruni (probably taken from his death mask), from Bruni's funeral monument by Bernardo Rossellino in the Church of Santa Croce, Florence. (See pp. 247-48.)

circulated widely in manuscript, was (apparently) the first Latin translation of a Greek Father's work to be printed, in 1470 or possibly 1471) in Venice,[17] soon to become Italy's leading printing center.

The enormous popularity of Basil's *Discourse*, not only because of its vindication of classical learning, but also because of its emphasis on the similarity of Christian and classical moral precepts and its praise for the classical literary style (especially its simplicity and directness), is indicated in that, before 1500, many incunabula editions (in Latin) were printed, including several Italian, German, Spanish, and even a Hungarian one.[18] It may, in fact, have been the first and only Greek Patristic work published in fifteenth-century Spain.[19] As for the Hungarian edition, it attests further to the range of Matteo Corvinus's humanistic patronage.[20] A chief source of information on which Greek Patristic works were first printed and why, is the prefatory letter of dedication customarily inserted at the beginning of each work by the editor and/or publisher.[21] Thus, in Bruni's prefatory letter to his translation of Basil's *Discourse*, dedicated to Florentine chancellor Coluccio Salutati (and which was repeatedly printed), the purpose of the translation—justification for Christian study of the classics—is clearly indicated. Such prefatory letters to printed editions naturally express praise for the person to whom the work is dedicated and, of course, explain the significance of the work printed. It is these letters, along with the text itself, which constitute our chief evidence for the attitudes of the editor and, perhaps, the publisher.

The second most popular Greek Patristic work published was, it seems, Eusebius' *Preparatio Evangelica*, and this again evidently on utilitarian grounds. Eusebius' remarkable affirmation that the Neoplatonic ideas of the Greeks were derived from the Hebrews, provided, for the humanists, still another argument for the study of the classics. Eusebius' case differed, however, from that of Basil in that he had long been subject to accusations of Arianism. In any event, the first to translate the *Preparatio* into Latin was the ubiquitous and irascible Cretan émigré, George of Trebizond, who had the work printed in Venice in 1470. In his prefatory letter, George, after praising his patron, Pope Nicholas V, tells us that, because of Eusebius' Arian proclivities, he (George) has, in his translation, "cut off the thorns from the work and left only the roses."[22] That George's translation, with its "corrective" editorial comments, was reprinted in numerous incunabula editions would seem to indicate the great

Portrait of George of Trebizond, from J. Boissard, *Bibliotheca sive thesaurus virtutis et gloriae in qui continente* . . . (Frankfurt, 1628). (See pp. 248-49.)

popularity of Eusebius' edition.[23] Still, certain editors preferred the original text to George's "rectified" version.[24]

George of Trebizond became deeply involved in the philosophic dispute over the respective merits of Plato and Aristotle, begun by the Greeks, especially Gemistos Pletho, at the Council of Florence. He made use, at least indirectly, of Eusebius' *Preparatio* to support the Aristotelian faction. Specifically, he tried through his edition of the *Preparatio* to demonstrate that the "wretched" Platonists had borrowed their "little wisdom" from the Hebrews.[25] How widespread this erroneous belief was in the Renaissance is not clear; nor is the opposite view of some later humanists—that the Greeks were older than Moses and could not, therefore, have borrowed from him. But a continuing repugnance for the Byzantines on the part of some Western humanists cannot be ruled out as a factor here.

Despite his heterodox views, Origen, as we have noted, came to enjoy considerable popularity in the Renaissance in Italy and also, later, in the North. However, researchers investigating the first editions of Origen must exercise caution in generalizing about the treatment of his views, especially the heretical ones, in the first printed versions. For, though the humanist Marsilio Ficino and others particularly fond of Origen were evidently discriminating in their use of his philosophy and theology, others, like Matteo Palmieri and Leonardo Dati, seem clearly (if secretly) to have accepted certain heretical views of Origen such as the preexistence of souls.[26]

In 1475 a Latin version of Origen's *Homilies* appeared and a few years later the Byzantine Theodore Gaza had Origen's *Contra Celsum* brought from Constantinople for Pope Nicholas V. The edition was dedicated to Pope Sixtus IV and the Venetian doge.[27] The translator of the work, Christopher Persona, in his preface of 1481, compares Sixtus to Origen in virtue and learning.[28] The attractiveness of Origen's views on such questions as the preexistence of souls for humanist proponents of Neoplatonism and of the esoteric and occult is understandable. But the fascinating question this brings up of the so-called rehabilitation of the heretic Origen is not without difficulties. We may recall, for example, the case of Pico della Mirandola, whose arrest was in part occasioned by several suspect theses he propounded, one of which affirmed that it was more reasonable to believe in Origen's salvation than in his damnation.

In their eagerness to disseminate knowledge of the Greek Fathers through the medium of the press and also to further acceptance of the classics in their educational and philosophical program, the Italian humanists were gradually enabled to view the Greek Fathers more accurately in their original historical context. Here one recalls the great Lorenzo Valla, whose critical acumen permitted him to demonstrate not only the spuriousness of the Donation of Constantine, and (remarkably) even to point out errors of translation in the version of Jerome's Vulgate Bible, but, more pertinently still, to air his suspicions, on philological-historical grounds, of the common Western view of Dionysius as the disciple of St. Paul. Work recently done on Valla's philological method[29] and the new edition of his *Annotationes*[30] indicate how the new type of philological analysis enabled Italian humanists to come gradually to a greater understanding not only of the text of many Greek Patristic works but also of the cultural ambience in which they were written. For as a result in no small part of the dogmatic disputes at the Council of Florence and of his contact with the Greek representatives there, Valla had become convinced of the inadequacy of the Scholastic method and the need to substitute for it an exegetical theology based primarily on philological and rhetorical analysis of the biblical text and derived, in the Byzantine manner, from the Patristic commentaries. In this development that went on in Valla's mind, Byzantine influence, as has recently been shown, played an important but hitherto overlooked role.

To turn briefly to northern Europe, the Patristic Greek editions of only two, but two of the greatest, humanists will concern us here— Lefèvre d'Etaples and Erasmus. The French-born Lefèvre differed from the earlier Italian humanists in that he was more concerned with the Greek Apostolic Fathers of the first and second centuries A.D. than with the later, better-known figures of the fourth and early fifth centuries. As he affirms in his prefatory letter to his *Theologia Vivificans* (containing letters of Polycarp and Ignatius and Ambrogio Traversari's translation of the Dionysian corpus—not, surprisingly, that of Ficino),[31] he preferred the Apostolic Fathers because they lay at or near the very sources of the Christian faith.[32] Lefèvre, who seemed to dislike Neoplatonism, viewing it as a corruption of Christianity, disputed Ficino's view that Dionysius was the "crown of Christian theology" and the "summit of Platonic learning."[33] It is interesting, nonetheless, that he believed that Dionysius should be considered not so much a Platonist as an immediate follower of Jesus and Paul—and in that lay his importance. Which raises the specific question whether, or to what extent, Lefèvre knew Byzantine theol-

Portrait of Erasmus, from J. Boissard, *Bibliotheca chalcographica* (Heidelberg, 1669). (See pp. 248-50.)

Portrait of Lorenzo Valla, from J. Boissard, *Bibliotheca sive thesaurus virtutis et gloriae in qui continente* . . . (Frankfurt, 1628). (See pp. 250-51.)

ogy (actually he knew little Greek) and, in particular, whether or not he used the Byzantine Maximos the Confessor's exegesis of Dionysius, with its more systematic organization and greater emphasis on the person of Christ.[34]

For the cosmopolitan Erasmus, the Greek Fathers were especially important in furthering his cherished program of "Christian humanism." Remarkably, they were of greater significance in his mind than the Latin Fathers. Indeed, it appears that Erasmus even borrowed his famous phrase "philosophy of Christ" from the Greek Fathers, the Apologists and Alexandrians.[35] Like Lefèvre, Erasmus was vitally interested in the question of Christian origins and especially in the original teachings of Christianity. And yet, again like Lefèvre, he was not particularly drawn to Dionysius. Indeed, in 1505 he had published the works of Valla in which Valla questioned the authenticity of the Dionysian writings.[36] Erasmus's views of the relative importance of the principal Greek and Latin Fathers show surprising perspicacity as well as an independence of judgment remarkable for his time.[37] Of the greatest Greek Fathers (for whom Erasmus had only the highest esteem) he calls Basil clear and natural, Chrysostom persuasive, and Gregory of Nazianzus, a writer with finesse. On the other hand, though he had tremendous regard and affection for Jerome in particular, Erasmus criticized the Latins Ambrose as obscure, Tertullian as difficult and gossipy, and Augustine as too digressive "like the Africans in general."[38]

Erasmus read the Greek Fathers, Chrysostom for instance, not only for their moral teachings but, it would seem, to further his never-faltering ideal of a united Christendom, particularly at a time when the unity of Christendom was in grave jeopardy. (We may recall the parallel views of the earlier Byzantines Cydones and Planudes with respect to the Latin Fathers Augustine and Thomas.) Knowledge of the Greek Fathers was particularly useful to Erasmus in his dispute with Luther. Indeed, it seems safe to say that, in his view, the writings of the Greek Fathers, many of whom were even closer in time than the Latins to the fountainhead of Christianity, strongly exemplified and reflected the unity of the church. Why, then, should Luther be permitted to shatter this traditional unity, especially when several of his chief views were directly based on certain ideas of Augustine which, or at least Luther's use of which, Erasmus did not look upon with favor?

Erasmus, moreover, seemed to have found in the Greek Fathers confirmation for his condemnation of papal claims to temporal power and for his views on the nature and unity of the church.[39] Strikingly, Erasmus considered Origen, that is, the "rehabilitated" Origen, to be the greatest of the Greek Fathers. (One may recall Erasmus's remark that one page of Origen is worth more for Christian philosophy than ten of Augustine.)[40] Nevertheless, despite his great enthusiasm for the ancient Greek Fathers, it does not seem that Erasmus had too high a regard for the late Byzantine theologians— whose empire he, like other humanists of the West such as Reuchlin, believed had fallen to the Turks as divine punishment for breaking away from the Roman church. And yet when he defines the church as "the consensus of the Christian people throughout the world," he seems, at least by implication, to include the Greeks.[41]

In any synoptic treatment of Greek Patristic first editions, Erasmus must occupy an important, if not the chief, place. For his editions mark, in certain ways, the climax to the entire movement. Scholars have, to be sure, extensively investigated aspects of his work in this regard. But the results have not always been used, as they should be, to throw light on the sources of his Christian humanism. Nor have they been integrated into a larger, comprehensive account of Greek first editions. This is significant, for when viewed in the light of the whole development, research on individual Greek Fathers takes on an added, sometimes even a rather different, meaning.

After Erasmus's death in 1536, and especially during the last part of the sixteenth century, his aims seemed to predominate in the printing of Patristic Greek editions. More complete texts were sought out, greater textual accuracy was striven for, and editions of hitherto unprinted Fathers appeared: Gregory of Nyssa, Clement of Alexandria, Epiphanius, and others.[42] Soon even certain late Byzantine theologians began to be published, for example, George Scholarios (Gennadios), the last Byzantine patriarch and the first under the Turks.[43] (As we have seen, already in the early fifteenth century Traversari had translated the work of the fourteenth-century Byzantine Latinophile theologian, Manuel Calecas, on the procession of the Holy Spirit [filioque] but this had been largely in order to help refute the Orthodox position.)[44] By the late sixteenth century, however, with publication of most of the corpus of the Greek Fathers, the chief criterion for publication seems to have become less the consideration of utility than scholarship—that is, philology.[45]

It should be noted that it was not until the 1550s that publication of the Fathers in the original *Greek* text became general; previously, almost everything published had been in *Latin* translation. (No part of Origen's work, for example, appeared in Greek until 1602.) This may most easily be explained by the greater exigencies of Greek scholarship. But not to be overlooked is the interesting fact that in 1567, when Pope Pius V declared St. Thomas a Doctor of the Church, he shortly thereafter (in 1568) also officially exalted four Greek Fathers—Basil, Gregory of Nazianzus, Chrysostom, and Athanasius—also declaring them Doctors of the Church.[46]

To turn, in conclusion, exclusively to the role of the Byzantine scholar-exiles in the West, how they catered to Western humanist tastes by translating, editing, and publishing first editions of *classical* Greek works is by now well known. But given the increasingly strong (but still all too insufficiently recognized) Western humanist interest in the Greek Fathers (already in 1499 Aldus Manutius had the Cretan Marcus Musurus edit several letters of St. Basil's for his press),[47] it would seem only logical that these exiles would have published, besides classical works, Patristic writings, not only to cater to rising interest among Latin readers, but also for the benefit of their own fellow Greeks. I have on several occasions quoted the prophetic words of Bessarion, who left his great library of Greek manuscripts to Venice not only for the use of Western scholars but, as he elsewhere so clearly implied, to benefit his own countrymen who, under the Turks, were in grave danger of becoming not only slaves but culturally barbarized.[48] There is no doubt that a feeling of patriotism also motivated other Greek exiles of the late fifteenth and early sixteenth centuries—such as George of Trebizond and Zacharias Calliergis in Italy, and Demetrius Ducas in Spain and Italy—to edit and publish first editions of Greek Fathers, of the Greek New Testament text (see chap. 9 for Ducas' vital role in editing Ximenes' Polyglot Bible), and of Orthodox liturgical books for the practical, daily worship of their fellow Greeks in the West.[49]

Of cardinal importance, then, as the last step in relations between the Byzantine and Western Renaissance worlds, was the rising interest among Western humanists in the Greek Church Fathers. Not only did this indicate increasing Western appreciation for a neglected but truly fundamental aspect of their own Christian heritage, but it demonstrated that even in the religious sphere, so long marked by controversy, some theologians and humanists of the Latin kindred culture, by emphasizing translations and original Greek texts of the Fathers, were able to foster a deeper awareness of the underlying cultural and ecclesiastical unity of the two great halves of Christendom.

Epilogue: The "Sibling" Cultures and the Effects of the Acculturative Process

The preceding chapters, focusing on societies, institutions, and individuals, have served to illumine the contours of an extraordinarily long and intricate interaction of the Byzantine and Latin cultures. As we have seen, the patterns of their relationship first took shape in the early fourth century when the sibling civilizations began to separate out of the Christianized late Roman Empire. Though the two peoples possessed a certain common heritage, it was this very circumstance which sometimes made it all the more difficult for them to tolerate even apparently minor cultural differences. This was especially true of problems that served to obscure deeper differences fundamental to the uniqueness of the respective societies.

At the outset, in the fourth century the two cultures were more or less equally advanced—that is, on a par intellectually speaking. But in the West, because of political, social, and economic forces, a gradually worsening cultural lag (usually referred to as the "Dark Ages") set in, marked by an increasing diminution of secular interests, and notably the disappearance of Greek learning.[1] These forces in turn resulted not only in an infrequency of cultural contacts, but even in certain respects (political and religious schism in particular) in the gradual development of a genuine rivalry between the two societies.

Rendering the problem of cultural interaction more complex was the fact that various strata in the same society might react differently in response to the same stimuli. With the changes in the political and military status of each civilization vis-à-vis the other, came modifications in the attitudes of groups within each society toward the other culture. When the Byzantine state and society were dominant, most Byzantines tended naturally to feel superior and secure socially, emotionally, and culturally. But when, in later centuries, the Western states and their society began to revive and even to challenge the Greek, the Byzantines began to feel increasingly on the defensive, while clinging even more tenaciously than ever to their belief in their cultural superiority. Indeed, as we have seen, the more the framework

281

of their society collapsed, the more culturally and religiously threatened the Byzantines felt.

The Latins, on the other hand, in time became hardly less antagonistic toward the Byzantines. Accusing the latter of treachery in the Crusades and irritated by two Greek rejections of ecclesiastical union (signed at Lyons in 1274 and again in Florence in 1439—see chaps. 8 and 11), most Westerners (with certain exceptions) became more and more contemptuous of what their chroniclers were wont to call the "perfidious, cowardly, schismatic" Greeks. All these factors were reflected, on both sides, in tendencies toward cultural attraction or repulsion. And it is these considerations which constitute, perhaps, the most subtle, elusive factor in any attempt to reduce to meaningful patterns the cultural relations between the two at once similar and yet disparate societies in the vast period under discussion.

In the Prologue, two approaches to the problem of cultural interaction were taken: (1) the historical unfolding of events from a chronological point of view, and (2) the presentation of a schema in terms of modes of acculturation.[2] Of the four chronological stages of interaction as delineated in the Prologue, the long first phase (330–1096) was marked, not surprisingly, by an increasing degree of Latin borrowing from Byzantine civilization. This, as observed (especially in chap. 3), was with few exceptions an almost entirely one-sided proposition, the West, then vastly inferior culturally, being the main and in most respects the sole beneficiary. Suffering for long from the chaos resulting from the waves of invasions—not to mention internal anarchy—the West, in its semibarbarian state, was hardly in a position to influence the East except in certain minor, usually rather superficial, respects. Nevertheless, the fact that the West was undergoing the tortuous process of integrating its own cultural elements—especially the most alien, the Germanic—into one organic synthesis, served to give rise to new tendencies in the West which themselves led to different attitudes toward government and socioeconomic life. With respect to ecclesiastical discipline and ritual in particular, the West, with the passing of the centuries, became more flexible in its approach than the East, which remained in many ways more conservative—a fact that was at once the Byzantine church's chief strength and sometimess its weakness.[3]

In the second chronological phase (1096–1261), culminating after 1204 in the Latin Crusader occupation of most of the Byzantine Empire, the Westerners exerted pressures against and soon came to dominate the East politically, militarily, and at times ecclesiastically, but did not, consciously or otherwise, transform it culturally. Inevitably, however, because of the mass settlement of Latins in the East, a certain accommodation, or social and cultural symbiosis, took place after 1204, though by no means can it be said that any true integration of cultures resulted. For although the two societies usually managed to live at peace with one another in the East, friction in the primary areas of social relations—marriage, religious beliefs and practices, questions relating to citizenship and political allegiance, etc.—did not disappear. For example, we know that in the Latin-occupied Morea (as later in the Catalan Duchy of Athens) mixed marriages were at first forbidden by the ruling Western feudal class, virtually all the Greeks being considered second- or third-class citizens.[4]

Nevertheless, in Byzantium certain classes of Greeks and Latins—nobles, merchants, and frequently *politique*-minded statesmen—often got along better than did the common people, who in general clung more tenaciously to the prejudices of centuries. Above all, however, it was the Greek monks who acted as the conservative religious, and sometimes even cultural, "conscience" of their people.[5] And yet despite, or on occasion even because of, Latin coercion exercised in the political and religious spheres, some aspects of the disparaged Western culture managed to seep into the Greek East. One specific example we have noted is the Byzantine adoption of, or rather momentary recourse to, the Western legal practices of ordeal by fire and judicial duel.

With masses of Westerners living in the East and associating daily with the Byzantines, cultural influences still largely flowed from Greeks to Latins. Thus, in the period of the Crusades, Latin merchants and knights who returned to the West brought back not only new political and social ideas (a view of the workings of a centralized state and certain new writings of Aristotle, for instance) but new techniques to be utilized in such activities as fortress-building, glass-making, or silk manufacture.

For the social scientist, the third chronological phase (1261–1453) is undoubtedly the most interesting one for the study of social change and cultural interaction. For now Latin culture, in part through Eastern tutelage during the first and second phases and in part as a result of its own maturation through integration of its cultural elements, had finally achieved parity with, in a few instances even superiority over, the East. The inevitable result was a direct confrontation of two advanced societies and their cultures—a type of phenomenon as noted, not yet carefully studied by sociologists. Since the period of the earlier Crusades, when large groups from the two peoples were first brought together en masse in the East, contacts were becoming more and more frequent. Economically, up to and even beyond 1453, the Italian maritime powers continued to try to expand, or at least to maintain control over, the lucrative Eastern markets, to the increasing detriment of the Byzantine economy. Ecclesiastically, the developing Turkish threat brought the need for more frequent negotiations for religious union. Intellectually, as the movement of the Renaissance in the West with its growing mania for ancient manuscripts progressed, Italian humanists began to scour the East for every remaining vestige of ancient Greek learning.[6] Yet most Westerners continued to draw a gratuitous distinction between the ancient Hellenes and the contemporary Greeks (that is, Byzantines), as is reflected in the humanist Petrarch's famous statement expressing preference for the enemy Turks over the "schismatic Greeks who are worse than enemies and fear and hate us with all their souls." Pope Pius II put it more sympathetically after Constantinople's fall in 1453, when he stressed that "this is the second death of Homer and Plato." Nevertheless, to most Italian humanists the fate of medieval Byzantium was of only secondary concern.[7]

In this same third period, as we have noted more than once, pressures were exercised, directly or indirectly, by the West (the papacy and Latin missionaries in particular) on the East for conformity, particularly in the religious sphere. So coercive and distasteful did these pressures seem that a large segment, especially from among the lower, less literate class of Byzantine society, became alienated from its leaders, who often, as noted, pursued a policy of appeasement or, as the group itself perceived it, of a kind of "religious acculturation" toward Rome. And it was this intransigent resistance of the tenaciously conservative common folk and the even more fanatically antiunionist monks that erupted into what we have termed a "nativistic reaction." This "nativistic reaction" on the part, it should be noted, of the less educated Byzantines, usually stressed the traditional liturgical forms of Orthodox worship (use of unleavened bread in the Eucharist, for example—see especially chap. 8).

This phenomenon in the lower classes found a more sophisticated analogue in certain upper-class, more educated social groups, which likewise wished to preserve the integrity of their state and culture. Their response to the dual challenge of the Turks and especially the West during the last two centuries became increasingly expressed in a desire not only to preserve traditional forms of worship but also to turn back to and revivify the theological pronouncements of the seven ecumenical councils and the writings of the fourth- and fifth-century Greek Church Fathers. But, as we have seen in the Prologue, this antiunionist group of the intellectual elite at the same time included those who also stressed a reversion to the writings, literary and philosophic, of *ancient* Greek culture—a development that must be viewed in the context of a Byzantine state now shorn of its multinational character and consisting exclusively of a Hellenic society and culture (see chap. 2). It was this phenomenon of a more intensive return, even proud appeal, to *ancient* Greek scholarship, expressed in a heightened sense of Hellenic, not Roman (Byzantine) patriotism, that played an important part in helping to spark the so-called Palaeologan Renaissance.

This cultural-ethnic response on the part of the upper-class intellectuals was certainly not the only factor in the etiology of the Palaeologan Renaissance, with its stress on a return to past roots. For of course ancient Greek literature and philosophy had always been a staple of Byzantine education, though sometimes, as in the eleventh century, it was accepted only with serious reservation by ecclesiastical authorities because of its pagan content.[8] The increasing Latin influence in the period of the Palaeologan Renaissance may, for its part, have had a positive as well as a negative side. Through its challenge to, sometimes cross-fertilization with, or at least "shaking up" of, Byzantine cultural elements, it may have provided a part of the impetus for a "revitalization," a new burst of life and creativity in aspects of Byzantine civilization such as painting, mystical thought, and a more intensive, now synthetic study of ancient Greek literature.

Some Greeks were convinced that Byzantine cultural and religious patterns would survive better under Turkish than Latin domination. True, the widespread supplantation of Greek culture in Asia Minor by Islam was clearly manifest by the fifteenth century, if not earlier. But at least up to the beginning of the fourteenth century, the Turkish conquerors of Asia Minor generally had exhibited marked tolerance toward Greek religion and culture.[9] Indeed, as early as the late twelfth century a Greek patriarch had voiced to the Latinophile emperor Manuel I Comnenus the view that subjugation to the

Muslims would not force conversion to Islam, but "under Frankish rule and union with the Roman Church I may have to separate myself from my God."[10]

To many Byzantines of the last two centuries before 1453 the prospect of aid from the West seemed very uncertain—witness the constant internecine struggles of the Italian states, the Hundred Years War between France and England, and the intransigent papal attitude with respect to religious negotiation and military assistance. Worse, papal aid in the form of the coming of armies and numerous Latin clerics to their land to oppose the Turks was felt by these Greeks to be even more insidious, for in their view it might result not only in renewed political and ecclesiastical domination, but ultimately in large-scale assimilation, possibly even absorption, of most of Byzantine culture into the Latin.

Our fourth chronological phase (ca. 1453–1600), in large part post-Byzantine, witnessed the exportation of the intellectual harvest of the Palaeologan Renaissance by Byzantine intellectuals and painters who carried it to the West in an emigration that we have termed a Greek diaspora. Despite the numbers of Greeks who went westward and the remarkable success of some émigré-scholars in securing professorial chairs in Latin universities, it cannot be said that any genuine integration of the various Greek communities established in the West into the mainstream of Western society took place. Even the Greek colony of Venice, the most significant of all, always remained an ethnic subculture of the Venetian. Thus the inhabitants of this colony were not considered to possess all the rights of Venetian citizens, though honorary citizenship—witness the case of Demetrius Cydones[11]—was sometimes bestowed upon the more noted of the Greek scholars. The most significant of the Byzantine savants generally lived with their Italian patrons or in a university setting outside the Greek colony, but this was primarily for professional reasons. In spite of their coexistence, both peoples were aware that the Greeks were not fully accepted by the host society, certainly not into the stratum of the latter's power elite.[12]

Given the Western reception of important aspects of the Palaeologan intellectual Renaissance, the chief cultural beneficiary in this, our fourth and last chronological period, was again the West. But this is not to diminish the significance of the growth of Western civilization, which by now had developed an even more remarkable creativity of its own. Indeed, the principal institutions or monuments of

Western medieval civilization at its height earlier in the thirteenth century—for example, parliaments, Gothic cathedrals, centralized feudalism, and universities—owed little or nothing to Byzantine institutions or culture. Yet at the same time, it seems clear (see chap. 13) that without the later contacts of the Italian humanists with the intellectual émigrés from the Byzantine East, the development of the Italian Renaissance, certainly in Quattrocento Florence, would have taken another course.

As for the converse question, Latin cultural influence on the Greek East did, as has been shown (in chap. 4 especially), pervade certain aspects of Byzantine thought during the thirteenth to fifteenth centuries. Yet neither Western theology nor philosophy was able, organically, to penetrate Byzantine thought: the core of Byzantine culture remained entirely Greek. Thus, in this most crucial encounter in the Greek homeland, despite virtual Western saturation of Byzantine *society*, Greek *culture* proved itself the stronger.[13] In the long run the only near-permanent inroads made into Greek culture were in the areas of Venetian-dominated Crete and the Ionian isles.[14] And with the Turkish conquest of Crete in 1689, it too reverted to traditional Greek patterns of life and thought.

Having briefly summarized the principal characteristics of each chronological period, what conclusions may be drawn with respect to the three modes, or tripartite typology, of cultural influence suggested in the Prologue?* I must at once emphasize, as should have been apparent in some of the chapters, that these various modes of acculturation do not necessarily coincide with any particular chronological order. Nor, in fact, are they mutually exclusive; two or more modes sometimes coexisted, if in different strata of society. To take an extreme case, our third chronological period (1261–1453), reflects not only the third mode of cultural interaction—confrontation of two advanced societies—but also the first mode, in the form of certain aspects of increasing political, economic, and ecclesiastical "hegemony" (dominance) of one society (Latin) over the other (Greek).

Moreover, as already noted, this third period, in the variety of responses elicited to the challenge of the West, reflects at least two

---

*(1) Dominance of one culture with assimilation of cultural elements by the other; (2) amalgamation producing a new type of cultural synthesis; and (3) confrontation of two culturally advanced societies. "Nativistic reactions" and "revitalization movements" may result as responses to any or all three of these modes.

important and differing social phenomena—a "nativistic reaction" on the part of the large, vigorously dissenting segment of the common people, monks, and lower clergy, and many of the middle class, and also "revitalization movements" on the part of the higher classes, especially among the intellectual elite. While the lower classes blindly rejected the Western religious and cultural challenge, the reaction of the upper, more sophisticated strata was a seeking somehow to come to terms with it without sacrificing what each group considered fundamental to its religious and cultural values.

The best example of our first mode or type of acculturation, the dominance over or strong influence of one society or culture upon another, is found in the first chronological period (330–1096) when, after initial parity, an increasing cultural lag occurred in the West. But as we have seen, this dominance was not uniform, for Byzantine influence was then exercised only piecemeal—by infiltration, so to speak. At this time the "contact situations" between the two societies were rarely of a prolonged nature, but were rather sporadic and were exercised largely through individuals (merchants, mercenaries, pilgrims, ambassadors, or even wandering scholars). It should not be forgotten that in the earlier centuries Western society was simply not ready to accept the more sophisticated ideas and practices of the East. However, when later the Westerners were in a position to understand Byzantine cultural phenomena, they generally absorbed them with little resistance. One reason for the ease of Western receptivity, given the pervasive influence of religion in this age, was that until 1054 the churches, despite an occasional quarrel (most notably that known as the "Photian schism" of the later ninth century)[15] were still in communion, and therefore other aspects of life had not yet been unduly affected by religious enmity.

Our second mode of acculturation, that of the amalgamation or fusion of cultures to produce a new kind of cultural synthesis, does not seem to be identifiable in any really clear form. Something akin to it, however, may perhaps be distinguished in our fourth chronological period (before 1453 to 1600), in the interaction of the two cultures taking place on Western soil. At that time, as a result of the Greek diaspora (and the fact that no "ethnic" or religious threat was posed to *Western* culture), Byzantine scholars made a crucial contribution to the development of the Italian Renaissance in the form of the original texts of classical Greek authors and Byzantine interpretations thereof—recall our emphasis on Byzantium's role as a cultural filter from antiquity. This Byzantine contribution was instrumental in producing not a truly new synthesis but a restructuring of the principal components of Western humanism. As a result, the orientation of Italian, in particular Florentine, humanism was shifted from a purely Latin rhetorical movement in its earlier phase to a movement primarily emphasizing Greek philosophy and literature (see chap. 13).[16] This new orientation had no little effect on the development of the Renaissance in northern Europe as well. Nonetheless, no complete cultural fusion ever seems to have taken place between the Byzantine and Latin societies, except, as we have noted, in seventeenth-century Crete, where a kind of hybrid Cretan-Venetian cultural synthesis did for a time emerge.[17]

But it is our third mode of acculturation, neglected by historians and sociologists a like, that requires the most clarification and amplification—the encounter of two major, more-or-less equally advanced, cultural traditions, a phenomenon manifested especially in our third chronological period. In this third period (1261–1453), when the West first sought to reconquer Constantinople from the Byzantines and then, beginning in the mid-fourteenth century, rather to "save" it from the Turks, most Greeks could never be convinced of the genuineness of Western concern for their welfare.[18] Because the Byzantines were now much weaker politically and militarily than the Latins—on the defensive with their backs to the wall—they felt that Western culture, now seemingly more dynamic theologically and superior technologically to that of the East, posed a more ominous threat to the existence of Greek culture than ever before. This feeling was confirmed by repeated Western proposals to convert the Byzantines to "Catholicism" by means of educating large groups of young Greek boys not only in the Latin faith but in Latin letters and Latin customs.

It was precisely this kind of penetration, the most effective means— as many Greeks sensed—of cultural transformation, that the Byzantines above all feared.[19] Indeed, it may be said that the bulk of the Greeks believed, or intuitively felt, that religious conversion would lead not only to ecclesiastical and political domination but to a gradual process of "cultural" Latinization as well. Reflecting the conflation in the Greek mind of faith and culture is the remark of one Greek prelate at the Council of Florence: "I will not accept the *filioque* and be Latinized."[20] And earlier in 1274, after the Council of Lyons, when the several legates of the Greek emperor returned to

Constantinople, it was (and this deserves repetition) the Constantinopolitan rabble, the lowest stratum of society, that articulated this
underlying anxiety of the Greeks by shouting, "Effrangepses!"
("You have become a Frank!"—in other words, by changing your
religion you have changed your culture and "nation"). One might
take note also of the story told by Syropoulos, the "nationalistic,"
rabidly antiunionist Greek historian of the Council of Florence who
seems best to expose the inner feelings of most of his countrymen.
Thus he tells of the Greek parish priest who was accused by his Greek
parishioners of "becoming pro-Latin" (*"Latinizon"*) because, after
the signing of union at the council, he had concelebrated with the
Greek prounionist patriarch, Metrophanes.[21] It was, then, this
mixed but largely lower-class group of Byzantine society (including
of course the monks) which clung most tenaciously to the traditional
orthodox forms of liturgical worship.

In contrast to the more numerous, ignorant, lower classes,
almost totally caught up in the "nativistic reaction," the upper,
educated classes responded in a variety of ways, depending primarily
on which threat they considered to be more serious for the preservation of their ethnic and cultural identity. One upper-class group
opposed religious union under any circumstances, preferring, like
some among the lower classes, a Turkish conquest to religious and
cultural capitulation to the hated Latins. Another group, more
politically sophisticated, favored ecclesiastical union with Rome for
the sake of political expediency—that is, it supported application of
the concept of *economia* to church affairs (see especially chaps. 2 and
8) in order to preserve the life of the state.

Still a third, very important upper-class segment of the intellectual
elite, while strongly opposing religious union, drew its inspiration not
only from reaffirmation of the roots of the Greek church but, notably,
also reemphasis on, and more intensive and systematic study of,
ancient Greek literature, philosophy, and even science. This reaching
back to Byzantium's past roots in ancient Greek culture, the works of
which were now in the Palaeologan Renaissance used in a more
creative manner than before, allows us to call this group, in modern
terminology, a "revitalization movement."

Finally, a fourth (the smallest) group, also of the intellectual elite,
saw considerable virtue even in Latin culture and Western forms of
worship, thereby going beyond supporting religious union simply
for political reasons. This group, unafraid of union, was able to

perceive clearly in certain aspects of medieval Latin culture, especially in Thomistic theology and philosophy, its Greek, Aristotelian roots. So impressed were they by what they considered this more constructive Western use of Greek classical learning, compared to what seemed the more static, traditional Byzantine interpretation of this ancient Greek legacy, that many of the group espoused the Latin faith from genuine religious and intellectual conviction.

Of all the upper-class intellectual groups mentioned, those characterized by anti-Latin feeling sometimes (though not always) supported the Hesychast movement, the ascetic, contemplative practices of which often came to be identified with a sense of Greek ethnicity or "nationalism"—a feeling exacerbated, perhaps, by the West's out-of-hand rejection of Hesychasm and Palamism as doctrinally innovative and therefore heretical. Other Greek anti-Latin intellectuals, however, vigorously opposed the views of Hesychasm as not being consistent with traditional Byzantine theology. As for the Byzantine Latinophile groups (drawn from the prelates and bureaucracy as well as a few of the upper middle class), they saw in religious union with Rome not only the best solution to the Turkish peril but, more important, were able to distinguish the classical Greek elements at the roots of Western Scholasticism and thus to regard it, in effect, as a "revitalization" of ancient Greek learning—the latter, of course, a very significant component of their own cultural inheritance.

The differing responses on the part of the various strata of Byzantine society to what seemed basically an ineluctable choice between Turkish conquest or religious and, ultimately, cultural assimilation by the Latins, are very difficult to categorize with regard to the specific social classes, since in many cases views overlapped. It is far easier to cite the names of individual leaders of the anti-Latin or pro-Latin groups: for instance, the aristocratic Lucas Notaras, who was grand duke (and supposedly said, "Better the turban of the Turk in Constantinople than the tiara of the pope");[22] the intransigent antiunionist Mark of Ephesus, who was a monk of probable Hesychast, if not Palamite, views; the Thomistic yet later violently antiunionist scholar and judge, George Scholarios, who came from the middle class and was to become the first patriarch under the Turks; the opponent of union (as well as of Hesychasm), the anti-Latin Nicephorus Gregoras, who played an important part in the Palaeologan intellectual Renaissance; and, finally, the high church dignitary John Bessarion, a leading prounionist and admirer of Latin culture who held the archbishopric of Nicaea.[23] Although class distinctions with respect to these various views were often unclear, it may be said in general that virtually all sectors of the Byzantine populace belonged to one or the other of two major camps—those who because of apprehension over Latinization and loss of "national" identity feared the Latins more and the Turks less, and those (this camp was far smaller) who feared the barbaric Turks more and the culturally kindred Latins less.

With the Byzantine social and political structure breaking down, it is certain that Byzantines of widely different classes shared the view that their best hope for survival as a people lay in the careful and meticulous preservation of the traditional Greek religion and culture. The growing hostility between East and West, nurtured for long centuries and exploding into the open in 1204, had become too deep to be overcome even in so fatal a crisis for Christendom as the imminent Turkish conquest of Constantinople. By the last two centuries of Byzantium's existence, the vast majority of Greeks had in fact become almost paranoid about even the symbol of things Latin. And this near-paranoia seems in the final analysis to have been based on the fear—perhaps subconscious, perhaps in part even irrational—ultimately of complete or nearly complete cultural absorption. To put it in modern terms, what the Byzantines seemed most apprehensive about was the imminent possibility of the disappearance, through "assimilation," of an identifiable Greek culture which could guarantee continuity of life and a distinct historical existence.[24]

And yet a few learned—one might venture to say enlightened—Greeks, such as the Latinophiles Grand Logothete Demetrius Cydones and later John Bessarion, were able to rise above the prejudices of centuries, to separate their ethnic feelings as "Greeks" from their religious convictions, and to accept what they envisioned as being the higher ideal of a larger, ecumenical community of Christendom in preference to what they considered the narrower view of their coreligionists.[25] But let the reader judge who was right, the adamant Byzantine antiunionist, Mark of Ephesus who, at the Council of Florence, rejected the *filioque* on doctrinal grounds and probably in the implicit conviction that it would ultimately lead to cultural as well as religious "Latinization," or his Byzantine opponent, the irenic prounionist Bessarion, who believed that, while accepting papal supremacy, his people could nonetheless maintain intact their revered Byzantine religious tradition and the legacy inherited from their ancient forebears—Hellenic culture.[26] One prounionist near-contemporary of Bessarion, the post-Byzantine scholar Demetrius Ducas, was quite definite regarding the relative importance of the two elements, affirming that the Byzantine theological legacy from the Orthodox Church Fathers was of a higher order of importance than their intellectual inheritance from the ancient Greeks.[27] But he, it should be observed, was a scholar of the diaspora living *after* 1453 in the West.

The views of Bessarion are frequently misunderstood today. It is not, as many modern historians put it, that he was genuinely "pro-Latin" (the word *Latinophron* means "of Latin mind") and therefore anti-Greek. Rather, he believed that coexistence, even an amalgamation of cultures, was possible and that it was not necessary for one culture to obliterate the other. Indeed, shortly before Constantinople's fall in 1453, he, like his teacher, the Neoplatonist philosopher Gemistos Pletho, impressed by the advances in Latin technology and social organization, proposed that in order to revivify the remnants of the Byzantine state (in particular the Peloponnesus) young Greeks should be sent to the West to learn such useful industrial techniques as ironworking and shipbuilding.[28] Still Bessarion always continued to emphasize the significance of the Greek inheritance from *both* the ancients and the Greek Fathers.

By the time the interaction of the two societies in the Middle Ages and the Renaissance came effectively to an end about 1600, ancient Greek letters had been successfully diffused throughout almost the entire Western world. And in this last major phase of the Western reception of classical Greek learning and Byzantium's creativity, the intellectual Byzantine exiles, though far from their homeland, played the major role.[29] It was a fitting climax to the many valuable Greco-Byzantine contributions to Western thought—a virtually unbroken process of acculturation extending from the "piecemeal" Byzantine contact with and filtering into Western culture in our lengthy first chronological phase, through the Greco-Latin social and cultural collisions and mutual borrowings of the second and third periods, to the more immediate and intensive Byzantine influence on the Italian Renaissance in the fourth and final period.

For now, to the medieval synthesis of Western culture—Roman Christianity, Latin learning, and the finally "domesticated" Germanic element—there was at last added perhaps the most inspirational influence of all, virtually the entire corpus of ancient Greek learning in the original language. What served as the capstone to this entire phenomenon, as the concluding step in the long process of cultural interaction—despite long-ingrained Western suspicion of the Byzantine church—was the reception and printing, by "Christian humanists" of the Western Renaissance, not only of the seminal Eastern Church Fathers but even of some of the later *Byzantine* theological and mystical writings as well (see chap. 14).

What is truly ironic is that by 1600 a reversal of cultural roles had taken place. It was now the Greeks who, under the oppressive and stultifying Turkish occupation, had declined in civilization and were suffering from a cultural lag. Indeed, as we have seen, after 1453 Greece gradually became a cultural wasteland. Already in 1455 this was foreseen by Bessarion himself, when in his commission to his protegé, the Byzantine humanist Michael Apostolis, to gather up Greek manuscripts, he stated, not without prescience, that he felt it his duty to preserve the ancient heritage for the benefit not of himself but of future generations of Greeks, "who, otherwise, would differ in no way from barbarians and slaves." For, with the Turkish oppression in Greece and the closing of virtually all schools (with the exception of a few serving the patriarch), most Greek intellectuals were abandoning the East and bringing their learning to the West. As we have already observed in chapter 9, it was these very Greek exiles of the diaspora who would later play a significant (and hitherto unappreciated) role in the resurrection of the modern Greek nation.[30]

I realize that the tripartite typology of modes of acculturation as set forth in this book will not please all sociologists, especially those who are "terminologically" oriented. The most recent sociological research seems, rather, to point to theories of pluralism, that is, to the use of many typologies to explain sociocultural phenomena.[31] Nevertheless, while recognizing that what has been presented here constitutes only one possible macroscopic typology of acculturation, I hope that cultural historians and sociologists alike will find some value in the combination of chronology and modes of cultural influence which the Prologue and Epilogue have offered as a framework for the chapters explaining the long and complex interaction between the "sibling" Byzantine and Latin worlds. For, as is still rarely realized, it was the melding of the Germano-Latin, Christian synthesis on the one hand, together with ancient Greek learning (as pres-

served and transmitted by Byzantium) and strains of Eastern Orthodox religious creativity and tradition on the other, that constituted
two of the primary components in the formative period of what
came to be called "modern Western civilization."[32]

Appendix:

Latin Text of Chalcondyles' Discourses

Folio 1ᵛ   Iste Grecus fuit Demetrius Atheniensis qui publice padue primo Erothimata deinde Hesiodum nobis exposuit.

Marsilius Ficinus in prohemio operum platonis de isto Demetrio mencionem facit eo modo.

Ne forte putes amice lector tantum opus editum temere, scito cum iam composuissem antequam ederem me censores huic operi pulures adhibuisse Demetrium Atheniensem non minus philosophia et eloquio quam genere Athicum Georgium Antonium, Joanem Baptistam, Florentinos viros latine lingue greceque peritissimos etc.

Folio 2ʳ   Oratio Greci, viri clarissimi habita in principio sue lecture: Anno domino мссссlхiii Padue Preambulum.

Et si ego de studiis litterarum Grecarum orationem neque rei dignitate neque auribus vestris dignam, Magnifice Rector, doctores celeberrimi ceterique viri eruditissimi, non me videam habere posse cum magnitudine rei tumque ego parum admodum in huiuscemodi rebus exercitatus, parvo preterea ingenio et doctrina modica vobis doctissimis sapientissimisque viris nullo pacto satisfacere possem. Tamen quia rei novitas ac potissimum principiorum consuetudo hoc efflagitare videntur pingui (ut aiunt) Minerva hanc provinciam aggressus sum. Vos vero humanissimi ac sapientissimi viri cum in omnibus summan humanitatem atque mansuetudinem gerere consuevistis eandem ipsam vel mihi nullam homini novo et in litteris latinis mediocriter erudito prestare propicioque et ylari fronte meum

Folio 2ᵛ   audire/ sermonem velitis. Cum igitur ab illustrissimo ac inclito venetorum dominio rogatu Reverendissimi domini mei Cardinalis sedisque Apostolici legati de latere favoreque et auxilio magnifici Rectoris et egregiorum scolarium, ut ergo litteras Grecas publice legerem constitutus sum, idcirco quantum utilitatis ornamenti perfectionisque studia litterarum latinis afferant quantumque illustraverint et illustrent, non ab re aliquid dicere visum est.

Aliud preambulum eiusdem Greci anno sequenti, videlicet мссссlхiiii in studio paduano.

Hodiernum diem mihi iocundissimum simul et horrendum esse existimo. Iocundissimum quidem quod frequencia tanta virorum clarissimorum doctissimorumque mee orationi interesse dignati fuerint. Que si quoquo modo auribus vestris digna grataque fuerit, nihil mihi felicius, nihil suavius ac magis optabile esse profecto duxero. Horrendum vero quod ego tam parvo ingenio doctrina modica tamque tenui et exigua eloqencia mea apud viros ubique terrarum ingeniis sapiencia omni genere doctrina et

Folio 3ʳ   eloquen/ tia celeberrimos prestantissimosve oracionem sum habiturus. Quis esset vel adeo eloquens adeoque ingenio periciaque valens, qui in conspectu vestro omni gravitate ac sapiencia referto non obstupesceret, horreret hesitaretque. Verum cum ego animadverto vestram scienciam humanitatem et mansuetudinem erga omnes, haud dubitavi quod etiam in homine novo ac poenitus inconsueto parumque admodum in huiuscemodi rebus exercitato et litteris latinis ne mediocriter erudito propicios vos prebueritis et benignos, tametsi sermo meus exilis nec dignus neque rei dignitate de qua aliqua dicere[1] animus est neque sapientia fuerit. Cum igitur ego ab illustrissimo et inclito dominio venetorum rogatu Reverendissimi domini mei Cardinalis et legati de latere favoreque auxilio voluntate et consensu insignis rectoris et egregiorum scolarium ut litteras grecas legerem publice constitutus sum, quantum utilitatis ornamenti perfeccionisque afferent quantumque litterarum grecarum studia latinarum litterarum illustraverunt illustrantque, non ab re dicere aliquid visum est. Quare velim, magnifici ac humanissimi viri, parumper animum[2] huc animadvertetis benignoque fronte

Folio 3ᵛ   ac hilarique pro consuetudine vestra sermonem/ meum[3] audire velitis.

Incipit oratio Greci insignis habita in principio lecture in inclito gymnasio Patavino.

Nemini credo vestrum esse ignotum omne genus liberalium artium a grecis latinos accepisse et cum auctores omnium istarum arcium grecos et ipsa nomina artibus indicta greca fuisse constat. Nam ut ab ipsis infimis incipiam et ipsorum elementorum et grammatice poesis oratorie artis ac hystorie logice mathematicorum philosophie naturalis medicine ac ipsius denique divine science, quis idem mediocriter eruditus ignorat eos inventores fuisse, aut omina aut aliqua ex his ab aliis accepta ipsos meliora perfectioraque reddidisse, at[4] postea latinis tradidisse. Qui adeo in omni genere virtutis doctrinaque viguere ut nemini ea tempestate qua florebant in nulla re cessisse compertum est. Hos latini ad unguem sequuti usque ad ipsa litterarum elementa merito antecelluisse ceteris gentibus tam in omni genere doctrine quam etiam in re militari existimantur.

Folio 4ʳ   Cum itaque et studia litterarum et omnes artes ab/ eis ac-

cepissent[5] auctoresque ipsos sequuntur, nemo inficias ibit,
quin studia litterarum grecarum plurimum fructus latinis in
omni genere doctrine afferant. Et enim ut de iis in primis
quae ad grammaticam attinent aliquid dicam, cum gram-
matica latina grece coniuncta est et ab ipsa dependere videtur,
quomodo quisquam cognitionem plenam eius habere puta-
verit nisi litteras grecas noverit Neque enim derivacionem
complurium vocabulorum et significatus proprios neque
declinacionem multorum nominum quantitatesque sil-
labarum scire aut denique recte ac eleganter loqui voluerit,[6] si
eas ignoraret. Nec recte ut puto dici posset quod non nulli
auctores latini aliqua documenta his rebus tradidissent, id
circo non opus esset litteris grecis. Nam et illi ita de his loqu-
untur ut discentes cognitionem earum habeant, non ut
prorsus ignorent. Ad hoc nequaquam ita perfecte ex his qui
admodum tetigerint eo sicut ex ipso fonte (ut ita dicam)
dicere possent, veluti si aliquis sitim suam explere cupiens non
stagnum pocius quam fontem peteret neque exuriens[7] belaria
pro cibis solidis habere mallet. Pariter quoque dicendum
censeo/

Folio 4ᵛ   de his que ad poetas atque artem oratoriam et omne genus
dicendi spectare videantur, cum neque poema neque
oracionem sine nominibus atque recta loquucione figuris
coloribus argumentisque aliquis confici posse existimaret.
Cumque ars utriusque abunde et copiose ab his tradita et in
eorum poematibus ac orationibus ac hystoriis quam plene
perfecteque digesta sit, confirmant sentenciam meam veteres
auctores latini tam poete quam oratores et qui historias
conscripsere. Quorum nullum ignarum litterarum grecarum
fuisse constat. Quin complures eorum adeo bene pleneque eas
venerasse, ut dubium esset an litteras grecas vel latinas melius
scirent. Fertur M. Ciceronem in grecia optime grece orasse,
et inscriptis suis ipsemet fatetur greca latinis semper ad
utilitatem suam coniunxisse. Nullamque differentiam inter
cognicionem lingue[8] latine et grece facere, quemadmodum
vos me longe melius hec scire potestis. Brutumque epistolas
graece scriptas elegantissime gravissimas sentenciosissimasque
posteris reliquisse constat. Favorinum preterea virum latinum
ut Philostratus in libro suo quem de vitis sophistarum edidit
egregium oratorem extitisse

Folio 5ʳ   testatur, multos adeo alios,/ quorum nomina recensere longum
esset, peritos[9] admodum litterarum graecarum videri evasisse.
Non igitur illi viri doctissimi tantam operam hiis litteris im-

pendissent, nisi magnum fructum inde posse, capere sese existi-
massent magnoque adiumento et ornamento eas litteras latinis
suisque operibus esse perspicerent. Ut etiam ex sententia Oratii
poete gravissimi atque optimi aperte animadverti potest
qui sic de graecis loquitur. "Graiis ingenium, Graiis dedit
ore rotundo musa loqui."[10] Et alibi hortando latinos ad haec
studia admonet: "Vos exemplaria greca nocturna versate manu,
versate diurna."[11] Quid dicam de ipsa philosophia in qua et si
nullum alium ex hiis studiis fructum aliquis capere posset,[12]
tamen ob ipsos textus Aristotelis qui in latinam linguam satis
male inepteque conversi sunt, ut eos plenius rectiusque in-
telligerent, in proprio fonte philosophie potissimum in-
cumbentes has litteras discere debent. Omitto dicere quantum
etiam succi et fructus in hac philosophia copiose ex aliis
voluminibus grecis capere quantumve melius pleniusque
sentencias aliorum philosophorum atque opiniones ex ipsis
grecis autoribus intelligere possent. Quas modo veluti sub
umbra videre tenebre videntur.[13] Itidem de medicina et

Folio 5ᵛ astrologia ceterisque artibus dicere possem, quum/ et
omnium istarum[14] auctores greci fuisse asserant cumque plura
ut arbitror in hiisce scientiis sint, que nisi quis has litteras
teneat hadud facile intelligere posset. Quare egregii et eruditi
adolescentes qui virtutibus liberalibusque artibus operam
impensius datis, exemplis veterum auctorum vestrorum
multisque rationibus ducti velitis cunctis viribus his incumbere litteris fructumque ex his iocundum animum
alentem consequi, quod si prompto alacriorique animo
feceritis, sencietis profecto me recte vobis consuluisse. Nec vos
post hec (ni fallor) magis poenitebit incoepti quam pigebit
quod tardiuscule has litteras discere inceperitis. Nec preterea
magnam difficultatem, ut forte existimabatis, in hiis discendis
habebitis, cum haud parvam conformitatem et propinquita-
tem cum litteris latinis habere videantur. Quas etsi difficiles
cognitu quoqo modo aliquis existimaret, tamen proter spem
fructus et utilitatis ex hiis habende[15] nullum laborem aut
aliquam arduitatem vita re debetis. Illud presertim con-
siderantes quod nulla res in se virtutis aliquid habens sine
labore difficultateque comparari potest ut et Hesiodus ait
poeta.

ΑΡΕΤΗΣ ΔΡωΣΑΤΕ απρο πεδεν ἔθασκα την
μεν τι κακο της ηκε ικηνις σνελεθα[16]

quos versus sic aliquis interpretari posset: "virtuti multum
superi junxere sudorem."

Aretis drosathe apro peden ethaska tin men ti kako tis ike ἰκίνις sneletha.

Folio 6ʳ Quis simul et vitium quamquam sibi sumere potest." Ego vero qui vos his litteris deo dante instructurus sum, etsi non cognosco me eam habere doctrinam, ut alciora ac magis ardua vos doceam, tamen omnibus viribus evitar in hiis principiis gramatice et in poetis ac oratoribus vobis satisfacere, viamque quoad possum breviorem melioremque in adipiscendis his litteris patefacere, denique omnem meam operam ac studium prestiturum me in hiis vobis polliceor. Superest ut animum vestrum hiis studiis intendatis solerciaque vestra ac vigilancia me prompciorem alacrioremque in docendo vos efficiatis. De hac autem lectura que denuo[17] huic celebri universitati adiuncta est ad honorem amplificacionem utilitamque eius vos et ego una ingentes in primis ac immortales[18] gracias illustrissimo et inclito dominio venetorum. Quod sua liberalitate de hac lectura rogatum facile concesserat habere debemus. Deinde Reverendissimo domino Cardinali ac Patriarche[19] Constantinopolitano sedisque apostolice legato de latere et meo singularrissimo domino. Qui cum doctissimus in utraque lingua atque sapientissimus sit intelligatque quantum fructus hec littere afferant exibeant[20] pariant quam primum voluntatem universitatis accepit

Folio 6ᵛ omni mora sublata haud quaquam rogare Illustrissimum/ dominium ac simul impetrare neglexit, quod deus omnipotens una cum ipso incolume[21] atque fortunatum[22] semper conservet[23] cum ob eorum in se observacionem et pietatem, tum ob optimam voluntatem et animum quem gerunt adversus teterrimos immanissimos atque impios barbaros thurcos pro fide ac utilitate omnium christianorum ac pro recuperacione grecie misere quae crudelissime ab illis subacta oppressaque supplex auxilium implorat omnium christianorum et maxime latinorum abhiisque hanc remuneracionem exposcit. Ut quemadmodum[24] ipsa omnes res suas preciosissimas atque prestantissimas liberaliter et absque aliqua parsimonia iis erogaverat suaque manu ac virtute armorum Italiam olim a Gothis oppressam in suum statum restituerat. Ita nunc iacentem atque afflictam[25] elevare et armis a manibus barbarorum liberare velint. Quod potissimum sese impetraturam[26] ab illustrissimo venetorum dominio per cuius potenciam et voluntatem sanctissimam et piissimam ab infidelibus liberata Deo propicio et auxiliante et in pristinum statum redacta immortales ei gracias pro tali beneficio perpetuo aget, idque non secus ad salutem suam apparuisse existimabit ac illi[27] qui a malo ut[28] in inferno Dantis[29] Christum pro sua liberatione in infernum descendisse viderant.

Folio 7ʳ   Hec in conspectu verstri pro parvitate doctrine/ingenii mei dixisse volui, non ut[30] vos deceam aut quia vos haec ignorare existimo, sed ut consuetudinem in huiuscemodi principiis servare,[31] meumque officium ad haec studia iuvenes hortandi haud pretermisisse viderer. Vos vero etsi ego nihil dignum neque expectatione neque dignitate vestra fecerim, tamen pro humanitate ac consuetudine vestra veniam dabitis mihi qui variis casibus ac infortuniis agitatus neque mediocrem quidem doctrinam adeptus sum neque, si vel longe maiorem doctrinam magisque ingenium valens[32] haberem, existimarem me unquam tantis viris satisfacere posse. Graciasque quas possum vobis quod me adeo benigne ac perhumane viri tante sapiencie ac dignitatis audire volueritis.

Finis Orationis prime viri prestantissimi Greci.

Folio 7ᵛ   Oratio Secunda Greci Initio Studii habita Padue. Anno domini die x Novembris MCCCCLXXIIII[33]

Vellem Magnifice Rector, Doctores celeberrimi ceterique viri ornatissimi, ut mihi ingenii vires essent eaque doctrina simul et eloquencia, ut aliqua de litterarum grecarum studiis, que hiis congrua, vestra vero expectacione digna essent dicere possem hoc enim modo et eorum dignitas studiorum atque utilitas satis explanari posset et sapientiis vestris quodammodo satisfactum putarem. Sed cum exile ingenium, exiguam doctrinam tenuem admodum eloquenciam in me esse perspiciam, vereor ne in dicendo vobis viris gravissimis ac in eius[34] scientiarum genere peritissimis ineptus esse videar, ut ne deterius quam rei causa postulet dicam. Verum cum considero quam vos humanos quamque benignos omnibus hic dicere solitis prebere consuevistis, quod tantum benignitatis unicuique tribuitis, quantum et ingenium et facultas cuiusque exposcere videtur. Fruens et ego humanitate

Folio 8ʳ   vestra, non mea eruditione, aliqua dicenda de hiis/studiis censui, cum presertim consuetudinem in hiis principiis longo iam tempore observatam et approbatam vel me sequi oporteat. Ut igitur hic initium faciam, litterarum grecarum studia magne utilitati et ornamento in primis generi humano fuisse neminemque aliqua litterarum disciplina imbutum ignorare existimo. Quis enim esset tam expers tamque rudis liberalium artium qui omne[35] scientiarum genus maxime apud graecos viguisse et excultum fuisse nesciret? Nam qui auctores omnium ferme scientiarum atque cultores fuere? Quantique eos omnes terrarum nationes faciant, quanta veneratione prose-

quantur facile quisque animadvertere potest. Que nisi[36] de
hiis litteris eruditi fuissent, numquam (ni fallor) perfeccionem
scientiarum attigisse valuissent, quippe ubi in hiis litteris
fundamenta et principia scientiarum omnium iacta eaque
discussa ac digesta poenitus sint. Quanto homines doctiores
peritioresque in hiis scienciis erant, tanto magis harum studio
litterarum flagrabant. Quod quidem Romani qui non minus
forte in liberalibus artibus quam in armis superiori tempore
claruere plane demonstrant. Nam hii omnes ferme non
minus linguam propram quam grecam callebant affectusque
animi ac rerum

Folio 8ᵛ   vim et naturam grecis nominibus magis quam latinis
aptius exprimere malebant. Volumina enim pene omnium
dignissimorum auctorum dictionibus atque sententiis grecis
referta hoc indicare nemo[37] ut puto animum advertens
ambigeret, nec solum hunc fructum ex litteris grecis
consequi posse, verum etiam pleniorem cognicionem
proprie lingue[38] inde habere perspexerunt, cum latinam
eloquucionem ex greca originem traxisse eamque veluti
parentem habuisse nullus[39] illorum inscius esset. Quid dicam
de viris in quavis facultate peritis, qui aliquid in sua quisque
arte componere atque in lucem producere vellent? Quantum
fructum quantamve ubertatem a fontibus grecorum, ut divus
Cicero clamat, haurire possent. Que quidem cum unusquis-
que animo revolvere possit exemplaque tam dignissima
illorum clarorum priscorum pre oculis habeamus, satis profecto admirari nequeo, cur tanta ignavia tantaque desidia
hii omnes obstiti sunt, ut harum litterarum studia poenitus
negligant. Quod si indocti imperitique litterarum bonarum
facerent nec artibus liberalibus delectarentur aut ingenium
extollere nollent, non utique mirum videretur. Huiusmodi
namque homines haud facile adherere litterarum studiis
amant. Quin eis cuncta studia oneri maximo esse videntur,
nec ea secus abhorrent

Folio 9ʳ   ac frenesi capti peritos medicos aut quoscumque alios sue
saluti consulere volentes. Sed cum homines eruditos atque
doctos hoc facere video, in admirationem sane maximam
ducor. Nam per deos immortales cum haec littere et
cognitionem et finem (?) pleniorem ac[40] certe firmiorem
et fructum in omnibus scientiis non mediocrem afferre
possint, adde etiam ornamentum et copiam et plurium rerum
atque hystoriarum, quid est quod ab hiis studiis amovere
faciat? Scilicet[41] labor ne et rei difficultas, an locorum maxi-

ma intervalla? at turpe est viris virtute preditis atque peritis aliquid bonum virtutemque[42] propter horum aliquid fugere velle. Nam etsi nulla alia re, exemplis tum illorum antiquorum ac clarissimorum virorum, quos recensui[43] tam latinos quam grecos, ad hoc incitari[44] debemus, qui discendi causa nullo labore, nullo periculo perterriti totum pene peragraverunt orbem. Romani etiam qui terre marisque domini extitere docti preterea domique ludis omnium ferme scientiarum existentibus suos liberos Athenas mittere consueverunt. Vos vero qui non magnum laborem, neque longam peregrinationem horum causa studiorum subire opus sit, adhuc arripere negligitis, adhuc hesitatis? Barbaris hec ignavia, barbaris inquam omnium bonarum artium inexpertis hec inertiam permittatur.[45] Nec mihi velim hoc arroganter

Folio 9ᵛ   dictum aut/ de me ipso haec dicere me existimaretis. Non enim tantam mihi arrogo provinciam nec adeo elatus sum ut me ipsum aliquantulum non cognoscere valeam. Sed hec ideo dixi ut ostenderem illos priscos ac pene divinos viros nullum laborem, nullum tam longissimum intervallum locorum virtutis causa declinasse. Nos tantum distare ab illis videmur, ut que illi procul a suis patriis posita atque inventa omnibus viribus enixi sunt capere, nos interdum prope[46] admodum locata reicere atque contemnere videmur. Nec preterea res ita ardua est, ut quivis his litteris incumbere volens brevi multum proficere non possit. Quippe que tantam convenientiam tantamque (ut ita dicam) necessitudinem cum latinis habeant, ut qui alteras sciat facilime alteras consequatur. Quod etiam multis experienciis compertum habemus. Nam cum nonnulli viri externi has litteras discere voluerunt, qui magis ab hiis alieni videntur, brevi admodum spacio temporis non parum in hiis litteris profecere. Quamobrem vos adolescentes, qui in florentissima estis etate, in qua multa discre potestis, quisque omni genere

Folio 10ʳ   disciplinarum flagratis, agite et haec studia cum vestris coniungite et vestros maiores in hoc imitari velitis, fructumque ex hiis litteris vobis oblatum alacri accipite animo. Me enim in hiis tradendis[47] litteris promptissimum ut vobis libuerit semper invenietis, et ingeniolum meum quantumcumque sit ac doctrinam litterarum istarum et omnes denique vires intus que sint libentissime impendere pro certo habetote quo[48] vos eruditos in hiis studiis litterarum efficiam brevique harum cognicionem forte non medicorem tradam. Et pro beneficio quod mihi haec preclara universitas contulit cuius consensu

et rogatu, ac intercessione serenissimi domini mei singularissimi ac sapientissimi Cardinalis Niceni ab Illustrissimo ac
munificentissimo Dominio venetorum lecturam istam obtinui
hanc remunerationem et gratiam plenissime pro viribus
reddam. Tibi vero Magnifice ac humanissime Rector cui
me ob tuas singulares virtutes tuamque precipuam doctrinam[49] devinctum semper fatebor vobisque doctores sapientissimi et reliquis in me[50] benignitatem ac et studium pro impetratione huius mee lecture viris cum virtute ac doctrina
praeditis quas possum, non quas debeo gracias ago quod
me tam benigne

Folio 10ᵛ   tamque equo ani/ mo audire dignati estis.

ΤΕΛΟΣ

Finiunt foeliciter Orationes Desiderii[51] viri clarissimi Greci preceptoris
mei in studio paduano ac principio sue lecture lepidissime recitate.

Scripsi ego Hartmannus Schedel de Nuremberga artium ac medicine
doctor Patavinus, in primordio studii de manu prefati Greci dum initia
litterarum grecarum edocuit.

Laus Deo

Notes to Appendix

1. diceret, *cod.*   2. animum, *cod.*   3. aliter orationem meum, *suprascripsit cod.*
4. *malim* et.   5. (accep)erint, *supram cod.*   6. *malim* posset.   7. i.e. *esuriens.*   8.
ligue *cod.*   9. peritis *cod.*   10. Horace, *Ars Poetica*, 323–24.   11. Ibid., 268 –69.
12. arbitraretur, *in margine add. cod.*   13. sine, *cod.,* tenere, *cod.,* vident, *cod.*   14.
istorum, *cod.*   15. habunde, *cod.*   16. The Greek original from Hesiod is doubtless
the following line: τῆς δ'ἀρετῆς ἰδρῶτα θεοὶ προπάροιθεν ἔθηκαν ἀθάνατοι. (*Works
and Days,* Loeb ed., l. 289). For those unfamiliar with Greek, Schedel inserts at the
bottom of this page a Latin transliteration of Hesiod.   17. de novo, *in margine.*   18.
mortales, *cod.*   19. Patriarcha, *cod.*   20. exibent, *cod.*   21. incolumis, *cod.*   22.
fortunatis, *cod.*   23. conservat, *cod.*   24. liberalissime, *in margine.*   25. afflictam,
cod.   26. *in margine,* consequuturam (*lec. var.* pro impetraturam).   27. illo, *cod.*
28. vi, *cod.*   29. Danti, *cod.*   30. ut, *addidi.*   31. *in margine,* sequi (*lec. var.* pro
servare).   32. *in margine,* pollens.   33. 1464? *in margine, recente manu.*   34. *malim*
eiusmodi.   35. omnium, *cod.*   36. nihi, *cod.*   37. venio, *cod.*   38. ligue, *cod.*
39. nullius, *cod.*   40. at, *cod.*   41. labor scilicet, *cod.*   42. virtuteque, *cod.*   43.
recensere, *cod.*   44. incitare, *cod.*   45. omittatur, *cod.*   46. proprie, *cod.*   47.
tratradendis, *cod.*   48. ut, *supram cod.*   49. doctrinam *addidi.*   50. *malim* propter.
51. Desiderii, *cod.* (*malim* Demetrii). Desiderii was added later, in another hand.

Notes

1. No studies, to my knowledge, have focused primarily on the problem of the interaction or "acculturation" of the Byzantine and Latin societies through their long history of relations. In the Prologue and Epilogue, *acculturation* is taken to mean not only the interaction of the two cultures discussed but particularly the influence or rejection of elements or aspects of either culture on the part of the other, emphasizing attitudes of receptivity and repulsion. *Acculturation*, for sociologists, does not refer only to culture in the narrow sense (art, literature, theology) but, even more importantly, is concerned with the general ethos or "ambience" of society. R. Linton, "The Distinctive Aspects of Acculturation" in D. Walker, *The Emergent Native Americans* (Boston, 1972), p. 6, gives this definition: "[Acculturation] comprehends the phenomena resulting when groups of individuals with different cultures come into continuous first-hand contact, with subsequent changes in the original culture pattern of either or both groups." Given the lack of sociological studies (so I am told by several sociologists) on two equally advanced societies (as the Byzantine and Western after some centuries became), I have here formulated my own criteria, that is, my own typology for outlining the process of Byzantine-Latin acculturation.

    Sociological works of a general nature which have been of help to me in one way or another are the following: W. Newman, *American Pluralism: Attitudes of Minority Groups and Social Theory* (New York, 1973); B. Malinowski, *The Dynamics of Cultural Change* (New Haven, 1961), which emphasizes the agents of cultural change, especially the role of missionaries; M. Gordon, *Assimilation in American Life* (New York, 1964), exclusively on America; C. Geertz, *Islam Observed* (New York, 1968), on religion and cultural change; R. Bellah, *Tokugawa Religion* (Glencoe, Ill., 1957); C. Darlington, *The Evolution of Man and Society* (New York, 1969), esp. pp. 371–80 which stress especially the power of the state and the role of the eunuchs in the earlier Byzantine government; S. Lipset, *The Radical Right* (New York, 1969), who uses the term "nativistic reaction"; R. Nichols and G. Adams, eds., *American Indian: Past and Present* (Waltham, Mass, 1971), esp. the chapter by R. Berkhofer, "Protestants, Pagans, and Sequences, 1760–1860," on the acculturation of the Indian to Protestant ideals; the old but still useful works of L. Gumplowicz, *Der Rassenkampf, Soziologische untersuchungen* (Innsbruck, 1883) and G. Ratzenhofer, *Soziologie. Positiv Lehre . . .* (Leipzig, 1907); C. Russett, *The Concept of Equilibrium in American Social Thought* (New Haven-London, 1966); R. Park, *Race and Culture* (New York, 1970) concentrating on Blacks in America and problems of the mulatto—which might also shed light on those of the Byzantine, half-breed Gasmule; W. Connolly, *The Bias of Pluralism* (New York, 1969); A. Smith, *Theories of Nationalism;* J. Wach, *Sociology of Religion* (Chicago, 1971); several works of G. von Grünebaum, including *Medieval Islam: A Study in Cultural Orientation* (Chicago, 1946) and his *Modern Islam: The Search for Cultural Identity* (Berkeley, 1962).

Socio-historical studies that have hitherto been done on Byzantium have primarily dealt with the following basic problems: (1) the decline and collapse of central authority in the empire: see the articles of Charanis, Ostrogorsky, and Diehl included in S. Eisenstadt, *The Decline of Empires* (Englewood Cliffs, N.J., 1967); (2) problems of the social structure of the empire (e.g. see P. Charanis, "The Aristocracy in Byzantium in the Thirteenth Century," ed. P. Coleman-Norton, *Studies in Roman Economic and Sociological History* (Princeton, 1951); (3) problems of land tenure and central authority (i.e. "feudalism"): see G. Ostrogorsky, *Pour l'histoire de la féodalité byzantine* (Brussels, 1954); and A. Kazdan, *Drevnja i gorod v Vizantii IX-X vv* (Moscow, 1960); (4) urban problems in Constantinople, e.g. D. Miller, *Imperial Constantinople* (New York, 1969); Kazdan, idem; and T. Rice, *Everyday Life in Byzantium* (London-New York, 1967), essentially concerned with Constantinople.

On Byzantine culture *in general* very few works of *synthesis* have appeared, notably the recent work of H. Haussig, *History of Byzantine Civilization*, trans. J. Hussey (London, rpt. 1971); the earlier work of S. Runciman, *Byzantine Civilization* (New York, 1933; rpt. 1959); H. Hunger, *Der Christliche Geist der Byzantinischen Kultur* (Graz, Austia, 1965); A. Kazdan, *Byzantiyskaya Kultura* (Moscow, 1968); and K. Wessel, *Die Kultur von Byzanz* (Frankfurt-am-Main, 1970) but without footnotes. The *New Cambridge Medieval History*, Vol. 4, pt. 2 (1967) is a collection of essays on Byzantine government, church, and civilization. Special mention should be made of D. Obolensky, *The Byzantine Commonwealth, Eastern Europe, 500–1453* (New York, 1971), esp. chap. 9, on factors of cultural diffusion, which deals with Byzantine-Slavic relations, with observations on Slavic attitudes toward Byzantine culture. See, finally, A. Toynbee, *Constantine Porphyrogenitus and his World* (London, 1973) esp. pp. 510 ff. For specific references to works cited here as well as others, sociological or cultural (e.g. on Byzantine-Latin ecclesiastical, political, literary, or artistic relations), see notes below to the Prologue, Epilogue, and the individual chapters of this book. Also see Bibliography.

2. On "nativistic movements" or reactions, see e.g. R. Linton, "The Distinctive Aspects of Acculturation," pp. 7 ff., and Prologue, below, n. 34. Also S. Lipset, *Radical Right* (New York, 1969), and W. Newman, *American Pluralism: A Study of Minority Groups and Social Theory* (New York, 1973). Other scholars also use the term, sometimes slightly differently. Cf. also A. Wallace, "Revitalization Movements," *American Anthropologist* 58 (1956): esp. 267, 278.

3. See the recent article of D. Jacoby, "The Encounter of Two Societies: Western Conquerors and Byzantines in the Peloponnesus after the Fourth Crusade," *American Historical Review* (1973), esp. pp. 891 and 903 ff., who perhaps makes the first attempt to analyze systematically from a sociological

and a historical viewpoint, the problem of social interaction between By-zantines and Latins in a given period and a definite area (the Morea, partic-ularly between the Frankish conquerors and the subjugated Byzantine populace). One of his remarks is especially pertinent here: "Further study of the Byzantine-Latin encounter in the Peloponnesus might enable us to discover the mental patterns underlying the attitudes and behavior of individuals, and especially of social classes and societies reacting to each other in conquered areas." This remark expresses a basic aim of the Prologue and Epilogue of this book.

4. On the sense of community in Christendom, see below, esp. chaps. 2, 4, 6, 8. On the principal ecumenical-minded Greeks of the fourteenth and fifteenth centuries, Cydones and Bessarion, see chap. 4, also Epilogue; and on Maxi-mos the Confessor of the seventh century, see chap. 6.

5. On Byzantine Christianity see esp. chap. 1 and passim.

6. On "contact situations," esp. helpful has been the article of R. Berkhofer, "Protestants, Pagans, and Sequences, 1760–1860," ed. R. Nichols and G. Adams, *American Indian: Past and Present* (Waltham, Mass., 1971). See also R. Linton, "The Distinctive Aspects of Acculturation," in D. Walker, ed., *The Emergent Native Americans* (Boston, 1972), p. 69 and passim.

7. On all these, see below, chaps. 3, 4, and 13. Also on Chrysoloras, see D. Geanakoplos, *Greek Scholars in Venice* (Cambridge, Mass., 1962), pp. 26 ff. (reprinted as *Byzantium and the Renaissance* [Hamden, Conn., 1972]).

8. These contact situations have never been delineated systematically and in detail.

9. This is not to minimize the importance of the Oriental tradition, largely Semitic. On this, see the beginning of chap. 3.

10. See chap. 9.

11. Cf. chap. 4 on this, and R. Southern, *Making of the Middle Ages* (London, 1953), pp. 210, 220, who says that Latin scholars first reflected on their past "comfortably" ca. 1230.

12. Including esp. chaps. 4, 7, and 13.

13. See below, esp. chap. 3, n. 17, and J. Hussey, *Church and Learning in the Byzan-tine Empire* (New York, 1963, reissued), esp. p. 203.

14. For an attempt to trace the growing religious schism between East and West, see D. Geanakoplos, "Edward Gibbon and Byzantine Ecclesiastical History," *Church History* 35 (1966):1–14. Cf. also D. Nicol, "The Byzantine View of Western Europe," *Greek, Roman, Byzantine Studies*, vol. 8 (1967).

15. On the famous problem of the "two emperors," see below, chap. 3, and (from the extensive literature) W. Ohnsorge, *Das Zweikaiserproblem im früheren Mittelalter* (Hildesheim, 1947). Also, my *Byzantine East and Latin West: Two Worlds of Christendom* (Oxford, 1966), p. 19, with bibliography; W. Ohnsorge, *Abendland und Byzanz* (Darmstadt, 1958), esp. pp. 1 ff., 64 ff., 79 ff.; and G. Ostrogorsky, *History of the Byzantine State* (New Brunswick, N.J., 1969), passim.

16. The armies were, of course, soon followed by other Latins—merchants, priests, colonists, etc. Obviously, the Crusader army did not fully represent Western culture.

17. See Robert of Clari, *La conquista di Costantinopoli*, critical study, translation,

and notes by A. Nada Patrone (Genova, 1972). That twenty years before this not all Latin civilians hated the Greeks, seems evident in William of Tyre, who says some Latins would not join in the slaughter of Greeks in 1182 "because they were Christians." See R. Davis, "William of Tyre," *Relations between East and West* . . . ed. D. Baker (Edinburgh, 1973), p. 76.

18. See my two chapters, "Byzantium and the Later Crusades," in K. Setton, ed., *A History of the Crusades*, vol. 3 (Madison, Wis., 1975), pp. 30–31.

19. On the Gasmules, see Geanakoplos, *Emperor Michael Palaeologus and the West* (Cambridge, Mass., 1959), pp. 127, 132. Cf. D. Nicol, "Mixed Marriages in Byzantium in the Thirteenth Century," *Studies in Church History*, vol. 1, (1965) and H. Haussig, *A History of Byzantine Civilization* (London, 1966), pp. 361, 369. The Gasmules were able to pass as either Greeks or Latins, though in most cases they preferred to be Latins (who in later centuries became superior to the Greeks militarily and often socially).

20. On all these phenomena, see below, esp. chaps. 3 and 4.

20a. See papal documents (dated 1205, 1248, in H. Wieruszowski, *The Medieval University* [New York, 1966], pp. 144, 153–54), who believes nothing came of the plan except perhaps the establishment of a college in Paris called "of Constantinople." Whether it ever educated Greek youths in Latin and in the ritual of the Roman church is, according to Wieruszowski, unknown. Yet the main purpose, as noted and as the 1205 document reads, was "to propagate the Christian religion in the East."

21. See Choniates' quotation in R. Jenkins, *The Imperial Centuries* (New York, 1966), p. 383; for Cinnamos, cf. R. Lopez, "Foreigners in Byazntium," *Bulletin de l'institut historique belge de Rome* 44 (1974) : 350.

21a. On the term *Latinization*, see next note and esp. Epilogue and chap. 2. On the problem of union and the council, see chaps. 8 and 11. Also my chapters "Byzantium and the Later Crusades," ibid., pp. 90–92, and D. Nicol, "Byzantine Requests for an Oecumenical Council in the Fourteenth Century," *Annuarium Historiae Conciliorum* 1 (1969) : 69–95.

22. On the Greek fear of Latinization, see below, esp. chaps. 2, 3, 4, and 8. Also, my *Emperor Michael Palaeologus and the West,* esp. pp. 270–72, 315–16; my *Byzantine East and Latin West*, pp. 2–3, 103, and esp. pp. 106 and 18, on Latin practices imposed on the Greek church after 1204. Important for the question of Latinization is Vacalopoulos, *Origins of the Greek Nation 1204–61* (New Brunswick, 1970) who fully appreciates the implications of this fear on the part of the Byzantines. This Greek fear, or deep apprehension, is often not understood or is minimized by Western historians (J. Gill, *The Council of Florence* [Cambridge, 1969], for example). But cf. Y. Congar, *After Nine Hundred Years* (New York, 1959), pp. 29–48, who perhaps best of all Western, non-Orthodox church historians understands this phenomenon. See also I. Sevčenko, "Intellectual Repercussions of the Council of Florence," *Church History* (1955), p. 295, who correctly maintains that Greek insistence on what were called "trifles" by the Latins (the patriarch's allusion to the pope at Florence as "brother," the Greek refusal to uncover their heads before the papal legate, etc.) were "not trifles at all but reflected Greek cultural and ethnic pride."

23. See below, esp. chap. 4.

24. On Cydones see below, esp. chap. 4, which cites the article of R. Loenertz, "Lettre de Demetrius Cydonès à Andronic Oeneote . . . .," *Revue des études byzantines* (1971), pp. 303–05. Also on Bessarion, see chap. 4 and "The Council of Florence and the Union between the Greek and Latin Churches," in my *Byzantine East and Latin West* (Oxford, 1966), pp. 100, 106, 112, 115, etc., with bibliography. Also Vacalopoulos, *Origins of the Greek Nation*, esp. pp. 241–45.

25. For an example of the common use of this Byzantine religious and ecclesiastical term *patroparadoton*, see my *Byzantine East and Latin West*, p. 106, n. 86, which cites Greek use of the term at Florence supporting Byzantine use of the "enzymes" in the ritual and objecting to the Latin azymes. Cf. *Acta Graeca*, ed. J. Gill (Rome, 1953), p. 446 (Mansi, *Concilia*, 31a, col. 1012) for a similar use of the term.

26. I. Dujčev, "Le Patriarche Nil et les invasions turques vers la fin du XIVe siècle," *Mel. Arch. et d'hist.* 88 (1966): 213.

27. See Guillaume d'Adam, *Directorium ad passagium faciendum* (wrongly attributed to Brocardus), printed in *Recueil des Historiens des Croisades, Documents Arméniens*, 2 (1906): 367 ff. (cf. my *Byzantine East and Latin West*, p. 2, n. 3); see also Sevčenko, "Intellectual Repercussions of the Council of Florence," *Church History* (1955), p. 293.

28. Dubois, *De Recuperatione terre sancte*, ed. V. Langlois, in *Collection de textes pour servir à l'étude de l'histoire* (Paris, 1891), chap. 6, pp. 51–52.

29. The letter (which has been apparently unused in this connection) is printed in L. Mehus, *Epistolae . . . S. Ambrogii Traversari* (Florence, 1759), 1:26. (On Traversari, see below chap. 14.) Cf. many other such plans to "Catholicize" (the Greeks would have said to "Latinize") them. See above, text and n. 20a

30. See my *Byzantine East and Latin West*, p. 106, quoting N. Kalogeras, *Mark Eugenikos and Cardinal Bessarion* (Athens, 1893; in Greek), p. 70. Also, my "Byzantium and the Later Crusades," in K. Setton, ed., *A History of the Crusades* (Madison, Wis., 1975). Cf. a little later the (supposed) advice of Lucas Notaras, the Byzantine "prime minister," to disavow the Union of Florence on the grounds that the "Latin armies of King Ladislas of Hungary were more interested in conquering Byzantine lands than aiding the Greeks against the Turks" (Sevčenko, "Intellectual Repercussions," see n. 27).

31. See A. Demetrakopoulos, *Historia Schismatis* (Leipzig, 1867; in Greek) and his *Graecia Orthodoxa* (1872; in Greek), p. 168 (as quoted in my *Byzantine East and Latin West*, p. 106, n. 84). A curious passage in the fifteenth-century Byzantine historian Sphrantzes (Bonn ed.), pp. 418 ff., written to the tutor of the children of the last representative of the Byzantine imperial family, instructs them to live in all respects as Latins, wearing Latin clothing, attending Latin churches, and even praying in the Latin manner. Cf., finally, my Epilogue to this book on Bessarion and his attitudes.

32. For an interesting discussion by a Byzantine and a Latin cleric (an "azymyta," as the Greeks said), see A. Vassilief, *Anecdota graeco-byzantina* (Moscow, 1893), pp. 179–88 (cf. Pachymeres [Bonn] 1: 491–92). This colloquy con-

stitutes chap. 8 of this book. For other Greek epithets directed against the Latins, and on the well-known Latin accusation of Greek "perfidy" and Greek "schismatics," see esp. chap. 2; also, my *Byzantine East and Latin West*, pp. 2–3 and 5 (see, for example, the account of Odo of Deuil, the twelfth-century crusader-chaplain of the French king, who calls the Byzantines "perfidious" and "inferior to the Latins.") To the Latin nobles, valor in battle was the prime virtue, a quality toward which the Greeks, as a far less military-minded people, had a different attitude (see MGH, *Scriptores*, 26:66). Petrarch, who prized ancient Greek learning, later even termed the Greeks "worse than the Turks" (*Lettere Senili di F. Petrarcha* [Florence, 1869], pp. 422–24).

33. On Humbert of Romans, see his irenic *Opus Tripartitum*, in Mansi, *Concilia*, vol. 24, cols. 106–36 (cf. my *Emperor Michael Palaeologus and the West*, p. 227). On Barlaam see my two chapters on "Byzantium and the Later Crusades," cited above, and G. Schirò, *Barlaam Calabro: Epistole greche, i primordi episodici e dottrinari delle lotte esicaste* (Palermo, 1954). Also of importance is M. Viller, "La question de l'union des églises entre Grecs et Latins," *Revue d'histoire ecclésiastique*, 16 (1921): 260–305, 515–32; 18 (1922): 20–60. Further, on Barlaam see my *Byzantine East and Latin West*, p. 68; and below, chap. 4.

34. The term "nativistic reaction" is used in S. Lipset, *Radical Right* (Cambridge, 1969), to refer to the reaction of white Anglo-Saxon Protestants against a new wave of southern Europeans (Catholics and Orthodox) emigrating to America and who might change the sociocultural balance. On "nativistic" movements, cf. also R. Linton, "The Distinctive Aspects of Acculturation," in D. Walker, ed., *The Emergent Native American* (Boston, 1972). Other scholars also use the term. On "revitalization movement," see A. Wallace, "Revitalization Movements," *American Anthropologist* 58 (1956): esp. 267, 278.

35. On Byzantine use of *Hellene* as "pagan," see chaps. 7 and 9, esp. nn. 9 and 65; and now esp. Vacalopoulos, *Origins of the Greek Nation*, passim. Also see S. Runciman, "Byzantine and Hellene in the Fourteenth Century," *Tomos Harmenopoulos* (1951), pp. 29–30. A few instances of the term *Hellene* had appeared already in Byzantine Nicaea in the thirteenth century. But the term became much more common in the fourteenth and fifteenth centuries.

36. See G. von Grünebaum, works cited in n. 1. Also see n. 34 above, the important work of Wallace.

37. On Hesychasm, see chap. 4 and also the authoritative work of J. Meyendorff, *Introduction à l'étude de Grégoire Palamas* (Paris, 1959), translated as *A Study of Gregory Palamas*, by G. Lawrence (London, 1965); also Meyendorff's, *St. Grégoire Palamas et la mystique orthodoxe* (Bourges, 1959); V. Lossky, *The Mystical Theology of the Eastern Church* (London, 1957); and for an excellent, convenient summary of Byzantine mysticism, S. Runciman, *The Great Church in Captivity* (Cambridge, 1958), pp. 128–58.

38. On the controversial question of the origins of the Palaeologan artistic Renaissance and its relation to the Italian Renaissance, there is a growing literature. See A. Grabar, *Byzantine Painting* (Switzerland: Skira, 1953), pp. 44–45, and his *Byzantine Art in the Middle Ages* (London, 1963). More recent is

O. Demus, *Byzantine Art and the West* (New York, 1970), esp. pp. 218–40; J. Beckwith, *The Art of Constantinople* (London-New York, 1961); and D. Rice, *Byzantine Painting: The Last Phase* (New York, 1968). See also the old but still useful A. Vasiliev, *History of the Byzantine Empire* (Madison, Wis., 1961) 2: 709 ff. Most persuasive is E. Kitzinger, "The Byzantine Contribution to Western Art of the Twelfth and Thirteenth Centuries, *Dumbarton Oaks Papers* 17 (1963): 25–48. See now also S. Runciman, *Byzantine Style and Civilization* (Harmondsworth, 1975), pp. 165–212, which is remarkably forceful and objective.

39. Cf. the "effusions" of the sociologist D. Darlington, *The Evolution of Man and Society* (New York, 1969), p. 373: "And in the sunset days of the fourteenth century the doctrines or "hallucinations" (my quotations) of Gregory Palamas, archbishop of Salonika, helped to renew the feeling of ecstasy in the people of the dying empire [!] See on this disputed problem of Byzantine art and Hesychasm, the objective judgment of D. Obolensky, *Byzantine Commonwealth*, pp. 358–59, who discusses especially the influence of Hesychastic views on Palaeologan art. He affirms that the arguments for such influence are not yet conclusive for scholarship except in the case of the theme and iconography of the Transfiguration, which figures prominently in Palamas' Hesychastic theology: see below, esp. chaps. 4 and 7. Cf. Rice, *Byzantine Painting*, pp. 178–89, and Haussig, *Byzantine Civilization*, pp. 363–64, both emphasizing Hesychastic influence on art.

40. On the Palaeologan revival of classical letters, see chap. 1 3 and Geanakoplos, *Byzantium and the Renaissance*, passim, with bibliography. Also recently, S. Runciman, *The Last Byzantine Renaissance* (Cambridge, 1950), which deals with events from the Byzantine side and not from the Italian; H. Hunger, *Johannes Chortasmenos, 1370–1436/7* (Vienna, 1969); and J. Verpeaux, *Nicéphore Choumnos* (Paris, 1959); see below, n. 42, for Sevčenko's recent article. On the "first" Byzantine "renaissance" (of the ninth and tenth centuries, the age of Photius, Arethas, and Constantine VII), see now P. Lemerle, *Le premier humanisme byzantin* (Paris, 1971).

41. The Palaeologan classical revival is a complex phenomenon, all the implications of which have not yet been clarified. Of course, to repeat, Byzantium had never lost its interest in the ancient classical Greek works (hence a true "renaissance" was, fundamentally, impossible), but, earlier, hostile or semi-hostile attitudes of the church and other factors had sometimes prevented these classical interests from emerging nearly as forcefully and clearly as in the Palaeologan "renaissance." See below, n. 46, the remark of Beck on the church and ancient learning.

42. It should be noted that at this time in Byzantium there was also a rather substantial, if less significant, interest in science, as seen in such figures as Theodore Metochites, Chrysokokkes, Planudes, and others: see Runciman, *Last Byzantine Renaissance*, pp. 52 ff., 63 ff.; I. Sevčenko, "Théodore Metochites, Chora, et courants intellectuels" (Venice, 1971); D. Nicol, *The Last Centuries of Byzantium* (New York, 1972), pp. 429–30; and his "The Byzantine Church and Hellenic Learning in the Fourteenth Century," *Studies in Church*

History 5 (Leiden, 1969): 23–57. Also R. Browning, "Byzantine Scholarship," in *Past and Present* 28 (1964): 3–20. Cf. below, chap. 4, text and n. 17, for Byzantine interest in mathematics and Arabic numerals.

43. E.g. A. Grabar, *Byzanting Painting* (1953), p. 45. For the remark, see Kitzinger p. 47 (cf. note 38).

44. E.g. see A. Vasiliev, *History of the Byzantine Empire,* pp. 562–63, 709–11.

45. See D. Obolensky, *The Byzantine Commonwealth* (London, 1971), pp. 336–43. and G. Maloney, *Russian Hesychasm. The Spirituality of Nil Sorskij* (The Hague, 1973). On Hesychasm as a conservative force in art, see Runciman, *Byzantine Style and Civilization,* p. 200; cf. Rice, *Byzantine painting,* pp. 178–92 and Haussig, *Byzantine Civilization,* p. 364.

46. See H. G. Beck's fascinating remarks in his chapter "Intellectual Life in the Late Byzantine Church," in *Handbook of Church History,* ed. H. Jedin, vol. 4 (1968), esp. pp. 505 ff.: "For the first time in Byzantine intellectual history even the churchmen no longer regarded the legacy of antiquity as mere decoration and merely to be tolerated for possible use." The new emphasis on Greek learning was more "secular" in the sense that it was usually "outer" (nontheological) learning, not "inner" (theological). And yet these humanists were still guided by Christian categories of thought.

47. See chaps. 9–14.

48. See chap. 9.

49. See below, e.g. chap. 3, n. 27. Also R. Walzer, *Greek into Arabic* (Cambridge, Mass., 1962), pp. 60–113.

49a. L. Mohler, *Aus Bessarions Gelehrtenkreis* (Paderborn, 1952), p. 481. Apostolis lived mainly in Venetian Crete.

50. See chap. 9.

51. See chap. 10.

52. See chap. 13, esp. on Chalcondyles' teaching at Padua University and his (Latin) inaugural address, which is here printed in its entirety.

53. See below, esp. chaps. 2 and 9.

54. On this reorientation, esp. in early fifteenth-century Florentine humanism, from the Latin rhetorical emphasis (esp. on Cicero) to the philosophical, with stress on Plato's metaphysical thought, see chap. 13 and esp. G. Holmes, *The Florentine Enlightenment* (New York, 1969), chap. 8, "The Return to Metaphysics," pp. 242–66, which emphasizes the importance of the teaching of Argyropoulos in Florence for the transformation. Cf. also J. Seigel's article, "The Teaching of Argyropoulos and the Rhetoric of the First Humanists," *Action and Conviction in Early Modern Europe* (Princeton, 1969); and very recently, E. Garin, *Portraits form the Quattrocento* (New York, 1973), esp. pp. 70 ff.; and P. Kristeller, *Renaissance Concepts of Man* (New York, 1972), chaps. 4–5. See now also D. Geanakoplos' article "The Italian Renaissance and Byzantium: The Career of the Greek John Argyropoulos, Humanist Professor in Florence and Rome," in *Conspectus of History,* 1, no. 1 (1974), *Focus on Biography* (Muncie, Ind., 1975), pp. 12–28.

Notes to Chapter 1

1. On Constantinople's population at its height, most scholars have cited the

figures given (see A. Andreades, "De la population de Constantinople," *Metron*, 1, no. 2 [1920]: 7, nn. 1, 32): 700,000 to 800,000 in the fourth century, certainly more later. See also T. Chandler, *Cities of the World* (New York, 1940). Cf. P. Charanis, "Byzantine Population," *Proceedings of the 13th International Congress of Byzantine Studies*, Oxford, 1966 (London, 1967), pp. 448–49, who fixes on some 500,000 (see his extensive notes with bibliography). See also D. Miller, *Imperial Constantinople* (New York, 1969), p. 6, which cites the various opinions, and T. Rice, *Everyday Life in Byzantium* (London, 1967), p. 144: 1 million.

2. Cf. my study, "Byzantium," in N. Cantor, ed., *Perspectives on the Past* (New York, 1972,) p. 139.

3. In many chapters below, esp. 3.

4. See W. Jaeger, *Early Christianity and Greek Paideia* (Cambridge, Mass., 1965), p. 11.

5. On the Greek Fathers see below, chap. 3, beginning section, and chap. 14. Also see: Jaeger, passim; R. Payne, *The Holy Fire* (London, 1958)—rather popularized; and J. Pelikan, *The Emergence of the Catholic Tradition* (Chicago, 1971), pp. 211–25, and his *The Spirit of Eastern Christendom* (Chicago, 1974).

6. See his "Address to Young Men on the Right Use of Greek Literature," trans. F. Padelford (New York, 1902), pp. 97–120. See below, chap. 14.

7. For a description of "apophatic" theology, see chaps 3, 4, and 6. See also *New Catholic Encyclopedia* (under that entry) and, for the Orthodox view, V. Lossky, *The Vision of God*, trans. A. Moorhouse (Clayton, Wisc., 1963), pp. 122 ff., etc. and (in Greek) *Religious and Ethical Encyclopedia* (Athens), under "apophatic."

8. For a convenient treatment of the emperor's authority over the church (and esp. his liturgical privileges, frequently misunderstood), see D. Geanakoplos, "Church and State in the Byzantine Empire: A Reconsideration of the Problem of Caesaropapism" (with bibliography, pp. 195–96), in *Byzantine East and Latin West: Two Worlds of Christendom* (Oxford, 1966), pp. 58–84.

9. On the archons and the Byzantine church, see esp. L. Bréhier, *Les Institutions de l'Empire byzantin* (Paris, 1949), esp. pp. 506 and 495–506 passim. On archontes in the post-Byzantine period, see N. Iorga, *Byzance après Byzance* (Bucharest, 1971, reprint) pp. 117–29. On their role in the fifteenth century, see *Les 'Mémoires' de Sylvestre Syropoulos sur le concile de Florence*, ed. V. Laurent (Paris, 1971), p. 384. Also now cf. J. Darrouzès, *Recherches sur les Offikia* (Paris, 1970), under archon.

10. On the Slavic conversion, see esp. Dvornik, *Byzantine Missions among the Slavs* (New Brunswick, N.J., 1970), and D. Obolensky, *The Byzantine Commonwealth* (London, 1972), esp. chaps. 3–4, 10.

11. On this (occasional) Byzantine objection to the liturgy in the vernacular, see esp. G. Soulis, "The Legacy of Cyril and Methodius to the Southern Slavs," *Dumbarton Oaks Papers* 19 (1965): 34.

12. On Byzantine Hesychasm, see esp. chaps. 4 and 11 (citing Meyendorff in particular). On the Russians see Obolensky, *Byzantine Commonwealth*, pp. 301–08, 336–43; and Maloney's book *Russian Hesychasm* (The Hague, 1973).

13. See below, chap. 3. Also on the liturgy, see esp F. Brightman, *Liturgies Eastern and Western*, vol. 1 (Oxford, 1896), and W. Lethaby and H. Swainson, *The*

Church of Sancta Sophia (London, 1894). See below, sect. 9 of Bibliog.

14. See below chap. 3, citation of E. Wellesz, *History of Byzantine Music and Hymno-graphy* (rev. ed., Oxford, 1961), and esp. his *Eastern Elements in Western Chant* (Oxford, 1947). See also N. Tomadakes, *Introduction to Byzantine Literature* (Athens, 1958), pp. 171 ff. (in Greek).

15. For English trans. (with Greek text) of the Akathistos, see *The Acathistos Hymn*, ed. G. Meersseman (Fribourg, Switzerland, 1958).

16. On Byzantine stained glass, see esp. A. Megaw, "Notes on Recent Work of the Byzantine Institute in Istanbul," *Dumbarton Oaks Papers*, 17 (1963): esp. 364. On Byzantine painting especially, see below, chap. 3 and also Prologue text and 37–43, on the Palaeologan artistic Renaissance. On "Macedonian" and "Cretan," terms invented by G. Millet, *Recherches sur l'iconographie de l'Evangile . . . d'après les monuments de Mistra, Macédoine, et du Mont-Athos* (Paris, 1916), but now discarded as unclear, see T. Rice, *Byzantine Painting: The Last Phase* (London, 1968), pp. 181 f., and the pioneer but now dated work of R. Byron and T. Rice, *The Birth of Western Painting* (London, 1930), passim. See recently O. Demus, *Byzantine Art and the West* (New York, 1970), pp. 70 and 179.

17. Cf. A. Haussig, *History of Byzantine Civilization* (London, 1971), p. 361.

18. On these colors, see, for example, A. Grabar, *Byzantine Painting* (Skira ed., 1953), pp. 45–46; and on elongation, S. Cirac, "L'hellénisme de D. Theoto-kopouli Crétois," *Kretika Chronika* 2 (1961): 213 ff.

19. On the great Byzantine painter (probably of the fourteenth century), see now A. Xyngopoulos, *Manuel Panselinos* (Athens, 1956), in Greek.

20. V. Lazarev. *Feofan Grek* (Moscow, 1961), pp. 81–87, 98–100. (in Russian).

21. Formerly it was believed he went to Venice at the age of eighteen, with great effect, therefore, on his artistic formation. For bibliography on El Greco, see below, chap. 3.

22. See Paul the Silentiary's poem, in P. Friedlander, *Johannes von Gaza und Paulus Silentiarius* (Leipzig-Berlin, 1912), pp. 227–65.

23. See text translation in G. Vernadsky, *Source Book for Russian History*, 1 (New Haven, 1972): 25–26.

24. *De Cerimoniis, Le Livre de Cérémonies* ed. A. Voigt. (Paris, 1939) and Pseudo-Codinus, *Traité des offices* ed. J. Verpeaux (Paris, 1966).

25. On Byzantine titles, see esp. L. Bréhier, *Les Institutions de l'Empire Byzantin* (Paris, 1949), pp. 138–53 and 495–506 especially.

26. For the liturgy and "The Emperor as Builder," see G. Downey, *Constantinople* (Norman, Okla., 1960), esp. p. 113. and also cf. my chap. 5.

27. See S. Runciman, *The Great Church in Captivity* (Cambridge, 1968), pp. 182–85 and T. Papadopoulos, *Studies and Documents Relating to the History of the Greek Church and People under Turkish Domination*, vol. 1 (Brussels, 1952).

28. On these ecclesiastical offices, see esp. Bréhier, *Les Institutions*, section on same, esp. pp. 498–506, and E. Villas, "Titles and Offices of the Patriarchal Order of St. Andrew" (New York: Greek Archdiocese, 1967; brochure).

29. On the relics seized, see P. Riant, *Exuviae Sacrae Constantinopolitanae*, 2 vois. (Geneva, 1876); also N. Baynes, "The Supernatural Defenders of Constantinople," esp. pp. 248–60. For Villehardouin, see M. Shaw, trans., *Chronicles*

of the Crusades (London, 1963), p. 90–91 (for brief mention); but esp. Robert of Clari, *The Conquest of Constantinople*, ed. E. McNeal (New York, 1936), pp. 102 ff.

30. On the relics of the Virgin, esp. her mantle and girdle (the city's palladia), see Baynes, "Supernatural Defenders," pp. 248–60.

31. Again on these officials, Bréhier, *Les Institutions,* and Villas, "Titles and Offices." See also now Darrouzès, *Recherches Sur les Offikia de l'église byzantine,* on these offices.

32. On the university, see the old work of F. Fuchs, *Die höheren Schulen von Konstantinopel im Mittelalter* (Leipzig-Berlin, 1926); also now esp. P. Lemerle, *Le premier humanisme byzantin* (Paris, 1972); M. Kyriakes, "The University: Origin and Early Phases in Constantinople," *Byzantion* 41 (1971): 161–182; the old works of L. Bréhier, "Notes sur l'histoire de l'enseignement superieure à Constantinople," *Byzantion* 4 (1927—28): 14–28, and his "L'enseignement superieure à Constantinople du XIe siècle," *Revue International de l'Enseignement* 38 (1899): 97—112. On the patriarchal school in particular—which involves unsolved questions—see my *Byzantine East and Latin West*, p. 168; R. Browning, "The Patriarchal School at Constantinople in the Twelfth Century," *Byzantion* 23 (1962): 84–186; Bréhier, idem; and M. Paranikas, *Schediasma . . . peri ton Grammaton* (Constantinople, 1867) pp. 153 ff. (in Greek). On the patriarchal school under the Turks, see Runciman, *Great Church in Captivity*, pp. 208 ff., and bibliography; and on Koraes, see Runciman, idem, pp. 392–93. On the patriarchal titles cited, see also Villas, "Titles and Offices."

33. On this hospital-orphanage (of the Pantocrator), see esp. D. Constantelos, *Byzantine Philanthropy and Social Welfare* (New Brunswick, N. J., 1968), pp. 171–79, 249–50, with bibliography.

34. See above, n. 24, citing *De Cerimoniis* and Pseudo—Codinus; cf. Bréhier, *Institutions*, pp. 498–506; and now Villas, "Titles and Offices."

35. Cf. Runciman, *Great Church*, p. 39; and Bréhier, esp. pp. 495–506.

Notes to Chapter 2

1. On Jews in the empire, see J. Starr, *The Jews in the Byzantine Empire* (Athens, 1939), esp. pp. 1–10. Also P. Charanis, "The Jews in the Byzantine Empire under the First Palaeologi", *Speculum* 22 (1947): 75–77; and A. Andreades, *The Jews in the Byzantine Empire* (Athens, 1929). Finally, see now A. Sharf, *Byzantine Jewry from Justinian to the Fourth Crusade* (London, 1971), whose thesis is that the Jews, within limits, were tolerated though they were in effect second-class citizens. Byzantine Jews usually lived in their own communities.

2. On the Armenians, see P. Charanis, *The Armenians in the Byzantine Empire* (Lisbon, 1963).

3. On the Slavs inside and outside the empire, see esp. recently D. Obolensky, *The Byzantine Commonwealth, 500–1453* (New York, 1972), passim, and esp. chap. 9.

4. On the emperor and the Monophysites, see G. Ostrogorsky, *The Byzantine State* (New Brunswick, N.J., 1969), esp. pp. 58 ff., 64 ff., 107–09.

5. Set Ostrogorsky, *Byzantine State*, esp. p. 60; "Monophysitism was an outlet for political separatist tendencies of Egypt and Syria." Also A. H. M. Jones, *Were Ancient Heresies Disguised Social Movements?* (Philadelphia, 1966).

6. On Eusebian theory, see D. Geanakoplos, *Byzantine East and Latin West* (Oxford, 1966), chap. 2 on church and state, and bibliography listed.

7. See chap. 5, "Church Construction and Caesaropapism," and Epilogue.

8. P. Charanis, *The Religious Policy of Anastasius the First* (Madison, 1939); also Geanakoplos, *Byzantine East and Latin West*, p. 58.

9. Geanakoplos, p. 61.

10. On Bulgars and Russ, see Obolensky, *Byzantine Commonwealth*, pp. 83–98 and 274–75, esp. 200–01: "Vladimir and his successors were wholly independent of Byzantium in political matters [but] they all . . . recognized that the Emperor as the head of the Orthodox Christian community, possessed by divine right a metapolitical jurisdiction over Russia"; G. Ostrogorsky, "The Byzantine Emperor and the Hierarchical World Order," in *The Slavonic and East European Review* 35 (1956–57): 1–14.

11. "Commonwealth" is Obolensky's term (*Byzantine Commonwealth*, passim). Also on the Byzantine "Family of Princes," see A. Grabar, "God and the Family of Princes presided over by the Byzantine Emperor," *Harvard Slavic Studies* 2 (1954):117–23.

12. Obolensky, pp. 284–85. Cf. the analogy of the West and Byzantine culture in my Epilogue.

13. On Varangians, see below, chap. 7, n. 37, their commander being Michael Palaeologus.

14. On mosques in Constantinople, see *New Cambridge Medieval History*, vol. 4, pt. 1, pp. 734, 726, and 283, for various periods. On the Amalfi monastery, see A. Pertusi, "Monasteri e monaci italiani all'Athos nell'alto Medioevo," *Le Millénaire du Mont Athos*, 1 (Chevtogne, 1963): 217–53; also P. Lemerle, "Les archives du monastère des Amalfitains au Mont Athos," *Ep. Het. Byz. Spoudon* 23 (1953): 548–66. Cf. also now R. Lopez, on "Foreigners in Byzantium," *Miscellanea C. Verlinden* (1974), pp. 348–49, for Arabs, Armenians, Italians, and others.

15. On the Paulicians, see D. Obolensky, *The Bogomils* (Cambridge, 1948), and his *Byzantine Commonwealth*, pp. 119–22, 215–16; and S. Runciman, *The Medieval Manichee* (Cambridge, 1947).

16. P. Alexander, "The Strength of Empire and Capital as seen through Byzantine Eyes," *Speculum* 37 (1962): 341–57.

17. Cf. P. Lemerle, *Le prémier humanisme byzanlin* (Paris, 1972).

18. "On Iconoclasm there is a large literature. I cite only the recent M. Anastos, "Iconoclasm and Imperial Rule," in *Cambridge Medieval History*, vol. 4, pt. 1, pp. 61–103; and pp. 66–67 on the Arab ruler. The latest article is P. Brown, "A Dark-Age Crisis: Aspects of the Iconoclastic Controversy," *English Historical Review* 346 (1973): 1 ff.

19. On "icon of Christ," see Geanakoplos, *Byzantine East and Latin West*, esp. p. 59. On Moses and Aaron, see G. Ostrogorsky, "Relations between Church

and State," *Sem. Kond.* 4 (1933): 121 ff. (in Russian); and Geanakoplos, *Byzantine East*, p. 63.

20. On exceptions to this policy of tolerance, see below, chap. 1, n. 11.

21. J. Erickson, "Leavened and Unleavened: Some Theological Implications of the Schism of 1054," *St. Vladimir's Theological Quarterly* 14 (1970): 3–23. While the West used "azymes," it sometimes grudgingly tolerated the Greek "enzymes." But the Greeks always condemned the Latin "azymes."

22. On Charles, see D. Geanakoplos, *Emperor Michael Palaeologus* (Cambridge, Mass., 1959; rpt. Hamden, Conn., 1972), pp. 189 ff.

23. Ibid., p. 271; esp. M. Laurent, *Le bienheureux Innocent V* (Vatican, 1947), p. 424, n. 23. On Latinization, see Prologue and Epilogue, nn. 20 ff.

24. On Michael, see esp. Geanakoplos, *Emperor Michael*, pp. 269–71; on 1453, see below, chap. 11, n. 20.

25. Geanakoplos, *Emperor Michael*, p. 270.

26. Quoted in Geanakoplos, *Byzantine East*, pp. 3–4, and cf. p. 104, n. 77.

27. Ibid., p. 2 and n. 3.

28. N. Kalogeras, *Mark Eugenikos and Cardinal Bessarion* (Athens, 1893), p. 70.

29. Cited in Geanakoplos, *Byzantine East and Latin West*, p. 106 and n. 84.

30. On this, see chap. 9 below, passim.

31. On Cydones, see below, chap. 4; also Prologue and Epilogue.

32. A. Vacalopoulos, *Origins of the Greek Nation*, vol. 1 (New Brunswick, N.J., 1970), esp. pp. 126–35 and 172–78.

33. Cf. Obolensky, *Byzantine Commonwealth*, pp. 257 ff.

34. Ibid., p. 363, on Russ view that Greek sins brought on the catastrophe of 1453. S. Runciman, *Great Church in Captivity* (Cambridge, 1968), pp. 159–61.

35. Passim, esp. nn. 15 ff.

36. See D. Geanakoplos, *Greek Scholars in Venice* (Cambridge, 1962), p. 81 (rpt. as *Byzantium and the Renaissance* [Hamden, Conn., 1971]); cf. chap. 9, n. 1, below.

37. On Nicousios, see Bibliog. in Geanakoplos, *Byzantine East*, esp. p. 179 and n. 28.

38. On Maxim the Greek, see esp. V. Ikonnikov, *Maksim Grek i ego vremia*, 2 vols. (Kiev, 1915); and also my forthcoming monograph on him. Cf. R. Billington, *The Icon and the Axe* (New York, 1970), pp. 87–95.

39. Cf. recently, G. Arnakis, *The Ottoman Empire and the Balkan States to 1900* (Austin-New York, 1969), chaps. 5–6. On education, cf. chap. 9, below.

40. On this term, see my Prologue, n. 2, and Epilogue, nn. 21 ff.

41. On nationalism, see below, chap. 9. Also on "Hellene," Vakalopoulos, *Origins of the Greek Nation*, passim. On Pletho's paganism, see F. Masai, *Pléthon et la Platonisme de Mistra* (Paris, 1956). An early reference to "Hellenes" is in A. Lepathenos' letter to Gregoras, ca. 1355: S. Runciman, "Byzantine and Hellene in the Fourteenth Century," *Tomos Harmenopoulos* (1952), pp. 27–33; and his *Last Byzantine Renaissance*, pp. 18–23. Also C. Patrinelis, "An Unknown Letter of D. Cydones," *Greek Roman Byzantine Studies* (1973).

42. On Latinization, see this book, Prologue and Epilogue; Geanakoplos, *Emperor Michael*, passim; my *Byzantine East*, p. 104, n. 79, p. 106, n. 84; T. Congar, *After Five Hundred Years* (New York, 1959), pp. 29–48.

43. See quotation in Obolensky, *Byzantine Commonwealth*, p. 264.

Notes to Chapter 3

1. E.g. N. Baynes, *Byzantine Studies and Other Essays* (London, 1955), pp. 71-73.

2. MSS survive, for example, of a bilingual grammar of Dositheos Magister (probably third to fourth-century), used by Greeks to learn Latin (one is at St. Gall).

3. The sense of community is a main theme of this book (see esp. Prologue); also, P. Lemerle, "L'Orthodoxie byzantine et l'oecumenisme médiéval: les origines du "schisme" des églises," *Bulletin Association G. Budé* (1954), pp. 228-46; also, I. Sevčenko, "Intellectual Repercussions of the Council of Florence," *Church History* (1955), p. 295. Now Southern, cited in next note.

4. On the differing theological approaches of East and West in the fourth and fifth centuries, see J. Pelikan, *The Spirit of Eastern Christendom* (Chicago, 1974), chap. 4. and the chapter of R. Southern, "The Divisions of Christendom," esp. pp. 53-67, in *Western Society and the Church in the Middle Ages* (Middlesex. Eng., 1970).

5. The Latin aristocracy and middle class of the early empire were generally bilingual. In the East the lingua franca was *koiné* Greek.

6. See *New Catholic Encyclopedia* (entry "Jerome") on Jerome's visit to Constantinople in A.D. 330. Also the biography of P. Gallay, *La vie de St. Grégoire de Nazianze* (Lyons, 1943), and the seventh-century biography by a priest, Gregorius (*MPG*, 35, cols. 243-304).

7. See below, this chapter.

8. On Gregory's rhetorical skill, see P. Gallay, *Langue et style de Saint Grégoire de Nazianze* (Paris, 1933). Also R. Payne, *The Holy Fire* (London, 1958), pp. 196-222 (a rather popular treatment). On ancient rhetoric in general, see H. Marrou, *Histoire de l'éducation dans l'antiquité* (Paris, 1948).

9. Especially by W. Jaeger and his students. See Jaeger, *Early Christianity and Greek Paideia* (Cambridge, Mass., 1965), and his *De instituto Christiano, Greg. Nyss. Opera* (Leiden, 1952). Also Gregory of Nyssa's *Contra Eunomium* (*Opera*, ed. W. Jaeger), vol. 2 (Leiden, 1950), etc. Cf. J. Danielou, "Platonisme et théologie mystique, essai sur la doctrine spirituelle de Grégoire de Nyssa...," *Trierer theologische Zeitschrift* (1953), pp. 338, etc., and cf. J. Quasten, *Patrology* 3 (Utrecht, 1966), bibliography on pp. 291-92. Also see H. Musurillo, ed., *From Glory to Glory* (London, 1962).

10. On Dionysius there is a large literature. For a brief account (in English), see Payne, *Holy Fire*, pp. 263-80. For a more scholarly account, see H. Beck, *Kirche und Theologische Literatur im byzantinischen Reich* (Munich, 1959), pp. 348 f., 366 f., etc.

11. See his *Mystical Theology* (English ed., Surrey, 1949), p. 14. On Eastern apophatic theology and mysticism, see, e.g., V. Lossky, *The Mystical Theology of the Eastern Church* (Cambridge-London, 1957), esp. chap. 2.

12. On the flight of Greek monks to the West in these periods (as many as 50,000 came in the eighth and ninth centuries, according to L. White, *Latin Monasticism in Norman Sicily* [Cambridge, Mass., 1938], pp. 15-17); cf. J. Gay, *L'Italie méridionale et l'empire byzantine* (Paris, 1904), Also K. Setton, "The

Byzantine Background to the Italian Renaissance," *Proceedings of the American Philosophical Society*, 100 (1956): 7.

13. On John's influence on the West, see esp. M. Anastos, "Some Aspects of Byzantine Influence on Latin Thought," *Twelfth-century Europe and the Foundations of Modern Society* (Madison, 1961), pp. 149–63, with bibliography. Also E. Gilson, *History of Christian Philosophy in the Middle Ages* (New York, 1955), pp. 91–92.

14. On such monasteries, see J. McNulty and B. Hamilton, " 'Orientale Lumen' et 'Magistra Latinitas,' Greek Influences on Latin Monasticism," *Le Millénaire du Mont Athos* (Chevtogne, 1963), p. 131. Also B. Hamilton, "The City of Rome and the Eastern Churches," *Orientalia Christiana Periodica, 27* (1961): 2–26.

15. Even had the Greeks and Latins been able to comprehend one another's languages, it still would have been hard successfully to communicate theologically because of the growing mutual hostility. On the difficulties in translating each other's theological terms—especially *prosopon, hypostasis, substantia, vicarius, aitia,* and *metanoia*—see Y. Congar, *After 900 Years* (New York, 1959), p. 31.

16. On the common view, see esp. E. Dekkers, "Les traductions grecques des écrits patristiques latins," *Sacris Erudiri* 5 (1953): 214 ff. Now cf. J. Ryan, ed., *Augustine's Confessions* (Garden City, N.Y., 1960), pp. 214 ff., introduction, which affirms that Augustine, while not acquiring a thorough mastery of Greek as a young man, later went on to much improve his knowledge, and thus in later life, when he did most of his theological writing, knew a considerable amount of Greek. Ryan also believes that Augustine might have read Plato in the original.

17. J. Hussey, *Church and learning in the Byzantine Empire* (New York, 1937), p. 203.

18. See below, chap. 4.

19. See under "Gregory the Great," in *New Catholic Encyclopedia*. Gregory seems to have disliked the Byzantine court as hypocritical. See esp. below, chap. 4.

20. See below chap. 14.

21. On the Lyons and Florence councils, see chapters 8 and 11.

22. See esp. my chaps. 4 and 14.

23. On Traversari, see esp. L. Mehus, *Ambrosii Traversarii . . . latinae epistolae* (Florence, 1959). Also D. Traversari, *Ambrogio Traversari e i suoi tempi* (Florence, 1912), and this book, chap. 14. On Manuel Calecas, see chap. 4 below and esp. summary biography in R. Loenertz, *Correspondance de Manuel Calecas* (Vatican City, 1950).

24. On Valla, see esp. the new work of S. Camporeale, *Lorenzo Valla. Umanesimo e Teologia* (Florence, 1972); and also cf. Geanakoplos, *Byzantium and the Renaissance*, pp. 238–46, on Ducas' (usually overlooked) application of philology to the *New Testament* (see chap. 10). Also see A. Perosa, *Collatio Novi Testamenti* (Florence, 1970) on Valla's use of Greek knowledge for his edition of the New Testament; and on philology and humanism in general, see below, chaps. 13–14. (esp. on Traversari and Valla's dislike for scholasticism).

25. See an even stronger statement by E. Gilson, in *History of Christian Philosophy in the Middle Ages* (New York, 1955), p. 541: "Practically every notable event in the history of Western thought in the Middle Ages is tied up with the presence of a man who had studied in Greece, or who knew Greek and had translated some Greek philosophic writings or had access to such translations."

26. On Muslim interpretation and the admixture of Aristotelian and Neoplatonic thought, see T. Arnold and A. Guillaume, *The Legacy of Islam* (Oxford, 1931), pp. 240–41; and P. Hitti, *History of the Arabs*, p. 307. See now R. Walzer, *Greek into Arabic* (Cambridge, Mass., 1962), pp. 60–113.

27. C. Haskins, *Renaissance of the Twelfth Century* (New York, 1968), p. 292.

28. John died ca. A.D. 750. He was in the employ of the Arab caliph.

29. On Cerbanus, A. Urbansky, *Byzantium and the Danube Frontier* (New York, 1968); A. Bryer, "Cultural Relations . . . in the Twelfth Century," in *Relations between East and West* (Edinburgh, 1973), p. 81.

30. On Moerbeke's translation of the *Politics*, see E. Barker, *Social and Political Thought in Byzantium* (Oxford, 1957), p. 136. From the end of the twelfth to the end of the thirteenth century, the proportion of translations made from Greek to those made from the Arab, at second hand, gradually increased. It is not usually known that Moerbeke also translated the *Poetics* of Aristotle (P. Kristeller, *Studies in Renaissance Thought and Letters* [Rome, 1956], pp. 340–41 and 23.) The *Poetics* was thus known to the thirteenth-century Western world. On Aquinas and John of Damascus, see Gilson, *History of Christian Philosophy*, p. 92. Thomas himself cites John (see *Summa Theologica*, pt. 1, quaestio 36, art. 2 ad tertium). The degree of Thomas's knowledge of John of Damascus' work has not been established.

31. Yet, see previous note on the *Poetics* of Aristotle.

32. Geanakoplos, *Greek Scholars in Venice,* passim, esp. pp. 284–86.

33. On Erigena, see M. Cappuyns, *Jean Scot Erigène, sa vie, son oeuvre, sa pensée* (Louvain, 1933).

34. Dionysius had first been brought to the West in the ninth century through Abbot Hilduin of St. Denis. See M. Viller and K. Rahner, *Askese und Mystik in der Väterzeit* (1939).

35. F. Masai, *Pléthon et le platonisme de Mistra* (Paris, 1956).

36. On Valla see n. 24, above.

37. See below, chap. 13. Also A. della Torre, *Storia dell'Accademia Platonica di Firenze* (Florence, 1902).

38. Apparently Ficino did not use the works of Pletho.

39. On this important conflict, see esp. E. Burtt, *Metaphysical Foundations of Modern Physical Science* (London, 1925), pp. 40 ff., who emphasizes the importance of the mathematical type of thinking in Plato (via Pythagoras) to be found in Neoplatonic thought. This, he says, led to the Copernican theory. Burtt is opposed by E. W. Strong, *Procedures and Metaphysics* (Berkeley, 1936) and J. Randall, "Development of Scientific Method in the School of Padua," *Journal of History of Ideas* (1940), pp. 176–206, who emphasizes, rather, the method (Aristotelianism) of Padua University for the rise of modern science. See also J. Randall, *The School of Padua and the Emergence of Modern Science*

(Padua, 1961) ; P. Duhem, *La système du monde* (Paris, 1954), vols. 7–8.

40. See below chap. 9, n. 18.

41. See A. Vasiliev, *History of the Byzantine Empire* (Madison, Wis., 1952), p. 491. The Latin version had been translated from the Greek in 1160 in Sicily. In 1175, Gerard of Cremona translated the work from the Arabic at Toledo. See now, A. Bryer, "Cultural Relations between East and West . . ." in *Relations between East and West*, ed. Baker (Edinburgh, 1973), p. 80.

42. P. Rose, "The *Mechanica* in the Renaissance," *Studies in the Renaissance* 18 (1971) : 76–77.

43. See, in N. Baynes and H. Moss, *Byzantium: An Introduction to East Roman Civilization* (Oxford, 1961), the essay by F. Marshall and J. Mavrogordato, "Byzantine Literature," pp. 221 ff. Also cf. R. Jenkins, "The Hellenistic Origins of Byzantine Literature," *Dumbarton Oaks Papers*, 17 (1963) : esp. 39 and 52; and N. B. Tomadakes, *Introduction to Byzantine Literature*, 1 (Athens, 1958) : esp. 16 ff. (in Greek).

44. A Pertusi, *Leonzio Pilato fra Petrarca e Boccaccio* (Venice, 1964). See G. Cammelli, *Manuele Crisolora* (Florence, 1941), pp. 8, 44, etc.

45. Cammelli, and Geanakoplos, *Greek Scholars*, p. 24.

46. On the problem of origins and the romance, see bibliography in K. Setton, "The Byzantine Background to the Italian Renaissance," pp. 38–39. Also see the *Basic Library* (Athens, 1955) anlaysis of E. Kriaras (in Greek). Cf. U. Holmes, *A History of Old French Literature to 1300* (New York, 1937), pp. 146–49.

47. On Salerno's origins, see *History of Science Ancient and Medieval*, ed. R. Taton, English trans. (New York, 1963), article by G. Beaujouan, p. 476. On Roger see A. Crombie, *Medieval and Early Modern Science* (New York, 1959), 1 : 232–36. Also see P. Kristeller, "Ancient Philosophy at Salerno in the Twelfth Century" (unpublished paper), where it is shown that in the eleventh century a certain Bartholomaeus knew Greek there. On early Western medicine, see L. MacKinney, "Tenth-Century Medicine," in "Symposium in the 10th century," *Medievalia et Humanistica* 9 (1955) : 10–13.

48. Ch. Diehl, *La société byzantine à l'époque des Comnènes* (Paris, 1929), pp. 51–56, and G. Schreiber, "Byzantinisches und abendländisches Hospital," *Gemeinschaften des Mittelalters* 1 (1948) : esp. 42 ff.

49. Crombie, *Medieval and Early Modern Science*, 1 : 234.

50. See J. Theodorides, "Byzantine Science," *History of Science Ancient and Medieval* ed. R. Taton, trans. A. Pomerans (New York, 1957), pp. 440 ff. Ibid., 1 : 220. MacKinney, "Tenth-Century Medicine," p. 12. E. Nordensköld, *History of Biology* (New York, 1942). On Musurus, see D. Geanakoplos, *Greek Scholars in Venice*, p. 162.

51. G. Sarton, *An Introduction to the History of Science* (Baltimore, 1931), p. 171. F. Chalandon, *Les Comnènes* (Paris, 1912) 2 : 317 ff. On the Byzantine silk industry, see esp. R. Lopez, "Silk Manufacture in the Byzantine Empire," *Speculum* 29 : 1 ff.

52. H. Bloch, "Monte Cassino, Byzantium, and the West in the Earlier Middle Ages," *Dumbarton Oaks Papers*, 3 (1946) : 163–224. In the tenth century,

bronze doors were cast at Hildesheim for Bishop Bernard, who had them copied from the Byzantine-inspired doors made at Aachen for Charlemagne. See F. Tschan, *St. Bernard of Hildesheim*, 2 (Notes Dame, 1942): 142, 168–69, and 200, n. 6.

53. See Theophilus Presbyter, *Schedula Diversarum Artium*, ed. H. Hagen (Vienna, 1874), esp. pp. 114–17. Also, A. Megaw's report in *Dumbarton Oaks Papers*, 17 (1963): 362.

54. See esp. E. Kitzinger, "On the Portrait of Roger II in the Martorana in Palermo," *Proporzioni* (1950), 3, pp. 30–34, who emphasizes the fact that Roger wore the costume of a Byzantine emperor (as he does on several coins and seals) and was addressed as Basileus, but also that the German imperial imagery of the Ottonians provides a precedent for Roger's face done in imitation of Christ. On the Norman rulers and Byzantine theocracy, see also A. Marongiu, "Lo spirito della monarchia Normanna della Sicilia," *Arch. stor. sic.*, ser. 3, vols. 50–51, pp. 115 ff.; and L. R. Ménager, "L'institution monarchique dans les états normandes d'Italie," *Cahiers des civilizations mediévales* (1959): 2 303 ff., who opposes such theories.

55. On Nilus Doxopatres, see the article of V. Laurent in *Dictionnaire d'histoire et géog. eccl.*, 14, cols. 769–71. Also Ch. Diehl, *Byzantium, Greatness and Decline*, pp. 285–87.

56. See G. Ferrari dalle Spade, "La legislazione dell'impero d'Oriente in Italia," *Italia e Grecia* (Florence, 1939), pp. 225–53. Cf. Dölger, "Byzanz und das Abendland vor den Kreuzzügen," p. 109.

57. G. Ostrogorsky, *History of the Byzantine State* (New Brunswick, N.J., 1957), pp. 216 ff. Also R. Lopez, "Byzantine Law in the Seventh Century and its Reception by the Germans and Arabs," *Byzantion* 16 (1942–3): 445 ff. Byzantine law was in force in Byzantine Sicily and southern Italy but evidently had no lasting influence there; yet it was known to, and did, affect the Franks (Latins) living in the East. The influence of Germanic law was probably responsible for the curious appearance of the ordeal by fire in 1253 at the trial of Michael Palaeologus: see below, chap. 7.

58. H. Scheltema, *New Cambridge Medieval History*, vol. 4. no. 2, pp. 71–73.

59. On Rhodian sea law, see W. Ashburner, *Rhodian Sea Law* (Oxford, 1909). Also W. P. Gormley, "The Development of the Rhodian-Roman Sea Law to 1861," *Inter-American Law Review* 3 (1961): 319 ff. On Byzantine navigational terms and the West, see H. and R. Kahane and A. Tietze, *The Lingua Franca in the Levant* (Urbana, Ill., 1958). esp. pp. 571, 503, 552, etc. For *dreki*, see S. A. Anderson, *Viking Enterprise* (New York, 1936). p. 62, and W. Vogel, "Nordische Seefahrten im früheren Mittelalter," *Meereskunde*, vol. 1, pt. 7, p. 25. Cf. J. De Vries, *Altnordisches Etymolog. Wörterbuch*, who says the German *Drache* (dragon) comes from Latin *draco*, itself from ancient Greek. Now see R. Lopez "Foreigners in Byzantium," p. 350, on the increasing Byzantine disinclination to engage in trade, which was left to the Italian cities.

60. F. Lane, *Venetian Ships and Shipbuilders of the Renaissance* (1934). p. 56.

61. There has been little done on Byzantine diplomacy. F. Dölger, *Byzantinische Diplomatik* (Ettal, 1956) contains documents and analysis; also see D. Obolensky, "The Principles and Methods of Byzantine Diplomacy," *XIIe Congrès*

International des études byzantines (Ochrida, 1961). A growing number of monographs exist, of course, on the diplomacy of individual emperors.

62. E. Freshfield, ed., *Roman Law in the Later Roman Empire: Book of the Eparch* (Cambridge, 1938). A recent article on the guilds is S. Vryonis, "Byzantine 'Demokratia' and the Guilds in the Eleventh Century," *Dumbarton Oaks Papers*, 17 (Washington, 1963); 289–314; see esp. pp. 289–93 and bibliography in nn. 5 and 13. Also Lopez, "Silk Industry in the Byzantine Empire," *Speculum*, 20 (1945): 184 ff.

63. On the round towers, see S. Toy, *A History of Fortification* (London, 1955), pp. 86 ff. On the Normans, see H. Brown, *The English Castle* (London, 1936), p. 23, The Arabs learned fortification from the Greeks, and the West also learned from Byzantium via the Arabs. A. Choisi, *L'art de bâtir chez les byzantins* (Paris, 1883), is not helpful here.

64. A. Kelly, *Eleanor of Aquitaine and the Four Kings* (Cambridge, Mass., 1950).

65. L. Bréhier, *Civilization Byzantine*, 2d ed. (Paris, 1970), pp. 51–52; also Runciman, *Byzantine Civilization*, p. 237; and on Damiani, see A. Capecelatro *Storia di San Pier Damiani* (Florence, 1862). L. Salzman, *English Industries of the Middle Ages* (Oxford, 1923), p. 171, says that as late as the thirteenth century forks, though known in the West, were seldom provided; the diner used his own knife, and spoons were commonly used.

66. For these terms I am grateful to my friends Henry and René Kahane of the University of Illinois. On the Spanish *quemar* specifically, see J. Corominas, *Breve Diccionario Etimologico de la lengua castellana* (Madrid, 1961). For musical instruments, see K. Sachs, *History of Musical Instruments*.

67. On these terms, also H. and R. Kahane, "Cultural Criteria for Western Borrowing from Byzantine Greek," *Homage to A. Tovar* (Madrid, 1972), pp. 205–29.

68. On the hymns, see esp. E. Wellesz, *History of Byzantine Music and Hymnography*, 2d. ed. (Oxford, 1961); G. Reese, *Music in the Middle Ages,* pp. 157 ff., 79; and N. Tomadakes, *Introduction to Byzantine Literature* (Athens, 1958) pp. 171 ff., 187 ff. (in Greek). On the Akathistos, see next note.

69. On the trisagion, see K. Levy, "The Byzantine Sanctus and its Modal Tradition in East and West," *Annales Musicologique* 6 (1958–63); 7–67; E. Wellesz, *Eastern Elements in Western Chant* (Oxford, 1947), p. 13. On authorship of the Akathistos, see bibliography in C. del Grande's edition of *L'Inno Acatisto* (Florence, 1948), pp. 30–31. Now E. Wellesz, "On Authorship of the Akathistos," *Dumbarton Oaks Papers*, no. 18 (1967), pp. 51-52. On the Grottaferrata hymn-writing, see Wellesz, *History of Byzantine Music*, p. 130, and L. Tardo, *L'antica melurgia bizantina* (Grottaferrata, 1938).

69a. See text in *Liber officialis,* 2. 1, in *Amalarii Episcopi Opera liturgica omnia,* 2, J. Hanssen, ed. (Vatican, 1948), p. 197. Also see Remegius, *De celebratione missae,* MPG v. 101, col. 1248, esp. "ut unum ejus populum nos esse ostendamus, unumque Deus utrumque populum credere, Kyrie Domine, eleeson miserere." See Yale Ph. D. dissertation of my student, B. Kaczynski, "Greek Learning in the Medieval West: A Study of St. Gall, 816–1022" (1975), p. 254.

70. On all this, see esp. Wellesz, *Eastern Elements in Western Chant,* p. 201.

71. On Notker, see *Einhard and Notker the Stammerer*, trans. L. Thorpe (Harmondsworth, 1969), pp. 142–43. Cf. Wellesz, ibid., pp. 168, 201. Also see G. Gray, *The History of Music* (London, 1928), p. 17. On the Arab influence on Charlemagne's court, see H. G. Farmer, *Historical Facts for the Arabian Musical Influence* (London, 1929).

72. See Aurelian, *The Discipline of Music*, trans. J. Ponte (Colorado Springs, 1968) pp. 24–25.

73. On the *echoi*, see Reese, *Music in the Middle Ages*, p. 90. Also on Gregory, see ibid., pp. 73, 90 and, Wellesz, *Eastern Elements*.

74. Reese, p. 120. G. Frotscher, *Geschichte des Orgelspiels*, vol. 1 (Berlin, 1935). The gift was evidently that of a hydraulic organ. See Notker, *Einhard and Notker*, p. 143. affirming that Byzantine envoys presented Charlemagne with several kinds of organs and other instruments. William of Malmesbury describes a hydraulic organ made by Gerbert (d. 1003), implying that this was still unique in the West as late as the eleventh century (see *Chronicle of the Kings of England*, trans. J. Giles [London, 1847], p. 175).

75. I. Young, "Franchinus Gaforius, Renaissance Theorist and Composer" (Ph.D. dissertation, University of Southern California, 1954).

76. S. Runciman, *Eastern Schism* (Oxford, 1955), pp. 159 ff. Y. Congar, *After Nine Hundred Years* (New York, 1959).

77. See discussion and bibliography in D. Geanakoplos, "On the Schism of the Greek and Roman Churches: A Confidential Papal Directive for the Implementation of Union," *Greek Orthodox Theological Review* 1 (1954): 16 ff. Also L. Bréhier, "Normal Relations between Rome and the Churches of the East before the Schism of the 11th century," *Constructive Quarterly* 4 (1916): 669 ff. D. Nicol, in his introduction to *Relations between East and West in the Middle Ages* (Edinburgh, 1973), says, "after 975 and 1018 a flood of Westerners, mainly pilgrims, passed through Byzantium."

78. See, for background of possible Byzantine influences on the Cluniac Reform Movement, R. Weiss, "The Greek Culture of South Italy in the Middle Ages," in *Proceedings of the British Academy* (1951), pp. 23–50, and esp. McNulty and Hamilton, ' "Orientale Lumen' et 'Magistra Latinitas,' " pp. 181–216.

79. See esp. R. Southern, *Making of the Middle Ages* (New Haven, 1953), pp. 246–56. Recent works helpful here are, for the Greek viewpoint, J. Kalogerou *Mary, the Perpetual Virgin Theotokos according to the Orthodox Faith* (in Greek; Salonika, 1957) and J. Anastasiou, *The Presentation of the Theotokos: History, Iconography and Hymnography* (in Greek; Salonika, 1959). For the Catholic view M. Gordillo. "Mariologia Orientalis," in *Orientalia Christiana Analecta*, p. 141 (Rome, 1954) and M. Jugie, *L'Immaculée Conception dans l'Ecriture Sainte et dans la Tradition orientale* (Rome, 1952), pp. 225–40. Also see articles of G. Florovsky and V. Lossky, in E. Mascall, ed., *The Mother of God. A Symposium* (London, 1949); p. Sherwood, "Byzantine Mariology," *Cath. Theol. Society* 15 (1960): 107–34.

80. Ch. Diehl, *Une République patricienne: Venise* (Paris, 1928). Geanakoplos, *Greek Scholars in Venice*, p. 35. Especially, see chap. 9. below.

81. The Byzantine monuments of Torcello, Venice's original settlement, date back to the seventh century, and especially the twelfth. Also see Tschan, *St. Bernard of Hildesheim*, 2: 142, 168–69, and 200, n. 6.

82. T. Rice, *Byzantine Art*, pp. 229–32; Runciman, *Byzantine Civilization*, p. 238. Cf. O. Demus, *Byzantine Art and the West*, pp. 154 ff., on England.

83. Bloch, "Montecassino, Byzantium and the West," p. 194. It is believed that the mosaics in the Baptistery of Florence were decorated by Byzantine or Byzantine-trained craftsmen in the thirteenth century. Cf. J. Beckwith's *The Art of Constantinople* (London, 1961), p. 137. Also Kitzinger, "Byzantine Contribution to Western Art of 12th and 13th Centuries," p. 35–44.

84. The church of Cluny was begun in 1089 and dedicated in 1131. See J. Gay, "L'abbaye de Cluny et Byzance au début du XIIe siècle," *Echos d'Orient*, 30 (1931): 84–90. On twelfth-century Byzantine-Western artistic relations, see E. Kitzinger, article in *Dumbarton Oaks Papers* 17 (1963): 47:"a vast field of further inquiry."

85. On stained glass, see above, chap. 1, n. 16, Megaw's article.

86. See P. Schweinfurth, "Die Bedeutung der byzantinischen Kunst für die Stilbildung der Renaissance," *Die Antike* 9 (1933): 2. Also cf. the old work of R. Byron and T. Rice, *The Birth of Western Painting* (London, 1930), and C. Diehl, *Manuel de l'art byzantin*, 2d ed. (Paris, 1925-26), pp. 743–44. Also see next note, and esp. cf. my Prologue. Most important, see now Kitzinger, "Byzantine Contribution," pp. 25–48.

87. Cf. A. Grabar, *Byzantine Painting* (Geneva, 1953), pp. 45–46. Diehl, *Manuel*, pp. 743–44; and V. Lazarev, "Duccio and 13th-Century Greek Icons," *Burlington Magazine* 59 (1931): 159. Cf. now O. Demus, *Byzantine Art and the West*, pp. 238–239, who shows Byzantine ("Hellenistic") influences on El Greco, esp his later painting. Until recently art historians distinguished, in the Palaeologan artistic Renaissance, between the so-called Macedonian and Cretan schools of painting. "Macedonian" was taken to refer in general to the shorter-lived, more realistic art of the fourteenth century, radiating primarily from Thessalonika. And "Cretan" referred to the reversion to (or in some cases continuation of) the more traditional Byzantine modes of painting, found especially at Mt. Athos or on Crete, and extending through the sixteenth century and later. But recently scholars have become more aware of the complexity of Byzantine painting in this period (see e.g., the Prologue to this work, referring to "realism" in fourteenth-century Byzantine art, to the Hesychast influence, and other factors), and have therefore dropped the use of the two terms, at least as opposed to each other. The two terms, Macedonian and Cretan, were originally coined by G. Millet, *Recherches sur l'iconographie de l'Evangile . . . d'après les monuments de Mistra, Macédoine, et du Mont-Athos* (Paris, 1916). Cf. T. Rice, *Byzantine Painting: The Last Phase* (New York, 1968), pp. 103, 109 ff., and O. Demus, *Byzantine Art and the West* (New York, 1097) on these terms. Also now S. Runciman, *Byzantine Style and Civilization* (Harmondsworth, Eng., 1975).

88. T. Rice, *Byzantine Art*, p. 256, and his *Art of the Byzantine Era* (New York, 1962), p. 232; R. Byron, *The Byzantine Achievement* (London, 1929), pp. 38,

218; F. Rutter, review in *Burlington Magazine* 9 (1932): 274; J. Willumsen, *La Jeunesse du Peintre El Greco* (Paris, 1927), pp. 161 ff., etc. For more on El Greco, see chap. 1 above and chap. 10 below, with bibliography.

89. See C. Mertzios, "Gleanings from the records of the Notary Michael Mara," *Kretika Chronika* 1 (1961–62): 302 ff. (in Greek).

90. On El Greco's similarities to Palaeologan painting, see esp. Rice *Byzantine Painting*, pp. 191–92. Also see W. Wolfflin, *Principles of Art History* (New York, 1929), pp. 14–15 on depreciation of line in art. Cf. chap. 1, text and nn. 17–21.

91. U. von Wilamovitz-Moellendorff, *Euripides-Herakles* (Berlin, 1889) 1: 194, and Geanakoplos, *Greek Scholars in Venice*. pp. 288, 290.

Notes to Chapter 4

1. I hope soon to publish a separate monograph dealing with Western infuences on Byzantium. See now D. Geanakoplos, *Byzantine East and Latin West* (New York, 1966), p. 5. Also below, chap. 7, on German law and Byzantium.

2. E. Gibbon, *Decline and Fall of the Roman Empire*, ed. J. Bury (New York, 1914) 6:366–67 (chap. 60). Cf. my article, "Edward Gibbon and Byzantine Ecclesiastical History," *Church History* 35 (1966): 1–16.

3. See esp. W. Ohnsorge, *Das Zweikaiserproblem im früheren Mittelalter* (Hildesheim, 1947).

4. E. Gilson, *History of Christian Philosophy in the Middle Ages* (New York, 1955), p. 540 and cf. p. 542. On Byzantine attitudes to the West in the fifth century (esp. A.D. 410 and 476), see W. Kaegi, *Byzantium and the Decline of Rome* (Princeton, N. J., 1968).

5. J. Hussey, *Church and Learning in the Byzantine Empire* (New York, 1937), p. 203. See Kaegi, esp. pp. 240–41, for the little Byzantine knowledge of Augustine.

6. See Pauly's *Real-Encyclopädie der class. Altert.*, Vol 6 (1909), cols. 2508 ff. on Virius Nicomachus Flavianus's *Annales*, reaching to ca. A.D. 366; also vol. 10, col. 1314–29; F. Dölger, "Rom in der Gedankenwelt den Byzantiner," *Byzanz und die Europaische Staatenwelt* (Etal, 1953). pp. 70–115.

7. See E. Dekkers, "Les traductions grecques des écrits patristiques latins," *Sacris Erudiri*, 5 (1953): 214–15. A. Turyn, *Dated Greek Manuscripts of the 13–14th Centuries*, 1 (Urbana, 1972): 117.

8. On Leo of Naples's translation of Pseudo-Callisthenes' Alexander story, see W. Buchwald, A. Hohlweg. O. Prinz, *Tusculum Lexicon* (Munich, 1963), p. 297.

9. Check esp. F. Dölger, *Regesten der Kaiserurkunden des Oströmischen Reiches*, 5 vols. (Munich-Berlin, 1924–65) for references to such Latins. On the Spaniard mentioned, see C. Will, *Acta et Scripta* (Frankfurt-am-Main, 1861), p. 161. On reciprocal ignorance of Latin and Greek, see M. Jugie, *Le Schisme byzantin* (Paris, 1941), pp. 39–42; and S. Runciman, "Byzantine Linguists," *Prosfora to S. Kyriakedes* (1953), p. 577 (in Greek).

10. See F. Füchs, *Die höheren Schulen von Konstantinopel* (Amsterdam, 1964), p. 26.

11. On the two brothers, see esp. M. Anastos, "Some Aspects of Byzantine In-

fluence on Western Thought," *Twelfth-Century Foundations of Modern Europe* (Madison, 1961), pp. 138, 140–49, and bibliography cited.

12. On Byzantine libraries, see recently N. Wilson, in *Greek Roman Byzantine Studies*, 8 (1967):53–80; and L. Reynolds and N. Wilson, *Scribes and Scholars* (Oxford, 1968), pp. 50–53, 60–63. On Western knowledge of Greek patristic literature to 1200, see A. Siegmund, *Die Ueberlieferung der griechischen Literatur in der lateinische Kirche* (Munich-Pasing, 1949).

13. On Anselm of Havelberg, see Migne PL, vol. 188, cols. 1119–1248. On John, see above, chap. 3, n. 30; see also M. Anastos, in *Twelfth-Century Europe and the Foundations of Modern Society*, ed. M. Clagett, G. Post, R. Reynolds (Madison, 1961), pp. 149–63.

13a. On Greek translations of the Roman mass, see Lumpe, "Abendländisches im Byzanz," col. 322 (in W. Berschin, "Griechisches im lateinisches Mittelalter," *Reallexikon der Byzantinistik*, A. 1. 3–4 [Amsterdam, 1970] pp. 227–304); and A. Strittmater, "Liturgical Latinisms in a Twelfth Century Greek Euchology," *Miscellanea G. Mercati* 3 (Vatican, 1946), pp. 41–64. Cf. this book, Epigraph quoting Anonymous of Tours.

14. See on Lyons: D. Geanakoplos, *Emperor Michael Palaeologus and the West* (Hamden, Conn., 1972, new ed.), pp. 258–76, esp. p. 260, n. 8a, on Bonaventura and Aquinas; also M. Roncaglia, *Les frères mineurs et l'église grecque orthodoxe au XIIIᵉ siècle* (Cairo, 1954); B. Roberg, *Die Union . . . auf den Konzil von Lyon* (Bonn, 1964); and P. Franchi, *Il Concilio II di Lione* (Rome, 1965); finally, see below, chap. 11, on Bernardino, discussing Lyons, esp. n. 1, citing my new article.

15. See esp. Geanakoplos, *Emperor Michael Palaeologus*, esp. chaps, 9–11.

16. G. Hofmann, "Patriarch Johann Bekkos and die lateinische Kultur," *Orientalia Christiana Periodica*, 11 (1945):141–64.

17. On Planudes there is a growing literature: see esp. M. Treu, *Maximi monachi Planudis, Epistulae* (Breslau, 1890); C. Wendel, "Planudes," in Pauly-Wissova *Real-Encyclopädie*, vol. 20 (1950), cols. 2202–53; and S. Runciman, *The Last Byzantine Renaissance* (Cambridge, 1970), pp. 59–60. Plandues used the Arab-Hindi zero and the decimal system (which had been brought to the West by Ficcabono [Leonard of Pisa]). In Byzantium Arabic numerals were almost never used for dates. Cydones probably learned Arabic numerals in Italy. On Planudes and mathematics, esp. at the Chora monastery, see I. Sevčenko, 'Théodore Metochites, Chora, et les courants intellectuels de l'époque," *Arte et Société à Byzance sous les Paléologues* (1971), pp. 29 f. Cf. below, n. 56.

18. On Ovid and the Greeks, see W. Schmitt, "Lateinische Literatur in Byzanz," *Jahrbuch der Österreichischen byzantinischen Gesellschaft*, 17 (1968): 127–47, esp. 129 and 139. On Augustine's *De Trinitate*, see below n. 27; also C. Wendel, "Planudes," *Byz. Zeitschrift*, 40 (1940): 406–45.

19. On the Pera monastery, see R. Loenertz, Les établissements dominicains de Péra-Constantinople," *Echos d'Orient* 34 (1935):332–49. Also R. Loenertz, "Les dominicains byzantins Theodore et André Chrysoberges. . . . ," *Arch. Frat. Praed,* 9 (1939):5–61 and 338; and A. Altaner, "Die Kenntnis des Griechische in den Missionsorden während des 13. und 14. Jahrhunderts," *Zeitschrift für Kirchengeschichte* 53 (1934): 436 ff. Manuel Calecas learned Latin at the Pera convent under the Italian, Angelo de Scarperia.

20. On the Cydones brothers, see G. Mercati, *Notizie di Procoro e Demetrio Cydone, Manuele Caleca, e Teodoro Meleteniota, Studi e Testi*, vol. 56 (Vatican City, 1931). On Cyparissiotes, see this book chap. 6. On Manuel Calecas, see R. Loenertz, *Correspondance de Manuel Calecas* (Vatican City, 1950). On Mammas, see my two articles, "Byzantium and the Later Crusades," esp. chap. 3, text and n. 113, in *A History of the Crusades*, vol. 3 (Madison, Wis., 1975) and Runciman, *Great Church in Captivity*, p. 168.

21. See A. Dondaine, "Contra Graecos. Prémiers écrites polémiques des dominicains d'Orient," *Archivum fratrum praedicatorum*, 21 (1951; new ed., Leonine Commission, Vatican, 1967): 387 ff. See also Migne, PG, vol. 140, cols. 487–574.

22. For Cantacuzene's view of Barlaam, see Migne PG, vol. 160, cols. 1083–1301. On Barlaam, see esp. G. Schirò, *Barlaam Calabro, Epistole Greche* (Palermo, 1954) and his *Barlaam and Philosophy in Thessalonika in the 14th Century* (Thessalonika, 1959) (in Greek). On Palamas, see J. Meyendorff, *A Study of Gregory Palamas* (London, 1964) and esp. his *Grégoire Palamas. Les Triades pour la défense de Saintes-hésychastes* (Louvain, 1959). Also see B. Laourdas, "Classical Philology in Thessalonike," *Hellenika* (in Greek).

23. My view. Besides those modern Western scholars who insist that Barlaam was a Nominalist of the Occamite school, others (Schirò, for example) tell me he was, rather, a Scotist. Palamas' views were approved as being in the tradition of the Greek fathers by the Byzantine Hesychast Council of 1361. See A. Papadakes, "Gregory Palamas at the Council of Blachernae, 1351," *Greek Roman Byzantine Studies* 10 (1969): 337–42. M. Jugie, under "Palamas," *Dict. Theol. Cathol.*, affirms the essentially standard Western position that Palamas' theological opinions (on the divine light and the energies of God, etc.) were unknown in Patristic times, and were therefore innovations." This also accords with the view of some of Palamas' Greek opponents. On Palamism at the Council of Florence, see below, chap. 11, nn. 29–33.

24. On the theology involved, see esp. Meyendorff, *A Study of Gregory Palamas*, pp. 116–242; also B. Krivocheine, "Ascetic and Mystical Teaching of St. Gregory Palamas," *Eastern Churches Quarterly* (1938), no. 4.

25. Printed in Migne PG, vol. 152, cols. 737 ff. Cf. this book chap, 6. text and nn. 28 ffff.

26. Dekkers, "Les traductions grecques des écrits patristique latins," pp. 193–233. There are probably more exceptions than realized.

27. See Mercati, *Notizie di Procoro*, etc., esp. pp. 30, 159, 160, 239, 429, and C. Wendel, "Planudes," in *Byz. Zeit.* 40 (1940): 406–45.

28. For Calecas' treatise, see Migne PG, vol. 152, cols. 429–661, esp. cols. 536–53; cf. J. Gouillard, "Les influences latines dans l'oeuvre de M. Calecas," *Echos d'Orient* (1938), pp. 37–40.

29. Cf. esp. R. Loenertz, *Demetrius Cydonès Correspondance*, 2 vols. (1956–60); and Runciman, *Great Church in Captivity*, pp. 74–75.

30. Cf. views of Cydones himself in his "Autobiography," pp. 359–403 (Mercati, *Notizie*). See R. Loenertz, "Les établissements dominicains de Péra-Constantinople," *Echos d'Orient* 34 (1935): 332–49. See Loenertz, p. 82 and *Echos d'Orient* 34 (1935): 332. Cydones himself tells us that he wanted to learn Latin

because when he was in charge of the imperial correspondence he found too many points garbled by the Greek translators. See his "Apologia," in Mercati, *Notizie*, pp. 359 ff. His words in Greek are: "ei me pros tas eteran apoblepetai glossas all'autos emauto hromen mathon latinizein." (Note the word *Latinizing* here.) Also cf. ibid., p. 162. See in addition G. Cammelli, *Démétrius Cydones Correspondance* (Paris, 1930), pp. xv-xvii and 145–46.

31. See Cydones, "Autobiography" (Mercati, *Notizie*, p. 159). Also, on the *filioque* and his translations from Thomas, see E. Bouvy, "Saint Thomas: Ses traducteurs byzantins," *Revue Augustinienne* 16 (1910): 404. The *De Potentia* (a *quaestio disputata* by Aquinas on the *filioque*) is no. 10, article 4. See now also S. Papadopoulos, *Hellenikai metaphraseis Thomistikon Ergon* (Athens, 1967; in Greek).

32. See Mercati, *Notizie*, pp. 359–435, esp. 362.

33. See Cydones, in Mercati, *Notizie*, p. 159.

34. See Dekkers, "Les traductions greeques," and also M. Rackl, "Die griechischen Augustinusübersetzungen," *Misc. F. Fhrle*, 1 (Rome, 1924): 1–38.

35. On Margounios, see Geanakoplos, *Byzantine East and Latin West*, pp. 165 ff. To these two names should be added that of Nicephoros Blemmydes of the thirteenth century.

36. See my "Byzantium and the Later Crusades," chap. 3, p. 72, in *A History of the Crusades*, vol. 3 (Madison, Wis., 1975). Also D. Zakythinos, "Démétrius Cydonès et l'entente Balkanique au XIVe siècle," *La Grèce et les Balkans* (Athens, 1947). Important on Cydones is R. Loenertz, "Lettre de Démétrius Cydonès à Andronic Oenéote Grand Juge des Romains (1369–1371)," *Revue des études byzantines* 29 (1971): 303–08.

37. Cf. G. Mercati, Cydones' "Apologia," pp. 362, ff. 366, 372, 389, 402; German trans. by H. G. Beck, "'Die 'Apologia pro vita sua' des Demetrios Kydones," *Ostkirchlichen Studien*, vol. 1 (1957).

38. Text in Migne PG, vol. 154, cols. 952B. See G. Papadopoulos, "Byzantine Theology: Relations with the West" (in Greek) in *Encyclopedia of Religion and Ethics*, vol. 3, p. 1095.

39. For example, Papadopoulos, "Byzantine Theology," p. 1095. This is the standard Greek criticism of the *filioque*.

40. Cf. also St. Thomas, *Summa Theologica*, pt. 1, 27; actually combined from Augustine, *De Trinitate*, bk. 6, chap. 10 (cf. bk. 15) and from Thomas, *Summa Theologica*, pt. 1, Q. 39: "potestas, sapientia, bonitas," but Thomas and Augustine equate *sapientia* with *verbum* (*logos*), and *bonitas* with *caritas*.

41. On the Thomist circle, see esp. M. Jugie, "Démétrius Cydonès et la théologie latine à Byzance du XIVe et XVe siècles," *Echos d'Orient* 31 (1928): 385–402. On Prochoros' work, see Mercati, *Notizie*, p. 287.

42. For Calecas' works, see Migne PG, vol. 152, cols. 429–661. Cf. now W. Schmitt, "Lateinische Literatur in Byzanz," *Jahrb. Osterr. byz. Gesellschaft*, 17 (1968): 127–47, who questions the translation of Anselm's *Cur Deus Homo*.

43. For text see Migne PG, vol. 152, esp. col. 568B.

44. For Scholarius' summary of the Orthodox faith, see his "Contre Judaeos," *Oeuvres Complètes*, 8 vols. (Paris, 1928–30). On his opposition to both Cydones and his pupil Calecas, see Mercati, *Notizie*, p. 449, n. 2, to the effect that

Cydones and Calecas had accepted Latin Christianity because they had been expelled from the Greek church on account of their attachment to doctrines of Barlaam and Acyndinos.

45. On Greek insistence on the convocation of an ecumenical council to debate union, see Geanakoplos, "Byzantium and the Later Crusades," chap. 3, pp. 90–92. Also M. Viller, "La question de l'union des églises entre Grecs et Latins," *Revue d'histoire ecclésiastique* 15 (1921): 260–305, 515–32, 18 (1920): 20–60; and D. Nicol, "Byzantine Requests for an Ecumenical Council in the 14th Century," *Annuarium Historiae Conciliorum* 1 (1969): 69–95.

46. See F. Masai, *Pléthon et le Platonisme de Mistra* (Paris, 1956), pp. 338–39 (original text edited in Paris in 1541).

47. On the presumed Greek inadequacy in debate, see the views of J. Gill, *The Council of Florence* (Cambridge, 1959), pp. 228–29, who also cites the emperor's words (*Acta Graeca*, pp. 418, 421). On George Scholarius, see his *Opera* (Paris, 1928) 1: 299, where he complains that the Greeks no longer had qualifications to compete with the Latins. Cf. P. Sherrard, *Greek East and Latin West* (London, 1959) pp. 168 f. But now see S. Camporeale, *Lorenzo Valla. Umanesimo e teologia* (Florence, 1972), who discusses what Valla learned about exegetical methodology in Florence from Greeks. To support a theological interpretation, the Greek method was to present a "chain" of evidence from writings of the Fathers; the Latins, however, now generally used a "syllogistic" approach.

48. On Pletho, see esp. Masai, *Pléthon et le Platonisme de Mistra*, and also A. Vacalopoulos, *Origins of the Greek Nation: The Byzantine Period* (New Brunswick, N. J., 1970), esp. pp. 126–35. Also this book Prologue and Epilogue.

49. See Runciman, "Byzantine Linguists," *Prosfora to S. Kyriakedis* (1953), p. 577 (in Greek). Also Geanakoplos, *Byzantine East and Latin West*, esp. pp. 1–4, for a summary of "national" Greek and Latin attitudes. Esp. see Pope Nicholas I's letter to the Byzantine court objecting to the Greeks' calling the Latin language "barbarian" (in F. Dvornik, *The Photian Schism: History and Legend* [Cambridge, 1948] pp. 105–09).

50. Michael Psellus, *Chronographia*, ed. E. Sewter (New Haven, 1953). According to Psellus, in his *De Omnifaria Doctrina*, ed. L. Westerink (1948), p. 90, he memorized the *Iliad* as a child.

51. See R. Henry, *Photius Bibliothèque* (Paris, 1959). Also Dekkers, "Les traductions grecques," pp. 208, 214–16, who shows that Photius mentions Augustine and Gregory the Great. Now see also P. Lemerle, *Le prémier humanisme byzantin* (Paris, 1972).

52. For Latin knowledge of Greek Christian literature (up to the twelfth century), see A. Siegmund, *Die Uberlieferung der griechischen christlichen Literatur in der lateinische Kirche* (Munich-Pasing, 1949).

53. I am told this by the palaeographer M. Naoumides, professor of Greek at the University of Illinois. Cf. above, chap. 3, n. 2.

54. See translation of F. Wright, *Liudprand of Cremona* (1930), "The Embassy to Constantinople," chap. 31: chap. 47.

55. On Constantine see above, n. 10.

56. On Petrus Hispanus see *Enciclopedia italiana* under that entry; also the curious work of C. Prantl, *Michael Psellus und Petrus Hispanus* (Leipzig, 1867). On Planudes' translations see above, n. 17; and now W. Schmitt, "Lateinische

Literatur in Byzanz," *Jahrb. Osterr. byz. Gesellschaft* 17 (1968): 127–47. A. Turyn informs me that the view that Planudes translated Caesar's *Bellum Gallicum* is false. The latest work on Planudes is P. Stadter, "Planudes, Plutarch and Pace of Ferrara," *Italia medievale e umanistica* 16 (1973): 137–62.

57. On Planudes in Venice (where he was sent precisely because of his fine knowledge of Latin), see Geanakoplos, *Greek Scholars in Venice* (Cambridge, 1982), p. 27 and n. 48; also Wendel in *Byz. Zeit.* 40 (1940): 406 ff.

58. See esp. G. Mercati, *Notizie,* as cited above in n. 27. Also Stadter, p. 158.

59. Moschopoulos' even more brilliant pupil was Marcus Musurus. On Moschopoulos, see Geanakoplos, *Greek Scholars in Venice,* esp. pp. 23, 220, 286–88; and A. Turyn, *The Byzantine Manuscript Tradition of the Tragedies of Euripides* (Urbana, Ill., 1959), passim. On other students of Planudes, see Stadter (above, n. 56), pp. 158, 139, mentioning John and Andronikas Zarides, and Planudes' class.

60. See Augustine, *De doctrina christiana,* bk. 4, who suggests using the classics but not enjoying them; St. Jerome also suggested the same thing, as later, in effect, did St. Basil in his famous "Discourse to the Youth on the Reading of Classical Literature." See below, chap. 14 and esp. Epilogue, n. 8, work of Wilson.

61. See R. Henry, *Photius Bibliothèque* (Paris, 1959).

62. On all these figures, see Geanakoplos, *Greek Scholars in Venice,* and esp. E. Legrand, *Bibliographie hellénique . . . au XVe et XVIe siècles,* vols. 1–2 (Paris, 1935 ff.). Esp. cf. below, chap. 13.

63. D. Geanakoplos, "A Byzantine Looks at the Renaissance: The Attitude of Michael Apostolis Toward the Rise of Italy to Cultural Eminence," *Greek and Byzantine Studies* 1 (1958): 157–62.

64. For influences of medieval Latin romances on Byzantine literature, see below, chap. 3.

65. See below, chap. 13, text and note that indicates Demetrius Chalcondyles' reference to the *Divine Comedy* of Dante.

66. See Vacalopoulos, *Origins of the Greek Nation,* pp. 241–45, esp. 244, quoting Bessarion's words that Greek youth should learn the techniques of Italian engineering (ironworking) and shipbuilding to help the Greek nation. See below, Epilogue.

67. N. Kalogeras, *Markos Eugenikos and Cardinal Bessarion* (Athens, 1893), p. 70, prints a quotation from Joseph Bryennius (from 1400, published in Leipzig in 1478) which reads: "Do not be deceived . . . If Latin allied troops come to aid us against the Turks they will take arms in order to destroy our city, our race, and our name" (earlier quoted here in Prologue).

68. On the period of Turkish domination in Greece, see below, chap. 9; also T. Papadopoulos, *Studies and Documents relating to the History of the Greek Church and People under Turkish Domination* (Brussels, 1952); and S. Runciman, *The Great Church in Captivity* (Cambridge, 1968), pp. 168, 208 ff.

Notes to Chapter 5

1. Eusebius, *Laus Constantini, Eusebius Werke,* ed. I. A. Heikel, 1 (Leipzig, 1902): 199. For the importance of Eusebius in Byzantine political theory, see D.

Geanakoplos, "Church and State in the Byzantine Empire: A Reconsideration of the Problem of Caesaropapism," *Church History* 34 (1965): 385. On Eusebius' political thought, see esp. N. Baynes, "Eusebius and the Christian Empire," *Annuaire de l'Institut de philologie et d'histoire orientales* 2 (1933–34): 13–18; E. Schwartz, *Kaiser Constantin und die christliche Kirche* (Leipzig, 1936); F. Cranz, "Kingdom and Polity in Eusebius of Caesarea," *Harvard Theological Review* (1952), p. 47–66; cf. Ph. Sherrard, *Greek East and Latin West* (London, 1959), pp. 92 ff.

2. On this problem, see Geanakoplos, "Church and State," 385 ff. with bibliography. See also K. M. Setton, *Christian Attitude Towards the Emperor in the Fourth Century, Especially as Shown in Addresses to The Emperor* (New York, 1941), pp. 48 ff., 79 ff.

3. G. T. Armstrong, "Imperial Church Building and Church-State Relations, A.D. 313–63," *Church History* 36 (1967): 3–17. On views of the work of Eusebius, *Vita Constantini*, see below passim, especially n. 19. Also recently, R. MacMullen, *Constantine* (New York, 1969), pp. 211 ff.

4. N. Baynes, *Constantine the Great and the Christian Church* (London, 1932), p. 29.

5. Zosimus, *Historia Nova*, ed. Bekker (Bonn, 1837), pp. 97 ff., mentions the temple of the Dioskouroi and the Tycheion. Socrates, *Ecclesiastical History* (Migne, PG 67 [Paris 1864], col. 409), notes that Emperor Julian worshipped the image of Tyche in a building called a *basilike*. For Constantine's temple in Umbria, see *Corpus Inscriptionum Latinarum* XI.2.1. 5265. This inscription from Hispellum, dating from the last year of his reign, prohibits the use of the temple for pagan worship. See also A. H. M. Jones, *Constantine and the Conversion of Europe* (New York, 1962), pp. 89, 175.

6. On Marme, see Eusebius, *Vita Constantini* (*Eusebius Werke*, ed. Heikel, 1 [Leipzig, 1902]: 99–104, where Eusebius tells of the order to build a church building in place of the pagan altar at Marme, and mentions the destruction of temples at Aphaca on Mt. Lebanon in Phoenicia and at Aegae in Cilicia. He also reports that a shrine of Aphrodite was removed from the location where the Church of the Holy Sepulcher was built (pp. 89 f.).

7. *Vita Constantini*, pp. 104 f.

8. *Codex Theodosianus*, 9.16. 1–2 and 16.10.2, ed. T. Mommsen and P. M. Meyer, in *Theodosiani libri XVI cum constitutionibus sirmondianis* (Berlin, 1905), I.1, 459 f. and I.2, 879. Cf. Eusebius, *Vita Constantini*, pp. 59 f. and 98.

9. Eusebius, *Vita Constantini*, pp. 101 f.; also Eusebius, *Laus Constantini*, p. 216.

10. Eusebius, *Vita Constantini*, pp. 60 f. For Constantine's own views, see a letter recorded by Eusebius in *Vita Constantini*, pp. 61 f., and his edict preserved by Eusebius, *Ecclesiastical History*, ed. E. Schwartz, *Eusebius Kirchengeschichte*, ed. min. (Leipzig, 1908), pp. 388–91.

11. Eusebius, *Laus Constantini*, p. 220, indicates that one aspect of the emperor's task was to foster unity by constructing houses of prayer. Baynes, *Constantine the Great* (supra, n. 4) pp. 12–30, convincingly argues that the necessity for ecclesiastical unity was a determining factor in Constantine's religious policy.

12. Letter of Constantine to Celsus, his Vicar of Africa, in *S. Optati Milevitani libri VII*, ed. C. Ziwsa, in *Corpus scriptorum ecclesiasticorum latinorum*, 26 (Vienna, 1893): 211–12 (app. 7).

13. A fine survey of these documents is found in Baynes, *Constantine the Great*, pp. 12–17, with notes. Cf. Jones, *Constantine and the Conversion of Europe*, pp. 91–104, who labels Constantine's emerging attitude "Caesaropapism" (p. 103).

14. Letter of Augustine to Januarius, in *S. Aureli Hipponiensis episcopi epistulae*, ed. A. Goldbacher, in *Corpus scriptorum ecclesiasticorum latinorum*, 34 (Vienna, 1895): 408 f. Jones, pp 104 ff., suggests that the order for confiscation was revoked after about three months, early in 321. Eusebius, *Vita Constantini*, pp. 112 f., records part of an edict designed to remove from heretical control every building used as a place of prayer. Neither Donatists nor Arians are mentioned in this context, but Novatians, Valentinians, Marcionites, and Paulianists are (p. 111).

15. Letter of Constantine to the bishops of Numidia, in *S. Optati Milevitani* pp. 213–16 (app. 10).

16. Ibid., p. 215 (app. 10).

17. On Constantine's motives for building, see Eusebius, *Laus Constantini*, pp. 220 f., 224, 259, and n. 24 below. Eusebius, *Vita Constantini*, pp. 131 f. also tells of Constantine's order for fifty copies of the Holy Scriptures, to meet the needs of the growing number of churches. On Constantine's enlarging of existing churches, see test for n. 21 below.

18. The best recent study of Constantine's churches is by L. Voelkl, *Die Kirchenstiftungen des Kaisers Konstantin im Lichte des römischen Sakraltechts* (Cologne and Opladen, 1964). Cf. G. T. Armstrong, "Imperial Church Building in the Holy Land in the 4th Century, *Bibl. Arch.* 30 (1969): 90–102, and his related "Church and State Relations. The Changes Wrought by Constantine," *Journal of Bible and Religion* 32 (1964): 1–7.

19. I accept the view of A. H. M. Jones, who holds the *Vita Constantini* to be a reliable source and an authentic work of Eusebius: see his recent "Notes on the Genuineness of the Constantinian Documents in Eusebius' Life of Constantine," *Journal of Ecclesiastical History* 5 (1954): 196-200. See also Baynes (supra, n. 4) pp. 40–49, who is in essential agreement with Jones, although he holds that the *Vita Constantini* "never received final revision at its author's hands" (p. 49); and G. Downey, "The Builder of the Original Church of the Apostles at Constantinople: A Contribution to the Criticism of the *Vita Constantini* attributed to Eusebius," *Dumbarton Oaks Papers*, 6 (1951): 58–72, who holds that certain problematic passages in the *Vita* are later interpolations in an otherwise reliable and authentic work. Cf. the most radical view of the *Vita Constantini* hy H. Grégoire, "Eusebe n'est pas l'auteur de la *Vita Constantini* dans sa forme Actuelle et Constantin n'est pas converti en 312," *Byzantion* 13 (1938): 561 ff.

20. *Vita Constantini*, pp. 91 f. On the churches of Constantine in Palestine, see J. W. Crowfoot, *Early Churches in Palestine* (London, 1941).

21. For this famous passage, see *Vita Constantini*, p. 60. On the heightening and enlarging of existing church buildings, see L. Voelkl, "Die konstantinischen Kirchenbauten nach Eusebius," *Reallexikon für Antike und Christentum* 29 (1953): 60–64.

22. The question of the origin of the basilica has produced considerable literature with very varied interpretations. See especially J. B. Ward Perkins, "Con-

stantine and the Origins of the Christian Basilica," *Papers of the British School at Rome*, 22 (1954): 69–90, and W. MacDonald, *Early Christian and Byzantine Architecture* (New York, 1962), with bibliography. See also E. Swift, *Roman Sources of Christian Art* (New York, 1951). For a short survey of opinions, see W. Lowrie, *Art in the Early Church* (New York, 1947), pp. 87–110.

23. *Vita Constantini*, pp. 101–04, and *Laus Constantini*, p. 216. The practice of opening the temples for public inspection and even displaying the contents was revived in Theodosius I's day: see Sozomen, *Ecclesiastical History*, ed. J. Bidez (Berlin, 1960), pp. 319 ff.

24. For the use of the term *basilike* to apply to secular imperial structures before Constantine's conversion, see the survey by Ward Perkins (above, n. 22), pp. 69–76 with notes, and Swift (above, n. 22), pp. 9–30. Cf. L. Voelkl (above, n. 21), pp. 60 ff. We mention here terms applied by Eusebius to early church buildings, some already noted, others unemphasized. For example, for usages of *ekklesia, efkterios neos*, and *efktenos oikos*, see *Vita Constantini*, pp. 98–99; for *prosefkterion*, see *Ecclesiastical History*, ed. Schwartz, p. 370; and for the first occurence of *kyriakon oikeion*, see *Ecclesiastical History*, ed. Schwartz, p. 363. The church building in Tyre, dedicated ca. 314 (see Setton [above n. 2], p. 44) is referred to in Eusebius' panegyric as a *basileios oikos* (*Ecclesiastical History*, p. 381). See also n. 5 above. Constantine's churches in the Holy Land are characterized by Eusebius as *basilikes dianoias basilika megalourgemata* ("imperial monuments of an imperial spirit"), who calls them trophies to the victory of the heavenly Basileus (*Leus Constantini*, pp. 220, 224, esp. 259). On the basilica in general, see R. Krautheimer, *Early Christian and Byzantine Architecture* (Harmondsworth, 1965) and esp. his (with S. Corbett and W. Frank) *Corpus Basilicarum Christianarum Romae*, vol. 4 (Vatican, 1970).

25. Setton, *Christian Attitude* (above, n. 2), pp. 53 ff., 71 ff., and n. 26 below.

26. On the attitudes of Constantine's contemporaries, see Setton, pp. 40 ff., and n. 30 below. On Constantine's benefactions to the bishops, see, for example, the documents preserved in Eusebius, *Ecclesiastical History*, pp. 394–95.

27. See sources cited above in nn. 6, 10, and 23 for Constantine's attitude toward the pagans; also his letter to the Persian king on behalf of Christians, in Eusebius, *Vita Constantini*, p. 121. On Constantine's view of his proselytizing as a duty, see Baynes, *Constantine the Great*, pp. 25 ff.

28. See Stein, *Geschichte des spätrömischen Reiches*, 1 (Vienna, 1928): 226 f. and Setton, *Christian Attitude*, pp. 71 ff.

29. Setton, p. 82.

30. Cf. G. H. Williams, "Christology and Church-State Relations in the Fourth Century," *Church History* 20 (1951): no. 3, pp. 8–14 and no. 4, pp. 15 ff. The statement from Athanasius is found in his *Historia Arianorum, MPG*, 25 (Paris, 1884), col. 729.

31. On the mosaics of Sant' Apollinare Nuovo and San Vitale, see O. M. Dalton, *Byzantine Art and Archaeoloy* (Oxford, 1911), pp. 350 ff. and esp. 358 ff. (on the various interpretations of the San Vitale mosaics), and A. Grabar, *Byzantine Painting* (Geneva, 153), pp. 52 ff. and esp. 68 (on San Vitale). For a comparison between Arian and Orthodox ornamentation, see views of W. Fleming, *Arts and Ideas* (New York, 1963), p. 146.

32. *MPG*, 67, cols. 380–81.

33. Socrates, *Ecclesiastical History*, PG 67, col. 196, reports Constantius' completion of the church at Antioch ten years after Constantine started it. Regarding the Holy Apostles, G. Downey (supra, n. 19), pp. 77 ff., concludes, in agreement with Procopius, *De Aedificiis*, ed. J. Haury and G. Wirth, in *Procopii Caesariensis Opera Omnia*, 4 (Leipzig, 1964), p. 25, that Constantius founded the church—a view I find convincing; but cf. J. Vogt, "Der Erbauer der Apostelkirche in Konstantinopel," *Hermes* 81 (1953): 111 ff.

34. See Setton's discussion of Firmicus, *Christian Attitude*, p. 64; also H. Lietzmann, *A History of the Early Church*, trans. Wolf. 3 (New York, 1961): 255.

35. Ammianus Marcellinus, *Rerum Gestarum libri qui supersunt*, ed. C. U. Clark 1 (Berlin, 1910): 257. Sozomen, *Ecclesiastical History*, ed. Bidez, p. 195. Socrates, *Eccl. Hist.*, *PG* 67, col. 337.

36. An example of the violence that erupted early in Julian's reign is given in Theodoret, *Ecclesiastical History*, ed. L. Parmentier and F. Scheidweiler, (Berlin, 1954): 182 ff.

37. Theodoret, pp. 198 ff. Sozomen, pp. 229 ff. Ammianus Marcellinus, ed. Clark, 1: 296. Rufinus, *Ecclesiastical History*, ed. Migne, *PL* 21 (Paris, 1849), cols. 505–06. See Lietzmann, *History of the Early Church*, 3: 282, for an evaluation of Julian's policy toward the Jews.

38. Socrates, *Ecclesiastical History.*, *PG* 67, col. 327. To be sure, it was believed that the Anastasia was constructed of the materials which had once been hauled from the site to construct a church in Sycae but which was now dismantled and brought back.

39. The church was originally destroyed during the reign of Constantius; Sozomen, pp. 200 and 214. Socrates, *PG* 67, col. 409.

40. Sozomen, pp. 239 f. Socrates, *PG* 67, col. 449. Theodoret, p. 216.

41. *Codex Theodosianus* 16.10.10-11, ed. Mommsen and Meyer, Vol. 1, no. 2, pp. 899 f.

42. Destruction of pagan temples was largely a local task. Under Theodosius, e.g., the Eastern Prefect Cynegius sponsored the destruction of temples in his area, especially at Edessa and Apamea; see Lietzmann, *History of the Early Church*, 4:85–86. It is likely, as J. B. Bury in *History of the Later Roman Empire*, 1 (New York, 1958): 365 says, that Theodosius intended only to secularize, not to demolish, pagan temples. The subsequent edicts of Arcadius in 399 and 407 indicate that only those temples in rural districts were to be razed, and even this was prohibited in 407: *Codex Theodosianus* 16.10.15, 16, 18, 19, ed. Mommsen and Meyer, vol. 1, no. 2, pp. 901 ff. C . also Theodoret, *Eccl. Hist.*, ed. Parmentier, pp. 329 f., who notes that John Chrysostom secured funds from rich Christian women to pay the expenses of razing temples in Phoenicia.

43. Roger Thynne, *The Churches of Rome* (London, 1924), p. 63.

44. Ambrose, *Epistolae* 40 and 41, in Migne *PL*, 16 (Paris, 1845), cols. 1101 ff.

45. M. Pavan, *La politica gotica di Teodosio nella publicistica del suo tempo* (Rome, 1964); see my review, *American Historical Review* 71 (1965): 131 f.

46. Zosimus, *History.*, ed. Bekker, pp. 269 ff. Sozomen, *Eccl. Hist.*, ed. Bidez, pp. 355 ff. Socrates, *Eccl. Hist.*, *PG* 67, cols. 675 ff. Theodoret, *Eccl. Hist.*, ed. Parmentier, p. 330. See also Stein, (supra, n. 28) 1: 361 f.

47. Ed H. Grégoire and M. Kugener, *Marc le Diacre, Vie de Porphyre, Evêque de*

Gaza (Paris, 1930), pp. 44, 71. See also M. Avi-Yonah, "The Economics of Byzantine Palestine," *Israel Exploration Journals* 8 (1958): 42, and G. Downey, *Gaza in the Early Sixth Century* (Norman, Okla., 1963), pp. 22 ff.

48. Mark the Deacon, *Life of Porphyry*, ed. Grégoire and Kugener, p.35. In their introduction (pp. xliii-xliv), the editors compare the use of *evgnomeneo* ("to be of good feeling") regarding the willingness of the people of Gaza to pay their taxes, with the term *evgnomosyne* ("loyalty"), used by Justinian regarding the loyalty of the people of Caesarea—see his Novel 103 (in *Corpus Iuris Civilis*, ed. R. Schoell and W. Kroll 3 [Berlin, 1912], pp. 469–70). Arcadius' hesitation to destroy the Marneion in the center of the city was in line with a general policy to secularize rather than destroy all city temples (see above, n. 42).

49. Evagrius, *Eccl. Hist., MPG*, 86.2 (Paris, 1865), cols. 2469, 2472, mentions churches in Antioch named for Rufinus, Prefect of the East under Theodosius I; for Zoilus and Callistus, each at one time *Consularis* of Syria; and for Anatolius, a *strategos*. See also M. Avi-Yonah, "Economics of Byzantine Palestine," pp. 43 ff. and 50–51 for a list of private benefactors in Palestine.

50. Avi-Yonah, p. 44. Evagrius, *Eccl. Hist., PG* 86.2, cols. 2476–84.

51. P. Charanis, *Church and State in the Later Roman Empire: The Religious Policy of Anastasius I* (Madison, Wis., 1939), p. 12.

52. M. Anastos, "Justinian's Despotic Control over the Church as Illustrated by his Edict on Theopaschite Formula and Letter to Pope John in 533," *Zbor. Rad. Viz. Inst.*, no. 312 (= Mélanges Ostrogorsky, 2 [1964]: 1–11). See Geanakoplos, "Church and State," pp. 392–94, 397–98.

53. Bury, *History of the Later Roman Empire*, 2: 23 ff., 360 ff., and 392. E. Stein, *Histoire du Bas-empire* (Paris, 1949), 2: 278–79. See now W. Frend, "Old and New Rome in the Age of Justinian," in *Relations between East and West in the Middle Ages*, ed. D. Baker (Edinburgh, 1973), pp. 11–29.

54. W. Ensslin, "The Emperor and the Imperial Administration," *Byzantium: An Introduction to East Roman Civilization*, ed. N. Baynes and H. Moss (Oxford, 1961), p. 275, points out that both Theodosius II and Justinian were greeted as *archierefs* and that Marcian was acclaimed *hierefs* and *basileus* at the Council of Chalcedon.

55. See Geanakoplos, "Church and State," pp. 390–92, with bibliography (citing Mitard and Diehl). As Procopius puts it, *De Aedificiis*, ed. Haury-Wirth, 4: 6, Justinian closed all paths leading to error and established religion firmly upon a single foundation of the faith.

56. Evagrius, *Ecclesiastical History, PG* 86.2, cols. 2736–37. See n. 58 below for the churches in that area specifically mentioned by Procopius.

57. MacDonald, (supra, n. 22), p. 32, and Fleming, (supra, n. 31), p. 147. Cf. Bury, (supra, n. 42), 2: 284 f.

58. Procopius, *De Aedificiis*, ed. Haury-Wirth, 4: 185. In addition to the church at Septum, modern Ceuta, five churches at Leptis Magna, modern Ledba (p. 177), a church at Sabratha, modern Tripoli Vecchia (p. 178), and two churches and a monastery at Carthage are mentioned (p. 180). A. A. Vasiliev *History of the Byzantine Empire*, 1 (Madison, 1964): 138 f., mentions archaeo-

logical evidence of apparently Justinianic churches in Spain and in the Crimea (at Dory).

59. See Bury, 2: 371. These churches were built in Phrygia, Lydia, and Caria; fifty-five were paid for by the imperial treasury and forty-one were built by the proselytes out of their own funds. Two monasteries were also built. Procopius makes no attempt to list all Justinian's buildings (see *Aedificiis*, ed. Haury-Wirth, 4: 38, 186); yet he does name or imply the presence of church building(s) at over seventy different sites. Twelve of the churches or shrines mentioned were dedicated to the *theotokos* (*loc. cit.*, p. 20, and passim). In Constantinople and the adjoining areas he built over twenty new churches, shrines, and sanctuaries, and rebuilt or enlarged over half that many. Cf. G. Downey, *Constantinople in the Days of Justinian* (Norman, Okla., 1960), p. 100. Procopius' statement (*Aedificiis*, p. 34) that no churches were built anywhere in the empire *without* imperial sanction, should be read in the light of statements in his *Historia Arcana* (original title, *Anekdota*), ed. J. Haury and G. Wirth, *Procopii Caesariensis Opera Omnia* (Leipzig, 1963) 3: 158 f., 164, regarding the emperor's many exactions and control over local spending. On churches built in the Holy Land in this period, see G. Armstrong, "Fifth and Sixth Century Church Building in the Holy Land," *Greek Orthodox Theological Review* 14 (1969): 17–30.

60. E. B. Smith, *The Dome: A Study in the History of Ideas* (Princeton, 1950), esp. pp. 77 ff. Procopius, *Aedificiis*, ed. Haury-Wirth, 4: 30, writes that Justinian expressed his gratitude for a miraculous cure received from Saints Cosmas and Damian, the Christian counterparts of Castor and Pollux, by rebuilding and enlarging their shrine at Constantinople. The association between the Christian saints and the pagan twins is also suggested by Bury, 1: 373. Cf. Swift, (supra, n. 22), pp. 80–84, 107–08, who argues that the domes of St. Sergius and Bacchus and St. Sophia were inspired by domes in Rome which Anthemius of Tralles is supposed to have studied. There seems little doubt that the imagery of the dome suggesting heaven, and the analogy between the emperor's authority over the earth with that of God in heaven, was important in Justinian's adoption of the dome for St. Sophia. See especially Fleming's statement, n. 71 below.

61. Paulus Silentiarius, *Descriptio S. Sophiae*, ed. Bekker (Bonn, 1837), p. 25, ll. 489–91. Note also ll. 529 f. (p. 27) where the dome is described by the words "the roof rises like a beautiful high-crowned helmet."

62. Ed. Haury-Wirth, 4: 8.

63. Constantine had despoiled temples: see above, nn. 6 and 23. Justinian despoiled Arian churches, according to Procopius, *Historia Arcana*, ed. Haury-Wirth, 3: 72 ff.

64. Justinian's words are recorded in an anonymous account preserved by Banduri and other editors: see *Relation on the Construction of the Great Church of God called St. Sophia* (in Greek), § 27, ed. T. Preger, *Scriptores Originum Constantinopolitanarum*, 1 (Leipzig, 1901): 105.

65. Paulus Silentiarius, *Descriptio S. Sophiae,* ed. Bekker (Bonn, 1837), p. 3, l. 2.

66. Procopius, *Aedificiis*, 4: 55.

67. G. Downey, "Imperial Building Records in Malalas," *Byz. Zeit.*, 38 (1938): 1–11, esp. 10 and n. 3.

68. Procopius, *Aedificiis (Peri Ktismaton)*, ed. Haury-Wirth, 4: 134, concludes his discussion here of all Justinian's buildings *(ktiseis)* in Constantinople, ecclesiastical and secular.

69. Constantine Porphyrogenitus, *De Cerimoniis Aulae Byzantinae*, ed. Reiske (Bonn, 1830), p. 521. See also E. Kantorowicz, *Laudes Regiae* (Berkeley, 1946), p. 50.

70. Procopius, *Aedificiis*, 4: 92.

71. G. Armstrong (supra, n. 3) for the term "propaganda" follows the usage of B. Rubin, *Das Zeitalter Iustinians*, 1 (Berlin, 1960): 139–45. Fleming (supra, n. 31), pp. 171 f., suggests that centralized churches like San Vitale and St. Sophia, with their "sharp hierarchical divisions that set aside a place for men and women, clergy and laity, aristocrat and commoner, were admirably suited to convey the principle of imperial authority [such structures inspired an attitude of reverence] not only to God, but also to His viceroys on earth. . . . The majesty of God was felt through the infinite power of government. . . . Both spiritual and secular authority were imposed on man from above [fostering his acceptance of] the unified ideal of one Christian empire with one church, one emperor, and one body of laws." See also n. 67 above.

72. *Historia Arcana*, ed. Haury-Wirth, 3: 51, 120–21, and esp. 162.

73. *Codex Justinianus*, 1.17.1, ed. Krueger, *Corpus Iuris Civilis*, 3: 69. For further analysis of Byzantine church-state ideology, see my *Byzantine East and Latin West: Two Worlds of Christendom in Middle Ages and Renaissance* (Oxford, 1966), pp. 33, 86, 96 ff; cf. G. Mathew, *Byzantine Aesthetics* (London, 1963), esp. pp. 59–64, 86, and 93, which deals peripherally with some questions discussed in this chapter. Also now see S. Runciman, *Byzantine Style and Civilization* (Harmondsworth, Eng., 1975).

Notes to Chapter 6

1. H. Beck, *Kirche und theologische Literatur im byzantinischen Reich* (Munich, 1959), pp. 436 and 91. Cf. A. Vasiliev, *History of the Byzantine Empire*, 1: 231 "[Maximos] was one of the most remarkable Byzantine theologians." (It should be noted that some would perhaps call Gregory Palamas the last really outstanding Byzantine theologian.) Eastern works on Maximos are by E. von Ivanka, *Maximus der Bekenner: all-eins in Christus* (Einsiedeln, 1961), with excerpts from the earlier *Ambigua* and *Ad Thallasium*; V. Grümel, "Notes d'histoire et de chronologie sur la vie de S. Maxime," *Echos d'Orient* 26 (1927): 24-32, and his "Maxime de Chrysopolis," *Dict. Theol. Cath.* 10: 448–59; H. Beck, idem, pp. 330, 353, 357, passim; A. Brilliantoff, *The Influence of Eastern Theology on Western as Evidenced by Works of John Scotus Erigena* (St. Petersburg, 1898; in Russian); S. Epifanovic, *Materials to Serve in the Study of the Life and Works of St. Maximus the Confessor* (Kiev, 1917; in Russian); I. Hausherr, *Philautie, de la tendresse pour soi à la charité selon S. Maxime le Confesseur* (Rome, 1952); "Massimo il Confessore," in *Enciclopedia Cattolica*, 8 (1952): 307; article on him in (Greek) *Religious and Ethical Encyclopedia*, 8,

col. 614–24. I. H. Dalmais, at the Oxford Patristic Congress (1963), established a connection between Maximos and Erigena. See also H. Dalmais, "Place de la mystagogie de St. Maximus le Confesseur dans la théologie liturgique byzantine," *Studia Patristica* 5 (1963): 277–83. I. Zizoulias, Ph. D. dissertation, Harvard University (1964), on the Christology of Maximos; M. Candal, "La gracia increada del 'Liber Ambiguorum' de San Maximo," *Orientalia Christiana Periodica* 27 (1961): 38–45, and J. Meyendorff, *Christ in Eastern Christian Thought* (Washington, D.C., 1967), chap.7

Other significant works in whole or in part on Maximos, esp. by westerners, are (most importantly) by P. Sherwood, *St. Maximus the Confessor, The Ascetic Life, The Four Centuries on Charity* (London, 1955); his "Survey of Recent Work on St. Maximus the Confessor," *Traditio* 20 (1964): 428–37; J. Dräseke, "Maximus Confessor und Johannes Scotus Erigena," *Theologische Studien und Kritiken* 84 (1911): 20–60; M. Cappuyns, *Jean Scot Erigène* (Louvain-Paris, 1933); B. Altaner, "Die Kenntnis der Greiechischen in den Missionsorden während des 13. und 14, Jahrhunderts: Ein Beitrag zur vorgeschichte des Humanismus," *Zeitschrift für Kirchengeschichte* 13 (1934); E. Gilson. *The Mystical Theology of St. Bernard*, trans. A. Downes (New York-London, 1940), esp. pp. 25–28; and, most recently, J. Pelikan, "Council or Father or Scripture: The Concept of Authority in the Theology of Maximus Confessor," *Orientalia Christiana Analecta* 195 (1973): 277–88.

2. The view is often expressed that Maximus "put Christ at the center of Dionysian thought."
3. Anna Comnena says the court of her father Alexius read Maximos: E. Dawes trans. of *Alexiad* (New York, 1967), p. 135. On Symeon, "the New Theologian," see *Oxford Dictinary of the Christian Church* (London, 1958), p. 1256. Pachymeres is, after Maximos, the most important Byzantine paraphraser of and commentator on Dionysius. He wrote a *paraphrasis* on Dionysius' epistles: *MPG*, 4, cols. 433 ff. The *Oxford Dictionary of the Christian Church* (London, 1958), p. 403, says Pachymeres and Andrew of Crete wrote commentaries on Dionysius. For other influences, see P. Sherwood, "Survey of Recent Work on Maximos the Confessor," *Traditio* 20 (1964): 435 ff. On Nicholas Cabasilas, see his *Explication de la divine liturgie*, trans. and notes by S. Salaville Paris, 1967) (*Sources chrétiennes*, no. 4). On Cyparissiotes, see below.
4. He wrote scholia to the four great works of Dionysius, and to his epistles, plus a prologue and glossary of terms usd by Dionysius, *MPG*, vol 4. It should be noted that the scholia on Dionysius attributed by Western scholars to Maximos the Confessor, were in part the work of Maximos' near contemporary, John of Scythopolis (see esp. H. U. von Balthasar, "Das Scholien Werk des Johannes von Skythopolis," *Scholastik* 15 (1940): 16 ff.
5. *The New Catholic Encyclopedia*, 7: 1073, under John Scotus Erigena by L. Lynch, says Erigena's translation of the *Ambigua* of Maximos consisted of a preface, two poems, and sixty-seven chapters, of which only the first five and the beginning of six have been printed. On the *Earlier Ambigua*, see Sherwood, "The Earlier Ambigua of Maximos," *Studia Anselmiana* 36 (1935): 1–22; M. Cappuyns, "La 'Versie Ambiguorum Maximi,' de Jean Scot Erigena,"

Recherches de Théologie ancienne et médievale 30 (1963): 324–29, and his "Gloss
inédite de Jean Scot sur un passage de Maximi," idem, 31 (1964): 320–24.

6. Erigena translated into Latin the four great mystical works of Dionysius. At
the Oxford Congress (1963) Dom Meyvaert announced (see *Sacris Erudiri*
14 [1963]: 130–48) the discovery of a translation of Maximos' *Ad Thalassium*
by Scotus Erigena. See more recently, M. Cappuyns, "Jean Scot Erigène et
les 'Scholia' de Maxime le Confesseur," *Recherches le Théologie ancienne et
médievale*, 31 (1964): 122–24.

7. See Dondaine (cited in n. 15). Anastasius, in fact, preserved in Latin a fragment of a letter of Maximos sent to a certain Peter concerning the primacy
of the pope; see *MPG*, 91, cols. 141–44. K. Krumbacher, *Geschichte der byzantinischen Litteratur* (Munich, 1897), p. 63, says Maximos is known in the West
as "The Interpreter" of Dionysius.

8. In *The Mystical Theology of St. Bernard* (New York–London, 1940), p. 25, E.
Gilson says Bernard was influenced by Dionysius through Maximos in
Erigena's translation. Gilson says Bonaventure was also influence by Maximos. The *Dict. Theol. Cath.*, 7 pt. 1, col. 246 (under Hughes de Saint-Victor),
says Dionysius is mentioned twice in Hughes, who wrote a commentary on
the *Celestial Hierarchy*. See also on the *Theologia Mystica*, M. Honecker, "Nikolaus von Cues und die griechische sprache." *Sitz. Heidelb. Akad. Wissen.*,
Phil, Hist. Kl., 28 (1938): 26, n. 92. Cerbanus, the twelfth-century Western
monk, knew the *Centuries on Charity*. See n. 57 below.

9. Albert the Great wrote commentaries on Dionysius' *Celestial Hierarchy, Ecclesiastical Hierarchy, Mystical Theology*, and *Epistles*. Doubtless he must have
read the Anastasian corpus. I can find no record of Albert's use of the *Ambigua*. But see J. Bach, *Des Albertus Magnus Verhältniss zu der Erkenntnisslehre
der Griechen, Lateiner, Araber, und Juden* (Vienna, 1881).

10. See A. Pegis, ed., *Basic Writings of Saint Thomas Aquinas*, vol. 2 (New York,
1945), index of authors, p. 1174 under Maximos (esp. concerning angels,
their intellectual powers, and their nature, vols. 1-2, pp. 50, 6, Obj. 1 and
Obj. 2).

11. D. A. Callus, ed., *Robert Grosseteste, Scholar and Bishop* (Oxford, 1955), pp. 34,
56–57. See E. Francheschini, "Grosseteste's translation of the Prologos and
Scholia of Maximos to the writings of the Pseudo-Dionysius the Areopagita,"
Journal of Ecclesiastical History 34 (1933); 353–63, esp. 356–57. Francheschini
states that Grosseteste did not know these scholia were by Maximos. Anastasius Bibliothecarius had translated them and sent them with a dedicatory
letter to Charles the Bald in 865. No evidence shows that Grosseteste knew
this version. R. R. Bolgar, *The Classical Heritage and Its Beneficiaries* (Cambridge, 1958), p. 243, suggests a strong influence of Dionysius (perhaps of
Maximos too) on Pico and Ficino.

12. On Nicholas and Balbus, see below. As noted above, Maximos is important
to the West as the interpreter of Pseudo-Dionysius.

13. See W. Sparrow-Simpson, in C. Rolt, ed., *Dionysius the Areopagite on the Divine
Names and the Mystical Theology* (SPCK: New York, 1951), p. 203, who says
that the Greek writings of Dionysius were sent to the Gallican church in 757
by Pope Pascal and remained unread for nearly a century in the abbey of

St. Denys until Charles the Bald asked Erigena to translate them into Latin (all four principal works). Cf. Dondaine p. 25, n. 15, who says this is not historically corroborated, and that the first exemplar of Dionysius we can trace is the one sent from Byzantium by Emperor Michael II.

14. P. Sherwood, *St. Maximus the Confessor* (in *Ancient Christian Writers*, no. 21), pp. 24–28. Also see his article cited in *Studia Anselmiana* 30 (1952): 1–22.

15. H. Dondaine, in *Le Corpus Dionysien de l'Université de Paris au XIIIe siècle* (Rome 1953), pp. 25–26, says Hilduin probably had the MS of Dionysius (which had lain there unread in its library for a time) read by someone who knew Greek, then translated orally by another into Latin, and finally written down by still another. Inevitably, then, many errors occurred, making for a very faulty translation.

16. Maximos probably used Dionysius' thought in order to comment on Gregory of Nazianzus. Erigena may have also translated *Ad Thalassium*. See n. 6, above.

17. See *Versio Maximi, MPL*, vol. 122, cols. 1193 ff., esp. 1195A: "nisi viderem, praefatum beatissimum Maximum saepissime in processu sui operis obscurissimas sanctissimi theologi Dionysii Areopagitae sententias, cujus symbolicos theologicosque sensus nuper Vobis similiter jubentibus transtuli., . . . quae illuminat abscondita tenebrarum." Also see M. Cappuyns, *Jean Scot Erigène, Sa vie, son oeuvre, sa pensée* (Paris-Louvain, 1933), p. 162.

18. *MPL*, v. 122, cols. 1027–28; also H. Bett, *Johannes Scotus Erigena*, (Cambridge, 1925), p. 17.

19. See *MPL*, vol. 122, cols. 1194 D–1195 A: "hoc est intellectu difficilium . . . de Graeco in Latinum vobis jubentibus edidi, etc." Cf. Bett, *Erigena*, p. 17, n. 2.

20. *MPL*, v. 122, col. 1197D (footnote of Latin text no. D); cf. Bett, *Erigena*, p. 17, n. 2. J. Dräseke, article cited above, n. 1, commenting on Erigena's Greek, says it was easier for him to read Gregory of Nyssa than Maximos because the latter's style and thoughts are more difficult.

21. From *MPG*, vol. 91, col. 1113 B. Cf. H. Bett, *Erigena*, pp. 24–25. Cf. Erigena's quotation from Maximos (*MPL*, vol. 122, col. 494C, *De Divisione Naturae. . . :* "ut ait Maximus, humanus intellectus ascendit per caritatem, in tantum divina sapientia descendit per misericordiam." See T. Gregory, "Note sulla dottrina della 'teofanie' in Giovanni Scoto Eriugena," *Studi Medievali*, ser. 3, vol. 4, pt. 1, pp. 75–91. See also Gilson's book on Bernard, *Mystical Theology of St. Bernard*, (cited in n. 1), esp. pp. 25–28.

22. Summarized in Bett, *Erigena*, p. 25, from *MPL*, Erigena's *De Divisione Naturae*, vol. 122, col. 451.

23. Maximos' *Ambigua, MPG*, vol. 191, cols. 1285–88.

24. See *MPL*, *Erigena*, vol. 518A, and *MPG*, vol. 91, Maximos' *Ambigua*, col. 1185B.

25. *MPG*, vol. 90, col. 672C, and *MPG*, vol. 91, col. 136B, where Maximos formulated the term *dia tou uiou*. Cf. Beck, *Kirche und theologische Literatur*, pp. 308 ff. On the Council of Florence and views on the "procession," see D. Geanakoplos, *Byzantine East and Latin West* (Oxford, 1966), pp. 99–102, and J. Gill, *Council of Florence* (Cambridge, 1959), pp. 151–52, 212–13, etc; and

on Margounios and Maximos the Confessor, see Geanakoplos, idem, esp. p. 171, and also F. Dvornik, *Byzantium and the Roman Primacy* (New York, 1966), pp. 12–13.

26. See preceding note, esp. based on Maximos' phrase *dia tou uiou*. Also Bett, *Erigena*, pp. 30, 108 and n. 5. Unlike Augustine and Tertullian, Erigena did not use *a patre per filium*. (*De Trin*, 15: 48, and *Adversus Praxeam*, p. 4).

27. See D. Geanakoplos, *Byzantine East and Latin West*, p. 171. Also cf. G. Fedalto, *Massimo Margounio e la sua opera per conciliare la sentenza degli orientali e dei latini sulla processione dello Spirito* Sancto (Padua, 1961) p. 51, and his *Massimo Margunio e il suo commento al De Trinitate di S. Agostino* (Brescia, 1968). Cf. now A. Papadakes, "Gregory II of Cyprus and an unpublished report to the Synod," *Greek Roman Byzantine Studies* 16 (1975): 227–28, for similar usage.

28. See A. Mercati, "Giovanni Ciparissiota alla corte di Gregerio XI," *Byz. Zeit.*, 30 (1929/30): 496–501, and B. Dentakis, *John Cyparissiotes, the Wise, and the Philosopher* (Atens, 1965; in Greek). Also on Cyparissiotes, Beck, *Kirche und theologische Literatur*, pp. 330, 727, 738, 749 ff., 789.

29. Latin title (given by editor Turrianus) is *Expositio materiaria eorum quae de Deo a theologis dicuntur, in decem decades partita*: *MPG*, vol. 152, cols. 737 ff. His earlier work is his "Against the Errors of the Palamites" (for Latin title see *MPG*, vol. 152, cols. 663 ff., given by ed. Fr. Combefisius, *Palamiticorum Transgressionum liber primus*).

30. B. Dentakis, *John Cyparissiotes, The Wise, and the Philosopher* (Athens, 1965), pp. 62 ff., esp. 67 (in Greek). H. Beck, *Vorsehung und Vorherbestimmung in der theologischen Literatur der Byzantiner* (Rome, 1937), *Orientalia Christiana Analecta* 114: 171–75, demonstrates a doctrinal relationship between Cyparissiotes and the commentators of Dionysius. The ten Decades of Cyparissiotes take up the symbolic and negative theology of the East from Clement of Alexandria to Dionysius and his commentators.

31. B. Dentakis, *The Nine Hymns to the Logos of God Attributed to John Cyparissiotes* (Athens, 1964;) in Greek), p. 13 ff.* (asterik is part of page number in Dentakis' book); and *MPG*, vol. 152, col. 741–992.

32. *MPG*, vol. 152, col. 746.

33. See e.g. *MPG*, vol. 152, col. 751: "Quod symbolicae theologiae quae in specie sub sensum cadente versatur."

34. *MPG*, vol. 152, col. 767A, chap. 4.

35. See *MPG*, vol. 90, col. 1083, with slightly inverted word order in Latin: "Capita ducenta ad theologiam Deique Filii in carne dispensationem spectantia."

36. Cyparissiotes in *MPG*, vol. 152, col. 767.

37. Beck (see n. 30).

38. *MPG*, vol. 152, col. 778 (cf. n. 1 of scholia) taken from Maximos' *Ambigua*.

39. Quoting from Maximus' work in explanation of Gregory Nazianzenus, *MPG*, vol. 152, col. 778.

40. *MPG*, col. 152, col. 887A-B.

41. *MPG*, vol. 152, col. 899; pasage taken from Maximos' work on *Centuries on Theology*, chap. 35, col. 1094, with slightly altered wording.

42. From MPG, vol. 152, col. 956C. Taken from Maximos, *Centuria* 4, cap. 1.

43. *MPG*, vol. 152, col. 959A.

44. On the originality of Cyparissiotes, see in *Dictionnaire de spiritualité ascetique*, 18 (Paris, 1964), col. 314.

45. Beck, *Kirche und theologische Literatur*, p. 739. B. Dentakis, *The Nine Hymns to the Logos of God Attributed to John Cyparissiotes* (Athens, 1964), p. 13 (in Greek).

46. See Bett, *Erigena*, p. 11.

47. *MPL*, vol. 122, col. 1194B.

48. P. Sherwood, "Survey of Recent Work on Maximus the Confessor," *Traditio* 20 (1964): 438 ff.

49. See Bett, *Erigena*, p. 192.

50. I find no mention of Nicholas' use of Maximos in M. Honecker, *Nikolaus von Cues und die griechische Sprache* (cited above), pp. 26–27, though there are many mentions of Dionysius and translations of him in Hugh of St. Victor, Grossteste, and Thomas Gallo. (It seems that Nicholas brought back from Constantinople a Greek MS of Dionysius the Areopagite).

51. See Bett, *Nicholas of Cusa*, p. 93, n. 4. But this is Bett's only mention of Balbus, who had dedicated to Cusanus his translation of Alcinous, *Epitome of Plato*.

52. D. Konstaninos, "Krētikē analusis tēs meletēs tou M. Reding: Die Akualität des N. Cusanus" (Berlin, 1964), *Theologia* (in Greek) 3 (1966): 138 ff.

53. M. de Gandillac, *Nikolaus von Cues* (Düsseldorf, 1953), pp. 250–51. See the *Dizionario biografico degli Italiani*, 5: 379, on the MS of Balbus's Latin translations of Maximos. According to an indirect testimony of Ughelli, there should be other MSS at the Biblioteca Capitolare of Capua, an unspecified sermon of Maximos and forty chapters of Maximos' *De caritate* (instead of the eighteen of the Florence MS). V. Capialbi, *Mémoire per servire alla storia della santa chiesa tropeana* (Naples, 1952), p. 36, cites Ughelli (*Italia Sacra*) as noting that in the Tesoro of Capua Cathedral are MSS with Balbus's translations from Greek to Latin, including "s. Maximi Sermo per dialogum ad Sixtum IV." Pietro Balbus studied Greek, incidentally, with the famous Vittorino da Feltre.

54. E. Van Steenbergh, *Le Cardinal Nicolas de Cues* (Paris, 1920), and M. de Gandillac, *Nikolaus von Cues* (Düsseldorf, 1953), esp. p. 288, where it is suggested that the words *unitas* and *entitas* correspond to the unusual Greek term *ontotes* to be found in Maximos' *Cent. gnost.* 1: 48 (*MPG*, vol. 90, 1101B). But Gandillac does not specifically say that Nicholas knew Maximos' work.

55. Beck, *Kirche und theologische Literatur*, p. 436.

56. B. Dentakis, *John Cyparissiotes, The Wise, and the Philosopher* (Athens, 1965) p. 69 (in Greek).

57. Cerbanus's translation of *De Caritate* (Cerbanus, a Venetian, lived for a time in Constantinople), is an interesting example of the twelfth-century revival of Greek thought in the West (P. Sherwood, *St. Maximus the Confessor*, pp. 101–02). Cerbanus also apparently was the first to make even a partial translation of John of Damascus: N. M. Haring SAC, *The First Traces of the So-Called Cerbanus translation of St. John Damascene 'De Fide Orthodoxa,'* 3: 1–8, in *Medieval Studies* 12 (1950): 214–16. Cf. E. Gilson, *History of Christian*

Philosophy, p. 600; and on Cerbanus, also see my chap. 3, above, text and n. 29.

58.   Ficino's translation of Dionysius was completed in 1492 (P. Kristeller, *The Philosophy of Marsilio Ficino* [New York, 1943], p. 18). Thomas Gallus did a paraphrase of Dionysius, not a translation. John Sarazenus's famous translation of Dionysius did not include a new translation of Maximos' scholia on Dionysius.

Notes to Chapter 7

1.   Along with Epirus and Trebizond.

2.   George Acropolites, *Opera*, ed. A. Heisenberg (Leipzig, 1903), 1: 98 (hereafter cited as Acrop.).

3.   George Sphrantzes, *Annales*, ed. I. Bekker (Bonn. 1838), p. 9. Cf. more recent edition of J. Papadopoulos, *Chronikon*, vol. 1 (Leipzig, 1935).

4.   Demetrios Chomatianos, *Analectb Sacra Spicilegio*, ed, J. Pitra (Paris, 1891), 7: 3g9–90.

5.   *Byzantinon bios kai politismos* (Athens, 1949), 3:356 ff., and 357 n. (in Greek). G. Glotz, *L'Ordalie dans la Grèce Primitive* (thesis, Paris, 1904), p. 109, states that the ancient Greek ordeal "existait encore dans la periode byzantine." However, he adduces no evidence for his opinion.

6.   Sophocles, verses 264–65.

7.   There is always the possibility, of course, that other evidence may be found in unpublished documents Cf. below, n. 41.

8.   *Byzantinon bios* 3: 357.

9.   See this book, Prologue and Epilogue, for gradual identification of ancient Hellenes and Byzantines in the fourteenth and fifteenth centuries.

10.   Constantine Sathas (d. 1914) was a pioneering, zealous scholar who published many Byzantine and modern Greek sources for the first time.

11.   *La tradition hellénique et la legende de Phidias de Praxitèle et de la fille d'Hippocrate au Moyen Age* (Paris, 1883), pp. 23 ff.

12.   There seems to be no mention of his Albanian descent in the Byzantine sources. Furthermore, 1 know of no evidence for the presence of Albanians in Thrace at this time. Sathas discovered and printed the Vulgar Greek Cypriot translation of the Assizes of Romania. See n. 26, below.

13.   P. Michalopoulos, in his commemorative brochure on Sathas' life, *Konstantinos Sathas, 1842–1914* (Athens; in Greek, 1949) p. 8, writes: "All, almost all the scientific theses that Sathas propounded on various ideological, linguistic, and philological matters . . . cannot bear proof."

14.   Acrop., p. 96.

15.   See *La tradition hellénique et la legende de Phidias*, etc., p. 28.

16.   The *Mirabilia Romae* is a medieval collection of works (largely anonymous) concerned with the wonders of Rome. It describes the two colossal statues of Castor and Pollux whose bases bore the names of Phidias and Praxiteles. The two sculptors were believed to have come to Rome during the reign of the emperor Tiberius and to have promised to reveal certain things to him if he would build a monument to them—hence the statues, nude in order to

symbolize "that all human knowledge was naked to their eyes." *Mirabilia* is published in H. Jordan. *Topographie der Stadt Rom in Alterthum* (Berlin, 1871), 2: 619 ff. See also A. Hare, *Walks in Rome* (London, 1878), 1: 447.

17. For a review of Sathas' article, see the work of the Greek scholar N. Politis: *Hellenikoi Mesaionike Mythoi . . . Laografika Symmeikta* (Athens, 1921), 2: 7 ff. He is severe toward Sathas for lack of evidence regarding the Phidias-Praxiteles story. Politis points out that Michael Palaeologus, in his remarks mentioning the sculptors, did not say (as Sathas would have us believe) that one could not escape being burned "unless he were Phildias or Praxiteles," but that one could not avoid burning "unless he were a statue *fashioned* by those sculptors."

18. See C. Ducange, *Glossarium Mediae et Infimae Latinitatis* (Paris, 1843), 3: 238.

19. *Superstition and Force* (Philadelphia, 1892), p. 299.

20. *The Lascarids of Nicaea* (London, 1912), p. 192. Now also M. Angold, *A, Byzantine Government in Exile: Government and Society under the Lascarids of Nicaea* (London, 1975), who believes the ordeal came from the West. My book was in press when Angold's appeared.

21. *Les Institutions de l'Empire Byzantin* (Paris, 1949), p. 243.

22. *Geschichte des Römaischen Rechts* (Leipzig, 1894), 3: 407.

23. *Historia tou Basileiou tes Nikaias . . .* (in Greek; Athens, 1898), p. 406; "It came to the Byzantines from the Western peoples," meaning the Latins. See also A. Siatos, *Mia poineke dike kata Michael Palaiologou* (Athens, 1938), p. 29, who agrees on Latin provenience. His article is a popularized account of the trial.

24. *Histoire du droit Byzantin* (Paris, 1843–47), 3: 197 ff. and 208.

25. "Studien zum Hochverrätsprozesse des Michael Paläologos im Jahre 1252," *Byzantinisch-Neugriechische Jahrbücher* (Athens, 1929–30), 8: 59–98.

26. Sathas first published the Greek version, *Assizes of the Kingdom of Jerusalem and Cyprus* (in Greek), *Bibliotheca Graeca Medii Aevi* (Paris, 1877), 6: 1.

27. Czebe, "Studien," pp. 86–87.

28. George Pachymeres, *De Michaele et Andronico Palaeologis*, ed. I. Bekker (Bonn, 1835), p. 33.

29. Acrop., p. 396.

30. Sphrantzes, *Annales*, p. 8.

31. See above, n. 6.

32. *Annae Comnenae Alexiadis, Corpus Scriptorum Historiae Byzantinae* (Bonn, 1839), 1: 243.

32a. Cf. K. Hadjipsaltes, "The Church of Cyprus and the Ecumenical Patriarchate in Nicaea," *Kypriakai Spoudai* (in Greek), 28 (1964): 14–68, on certain Greek ecclesiastical connections.

33. C. Diehl, *La Société byzantine à l'époque des Comnènes* (Paris, 1929), affirms that "Western customs penetrated the East in the 12th century, like the judicial duel or appeals to the judgment of God." But he, too, cites no evidence.

34. See *Les Assises des Romanie*, ed. G. Recoura (Paris, 1930), pp. 146–53; cf. also J. Lamonte, "Three Questions concerning the Assizes of Jerusalem," *Byzantina Metabyzantina* (New York, 1946), p. 210. P. Topping, *Assizes of Romania* (Philadelphia, 1949), p. 170, n. 20, says that Palaeologus, after declining

to undergo the ordeal by fire, received a trial "according to the usual Byzantine forms." In point of fact, Michael never had a genuine trial, since he was never formally accused of any charge.

35. Acrop., p. 85.

36. Acrop., p. 104; N. Gregoras, *Byzantina Historia* (Bonn, 1829), 1: 45; Mathew Paris, *Chronica Majora*, ed. Luard (London, 1872–73), 5: 408.

37. Acrop., p. 99.

38. See the Registers of Innocent III, *Migne Patrologia Latina*, vol. 216 (Paris, 1891), cols. 353–54.

39. Pachymeres, *Michaele et Andronico*, p. 21.

40. Czebe, "Studien," p. 88.

41. Pachymeres, *Michaele et Andronico*, p. 33. Cf. H. Lea, *Superstition and Force*, pp. 253–63.

42. See n. 32, supra.

43. See Nicetas Choniates, *Historia, Corpus Scriptorum Byzantinae* (Bonn, 1835), p. 43. See also C. Diehl, *L'Europe Orientale*, etc., p. 48; and S. Dragumis, *Hoi diadoratismoi para tois Byzantinois* (in Greek; Athens, 1909), p. 700.

44. Acrop., p. 98.

45. Acrop., p. 99.

46. See Recoura, *Assises de Romanie*, par. 157; Topping, *Assizes*, p. 163, n. 12; also cf. Topping's appropriate remark, p. 170, n. 20: "Trial by battle was accepted among the Byzantines as less degrading to their sense of superiority as Graeco-Romans."

47. Acrop., p. 98.

48. Acrop., p. 96; Czebe, "Studien," p. 97.

49. Acrop., pp. 99–100, who notes that before his release Michael had to take an oath of loyalty to the emperor.

50. "Livre de Jean d'Ibelin," *Recueil des Historiens des Croisades, Lois I, Assises de Jerusalem, Assise de la haute cour*, ed. M. Beugnot (Paris, 1841), 1: 165–74.

51. Acrop., p. 95; "Livre de Jean d'Ibelin," pp. 165–74.

52. Ibid.

53. Acrop., p. 98; "Livre de Jean d'Ibelin," pp. 165–74.

54. Pachymeres, *Michaele et Andronico*, 1: 33.

Notes to Chapter 8

1. On the Council of Lyons, see now D. Greanakoplos, "Bonaventura, the Mendicant Orders, and the Greeks at the Council of Lyons," in *The Orthodox Churches and the West: Studies in Ecclesiastical History*, 13 (Oxford, 1976); and my *Emperor Michael Palaeologus and the West*, Chaps. 11–12. Also B. Roberg, *Die Union zwischen der griechischen und der lateinischen Kirche auf dem II. Konzil von Lyon* (Bonn, 1964); A. Franchi, *Il Concilio di Lione (1274) secondo la Ordinatio Concilii generalis Lugdunensis* (Rome, 1965); and H. Wolter and H. Holstein, *Lyon I et Lyon II* (Paris, 1965).

2. Pachymeres, *De Michaele Palaeologo* (Bonn ed.) 1: 491–92, discusses such *libelil* and the penalties for reading them or even having them in one's possession.

3. The document is printed in several places (see H. Beck, *Kirche und theologische Literatur im byzantinischen Reich* [Munich, 1959], p. 680). I have used the text printed in A. Vassilief, *Anecdota graeco-byzantina* (Moscow, 1893), pp. 179–88. For completion of the text, see M. Concasty, "La fin d'un dialogue contre les Latins azymits d'après le Paris Suppl. gr. 1191," *Akten des XI. intern. byzantinistenkongresses München 1958* (Munich, 1960), pp. 86–89. The text of this document has not hitherto been translated or analyzed (except for a few passing remarks by historians). For remarks on Vassilief's edition, of which the ending is missing, see Concasty, idem. Vassilief, idem, p. xli, says the *libellus* was written in 1274 by an anti-unionist opponent of Michael Palaeologus, probably soon after the return of Michael's envoys from Lyons. Concasty presents two possible dates: 1275 (after the official proclamation of union in Constantinople in January 1275) and 1278 (after a local Greek, antiunionist schismatic council held in Thessaly), but both dates raise several problems. For modern works mentioning the *libellus*, see also D. Nicol, "The Byzantine Reaction to the Second Council of Lyons, 1274," *Church History VII, Councils and Assemblies*, ed. C. Cuming and D. Baker (Cambridge, 1971), pp. 134–35, and his observations.

4. On Euphrosynus' identity, see Concasty, "La fin d'un dialogue," p. 86, who identifies him with a Byzantine consul named in the exordium to the work (cf. Vassilief, *Anecdota*, p. 179).

5. On Parastron, see esp. Geanakoplos, *Michael Palaeologus*, pp. 259–60, 267–68, and now esp. Geanakoplos, article cited in n. 1. above. Also source material in Pachymeres, 1: esp. 372.

6. Vassilief, p. 179.

7. On the *straordienst* and Michael's performance before Arsenios, see Geanakoplos, *Emperor Michael*, pp. 44–45.',

8. See below, passim, on the "azyma," which is central to this *libellus*.

9. On these persons see Pachymeres, 1: 489 ff; cf. Geanakoplos, pp. 275, 320.

10. On Holobolos' tortures by the emperor, see Pachymeres, 1: 192–93; Geanakoplos, p. 275.

11. Greek text: "akrovystian synteresas."

12. See most recently on the "azyma," the acute article of J. Erickson, "Leavened and Unleavened: Some Theological Implications of the Schism of 1054," *St. Vladimir's Theological Quarterly* 14 (1970):3–24.

13. See above, Prologue to this book.

14. Some of the Psalms (usually attributed to David) are prophetic in nature.

15. Text in Vassilief, p. 181. Cf. the Psalms, especially 75:9, which mentions an "emptying." The Psalms were very popular in the Greek church. Recall also the expression of St. Paul (Philippians, 2:7), who speaks of Christ as God emptying Himself (*kenosis*) when taking the form of a slave (a man), though this did not diminish his divinity.

16. Vassilief, p. 181.

17. See, on Mary's perpetual virginity, W. Burghardt, "Mary in Eastern Patristic Thought," *Mariology*, vol. 2, ed. J. Carol (Milwaukee, 1957), esp. pp. 102 ff., where the analogy is made between Christ's issue from Mary's womb and Ezekiel's "Gate of the Lord," where the Lord goes in and out and still the

gate is closed. On Proklos' (later bishop of Constantinople) famous sermon on the virgin birth and Mary's perpetual virginity, see F. Bauer, *Proklos von Konstantinopel* (Munich, 1919).

18. Vassilief, p. 181.

19. On doves, see G. Lampe, *A Patristic Greek Lexicon*, under *peristera*, p. 1072; on tortoises (*helone*), see Liddell and Scott, *Greek-English Lexicon*, 2: 1967.

20. Greek text, Vassilief, p. 181. In Genesis 1, it is suggested that the world (firmament) is made of beaten metal (see also Job, 38:30). Cf. views ascribed to Muslims in Christian polemics against them, that God is "all spherical" (*holosphairos*) and "made of solid beaten metal" (*holosphyros*). See J. Pelikan, *The Spirit of Eastern Christendom* (Chicago, 1974), p. 233.

21. Cf. a somewhat similar description in Exodus, 20:4, on the tripartite division of the universe into: (1) the waters over the firmament; (2) the waters under the firmament; (3) the earth beneath, with Hades below the earth. This depiction of the area below the earth, that is hell, is in some ways carried over into the Fathers of the church, both Eastern and Western.

22. For Cosmas Indicopleustes, *Christian Topography*, ed. E. Winstedt (Cambridge, 1909); see e.g. 2 (92B).

23. Text, Vassilief, p. 182, esp. l. 25. See *De Principiis* of Origen, 1:8 (ed. Koetschau) on angelic battalions (or orders). Cf. on numbers cited, Apocalypse 5:12 and 14:1, which specifically refer to 144,000 people standing with the Lamb (Christ) on Mt. Sion, "who had His name and His Father's name written on their foreheads." Also cf. Apocalypse 7:1–8. One hundred and ninety-four thousand is the square of 12 multiplied 1,000 times and is thought to be symbolically representative of the sum total of the elect of Israel, or the sum total of Christianity. See H. Halley, *Bible Handbook* (Minneapolis, 1973), p. 591. Also on similar numbers, see Apocalypse 5:11–13, which says that in heaven $10,000 \times 10,000$ angels sing and the whole redeemed creation joins in the chorus.

24. Cf. the view of Vassilief, p. xl. Note the possible influence also of Arabic astronomy and astrology, which itself was drawn from the Hebrew and ancient Greek.

25. See passim in Dionysius, *Celestial Hierarchy* and *Ecclesiastical Hierarchy*. See also above, n. 23, on Origen's division of the angelic hosts. Interestingly, there is a somewhat similar division of society in *The Everlasting Gospel* of the contemporary, thirteenth century, south Italian mystic, Joachim of Flora, who is sometimes regarded as having been influenced by Byzantine apocalyptic ideas. Also, see the Apocalypse, which in several places makes a certain separation of groups of people.

26. Text, Vassilief, p. 183. Cf. passage in Chrysostom, Homily on John 76:3. One of the early Western councils said heaven and earth were created *simul*, which usually means "at the same time," but it may also mean "as well as." See H. Denzinger, *Enchiridion Symbolorum* (Freiburg, 1955), pp. 428, 1783. Neither Greeks nor Latins ever pronounced officially on whether God created heaven *before* the earth. On heaven and earth, see also Cosmas Indicopleustes, *Christian Topography*, 7 (341D).

27. On the four rivers, each binding a side of Paradise (hence "four sides"), see below, text and n. 29.

28. See Genesis 2:4–13. Also Apocalypse, e.g. 2:7.

29. Genesis 2:10–14.

30. Cf. in the Old Testament (1 Kings 20:9–13), there was an earthquake, a whirlwind, and a fire, and the voice of God was in none of these, but His voice was a tiny whispering sound.

31. See Apocalypse 4:6 ff.

32. Is it possible that Aristophanes' *Clouds* had an influence here?

33. Text, Vassilief, p. 184. I cannot find this passage in Hermogenes. (Cf. Moschopoulos' grammatical work, *Peri Schedon*.) On Hermogenes, see A. Turyn, *Dated Greek Manuscripts of the 13th and 14th Centuries* (Urbana, Ill., 1972), pp. 190, 196 and my chap. 13, below.

34. Achilles may well be a Greek pagan writer, perhaps Achilles Tatias, the only Achilles I can find. Both Demosthenes and Achilles may be referred to here from epitomes of their works, now lost. On Byzantine mathematics and astronomy, see K. Krumbacher, *Geschichte der byzantinischen Literatur* (Munich, 1897), pp. 620–30, and esp. *New Cambridge Medieval History*, 4, pt. 2, chap. 28, by K. Vogel.

35. In Apocalypse 17:9, the Whore of Babylon (!) is represented as sitting on seven hills. Seven may also be a reference to the seven hills of pagan Rome.

36. See above, chap. 4, n. 24. Hesychasts earlier than Palamas had also expressed these kinds of views.

37. On Christ's washing away of human sin with His blood, see Apocalypse 1:19–20 and 5:5. There are, of course, many such expressions in the Fathers, referring to the pelican and also to Christ. The pelican was a medieval symbol for Christ in both East and West.

38. On Byzantine Mariology, see my chap. 3, text and n. 79.

39. Cf. on the wearing of Christ over the heart, St. Paul in Galatians, 3:27.

40. On Latin and Greek ways of making the sign of the cross, see F. Cabrol and H. Leclercq, *Dictionnaire d'archéologie Chrétienne et de Liturgie*, III², col. 343. The Christian monks in the eighth century started making the sign of the cross with three fingers of the right hand (the others being kept closed) and touching the forehead, breast, and first the right than the left shoulder—the method still used in the Greek church. Cf. *New Catholic Encyclopedia*, 4: 475, which says that Pope Innocent III (d. 1216) directed that three fingers be used and that the direction be from right to left shoulder. In the thirteenth century (evidently *before* this *libellus* was composed), a change had come about in the Latin usage, all fingers being joined and extended, and the left shoulder being touched before the right.

41. Recall, at the early Council of Jerusalem (Acts 15:20 esp. 28–29), the dispute between St. Paul and St. Peter, when it was decided (against Peter and the "Judaizers") that the Christians did not have to be circumcised, though they must not eat strangled meat (that is, meat killed without drawing blood). Cf. also Paul's Epistle to the Galatians.

42. The medieval Latins believed that the body produced an oversupply of blood; hence "bleeding" was resorted to.

43. See J. Koncevicius, *Russia's Attitude towards Union with Rome* (Washington, D. C., 1927), pp. 97, 69–70. The Russians probably inherited this accusation from the Greeks.

44. See Acts 11 :8–10.
45. Actually, the Catholics do not chant the Hallelujah until Holy Saturday. (The Greeks also do not chant Hallelujah on Holy Friday.) Possibly the difference of the Easter date had something to do with the discussion here.
46. On Holy Thursday the Greeks move the Cross to the center of the church (that is, on the night of the reading of the twelve Bibles—a ceremony the Latin church does not have).
47. Text, Vassilief, p. 187.
48. *Efantasteka* in colloquial modern Greek also means "I had a nocturnal emission."
49. Text, Vassilief, pp. 187–88.
50. The Paris MS is Paris Suppl. gr. 1191 (cf. mention in H. Omont, *Catalogue des manuscrits grecs . . .* E. Miller [Paris, 1897], pp. 50–52). On completion of the Greek text, see esp. Concasty, "La fin d'un dialogue contre les Latins azymites . . . ," p. 88. In her article, Concasty also discusses other (incomplete) Slavic versions previously published by A. Popov, *Istoriko-literaturnyi obzor . . .* (Moscow, 1875), pp. 251–86, comparing them with Vassilief, and the completed Paris MS.
51. Printed in Roberg, *Die Union*, pp. 229–31. For this report, and especially for an analysis of the role of leading personalities at Lyons, see my forthcoming article, "Bonaventura, the Mendicant Orders, and the Greeks at the Council of Lyons," cited above, n.1.

Notes to Chapter 9

1. See D. Geanakoplos, *Greek Scholars in Venice* (Cambridge, Mass., 1962), p. 81 (reprinted as *Byzantium and the Renaissance* [Hamden, Conn., 1972], with references).
2. I. Tertsetis, *Ta Hapanta* (Athens, 1953), 3:236 (in Greek).
3. See K. Demaras, *Historia tes Neohellenikes Logotechnias*, 4th ed. (Athens, 1968); also Demaras, *La Grèce au temps de Lumière* (Geneva, 1969); S. Xydis, "Medieval Origins of Modern Greek Nationalism," *Balkan Studies* 9 (1968):1–20; P. Topping, "Greek Historical Writing in the Period 1453–1914," *Journal of Modern History* 33 (1961):157–73, esp. 162, 159; G. Arnakis, *The Ottoman Empire and the Balkan States to 1900* (Austin-New York, 1969). Cf. I. Moles, "Nationalism and Byzantine Greece," *Greek, Roman and Byzantine Studies* 10 (1969):95–108.
4. See K. Sathas, *Tourkokratoumene Hellas* (Athens, 1869; in Greek); also A. Vacalopoulos, *The Origins of Modern Greece* (New Brunswick, N.J., 1971) and his "Byzantinism and Hellenism," *Balkan Studies* 9 (1968): 100–26. T. Papadopoulos, *History of Greek Church and People Under the Turks* (Brussels, 1952), believes the Greek church most responsible for preserving the Greek sense of nationalism.
5. See Arnakis, *The Ottoman Empire*, p. 74. See S. Runciman, *The Great Church in Captivity* (Cambridge, 1968), esp. pp. 219–20. See below, n. 84. for statement by the sixteenth-century German scholar Martin Crusius on the sad state of general illiteracy in Greece.

6. See below, pp. 17–18 and 24–27, text and nn.
7. Quoted in D. Geanakoplos, *Byzantine East and Latin West* (Oxford, 1966), p. 111.
8. See, on the more recent colonies now, *Ho Hellenismos eis to Exoterikon* (in Greek), ed. J. Irmscher and M. Mineemi, *Berliner Byzantinischen Arbeiten* 40 (Berlin, 1968), containing K. Kyrris, "Cypriote Scholars in Venice in XVI and XVII Centuries," pp. 183–272. Cf. K. Kyrris, *Balkan Studies* 10:377–92 (review).
9. See esp. Geanakoplos, *Greek Scholars in Venice.*
10. On the origins of the Greek Venetian colony, see Geanakoplos, *Greek Scholars,* esp. chap. 3 (and bibliography cited). Also, the old work of J. Veludes, *Hellenon Orthodoxon Apoikoia en Venetia,* 2d ed. (Venice, 1893).
11. S. Antoniadou, "Porismata apo ten meleten procheiron diacheiristikon biblion ton eton 1544–47 kai 1549–54 . . . " (in Greek,) *Praktika tes Akademias Athenon* 33 (1958): 468–70; and M. Manousakas, "The First Permit of the Venetian Senate for the Church of the Greeks . . . ," *Thesaurismata* (Venice, 1962), pp. 109–18.
12. On the church, see Geanakoplos, *Greek Scholars,* pp. 65–68, and also his *Byzantine East,* pp. 132–33. On the paintings, see E. Chatzidakis, *Historical Sketch of Religious Painting after the Conquest* (Athens, 1957; in Greek), esp. pp. 80–190.
13. Geanakoplos, *Greek Scholars,* p. 70.
14. Ibid., pp. 60–61, also citing a statement of the Greek Andreas Darmarios, in 1580, that 15,000 Greeks lived in Venice (cf. E. Legrand, *Notice Biographique sur Jean et Theodose Zygomalas* [Paris, 1889], pp. 254, 255). Also, N. Tomadakes, "He Symbole ton Hellenon Koinoteton tou exoterikou eis ton agona tes eleutherias," speech to University of Athens, 1952 (Athens, 1953), p. 12, citing 10,000 people in the Greek colony of Venice.
15. Shown in Geanakoplos, *Greek Scholars,* passim.
16. On Musurus' living for a time within the Greek colony, see M. Manousakas, "La date de . . . Musurus," *Studi Venezian* (1970), p. 463 n. Cf. below, chap. 12.
17. On Apostolis, see Geanakoplos, *Greek Scholars,* pp. 73–111 (and on Frederick III, esp. pp. 97–99).
18. On Musurus' career, see Geanakoplos, *Greek Scholars,* pp. 111–67 (esp. pp. 150–57 for his "Hymn to Plato").
19. Ibid., p. 123.
20. On Calliergis and the Venetian-Greek printing of liturgical books, see Geanakoplos, *Greek Scholars,* p. 212, and his *Byzantine East,* esp. p. 130. For the list of books printed, see E. Legrand, *Bibliographie Hellénique ou description raisonné des ouvrages publiés en grec par des grecs au XVe et XVIe siècles,* 4 vols. (Paris, 1885–1906). Also his *Bibliographie Ionienne.* See also article of Tomadakes, cited below, chap. 14, n. 49.
21. On Sukhanov, see S. Bielokurov, *Arsenii Sukhanov I Biografiya Arseniya Sukhanova* (Moscow, 1891); Geanakoplos, *Byzantine East and Latin West,* p. 179.
22. Geanakoplos, *Byzantine East,* pp. 130–31.
23. The sole biography on Ducas is in Geanakoplos, *Greek Scholars,* pp. 223–56.

On Arsenios Apostolis, see *Greek Scholars*, pp. 167-201. And on Portus, Geana-koplos, *Byzantine East*, pp. 158-60.

24. On Chalcondyles, see below chap. 13. Also, the older work of G. Cammelli, *Demetrio Calcondila* (Florence, 1954).

25. On these patriotic appeals by Greek humanists abroad, see Geanakoplos, *Greek Scholars*, pp. 151-52. For a survey of such appeals, see also M. Man-ousakas, "Ekkleseis (1453-1535) ton Hellenon Logion tes Anagenneseos pros tous Hegemones tes Europes gia ten apeleftherose tes Hellados," discourse on March 25, 1963 to the University of Thessalonika (Thessalonika, 1965). On Bessarion, see Manousakas, idem, pp. 12-15. Bessarion sent many of his appeals, in manuscript, to the rector of Paris University, Guglielmo Fichet, who printed and sent them to Louis XI of France, Edward III of England, Emperor Frederick III, and Duke Amadeo IX of Savoy (see documents in E. Legrand, *Cent-dix lettres grecques de François Filelfe* [Paris, 1892], pp. 223-89). On Eparchos, see Manousakas, pp. 27-28.

26. Geanakoplos, *Byzantine East*, p. 148, and Manousakas, "Ekklescis," pp. 23-24.

27. Cf. below, text and n. 46.

28. Geanakoplos, *Byzantine East*, pp. 156-57.

29. On the *estradioti*, see Geanakoplos, *Greek Scholars*, pp. 55-56, and his *Byzantine East*, pp. 119-23. Also, M. Sanuto, *I diarii di Marino Sanuto*, ed. R. Fulin, 58 vols. (Venice, 1879-1903) passim; and esp. K. Sathas, "Hellenes stratiotai en te Dysei," *Hestia* 19 (1885): 370-76 and later issues (in Greek).

30. See below, text and n. 55.

31. See below, text and n. 51. Also, Geanakoplos, *Byzantine East*, pp. 132-35.

32. See esp. K. Mertzios, "Thomas Flanginis kai ho Mikros Hellenomnemon," *Pragmateiai tes Akademias Athenon*, 9 (1939): 47-52. and passim; also, Geana-koplos, *Byzantine East*, p. 124.

33. See below, text and n. 88.

34. On the colony's later fortunes, see esp. Veludes, *Hellenon Orthodoxon Apoikia*.

35. On the Greek community of Naples, standard for long on its ecclesiastical relations has been G. Meola, *Delle Istoire della Chiesa Greca in Napoli Esistente* (Naples, 1740). See also now J. Hassiotis, "La communità greca di Napoli e i moti insurrezionali nella penisola Balkanica meridionale durante la seconda metà del XVI secolo," *Balkan Studies* 10 (1969): 279-88 and bibliography listed there, p. 280, n. 3, and 281.

36. Hassiotes, "La communità greca." Also his *Scheseis Hellenon kai Hispanon sta Chronia tes Tourkokratias* (Thessalonika, 1969), pp. 40 ff.

37. Cited in Hassiotes, "La communità greca," esp. p. 283.

38. Hassiotes, "Makarios, Theodoros, kai Nikephoros hoi Melissenoi" (Thes-salonika, 1966; in Greek).

39. On the Greek college, see esp. R. Netzhammer, *Das griechische Kolleg im Rom* (Salzburg, 1905) and in general A. Fortescue, *The Uniate Eastern Churches* (London, 1923), pp. 151-59.

40. Hassiotes, "La communità greca," p. 283. The Turks tried to prevent young Greeks from the mainland from studying in the West.

41. On Chimara, see ibid., p. 284. and Hassiotes's "He epanastases ton Himarioton sta 1570," *Epieirotike Estia* 15 (1968): 265–76. On Longos and Combis, see Hassiotes "La communità greca," pp. 284–85. Also, his "Ho Archiepiskopos Achrithos Hioakeim kai Hoi Synomotikes Kineseis ste Boreio Epiro," *Makedonikon* (1964), pp. 237–55; and his *Scheseis Hellenon kai Hispanon*, p. 39.

42. Hassiotes, "La communità greca," pp. 285–86.

43. See the old work of L. Conforte, *I Napoletani a Lepanto* (Naples, 1886), pp. 46–55; and now on Lepanto in general, see Hassiotes," Anekdoto 'Brachy Chroniko' gia te naumachia tes Nafpaktou (1571): Hena Hithiotypo Eikonografemeno Keimeno tou Hioannou Hagiomaura (1578)," *Hellenika*, 19 (1966):105–13.

44. Hassiotes, "La communità greca," p. 287, and esp. his *Scheseis Hellenon kai Hispanon*, p. 41, on the appeal by the Greek patriarch to Philip III to aid a Greek mainland revolt against the Turks.

45. On these men, see esp. Geanakoplos, *Greek Scholars*, and K. Setton, "The Byzantine Background to the Italian Renaissance, pp. 12 and 40 ff.

46. On Constantine Lascaris, see A. de Rosalia, "La vita di Costantino Lascaris," *Archivio storico siciliano*, 3 (1957–58): 21–70. Also, Geanakoplos, *Greek Scholars*, pp. 1, 57.

47. Geanakoplos, *Byzantine East and Latin West*, p. 144; also p. 174, n. 13, citing A. Pertusi, "Erotemata," *Italia Medioevale e Umanistica*, 5 (1962): 324, on the Erotemata as a Byzantine grammatical genre.

48. Hassiotes, *Scheseis Hellenon kai Hispanon*, p. 69. Cf. below, n. 82.

49. On the Macedonian regiment, Hassiotes, *Scheseis Hellenon kai Hispanon*, p. 60, and on Spanish Philhellenism, p. 61.

50. Geanakoplos, *Byzantine East and Latin West*, p. 149, and K. Kyrris, "Cypriote Scholars in Venice" (see n. 8).

51. Geanakoplos, *Byzantine East*, pp. 151–52. The painters were Nicholas Greco and Pedro Greco.

52. See now G. de Andres, *El Cretense Nicolas de la Torre Copista Griego de Felipe II* (Madrid, 1969), esp. pp. 24–25, 65–66.

53. Geanakoplos, *Byzantine East*, p. 135; and P. Kelemen, *El Greco Revisited* (New York, 1961), pp. 100–01.

54. The only biography of Ducas is in Geanakoplos, *Greek Scholars*, pp. 223–55. See there for theories on the New Testament edition and on his first published Greek books.

55. On Marullus, see D. Zakythinos, "Michael Maroullos Tarchaniotes," *Ep. Het. Byz. Sp.* 5 (1928): 202. For his poetry, A. Perosa, *Michaelis Marulli, Carmina* (Verona, 1951), and for his attitude, M. Manousakas, "Ekkleseis ton Hellenon Logion tes Anagenneseos, etc.," pp. 16–17. See now Vacalopoulos, *Origins of the Greek Nation*, pp. 261–63. On Greek merchants in Ancona as early as 1514 see T. Stoianovich, "The Conquering Orthodox Balkan Merchant," *Journal of Economic History* 20 (1960).

56. On John Gemistos, see Manousakas, "Ekkleseis," pp. 20–22.

57. On Livorno, see N. Tomadakes, "He Symbole ton Hellenikon Koinoteton tou Exoterikou eis ton agona tes eleutherias," address at University of Athens,

March 25, 1952 (Athens, 1953), p. 15. Also his "Naoi kai Thesmoi tes Hellenikes Koinotetos tou Livornou," *Epeteris Hetaireias Byzantinon Spondon*, 16 (1940):81–127 and bibliography cited. Also on Livorno, *Megale Hellenike Enkeklopaideia*, 10.

58. On Trieste, see esp. *Cenni istorici della communità greco-orientale di Trieste* (Trieste, 1882), and Tomadakes, "He Symbole ton Hellenikon Konioteton," bibliography, p. 34. With respect to Rome, we recall the famous Greek Uniate and librarian of the Vatican, Leon Allatius (b. 1586) from Chios. See A. Culter, *The Newer Temples of the Greeks* (University Park, Ill., 1969). Today a "borgo dei Greci" still exists in Florence.

59. See esp. G. Cecchini, "Anna Notaras Paleologa: Una principessa greca in Italia e la politica senese di ripopolamento della Maremma," *Bolletino Senese di Storia Patria* 16 (1938):1–41. Also, Geanakoplos, *Byzantine East*, p. 118, and his *Greek Scholars*, p. 62 and n. 26, with more recent bibliography. Hassiotes, *Scheseis Hellenon kai Hispanon*, p. 44, finds evidence of plans for the foundation of a Greek colony in Andalusia, Spain (to replace the Moriscos of Granada).

60. On the importance of these appeals, see esp. Geanakoplos, *Greek Scholars*, pp. 151–52. Many appeals are discussed in Manousakas, "He Symbole ton Hellenikon Konioteton."

61. See A. Keller, "A Byzantine Admirer of Western Progress, Cardinal Bessarion," in *Cambridge Historical Journal* 11 (1953–55): 343–48; and Vacalopoulos, *Origins of the Greek Nation*, pp. 175–78.

62. On Pletho, see esp. F. Masai, *Pléthon et la platonisme de Mistra* (Paris, 1956). Now cf. Vacalopoulos, *Origins of the Greek Nation*, p. 256.

63. Cited in Masai, *Plethon*, p. 337, n. 2, pp. 320, 332–33.

64. Masai, pp. 270–314 and M. Anastos, "Pletho's Calendar and Liturgy," *Dumbarton Oaks Papers*, 4 (1948):183–305.

65. Vacalopoulos, *Origins of the Greek Nation*, pp. 256 f. Also, S. Xydis, "Medieval Origins of Modern Greek Nationalism," *Balkan Studies* 9 (1968) and Vacalopoulos, "Byzantinism and Hellenism," *Balkan Studies* 9 (1968):112 ff.

66. On silk and the Greeks of Lyons, see P. Rudier, *The Romance of French Weaving* (New York, 1931), pp. 172–75 and bibliography Also, P. Kelemen, *El Greco Revisited*, p. 87.

67. On Hermonymos, see Geanakoplos, *Greek Scholars*, p. 258, his *Byzantine East*, pp. 154–57, and idem., pp. 155–56 on Vergikios and Eparchos.

68. On Columbus and Bissypat, see the "popular" work of S. Canoutas, *Christopher Columbus, A Greek Nobleman* (New York, 1943), p. 189.

69. On Fitzstephen, I am planning to publish an article.

70. On Philarges, see Geanakoplos, *Byzantine East*, p. 153, and on Manuel II, J. Barker, *Manuel II Palaeologus (1391–1425): A Study in Late Byzantine Statesmanship* (New Brunswick, N.J. 1969), pp. 177–81.

71. Geanakoplos, *Byzantine East*, p. 157, and esp. R. Weiss, *Humanism in England during the Fifteenth Century* (Oxford, 1941), pp. 144–48; G. Cammelli, "Andronico Callisto," *Rinascità* 23–24 (1942):3–64.

72. See S. Runciman, *The Great Church in Capitivity* (Cambridge, 1968), pp. 292–

96 and 300–04. On other Greeks in England, see now R. Browning, "Some Early Greek Visitors to England," *Essays in Memory of Basil Laourdas* (Thessalonika, 1975), pp. 387–95.

73. I hope to publish a document, dated 1590, referring to trade in a cloth called "carisée."

74. Geanakoplos, *Byzantine East*, pp. 150–51.

75. Ibid., p. 174.

76. See recently, Runciman, *Great Church in Capitivity*, pp. 222–24.

77. E. Layton, "Nikodemos Metaxas, the First Greek Printer in the Eastern World," *Harvard Library Bulletin* (April, 1967); Runciman, p. 222.

78. On Margounios, see Geanakoplos, *Byzantine East*, pp. 165–94. Recall also the Metropolitan Theophilus Carydalaeus, who did work in education in the Balkans: C. Tsourkas, *Les Debuts de l'Enseignement philosophique et de la Libre Pensée dans les Balkans* (Thessalonika, 1971).

79. Recent on this is Arnakis, *The Ottoman Empire and the Balkan States to 1900*, pp. 146–47.

80. K. Paparegopoulos, *Historia tou Hellenikou Ethnous*, 5th ed. (Athens, 1932; in Greek), vol. 5, pt. 2, p. 163.

81. On the patriarchal school see Geanakoplos, *Byzantine East*, p. 167. Also Paparegopoulos, *Histonia tou Hellenikou, Ethnous,* vol. 5 pt. 2, p. 163, Runciman, *Great Church in Capitivity*, pp. 215–16.

82. Tomadakes, "He Symbole," pp. 10–11, notes that, though most of the diaspora communities had relations with the patriarch, occasionally some, for political reasons, would forbid the community priest from communication with the patriarch (as at Livorno).

83. A. Toynbee, *History of Civilization*, 2 (New York, 1946, abridged ed.), p. 176.

84. This cultural deprivation of Greece is emphasized in Vacalopoulos, *Origins of the Greek Nation* pp. 231, 254; G. Arnakis, *The Ottoman Empire and the Balkan States to 1900* (Austin, 1969); and by Paparegopoulos, *Historia tou Hellenikou*, p. 163, M. Crusius, in his *Germano-graecia* (Basle, 1585), p. 18, says: "In all Greece, studies nowhere flourish; they have no public academies or professors except the most trivial schools (ecclesiastical)." Quoted in Runciman, *Great Church in Captivity*, p. 209.

85. J. Kakrides, "The Ancient Greeks and the Greeks of the War of Independence" (in Greek), *Balkan Studies* 4 (1963): esp. 255–57.

86. Ibid., pp. 255–59.

87. Paparegopoulos, *Historia*, vol. 5, pt. 2, p. 163.

88. See ibid., pp. 163–67. Also on the schools, Tomadakes, "He Symbole," esp. pp. 11–21.

89. See esp. K. Mertzios, "Thomas Flanginis kai ho Mikros Hellenomnemon" (in Greek), *Pragmateiai tes Akademias Athenon* 9 (1939): 47–52, passim.

90. On Padua University, see esp. Geanakoplos, *Greek Scholars*, passim, and Runciman, *Great Church in Capitvity*, pp. 212–13. Vienna established schools in (northern) Greece from 1793 on (Tomadakes, p. 17).

91. J. Veludes, *Hellenon Orthodoxon apoikoia en Venetia*, 2d ed. (Venice, 1893) 2:

esp. 107–08, noting a document of the Venetian Greek colony (in 1593) that links education and the military art as the best expressions of the Greek "nation." Also, Paparegopoulos, *Historia*, Vol. 5, pt. 2, p. 165.

92. This is, of course, not to forget the "Rum millet." or "Greek nation" under the patriarch. But it was not free, since its superior above the patriarch was the Ottoman sultan. See Runciman, *Great Church in Captivity*, pp. 167–68. After this chapter was written, the author saw G. Henderson, *The Revival of Greek Thought* (Albany, 1970), which has some interesting ideas on education; cf. esp. pp. 1–11.

Notes to Chapter 10

1. I am preparing an entire monograph on the life and career of Peter Philarges (Alexander V).

2. On Atumano, see recently G. Fedalto, *Simone Atumano Monaco di Studio* (Brescia, 1968). Also see bibliography cited there and in Geanakoplos, *Byzantium and the Renaissance*, p. 24; cf. Setton, "Byzantine Background to the Italian Renaissance," pp. 49–51.

3. On Chrysoloras, see esp. G. Cammelli, *Manuele Crisolora* (Florence, 1941); C. Patrinelis, "An Unknown Discourse of Chrysoloras addressed to Manuel II Palaeologus," *Greek, Roman, Byzantine Studies* (1973), pp. 497–502. Chrysoloras wrote a remarkable comparison between Old and New Rome (Rome and Constantinople): see Epigraph to this book; also discussion in G. Holmes, *The Florentine Enlightenment, 1400–1450* (New York, 1969), pp. 231–32. (For translation of an important letter of Chrysoloras [who, according to Holmes, also helped to inspire the humanists' interest in art], see M. Baxandall, "Guarino, Pisanello, and M. Chrysoloras," *Journal of Warburg and Courtauld Institutes* 28 [1965]:197–98).

4. On the Florentine period of primacy in Greek Studies, see (from the large bibliography) most recently Holmes, *Florentine Enlightenment*, passim; P. Kristeller, *Renaissance Concepts of Man* (New York, 1972), section on "The Renaissance and Byzantine Learning," pp. 64–109; and, most recently, E. Garin, *Portraits from the Quattrocento*, trans. V. and E. Velen (New York, 1973), passim, esp. chap. 3, dealing with the important Byzantine humanist Argyropoulos. On the Roman phase under Bessarion (under Pope Sixtus IV), there is less bibliography. See esp. H. Vast, *Le Cardinal Bessarion* (Paris, 1878). Also Holmes, pp. 255 ff. Finally, on Bassarion see Prologue, n. 49a.

5. For the intellectual side, see esp. my *Byzantium and the Renaissance*, with bibliography, passim. For the juridical aspects of the Greek community, see now G. Fedalto, *Ricerche storiche sulla posizione giuridica ed ecclesiastica dei Greci a Venezia nei secoli XV e XVI* (Florence, 1967).

6. On Aldus, see Geankakoplos, *Byzantium and the Renaissance*, (Hamden, Conn., 1972, rpt. of *Greek Scholars in Venice*), esp. pp. 128–58; also the old work of A. Firmin-Didot, *Alde Manuce et l'hellénisme à Venise* (Paris, 1875); and C. Dionisotti, "Aldo Manuzio Umanista," *Umanesimo Europeo e Umanesimo Veneziano* (Florence, 1963), pp. 213–43.

7. On the Cretan emigration, see above, chap. 9, and my *Byzantium and the Renaissance*, pp. 41–52. See the recent article of M. Manousakas, "Rapid

Overview of Research on Venetian-held Crete," *Kretika Chronika*, 23(1971): 245 f. (in Greek). The basic source for the Venetian hegemony in Crete is G. Gerola, *Monumenti veneti dell'isola di Creta*, 4 vols. (Venice, 1905–32).

8. This theory is generally accepted, but two Greek psalters were published earlier in Venice. See A. Pertusi, "Erotemata," in *Italia medioevalia e umanistica* 5(1962): 324.

9. On Calliergis, see biography in my *Byzantium and the Renaissance*, pp. 201–23.

10. So I am told by the eminent philologist, my good friend A. Turyn (cf. Turyn, *De codicibus pindaricis* [Cracow, 1932]). On Aldine publications, see esp. A. Renouard, *Annales de l'imprimerie des Alde*, 3d ed., 3 vols. (Paris, 1834) and V. Scholderer, *Greek Printing Types, 1465–1926* (London, 1927).

11. On Musurus' career, see most recent biography (with bibliography) in Geanakoplos, *Byzantium and the Renaissance*, pp. 111–67. Cf. the older R. Menge, *Vita Marci Musuri Cretensis Vita*, etc., in M. Schmidt, ed., *Hesychii Alexandrini Lexicon*, 5 (Jena, 1868):1–57.

12. For evaluation of Musurus' emendations, see A. Turyn, *The Manuscript Tradition of the Tragedies of Euripides* (Urbana, Ill., 1957), p. 375; and L. Reynolds and N. Wilson, *Scribes and Scholars* (Oxford, 1968), pp. 131–33. See also Turyn's thorough recent study, "Demetrius Triclinius and the Planudean Anthology," *Festschrift N. Tomadakes* (Athens, 1973), pp. 403–50.

13. On qualitative vs. quantitative (involving the so-called Erasmian pronunciation of Greek), see bibliography in my *Byzantium and the Renaissance*, pp. 273–75 and my "Erasmus and the Aldine Academy of Venice: A Neglected Chapter in the Transmission of Graeco-Byzantine Learning to the West," *Greek, Roman, and Byzantine Studies* 3 (1960):129–30 and notes.

14. Opinion of E. Legrand, *Bibliographie hellénique* ... , 1:CVXI. For translation of part of Musurus'poem, see W. Roscoe, *The Life and Pontificate of Leo X*, 2: 241–47.

15. See besides my *Byzantium and the Renaissance*, p. 137, also J. Hutton, *The Greek Anthology in Italy to the Year 1800* (Ithaca, 1935), p. 155.

16. For enumeration of students, see Geanakoplos, *Byzantium and the Renaissance*, pp. 135–38.

17. Cf. Geanakoplos, "Erasmus and the Aldine Academy of Venice," pp. 122–23.

18. On Hermogenes' importance, see below, chap. 13 and now see A. Patterson, *Hermogenes and the Renaissance. Seven Ideas of Style* (Princeton, 1970) a useful work stressing the later Renaissance period but with nothing on the Byzantine transmission.

19. On both Michael and Arsenios Apostolis, see biographies with bibliography in Geanakoplos, *Byzantium and the Renaissance*, pp. 73–111 and 167–201.

20. Politian would have contested this evaluation, believing that his knowledge equaled or surpassed that of any Greek exile: see below, chap. 13; Geanakoplos, *Byzantium and Renaissance*, p. 291; E. Garin, *Portraits from the Quattrocento* (New York, 1963), esp. pp. 171–75; Holmes, *Florentine Enlightenment*, p. 263; and Reynolds-Wilson, *Scribes and Scholars*, pp. 119–21.

21. See, on Margounios, the recent biography in Geanakoplos, *Byzantine East and Latin West*, pp. 165–93, and esp. bibliography pp. 199–200; including works of Fedalto.

22. For biography of Ducas, see Geanakoplos, *Byzantium and the Renaissance*, pp. 223–55. Legrand, *Bibligraphic hellénique*, has only scattered references.

23. See texts in the original Complutensian Bible (cf. Geanakoplos, *Byzantium and the Renaissance*, pp. 238–44.)

24. Cf. ibid., pp. 238–44.

25. See Legrand, *Bibliographie hellénique*, 1: 192 ff., and cf. ibid., p. 247.

26. Legrand, vol. 1. For MSS copied by him, see A. Martini and D. Bassi, *Catalogus codicum graecorum Bibliothecae Ambrosianae*, 2 (Milan, 1906): 981–82ff., and cf. Patrinelis, "Greek Codicographers in the Renaissance" (in Greek), *Epeteris tou Mesaionikou Archeiou* (Athens, 1961). On liturgical editions, see now below, chap. 14, n. 49.

27. On this disputed question, see above, chap. 3, text and notes.

28. Found and published by C. Mertzios, "Gleanings from the records of Notary Michael Mara" (in Greek), in *Kretika Chronika* 1 (1961–62): 302 ff. Also on this disputed matter of El Greco's youth and training, see now my *Byzantine East and Latin West*, summary on pp. 133–35, with extensive bibliography. Cf. below, n. 35, work of Andres, for new source material on El Greco.

29. I was told by S. Cirac in Barcelona several years ago, that El Greco's elongated type of figure is prominent on Mt. Athos and in Crete (see Cirac, "L'hellénisme de D. Theotokopoulos," *Kretika Chronika* [1963], pp. 213–27); cf. K. Kalokyris, *Byzantine Wall Paintings of Crete* (Athens, 1957; in Greek). On recent objections to terms *Cretan* (and *Macedonian*) applied to art styles, see above, esp. chap. 3, n. 87.

30. On his famous (unpublished) *Commentaries* on Peter Lombard's *Sentences*, see F. Ehrle, *Der Sentenzen Kommentar Peters von Candia* (Münster, 1925); Geanakoplos, *Byzantine East*, pp. 133–34.

31. On J. Lascaris, see B. Knös, *Un ambassadeur de l'hellénisme: Janus Lascaris et la tradition greco-byzantine dans l'humanisme français* (Uppsala-Paris, 1945), and new material in Geanakoplos, *Byzantine East and Latin West*, p. 149 and n. 25.

32. See my work, *Byzantine East*, pp. 155–57, and cf. Legrand, *Bibliographie Hellénique* 1: CLXXV-CLXXXVI.

33. On England and Greek scholars, see, besides Legrand, R. Weiss, *Humanism in England in the 15th Century* (Oxford, 1951).

34. I have a document referring to Cretan trade in a special type of cloth.

35. Cf. Patrinelis, "Codicographers," for names of other Cretan copyists; also Geanakoplos, *Byzantine East*, pp. 154. ff Important now is the recent work of G. de Andres, *El Cretense Nicolas de la Torre* (Madrid, 1969).

36. See W. Regel, *Analecta Byzantino-Russica* (Petrograd, 1891), letters of Pegas, on pp. 92–115.

37. On Portus, see esp. Legrand, *Bibliographie hellénique*, 2: and cf. Geanakoplos, *Byzantine East*, pp. 158–60, esp. bibliography on 160; and A. Embiricos, *La Renaissance Crétoise* (Paris, 1960). Note mention of Portus's edition of Hermogenes.

38. On Lucaris, see S. Runciman, *The Great Church in Captivity*, pp. 259–88; cf. W. Adeney, *The Greek and Eastern Churches* (Clifton, N. J., 1965), pp. 309–24.

39. Legrand, 2: XXI-XXII.

40. For example, Emmanuel Adramyttenos, who taught Greek to the great Pico

della Mirandola. See recently, on Cretans, the extensive bibliography in the article of M. Manousakas, "Rapid Overview of Research on Venetian-held Crete" (in Greek), *Kretika Chronika* 23 (1971): 245–97.

41. See above on this, chap. 9.

42. On seventeenth-century cultural developments—which were clearly borrowings from Venice that appeared on Cretan soil, producing a true hybrid, Cretan-Venetian culture, as it were—see A. Embiricos, *La Renaissance Crétoise*, 1–2, and references Also see J. Tulard, *Historie de la Crète* (Paris, 1962), pp. 95–109. There is a large modern Greek literature on this subject. Important poems (the *Erotokritos*) and plays imitating the Italian *commedia dell' arte* were produced. See e.g., A. Mirambel, *La littérature grecque moderne* (Paris, 1953), chap. 1, and esp. M. Manousakas, "La litterature crétoise à l'époque Vénitienne," *L'hellénisme contemporain* (1955), pp, 95–120.

Notes to Chapter 11

1. K. Setton, "Byzantine Background to the Italian Renaissance," in *Proceedings of the American Philosophical Society*, 100 (1956): 71.

2. See on this question, I. Origo, *The World of San Bernardino* (New York, 1962), pp. 202–04, which is rather inadequate. Also the recent Ph. D. dissertation of my student, J. Bernard, "San Bernardino of Siena: His Relation to the Humanist World of the Early Renaissance" (Yale University, 1972).

3. J. Gill, *The Council of Florence* (Cambridge, 1959), p. 51, only mentions him, as do a few specialists on Bernardino or on the Franciscan order: I. Origo, *World of San Bernardino*, p. 203; and J. Moorman, *A History of the Franciscan Order* (Oxford, 1968), p. 465.

4. On Bernardino there is a large literature. See n. 2 above (and bibliographies cited there); also A. Howell, *San Bernardino of Siena* (London, 1913), esp. pp. 188–89, and V. Facchinetti, *San Bernardino da Siena, mistico sole del secolo XV* (Milan, 1933).

5. See D. Geanakoplos, *Emperor Michael Palaeologus and the West* (Cambridge, 1959), p. 260; and M. Roncaglia, *Les Frères Mineurs el l'église grecque orthodoxe au XIIIe siècle* (Cairo, 1954), pp. 175–78. The article of L. De Simone, "S. Bonaventura al concilio di Lione II e l'union con i Greci," *Asprenas* 9 (1962): 418–28 is of little value. See also bibliography above, in chap. 8, n. 1.

6. See Roncaglia, *Les Freres Mineurs et l'eglise grecque*; also my article on the Lyons council, above, chap. 8, n. 1.

7. See Geanakoplos, *Emperor Michael Palaeologus*, pp. 264–79. Also in this book, Prologue, chap. 8, and Epilogue, on the Greek reaction to the question of union with Rome; and Geanakoplos, "Byzantium and the Later Crusades," chaps. 2 and 3, in *History of the Crusades*, vol. 3, ed. K. Setton (Madison, Wis., 1975).

8. See D. Geanakoplos, "The Council of Florence and the Problem of Union between the Greek and Latin Churches," in *Byzantine East and Latin West* (Oxford, 1966), pp. 84–111.

9. Recently edited by V. Laurent, "*Les 'Mémoires' de Sylvestre Syropoulos sur le concile de Florence*" (Paris, 1971). Cf. Geanakoplos, *Byzantine East and Latin*

West, p. 88, discussing the old translation of R. Creyghton, *Vera Historia unionis non verae inter Graecos et Latinos* (The Hague, 1660).

10. "Vita Sancti Bernardini Senensis, Ordinis Minorum ab ejus quodam contemporaneo, fideliter conscripta sed stylum Laur. Surius mutabit natus anno 1380 ob. 1444," in Surius, *Historiae seu Vitae sanctorum*, 5 (Turin, 1876): 618–59. Also see Lucas Waddingus, *Annales Minorum*, (Quarrachi, 1931–41): 11: 67.

11. "Tum suae [Bernardini] vitae exemplo, tum privatis colloquiis et publicis praedicationibus Graecis ad unionem alliciendo . . . . Mos ferventi spiritu, multa in Deum fiducia, ascendit suggestum graeceque concionatus est, de Catholica fide Graecos summo studio erudiens: ita ut mirarentur omnes dicerentque eum, non minus probe graece, quam si in Graecia natus esset; sed Deus movebat linguam ejus et loquebatur per eum" (quoted by Surius, in Waddingus, *Annales Minorum*, 11: 67). Waddingus adds that "[Bernardino] thereafter remained as ignorant [of that language] as he had been before."

12. See thesis of Bernard, p. 195, n. 71, citing evidence that a contemporary of San Bernardino, Timoteo Maffeo, in a work entitled "In sanctam religionem litteras impugnantem ad Nicolaum V Pontificem Maximum" (printed in L. Mehus, *Ambrorii Traversarii epistolae* [Florence, 1789], p. 384), asserts that Guarino had once been Bernardino's master of eloquence. Also a note, in the hand of Battista Guarino, son of the great Guarino, reads: "Among the many students, Bernardino, the preacher of God, has been overlooked. Of an advanced age and already long in the religious life, Bernardino was not ashamed to have Guarino of Verona as a teacher in the liberal arts." ["Omissus est inter plures alunnos dei (*sic*) praeco Bernardinus qui etate iam ac religione provectus non erubuit Verone Guarinum ipsum in optimis artibus habere praeceptorem."] In C. Valori, "La cultura profana di San Bernardino," *Bolletino di studi bernardiniani* 3 (1937): 32 n. 2.

13. C. Cenci, my good friend at the monastery of San Bonaventura at Grottaferrata in Italy, tells me he believes that Guarino's knowledge of Greek was very slim. Cf. also A. Howell, *S. Bernardino of Siena* (London, 1913), appendix 3: ". . . tending to show that he had some knowledge of Greek, but did not extend very far."

14. See in *Collectanea Anglo-Minoritica Or A Collection of the English Franciscans*, ed. A. Parkinson (London, 1726), pt. 1, p. 162, on "Brother John of England . . . a zealous Franciscan, who was sent a Missionary into Sclavonia, where he preached the Word of God in the Illyrick language by the Inspiration of the Holy Ghost, having no other knowledge of that tongue. . . . He wrought great conversions of that People too by a miraculous Operation of the Holy Ghost, who inspired either the Preacher with the Gift of Tongues, or the Hearers with the Gift of Understanding."

15. We cite only the well-known cases (of miracle-story transferring), as seen in Gregory the Great's *Dialogi* (on St. Benedict) and of Martin of Tours by Sulpicius Severus.

16. On Secundinus, see recently P. Mastrodimitri, *Nikolaos Sekoundinos* (Athens, 1970; in Greek); and on Bessarion, esp. H. Vast, *Le Cardinal Beassarion* (Paris,

1878). On Andreas of Rhodes, see R. Loenertz, "Les Dominicains byzantins Theodore et André Chrysobergès et les negociations pour l'union des églises," *Arch. Frat. Praed.* 9 (1939): 9 ff.

17. Valla's treatise is printed by G. Zippel, "Lorenzo Valla e le origini della storiografia umanistica a Venezia," *Rinascimento* 7 (1956): 99. Cf. also, recently, G. Holmes, *The Florentine Enlightenment* (New York, 1969), pp. 134, and esp. S. Camporeale, *Lorenzo Valla. Umanesimo e teologia* (Florence, 1972), pp. 245 ff.

18. On Bessarion, see Vast, *Cardinal Bessarion*, p. 154, and for Valla's quotation, see Setton, "Byzantine Background to the Italian Renaissance," p. 73; on Bernardino's canonization in 1450 under Nicholas V, see Vast, idem, pp. 161–62.

19. On Laonikos Chalcondyles' style, see W. Buchwald, A. Hohlweg, O. Prinz, eds., *Tusculum Lexikon Griechischer und Lateinischer Autoren des Altertums und des Mittelalters* (Munich, 1963), p. 97.

20. On Greek "sins," see my "Byzantium and the Later Crusades," in *History of the Crusades*, vol. 3, chaps. 2 and 3, esp. pp. 100 ff.; I. Sevčenko, "Decline of Byzantium . . . ," *Dumbarton Oaks Papers*, 15 (1961): 179. Also cf. the similar Russian Orthodox reaction, in G. Vernadsky, *A Source Book for Russian History* (New Haven, 1972), 1: 126.

21. *MPG*, vol. 159, col. 420: "kai naous anoikodomon ouk oliga ana ten Italian agalmata" (in Greek).

22. See below in this book, chap. 13, on Demetrius Chalcondyles.

23. Laonikos Chalcondyles (1423–90), *De origine ac rebus gestis Turcorum*, in *MPG*, vol. 149, cols. 419–20, esp.: "es ta prota anekon sofias kai theorias."

24. On Greek viws of the Latin clergy, see Syropoulos, *Mémoires*, passim; and cf. my book, *Byzantine East and Latin West*, p. 45. Also n. 27, below.

25. Vespasiano, *Renaissance Princes, Popes, and Prelates*, trans. W. George and E. Waters (New York, 1963), p. 164.

26. On Bernardino's views, which are well known, see esp. J. Moorman, *History of the Franciscan Order* (Oxford, 1968), esp. pp. 45—66 and bibliography, p. 603; also works cited above of Howell and Origo.

27. See above, n. 24; also E. Gibbon, *Decline and Fall of the Roman Empire*, chap. 54, p. 123; my article, "Edward Gibbon and Byzantine Ecclesiastical History," *Church History* 35(1966): 1–16; H. Grégoire, "The Byzantine Church," in *Byzantium: An Introduction to East Roman Civilizalion*, ed. N. Baynes and H. Moss (Oxford, 1961), pp. 86–135; and Y. Congar, *After Five Hundred Years* (New York, 1959), p. 27. who stresses Greek reproaches against Latin "taste for domination, power and unchecked proselytism."

28. See above, n. 11.

29. See, on the lingering partisans of Hesychasm after the death of its greatest protagonist, the fourteenth-century monk and bishop, Gregory Palamas, in D. Obolensky, *The Byzantine Commonwealth* (New York, 1972), p. 301–08. Also, J. Meyendorff, *St. Grégoire Palamas et la mystique Orthodoxe* (Paris, 1959) pp. 135–77. On Mark and Hesychasm, esp. see K. Mamonis, "Mark Eugenicus' Life and Work," *Theologia* 25 (1954): 377–404, 521–75 (in Greek); and on the works of Mark, see *Patrologia Orientalis* vols. 15 and 17 (Paris, 1927

and 1923); and S. Runciman, *Great Church in Captivity*, p. 125, who implies that Mark was a (Palamite) Hesychast.

30. The more extreme views of the Palamites (e.g. on the Light of Tabor being seen by corporeal eyes) were, in the late fourteenth and fifteenth centuries, played down by most Hesychasts. See H. G. Beck's chapter, "Intellectual Life in the Late Byzantine Church," *Handbook of Church History* (1970) 4: 504.

31. On Florence and Hesychasm, see the references of J. Gill, *Council of Florence*, pp. 206, 225, 267, and 396. On the emperor's prohibition, see S. Runciman, *Last Byzantine Renaissance* (Cambridge, 1970), p. 48. It seems that at Florence the Latins sought to bring up Hesychasm for debate but that the emperor forbade the Greek clergy to answer (Gill, *Council*, p. 206).

32. See, e.g., F. Murphy, entry under "Jesus prayer," in *New Catholic Encyclopedia*, 7: 971. Cf. Chap. 3, text and nn. 69a, 73, and 78; also chap. 4, text and n. 13a; also see L. Gillet, *Un moine de l'église de l'Orient. L'invocation du nom de Jesus* (Chevtogne).

33. See above, chap. 4, and Meyendorff, *A Study of Gregory Palamas*, pp. 141 ff. and esp. Palamas's *Triads*, ed. Meyendorff, *Défense des saints hésychastes*, 2 vols. (Louvain, 1950). For Western use of words from the Greek liturgy (esp. *Kyrie eleeson*—in effect, the Greek "Jesus Prayer"), see above p. 79 and this book's epigraph, quotation from Anonymous of Tours.

34. On Mark's intransigence in this respect, see Geanakoplos, *Byzantine East and Latin West*, p. 100, where all the sources are cited; and Gill, *Council of Florence*, p. 67.

35. See L. Mehus, *Ambrosii Traversarii Latinae epistolae* (Florence, 1759), 13: 20, 22. Cf. mention of Bernardino, his trigram and Bessarion, in L. Valla, Perosa ed., *Collatio Novi Testamenti* (Florence, 1970), p. xlix.

Notes to Chapter 12

1. See D. Geanakoplos, *Greek Scholars in Venice* (Cambridge, 1969), (reprinted as *Byzantium and the Renaissance* [Hamden, Conn., 1972]), pp. 162–63. This chapter was originally prepared as a paper for the Second International Congress for Southeast European Studies, held in Athens in 1970. Since then, M. Manousakas, who also participated in the congress, has published an interesting article, "La date de la mort de Marc Musurus," *Studi veneziani* 12 (1970): 459–63, which also deals with one of the several problems discussed here—the precise date of Musurus' death. (He makes use of an overlooked article of A. Ferrajoli, "Il ruolo della corte di Leone X: Prelati domestici della corte di Leone X," *Archivio della Società di Storia Patria*, 39 [1916]: 544–45.) For the different emphases of each, see our two articles.

2. Geanakoplos, *Greek Scholars*, pp. 158–59; M. Manousakas, "The Presentation by Janus Lascaris of the First Students of the Greek School of Rome to Pope X (1514)," *Eranistes* 1 (Athens, 1963; in Greek): esp. 171.

3. See below.

4. Paolo Giovio, *Elogia virorum literis illustrium* (Basle, 1577), p. 67; and Lilio Gyraldi, *Le iscrittioni . . . degli huomini famosi* (Florence, 1552), p. 63. Also see G. Valeriano, *De Litteratorum infelicitate* (Venice, 1620), p. 11. N. Papadopoli, *Historia gymnasii Patavini*, 1 (Venice, 1762): 294, repeats the story almost

verbatim. Cf. R. Menge, *De Marci Musuri Cretensis vita* (Jena, 1868), pp. 42–43; and my *Greek Scholars*, p. 163 and n. 175.

5. See D. Geanakoplos, "The Council of Florence and the Union of the Greek and Latin Churches," in *Byzantine East and Latin West*, p. 153, and my forthcoming book on Pope Alexander V.

6. G. Cammelli, *Manuele Crisolora* (Florence, 1941), pp. 145 ff.; L. Pastor, *History of the Popes* (London, 1891 ff.); W. Roscoe, *The Life and Pontificate of Leo X* (Liverpool, 1805 ff.).

7. Gyraldi, *Dialogi duo*, pp. 63–64. Cf. Geanakoplos, *Greek Scholars*, p. 163.

8. Archivio di Stato, Archivio Proprio, Rome, Envelope 4 (1516–28), fols. 71r-72v. I am greatly indebted for the transcription of the two documents I have used here to the kindness of the late scholar, K. Mertzios, Greek consul in Venice, who found the documents in the archives many years ago and sent me the transcriptions which I have used here.

9. Marino Sanuto, *I diarii di Marino Sanuto (1497–1533)*, ed. R. Fulin, etc. (Venice, 1879 ff.), vol. 25, col. 66.

10. "XXVI Octobris 1517 perchè la vostra serenità per una sua [lettera] mi commette che debba intendere quando il reverendissimo Mousuro è per venire a Venetia alla sua lettera li significo, come lui grandemente desiderava, ritornare a leggere, né delle cose di qui molto si sodisfaceva, ma l'è piacuto al Nostro Signore Iddio di chiamarlo a Se, e domenica a ore X morse." Cf. my *Greek Scholars*, p. 159.

11. On the complex chronology, see esp. Manousakas, "La date," p. 462, Cf. M. Del Piazzo, *Manuale di Cronologia* (Rome, 1969), p. 18; A. Cappelli, *Cronologia, cronografia e calendario perpetuo* (Milan, 1931; new ed. 1965).

12. Sanuto, *Diarii*, vol. 24, col. 669, dated Sept. 10, 1517.

13. Geanakoplos, *Greek Scholars*, pp. 160–61. But May 26 (not June 19, 1516, as commonly believed) is the correct date of his appointment to the see of Monemvasia, according to the document of appointment, now filed under "Bembo" in the Morgan Library of New York (as P. Winckler writes me).

14. Register 18, Senato Mar, a. 1516, July 16. Same place, different letter (text unclear): "Si ragona di far Cardinali et il gran partito vien posto alla santità del pontifice oltre la necessità del danaro nella quale si ritrova, credo sia causa di far'questa nuova elettione, si ragiona esser dieci, che vogliono spendere da 40 in 60 ducati per uno, e tra l'altri è nominato un filio di Dom Francesco da Ramada . . . Reverendo Archiepiscopo di Napoli. L'auditor della Camera il copis [?] et alteri sin da reverendissimo il numero delli 72 apostoliche [last phrases are unclear]. Ma certamente è cosa di poca dignità di questo ordine perchè etre [oltre?] il gran numero la necessità che fatisco li fanno perdere ogni estimazione. Ma l'invenzione è bella al Pontefice." (The document containing Minio's report is apparently not clear enough to be read with absolute accuracy at this point.) Note that Paolo Giovio, *Elogia* p. 67; Gyraldi, *Le iscrittioni*, p. 63 (cf. Geanakoplos, *Greek Scholars*, p. 163), says that Leo, in one day, raised thirty men of different nations to the cardinalate.

15. A possible implication, to judge from the document.

16. On this, see Geanakoplos, *Greek Scholars*, p. 163, n. 175.

17. Geanakoplos, *Greek Scholars,* p. 169. Pio is referred to at that time as ambassador of the king of France; but he moved from French to German to other service. See under Pio, *Enciclopedia Italiana,* and P. Litta, *Famiglie nobili italiane* (Milan, 1819 ff.), 2 : 18.

18. See text above in n. 14.

19. *Diarii,* vol. 24, col. 669, and my *Greek Scholars,* p. 162.

19a. See letter of Bombasio to Erasmus, 6 December 1517, in Erasmus's *Opera Omnia* (Leiden, 1703) vol. 2, col. 274 (cf. E. Rodocanachi, Le *Premiere Renaissance au temps de Jules II et de Léon X* [Paris, 1912], p. 165).

20. Register 18, Senato Mar, a. 1516, July 16.

21. Manousakas, "La date de la morte," p. 462, concludes that his death occurred between October 24 and 25, basing his judgment primarily on Ferrajoli, "Il ruolo della corte," pp. 544–45, which had been overlooked.

22. See R. De Roover, *The Rise and Decline of the Medici Bank* (Cambridge, 1963), esp. chap. 14, on the decline of the bank. Much of the Medici income came from their handling of ecclesiastical revenues.

23. Archivio di Stato, Archivio Proprio, Rome, Envelope 4 (1516–28).

24. See below, n. 26.

25. On Pio, see Geanakoplos, pp. 125–26 and 169. Did the Portuguese king call himself "emperor" in the (Spanish) Leonese style of old? Cf. next note.

26. The passage from the document (see n. 23) reads: "Sono state all'ossequie oltre il gran numero di episcopi l'oratore dell'imperatore Portugallo, et ancora io i saluti per nome del reverendissimo cardinal di Medici del qual lui era familiare. Ha lassato suoi commissarii il signor Alberto da Carpi, e domino Zuan Lascari." For passage, see also Manousakas, "La date," pp. 462–63.

27. Archivio Proprio, Rome, Envelope 4, 26 October 1517. This document also gives conclusive proof (cf. Geanakoplos, *Greek Scholars,* p. 160 n., and also Manousakas, "La date de la mort," p. 122–23) that the Greek Manilius Rhalles was at this time promised that, at the next consistory, the bishopric of Monemvasia (in southern Greece), held previously by Musurus, would be conferred on him: "L'episcopato è stato promesso a D. Manilio Rali secretario del detto Reverendissimo Medici [the future Clement VII] e nel primo consistorio li sarà conferito ditto episcopato."

Notes to Chapter 13

1. On the importance of Greek learning in the Renaissance, one may best cite the views of the Western Renaissance humanists themselves: Petrarch, Salutati, Bruni, Guarino, Vergerio, Valla, Erasmus (see below, nn. 49, 51, 53; also this book, passim). See now E. Garin, *Portraits from the Quattrocento* (New York, 1973), pp. 69–85. Also P. Kristeller, *Renaissance Concepts of Man* (New York, 1972), pt. 2; Geanakoplos, *Byzantium and the Renaissance,* passim; and M. Gilmore, *The World of Humanism* (New York, 1952), pp. 190 ff.

2. On Chalcondyles' life, see G. Cammelli, *Demetrio Calcondila* (Florence, 1954), a pioneering work now rather dated and with very little on the Paduan tenure of his teaching. The older biography (in Greek) of D. Kampourouglou,

Hoi Chalkokondylai (Athens, 1926) is very outdated; see also A. Badini Confalonieri and F. Gabotto, eds., "Notizie biografiche di Demetrio Calcondila," *Giornale ligustico* (1892), pp. 241 ff. Also, sketch in E. Legrand, *Bibliographie hellénique*, 1 (Paris, 1885): XCIV-CI and, on Chalcondyles' teaching in Venice, W. Heiberg, *Beiträge zur Geschichte Georg Vallas und seiner Bibliothek* (Leipzig, 1896).

3. For these details, see esp. Cammelli, *Demetrio Calcondila*, pp. 4–19, and Kampourouglou, *Hoi Chalkokondylai*, pp. 179–80.

4. On Bessarion and his circle, see above, chaps. 9 and 10. Cammelli, p. 11; Geanakoplos, *Byzantium and the Renaissance*, passim; and Holmes, *The Florentine Enlightenment* (London, 1969), pp. 255–60. Also L. Mohler, "Aus Bessarions Gelehrtenkreis . . . ," *Quellen und Forschungen aus dem Gebiete der Geschichte*, vol. 24 (Paderborn, 1942).

5. On Gaza, see Cammelli, pp. 18–20.

6. On this conflict, see Geanakoplos, *Byzantium and the Renaissance*, pp. 86–87; Cammelli, p. 22; Holmes, *Florentine Enlightenment*, pp. 257–60; and esp. F. Masai, *Pléthon et le Platonisme de Mistra* (Paris, 1956), passim.

7. On these events, see Cammelli, pp. 30–38. On Schedel, see esp. R. Stauber, *Die Schedelsche Bibliothek* (Freburg i.B., 1908).

8. Legrand, *Bibliographic hellénique*, 1: xcv.

9. Cammelli, esp. pp. 39 ff.

10. Ibid., pp. 46–47.

11. Ibid., pp. 54–55. Cf. E. Motta, "Demetrio Calcondila editore," *Archivio Storico Lombardo* 20 (1893): 144.

12. Cammelli, *Demetrio Calcondila*, p. 57.

13. A. Della Torre, *Storia dell'Accademia Platonica di Firenze* (Florence, 1902), p. 562.

14. Cammelli, pp. 59–60. On the teaching of Plato in Florence by Argyropoulos, whom Garin considers the most influential Greek humanist in Italy, see his *Portraits from the Quattrocento* (New York, 1973), pp. 69–81; and J. Seigel, "The Teaching of Argyropoulos and the Rhetoric of the First Humanists," *Action and Conviction in Early Modern Europe*, ed. T. Rabb and J. Seigel (Princeton, 1969), pp. 237 ff. And now D. Geanakoplos, "The Italian Renaissance and Byzantium: The Career of the Greek Humanist-Professor John Argyropoulos in Florence and Rome (1415–87)," in *Conspectus of History*, vol. 1, no. 1 (1974), *Focus on Biography*, eds. D. Hoover-J. Koumoulides (Muncie, Ind., 1975), pp. 12–28.

15. Cammelli, pp. 64–69: "ad legendum lecturam philosophiae moralis . . . et ad aliam lecturam in greco sermone et docendum grecas auctores."

16. For his pupils, see Cammelli, pp. 70–83.

17. Ibid., p. 84.

18. Ibid., pp. 84–87. Paolo Giovio's "evil tongue" attacked everyone (see above, chap. 12, against Musurus). Actually, Poliziano boasted that his knowledge of Greek surpassed that of any Greek refugee (certainly he was the equal of most, but not all, of them).

19. See Geanakoplos, *Byzantium and the Renaissance*, pp. 57–58.

20. See E. Ferrai, *L'Ellenismo nello studio di Padova* (Padua, 1876), p. 29, n. 17.

21. Cammelli, pp. 91–92. For text of prefaces, see Legrand, *Bibl. hell.*, 1: 1–9.
22. Cammelli, p. 92; and E. Ferrai, *L'Ellenismo*, p. 30.
23. Cammelli, pp. 94 ff.
24. On Greeks at Milan, see N. Tomadakes, "I Greci a Milano: Nota," *Istituto Lombardo (Rendiconti, Classe di Lettere)* 101 (1967): 568–80.
25. On Constantine Lascaris, see esp. A. de Rosalia, "La Vita di Costantino Lascaris," *Archivio Storico Siciliano* 3 (1957–58): 21–70; cf. Cammelli, pp. 103–04.
26. Cammelli, p. 109.
27. On the secretary's letter, see A. da Badini Confalonieri and F. Gabotto, eds., "Notizie biografiche di Demetrio Calcondila," *Giornale Ligustico* 19 (1892): 321–22.
28. On his pupils in Milan, see Cammelli, pp. 117–19, and bibliography; also G. Trissino, *Tutte le opere* (Verona, 1729), 2: 269–70; Badini-Gabotto, "Notizie biografiche," pp. 323–26 (on Aldus).
29. On his publications, see Cammelli, pp. 122–27; Legrand, *Bibliographic hellénique*, 1: 16–17, 63; and Motta, "Demetrio Calcondila editore," pp. 163–65.
30. M. Sanuto, *Diarii*, ed. R. Fulin, etc. (Venice, 1880), vol. 3, cols. 90–91 and 353.
31. Cammelli, pp. 128–30; cf. Legrand, 1: 198.
32. The speech, uncatalogued, is in the Munich Staatsbibliothek: Codex Latinus Monacensis, 28. 128. I am indebted to P. Kristeller for pointing out this manuscript to me and helping to transcribe the more difficult passages. While this book was in press, a few small sections of the Latin text of this MS were published in my article, "The Discourse of Demetrius Chalcondyles on the Inauguration of Greek Studies at the University of Padua in 1463," in *Studies in the Renaissance* 21 (1974): 18–44. Essentially, therefore, the first publication of this MS is here in this book.
33. Cammelli, p. 28.
34. See Appendix above containing Latin text, MS fol. 2v.
35. On Besarion's library, see above, chap. 9.
36. On the custom, see P. Kristeller, *Renaissance Philosophy of Man* (Chicago, 1948), p. 198.
37. On Hartmann Schedel, see esp. R. Stauber, *Die Schedelsche Bibliothek* (Freiburg im B., 1908) and W. Wattenbach, "Hartmann Schedel als Humanist," *Forschungen zur deutschen Geschichte* 11 (1871): 351–74; also *Biographie Universelle*, 38: 256 ff.
38. Ficino began his translation of Plato in 1463, completed it ca. 1470 (M. Gilmore, *World of Humanism*, p. 191, says he finished it in 1468), and printed it in 1484. See P. Kristeller, *Supplementum Ficinianum*, 2 (Florence, 1937): 105, for this preface. According to Legrand, *Bibliographie hellénique* 1: CI, Ficino's preface appears in the Venice edition of 1491.
39. See text, fol. lv.
40. For Ficino's own words, see Legrand, *Bibliographie hellénique*, p. CI. Legrand (p. C) says that a portrait of Boerner shows Ficino, Christoforo Landino, Poliziano, and Chalcondyles conversing amicably in the countryside, probably at the Platonic Academy at Careggi. See Frontispiece.

41. See Ferrai, *L'Ellenismo nello studio di Padova*, p. 39, n. 16: "apud Bernardum Bembum . . . Antonio Chronico veneto ac Demetrio Attico."

42. On the knowledge of Hesiod in the West, R. Bolgar, *Classical Heritage and its Beneficiaries* (Cambridge, 1958), p. 279, says that though Hesiod was scarcely known in the first part of the fifteenth century, he was represented in Giorgio Valla's library (1493) by two copies of the *Works and Days*. And earlier, in the fourteenth century, we know that Greek monks of southern Italy were copying from Greek poets, especially Homer and Hesiod. On the first edition of the *Works and Days*, see Sandys, *History of Classical Scholarship*, vol. 2, p. 104. Niccolò de Valle first translated into Latin and published Hesiod. See Geanakoplos, *Byzantium and the Renaissance*, p. 264, for mention of Musurus' scholia on Hesiod, loaned to Erasmus in Venice. Sandys (*Hist. Class. Schol.* 2: 84), says that Poliziano, after 1482, composed a Latin poem on Hesiod.

43. None of the manuscripts of Ficino's translation of Plato contains this "Preface to the Reader" quoted by Schedel in this manuscript. It was taken, then, probably from the first printed edition of 1484. Therefore, unless the preface was added later by Schedel, the MS itself was probably copied *after* publication of Plato in 1484.

44. See above, text for nn. 13–14. Also see most recently J. Seigel, "The Teaching of Argyropoulos and the Rhetoric of the First Humanists," *Action and Conviction in Early Europe*, pp. 237 ff., and also G. Holmes, *Florentine Enlightenment*, esp. pp. 242 ff., and 262 ff. Now also, E. Garin, *Portraits from the Quattrocento*, pp. 70 ff. On the *Erotemata* (there were several written), see A. Pertusi, "Erotemata," *Italia medievalia e umanistica* 5 (1962): 324, and Geanakoplos, *Byzantium and the Renaissance*, pp. 219–20.

45. See MS fol. 2r.

46. Cf. Conrad Celtis's similar remark in his oration (as quoted in L. Spitz, *Northern Renaissance*, p. 25) that Cato studied Greek in his eighties in order to learn to speak Latin better.

47. R. Sabbadini, *Giovanni da Ravenna, Insigne figure d'umanista* (Como, 1914), p. 103, and cf. p. 220.

48. On Dominici, see Holmes, *Florentine Enlightenment*, pp. 32–35.

49. Geanakoplos, *Greek Scholars*, p. 39; V. Rossi, *Il Quattrocento* (Milan, 1938), p. 92. As late as ca. 1531, Pietro Bembo gave a speech before the Venetian senate extolling but also defending the Venetian study of Greek letters (Geanakoplos, idem, p. 279, n. 1).

50. Notice here how the Byzantine orders these subjects. Cf. below, n. 73.

51. See Erasmus's famous dictum, "Latin erudition, however ample, is crippled without Greek" (see Geanakoplos, *Greek Scholars*, p. 258). And see Guarino, in Woodward, *Vittorino da Feltre and Other Humanist Educators* (New York, 1963), p. 166, and Vergerius, idem, p. 106. Cf. also Guarino's statement (p. 166) that "I am well aware that those ignorant of Greek decry its necessity for reasons which are sufficiently evident."

52. Text fol. 4r.

53. This reminds one of Erasmus's remark: "We have in Latin at best small brooks and turbid pools, while the Greeks have the purest fountains and rivers running with gold" (Geanakoplos, *Greek Scholars*, p. 258).

54. Text, fols. 4r and 4v. One wonders what influence, if any, the seven categories of the most studied Byzantine rhetorician, Hermogenes, may have had on this listing of qualities. See G. Kustas, "Function and Evolution of Byzantine Rhetoric," *Viator, Medieval and Renaissance Studies* 1 (London, 1970): 64. Also on Hermogenes and his chief commentator, Aphthonius, see L Reynolds and N. Wilson, *Scribes and Scholars* (Oxford, 1968), p. 68.

55. MS fol. 4v.

56. Horace, *Ars Poetica* 11. 323–24.

57. Yet Legrand, *Bibliographie hellénique*, 1 : xcv, quotes a source saying that Chalcondyles was versed in Latin and Greek: "qui quanta sit et graecarum et latinarum litterarum eruditione refertus." But this was probably later.

58. According to Kustas, "Byzantine Rhetoric," pp. 64–65, prose was much more valued in Byzantine rhetoric because it was the proper medium of education.

59. In contrast, of all the Latins apparently only Guarino, Aurispa, and esp. Filelfo, ever learned both to read and *speak* Greek well. Cf. above, Prologue.

60. See Holmes, *Florentine Enlightenment*, pp. 113, 115 ff., cf. 262 ff. Argyropoulos criticized Bruni's translations of Aristotle as being too free and overly stressing eloquence. Recall also the Scholastic bishop of Burgos's criticism of Bruni's translations (Seigel, "Teaching of Argyropoulos, p. 246).

61. In L. Zdekauer, *Lo studio di Siena nel rinascimento* (Milan, 1894), there is mention of a chair of astrology at the Siena studium, meaning astronomy.

62. One might well compare the similar remarks on the difficulty of learning Greek made by Argyropoulos in 1456 to students at the Florentine studium.

63. See MS fol. 5v. The Greek original from Hesiod, *Works and Days* (Loeb ed., p. 289) is doubtless the following line: Τῆς δ'ἀρετῆς ἱδρῶτα θεοὶ προπάροιθεν ἔθηκαν ἀθάνατοι.

64. See MS fol. 6r.

65. Is Chalcondyles obliquely suggesting this by his words, "this lectureship is instituted at this famous university for its honor, enlargement, and its *utility*?"

66. See MS fols. 6v-7r.

67. See R. Lopez, "Il principio della guerra veneto-turco nel 1463," *Archivio Veneto*, ser. 5, 15 (1934): 45–131.

68. The "Anno domini MCCCCLXXIIII" should read 1463, as indicated in margin.

69. Note the use of the words *hystoriis* (fol. 4v) in the first oration and *hystoriarum* (fol. 9r) in the second oration.

70. The main episodes were the instruction of Chrysoloras at Florence, Guarino at Ferrara, Argyropoulos at Florence, Chalcondyles at Padua and Florence, and Musurus at Padua.

71. Possibly in 1484, because not until then was the preface of Ficino to Plato's *Dialogues* published, which preface Schedel mentions at the beginning of this document. The Latin text finishes with Schedel's statement: "Finiunt foeliciter Orations viri clarissimi Greci preceptoris mei in studio paduano ac principio sue lecture lepidissime recitate. Scripsi ego Hartmannus Schedel de Nuremberga artium ac medicine doctor Patavinus, in primordio studii de manu prefati Greci dum initia litterarum grecarum edocuit." Stauber,

Schedelschen Bibliothek, p. 49, believes Schedel could only have copied the speeches of Chalcondyles later, since he was not a Paduan doctor in 1463 or 1464. (The text of the speeches is attached to a printed book in Schedel's library.)

72. Other appeals of Bessarion (to Venice, France, and elsewhere) are well known (Vast, *Le Cardinal Bessarion*). This is the only reference to Dante (who wrote here in vernacular Italian) that I have been able to find in a Byzantine writer.

73. The eleventh-century Byzantine, Psellus, said one should study a combination of rhetoric and philosophy and then political action (Kustas, "Byzantine Rhetoric," p. 72). On the stages of Byzantine education and subjects studied, especially in the last century, see L. Bréhier, *Les Institutions Byzantines* (Paris, 1949), pp. 467–85. Baynes and Moss, *Byzantium* (Oxford, 1948), p. 205, say (correctly) that neither the names nor the sequences of different branches of Byzantine education are very clear to us. School and university subjects seem to overlap. See now E. Garin, quoting from Argyropoulos on the phases of (presumably) Byzantine study: from grammar to rhetoric to philosophy. It is noteworthy that Argyropoulos (whom Garin, *Portraits from the Quattrocento*, p. 78 ff., calls the most influential of all the Greek exile-humanists) had also studied at Padua University (p. 71) and therefore knew Western Scholasticism as well as Byzantine learning.

74. On history, see below, MS fols. 3v and 9r. The famous Latin phrase on history reverts back to Petrarch and is also found in Salutati and Vergerio (M. Gilmore, *Humanists and Jurists*, pp. 18–20). Cf. the ninth-century Byzantine Photius, who said, "History teaches events done in our midst that we can learn about now" (Kustas, "Byzantine Rhetoric," p. 71).

74. He is called "philosophus" in the document of appointment (now lost). See J. Facciolatti, *Fasti Gymnasii Patavini* (Padua, 1757), 1: 54.

76. See Baynes and Moss, *Byzantium: An Introduction*, p. 489. Also now, cf. E. Garin, *Portraits from the Quattrocento*, pp. 79 and 83.

77. See discussion of Hermogenes in Kustas, "Byzantine Rhetoric," p. 65. Hermogenes stresses clarity, loftiness, sincerity, beauty, conciseness, and above all, force (*deinotes*). Hermogenes' MSS were known in the West after 1425 and 1427, when Filelfo sent a list of MSS, including Hermogenes', to Florence (see A. Traversari, *Epistolae*, 24: 32). But strangely enough, the Florentine Platonic Academy was not affected by Hermogenes: see A. Patterson, *Hermogenes and the Renaissance* (Princeton, 1970), p. 8.

78. See on these figures, especially the excellent works of A. Turyn: (1) *The Manuscript Tradition of the Tragedies of Euripides*; (2) . . . *of Aeschylus*; and (3) . . . *of Sophocles*, passim. Also see, for some helpful material, works of G. Zuntz, *An Inquiry into the Transmission of the Plays of Euripides* (Cambridge, 1965); H. Hunger, etc., *Geschichte der mittelalterlichen Literatur*, vol. 1 (Zurich, 1961); Reynolds-Wilson, *Scribes and Scholars*, pp. 65–68; R. Browning, "Byzantine Scholarship," *Past and Present* (1964), pp. 320-21; Geanakoplos, *Byzantium and the Renaissance*, passim.

79. Ferrai, *L'Ellenismo*, p. 30, n. 18, and p. 31. Kustas, p. 56, n. 3. states, "The study of Byzantine rhetoric is still in its infancy."

80. For encomnia of cities, see W. Hammer, *Latin and German Encomia of Cities* (Chicago, 1937); E. Fenster, *Laudes Constantinopolitanae* (Munich, 1968); New *Cambridge Medieval History*, vol. 4, pt. 2, (1967) chap. 27.

81. See text fol. 9r. One might profitably compare this oration to the inaugural oration given in Florence in 1456 by Argyropoulos (see Seigel, "Teaching of Argyroproulos," pp. 257 ff.) Also, several more orations by Greek humanists are published in K. Müllner, *Reden und Briefe italienischer Humanisten* (Vienna, 1899).

Notes to Chapter 14

1. The few works even touching on the recovery and publication of the Greek Fathers in the Renaissance include E. Legrand, *Bibliographie hellénique ou description raisonnée des ouvrages publiés en grec par des grecs au XVe et XVIe siècles*, 4 vols. (Paris, 1885-1906) and his *Bibliographie hispano-grecque* (New York, 1915–17); P. Meyer, *Die theologische Literatur der griechischen Kirche im sechszehnnten Jahrhundert* (Leipzig, 1899); R. Sabbadini, *Le scoperte dei codici latini e greci nei secoli XIV e XV*, 2 vols. (Florence, 1905–14; reprinted 1967); J. Sandys, *A History of Classical Scholarship*, 3 vols. (Cambridge, 1903–08; reprinted 1958). I am greatly indebted to my former student and assistant (now professor) John Erickson for generously permitting me to use some ideas and bibliography from his unpublished paper, "The Greek Fathers in the Renaissance: Printed Editions of the Greek Fathers to 1575," written in 1968 for my seminar at Yale.

2. On medieval knowledge of Greek Christian literature, see esp. A. Siegmund, *Die Uberlieferung der griechischen cristlichen Literatur in der lateinischen Kirche bis zum zwölften Jahrhundert* (Munich, 1949).

3. On John of Damascus, see above, chap. 3, and on Pseudo-Dionysius, above, chap. 6.

4. On this episode, see G. Holmes, *The Florentine Enlightenment* (New York, 1969), pp. 115–17. It must be noted that the bishop preferred the literal translation, in part at least because he was vitally interested in theological terminology, which required a verbatim approach.

5. See E. Wind, "The Revival of Origen," in D. Miner, ed., *Studies in Art and Literature for Belle da Costa Greene* (Princeton, 1954), pp. 412–24. D. Walker, "Origène en France au début du XVIe siècle," *Courants religieux et humanisme à la fin du XVe et au début du XVIe siècle* (Paris, 1959).

6. For the finding of the *Praeparatio evangelica*, see preface of George of Trebizond, in Legrand, *Bibliographie hellénique*, 3: 8–9: "in Urbe forte reperta est"

7. On Traversari, see A. Dini-Traversari, *Ambrogio Traversari e il suo tempo* (Florence, 1912); and for his correspondence, L. Mehus, *Ambrosii Traversarii latinae epistolae* (Florence, 1959). (Prof. Charles Stinger is preparing an entire monograph on Traversari and Greek Patristics, a section of which he kindly let me see.) On chronology of letters, see F. Luiso, *Riordinamento dell'epistolario di A. Traversari*, 3 vols. (Florence, 1898–1903). Traversari translated into Latin more than twenty Greek Patristic works. Of Traversari's favorite, Chrysostom, he possessed some 17 to 18 manuscripts: see B. Ullman and P. Stadter, *The Public Library of the Renaissance: Niccolò Niccoli, Cosimo de' Medici*

and the Library of San Marco (Padua, 1972), p. 25. For Traversari's reference to his Greek, see L. Bertalot, "Zwölf Briefe des A. Traversari," *Römische Quartalschrift* 29 (1915): 101–02. Cf. Holmes, *Florentine Enlightenment*, p. 56.

8. On Scaranus, see esp. Mehus, *Ambrosii Traversarii*, p. 365; and G. and A. Mittarelli, *Annales Camaldulenses* (1755), 6: 270; cf. G. Cammelli, *Manuele Crisolora* (Florence, 1941), pp. 66, 143.

9. On libraries used by Traversari, see R. Blum, *La Biblioteca della Badia Fiorentina . . .* , in *Studi e Testi* (Vatican, 1951); Cammelli, *Manuele Crisolora*, p. 185; and Holmes, *Florentine Enlightenment*, p. 92.

10. See Mehus, *Ambrosii Traversarii*, esp. 8: 46.

11. See Cammelli, *Manuele Crisolora*, pp. 66–67.

12. On Calecas, see Dini-Traversari, *Ambrogio Traversari*, p. 124, and J. Gill, *The Council of Florence* (Cambridge, 1959), p. 164.

13. See L. Hain, *Repertorium bibliographicum in que libri omnes ab arte typographica inventa* (Stuttgart, 1826–38), 4 vols. Also Holmes, pp. 96–99, 122–24; and Cammelli.

14. Gill, pp. 141, 169, etc.

15. On Bruni, see now Holmes, passim, with bibliography.

16. See esp. W. Jaeger, *Early Christianity and Greek Paideia* (Cambridge, 1961).

17. Since most early editions were undated, it is often difficult to know exactly when Greek Patristic works were first printed, but this seems to have been the first. See *Gesamtkatalog der Wiegen drücke*, vol. 3 (Leipzig, 1928), no. 3700.

18. Gathered from *Gesamtkatalog*, vol. 3, nos. 3700–18; Sabbadini, *Scoperte*; V. Scholderer, *Catalogue of Books Printed in the Fifteenth Century now in the British Museum* (London, 1908–49); B. Botfield, *Praefationes et epistolae editionibus principibus auctorum veterum praepositae* (Cambridge, 1861); and J. Graesse, *Trésor de livres rares et précieux* (Dresden, 1859–69; cf. Erickson, "Greek Fathers," p. 11. In 1499 in Spain, the humanist Rodrigo de Santaella published a letter of St. Basil in his *Vocabularium ecclesiasticum* (see M. Bataillon, *Erasmo y España* [Mexico City, 1950], 1: 56–57).

19. For Spain, see Legrand, *Bibliographie hispano-grecque*. In 1519 Hernan Nuñez prepared an interlinear edition of Basil's *Discourse to the Youth* for his students; (Legrand, idem, p. 43), and in 1524 Francesco de Vergara at Alcalà University made a translation and edition of a theological treatise of the Greek Father, Gregory of Nyssa, who was largely bypassed by the Renaissance Christian humanists, especially of France, in part, perhaps, because of his confusion with Nemesios of Emessa(E. Rice, "The Humanist Idea of Christian Antiquity: Lefevre d'Etaples and his Circle," in W. Gundersheimer, *French Humanism* (New York, 1969), pp. 179–80).

20. On Corvinus, see *Mathias Corvinus König von Ungarn, 1458-90*, ed. W. Fraknól (Freiburg i. B., 1891).

21. For Bruni's preface, see *Gesamtkatalog*, vol. 3, no. 3711. Also Basil, *De legendis libris gentilium* (Leipzig: Kachelefen, ca. 1490–94). Cf. Erickson, "Greek Fathers," p. 12.

22. On the discovery of Eusebius and his *Praeparatio Evangelica*, see George of Trebizond's preface (Venice, 1470, printed by Nicholas Jenson).

23. Preface reprinted in Legrand, *Bibliographie hellénique* 3: 8–9; also 10.

24. Erickson cites an edition published at Treviso in 1480, from Hain, *Repertorium bibliographicum*, p. 6702.

25. V. Rossi, *Il Quattrocento* (Milan, 1897), pp. 68–69.

26. On all this, see esp. Wind, "Revival of Origen," and Holmes, *Florentine Enlightenment*, p. 97.

27. See Hain, p. 7947 for dedication to doge and pope. On recovery of the *Contra Celsum*, see Legrand, *Bibliographic hellénique*, 3: 51–52.

28. See Wind, pp. 414–15. Letter of Persona in *Origenis contra Celsum Libri Octo* (Rome, 1481), p. 20.

29. See Camporeale, *Lorenzo Valla: Umanesimo e teologia* (Florence, 1972), pp. 234–76.

30. A. Perosa, *Collatio Novi Testamenti*, Valla ed. (Florence, 1970).

31. He preferred the style of Traversari to that of Ficino.

32. For Lefèvre, see esp. A. Renaudet, *Preréforme et humanisme à Paris pendant les premières guerres d'Italie* (Paris, 1916), and C. Graf, *Essai sur la vie et les écrits de J. Lefèvre d'Etaples* (Geneva, 1970). (cf. Erickson, "Greek Fathers," p. 16). On the *Theologia Vivificans*, see edition of J. Higman and W. Hopyl (Paris, 1498–99). For background, see also E. Rice, *The Prefatory Epistles of Jacques Lefèvre d'Etaples and Related Texts* (New York, 1972), and for Greek learning, his "The Humanist Idea of Christian Antiquity: Lefèvre d'Etaples and his Circle," 163–80 (see n. 19, above).

33. See Marsilio Ficino, *Opera Omnia* (Basel, 1576), vol. 2, pt. 2, p. 1013.

34. See above, my chap. 6, on Maximos' influence. Also cf. E. Rice, "Lefèvre d'Etaples and his Circle," p. 179; and in same volume, L. Stevens, "A Re-evaluation of Hellenism in the French Renaissance," p. 189.

35. L. Spitz, *The Religious Renaissance of the German Humanists* (Cambridge, Mass., 1963), p. 214, says Erasmus placed the Latin Fathers below the Greek in exegetical skill—a talent much admired by Erasmus. See also Spitz, p. 235, for the phrase "philosophy of Christ".

36. Valla, *Annotationes in Novum Testamentum* (Paris, 1505), published by Badius. Now cf. Perosa, *Collatio Novi Testamenti* (Florence, 1970).

37. On Erasmus and the Greek Fathers little has been done, but see esp. R. Peters, "Erasmus and the Fathers: Their Practical Value," *Church History* 36 (1967): 254–61; R. Pfeiffer, "Erasmus und die Einheit der klassischen und der cristlichen Renaissance," *Historisches Jarhbuch* 74 (1954): 175–88; and C. Heckethorn, *The Printers of Basel in the 15th and 16th Centuries* (London, 1897). Important is H. S. and P. S. Allen, *Opus Epistolarum* (Oxford, 1906–47). Erasmus prepared editions of thirteen fathers; the Greek included primarily Irenaeus, Chrysostom, Athanasius, Basil, and Origen, his last work. The other most important humanist editors of Greek Fathers were Agricola and Pirckheimer in Germany. Erasmus ed. *in Greek* Chrysostom, and Basil, *ed. pr.*

38. Quoted in Peters, "Erasmus and the Fathers," p. 254, who refers to Erasmus's *De Ratione concionande*, *Opera Omnia* (Leiden, 1703–06), 5: 857.

39. L. Spitz, *The Religious Renaissance of the German Humanists*, p. 325.

40. See Erasmus's letter to John Eck (May 15, 1518) in Allen, *Opus Epistolarum*, 3:337 (cited in Wind, "Revival of Origen," p. 422).

41. See R. Bainton, *Erasmus of Christendom* (New York, 1969), p. 193.

42. For these editions, see handbooks listed above (n. 18), esp. Graesse, *Trésor de livres rares*.
43. Gennadius was much attracted to Thomas Aquinas. See A. Papadakes, "Gennadius II and Mehmet the Conqueror," *Byzantion* (1972), pp. 89–90.
44. See Holmes, *Florentine Enlightenment*, pp. 96–99, 122–24.
45. Erickson rightly stresses this point.
46. See *New Catholic Encyclopedia*, under "Doctor of the Church."
47. This was the first Greek Patristic publication to appear *entirely* in Greek, but consisted of some letters of St. Basil (see my *Byzantium and the Renaissance*, p. 122). The practice of printing the original Greek text did not become general until the 1550s.
48. See chap. 9 above, text and n. 1.
49. Liturgical works were needed by Orthodox Greeks in the West for purposes of worship. Venice was the primary (and almost exclusive) center for liturgical Greek publication for centuries. See now N. Tomadakes, "The Publications in Italy of Greek Ecclesiastical Works (primarily liturgical)," *Ep. Het. Byz. Spoudon* (in Greek 1969–70), pp. 3–22, which deals with publication only by Greeks. Cf. also Geanakoplos, *Byzantium and the Renaissance*, pp. 247–49, on Ducas' printing of the liturgies of Basil and Chrysostom, and pp. 212, 219, on Calliergis' *Octoechos*. Cf. above, p. 272, on Trebizond's Eusebius.

Notes to Epilogue

1. E. Gilson, *History of Christian Philosophy in the Middle Ages* (New York, 1955), p. 541, implies that a basic reason for the onset of the Western Dark Ages, culturally, was the loss of contact with, and stimulation afforded by, ancient Greek philosophy; conversely, the progressive rediscovery of Greek philosophy was of paramount importance for the revival of medieval Western philosophical thought.
2. Some sociologists and anthropologists have termed the historical unfolding of events, chronologically, the *horizontal* approach, and the modes of acculturation, the *vertical* approach.
3. Cf. J. Pelikan, *The Spirit of Eastern Christendom* (Chicago, 1974), p. 241.
4. D. Jacoby, "The Encounter of Two Societies, Western Conquerors and Byzantines in the Peloponnesus after the Fourth Crusade," *American Historical Review* (1973), pp. 891 f. Cf. on such marriages, D. Nicol, "Mixed Marriages in Byzantium in the 13th Century," *Studies in Church History* 1 (1964): 160–74.
5. This was particularly true in the later, Palaeologan period: see esp. on the Arsenite monks and the Zealots, intransigent opponents of religious union, V. Laurent, "Les grandes crises religieuses à Byzanz. La fin du schisme Arsénite," *Acad. Roumaine, Bull. sect. hist.*, 26 (1945): 1 ff., where the monks are shown to have wandered from place to place arousing the common people against the Latin union.
6. Such scholars as Guarino, Filelfo, Aurispa, and Tortelli, in the fifteenth century went to Constantinople itself either to study or search for MSS. See esp. the basic work of R. Sabbadini, *Le Scoperte dei codici latini e greci nei secoli XIVe-XVe*, 2 vols. (Florence, 1905–14).

7. For Petrarch, see above, chap. 2; Pius II, *Opera Omnia* (Basle, 1571), p.712.

8. See above, chap. 4. N. Wilson, in "The Church and Classical Studies in Byzantium," *Antike und Abendland* 16 (1970): 76, argues plausibly that the church usually fostered classical learning. (He deals with earlier centuries.) The Hesychasts, from the fourteenth century on, were generally hostile to ancient philosophic learning: see J. Meyendorff, "Society and Culture in the Fourteenth Century," *Actes du XIVe Congrès International des études byzantines* (1974), p. 114.

9. C. Cahen, *Pre-Ottoman Turkey* (New York, 1968), p. 326; and cf. S. Vryonis, *The Decline of Medieval Hellenism in Asia Minor and the Process of Islamization* (Berkeley, 1971).

10. See A. Bryer's article, in P. Whiting, ed., *Byzantium: An Introduction* (New York, 1971), p. 103; also, his "Cultural Relations between East and West in the 12th Century," *Relations between East and West in the Middle Ages* (Edinburgh, 1973), p. 80.

11. On honorary citizenship for Cydones, conferred in 1391 by Venice, see R. Loenertz, "Démétrius Cydonès, citôyen de Venise," *Echos d'Orient* 27 (1938): 125–26. Cf. my *Byzantium and the Renaissance*, pp. 27–28. On the legal position of the Greek colony in Venice after 1453, see next note.

12. Cf. Fedalto, *Ricerche storiche sulla posizione giuridica ed ecclesiastica dei Greci a Venezia.*, esp. p. 114.

13. See Haussig, *Byzantine Civilization*, esp. p. 370.

14. See above, chap. 4, and below, n. 17.

15. See above, chaps. 3–4.

16. See above, chap. 13, esp. p. 236, and Prologue, p. 23.

17. See esp. A. Embiricos, *La Renaissance Crétoise* (Paris, 1960); M. Manousakas, "La littérature crétoise à l'époque vénitienne," *L'hellénisme Cont.* 9 (1955): 106–07. For the twelfth century, Bryer, in his "Cultural Relations between East and West in the 12th Century," pp. 81–82, speaks correctly of areas of cultural "overlap"—Hungary, Serbia, South Italy, and Sicily. These, however, were ultimately to be separated from the true Greek homeland.

18. See D. Geanakoplos, "Byzantium and the Later Crusades," in *A History of the Crusades* (1975), pp. 27–103, esp. 31–33.

19. Interestingly enough, Emperor John V, in 1369, in order to guarantee the pope conversion of the Greeks to Catholicism, suggested a solution that itself reflected this basic Greek fear: he promised, among other things, to send his son Manuel to be educated by the pope, to have him learn Latin and be brought up in the Latin manner! (The negotiations came to nothing, however.) See O. Halecki, *Un Empereur de Byzance à Rome* (Warsaw, 1930), pp. 17–18.

20. See *Acta Graeca*, ed. J. Gill (Rome 1953), p. 400.

21. See above, chap. 2, "Religion and Nationalism," quoting from a report of the Greek legate George Metochites, to the pope, in M. Laurent, *Le Bienheureux Innocent V* (Vatican, 1947), p. 424. See also Pachymeres (Bonn ed.), 1: 401. Even more significant are the many passages in the historian of the Council of Florence Syropoulos (especially important for Greek attitudes and actions

behind the scenes). He uses the term *efrangepses* (or "becoming Latinized") in this sense, both religious and cultural (recent ed. by V. Laurent, *Les Mémoires de Sylvestre Syropoulos* [Paris, 1971]): see its index under Greek words *latinizo, latinismos, latinophron*, listed on p. 652. Note, among other things, the story told by Syropoulos (p. 524). Cf. I. Sevčenko, "Intellectual Repercussions of the Council of Florence," *Church History* (1955), p. 298.

22. See on Notaras, Geanakoplos, *Byzantine East and Latin West*, p. 117.

23. On these figures see I. Sevčenko's fascinating article, "Society and Intellectual Life in the Fourteenth Century," *Actes du XIVe Congrès international des études byzantines, Bucharest, 1971* (Bucharest, 1974), pp. 81–83, 86–87. On Scholarios, see also C. Turner "George Scholarius and the Union of Florence," *Journal of Theological Studies* 18 (1967) 83–103.

24. According to sociologists, this is a basic factor in fears of cultural absorption. If a society collapses, what remains is the "identifiable" culture, which can guarantee the continuity of life with a distinct historical existence. (I am indebted to sociology professor E. Vlachos for this information.)

25. On these two men and their ideas see above, esp. chap. 4.

26. See on Mark, above, esp. chap. 11, and N. Kalogeras, *Mark of Ephesus and Cardinal Bessarion* (Athens, 1893; in Greek). Also, cf. the recent views of A. Papadakes, "Gennadius II and Mehmet the Conqueror," *Byzantion* (1972), pp. 89–90. Though Bessarion would never even have considered separating Hellenic learning and Orthodoxy, it may well be that for him, whether he consciously realized it or not, Hellenic culture was the really underlying element. Cf. Vacalopoulos, *Origins of the Greek Nation*, p. 244, and esp. F. Masai, *Pléthon et le Platonisme de Mistra* (Paris, 1956), pp. 306–07 and *Kardinal Bessarion als Theologe, Humanist und Staatsman*, L. Mohler, ed. (Paderborn, 1942), vol. 3, pp. 68–69.

27. On Ducas, see Geanakoplos, *Byzantium and the Renaissance*, p. 248.

28. These ideas are expressed in Bessarion's letter written ca. 1444 to Despot Constantine Palaeologus of the Morea, printed in S. Lampros, *Neos Hellenomnemon* (Athens, 1906), 3: 15. Also A. Keller, "A Byzantine Admirer of Western Progress: Bessarion," *Cambridge Historical Journal* 11 (1953–55): 343. Cf. Vacalopoulos, *Origins*, p. 244. It is possible (although one cannot be certain) that, in modern sociological terms, Mark saw the reality of the Byzantine social disintegration more clearly than Bessarion and that this was, in part at least, a cause of his adamant anti-latin, anti-unionist attitude (cf. also on Bessarion, ch. 9, n. 1.)

29. See above, chap. 13, n. 16, text and nn. 34–35.

30. See above, chap. 9.

31. See, for example, M. Gordon, *Assimilation in American Life* (New York, 1964), p. 70, who remarks that assimilation is a multidimensional process consisting of seven different subprocesses (the first of which is "acculturation"). For Gordon, assimilation is the "umbrella" term. It is an ongoing process to be thought of in terms of degrees. In its ideal sense, in his view, assimilation marks the complete fusion of cultures. In my book the more traditional views of acculturation are followed.

32. Other "primary" elements in "modern Western civilization" are the Arab influence on medieval Western culture (based, however in considerable part on ancient Greek philosophy and science) and post-Renaissance, Western developments such as the thought of the Enlightenment and, of course, modern science.

Bibliography

*Organized according to theme. Not all works
included in the notes are listed here.*

I. SOCIOLOGICAL AND HISTORICAL WORKS
(NON-BYZANTINE) FOR THE STUDY OF "ACCULTURATION"

Berkhofer, R. "Protestants, Pagans, and Sequences, 1760–1860." In
American Indian: Past and Present. Edited by R. Nichols and G. Adams.
Waltham, Mass., 1971.

Connolly, W. *The Bias of Pluralism*. New York, 1969.

Darlington, C. *The Evolution of Man and Society*. New York, 1969.

Geertz, C. *Islam Observed*. New York, 1968.

Gordon, M. *Assimilation in American Life*. New York, 1964.

Grünebaum, G. von. *Medieval Islam: A Study in Cultural Orientation*.
Chicago, 1946.

———. *Modern Islam: The Search for Cultural Identity*. Berkeley, Calif.,
1962.

Linton, R. "The Distinctive Aspects of Acculturation." In *The Emergent
Native Americans*. Edited by D. Walker. Boston, 1972.

Lipset, S. *The Radical Right*. New York, 1969.

Malinowski, B. *The Dynamics of Cultural Change*. New Haven, 1961.

Newman, W. *American Pluralism: A Study of Minority Groups and Social
Theory*. New York, 1973.

Park, R. *Race and Culture*. New York, 1970.

Russett, C. *The Concept of Equilibrium in American Social Thought*. New
Haven–London, 1966.

Smith, A. *Theories of Nationalism*. London, 1971.

Wach, J. *Sociology of Religion*. Chicago, 1971.

Walker, D., ed. *The Emergent Native Americans*. Boston, 1972. (Contains
several useful articles.)

Wallace, A. "Revitalization Movements." *American Anthropologist* 58
(1956): 265–80.

II. BYZANTINE-LATIN RELATIONS
(ESPECIALLY CULTURAL)

A. Of a General Nature

Amantos, K. *Historia tou Byzantinou Kratous*. 2 vols. Athens, 1963 (reprint
1969).

Bréhier, L. *Le monde byzantin*. 3 vols. Paris, 1947–50. See esp. vol. 2, *La Civilisation byzantine*.

Charanis, P. "The Aristocracy in Byzantium in the Thirteenth Century." In *Studies in Roman Economic and Sociological History*, edited by P. Coleman-Norton, pp. 336–55. Princeton, 1951.

Diehl, C. "Byzantine Civilization." In *Cambridge Medieval History*, pp. 745–47. New York, 1927.

————. *Byzantium: Greatness and Decline*. New Brunswick, N.J., 1957.

Dölger, F. "Byzanz und das Abendland vor den Kreuzzugen." *Relazioni del X Congresso Internazionale di Scienze Storiche* 3: 67–112. Florence, 1955.

Ebersolt, J. *Orient et Occident, recherches sur les influences byzantines et orientales en France pendant les croisades*. Paris, 1954.

Eisenstadt, S., ed. *The Decline of Empires*. Englewood Cliffs, N.J., 1967. Includes articles of P. Charanis, G. Ostrogorsky, and C. Diehl.

Gay, J. *L'Italie méridionale et l'empire byzantin*. Paris, 1904.

Geanakoplos, D. J. *Byzantine East and Latin West: Two Worlds of Christendom in Middle Ages and Renaissance*. Oxford, 1966. Greek translation by K. Kyriazes, Athens, 1975.

————. "Byzantium." In *Perspectives on the Past*, edited by N. Cantor, pp. 137–65. New York, 1971.

————. "Byzantium and the Crusades." In *A History of the Crusades*, vol. 3, edited by K. Setton, pp. 27–103, chaps. 2 and 3. Madison, Wisc., 1974.

Haussig, H. *History of Byzantine Civilization*. Translated by J. Hussey. Reprint, London, 1971.

Hesseling, D. *Essai sur la civilisation byzantine*. Paris, 1907.

Hunger, H. *Der Christliche Geist der byzantinischen Kultur*. Graz, 1965.

Hussey, J. *The Byzantine World*. Reprint, London, 1971.

Kazdan, A. *Byzantyyskaya Kultura*. Moscow, 1968.

Laiou, A. "The Byzantine Aristocracy in the Palaeologan Period." *Viator* 4 (1973): 131–51.

Lamma, P. *Oriente e Occidente nell'alto Medioevo*. Padua, 1965.

Lange, R. *Imperium zwischen Morgen und Abendland*. Bongers, 1972.

Miller, D. *Imperial Constantinople*. New York, 1969.

Miller, W. *Essays on the Latin Orient*. Cambridge, 1921.

————. *The Latins in the Levant*. London, 1908.

Nicol, D. *The Last Centuries of Byzantium*. New York, 1972.

Obolensky, D. *The Byzantine Commonwealth*. New York, 1972.

Ohnsorge, W. *Abendland und Byzanz*. Darmstadt, 1958.

Ostrogorsky, G. *Pour l'histoire de la féodalité byzantine*. Brussels, 1954.

Runciman, S. *Byzantine Civilization*. London, 1933.

————. "The Place of Byzantium in the Medieval World." In *Cambridge Medieval History* 4–2, pp. 355–75. Cambridge, 1967.

Sherrard, P. *Greek East and Latin West.* London, 1959.

Skazkin, S. D., ed. *Istoriya Vizantii.* 3 vols. Moscow, 1967.

Turchi, N. *La civiltà bizantina.* Turin, 1915.

Uspensky, T. *Essays on the History of Byzantine Civilization.* Moscow, 1896. (In Russian.)

Vasiliev, A. A. *History of the Byzantine Empire.* 2 vols. Madison, Wisc., 1964.

Wessel, K. *Die Kultur von Byzanz.* Frankfurt-am-Main, 1970.

Whiting, P., ed. *Byzantium: An Introduction.* New York, 1971.

B. More Specialized Works

Adam, William. *Directorium ad Passagium faciendum.* In *Recueil des historiens des Croisades, Documents Arméniens,* vol. 2 (1906). (Primary source.)

Angold, M. *A Byzantine Government in Exile. Government and Society under the Laskarids of Nicaea (1204–1261).* London, 1975.

Ballard, M. "Les Génois en Romanie entre 1204 et 1261. Récherches dans les minutiers, notariaux génois." *Mélanges d'archéologie et d'histoire* 78 (1966): 467–501.

Barker, E. *Social and Political Thought in Byzantium from Justinian I to the Last Palaeologus.* Oxford, 1957. (Primary sources.)

Barker, J. *Manuel II Palaeologus (1391–1425): A Study in Late Byzantine Statesmanship.* New Brunswick, N.J., 1969.

Borsari, S. "I rapporti tra Pisa a gli stati di Romania nel duecento." *Rivista storica italiana* 67 (1955): 477–92.

Brand, C. *Byzantium Confronts the West, 1180–1204.* Cambridge, Mass., 1968.

Bryer, A. "Cultural Relations between East and West in the 12th Century." In *Relations between East and West in the Middle Ages,* edited by D. Baker, pp. 77–94. Edinburgh, 1973.

———. "The First Encounter with the West, A.D. 1050–1204." In *Byzantium: An Introduction,* edited by P. Whiting, pp. 85–110. New York, 1971.

Cessi, R. "Bizantinismo Veneziano." *Archivio Veneto* (1961): 3–22.

Charanis, P. "Byzantium and the West." In *Great Problems in European Civilization,* edited by K. Setton. New York, 1954. (Primary sources.)

Delaville Le Roulx, J. *La France en Orient au XIVe siècle.* Paris, 1886.

Diehl, C. *La Société byzantine à l'époque des Comnènes.* Paris, 1929.

Dubois, D. *De Recuperatione terre sancte.* In *Collection de textes pour servir à l'étude de l'histoire.* Edited by V. Langlois. Paris, 1891.

Fedalto, G. *La chiesa latina in Oriente.* Vol. 1. Verona, 1973.

Fotheringham, J. *Marco Sanudo, Conqueror of the Archipelago.* Oxford, 1915.

Gardner, A. *The Lascarids of Nicaea.* London, 1912.

Gay, J. *Le Pape Clément VI et les affaires d'Orient (1342–1352).* Paris, 1904.

Geanakoplos, D. *Byzantium and the Renaissance: Greek Scholars in Venice.* Hamden, Conn., 1972. (Reprint of *Greek Scholars in Venice.* Cambridge, Mass., 1962.) Italian translation by A. Martina, *Bisanzio e il Rinascimento,* Rome, 1967.

———. *Emperor Michael Palaeologus and the West: A Study in Byzantine-Latin Relations.* Cambridge, 1959; reprint Hamden, Conn., 1972. Greek translation by K. Polites, Athens, 1969.

Gerola, G. *Monumenti veneti dell'isola di Creta.* 4 vols. Venice, 1905–32. (Primary sources.)

Gill, J. "The Second Encounter with the West, A.D. 1204–1453." In *Byzantium: An Introduction,* edited by P. Whiting, pp. 113–33. New York, 1971.

Giunta, F. *Bizantini e bizantinismo nella Sicilia normanna.* Palermo, 1950.

Halecki, O. *Un Empereur de Byzance à Rome.* Warsaw, 1930.

Hecht, W. *Die byzantinische Aussenpolitik zur Zeit der letzten Komnenen Kaiser (1180–85).* Neustadt, 1967.

Heilig, K. *Ostrom und das deutsche Reich um die Mitte des 12. Jahrhunderts.* Leipzig, 1944.

Heyd, W. *Histoire du commerce du Levant.* Translated by F. Raynaud. 2 vols. Amsterdam, 1959.

Hiestand, R. *Byzanz und das Regnum Italicum im 10. Jahrhundert.* Zurich, 1964.

Hopf, C. *Chroniques Gréco-Romanes.* Berlin, 1873; new ed., Athens, 1961. (Primary sources.)

Jacoby, D. "The Encounter of Two Societies: Western Conquerors and Byzantines in the Peloponnesus after the Fourth Crusade." *American Historical Review* 78 (1973): 873–906.

Kaegi, W. *Byzantium and the Decline of Rome.* Princeton, 1968.

Keller, A. "A Byzantine Admirer of Western Progress, Cardinal Bessarion." *Cambridge Historical Journal* 11 (1953–55): 343–48.

Kyrris, C. "John Cantacuzenos and the Genoese, 1328–48." *Miscellanea storica ligure* 3 (n.d.): 3–48.

Laiou, A. *Constantinople and the Latins: The Foreign Policy of Andronicus II (1282–1328).* Cambridge, 1972.

Lamma, P. *Comneni e Staufer: richerche sui rapporti fra Bisanzio e l'Occidente nel secolo XII.* 2 vols. Rome, 1955–57.

Laurent, V. "Byzance et l'Angleterre au lendemain de la conquête normande, apropos d'un sceau byzantin trouvé à Winchester." *Numismatic Circular* 71 (1963): 93–96.

———. "La Croisade et la question d'Orient sous le pontificat de Grégoire X." *Revue historique du sud-est européen* 22 (1945): 106–37.

Lemerle, P. *L'Emirat d'Aydin, Byzance et l'Occident.* Paris, 1957.

Liudprand of Cremona. Edited by F. Wright. London, 1930. (Primary source.)

Loenertz, R. *Byzantina et Franco-Graeca*. Rome, 1970.

Longnon, J. *L'Empire latin de Constantinople et la principauté de Morée*. Paris, 1949.

Lopez, R. "East and West in the Early Middle Ages: Economic Relations." *Relazioni del X Congresso Internazionale di Scienze Storiche*, pp. 113–63. Florence, 1956.

———. "Foreigners in Byzantium." *Bulletin de l'institut historique belge de Rome* 44 (1974): 341–52.

———. "Le Problème des relations anglo-byzantines du septième au dixième siècle." *Byzantion* 18 (1948): 139–62.

Manousakas, M. "Rapid Overview of Research on Venetian-held Crete." *Kretika Chronika* 23 (1971): 245–308. In Greek.

Mayer, H. *The Crusades*. Oxford, 1972.

Meliarakes, A. *Historia tou Basileiou tes Nikaias*. Athens, 1898.

Meyendorff, J. "Society and Culture in the Fourteenth Century: Religious Problems." *Actes du XIVᵉ Congrès International des Études Byzantines*, pp. 111–29. Bucharest, 1911.

Mohler, L. *Kardinal Bessarion als Theologe, Humanist, und Staatsman*. Paderborn, 1923.

Nicol, D. "A Byzantine Emperor in England: Manuel II's Visit to London in 1400–01," *University of Birmingham Historical Journal* 12–2 (1971): 204–25.

———. "Mixed Marriages in Byzantium in the 13th Century." *Studies in Church History* 1 (1964): 160–74.

———. "The Byzantine View of Western Europe." *Greek, Roman, and Byzantine Studies* 8 (1967): 315–39.

———. "The Fourth Crusade and the Greek and Latin Empires, 1204–61." In *Cambridge Medieval History* 4–2, pp. 275–330. Cambridge, 1966.

Norden, W. *Das Papsttum und Byzanz*. Berlin, 1903.

Obolensky, D. "Byzantine Frontier Zones and Cultural Exchanges." *Actes du XIVᵉ Congrès International des Études Byzantines*, pp. 303–13. Bucharest, 1974.

Ohnsorge, W. "Byzanz und das Abendland im neunten und zehnten Jahrhundert. Zur Entwicklung des Kaiserbegriffes und der Staatsideologie." *Saeculum* 5 (1964): 194–220.

———. *Das Zweikaiserproblem im früheren Mittelalter*. Hildesheim, 1947.

———. "Die Auswirkung der byzantinischen staatlichen Siedlungsmethoden auf die Sachsenpolitik Karls des Grossen." *Niedersachsisches Jahrbuch für Landesgeschichte* 39 (1967): 86–102.

Pertusi, A. *Venezia e l'Oriente fra Tardo Medioevo e Rinascimento*. Florence, 1966. (Several articles on Venetian-Byzantine relations.)

Queller, D. *The Latin Conquest of Constantinople*. New York, 1971.

Riant, P. *Exuviae Sacrae Constantinopolitanae*. 2 vols. Geneva, 1876. (Primary source.)

Robert of Clari. *La conquista di Costantinopoli*. Edited by A. Nada Patrone. Genoa, 1972. (Primary source.)

Runciman, S. *A History of the Crusades*. Vol. 2. Cambridge, 1964.

————. *The Great Church in Captivity*. Cambridge, 1968.

————. *The Sicilian Vespers*. Cambridge, 1958.

Schramm, P. *Kaiser, Rom, und Renovatio*. 2 vols. Leipzig, 1929.

Setton, K. *Catalan Domination of Athens, 1311–88*. Cambridge, Mass., 1948.

Sevčenko, I. "Intellectual Repercussions of the Council of Florence." *Church History* 24 (1955): 291–323.

————. "Society and Intellectual Life in the Fourteenth Century." *Actes du XIVe Congrès International des Études Byzantines, Bucharest, 1971*, pp. 69–92. Bucharest, 1974.

Syropoulos, S. *Les 'Mémoires' de Sylvestre Syropoulos*. Edited by V. Laurent. Paris, 1971.

Thiriet, F. *La Romanie vénitienne au Moyen Age*. Paris, 1959.

Tomadakes, N. *Introduction to Byzantine Literature*. Athens, 1958. In Greek.

Toynbee, A. *Constantine Porphyrogenitus and His World*. London, 1973. (See especially pt. 4, pp. 510–74, on Byzantine civilization.)

Vasiliev, A. "The Opening Stages of the Anglo-Saxon Immigration to Byzantium in the 11th Century." *Seminarium Kondakovianum* 9 (1937): 39–70.

Weiss, R. "The Greek Culture of South Italy in the Middle Ages." *Proceedings of the British Academy* (1951), pp. 23–50.

Wolff, R., and Hazard, H., eds. *The Later Crusades 1189–1311* (vol. 2 of *A History of the Crusades*, edited by K. Setton). Madison, Wisc., 1969.

Zakythinos, D. *Le Despotat grec de Morée*. 2 vols. Paris, 1932–53.

III. Administration, Diplomacy, and Imperial Ceremonial

Ahrweiler, H., Glykatzi-. "Recherches sur l'administration de l'empire byzantin aux IXe aux XIe siècles," *Bulletin de Correspondance Hellénique* 84 (1960): 1–109.

Bréhier, L. *Les Institutions de l'Empire byzantin*. Paris, 1949.

Bury, J. *The Imperial Administrative System in the Ninth Century*. London, 1911.

Darrouzès, J. "Recherches sur les *officia* de l'église byzantine." *Archives de l'orient chrétien*. Paris, 1970.

Dölger, F. *Regesten der Kaiserurkunden des Oströmischen Reiches*. 5 vols. Munich-Berlin, 1924–65. (Primary sources.)

————. *Byzantinische Diplomatik*. Ettal, 1956.

Ensslin, W. "The Emperor and the Imperial Administration." In *Byzantium, An Introduction to East Roman Civilization*, edited by N. Baynes and H. Moss. Oxford, 1961.

————. "The Government and Administration of the Byzantine Empire." In *New Cambridge Medieval History* 4–2, pp. 1–55. Cambridge, 1967.

Obolensky, D. "The Principles and Methods of Byzantine Diplomacy." *XIIe Congrès International des études byzantines*. Ochrida, 1961.

Ostrogorsky, G. *History of the Byzantine State*. New Brunswick, N. J., 1969.

Treitinger, O. *Die oströmische Kaiser und Reichsidee*. Jena, 1938.

Verpeaux, J., ed. *Pseudo-Codinus, Traité des offices*. Paris, 1966. (Primary source.)

Voigt, A., ed. *De cerimoniis, Le livre de Cérémonies*. Paris, 1939. (Primary source.)

IV. Byzantine and Western Law
(including civil, canon, and "Germanic")

Alexander, P. "The Donation of Constantine at Byzantium and its earliest use against the Western Empire." In *Mélanges G. Ostrogorsky*, 1: 11–26. Belgrade, 1963.

Androutsos, C. *Dogmatics of the Orthodox Eastern Church*. Athens, 1956. In Greek.

Ashburner, W. *Rhodian Sea Law*. Oxford, 1909.

Chomatianos, Demetrios. *Analecta Sacra Spicilegio*. Edited by J. Pitra. Paris, 1891.

Collinet, P. "Byzantine Legislation from the Death of Justinian to 1453." In *Cambridge Medieval History* 4: 706–25. Cambridge, 1923.

Dvornik, F. *Byzantium and the Roman Primacy*. New York, 1966.

Ferrari dalle Spade, G. "La legislazione dell'impero d'Oriente in Italia." In *Italia e Grecia*, pp. 225–53. Florence, 1939.

Freshfield, E., ed. *Roman Law in the Later Roman Empire: Book of the Eparch*. Cambridge, 1938.

Gormley, W. "The Development of the Rhodian-Roman Sea Law to 1681." *Inter-American Law Review* 3 (1961): 319 ff.

Kotsonis, H. *Problemata ekklesiastikes oikonomias [Problems on ecclesiastical 'economia']*. Athens, 1957.

Koukoules, P. *Byzantinon Bios kai Politismos*. 5 vols. Athens, 1948–52.

Lopez, R. "Byzantine Law in the Seventh Century and its Reception by the Germans and Arabs." *Byzantion* 16 (1942–43): 445 ff.

Nikolaou, T. *The Ideas of G. Pletho on the State and on Law*. Thessalonika, 1974. In Greek.

Recoura, G., ed. *Les Assises de Romanie*. Paris, 1930. (Primary source.)

Rhalles and Potlis. *Syntagma ton Hieron Canonon*. Athens, 1852. In Greek. (Primary sources on canon law.)

Scheltema, H. J. "Byzantine Law." In *New Cambridge Medieval History* 4–2, pp. 55–78. Cambridge, 1967.

Topping, P. *Assizes of Romania*. Philadelphia, 1949.

Zacharia von Lingenthal, K. S. *Geschichte des Romaischen Rechts*. Leipzig, 1894.

Zepos, J., and Zepos, P. *Ius graeco-romanum.* Vol. 8. Athens, 1931.

V. Religion and "Nationalism" in the Byzantine Empire

Alexander, P. "The Strength of Empire and Capital as Seen Through Byzantine Eyes." *Speculum* 37 (1962): 341–57.

Angold, M. "Byzantine 'Nationalism' and the Nicaean Empire." *Byzantine and Modern Greek Studies* 1(1975):49–69.

Browning, R. *Greece—Ancient and Medieval. An Inaugural Lecture Delivered at Birkbeck College, 1966.* London, 1966.

Charanis, P. *The Armenians in the Byzantine Empire.* Lisbon, 1963.

———. "The Jews in the Byzantine Empire under the First Palaeologi." *Speculum* 22 (1947): 75–77.

Dölger, F. *Byzanz und die europäische Stattenwelt.* Ettal, 1933.

Grabar, A. "God and the 'Family of Princes' Presided over by the Byzantine Emperor." *Harvard Slavic Studies* 2 (1953): 117–23.

Irmscher, J. "Nikäa als Zentrum des griechischen Patriotismus." *Revue des études Sud-est Européenes* 8 (1970): 33–47.

Ivanka, E. *Hellenisches und christliches im frühbyzantinischen Geistesleben.* Vienna, 1948.

Jones, A. H. M. *Were Ancient Heresies Disguised Social Movements?* Philadelphia, 1966.

Kakrides, J. "The Ancient Greeks and the Greeks of the War of Independence." *Balkan Studies* 4 (1963): 251–63. In Greek.

Masai, F. *Pléthon et le platonisme de Mistra.* Paris, 1956.

Moles, I. "Nationalism and Byzantine Greece." *Greek, Roman, and Byzantine Studies* 10 (1969): 95–108.

Obolensky, D. "Nationalism in Eastern Europe in the Middle Ages." *Transactions of the Royal Historical Society,* 5th ser., 22 (1972): 1–16.

———. *The Bogomils.* Cambridge, 1948.

———. *The Byzantine Commonwealth, Eastern Europe, 500–1453.* New York, 1971.

Ostrogorsky, G. "The Byzantine Emperor and the Hierarchical World Order." *The Slavonic and East European Review* 35 (1956–57): 1–14.

Patrinelis, C. "An Unknown Discourse of Chrysoloras addressed to Manuel II Palaeologus." *Greek, Roman, and Byzantine Studies* 14 (1973): 497–502.

Runciman, S. "Byzantine and Hellene in the Fourteenth Century." *Tomos Harmenopoulos* (1951), pp. 27–33.

———. *The Medieval Manichee.* Cambridge, 1947.

Sharf, A. *Byzantine Jewry from Justinian to the Fourth Crusade.* London, 1971.

Starr, J. *The Jews in the Byzantine Empire.* Athens, 1939.

Vacalopoulos, A. "Byzantinism and Hellenism." *Balkan Studies* 9 (1968): 100–26.

———. *The Origins of the Greek Nation, The Byzantine Period*. New Brunswick, N. J., 1970.

Xydis, S. "Medieval Origins of Modern Greek Nationalism." *Balkan Studies* 9 (1968): 1–20.

VI. THE CHURCHES OF EAST AND WEST

A. Schism and Union, Ecclesiology and Doctrinal Differences

Baker, D., ed. *The Orthodox Churches and the West. Studies in Church History*, vol. 4. Oxford, 1976. Symposium papers read by D. Nicol, P. Brown, A. Mendieta, D. Geanakoplos, at the British Ecclesiastical History Conference, 1975.

Benz, E. *Wittenberg und Byzanz*. Marburg-Lahn, 1949.

Bréhier, L. "Attempts at Reunion of the Greek and Latin Churches." *Cambridge Medieval History* 4: 594–626. Cambridge, 1927.

———. *Le Schisme orientale du XIe siècle*. Paris, 1899.

———. "The Greek Church: Its Relations with the West up to 1054." *Cambridge Medieval History* 4: 246–273. Cambridge, 1927.

Cirac-Estopañan, S. "Ramon Lull y la union con los Bizantinos." *Cuadernos de Historia* (1954), pp. 9–66.

DeFries, W. "Die Päpste von Avignon und der christliche Osten." *Orientalia Christiana Periodica* (1964), pp. 85–127.

Demetrakopoulos, A. *Historia Schismatis*. Leipzig, 1867. In Greek.

Dölger, F. "Rom in der Gedankenwelt den Byzantiner." In *Byzanz und die europäische Staatenwelt*. Ettal, 1953.

Dondaine, A. "Contra Graecos. Premiers écrites polémiques des dominicains d'Orient." *Archivum fratrum praedicatorum* 21 (1951): 320–446. (New ed., Leonine Commission, Vatican City, 1967.)

Dvornik, F. *Byzance et la primauté romaine*. Paris, 1964.

———. *The Photian Schism: History and Legend*. Cambridge, 1948.

Erickson, J. "Leavened and Unleavened: Some Theological Implications of the Schism of 1054." *St. Vladimir's Theological Quarterly* 14 (1970): 3–24.

Every, G. *Misunderstandings between East and West*. London, 1965.

Franchi, A. *Il concilio di Lione (1274) secondo la Ordinatio Concilii generalis, Lugdunensis*. Rome, 1965.

Geanakoplos, D. J. "Bonaventura, the Mendicant Orders, and the Greeks at the Council of Lyons (1274)." In *The Orthodox Church and the West: Studies in Church History*. Vol. 4. Oxford, in press.

———. "Church and State in the Byzantine Empire: A Reconsideration of the Problem of Caesaropapism." In *Byzantine East and Latin West: Two Worlds of Christendom*, pp. 55–84. Oxford, 1966.

———. "Edward Gibbon and Byzantine Ecclesiastical History." *Church History* 35 (1966): 1–14.

———. *Emperor Michael Palaeologus and the West: A Study in Byzantine-Latin Relations*. Cambridge, 1959; reprinted Hamden, Conn., 1972.

———. "The Council of Florence and the Problem of Union between the Greek and Latin Churches." In *Byzantine East and Latin West*. Oxford, 1966.

Gianelli, C. "Un progetto di Barlaam Calabro per l'unione delle chiese." *Miscellanea G. Mercati (Studi e Testi)*, pp. 157–208. Vatican, 1946.

Gill, J. "The Church Union of the Council of Lyons portrayed in Greek Documents." *Orientalia Christiana Periodica* 40 (1974): 5–45.

———. *The Council of Florence*. Cambridge, 1959.

———. *Personalities of the Council of Florence*. Oxford, 1964.

Gouillard, J. "Les Influences latines dans l'oeuvre de M. Calecas." *Echos d'Orient* (1938): 37–40.

Grégoire, H. "The Byzantine Church." In *Byzantium: An Introduction to East Roman Civilization*, pp. 86–135. Edited by N. Baynes and H. Moss. Oxford, 1961.

Halecki, O. *Un Empereur de Byzance à Rome*. Warsaw, 1930.

Hergenröther, J. *Photius, Patriarch von Konstantinopel*. 3 vols. Darmstadt, 1960 (reprint).

Herman, E. "The Secular Church." *New Cambridge Medieval History* 4–2, pp. 105–34. Cambridge, 1967.

Jugie, M. "Demétrius Cydonès et la théologie latine à Byzance du XIVe et XVe siècles." *Echos d'Orient* 3 (1928): 385–402.

———. *De processione Spiritus Sancti ex fontibus revelationibus et secundum Orientales dissidentes*. Rome, 1936. (Primary source.)

———. "La Question du purgatoire au concile de Ferrare-Florence." *Echos d'Orient* 20 (1929): 322–32.

———. *Le schisme byzantin*. Paris, 1941.

———. *Theologia dogmatica Christianorum orientalium ab Ecclesia Catholica dissidentium*. 5 vols. Paris, 1926–35.

Kresten, O. *Das Patriarchat von Konstantinopel im ausgehenden 16. Jahrhundert*. Vienna, 1970.

Lemerle, P. "L'Orthodoxie byzantine et l'oecumenisme médiéval: les origines du schisme des églises." *Bulletin Association G. Budé* (1954), pp. 228–46.

Meyendorff, J. *Byzantine Theology: Historical Trends and Doctrinal Themes*. New York, 1974.

Meyendorff, J.; Afanassief, N.; Schmemann, A.; and Kouloumzine, N. *The Primacy of Peter in the Orthodox Church*. London, 1963.

Michel, A. *Humbert und Kerullarios*. Paderdorn, 1925–30.

Nicol, D. "Byzantine Requests for an Oecumenical Council in the Fourteenth Century." *Annuarium Historiae Conciliorum* 1 (1969): 69–95.

———. "The Byzantine Reaction to the Second Council of Lyons, 1274." *Church History VII, Councils and Assemblies*, edited by C. Cuming and D. Baker, pp. 113–46. Cambridge, 1971.

———. "The Greeks and the Union of the Churches. The Preliminaries to the Second Council of Lyons, 1261–74." In *Medieval Studies Presented to A. Gwynn*, pp. 454–80. Dublin, 1961.

Papadakis, A. "Gregory II of Cyprus and an Unpublished Report to the Synod." *Greek, Roman, and Byzantine Studies* 16 (1975): 227–39.

Papadopoulos, S. "Byzantine Theology: Relations with the West." In *Encyclopedia of Religion and Ethics*, vol. 3, pp. 1087–1103. Athens, 1963. In Greek.

Pelikan, J. "The Schism and Challenge of the Latin Church." In *The Spirit of Eastern Christendom*, pp. 148–98. Chicago, 1974.

Petit, L. "Documents relatifs au Concile de Florence. I: La question du Purgatoire à Ferrare." *Patrologia Orientalis* 15 (1920): 39–60; 108–51.

Roberg, B. *Die Union zwischen der griechischen und der lateinischen Kirche auf dem II. Konzil von Lyon (1274)*. Bonn, 1964.

Roncaglia, M. *Les Frères mineurs et l'église grecque orthodoxe au XIIIᵉ siècle*. Cairo, 1954.

Runciman, S. *The Eastern Schism*. Oxford, 1955.

Sherrard, P. *The Greek East and Latin West: A Study in the Christian Tradition*. London, 1959.

Southern, R. "The Divisions of Christendom." In *Western Society and the Church in the Middle Ages*, chap. 4. Middlesex, Eng., 1970.

Turner, G. "George-Gennadius Scholarius and the Union of Florence." *Journal of Theological Studies* 18 (1967): 83–103.

Viller, M. "La Question de l'union des églises entre Grecs et Latins." *Revue d'histoire ecclésiastique* 16 (1921): 260–305, 515–32; 18 (1922): 20–60.

Walter, H., and Holstein, H. *Lyon I et Lyon II*. Paris, 1965.

Will, C., ed. *Acta et Scripta*. Frankfurt-am-Main, 1861. (Primary source.)

Wolff, R. "Politics in the Latin Patriarchate of Constantinople, 1204–61." *Dumbarton Oaks Papers* 8 (1954): 225–303.

———. "The Organization of the Latin Patriarchate of Constantinople, 1204–61, etc." *Traditio* 6 (1948): 33–60.

Zachariades, G. *Tübingen und Konstantinopel. Martin Crusius und seine Verhändlungen mit der Griechisch-Orthodoxen Kirche*. Göttingen, 1941.

B. Mysticism, Spirituality, and Theological Speculation

Anastos, M. "Some Aspects of Byzantine Influence on Latin Thought." In *Twelfth-Century Europe and the Foundations of Modern Society*, pp. 131–88. Madison, Wisc., 1961.

Beck, H. G. *Kirche und theologische Literatur im byzantinischen Reich.* Munich, 1959.

Brightman, R. "Apophatic Theology and Divine Infinity in St. Gregory of Nyssa." *Greek Orthodox Theological Review,* vol. 18 (1973): 97–114.

Brilliantoff, A. *The Influence of Eastern Theology on Western as Evidenced by Works of John Scotus Erigena.* St. Petersburg, 1898. In Russian.

Brown, P. "A Dark Age Crisis: Aspects of the Iconoclastic Controversy." *English Historical Review,* vol. 346 (1973).

Burghardt, W. "Mary in Eastern Patristic Thought." In *Mariology,* vol. 2. Edited by J. Carol. Milwaukee, Wisc., 1957.

Cappuyns, M. *Jean Scot Erigène, sa vie, son oeuvre, sa pensée.* Louvain, 1933.

Dondaine, H. *Le Corpus Dionysien de l'Université de Paris au XIIIe siècle.* Rome, 1953.

Dräseke, J. "Maximus Confessor und Johannes Scotus Erigena." *Theologischen Studien und Kritiken* 84 (1911): 20–60.

Epifanovič, S. *Materials to Serve in the Study of the Life and Works of St. Maximus the Confessor.* Kiev, 1915. In Russian.

Francheschini, E. "Grosseteste's translation of the Prologos and Scholia of Maximus to the Writings of the pseudo-Dionysius the Areopagita." *Journal of Ecclesiastical History* 34 (1933): 355–63.

Gandillac, M. de. *Nikolaus von Cues.* Düsseldorf, 1953.

Gregory, T. "Note sulla dottrina della 'teofanie' di Giovanni Scoto Erigena." *Studi Medievali,* ser. 3, 4–1: 75–91.

Gregory of Nyssa. *From Glory to Glory: Texts from Gregory of Nyssa.* Edited by H. Musurillo. London, 1962.

Hausherr, I. *Philautie; de la tendresse pour soi à la charité selon S. Maxime le Confesseur.* Rome, 1952.

———. "Noms du Christ." *Orientalia Christiana Analecta* 57 (1960): 202–10.

Hussey, J. *Church and Learning in the Byzantine Empire, 867–1185.* London, 1937.

Hussey, J., and Hart, T. "Byzantine Theological Speculation and Spirituality." In *New Cambridge Medieval History* 4–2, pp. 185–206. Cambridge, 1967.

Jugie, M. "La Forme de l'eucharistie d'après G. Scholarios." *Echos d'Orient* 33 (1934): 289 ff.

———. "Palamas." In *Dictionnaire de théologie catholique.* Vol. 11. 1932.

Krivocheine, B. "Ascetic and Mystical Teaching of St. Gregory Palamas." *Eastern Churches Quarterly,* vol. 4 (1938).

Leclerq, J. " 'Sedere' à propos de l'Hésychasme en Occident." In *Le Millénaire du Mont Athos 963–1963,* 1: 253–64. Chevtogne, 1963.

Lossky, V. *The Mystical Theology of the Eastern Church*. Cambridge-London, 1957.

———. *The Vision of God*. Translated by A. Moorhouse. Clayton, Wisc., 1963.

Lot-Borodine, Myrrha. *Nicolas Cabasilas*. Paris, 1958.

Maloney, G. *Russian Hesychasm. The Spirituality of Nil Sorskij*. The Hague, 1973.

Masai, F. *Pléthon et le platonisme de Mistra*. Paris, 1956.

Mascall, E., ed. *The Mother of God: A Symposium*. London, 1949. (Especially the articles by V. Lossky and G. Florovsky.)

Meyendorff, J. *A Study of Gregory Palamas*. London, 1964.

———. *Byzantine Hesychasm: Historical, Theological and Social Problems*. London, 1974.

———. *Christ in Eastern Christian Thought*. Washington, D.C., 1969.

———. *Grégoire Palamas. Les Triades pour la défense de Saintes-hésychastes*. Louvain, 1959. (Primary source.)

———. *Introduction à l'étude de Grégoire Palamas*. Paris, 1959. (Translated as *A Study of Gregory Palamas*, by C. Lawrence. London, 1964.)

———. "Note sur l'influence dionysienne en Orient." *Studia Patristica* 2 (1957): 547–52.

———. *St. Grégoire Palamas et la mystique orthodoxe*. Bourges, 1959. English translation, New York, 1974.

Papadakes, A. "Gregory Palamas at the Council of Blachernae, 1351." *Greek, Roman, and Byzantine Studies* 10 (1969): 337–42.

Papadopoulos, S., trans. *Hellenikai metaphraseis thomistikon ergon. Philothomistai kai antithomistai en Byzantio*. Athens, 1967.

Pelikan, J. "Council or Father or Scripture: The Concept of Authority in the Theology of Maximus the Confessor." *Orientalia Christiana Analecta* 195 (1973): 277–88.

———. *The Spirit of Eastern Christendom*. Chicago, 1974.

Romanides, J. "Notes on the Palamite Controversy and Related Topics." *Greek Orthodox Theological Review* 6 (1960–61): 186–205; 9 (1963–64): 225–70.

Runciman, S. *The Great Church in Captivity*. Cambridge, 1958.

Schirò, G. *Barlaam Calabro: Epistole greche, i primordi episodici e dottrinali delle lotte esicaste*. Palermo, 1954. (Primary source.)

Sherwood, P. "Byzantine Mariology." *Catholic Theological Society* 15 (1960): 107–34.

———. "Survey of Recent Work on St. Maximus the Confessor." *Traditio* 20 (1964): 428–54.

Völker, W. "Der Einfluss des Pseudo-Dionysius Areopagita auf Maximus." *Universitas: Festschrift für Albert Stohr*, 1: 243–54. Mainz, 1960.

C. Monasticism (Including the Mendicant Orders in the East)

Altaner, B. *Die Dominikanermissionen des 13. Jahrhunderts.* Habelschwert, 1924.

Brown, E. "The Cistercians in the Latin Empire of Constantinople and Greece, 1204–76." *Traditio* 14 (1958): 63–120.

Constantelos, D. *Byzantine Philanthropy and Social Welfare.* New Brunswick, N. J., 1968.

Delehaye, H. "Byzantine Monasticism." In *Byzantium: An Introduction to East Roman Civilization*, pp. 136–65. Edited by N. Baynes and H. Moss. Oxford, 1949; 1961 reprint.

———. *Les Saints stylites* (= *Société des Bollandistes*). Brussels, 1923.

Hamilton, B. "The City of Rome and the Eastern Churches." *Orientalia Christiana Periodica* 27 (1961): 2–26.

Hussey, J. "Byzantine Monasticism." In *New Cambridge Medieval History* 4–2: 161–84. Cambridge, 1967.

———. *Church and Learning in the Byzantine Empire.* New York, 1937; 1963 reprint.

Laurent, V. "Les Grandes Crises religieuses à Byzanz. La fin du schisme Arsénite." *Académie Rumaine, Bulletin section historique* 26 (1945): 1 ff.

Leclerq, J. "Études sur la vocabulaire monastique du moyen âge." *Studia Anselmiana* 48 (1961): 35 ff.

———. "Les Relations entre le Monachisme Oriental et Occidental dans le haut Moyen Age." In *Le Millénaire du Mont Athos*, 2: 4–80. Chevtogne, 1965.

Lemerle, P. "Les Archives du monastère des Amalfitains du Mont Athos." *Epeteris Hetaireias Byzantinon Spoudon* 23 (1953): 548–66.

Loenertz, R. "Les Établissements dominicains de Péra-Constantinople." *Echos d'Orient* 34 (1935): 332–49.

McNulty, J., and Hamilton, B. " 'Orientale Lumen et Magistra Latinitas,' Greek Influences on Latin Monasticism." In *Le Millénaire du Mont Athos*, 1: 181–216. Chevtogne, 1963.

Pertusi, A. "Monasteri e monaci italiani all'Athos nell'alto medioevo." In *Le Millénaire du Mont Athos*, 1: 217–53. Chevtogne, 1963.

Raschella, D. *Saggio storico sul monachismo italo-greco in Calabria.* Messina, 1925.

Roncaglia, M. *Les Frères mineurs et l'église grecque orthodoxe au XIIIe siècle.* Cairo, 1954.

Scaduto, M. *Il monachismo basiliano nella Sicilia medievale.* Rome, 1947.

Van der Vat, O. *Die Anfänge der Franziskanermissionen und ihre Weiterentwicklung im nahen Orient.* Werl. in Westf., 1934.

White, L. *Latin Monasticism in Norman Sicily.* Cambridge, Mass., 1938.

VII. Architecture (Ecclesiastical) and its Relation to Aesthetics and Political Theory

Anastos, M. "Justinian's Despotic Control over the Church as Illustrated by his Edict on Theopaschite Formula and Letter to Pope John in 533." *Zbor. Rad. Viz. Inst.* 312 [= *Mélanges Ostrogorsky*] (1964): 1–11.

Armstrong, G. T. "Church and State Relations. The Changes Wrought by Constantine." *Journal of Bible and Religion* 32 (1964): 1–7.

———. "Fifth and Sixth Century Church Building in the Holy Land." *Greek Orthodox Theological Review* 14 (1969): 17–30.

———. "Imperial Church Building and Church-State Relations, A.D. 312–63." *Church History* 36 (1967): 3–17.

Baynes, N. "Eusebius and the Christian Empire." *Annuaire de l'Institut de philologie et d'histoire orientales* 2 (1933–34): 13–18.

Bodnar, E. *Cyriacus of Ancona and Athens.* Brussels, 1960.

Charanis, P. *Church and State in the Later Roman Empire: The Religious Policy of Anastasius I.* Madison, Wisc., 1939.

Dalton, O. M. *Byzantine Art and Archaeology.* Oxford, 1911.

Downey, G. *Constantinople in the Days of Justinian.* Norman, Okla., 1960.

———. *Gaza in the Early Sixth Century.* Norman, Okla., 1963.

———. "The Builder of the Original Church of the Apostles at Constantinople: A Contribution to the Criticism of the *Vita Constantini* attributed to Eusebius." *Dumbarton Oaks Papers* 6 (1951): 58–72.

Fleming, W. *Arts and Ideas.* New York, 1963.

Frend, W. "Old and New Rome in the Age of Justinian." In *Relations between East and West in the Middle Ages,* edited by D. Baker, pp. 11–29. Edinburgh, 1973.

Grabar, A. "Byzantine Architecture and Art." In *New Cambridge Medieval History* 4–2: 307–53. Cambridge, 1967.

Krautheimer, R. *Early Christian and Byzantine Architecture.* Harmondsworth, Eng., 1965.

Lowne, W. *Art in the Early Church.* New York, 1947.

McDonald, W. *Early Christian and Byzantine Architecture.* New York, 1962.

Mathew, G. *Byzantine Aesthetics.* London, 1963.

Perkins, J. B. Ward. "Constantine and the Origins of the Christian Basilica." *Papers of the British School at Rome* 22 (1954): 69–90.

Runciman, S. *Byzantine Style and Civilization.* Harmondsworth, Eng., 1975.

Schwartz, E. *Kaiser Constantin und die cristliche Kirche.* Leipzig, 1916.

Setton, K. *Christian Attitudes towards the Emperor in the Fourth Century.* New York, 1941.

Smith, E. B. *The Dome: A Study in the History of Ideas.* Princeton, 1950.

Thynne, R. *The Churches of Rome.* London, 1924.

Voelkl, L. "Die Konstantinischen Kirchenbauen nach Eusebius." *Reallexikon für Antike und Christentum* 29 (1953): 60–64.

Williams, G. H. "Christology and Church-State Relations in the Fourth Century." *Church History* 20, no. 3 (1951): 8–14; no. 4, pp. 15–28.

VIII. Painting and Mosaics

Baxandall, M. "Guarino, Pisanello, and M. Chrysoloras." *Journal of Warburg and Courtauld Institutes* 28 (1965): 197 ff.

Beckwith, J. *The Art of Constantinople.* London-New York, 1961.

Bloch, H. "Monte Cassino, Byzantium, and the West in the Earlier Middle Ages." *Dumbarton Oaks Papers* 3 (1946): 163–224.

Chatzidakis, E. *Historical Sketch of Religious Painting after the Conquest.* Athens, 1957. In Greek.

Delvoye, C. *L'Art byzantin.* Paris, 1967.

Demus, O. *Byzantine Art and the West.* New York, 1970.

———. *Byzantine Mosaic Decoration.* London, 1947.

———. "Die Entstehung des Paläologenstils in der Malerei." *Berichte zum XI. Intern. Byz.-Kongress*, vol. 4, pt. 2, pp. 33 ff. Munich, 1958.

———. *The Mosaics of Norman Sicily.* London, 1949.

Diehl, C. *Manuel de l'art byzantin.* 2d ed. Paris, 1925–26.

Grabar, A. *Byzantine Art in the Middle Ages.* London, 1963.

———. *Byzantine Painting.* Geneva, 1953.

Kalokyris, K. *Byzantine Wall Paintings of Crete.* Athens, 1957. In Greek.

Kitzinger, E. "The Byzantine Contribution to Western Art of the Twelfth and Thirteenth Centuries." *Dumbarton Oaks Papers* 17 (1963): 25–48.

———. *The Mosaics of Monreale.* Palermo, 1960.

Lazarev, V. *Storia della pittura bizantina.* Turin, 1967. Translated from Russian.

Mango, C. *The Art of the Byzantine Empire, 312–1453, Sources and Documents.* Englewood Cliffs, N. J., 1972.

Megaw, A. "Notes on Recent Work of the Byzantine Institute in Istanbul." *Dumbarton Oaks Papers* 17 (1963): 333–72.

Ménager, L. R. "L'Institution monarchique dans les états normandes d'Italie." *Cahiers des civilizations mediévales* 2 (1959): 303 ff.

Mertzios, K. "Gleanings from the Records of Notary Michael Mara." *Kretika Chronika* 1 (1961–62): 302 ff. In Greek.

Rice, T. *Art of the Byzantine Era.* New York, 1962.

———. *Byzantine Painting: The Last Phase.* New York, 1968.

———. *The Appreciation of Byzantine Art.* London, 1972.

Runciman, S. *Byzantine Style and Civilization.* Harmondsworth, Eng., 1975.

Stubbelbine, J. "Byzantine Influence in Thirteenth-Century Italian Panel Painting." *Dumbarton Oaks Papers* 20 (1966): 85–102.

Xyngopoulos, A. *Manuel Panselinos*. Athens, 1956. In Greek.

Zaloziecky, W. *Byzanz und Abendland im Spiegel ihrer Kunsterscheinungen*. Salzburg-Leipzig, 1936.

IX. BYZANTINE MUSIC: LITURGY AND HYMNOGRAPHY

Aurelian. *The Discipline of Music*. Translated by J. Ponte. Colorado Springs, 1968. (Primary source.)

Brightman, F. *Liturgies Eastern and Western*. Oxford, 1896.

Cabasilas, N. *Explication de la divine liturgie*. Translated and with notes by S. Salaville. Paris, 1967. [*Sources chrétiennes*, no. 4.]

Dalmais, H. *The Eastern Liturgies*. New York, 1960.

Denzinger, H. *Enchiridion Symbolorum*. Freiburg, 1955. (With primary sources.)

Downey, G. *Constantinople*. Norman, Okla., 1960.

Goldron, R. *Byzantine and Medieval Music*. New York, 1968.

Jungmann, J. *The Mass of the Roman Rite*. 2 vols. New York, 1951.

King, A. *The Rites of Eastern Christendom*. 2d ed. Rome, 1947.

Levy, K. "The Byzantine Sanctus and its Modal Tradition in East and West." *Annales Musicologiques* 6 (1958–63): 7–67.

Meersseman, G. *The Akathistos Hymn*. Fribourg, 1958.

Salaville, A. *An Introduction in the Study of Eastern Liturgies*. London, 1938.

Schmemann, A. *Introduction to Liturgical Theology*. London, 1966.

Strittmater, A. "Liturgical Latinisms in a 12th Century Greek Euchology." In *Miscellanea G. Mercati*, vol. 3, pp. 41–64. Vatican, 1946.

Tardo, L. *L'antica melurgia bizantina*. Grottaferrata, Italy, 1938.

Tillyard, H. *Byzantine Music and Hymnography*. 2d ed. Oxford, 1961.

Tomadakes, N. *Introduction to Byzantine Literature*. Athens, 1958. In Greek.

Ursprung, O. "Alte griechische Einflüsse und neuer gräzistischer Einschlag in der mittelalterlichen Musik." *Zeitschrift für Musikwissenschaft* 12 (1930): 193–219.

Ware, M., and Ware, K., trans. *The Festal Menaion*. London, 1969. (With primary sources.)

Wellesz, E. *Byzantine Music and Hymnography*. 2d ed. Oxford, 1961.

——. *Eastern Elements in Western Chant*. Oxford, 1947.

——. "On Authorship of the Akathistos." *Dumbarton Oaks Papers* 18 (1967): 51 ff.

X. SCIENCE AND MEDICINE

Beck, H. *Theodoros Metochites*. Munich, 1952.

Codellas, P. "The Pantocrator, the Imperial Byzantine Medical Center of the XIIth Century in Constantinople." *Bulletin of the History of Medicine* 12 (1942): 392–410.

Crombie, A. *Medieval and Early Modern Science*. 2 vols. New York, 1959.

Drake, Stillman. *The Science of Mathematics in Italy in the 15th and 16th Centuries*. Madison, Wisc., 1973.

Duhem, P. *La Système du monde*. Vols. 7–8. Paris, 1954.

Hunger, H. "Von Wissenschaft und Kunst der frühen Palaiologenzeit." *Jahrbuch der Osterreichen Byzantinistik* 8 (1959): 123–55.

Kristeller, P. "Nuove fonti per la medicina salernitana del secolo XII." *Rassegna storica salernitana* 18 (1957): 61–75.

MacKinney, L. "Tenth Century Medicine." In "Symposium in the 10th Century." *Medievalia et Humanistica* 9 (1955): 10–13.

Nordensköld, E. *History of Biology*. New York, 1952.

Randall, J. *The School of Padua and the Emergence of Modern Science*. Padua, 1961.

Rose, P. "Humanist Culture and Renaissance Mathematics: The Italian Libraries of the Quattrocento." *Studies in the Renaissance* 20 (1973): 48–105.

————. "The *Mechanica* in the Renaissance." *Studies in the Renaissance* 18 (1971): 76.

Sarton, G. *An Introduction to the History of Science*. Baltimore, 1931.

Schreiber, G. "Byzantinisches und abendländisches Hospital." *Gemeinschaften des Mittelalters* 1 (1948): 42 ff.

Temkin, O. *Soranus' Gynecology*. Baltimore, 1956.

Theodorides, J. "Byzantine Science." In *History of Science, Ancient and Medieval*. Edited by R. Taton; translated by A. Pomeranz. New York, 1957.

Vogel, K. "Byzantine Science." In *New Cambridge Medieval History* 4–2, chap. 28. Cambridge, 1967. (With exhaustive bibliography of Byzantine science.)

XI. Language as an Instrument of Cultural Transmission

Allgeier, A. "Exegetische Beiträge zur Geschichte des Griechischen vor den Humanismus." *Biblica* 24 (1943): 261–88.

Altaner, A. "Die Kenntnis des Griechischen in den Missionsorden während des 13. und 14. Jahrhunderts." *Zeitschrift für Kirchengeschichte* 53 (1934): 436–93.

Berschin, W. "Griechisches im lateinischen Mittelalter." In *Reallexikon der Byzantinistik*, A. 1.3–4, pp. 227–304. Amsterdam, 1970.

Bischoff, B. "Das griechische Element in der abendländischen Bildung des Mittelalters." *Byzantinische Zeitschrift* 44 (1951): 27–55.

Dain, A. "Le Moyen-Age occidental et la tradition manuscrit de la littérature grecque." *Association G. Budé, Congrès de Nice*, pp. 358–78. Paris, 1935.

Dawkins, R. "The Greek Language in the Byzantine Period." In *By-*

zantium: An Introduction to East Roman Civilization, pp. 252–67. Oxford, 1948 (reprint 1961).

Delaruelle, E. "La Connaissance du grec en Occident du Ve au IXe siècle." *Mélanges de la Société Toulousaine d'Études Classiques,* pp. 207–26. Toulouse, 1946.

Kahane, H., and Kahane, R. "Cultural Criteria for Western Borrowing from Byzantine Greek." In *Homage to A. Tovar,* pp. 205–29. Madrid, 1972.

Kustas, G. "Function and Evolution of Byzantine Rhetoric." *Viator, Medieval and Renaissance Studies* 1 (1970): 55–73.

Runciman, S. "Byzantine Linguists." In *Prosfora to S. Kyriakedes,* pp. 577 ff. Athens, 1953.

Shartau, B. "Observations on the Activities of Byzantine Grammarians of the Palaeologan Era." *Byzantinische Zeitschrift* 66 (1973): 435 ff.

Steinacker, H. "Die römische Kirche und die griechischen Sprachkenntnisse des Frühmittelalters." *Mitteilungen des Instituts für österreichische Geschichtsforschung* 62 (1954): 28–66.

XII. Humanism and Education: The Period of the Middle Ages

Beck, H. G. "Intellectual Life in the Late Byzantine Church." In *Handbook of Church History* 4 (1968): 505–12.

Bolgar, R. *The Classical Heritage and its Beneficiaries,* pp. 59–90. Cambridge, 1954 (reprint 1958).

Bréhier, L. "L'Enseignement supérieure à Constantinople du XIe siècle." *Revue International de l'Enseignement* 38 (1899): 97–112.

———. "Notes sur l'histoire de l'enseignement supérieure à Constantinople." *Byzantion* 4 (1927–28): 14–28.

Browning, R. "Byzantine Scholarship." *Past and Present* 28 (1964): 3–20.

———. "The Patriarchal School at Constantinople in the Twelfth Century." *Byzantion* 32 (1962): 166–202.

Fuchs, F. *Die höheren Schulen von Konstantinopel.* Amsterdam, 1964.

Gigante, M. "La cultura latina a Bizanzio nel sec. XIII." *La parola del passato* 17 (1962): 32–51.

Haskins, C. *Renaissance of the Twelfth Century.* New York, 1968.

Hunger, H. *Geschichte der mittelalterlichen Literatur.* Vol. 1. Zurich, 1961.

Hussey, J. *Church and Learning in the Byzantine Empire.* New York, 1937 (reprint 1963).

Jaeger, W. *Early Christianity and Greek Paideia.* Cambridge, Mass., 1965.

Jenkins, R. "The Hellenistic Origins of Byzantine Literature." *Dumbarton Oaks Papers* 17 (1963): 38 ff.

Kristeller, P. *Catalogus Translationum et Commentariorum; Medieval and Renaissance Latin Translations and Commentaries.* Washington, D.C., 1960.

Krumbacher, K. *Geschichte der byzantinischen Literatur*. Munich, 1897.

Kustas, G. "Studies in Byzantine Rhetoric." *Theologia* 45 (1974): 413 ff.

Laourdas, B. "Classical Philology in Thessalonika." Lecture, Institute for Macedonian Studies, 1960. In Greek.

Lemerle, P. *Le Premier Humanisme byzantin*. Paris, 1972.

Luttrell, A. "Greek Histories Translated and Compiled for Juan Fernandez de Heredia, Master of Rhodes, 1377–96." *Speculum* 34 (1960): 401 ff.

Marshall, F., and Mavrogordato, J. "Byzantine Literature." In *Byzantium: An Introduction to East Roman Civilization*, pp. 221–51. Edited by N. Baynes and H. Moss. Oxford, 1961.

Pertusi, A. "Bisanzio e l'irradiazione della sua civiltà in Occidente nell' alto medioevo." In *XI Settimana di Studi di Spoleto*. Spoleto, Italy, 1964.

Reynolds, L., and Wilson, N. *Scribes and Scholars*. Oxford, 1968.

Schirò, G. *Barlaam and Philosophy in Thessalonika in the 14th Century*. Thessalonika, 1959. In Greek.

Tatakis, P. *La Philosophie byzantine*. Paris, 1949.

Turyn, A. *Dated Greek Manuscripts of the 13th–14th Centuries*. Urbana, Ill., 1972.

Wilson, N. "Byzantine Libraries." *Greek, Roman, and Byzantine Studies* 8 (1967): 53–80.

———. "The Church and Classical Studies in Byzantium." *Antike und Abendland* 16 (1970): 68–77.

XIII. HUMANISM: THE PERIOD OF THE RENAISSANCE

Anastos, M. "Pletho's Calendar and Liturgy." *Dumbarton Oaks Papers* 4 (1948): 183–305.

Andrés, G. *El Cretense Nicolas de la Torre, Copista Griego de Felipe II*. Madrid, 1969.

Babinger, F. *Johannes Darius (1414–94). Sachwalter Venedigs im Morgenland und sein griechischer Umkreis*. 1961.

Bolgar, R., ed. *Classical Influences in European Culture, A.D. 500–1500*. Cambridge, 1971.

Cammelli, G. "Andronico Callisto." *Rinascita* 23–24 (1942): 3–64.

———. *Demetrio Calcondila*. Florence, 1954.

———. *Giovanni Argyropulo*. Florence, 1941.

Coccia, A. "Vita e opere del Bessarione." In *Il Cardinale Bessarione nel V Centenario della Morte*, pp. 23–51. Rome, 1974.

Della Torre, A. *Storia dell'Accademia Platonica di Firenze*. Florence, 1902.

Dionisotti, C. "Aldo Manuzio Umanista." In *Umanesimo Europeo e Umanesimo Veneziano*, pp. 213–43. Florence, 1963.

Enepekides, P. "Maximos Margounios an deutsche und italienische

Humanisten." *Jahrbuch der österreichischen byzantinischen Gesellschaft* 10 (1961): 93–145.

Fedalto, G. *Simone Atumano Monaco di Studio*. Brescia, Italy, 1968.

Ferrai, E. *L'ellenismo nello studio di Padova*. Padua, 1876.

Firmin-Didot, A. *Alde Manuce et l'hellénisme à Venise*. Paris, 1875.

Garin, E. "Donato Acciauoli, Citizen of Florence." In *Portraits from the Quattrocento*, chap. 3. Translated by V. and E. Velen. New York, 1973. (Primarily on Argyropoulos.)

Geanakoplos, D. J. "Erasmus and the Aldine Academy of Venice: A Neglected Chapter in the Transmission of Greco-Byzantine Learning to the West." *Greek, Roman, and Byzantine Studies* 3 (1960): 107–34.

———. "The Discourse of Demetrius Chalcondylas on the Inauguration of Greek Studies at the University of Padua in 1463." *Studies in the Renaissance* 21 (1974): 18–44.

———. *Greek Scholars in Venice: Studies in the Dissemination of Greek Learning from Byzantium to the West*. Cambridge, 1962. Reprinted as *Byzantium and the Renaissance*. Hamden, Conn., 1972.

———. "The Italian Renaissance and Byzantium: The Career of the Greek Humanist-Professor John Argyropoulos in Florence and Rome (1415–87)." *Conspectus of History* 1–1 (*Focus on Biography*) (1974): 12–28.

Heiberg, W. *Beiträge zur Geschichte Georg Vallas und seiner Bibliothek*. Leipzig, 1896.

Holmes, G. *The Florentine Enlightenment*. New York, 1969. (See especially chaps. 3 and 8, dealing, in part, with Greek learning.)

Hunger, H. *Johannes Chortasmenos, 1370–1436*. Vienna, 1969.

Hutton, J. *The Greek Anthology in Italy to the Year 1800*. Ithaca, 1935.

Irmscher, J. "Ovid in Byzantium." *Byzantinoslavica* 35 (1974): 28–33.

Knös, B. *Un Ambassadeur de l'hellénisme: Janus Lascaris et la tradition greco-byzantine dans l'humanisme français*. Uppsala-Paris, 1945.

Kresten, O. "Der Schreiber und Handschriftenhändler A. Darmarios." *Mariahilfer Gymnasium* (1968), pp. 6–11.

Kristeller, P. "The Renaissance and Byzantine Learning." In *Renaissance Concepts of Man*, pp. 64–110. New York, 1972.

———. *Studies in Renaissance Thought and Letters*. Rome, 1956.

Labowsky, L. "Bessarion Studies." *Medieval and Renaissance Studies* 5 (1961): 108–62.

———. "Il Cardinale Bessarione e gli inizi della Biblioteca Marciana." In *Venezia e l'Oriente fra tardo Medio Evo e Rinascimento*, pp. 159–82. Edited by A. Pertusi. Venice, 1966.

Legrand, E. *Bibliographie hellénique ou description raisonnée des ouvrages publiés en grec par des Grecs au XVe et XVIe siècles*. 4 vols. Paris, 1885–1906.

————. *Bibliographie hispano-grecque.* Vol. 1. New York, 1915.

————. *Cent-dix lettres grecques de François Filelfe.* Paris, 1892. (Primary source.)

————. *Notice biographique sur Jean et Theodose Zygomalas.* Paris, 1889.

Loenertz, R. "Pour la biographie du cardinal Bessarion." *Orientalia Christiana Periodica* 10 (1944) : 116–49.

Luttrell, A. "Coluccio Salutati's Letter to Juan Heredia." *Italia medievale e umanistica* 13 (1970) : 235–43.

Manousakas, M. "Ekkleseis (1453–1535) ton Hellenon Logion tes Anagenneseos pros tous Hegemones tes Europes gia ten apeleftherose tes Hellados." Discourse given on March 25, 1963, at the University of Thessalonika. Thessalonika, 1965.

————. "La littérature crétoise à l'époque Vénitienne." *L'Hellénisme Contemporain* (1955), pp. 95–120.

Masai, F. *Pléthon et le Platonisme de Mistra.* Paris, 1956.

Menge, R. *Vita Marci Musuri Cretensis.* In *Hesychii Alexandrini Lexicon.* Vol. 5. Edited by M. Schmidt. Jena, 1868.

Mercati, G. *Notizie di Procoro e Demetrio Cydone, Manuele Caleca, e Teodoro Meleteniota, Studi e Testi.* Vol. 26. Vatican City, 1931.

Mioni, E. "La biblioteca greca di Marco Musuro." *Archivio Veneto* 43 (1971) : 5–28.

Müllner, K., ed. *Reden und Briefe italienischer Umanisten.* Vienna, 1899. (Primary source.)

Nicol, D. "The Byzantine Church and Hellenic Learning in the Fourteenth Century." *Studies in Church History* 5 (1969) : 23–57.

Nucius, Nikandros. *The Second Book of the Travels of Nicander Nucius of Corcyra.* Edited by J. A. Cramer. London, 1841.

Patrinelis, C. "Greek Codicographers in the Renaissance." In *Epeteris tou Mesaionikou Archeiou.* Athens, 1961. In Greek.

Patterson, A. *Hermogenes and the Renaissance: Seven Ideas of Style.* Princeton, 1970.

Pertusi, A. "Leonzio Pilato a Creta prima del 1358–9. Scuole e cultura a Creta durante il secolo XIV." *Kretika Chronika* 15–16 (1961–72) : 363 ff.

————. *Leonzio Pilato fra Petrarca e Boccaccio.* Venice, 1964.

————. *Storiografia umanistica e mondo bizantino.* Palermo, 1967.

Renouard, A. *Annales de l'imprimerie des Alde.* 3d ed. 3 vols. Paris, 1834. (Primary source.)

Reynolds, L., and Wilson, N. *Scribes and Scholars.* Oxford, 1968.

Ricci, P. "La prima cattedra di Greco in Firenze." *Rinascimento* 3 (1952) : 159–65.

Rosalia, A. de. "La vita di Costantino Lascaris." *Archivio storico siciliano* 3 (1957–58) : 21–70.

Runciman, S. *The Last Byzantine Renaissance.* Cambridge, 1970.

Sabbadini, R. *Le scoperte dei codici latini e greci nei secoli XIV e XV.* 2 vols. Florence, 1905–14.

Sandys, J. *History of Classical Scholarship.* Vol. 2. New York, 1964.

Sathas, K. *Tourkokratoumene Hellas.* Athens, 1969.

Schirò, G. "Missione Umanistica di Massimo Margunio a Venezia." *Rivista di Studi Bizantini e Neoellenici* (1967), pp. 159–87.

Schmitt, W. "Cato in Byzanz." *Klio* 48 (1967): 330–34.

————. "Lateinische Literatur in Byzanz." In *Jahrbuch der österreichischen byzantinischen Gesellschaft* (1968), pp. 121–47.

Scholderer, V. *Greek Printing Types, 1465–1926.* London, 1927.

Seigel, J. "The Teaching of Argyropoulos and the Rhetoric of the First Humanists." In *Action and Conviction in Early Modern Europe*, pp. 237 ff. Edited by T. Rabb and J. Seigel. Princeton, 1969.

Setton, K. "The Byzantine Background to the Italian Renaissance." *Proceedings of the American Philosophical Society* 100 (1956): 1–76.

Sevčenko, I. *Études sur la polémique entre Théodore Métochite et Nicéphore Choumnos.* Brussels, 1962.

————. "Society and Intellectual Life in the Fourteenth Century." *Actes du XIVᵉ Congrès International des Études Byzantines, Bucharest, 1971*, pp. 69–92. Bucharest, 1974.

————. "Theodore Métochites, Chora et les courants intellectuels de l'époque." *Art et Société à Byzance sous les Paléologues.*

Stadter, P. "Planudes, Plutarch, and Pace of Ferrara." *Italia medioevale e umanistica* 16 (1973): 137–62.

Torre, A. della. *Storia dell'Accademia Platonica di Firenze.* Florence, 1902.

Turyn, A. *Dated Greek Manuscripts of the 13th and 14th Centuries.* Urbana, Ill., 1972. (Primary source.)

————. "Demetrius Triclinius and the Planudean Anthology." In *Festschrift N. Tomadakes*, pp. 403–50. Athens, 1973.

————. "Michael Lulludes (or Luludes), a Scribe of the Palaeologan Era." *Rivista di Studi Bizantini e Neoellenici* 10–11 (1973–74): 3–15.

————. *The Manuscript Tradition of the Tragedies of Aeschylus.* New York, 1943.

————. *The Manuscript Tradition of the Tragedies of Euripides.* Urbana, Ill., 1957.

————. *The Manuscript Tradition of the Tragedies of Sophocles.* Urbana, Ill., 1952.

Ullman, B., and Stadter, P. *The Public Library of the Renaissance: Niccolò Niccoli, Cosimo de' Medici and the Library of San Marco.* Padua, 1972.

Vasoli, C. "Su una Dialectica attribuita all'Argiropulo." *Rinascimento* (1959), pp. 157–64.

Vast, H. *Le Cardinal Bessarion.* Paris, 1878.

Verpeaux, J. *Nicéphore Choumnos. Homme d'état et humaniste byzantin.* Paris, 1959.

Weiss, R. *Humanism in England during the Fifteenth Century.* Oxford, 1941.

————. "Lo studio di Plutarco nel Trecento." *La parola del passato* 8 (1953): 322–24.

Wendel, C. "Planudes." In *Pauly-Wissova Realencyclopädie,* vol. 20, cols. 2202–53 (1950).

Woodward, W. *Vittorino da Feltre and Other Humanist Educators.* New York, 1963.

Zakythinos, D. "Michael Maroullos Tarchaniotes." *Epeteris Hetaireias Byzantinon Spoudon* 5 (1928): 200–42.

Zuntz, G. *An Inquiry into the Transmission of the Plays of Euripides.* Cambridge, 1965.

XIV. The Greek Fathers of the Church in the Italian and Northern Renaissance

Bainton, R. *Erasmus of Christendom.* New York, 1969.

Botfield, B. *Praefationes et epistolas editionibus principibus auctorum veterum praepositae.* Cambridge, 1861. (Primary source.)

Camporeale, S. *Lorenzo Valla. Umanesimo e Teologia.* Florence, 1972.

Dekkers, E. "Les Traductions grecques des écrits patristiques latins." *Sacris Eruditi* 5 (1953): 193–233.

Dini-Traversari, A. *Ambrogio Traversari e il suo tempo.* Florence, 1912.

Fedalto, G. *Massimo Margunio e il suo commento al 'De Trinitate' di S. Agostino.* Brescia, 1968.

Gesamtkatalog der Wiegendrücke. 3 vols. Leipzig, 1928.

Graesse, J. *Trésor de livres rares et précieux.* Dresden, 1859–69.

Graf, C. *Essai sur la vie et les écrits de J. Lefèvre d'Etaples.* Geneva, 1970.

Hain, L. *Repertorium bibliographicum in que libri omnes ab arte typographica inventa.* 4 vols. Stuttgart, 1826–38.

Heckethorn, C. *The Printers of Basel in the 15th and 16th Centuries.* London, 1897.

Legrand, E. *Bibliographie hellénique ou description raisonnée des ouvrages publiés en grec par des Grecs au XVe et XVIe siècles.* 4 vols. Paris, 1885–1906.

Mehus, L., ed. *Ambrosii Traversarii latinae epistolae.* Florence, 1759. (Primary source.)

Meyer, P. *Die theologische Litteratur der griechischen Kirche im sechszehnten Jahrhundert.* Leipzig, 1899.

Peters, R. "Erasmus and the Fathers: Their Practical Value." *Church History* 36 (1967): 254–61.

Pfeiffer, R. "Erasmus und die Einheit der Klassischen und der cristlichen Renaissance." *Historisches Jahrbuch* 74 (1954): 175–88.

Rackl, M. "Die griechischen Augustinusübersetzungen." In *Miscellanea F. Ehrle*, 1: 1–38. Rome, 1924.

Rice, E. "The Humanist Idea of Christian Antiquity: Lefèvres d'Etaples and his Circle." In *French Humanism*, edited by W. Gundersheimer, pp. 163–80. New York, 1969.

Siegmund, A. *Die Uberlieferung der griechischen cristlichen Literatur in der lateinischen Kirche bis zum zwölfte Jahrhundert*. Munich-Pasing, 1949.

Stevens, L. "A Re-evaluation of Hellenism in the French Renaissance." In *The French Renaissance*, edited by W. Gundersheimer, pp. 181–96.

Tomadakes, N. "The Publications in Italy of Greek Ecclesiastical Works (primarily liturgical)." *Epeteris Hetaireias Byzantinon Spoudon* (1969–70), pp. 3–22. In Greek.

Walker, D. "Origène en France du début du XVIe siècle." *Courants religieux et humanisme à la fin du XVe et au début du XVIe siècle*. Paris, 1959.

Wind, E. "The Revival of Origen." In *Studies in Art and Literature for Bella Costa Greene*, edited by D. Miner, pp. 412–24. Princeton, 1954.

XV. San Bernardino of Siena and the Greeks at the Council of Florence

Beck, H. G. "From the Second Council of Lyons to the Council of Florence." *Handbook of Church History*, 4: 488–98.

Camporeale, S. *Lorenzo Valla, Umanesimo e Teologia*. Florence, 1972.

Congar, Y. *After Five Hundred Years*. New York, 1959.

Facchinetti, V. *San Bernardino da Siena, mystico sole del secolo XV*. Milan, 1933.

Geanakoplos, D. J. "Edward Gibbon and Byzantine Ecclesiastical History." *Church History* 35 (1966): 1–16.

———. "The Council of Florence and the Problem of Union between the Greek and Latin Churches." In *Byzantine East and Latin West*, pp. 84–111. Oxford, 1966.

Gill, J. *The Council of Florence*. Cambridge, 1959.

Holmes, C. *The Florentine Enlightenment*. New York, 1969.

Howell, A. *San Bernardino of Siena*. London, 1913.

Laurent, M. *Les 'Mémoires' de Sylvestre Syropoulos sur le concile de Florence*. Paris, 1971. (Primary source.)

Loenertz, R. "Les Dominicains byzantins Théodore et André Chrysobèrgès et les négociations pour l'union des églises." *Archivum Fratrum Praedicatorum* 9 (1939): 5–61.

Mamonis, K. "Mark Eugenicus, Life and Work." *Theologia* 25 (1954): 377–404, 521–75. In Greek.

Mastrodimitri, P. *Nikolaus Sekoundinos*. Athens, 1970. In Greek.

Moorman, J. *A History of the Franciscan Order*. Oxford, 1968.

Origo, I. *The World of San Bernardino*. New York, 1962.

Sevčenko, I. "Decline of Byzantium as Seen through the Eyes of its Intellectuals." *Dumbarton Oaks Papers* 15 (1961): 291–323.

Ullman, W. "A Greek Démarche on the Eve of the Council of Florence." *Journal of Ecclesiastical History* 26 (1975): 337–52.

XVI. The Greek "Diaspora" to the West

Antoniadou, S. "Porismata apo ten meleten procheiron diacheiristikon biblion ton eton 1544–47 kai 1549–54 . . ." *Praktika tes Akademias Athenon* 33 (1958): 468–70. In Greek.

Browning, R. "Some Early Greek Visitors to England." In *Essays in Memory of Basil Laourdas*, pp. 387–95. Thessalonika, 1975.

Cecchini, G. "Anna Notaras Palaeologa: Una principessa greca in Italia e le politica senese di ripopolamento della Maremma." *Bolletino Senese di Storia Patria* 16 (1938): 1–41.

Cenni istorici della comunità greco-orientale di Trieste. Trieste, 1882.

Embirikos, A. *La Renaissance crétoise*. Paris, 1960.

Fedalto, G. *Ricerche storiche sulla posizione giuridica ed ecclesiastica dei greci a Venezia*. Florence, 1967.

Geanakoplos, D. J. *Byzantine East and Latin West*. Oxford, 1966. (See especially chaps. 4–6.)

————. *Greek Scholars in Venice: Studies in the Dissemination of Greek Learning from Byzantium to the West*. Cambridge, Mass., 1962. Reprinted as *Byzantium and the Renaissance*, Hamden, Conn., 1972.

Hassiotes, J. "Hellenikoi Epoikismoi sto Basileio tes Neapoles." *Hellenika* 22 (1969): 116–62.

————. "La communità greca di Napoli e i moti insurrezionali nella penisola balkanica meridionale durante la seconda metà del XVI secolo." *Balkan Studies* 10 (1969): 279–88.

————. *Scheseis Hellenon kai Hispanon sta Chronica tes Tourkokratias*. Thessalonika, 1969.

orgIa, N. *Byzance après Byzance*. Bucharest, 1971 (reprint).

Irmscher, J., and Nagel, P., eds. *Studia Byzantina*. Vol. 2. Berlin, 1973.

Kyrris, K. "Cypriote Scholars in Venice in XVI and XVII Centuries." *Berliner Arbeiten* 40 (1968): 183–272.

McNeil, W. *Venice, the Hinge of Europe*. Chicago, 1974.

Manousakas, M. "The First Permit of the Venetian Senate for the Church of the Greeks. . . ." In *Thesaurismata*, pp. 109–18. Venice, 1962. In Greek.

Meola, G. *Delle istorie della Chiesa Greca in Napoli esistente*. Naples, 1740.

Mertzios, K. "Thomas Flanginis kai Ho Mikros Hellenomnemon." *Pragmateiai tes Akademias Athenon* 9 (1939): 47 ff. In Greek.

Netzhammer, R. *Das griechische Kolleg im Rom.* Salzburg, 1905.

Paparegopoulos, K. *Historia tou Hellenikou Ethnous.* 5th ed. Vols. 4–5. Athens, 1932. In Greek.

Pseroukes, N. *History of the Greek Communities of Europe.* Athens, 1975. (Unavailable to me.)

Sathas, K. "Hellenes stratiotai en te Dysei." *Hestia* 19 (1885): 370–76; and later issues.

Tomadakes, N. "He Symbole ton Hellenon Koinoteton tou exotericou eis ton agona tes eleutherias." Speech given at Athens University, 1952, pp. 1–40. Athens, 1953.

———. "I Greci a Milano: Nota." *Istituto Lombardo (Rendiconti, Classe di Lettere)* 101 (1967): 568–80.

———. "Naoi kai Thesmoi tes Hellenikes Koinotetos tou Livornou." *Epeteris Hetaireias Byzantinon Spoudon* 16 (1940): 81–127.

Veludes, J. *Hellenon Orthodoxon Apoikia en Venetia.* 2d ed. Venice, 1893.

Index